ABBA EBAN

An Autobiography

ABBA EBAN

An Autobiography

WEIDENFELD AND NICOLSON
LONDON

To Suzy

*Life must be lived forwards but
can only be understood backwards.*
—KIERKEGAARD

Contents

CONTENTS

ABBA EBAN

An Autobiography

1

Divided Childhood

OUTWARDLY, EVERYTHING SEEMED NORMAL. MILLIONS WERE LIVING THEIR boyhood years at the same familiar rhythm. No drama disturbed the even flow.

The scene was London in the nineteen-twenties and thirties: more precisely, a small sector of the endless metropolitan sprawl, bordered by home and school south of the Thames. It was a gray district poised narrowly between austerity and squalor. But both home and school had detached themselves from their local condition as if determined to have nothing to do with their own environment. Home was a three-floor house in the Kennington Park Road, along which went a procession of swaying tram cars, buses and trucks, in a steady turbulence of noise and grime. The outer façade of Number 12 was stark, but inside, everything was redeemed by my mother's sense of harmony, into a modest but solid comfort. We were a newly constituted family learning to live together for the first time; my widowed mother, her new husband, Dr. Isaac Eban, and my elder sister, Ruth, and I, still far from our teens. Our roots were nowhere near Kennington Park Road. They lay behind us in a Lithuanian Jewish township, Yanushki, near Kovno, where my grandparents Eliahu and Bassya Sacks had produced eleven children, of whom, in the manner of the times, only four grew beyond infancy. My mother was the third of these. Her own survival in infancy had been so narrow that she was

3

hopefully named "Alta," the old one, in what turned out to be a successful persuasion of the fates to grant her length of life.

In their middle years Eliahu Sacks, like many Lithuanian Jews, moved his family away from East Europe in search of larger fortune, first to South Africa, then to London. He seems to have been the only Jewish immigrant from Lithuania to South Africa who achieved no affluence whatever. In a short time he was on the move again, this time to London, leaving my mother, now named Alida, behind in Cape Town, married to Abraham Meir Solomon, also an emigrant from Yanushki, but by now a solid merchant with a meticulous passion for founding Zionist societies wherever he went. Here my sister and I were born, and here a terrible doom struck our home. My father became afflicted with terminal cancer in 1916, the first year of my life, and sailed in hopeless search of cure to England. My mother would tremble in later years whenever she recalled the nightmare journey of the dying man with his young wife and two babies in a crowded, sweaty troopship through seas infested with submarines and mines. A few months later my father died in London. I was destined to live without any recollection of him beyond a few faded photographs from family albums and Zionist newspapers.

From the age of three I was farmed out to relatives or later to seaside kindergartens; once even dispatched to Ireland for shelter from the Zeppelin raids. The absence of her children, however poignant, did enable my mother to struggle for a living as a laboratory assistant to her brother Samuel Sacks. He was then a young physician battling a deadly flu epidemic in the East End of London, where Jewish immigrants were crowding in from Europe, bringing their Yiddish speech, their pieties and hopes, their tangy delicatessen stores, their tenacious family solidarities and their crowded synagogues and Hebrew schools.

In 1921 my mother was married again, this time to Isaac Eban, a physician of strong Jewish background and loyalties who had studied and taught mathematics in Scotland before embarking on a medical career. A physician's practice was found in Kennington Park Road and this was the solitary reason for us to live there. Here two Eban children, Carmel and Raphael, were born. The family was now of six human beings groping rather awkwardly toward cohesion in a London environment uncompromisingly alien to all their Jewish memories and dreams.

In the same measure, my school life was oblivious of its surroundings. St. Olave's was an Elizabethan foundation established in 1588 and subsequently housed in a building of heavy dignity, situated, for unknown reason, close to the dockyard area of the Tower Bridge, where there was no residential zone from which pupils could be recruited. All of us traveled some distance to and fro. The noises around were of cranes and heavy trucks with an occasional urgent hoot of a ship's siren demanding passage under the bridge. When this happened, traffic would stop and the road forming the bridge would split alarmingly, while each half rose impressively into the air, as though to create a deferential arch under which ships would pass in unchallenged priority. It was taken for granted that landborne traffic, however heavy, must always give way to seaborne vessels, however small. To my childish relief, the arms of the bridge would soon come down again, creak firmly into place and reconstitute the road. The uniformed man in the tower, who controlled all these movements with a wheel like a ship's helm, was my first symbol of virile omnipotence. At the age of eight I was, in my own mind, a ruthless aspirant for his job.

Of this dockland world, St. Olave's School took no notice at all. Its routine was of rigorous scholarship, focused mainly on classical literature. I do not recall that the natural sciences were actually persecuted; there was even a grudging tolerance for pupils of minor attainments who gravitated to a world of laboratories and classrooms with mathematical symbols on the board. But boys of higher perceptions and talents were monastically consecrated to Greek and Latin. My adolescent years were thus filled with Homer and Vergil, Xenophon, Horace, Herodotus, Thucydides, Lucretius, Plato, and later, more daringly, with Ovid, Pindar and Sappho, with an occasional obeisance to English poetry and the Bible. The business of education, in the Olavian view, was literature. Minds nourished with great ideas nobly expressed—so it was believed—would somehow adjust to the more specific claims of modernity and livelihood.

The moving spirit in this enterprise was the headmaster, H. G. Abel, a Cambridge scholar who combined a severe precision with an extraordinary capacity for esthetic emotion. I remember him reading a Greek lyric and suddenly coming close to tears when he encountered a phrase of special perfection, as if there were a latent sadness, as indeed there is, in all beauty that is fragile and of transient lease. Apart from a passion for classical learning, Abel had some eccentricities. He preached a strong Protestant religiosity, with the Deity invoked a little too often in support of whatever he chose to advocate or defend. To this he added, surprisingly, a candid support of socialism. This rare audacity was not likely to help him much in his career, but it did seem to bridge a gap between the school's élitist curriculum and the hard, clanging world of the docks a few yards away. Abel also had a bizarre hatred of motorcars. There is a particular monopoly of uninterrupted speech reserved for headmasters, judges and generals, and Abel used this prerogative to denounce the modern automobile, with frightening vehemence, as a source of private luxury and therefore of social decadence. Young as I was, I thought that a revolt against the seductions of the internal-combustion engine was a hopelessly lost cause, but when the Eban medical practice flourished to the point of needing a Rover car, I kept the guilty secret dark lest Abel's antimechanical conscience be too much offended. He was fond of Biblical quotation, especially of the Psalms. When anything went wrong he would declaim, "Thy Rod and thy Staff shall comfort me." In later years, most Olavians agreed that they found some comfort in Abel's capable Staff—none at all in his Rod.

So during the whole time between my eighth and eighteenth years I would ply between Kennington and the Tower Bridge in a closely circumscribed routine, stable and free of shock. But this normality was disrupted by the unusual fact that Kennington and St. Olave's were only a half of my existence. Unlike my school fellows, I lived both in their world and in another, clothed in mystery, far beyond their imaginings. For my maternal grandfather, Eliahu Sacks, had decided that his legacy of Hebrew scholarship must pass to me, and that the transmission of it would henceforth be his life's sole purpose. Every Friday after school until Sunday night or Monday dawn, I would be spirited away from Kennington and St. Olave's for an almost brutally intensive immersion at my grandfather's dingy house in Hackney, in a world dominated by the Hebrew language, whose alphabet I had learned at the age of five, before I knew the English script. Soon I was being guided through the Biblical literature by a mind never formally trained but lit up with an intuitive scholarship, and thence into modern Hebrew writing, with only a surprisingly short sojourn in the Talmud. This was not through any lack of grandfatherly competence; Eliahu Sacks was so learned that by sticking a pin into a standard Vilna edition of the Talmud text he would be able to tell you what was written at the corresponding position six pages ahead. But he was at heart a son of the "enlightenment," captivated by the Haskalah movement, which had stressed Hebrew studies more as a humanistic discipline than as a tool for ritual. His attitude to religious observance was correct but without fanaticism. And while he respected Zionism for the active reverence that it gave to the Hebrew language, he was not very sanguine about its political prospects. Back in 1916 he had told my mother that hair would grow in the palm of his hand before any government supported the Zionist dream. Nevertheless, when the Balfour Declaration was published he did not recant openly, for he was a proud and sensitive man. But late in 1917 he went to the Kingsway Hall, where Chaim Weizmann raised his arms aloft

6

to celebrate the great victory, and sitting at the back he broke into silent and uncontrollable tears.

Hebrew scholarship for him was an end in itself, a total destination, not an avenue to something else. He was never explicit about what he expected me to do with this heavy cargo of learning, except that he was implacably opposed to a rabbinic vocation. Whatever the intention, the consequence for me was formative to the ultimate degree. It was the weekend, not the weekday world that came to excite my deepest sources of feeling. The Jewish legacy was my close possession. St. Olave's belonged to its own English world, and Kennington Park Road was restrictively parochial. They could exist without me—and I without them. On the other hand, the Jewish domain was lived on an intimate level of personal experience. My own sufferings and suspense were of Isaac beneath Abraham's threatening knife. My sense of awe came to life in the "thunder and lightning and the trumpets exceeding loud" that accompanied Moses on Mount Sinai. My sense of nationhood was born with the parting of the Red Sea and the Israelite defiance of Egyptian tyranny. Pharaoh, in my adolescent days, was my own personal enemy. The frogs, the flies, the locusts and the cattle plague all served him right, although in my incorrigibly liberal mind I secretly felt that the slaying of the firstborn carried things a little too far. The rhetoric of the Prophets was frightening, but it captivated me for its concern with the human condition. I felt that Hebrew prophetic writing soared in thought and language even above the levels of my favorite Greek authors with their unconvincing gallery of trivial "gods" and their melancholy brooding on a golden age in the past, from which all history seemed to descend, in constant nostalgia, from a Paradise Lost. How could these superstitious folk compare with the Jewish minds which had the effrontery to conceive of a golden age in the future, so that all history would unfold forward and upward in progress and ascent?

As my grandfather guided me hour after hour through the modern Hebrew literature, my loyalties became linked with more recent dramas—the martyrdoms, inquisitions, massacres and pogroms, and most of all, with the quest for remedy and honor now being enacted by the Zionist pioneers, few and weak but supremely tenacious, hundreds of miles away. Before I passed my early teens, I was the captive of a Jewish destiny. Whenever anyone in our family said "we" or "us," we meant the Jewish people and none else.

For there was another special dimension in my boyhood experience, in addition to my grandfather's home, that set me apart from school and street. My mother, on arriving as a widow from Cape Town, had secured her first employment in 1916 as a secretary and translator at

7

the Zionist Office, newly established in 175 Piccadilly. At first it seemed to be no more than a job—and a precariously paid one at that. But in a short time it had flowered into an extraordinary adventure that was to leave its mark on her and on all of us. The moving spirit of the Zionist Office, Chaim Weizmann, had lived in Manchester for eight years as a university lecturer in biochemistry, with a relatively junior position in the world Zionist hierarchy. But he had a strong intuition that the war would end with Britain in control of Palestine, and that it would be possible to commit the British government to the fulfillment of the Zionist program. There was no real evidence at the time that Britain would in fact be on the winning side—still less that it would sponsor a Zionist movement which seemed to command no tangible power and which most practical politicians regarded as a charming but useless fad.

But Weizmann had a special capacity to believe and to convince others that the needs of Jewish history must ultimately prevail against all obstacles of rationality. He had swiftly gathered a few men around him, watched and nursed his chances, and then intervened in the central political arenas with such authority and sureness of timing as to change the whole direction of his people's history. The result was the Balfour Declaration of November 2, 1917, expressing Britain's obligation to promote the establishment of "a Jewish national home in Palestine."

My mother had watched this drama from close at hand as secretary to Nahum Sokolow, who was Weizmann's chief colleague in this adventure. In point of fact Sokolow, as a member of the elected Zionist World Executive, was senior to Weizmann in the Zionist hierarchy. He was also a famous figure in the Hebrew literary movement, a linguist and scholar of staggering versatility. But he did not have Weizmann's militant passion, and his gentle, skeptical realism was not congenial to strong leadership. To his immense credit, he accepted a subordinate role and gave crucial service in obtaining French and Italian acquiescence in Weizmann's dream of a British trusteeship for the future Jewish homeland.

On November 1, 1917, my mother had been occupied with my querulous two-year-old screamings when a call came from Sokolow insisting that she come to the office to translate "an important document" into French and Russian. She made what I have always described as a characteristically Zionist decision; she simply left her infant son to fend for himself and went off into the November fog. She found Weizmann, Sokolow and their few colleagues in a sort of ecstasy. The document was the text of the Balfour Declaration, transmitted to Weizmann by the British Foreign Office that day. The Jewish homeland was not quite a reality, but neither was it any longer a wild and hopeless dream.

The vibrations of this event were subsequently transmitted to me, through my mother's narrative, in waves of quiet but proud recollection. The experience, together with my grandfather's teachings, ensured that Zionism had conquered my inner world. Something quite unusual and exalting had flashed across my family's sky—and the glow of it would never be lost. Moreover, the contacts and friendships that my mother had formed, together with her own gift of hospitality, brought famous Zionist figures into our orbit and sometimes even into our home.

My grandfather died a little after my fourteenth birthday, having invested nine years of his life in my intensive "Hebraization." He succumbed to the kind of pneumonia infection that would today be remedied by two or three antibiotic injections. In retrospect, I see him as a strange figure, compassionate yet remote and of strongly concealed emotions. His own life had known very few successes, and young as I was, I had the vague feeling that he was seeking vicarious and posthumous vindication of himself by investing in my future. All his material scarcities notwithstanding, he conveyed an air of lineage. He was the sort of man to whom people would have intuitive recourse when in trouble. But for his habit of spending most of the day in a skullcap and well-worn woolen dressing gown, he could have been said to have a regal air. His photograph shows how easily he could have been mistaken for King George V or the last of the Russian czars; such was the effect of the balding pate, the well-cut Hanoverian beard and the eyes stern with authority. His nearest approach to frivolity was to play chess in total silence with one of his few neighborhood friends or relatives. He did not enjoy losing, and when defeat loomed close ahead, he would suddenly remember an appointment and break off the contest while there was some honor still to save.

It had not been Eliahu Sacks's intention to die when I was only fourteen, and he followed his own final illness with a detached air of disapproval rather than with any kind of self-pity. Only three weeks before, he had brought home a vast mass of old Hebrew books, including one formidable *Concordance of the Bible* by Fuerst, so unwieldy and massive that the bookseller had probably been glad to get rid of it. Apart from its value for reference, it was irreverently used to press trousers or for other household chores in which its enormous weight was an asset.

It began to occur to me at this time that unlike everyone else of my age, I had never known the taste of a free weekend, or a day in which to walk and live and play at leisure. The knowledge that there was deprivation in the acceptance of my grandfather's scholarly gifts never seemed to burst into resentment, but it must have been simmering, latent and potentially explosive. With my grandfather's death, there went a vast grief, a sense of void—and yet, at the same time, a guilty consciousness of freedom. Two out of the seven days of the week had suddenly and miraculously become my own. Yet all of us in the family knew that Eliahu Sacks's investment must not be squandered by discontinuity and neglect. We recalled that he had spoken well of a distinguished Hebrew scholar, Isidore Wartski, then the lecturer in modern Hebrew at the School of Oriental Studies in London University. Arrangements were made for me to take weekly periods of study with him at his home in North London.

This brought about a sudden transition from a predominantly Biblical preoccupation to the modern Hebrew literature of which Achad Ha'am and Chaim Nachman Bialik were the leading figures. Achad Ha'am was an essayist of sharp rationality who regarded Zionism as having a primarily spiritual vocation. His system of thought conceived of a "center" in Israel radiating influences outward, like spokes from a wheel, to Jews across the world. His skeptical temperament marked him off from his more rhapsodic colleagues in the Zionist and Hebrew movements. He had the irritating habit of knowing what was wrong and of saying so with relentless candor. He was the first leading Zionist writer to point out that the Land of Israel was not empty, and that despite a transient serenity, relations with the Arabs would ultimately loom, large and defiant, as the central predicament of Zionism.

Bialik had enchanted me with his long, mournful ballad "Hamatmid" (The Eternal Student), which told the poignant story of a young scholar in the Pale of Settlement, imposing a cruel discipline upon himself to the total destruction of his health and the strangulation of normal sensualities, so that the study of the Talmud became a kind of self-immolation in which all satisfactions of body and mind were denied. Although my own circumstances could not rationally be compared with the oppressive squalor in which Bialik's "Matmid" lived, there was, nevertheless, between me and him a common emotion of quiet grievance at the heavy price exacted by an assiduous scholarship, with no certainty of compensating reward.

At the age of seventeen I presumptuously entered public life, joining Zionist societies close to my home in which young people meeting in drafty halls discussed Israel's renaissance with unrelieved solemnity. We all developed a talent for rhetoric. Zionists have always been great talkers, eager to pour their themes and justifications into any ears that could be persuaded to listen.

By now the leading Zionists were no longer remote legends from my mother's early memory. Since London was the center of Zionist political activity, it also became the main destination of politicians, poets and writers from the Palestine Jewish community. One day the great Bialik himself arrived to address a mass meeting in the Jewish-populated East End of London. I crept into the back of the hall as a zealous hero-worshiper, and emerged at the end with a sense of disappointment. His poetry was deep and majestic in the portrayal of melancholy. The "tears of things" could be heard everywhere. He wrote of persecution, hunger, indignity and despair—of a Jewish abasement contrasting sharply with the ancient glory. I had expected him to be an emaciated ascetic with large, soulful eyes. But Bialik in real life turned out to be a bald, clean-shaven, well-nourished man with a prosperous, mercantile air. There was nothing afflicted about him. He reminded me of a kindly bank manager who, on the whole, would rather grant a loan than refuse it and would always give a customer the benefit of every doubt. What horrified me most of all was that Bialik, the greatest of all Hebraists, seemed to have difficulty in speaking Hebrew. He would lurch violently, and without transition, from one form of pronunciation to another, taking refuge, when all seemed lost, in a familiar Yiddish colloquialism. Far from being plunged in melancholy, Bialik appeared to be rather pleased with himself, at peace with the world around him, and prone to easy and engaging laughter.

Far closer to my imaginative picture of him was the second Hebrew poet, Shaul Tchernichowsky, whom I heard speak in the same East London hall. He seemed to have taken a great deal of trouble to look as a poet is expected to look. A chaotic mane of tangled hair crowned a large face, across which a thick black mustache crawled like an expanding silky forest. He recited some of his own poems with a kind of Hasidic ecstasy, as though he were undergoing the throes of composition for the first time at the very moment of declamation. The third poet in the Hebrew triumvirate, Zalman Shneour, actually visited our home in Kennington Park Road. (He himself never admitted to being "the third".) In him I saw no disparity between reality and image. Like his poetry, he was tempestuous, sensual, irascible. He seemed to give a great deal of scrutiny to any good-looking woman in the company; and one evening when my mother's cook was late in presenting dinner, he erupted into a vast, indignant rage which would have been inexcusable were it not, as we learned the next day, that

11

he suffered from diabetes, so that punctuality of nourishment was a need, not a mere convenience.

Between my classical studies at St. Olave's and my grandfather's Hebrew hothouse, it was inevitable that my beginnings should be precocious. I was still a secondary-school boy when I began to write articles in the *Young Zionist,* pontificating with solemnity, heat and occasional lucidity on the events that agitated the Jewish world. As I look back in the files, I find to my disconcerted humility that my writing has neither progressed nor deteriorated very much since those days, except that I may have learned to control a rhetorical violence that was forgivable in so young a journalist.

Just before going up to Cambridge, I became familiar with the principal Zionist orators. I recall Weizmann in large halls in East and West London, scornful of rhetorical device, pitching his voice on a low tone, as if to compel his audience to a reverent silence. It is difficult for later generations to conceive the special air of majesty that he diffused around him. One of his devices for promoting a Jewish state was to behave as though it already existed. His appearance—tall, and with a goatee and a prodigious bald pate—like a well-nourished Lenin, all his mannerisms, his air of tranquil superiority and of social ease, as well as his material habits such as riding around London in a chauffeured Rolls-Royce, were those of a chief of state engaged in a permanent summit conference. He addressed foreign statesmen as though his status were already equal to their own. They and he knew that this was not strictly true, but something in his bearing and in their own historic imagination forbade them to break the spell. With Jewish audiences he was at his best when addressing recent immigrants in Yiddish, which he commanded to the full scope of its irony, pathos and self-deprecation. His English was meticulously correct, yet extraordinarily accented considering the many years that he had spent in Britain. Compared with the more ardent performers among Zionist speakers, he revealed a scientist's economy of phrase and emotion, a hard sense of realities, and an almost cruel insistence on telling his Jewish audiences how difficult and complex their Zionist task was going to be. Just because his usual discourse was quiet, he was unbearably impressive on the few occasions when he broke out into rage or visionary ardor.

My mother's mentor, Nahum Sokolow, was venerable in every sense of the word. He had probably been "venerable" at the age of thirty. His learning was vast, perhaps too abundant for his own good, for his speech and writing overflowed profusely in every direction, like a river in flood, with no clearly defined banks. He was a man of real quality. He wore a small pointed beard, excellent clothes and, more wonderfully, a monocle. He gave out an air of rich Jewish humanism, together with a cultivated demeanor that one would have expected to find in a European ambassador with three or four diplomatic generations behind him. Zionism owes him far more than it has ever acknowledged.

There are two other personages whom I recall from this period. I met the first at a gathering of a large galaxy of Zionist dignitaries that included Chaim Arlosoroff, who had become head of the Political Committee of the Zionist Organization in his early thirties. In the only speech I heard him make, his words were charged with sharp conviction, but the nature of his daily work seemed to involve him in matters of detail to which he had to devote a disproportionate mass of energy. Today there is no city in Israel without a street in his name, but I have always felt that what Israelis celebrate is a potentiality lost in its prime rather than anything brought to fulfillment. His diaries and writings tell of patient negotiations with British high commissioners about immigration schedules and land purchases which, in any case, were ultimately decided in London, not in Jerusalem. There was, however, one document rising beyond the routine level. This was an impassioned letter to Weizmann in 1932 expressing dark pessimism about the prospect for Zionism to achieve a substantive result under the British Mandate. In the final resort, he said prophetically, it would have to win its way by resistance and revolt.

These revolutionary words seemed less familiar from Arlosoroff than from Vladimir Jabotinsky, whom I heard at a mass meeting in the London East End somewhere around 1933. He already had an air of frustration, as though he knew once and for all that he was not destined for the central place. He was small, swarthy, lacking every photogenic quality, yet peculiarly magnetic and compelling while in full flow. His style was denunciatory, vehement, intensely self-confident, and yet the grim, beetle-eyed glare and the stabbing hand seemed to me to indicate a careful prior rehearsal. While Weizmann talked about solid facts, Jabotinsky put great emphasis on demonstrative acts—mass petitions, high-sounding manifestoes and a belief that if Zionist leaders would only bang tables and slam doors, this would force powerful governments into submission. Western Jewry was never to be Jabotinsky's most successful arena. Its empirical mood left little scope for the sweeping messianic passions that Jabotinsky had been able to arouse among Jews in Russia. Yet I admired his capacity to elicit strong loyalties and to draw men to his obedience, if necessary, at the cost of sacrifice. Despite his maximalist slogans, he had an intuitive liberalism and tolerance, quite out of accord with the invective rancor for which some of his followers became known in later years. I remember that meeting at the East End with particular vividness, since I only had a one-way bus fare and had to return penniless across the Thames. I had at least two hours of walking through the foggy London night in which to run Jabotinsky's ideas through my seventeen-year-old mind.

With schooldays coming to an end, I began my attempts to reach Cambridge University. There was never any question of choice; the headmaster of St. Olave's never gave or allowed the impression that any other university existed. The family finances, although not strained to the point of hardship, would certainly not make it possible to finance a Cambridge career. I would have to win scholarships with emoluments sufficient to ensure my maintenance. After a year's intensive study of Arabic with a private tutor, Nakdimon Doniach, who was later to compose the *Oxford English-Arabic Dictionary*, I sat for a scholarship involving the princely sum of £110 a year—established at Queens' College in honor of an eminent Hebraist and theologian called Kennett, Bishop of Ely. One day in early August, while our family was vacationing at Birchington on the Kent seacoast, I walked at dawn into the village to buy *The Times*, in which my name stared at me out of a list of successful candidates for Cambridge distinctions. I went into residence at Queens' College, Cambridge, in October 1934. It had been founded in 1448 in memory of two English queens, not one, and successive generations of Queensmen have fought with despairing pedantry for the apostrophe to be accurately placed after, not before, the final *s*.

2

From Cambridge to Cairo 1934-1940

CAMBRIDGE MEANT ENLARGEMENT, FIRST OF ALL IN ESTHETIC OPPORTUNITY. There was a sudden majesty of buildings, river and verdure—a sharp contrast with the drabness of Kennington and Tower Bridge Road. Medieval architects had given to Queens' a more perfect symmetry than to any other Cambridge foundation. And the intellectual vistas of Cambridge as a whole were as broad, or as narrow, as anyone wanted them to be. There was, of course, a built-in defect—an élitist principle that had produced a society with no cross sections, no variety of shades and levels, so that reality could soon be lost in the sheltering ease. The compensation lay in the intense accessibility of cultural experience and the speed with which divergent minds could be put to work.

I lived some of those years in a building where Erasmus had taught in the fifteenth century. (The plumbing facilities had changed little since then.) But the scholarly lineage was not of the past alone. Across the meadow at King's, John Maynard Keynes led the Cambridge school of economists. In the murky Cavendish Laboratories, Ernest Rutherford and John Cockroft were taking a suspicious look at the alleged indivisibility of the atom, all in a philosophic spirit, with no thought of consequence. A. E. Housman and Quiller Couch were among the luminaries of literature. James Jeans and J. J. Thompson wore their laurels in astronomy and physics. Hersch Lauterpacht was codifying and teaching international law. George Macaulay Trevelyan, Denis Brogan and Kenneth Pickthorn were the historians.

My own vocation still lay in the classical and Oriental literatures, but there was nothing to prevent anybody from browsing in pastures far afield. I used to attend open lectures of the pundits and luminaries, probably in a subconscious revolt against the specialized confinements in which I had been long held. In my own field, the leading professorial figures were Cook and Cooke: A. B. Cook, the classicist at Queens', and S. A. Cooke, the Regius Professor of Hebrew, so called because appointment to that Chair, and a few others, was in the royal prerogative. The two Cooks spoiled no broth. With A. B. I used to translate *Times* articles into classical Greek prose—an art for which there was not likely to be a lucrative market in later life, so that no slur of "careerism" could be leveled. S. A. was a sharp philologist, but his approach to the Hebrew scriptures was obfuscated by the "higher criticism" that had become the scholarly vogue in continental Europe. The theory is that the Scriptural books are a kind of jigsaw puzzle with a different author responsible for every few lines. Thus the writer who refers to the Deity as Elohim is a different author (E) from the writer for whom God is JHWH (J). The field day of the higher critics came in their dissection of the Book of Isaiah into its two separate epochs and authorships. There would be no harm in this if it did not lead to the attribution of some of mankind's finest poetry to a monstrosity called "Deutero-Isaiah," an appellation that makes literary hero-worship impossible.

The trouble with the higher criticism was that the obsessive puzzle "Who wrote it?" tended to replace the more essential question: "What is the writer trying to say?" Yet S. A. Cooke was a sensitive scholar, sympathetically attuned to the strange Israelites who, with immense effrontery, dreamed their dreams of a universal order from a little backwater of a country squeezed between the great empires of the ancient world. He was fascinated by the solemn grace of Hebrew poetry, of which, however, I found his declamation abrasive, for he suffered from adenoids, a deficient dental structure and a total incapacity to enunciate Semitic gutturals. But when he recited the famous verses he was clearly enjoying himself, and since the resultant cacophony was beautiful in his own ears, I begrudged him nothing.

I soon found that the academic ambition of Cambridge students was to achieve a First in each part of the examinations held at the end of the second and third years. A Double First was a distinction that pursued its holder all his life, a dignity by which he was known in private and sometimes even introduced in public. My grandfather and my school had given me an intensely competitive approach to scholarship. By doubling my quota of studies and examinations, after three years I emerged with a monstrosity called a Triple First in Classics and Oriental languages. Moreover, my conscience forbade me to lay financial burden on a home in which there were three other children to educate. So, in my first year, aided and abetted by the Reader in Rabbinics, Herbert Loewe, I studied the *Cambridge Year Book* looking for prizes. Many donors throughout the centuries had founded scholarships which had fallen into oblivion and disuse. But any undergraduate had the right to request the appointment of examiners for any endowment that had not been abolished.

By a combination of pious cupidity and academic zeal, I emerged not only as a Triple First but also as Jeremy Septuagint Prizeman, Stuart of Rannoch Hebrew Scholar, Syriac Prizeman and Wright Arabic Scholar. This aggregate of dignities was apparently rare enough to justify notices in the Cambridge and London press about my academic career. Some learned pundits in clubs, with more leisure than was good for them, even wrote to newspapers estimating how often or rarely Triple Firsts had occurred. Of greater interest to me was the fact that I had conducted my university life without expense to my family, and that the result gave me an option for an academic career if I wanted it. I went on to win the E. G. Browne Research Fellowship at Pembroke College for Persian studies. This transported me to the first rung of the faculty ladder, and I began to give tuition in Arabic and Hebrew studies to undergraduates.

E. G. Browne, for whom my post was named, had been one of Europe's premier Iranologists. His *Literary History of the Persians* is a masterpiece of vibrant prose. As a condition for the post, I had to abandon the verdure and symmetry of Queens' and "migrate" to Pembroke College, which had been founded in the thirteenth century, but whose extant buildings were not comparable in grace or antiquity to Queens'. On the other hand, there was the chance of meeting a new common-room family, including the Master of Pembroke, Sir Montagu Butler, who had been governor of Bengal and whose son, R. A. Butler, was beginning to rise toward the summit in the Conservative Party.

Sir Montagu seemed to find the presidency of a Cambridge college less challenging than a turbulent Indian province. He was mild of character but had evidently been a determined hunter of big game. The rug on his floor was composed of a tiger skin and head with startling fangs and a look of indignant rage. The tiger had not taken to its assassination kindly. Indeed, I was never fully convinced that it was altogether dead, and the consumption of tea and muffins under its hostile gaze was a tense ordeal.

Toward the end of my undergraduate studies in Cambridge, the central theme was Arabic literature and history. I entered this field not merely because it was academically adjacent to Hebrew but also in deference to my Zionist principles. I had innocently believed that Jews who settled in Palestine, as I intended to do, would regard themselves not only as citizens of the Jewish nation, but also as the trustees of a regional patriotism that would make them want to know what was being read, said and written in the surrounding countries. It was only later that I realized how far political hostility had spilled over into a cultural alienation that persists to our own day.

Although I had entered the world of Arabic thought with a strictly pragmatic purpose, I came to be impressed by its large visions and exuberant resources. With the best will in the world I could not come to terms with the turgid declamations of the Koran, although I respected the faith of those who found inspiration there. But the pre-Islamic Arabic poetry and the histories, geographies and literary and philosophical treatises of the caliphate periods were intellectually and emotionally stirring. Islam provides a total context for the life of individuals and communities; and Arabic culture and Islamic art are broad enough to constitute a full humanistic discipline.

Since the Ottoman conquest in the sixteenth century, the Arab world had been cut off from the sensation of its original greatness. It became easy to contrast the old glories with present oppression. Yet I have never been able to think or talk of Arabs without respect for their literary heritage. The language is both their blessing and their peril. The blessing is in the dignity of its range and its challenge to diversity of thought. The danger is in its music, which tempts some writers and orators to say things because they sound good rather than because they express authentic thought or feelings. My deep immersion in that legacy made it impossible for me thereafter to adopt the routine Zionist stereotype that regarded the Arab nation with intellectual condescension. Every man of Arab speech holds the key to a vast reservoir of culture; and whether he uses it well or not, the very possession of the key gives him a particular stature.

It was natural that my twin preoccupation with Arab studies and Zionism should encourage contact with Arab students at Queens'. Two of them in particular, Auni Daoudi from Jaffa and Ahmed Khalil from Haifa, brought me face to face with the pathos of conflict between two nationalisms striving for fulfillment in the same country. I have never found consolation in Middle Eastern history as a guide to our contemporary problems. Some romantics like to dwell on "golden eras" of collaboration, especially in Spain, and to draw a corollary hope for coexistence in our own times. The trouble is that even in the best of past ages, the relations between Arabs and Jews were not equal. The Arabs were on top as the masters of power. The Jews were below, sometimes tolerated, sometimes not, but never on an equal level. Arabs and Moslems thus find no incentive in history for regarding the Arab-Jewish relationship as anything but an encounter between a dominant empire and its subject citizens. The idea that non-Arabs or non-Moslems are legitimate carriers of independence in the Middle East requires the Arab mind to make an effort at innovation, not of memory.

My Cambridge years were not occupied by Middle Eastern cultures alone. There was intense development in my Zionist vocation. I became president of the university synagogue, the Jewish Society and the Zionist Group. Although Palestine was not the central issue of preoccupation in a world darkened by Franco, Mussolini and Hitler, there were ample opportunities for me to defend my cause against its Arab and British opponents. By the time I left the university in my early twenties, I had contributed to most English-language Zionist journals and had written articles and letters in the *New Statesman* and *Spectator*. The Zionist office in London occasionally mobilized me for speeches within the university communities and beyond. I became a member of the Executive of the British Zionist Federation, and in 1935 I followed my socialist conscience away from general Zionism into the lowly movement called Poalei Zion. This was a very marginal and puny group in Britain and elsewhere in Europe, but in Palestine Jewry itself, Labor Zionism was becoming the dominant force.

During vacations, our home continued to be a destination for Zionist visitors. I came to know political leaders of Palestine Jewry, especially Moshe Sharett and Dov Hos. They were a different brand of Zionist spokesmen than I had met before. They gave off a scent of Palestinian soil and sun rather than of corridors, documents and briefcases. They were the first generation to have been educated at the Herzliya Gymnasia in Tel Aviv, and their Hebrew had a natural cadence. Zionism for them was not just an argument, a "movement" or a "problem," but a physical reality with a sense of place. I was won over to their conception because of its authenticity. Diaspora Zionism began to lose some of its attraction for me; I was disturbed by the gap between its sincere rhetoric and the superficiality of its concrete involvement.

One day Sharett brought to our home in Kennington Park Road a figure who was exotic in that setting but increasingly impressive in the causes for which I was to strive in later years. He was Berl Katzenelson, the spiritual guide of the Zionist pioneering generation. Removed from all secular ambition, his authority was expressed by personal influence, not by organized action. His only weapons were ideas, never abstract or particularly original, but strongly aligned with Jewish realities, always expressed without pomposity, with a balance between pugnacity and literary grace and tied to an elevating vision of human equality and dignity. Berl, with his untidy mustache, his tousled hair and his working-class cap, seemed very incongruous when he came once to Cambridge with the frank intention of capturing some of its prominent Jewish students for Zionist service. He and Sharett were in their own words "fishing for talent," and they spread their nets very wide. The catch was not abundant, but it included me. The two men felt that the Russian-born leadership of Zionism and Palestine Jewry would soon become out of tune with a new Middle East whose fate would be largely determined by the interplay of Arabs and Western powers. They thought that Western and Arabic culture would become more relevant and modern than the Yiddish and Slavic traditions in which the Zionist hierarchy had grown. Katzenelson and Sharett agreed that I would be more useful if I completed my academic career than if I joined them at once. But it was tacitly understood that I was firmly committed to their service.

A defense of Zionism against its detractors was the theme of my first speech in the Cambridge Union. It is not enough to describe the Oxford and Cambridge unions as "debating societies." Those who achieved renown there could often expect to rise in the political hierarchy of their countries. Former presidents of the Union included prime ministers, Cabinet ministers, parliamentarians and high officials. They rarely subsided into obscurity. The Cambridge Union hall was built as a replica of the House of Commons, with debaters facing each other across a gangway that polarized them into sharp definitions of position. The ritual and procedure imitated the dignity of Westminster. Debaters addressed themselves to the chair, referred to each other not by name but by college origin, avoided reading manuscripts, kept strictly to ordained time limits, and for the sake of training, defended or attacked causes according to what was demanded of them without much reference to their own convictions. Moreover, the debates were rarely confined to undergraduates alone; the custom was to bring visitors who stood eminent in politics, science or culture. The general pattern was for an undergraduate and a visiting dignitary to be aligned on either side of a proposition. Thus I found myself joining Harold Laski in defense of socialism; taking part with Lord Ponsonby against a fellow undergraduate and Lord Samuel in a discussion on "optimism and pessimism"; fulminating against the Chamberlain policy of appeasement in the company of Wickham Steed, a former editor of *The Times*. The Union debates were reported fully in the university journals. It was thus that I first knew the temptation of speakers, actors and musicians who open newspapers with trembling hands in hope of a good review. The youthful correspondents of these journals were more prone to critical chastisement than to sentimental eulogy. I therefore attached some significance to the fact that I found myself praised after the major debates. Sometimes the accolade was given with a typically languid Cambridge reserve: "I am getting tired of repeating all the time that Mr. Eban is the best speaker in the Union." It was at that moment that I ceased to be fanatically shy. The national press in those days also kept an occasional eye on Oxford and Cambridge Union debates, especially after the Oxford Union had caused alarm by adopting a resolution "that this House will not fight for King and country." When the war against Hitler came, those who had supported the resolution became embattled defenders of the anti-Fascist cause, many of them making the ultimate sacrifice on its behalf.

In March 1938, when I called, during a tense debate in the Cambridge Union, for collective resistance to Franco, Hitler and Mussolini, the *Cambridge Review* described the end of my speech in serious tone as a "great peroration." The times were grave and we were no longer deemed to be playing juvenile oratorical games. I began to feel that I might be developing a talent that could be put to the service of causes which commanded my fidelity. After a few years at Cambridge, I had a clearly defined system of loyalties. I was a Jew, a Zionist, a democratic socialist, an advocate of resistance to Fascism, a supporter of the Spanish Loyalists against Franco and an adherent of the League of Nations concept. All my future years were to fluctuate among those ideas.

A saving grace of the Cambridge Union was that in an attempt to avoid pomposity it insisted on a due ration of humor and self-deprecation. I found myself speaking on such motions as "This House resolves that work is the curse of the drinking classes" or "A marriage of love is superior to a marriage of convenience."

In later life I was to encounter many allies and adversaries of Union debates high in public life. This was especially true of those who used their Cambridge education for training in the art of expelling Britain from its imperial possessions. Thus, Cyril Keunemann became a leading minister in Ceylon; S. M. Kumaramangalam reached high office in the Cabinets of Nehru and Indira Gandhi; Offori Attah became a

Foreign Minister of the new Ghana; and when I, as Israel's Foreign Minister, first addressed the Council of Europe in 1970, I looked behind me to find the presidential chair occupied by Geoffrey De Freitas, who had been president of the Union when I first spoke there. On that occasion he had not called upon me before cautiously inquiring whether I was "fluent enough in English" to be worthy of the distinction. It may have been in memory of that skepticism that having taken one look at him, I addressed the Council of Europe in French.

I had prospered so much at Cambridge, both in personal relations and in intellectual fulfillment, that I had every reason to want to settle there. If I were not obsessed with the Jewish fate, I would probably have had no other ambition. But my tranquil Cambridge scene was overcast by the harsher world outside. The life of my generation was obviously not going to take a normal course. It was in fact about to erupt into flames. Freedom was an embattled cause with a strong prospect of collapse, and the Jewish people was very near to a volcano. It seemed intolerable for a young Jew to shut out these noises in order to pursue a monastic and, therefore, illusory peace. Hence, the call that was loudest in my ears was not to scholarship but to service in the context of my Jewish loyalties. The fact that our Cambridge serenity was nothing but a volcanic lull came strongly into my consciousness when, in 1936, I heard that my friend John Cornford had been killed fighting for the Loyalists in Spain. He had been my colleague in the University Socialist Society, although he had a more radical and uncompromising temperament than myself. Indeed, he ended up very close to a Communist allegiance. His father was a professor of classics, and his mother, Frances Cornford, a gifted poet. The pain of his abrupt and brutal death was sharpened by the pathos of his youth.

I was thus psychologically reconciled to the call of the arena when I was drawn into the Zionist Office political work in 1938. The political secretary of the Zionist organization, Arthur Lourie, had to leave his post for some months on urgent family grounds. It seemed that my speeches and writing had won me some kind of renown in the Zionist hierarchy. One day I received a summons, on the authority of Dr. Weizmann, to discuss the possibility of filling Lourie's place during his absences. I reverently made my way to Great Russell Street, where I was interviewed by one of Weizmann's chief collaborators, Professor Lewis Namier. Some years later Namier was to be ennobled by knighthood in recognition of his eminence as a historian. He was a meticulous specialist in the parliamentary history of the eighteenth century. In 1938 he was already a considerable figure in European scholarship, and it was an achievement for Weizmann to have brought him to a Zionist headquarters, populated for the most part by professional Zionists who, as Namier unhesitatingly reminded them, were intellectually less formidable than Namier himself.

I found myself being interrogated by a complex and forbidding character who seemed predisposed to think the worst of everything unless there was some compelling evidence in a favorable direction. Namier praised my Cambridge-attainments with what I thought to be a touch of snobbery, for he contrasted them too insistently with the careers of his Zionist colleagues. His adulation of Chaim Weizmann was particularly impressive, since he seemed to have a low view of the rest of mankind. He did not even seem to think very highly of Jews as such. And yet, here he was, devoting himself unselfishly to their redemption. He admired the manners, the culture and the rootedness of the English aristocracy, of which he spoke in a thick Central European accent, across a wide gulf of alienation. But once he put pen to paper, his English prose came out lucid, lean and of perfect craftsmanship. I was later to learn that struggling authors used to tremble when they heard that Namier was going to review their books. He was capable of such devastations as "the only good thing about this work is the quality of the paper." He was often abrasive beyond any call of necessity. One of his eccentricities was to react with revulsion to such courteous platitudes as "How do you do?" Rumor had it that this was liable to incur the curt reply "My health is no business of yours." Part of his frustration arose from the fact that he never believed himself to have been given sufficient eminence. He was certain that but for his foreignness, his professorial chair would have been at his beloved Oxford rather than in the damp exile of Manchester. I suspected that even his devotion to Zionism proceeded from a negative source. He hoped that if the Jews were redeemed from the humiliations of exile, they would perhaps become less embarrassingly strident, and might even develop an aristocratic tradition similar to that of the English country houses of the eighteenth century.

Whatever his asperities, his intellectual rank and self-confidence made him a powerful advocate of our cause. He would call ministers and Members of Parliament on the telephone and excoriate them in the most vehement terms if they fell short of fidelity to Zionist interests. His special contempt was reserved for Jews who sought to evade the duties of their inheritance. He called them "Members of the OTI" —the Order of Trembling Israelites. Most Jews in politics, big commerce and the House of Lords fell, in his view, in this category. At any rate, he was an unexpected apparition in the grimy surroundings of 77 Great Russell Street, where Zionist headquarters had been established, opposite the British Museum.

I emerged intact from Namier's scrutiny and went to work as acting political secretary of the Jewish Agency during the long Cambridge vacation, and again in December 1938. Sandwiched between these two periods was my first full term on the faculty at Pembroke College as a tutor and research fellow in Oriental literature. I was already experiencing the tug of war that was to afflict me all my life. On the one hand, the ease and leisure of research and teaching were always available, and some in my family thought me foolish to renounce them in favor of unfashionable, precarious Zionist work which could offer no "career." On the other hand, the cause in which my heart was engaged gave me endless grief and had the advantage of relevance.

There was also the chance of working close to Chaim Weizmann. All that time he was in somber mood. It was his habit to pass from ecstasy to exaltation and back again, without ever stopping at an intermediate ground of placidity. When I set out for Great Russell Street or his suite in the Dorchester Hotel each morning, I never knew whether I was going to be bathed in the sunshine of his contentment or plunged into one of his storms of frustration. My compensation lay in his immense prestige, his love of high quality in thought and behavior, his uncanny power of persuasion, and the sense of pride that he gave to the Jewish adventure. Surrounding him like courtiers in an enlightened monarchy, in addition to Namier, were people of diverse temperament. There was Blanche Dugdale, Lord Balfour's niece, a Scottish lady of strong character—lanky, awkward of movement, embarrassingly deficient in feminine attraction but exquisitely subtle in perception. She obviously had a strong persuasive power, for some British Cabinet ministers had the habit of confiding matters of state to her as soon as they were out of 10 Downing Street. She was our barometer. We knew through her what storms lay ahead.

Another member of the group was Selig Brodetsky, plump, kind and voluble, a professor of mathematics at Leeds University. From a humble East End background, he had achieved a glittering Cambridge career crowned by the position of senior wrangler, a distinction once given to the most prominent mathematician each year. Brodetsky had a shrewd intuition that his influence would decline if he became materially dependent on the Zionist movement. He therefore insisted on retaining his chair. But this meant that he was detached from Zionist business for large portions of the week and spent many exhausting hours on the trains between Leeds and London. The advantage of intimate and consecutive knowledge thus lay with Namier, who persecuted Brodetsky with the kind of implacable intensity known only to academic rivals.

Another colleague was Berl Locker, who represented the labor movement in Palestine. He was the only one of the group who shared Weizmann's intense Jewishness from its East European aspect, and he found common ground with the populist elements in the British Labour movement. He was small, perky, cheerful, mercurial and idealistic, but unformidable. His private virtues were his public defects. He was too amiable and genial to take politicians by storm.

Zionism already had able civil servants, including Joseph Linton, who was later to be Israel's ambassador in Tokyo and Canberra. And flying in and out of London with increasing frequency were leaders from Palestine Jewry, especially Moshe Sharett, who gave concrete realism to our discussions, which might otherwise have been concerned more with diplomacy than with reality.

During this period in London I made my first contact with David Ben Gurion. It was not his best hour. His position, though supreme in the Palestine Jewish community, was still subsidiary to that of Weizmann in the Zionist hierarchy. In London, detached from his power base, he seemed to be constantly brooding on grievances, resigning, withdrawing his resignations, resigning again, refusing to participate in sessions, and reacting all the time to Weizmann with a curious mixture of deference and envy. At that time his capacity to influence statesmen or large audiences was constricted in comparison with the potency that he was to develop later. Weizmann, like Theodor Herzl before him, had given Zionism a personalized image. Nobody at high levels of authority in the world considered that he had received a primary contact with Zionism unless he had heard from Weizmann at first hand. It was thus not easy for any other tree to grow in his shadow. Ben Gurion was already beginning to resent the atmosphere of monopoly and centralized privacy in which Weizmann worked—and which Ben Gurion, of course, was destined to promote with even greater intensity when his turn came in later years.

Sharett, a less tempestuous personality, was my direct mentor and guide. During my weeks at Great Russell Street in 1938, our task was to mobilize support among politicians and parliamentarians in Britain against the Chamberlain government's White Paper of 1939, which would have spelled the end of the Zionist dream. It proposed a limited Jewish immigration for ten years, its cessation thereafter, a stunted capacity for land purchase, and the ultimate establishment of a constitution in which the Jews would be a minority under Arab rule. The reason given by British governmental leaders for this hostility was candid: war was on the horizon. The vulnerable, overextended

25

British imperial domain would be threatened, and so would Britain itself. The Arabs had the option of joining the anti-British cause, whereas for Jewry, any alliance with Hitlerism was unthinkable. The Jews had no recourse except to the Western democracies and therefore did not have to be appeased. Thus the proud vision of a Jewish national home, and eventual statehood, was to be replaced by a stunted ghetto in which to be Jewish was to be a subject of discrimination, both in the right to immigrate and in the right to purchase land. The British Foreign Secretary explained this frankly and sanctimoniously to Jewish leaders. Lord Halifax was a man of principle, but one of his principles was expediency.

The only hopeful prospect was the idea of partition, which had been recommended in 1937 by a royal commission headed by Lord Peel. Weizmann had appeared in full prophetic anger before this group in Jerusalem. He had clearly stirred its conscience with his uncanny prediction of six million Jews doomed to extinction. At the same time, an incisive intellectual breakthrough had been made by one of the commissioners, Professor Reginald Coupland, an Oxford authority on constitutional history. Coupland later studied the communal dispute in India and arrived at the conclusion that the Hindu and Moslem communities held so few ends in common that a unitary framework of government was unthinkable. He became an acute critic of the "unitary myth" in mixed societies. In 1937 he applied himself with equally cruel realism to the relations between the Arabs and Jews in Palestine. He reached the same inexorable conclusion: the Jews were not strong enough to impose their authority over the Arabs, but they were powerful enough to frustrate Arab attempts to hold sway over them. Thus there were two national communities, neither of which should or could force a minority status on the other. The conclusion was that sovereignty—and territory—had to be shared, not monopolized. The two national movements were so disparate in their origins and aspirations that each had to have its own domain of fulfillment. The idea that there could be a single Palestinian citizenship was "a mischievous pretence." Accordingly, the commission recommended the establishment of a Jewish state in a small part of western Palestine. If this solution could not be put into effect, they proposed that the British Mandate be continued, but with a much more restrictive attitude toward Zionist development. They were clearly using a carrot and a stick to induce Jewish support of partition.

Like many other Zionists, I had been affronted both by the tiny area allotted for the Jewish state and by the commission's proposals on restricting Jewish development during whatever remained of the Mandatory period. I wrote vehemently against these aspects of the report in Zionist journals. At the same time, the logic of partition captivated me and I could not fail to be moved by the intuition that the Peel Commission brought to its analysis of Zionism. Despite its disappointing territorial provisions, it had given the idea of Jewish statehood a serious international resonance which was never likely to subside.

During the summer of 1937 I had gone to Zurich, where I combined a vacation with attendance at the Zionist Congress. It was one of the dramatic assemblies of Jewish history. The Partitionists and anti-Partitionists were ranged against each other in full solemnity like the armies in a Homeric epic. On the one hand stood Weizmann, Ben Gurion and Sharett, who saw high opportunity in the very fact that a Great Power had put the idea of a Jewish state on the international agenda, not as a mystical ideal as in the days of Theodor Herzl, but as a proposal for implementation. On the other hand, if the vision itself was large and audacious, the proposed scope of its fulfillment seemed parsimonious. Weizmann and Ben Gurion concluded that the congress should adopt the idea and work hard to expand its application.

On the other side, the opponents of partition were led by the American Zionist leaders, Stephen Wise and Abba Hillel Silver, and among the Palestinians by Menachem Ussishkin, Berl Katzenelson and the Religious Party. They were on strong ground when they criticized the weak points in the Peel Commission's proposal. But their arguments were more vulnerable when they presented their alternative program. After all, if we could not establish a Jewish state in accordance with an agreed partition, the only choice was the continuation of British rule in the hope that we could force London to apply the Mandate more favorably for Zionist interests than hitherto. There was not the slightest indication that this was feasible. The real choice therefore was not between partition and a Zionist version of the Mandate, but between partition and the strangulation of Zionism by the White Paper policy of the Mandatory power. The plight of German Jewry, with an even vaster tragedy in early prospect, weighed heavily for a solution that would bring immediate relief. I left the Zurich congress fully converted to Weizmann and Ben Gurion's position. I also learned something about the nature of the political choices that we would be called upon to make in later years. Edmund Burke was right when he said that most political decisions are a choice "between the disagreeable and the intolerable."

By 1938 the British government itself had shied away from partition, not under Jewish pressure but under Arab threat. The Jewish condition was now pitiable. We were being violently assaulted by our enemies and cravenly deserted by our friends. The work of the Zionist leadership consisted largely in voicing frenzied protest, and partly in trying to salvage what we could by way of immigration permits during the twilight years. For me the experience of Zionist political work was valuable in bringing me into an orbit in which high-level leaders made important decisions. It was a big elevation of sights compared with the pettiness and provincialism of the Zionist societies with which I had been familiar so far.

Like most of my contemporaries in their mid-twenties, I was living in an atmosphere of fragility. The war could not be very far away, and all available literature had taught us that the chances of individual survival for any of us might be small. Still, Cambridge managed to go its way, oblivious of the eruptions threatening all around it. I do not recollect that we were any less free in life or learning, in thought or passion, than young people living in a more stable atmosphere. And yet, the natural frivolity of our youth was overshadowed by the clouds ahead. It was at this time that Sharett and Berl began to speak to me more urgently of joining the Jewish Agency in Jerusalem as soon as I had completed the current stage of my studies and research. I was in the full throes of this decision when the summer of 1939 descended on my life like a curtain, separating past from future with utter finality.

At the Twenty-first Zionist Congress in Geneva in 1939 I was not a mere spectator but a full-fledged delegate, just beyond the qualifying age. Once again I combined the journey with an effort at vacation in which my mother and my sister Carmel joined me. The congress proceedings went on in a desultory rhythm. The real events that would shape our destiny were evolving elsewhere, more particularly in Moscow, where a British delegation attempted in vain to secure an Anglo-Russian understanding to contain Hitler. The effort came too late. The Soviet Union had made a different choice. I shall never forget the emotions that surged in me as I sat among the British Zionist delegates on August 24, 1939. News had come of the Molotov-Ribbentrop agreement. The Soviet Union had joined forces with Hitler. Poland was the immediate target of their joint assault. All of us knew that this meant war, which would bring grief and suffering to many nations but a particular doom to the Jewish people. Weizmann caught the sense of the hour when he rose to address the congress. A chill went through the room when he spoke his final words:

> *There is darkness all around us and we cannot see through the clouds . . . If, as I hope, we are spared in life and our work continues, who knows, perhaps a new light will shine upon us from*

*the thick, black gloom . . . The remnant shall work on, fight on,
live on until the dawn of better days. Towards that dawn I greet
you. May we meet again in peace.*

The war scare was already potent, and it was less easy to get out of
Switzerland than it had been to enter. After a crowded ride across
France, we found Paris in the throes of mobilization with thousands
of troops moving into trains and trucks with a slow apathy, the
full purport of which was only later to emerge. After crossing the
Channel, I went with my family to their cottage home in Felcourt,
near East Grinstead in Sussex. It was there, on September 3, that I
heard Chamberlain's weary broadcast declaring war and the disappointment of all he had hoped for. Here was a statesman announcing
a cataclysmic human tragedy as though it were a personal snub administered in bad taste by someone who "should have known better."

The sensation of anticlimax carried over into the next few months.
We had been conditioned to believe that the outbreak of a major war
would be followed by vast explosions of carnage and the total disruption of organized society. Instead, everything that was supposed to
collapse went on exactly as before. I volunteered for military service
before any obligatory mobilization could take effect. This involved an
endless filling in of forms declaring my date of birth, educational attainments, the similar details concerning my forbears for three generations, and any avowal that I wished to make concerning a whole
list of alarming diseases. Nothing ensued from any of this; indeed,
there appeared to be a national determination at every level to pretend that war had not been declared at all and that the First Lord
of the Admiralty, Winston Churchill, was sinking German ships off
the shores of Uruguay for the lonely gratification of his well-known
bellicosity. Thus, by October, I was back in Cambridge, whose population was now swollen by expectant mothers evacuated from London and students of other universities, including the London School of
Economics and the School of Oriental Studies, taking shelter from
London's anticipated ordeals. I renewed my contact with Harold
Laski, whom I had been accustomed to visit in his Hammersmith
home with other socialist students from many lands. We were all very
grateful for the time and benevolence that he showered upon us, the
more so since, according to his own story, he was constantly being
pressed by President Roosevelt, Churchill, Nehru, Anthony Eden,
French statesmen and the Labour leaders, to advise them on measures
to be taken for the survival of mankind. His weakness for fantasies of
eminence seemed curious to me, since he was in fact eminent enough to
make do with strict veracity without losing pride.

The presence of the School of Oriental Studies in Cambridge enabled me to pursue Persian studies with Vladimir Minorsky while continuing my own research and teaching. But all of this was intolerably irrelevant in terms of my own urgent instinct for public service, and I went up to London in hot temper to persuade Weizmann to seek my release to him by a letter to the Master of Pembroke.

Arriving in London from Cambridge in December 1939, I found that Weizmann had set up a kind of double command post at his apartment in the Dorchester Hotel and at the Zionist headquarters. This celebrated office was remarkable for its dinginess and lack of hygienic provision. But in these respects, it did not differ very much from one of the more aristocratic ministries in Whitehall.

It was a time for long-term plans, not for sudden victories. The Jewish prospect had been disfigured by the ugly enactments of the 1939 White Paper; it was, in fact, a total sentence of death on Zionist aims. This betrayal of Jewish national hopes had been simultaneous with the Munich settlement and congruous with it in all respects. Indeed, the day after Munich, Jan Masaryk had come to Weizmann's home after pacing London streets in despair, to predict a whole new series of Munichs. Small peoples were going to be sacrificed one by one as burnt offerings to appease the violent tyrannies which then seemed to be the supreme favorites of fortune.

The future of Palestine was not a major concern of the British people as it went about collecting its gas masks, recruiting its expeditionary force, evacuating its children from the cities and casting an anxious eye on its sprawling expanse of empire. Weizmann surveyed the field and defined Zionism's first objective. There was clearly no chance for a new and auspicious definition of the final political solution. Our aim must be to put the 1939 White Paper on ice and then to create conditions in which it would appear, after an Allied victory, as a grotesque and unseemly anachronism. The first goal was to get the Jewish people represented in its own identity among the armed forces to be mobilized for Hitler's defeat. Behind its flag, consecrated in battle, the Jewish people would rally after the victory to claim its national rights.

The idea of a Jewish brigade or division had occupied the Zionist leaders throughout the autumn weeks which I had been frittering away at Cambridge. I found that Weizmann had laid down a tense diplomatic bombardment. Between September and December, those who heard him expound his cause included Winston Churchill, Leopold Avery, Malcolm MacDonald, Lord Halifax, Robert Vansittart, Walter Elliott, Archibald Sinclair, Lord Chatfield; the Labour leaders Clement Attlee, Ernest Bevin, Arthur Greenwood and Tom

Williams; Conservatives such as Walter Monkton, R. A. Butler and the Duke of Devonshire; and every editor or politician who came within his grasp.

It was like 1917 again. Weizmann's energy cascaded everywhere. His health was resilient rather than robust, but it was sensitively attuned to his mood and spirit. The pace was urgent. From the Continent came fearful news of the "solution" that Hitler was preparing for the Jews of occupied countries. The Jewish army was becoming a moral necessity for Jewish history—a token of retribution, as well as the credential of future statehood.

By December, when I joined the effort led by Weizmann, Locker, Namier, Blanche Dugdale, Brodetsky and Linton, some progress had been made. The Foreign Secretary, Lord Halifax, had agreed with Weizmann that this was no time to enact new provisions under the White Paper. "It was impossible to have these things cropping up now," he had said in vague languidity. More substantively, Zionist pressure had made a dent on the minds of military leaders. On November 14 the Chief of the Imperial General Staff, General Sir Edmund Ironside, had told Weizmann of his resolve to release forty-three young Jews (including a young farmer named Moshe Dayan), whom the Palestinian government had sentenced to long imprisonment for indulging in military training. My own work at the Zionist headquarters that winter included a daily barrage of pressure to get the forty-three released. (Little did I know then that two of them— Moshe Dayan and Moshe Carmel—would one day be my colleagues in Israeli Administrations.) "Fancy," the general said, "they have condemned some of Wingate's lads to life imprisonment. They ought to have been given the Distinguished Service Order." When Weizmann said that the Colonial Secretary, Malcolm MacDonald, was obstructing the Jewish army project at every stage, the general replied, "Oh, I see, but the Jewish army will come all the same. Besides, if it is to be a better world after the war, the Jews must get Palestine."

The better world seemed far away. My own experience showed me how frustrating the prospect was. I went with Brodetsky to try to get MacDonald to agree to the rescue of 20,000 children in Poland and then to get visas granted to 169 Zionist leaders who had received permits to enter Palestine before the outbreak of the war. Each of these demands was refused. MacDonald sanctimoniously told us that he fully realized the tragic consequences of his refusal for those involved. It was the voice of a deep-seated moral decadence.

But there were other forces at work. Weizmann placed strong hope in Winston Churchill, who was straining at Chamberlain's leash, scarcely concealing his impatience with the sluggish policies by which the government "prosecuted" the war. On December 17 I was waiting at Great Russell Street for Weizmann to come back from a conversation with Churchill. My task was to formulate Weizmann's minutes for dispatch to Jerusalem a few hours before his departure for New York:

> Mr. Churchill was very cordial and deeply interested in Dr. Weizmann's forthcoming visit to America. He made optimistic observations on the progress of the war. Dr. Weizmann thanked Mr. Churchill for his unceasing interest in Zionist affairs. He said: "You stood at the cradle of this enterprise. I hope that you will see it through." Mr. Churchill asked what Dr. Weizmann meant by "seeing it through." Dr. Weizmann replied that after the war, the Zionists would wish to have a state of some three or four million Jews in Palestine. Mr. Churchill said: "Yes indeed, I quite agree with that."

Weizmann's departure on December 20 for a three-month trip to America left me with little to do in Great Russell Street, except to argue with Namier about the syntax of memoranda that we were sending to British Cabinet ministers. On the whole, Namier and I found common ground. We each developed a hatred of what we called "stammers." By this we meant words that were inserted into sentences like cotton wool for no reason except to fill them out or improve the rhythm. If some unfortunate Zionist official wrote a sentence beginning "It is unnecessary to emphasise," Namier would write in the margin "Don't emphasise it if unnecessary." If the stammer was "It is worth noting that," Namier would comment "Then for God's sake, note it." Such phrases as "In this connection it is worth pointing out that" were deleted with a furious hand. In later years I was to wield my red pencil in similar vein on the dispatches of Israeli ambassadors, many of whom probably bear their silent resentments to this day.

Early in January 1940 I was back at Cambridge again, this time only for a few days. The forms that I had filled out in quintuplicate since the first day of the war had begun to germinate within the military bureaucracy. I was required to report to Mytchett Barracks near Farnborough for training as an officer cadet in preparation for a commission in the intelligence service. I was, however, apologetically told that before carrying whatever duties came under the impressive heading "intelligence," I would have to train in good faith as an infantry officer together with others destined for similar service.

For the next four months, from February to May, I underwent the experience of basic training, the first part of it in conditions of intense cold. In my platoon there were other Oxford and Cambridge linguists destined for the General Staff but committed in the meantime to the humbler rigors of military training. One of them, I remember, was a distinguished Finnish scholar. Another was Con O'Neil, later a central luminary in the British Foreign Office. We were, I'm afraid, the despair of our drill instructors. Our academic attainments were cumulatively immense, but they seemed to be in inverse proportion to our physical mobility. Our training included a gruesome ceremony which required us to affix a bayonet to our rifle and impale a straw dummy like a human figure at vital anatomical points, with appropriate screams of frenzied aggression. I was apparently not very convincing at this. I can still hear the sergeant major's screams: "Stick it into his guts, Cadet Eban, stick it into his guts. For Christ's sake, imagine that you hate somebody!" At a ceremonial parade our platoon of "Distinguished Dons" distinguished itself by an excessive individuality. We quite simply marched at a different pace, in different steps and in different directions. Across the foggy air came the sergeant major's stentorian shout: "Between the lot of you, you know fifty bloody languages, but, Jesus, you can't march fifty bloody steps!" In spite of all this, I graduated as a second lieutenant in May 1940. It would normally have been a time for celebration. I remember going up to London, newly uniformed, and walking down Regent Street, astonished by grave salutes from even humbler military ranks.

Yet all personal satisfactions were stilled by horrendous news of the war itself. In the latter weeks of our training it had seemed as if the war would be won by Hitler even before we could get ourselves into it. Holland, Belgium and Luxembourg were overrun, and France was close to defeat. It was in a bleak, bare barracks near Aldershot that I heard Churchill's orations. For many years it had appeared that Britain would rather face ruin than allow Churchill to become Prime Minister. In the end, it settled for the latter "disaster." Soon the defiant roar resounded in our barracks. There was nothing to offer but blood, sweat, toil and tears. "We shall fight on the seas and oceans. We shall fight on the beaches. We shall fight on the landing grounds. We shall never surrender. We shall carry on the struggle until the new world steps forth to the rescue and liberation of the old."

The "new world" was all very well, but the old one still had its regulations and prejudices. When I reported to the War Office for my staff intelligence assignment, I was met by an elegant colonel in a state of high embarrassment. It seemed that the War Office had unexpectedly discovered my grandparents from Yanushki. A new regulation had provided that officers of non-British parentage would be ineligible for confidential staff work, especially if the non-British nationality was something as ominous as Lithuanian Russia. Since Eliahu Sacks had not moved out of the Kovno area early enough, it "followed" logically that his grandson could be an infantry commander but not an intelligence officer. I went to Great Russell Street to pour my heart out to Weizmann. He was paternally sympathetic but, for a change, without any ideas about action. Exactly the same answer had been given to his son Michael, who was eligible for active flying service, provided he got nowhere near the mysterious papers that flowed through the staff offices. I told Weizmann that what mattered to me was not the nature or category of my military service, but its arena and destination. It was vitally urgent for me to get out to Palestine as quickly as possible; otherwise I feared that the curtain of war would descend and cut me off for the duration. Weizmann dictated a letter to MacDonald's successor as Colonial Secretary, Lord Lloyd, giving a full list of my academic attainments and stating that it seemed "natural" that someone with these endowments should serve in an area of whose languages, cultures and history he had special knowledge. Later he received an unforgettable reply: "But, Dr. Weizmann, there isn't going to be any war in the Middle East." Four days later, in defiance of the lordly prediction, Italy attacked France in the Mediterranean and began to wrest the Egyptian Western Desert from Britain.

In the meantime, there was nothing for it but to be an infantry officer in England. This vocation took me first to the gentle farmland in Hereford, and then to a frigid and stormbound command post at Yarmouth on the east coast. The assignment sounded very marginal at the time, but the surprising fact was that Yarmouth was about as near to the active "front" as any place could be, with the exception of the expeditionary force operating under Lord Gort in Europe. As the intelligence officer of my regiment, I became the proud possessor of a motorcycle and my first relations with it were similar to those of young cowboys in Hollywood films who get thrown off the back of a horse whenever they mount the saddle. In the end, however, I mastered its use and gloried in my mobility. The possession of a motorcycle and of an imposing green intelligence armband around my sleeve gave me some advantage of prestige with the female population of Yarmouth which it would have been absurd not to exploit to the full.

It was believed, with good foundation, that a German invasion of the British coast was planned for the late fall or early winter. I was duty officer during a sunny weekend when a genuine panic developed on the communications system. Agitated voices across the wire bade us to get into a situation of "full alert." It was September 21, 1940, which, as I later learned, was the day on which a German crossing of the Channel and the North Sea was not only expected, but actually planned. My own prosaic task was to estimate which hostelries, bars and other places of assignation were likely to be frequented at that time by our absent brigadiers and colonels.

Like many others, I remember the period of the "phony war" as one of triviality and idle suspense. Here was a historic reality as dramatic as could be imagined—the defense of human values against the most monstrous barbarism of all times. Yet the defense was enacted in ways that were prosaic, apathetic and unconvincing. It may be that the British people saved its sanity by a studious lack of imagination; it would probably have done nobody any good to go around obsessed by too much reality. After the war I took Yarmouth with retrospective seriousness only when documents showed that Hitler's landing had been planned not far from the Norfolk-Suffolk coast.

Certain events did remind us not to take the war too frivolously. Instead of invasion by land, there came terrifying air attacks. One of these hit buildings near our own base and I saw the results of sudden death of women and children for the first time. From time to time on leave in London, I would see the graver effects of a real assault. Complete destruction was wrought on Kennington Park Road and other of my childhood scenes south of the river. My family had not fully escaped becoming a target by moving to Harrow, near the Kodak factory in which reconnaissance photographs were deciphered. The bombs came very close to them every night.

The impressive thing about Britain in those years was the matter-of-fact way in which it was understood without much ideological discussion or analysis that Hitler had to be destroyed. I was beginning to be demoralized by the prospect of endless vigil in a cold fishing village when deliverance unexpectedly came. It took the form of a belated response by somebody in the bureaucracy to what Weizmann had asked of Lord Lloyd. The Middle East was now a war theater in every sense of the term. One of the paradoxical results was that Weizmann's dream of a Jewish division, having been memorably accepted by the British government in 1939, was withdrawn in 1940.

Yet, on a personal level, the new situation worked out in my favor. The idea that people with a knowledge of Middle Eastern languages might be more useful in the Middle East than in East Anglia had suddenly dawned upon some massive intelligence in the War Department.

One day in early December 1941 I received orders to embark for the Middle East. The intermediate assembly point of my unit was, unexpectedly, Oxford. I spent an uncomfortable night in a cold set of rooms at Lincoln College, once occupied by Dr. Samuel Johnson. With my mother and sister I made a sentimental visit to an Oxford theater, watching a stupendously irrelevant musical by Ivor Novello. I said goodbye to them the next morning, not knowing when, or if, I would see them again. The next stop was Liverpool and thereafter several weeks of travel in unexpected luxury on the S.S. *Orcades,* bound for an eastern destination.

The journey illustrated one of the anomalies of war—peril coexisted with lavish normality. The officers aboard lived as first-class passengers on an expensive cruise, yet the seas through which we sailed were thick with possibilities of death. There were several weeks of tortuous weaving around, with warships in protective attendance. Then we reached our first port of call. It turned out to be Cape Town, which I had left at the age of seven months, more than two decades before. There was no way of giving anyone notice of my arrival. I stepped ashore during the four nights of anchorage in search of whatever relics of family history that I could find. In the telephone book I found the address of the Zionist headquarters. Walking into an empty building, I was emotionally crushed to see, on a central wall, the wedding picture of my mother and father presented to the Dorshei Zion Association, of which my father had evidently been the founder. The next day, uncles and aunts and cousins were discovered and bottles of champagne rapturously opened. I had not seen the city of my birth before and have not seen it since.

The troopship voyage had many aspects of nirvana, a total detachment from the storms and realities of the world. Yet the ship's radio gave us some news of events outside. It was aboard the *Orcades* that I heard of Pearl Harbor and listened to Churchill growling defiance to the Congress of the United States ("What sort of people do they think we are?"). There was Roosevelt's solemn declaration of war, not only on Japan but on Germany and Italy as well.

By the time we reached Cairo, two weeks later, the Allies had lost many naval battles in the Pacific waters, and Japanese power was expanding across most of eastern Asia. The Russians were falling back before the Nazi assault. The fighting lines in the Western Desert had been temporarily stabilized and the large military population in Cairo, mostly British, pursued a life of uninhibited hedonism as though the war were thousands of miles away. It was hard not to be shocked by the colonialist atmosphere of the city. Everything important seemed to be determined by the foreign "colonies" and the military staffs. Cairo seemed to have no reference to Egypt at all. I paid the penalty of my linguistic prowess by being assigned to a job of crushing tediousness in the Arabic censorship department. But it was this very fascination with the Arabic tongue that took me out of the military ghetto in search of contact with an Arab and Egyptian world.

The Road
to Jerusalem
1941-1945

MY WORK AS A CENSOR OF ARABIC LETTERS AND NEWSPAPERS HELD MY
interest for about forty-eight hours. There were, after all, very few
Arabic-writing soldiers in the Allied forces. So I was reduced to a
perusal of letters by Libyan soldiers in the Western Desert of Egypt,
each expressing simultaneous and exclusive devotion to a wide diversity of wives and girl friends. The press censorship was of greater interest. Newspapers, of which the galley proofs came before me, indicated a mood of simmering revolt beneath an outward surface of
docility. Clearly, Britain's status in Cairo was becoming less respected
in the measure that her armies retreated. There seemed to be no
ideological objection in Egypt or the Arab world to Nazism. Everything depended on who won. There was thus an inherent paradox in
the use by Britian of Egyptian territory for the purpose of defeating
Hitler.

I found no attraction in the social life of wartime Cairo, with its
emphasis on hard liquor and other manifestations of an incongruous
dolce vita. My main relief was in lectures and meetings with Arabic
scholars at universities; and on one rewarding day I was introduced to
Taha Hussein, a blind novelist then regarded by most Egyptians as the
greatest figure in modern Arabic letters. There was a great pathos in
his solitary darkness and in his gratitude to those who kept his mind
alive with conversation and ideas. But on the whole my consolations
were few, and my torments many. One of them came from the knowl-

edge that Jerusalem was only an hour's flight away. In a dejected mood, I wrote to Moshe Sharett. He replied with characteristic warmth, and also with the news that he might be able to get me eastward across Sinai in less than the forty years spent by our ancestors.

Egypt in those days had a separate national personality. It was detached from the passion of Arab anti-Zionism. Taha Hussein had just published his sensational book *The Future of Culture in Egypt,* in which he urged his compatriots not to look eastward into the desert but west and north across the Mediterranean, toward the centers of Hellenic and Latin civilizations with which Egypt had often been associated in her history. Other scholars evoked the Pharaonic era, which had given Egypt its fame long before the advent of Islam. The Egyptian nationalist struggle under the leadership of the Wafd Party, headed by Saad Zaghlul and Mustafa el-Nahas, had taken a separate path from that pursued by Arab nationalism in the north. The slogan of Egyptian nationalism was "Unity of the Nile Valley"; in other words, the national gaze was directed southward toward Sudan, not eastward into Arabia. Egypt's support of Arab anti-Zionism was perfunctory. There was no difficulty for Palestinian Jewish leaders or, for that matter, Zionists from abroad, or even institutions such as the Palestine Jewish Symphony Orchestra, to come to Cairo as often as they wished. The more eminent Zionists such as Weizmann used to sign the Visitors' Book at the Royal Palace and hold conversations with leading Egyptian statesmen. Thousands of Palestinian and Jewish troops serving in Allied forces were based in or near Cairo. A Jewish community headed by respected traditional families gave out an air of mercantile and professional success. Synagogues, schools and social organizations were well organized and supported. Urban Egypt was a pluralized maze of autonomous communities—Arab, Italian, Greek, French, British—and in this atmosphere of diversity, a Jewish community could flourish.

A new dimension of Jewish-Egyptian contact was now formed by Zionist leaders coming from Jerusalem to consult with the British High Command, British embassy officials, or even with Egyptian politicians. Thus it was not surprising to me when shortly after my letter to Sharett, Reuven Shiloah of the Jewish Agency came to Cairo and called me on the telephone.

I had previously got to know Reuven through his visits to London, either in the company of Sharett, or alone. Born in Jerusalem of an orthodox rabbinic family, he had become a trusted counselor of the Zionist leaders. His knowledge of the Arabic language and culture made him a valuable diplomat. He was also a born intelligence officer —shrewd, objective and free from any tendency to confuse his own wishes with harsh realities. As a leader of the Haganah he had, of course, been obliged to learn the methods of underground action. He had even developed an endemic air of conspiracy. Whenever he called me on the telephone he would immediately ask me my name, but was very slow to divulge his own. When he got into a taxicab in Jerusalem, Cairo or London, the driver would have to wait a long time before Reuven chose to give some hint of his destination. When we went to eat at a restaurant, he would study the menu with an air of sharp suspicion, as though convinced that it might harbor an obscure code. None of these quirks detracted from the strength of his personality. He was single-minded in his public devotion, without time or thought for anything that lay outside the national preoccupation. He gave his leaders a dogged fidelity and a self-abnegation which were to become less conspicuous in the Israeli public service as years went on.

The story that he conveyed to me on the terrace of the Continental Hotel would have lacked credibility in any other time and place. It belonged both to the duplicity of war and to the exotic traditions of Middle Eastern politics. On the one hand, the British government in London and Jerusalem was administering Palestine in accordance with the 1939 White Paper. It was hostile to the Jews of Palestine, whose cooperation in aiding the anti-Nazi cause was, anyhow, taken for granted. It was ineffectually obsequious toward the Arabs, most of whose rulers cared nothing whether Hitler triumphed or not. But while it was doing everything on the administrative level to prevent Palestinian Jewry from growing stronger, the British government was operating on another level, through its intelligence and Secret Operations agencies, with the single aim of helping to defeat Hitler. In this context, of course, the Jewish people was an ally and partner.

The British government, and especially Winston Churchill, had felt humiliated by the ease with which Allied positions had been surrendered at Singapore and Tobruk. The German-Italian movement across the Western Desert might well compel a British retreat from Egypt and Palestine. If this were to happen, it was resolved to make the price of occupation exorbitant for the Nazis and their allies. Palestinian Jewish units would be trained to carry out resistance and sabotage. They would make Palestine an inferno for any occupying Nazi army. Simultaneously, some Palestinian Jews would carry the war into enemy territory. Since there were Jews of German, Yugoslav, Hungarian and other East European nationalities, they could be trained as parachutists, saboteurs and agents to be dropped behind the German lines in occupied Europe.

These activities had led to a close organizational collaboration between the British intelligence units and the Jewish Agency. The immediate task was to establish a camp at Kibbutz Mishmar Ha-emek, in which some hundreds of Haganah members, especially its striking force, Palmach, would be trained for resistance activities. The result was that one branch of the British government would have to work against another. In Palestine itself, the high commissioner and his soldiers would swoop punitively on any Jews caught in the possession of weapons. At the same time, a more prestigious arm of the government in London would pour weapons and explosives into the hands of the most effectively trained and militant Jewish fighters.

War is able to transcend such anomalies. It was clear that for Churchill, the defense ministries and the office in charge of subversive operations, Special Operations Executive (which I later found out was supervised by the Labour leader and Minister of Economic Warfare, Hugh Dalton), the objective of winning the war against Hitler was paramount. It therefore justified the mobilization of the anti-Nazi fervor of Jews, whatever the local Palestine government might think or feel.

There was, to put it very mildly, an inherent complexity in this scheme. One of the problems was that the Haganah would inevitably have to reveal much about its personnel, leadership and structure to those who were going to arm and finance it. There was need of a liaison officer who would be trusted by both parties in this strange alliance. Sharett and Shiloah had suggested my name. All that was now required was that I should secure the approval of Wing Commander Domville, who commanded the Cairo headquarters of SOE.

The wing commander was known both for his gallantry in combat and for his prodigious capacity of alcoholic absorption. The important thing was to get at him early during the hours of his maximal lucidity. Accordingly, I arranged to be interviewed at ten in the morning. Although there was a large tumbler of Scotch on the table, ten o'clock was apparently only the dawn of a new day. Everything was clear and amiable, and I emerged with the impressive description of "Liaison Officer between SOE and the Jewish Agency for Palestine on Special Operations."

My sojourn in Cairo had lasted for only a few weeks. On an unforgettable morning toward the end of February, I set out by train toward the eastern Delta and El Qantara across the Sinai Wilderness —into the Promised Land.

All Jews who ever came to Israel with a Zionist purpose have tended to romanticize their first contact. Today the arrival is at an airport so similar to others that the very banality of it makes it difficult for any but the most rhapsodic immigrants to embrace the asphalt in obeisance. Many Zionist pioneers and immigrants used to describe how they slept under a clear sky on their first night after arrival, and how they met the early dawn in the Land of Israel as it came up, amid a yellow and purple radiance that repeated itself in the evening twilight. My own first contact with Israel's soil was outwardly less emotional, but the inner stirrings were deep. I was more aware at first of the natural scenery than of the human landscape. The coastal road to Jerusalem in those days was narrower, more tortuous, and flanked by fewer forests than now. But there was a cleanness of color and sharpness of light that contrasted with the grime and sweat of Egypt. Within the first week of my arrival I had gone through the country north and south, often recalling the words of George Adam Smith: "Men who looked at life under that lofty imagination did not always notice the details of their country's scenery. What failed them was the sense of space and distance, stupendous contrast of desert and fertility, the hard straight coasts with the sea breaking into foam, the swift sunrise, the thunderstorms sweeping the length of the land; and if these great outlines are touched here and there with flowers or a mist or a bit of quiet meadow or a quiet pool or an olive tree in the sunshine, it is to illustrate human beauty which comes upon the earth as fair as her wild flowers and as quickly passes away."

My first night in Jerusalem was spent unromantically and unJewishly in a modern stucco house on the Bethlehem Road. The house belonged to an Arab physician who had translated his affluence into the pink vulgarity of a marble-tiled bathroom. My companions were Major General B. T. Wilson, a North Irishman of simple pieties who had become converted to Zionism before I arrived; and Anthony Webb, then a captain on the General Staff, who was later to become the Chief Justice of Kenya. There was not much Zionist satisfaction in these surroundings, but scarcely had I taken stock of where I was than Shiloah took me to Tel Aviv to get a taste and smell of our new Jewish society.

Having patriotically overcome the stunning shock of Tel Aviv's architecture, I entered quickly into the pulse of the city's life. My first visit was to Berl Katzenelson, whom I found in the headquarters of the *Davar* newspaper, scarcely visible behind a table piled with books tumbling in disorder to the floor. Every twenty minutes some guest, uninvited, would arrive—a secretary of a kibbutz or of a Histadrut (National Labor Federation) committee or some other dignitary seeking inspiration from his movement's "teacher." Berl evoked our meetings in London, spoke with staccato rapidity about recent books and papers, and interrogated me sharply about the prospect that I would enter the Zionist service as soon as military conditions would allow.

My next stop was at the home of David Ben Gurion. He sat behind a bare wooden table, looking even smaller than he was, the white tufts of hair springing belligerently and disconnectedly from his massive pate. His conversation was disjointed. It came in a series of barks and grunts with which I was to become familiar in later years. At one point he would appear to be deeply involved in what I was saying; at the next he would begin writing busily in a notebook as though I were not in the room at all. It later emerged that he used to make verbatim records of conversations in the very course of their evolution.

I went on to Rothschild Boulevard—a quietly tranquil street, but less magnificent than the two words would indicate. Here I had a meeting with Eliahu Golomb, head of the Haganah organization. I had met Eliahu once or twice in London, where his extreme taciturnity barred my understanding of his rich world of thought and passion. Here at his home, clad in a quaint Russian *rubashka* shirt, he was more at ease. He was close to his own vocation. His business was to ensure that Jews could survive in the elementary physical sense. The work that I was doing in SOE was of great relevance to him. If it succeeded, two results would be achieved. The Palmach would get an intensive training far beyond its own resources, as a result of its cooperation with the British military staff. And a further dimension would be added to the Jewish war against Hitler. The Palestine Jewish leaders were willing to contribute manpower lavishly to the British High Command. But they also sought a recognizable military performance by Palestinian Jews in their own identity. The tension between these two objectives was expressed in a certain rivalry between those who favored maximal mobilization in the British army, and those who wished to keep the best Jewish manpower in reserve for specific national tasks.

For the next fourteen months—from February 1942 to April 1943—my life was lived in a familiar duality between military duties and a growing intimacy with the Zionist leadership. The meetings of our intelligence group with Shiloah and his colleagues at the Bethlehem Road house aroused speculation in that totally Arab neighborhood. Accordingly General Wilson, Captain Webb and I moved our SOE headquarters to Talbiah, more centrally placed for simultaneous contacts with Jewish, British and Arab communities. Wilson and Webb were soon replaced by Ringrose and Grant-Taylor. The former was a quick-witted colonel of easy temperament who managed to be reasonably industrious amid the hedonistic attractions available at a behind-the-lines base, for in Jerusalem, as in Cairo, the proximity of danger went together with a provisional but lavish comfort. Hitler's armies might overrun Egypt and Palestine at any moment, in which case everything would fall in ruin. But meanwhile there was an "eve of Waterloo" euphoria which provided many Allied officers and officials with pleasant recollections of Cairo and Jerusalem when they were restored in later years to their distant and uneventful homes. Indeed, Jerusalem had a kind of cosmopolitan florescence during the war; Jews, Arabs, British, American, Australian, Free French, exiled Poles, all moved through a united city in a varied social rhythm.

But while for the British, Palestine was one of many interests, and for Arabs one of several arenas of life and struggle, it was for the Jews the last and only destination. It now became the sole chance of saving their identity, for early in 1943 we began to receive such horrifying reports about the fate of European Jewry that the limits of credulity were strained. We now know that the "final solution" of the Jewish problem by mass extermination was decided on January 20, 1942. It took some months before the news reached Jewish leaders in Palestine with enough detail to command belief. The facts were hideous, but inescapable. Millions of Jews—men, women and children, in the communities of Europe all the way from Norway to Greece, across France, Germany, Holland, Belgium, Luxembourg, Italy, Austria, Yugoslavia and especially the densely populated Jewish centers in Poland, Rumania and the western parts of the Soviet Union—were being herded together like cattle, shipped off in sealed railway cars to special camps and there simply destroyed like useless rubbish.

Not even this terrifying, convulsive and revolutionary event had any effect on the British bureaucracy in Palestine, which continued to woo an Arab world that had for the most part taken sides with the Nazis. There was intense sympathy with the Jewish plight in London, where in a moment without parallel in parliamentary history, the House of Commons was brought to its feet in silent mourning for European Jews. This was done on the initiative of James de Rothschild, MP, son of Baron Edmond. But, together with this gesture, there was a relentless assault on the Jewish national home, which was clearly the only Jewish hope of refuge and asylum.

In my own small world the news of this infinite tragedy had two effects. It put an end to any hesitations in my mind about my dedication to Zionism rather than to a renewed academic career; and it even gave a tang of significance to the particular enterprise on which I was engaged in SOE. Within its limited frame of reference, this project was one of the few which seemed likely to bring Jews into head-on physical confrontation with their terrible foe: if Palestine was over-run, the Jews would sell their lives dearly; if, as seemed likely, Mont-gomery's forces would protect them against such contingencies, the parachutists and partisans whom we were training at Mishmar Ha-emek might bring some relief and organized resistance to whatever remained of European Jewry at the end of the war.

There is no doubt that the Palmach benefited greatly from the varied training received under the auspices of SOE, safe from govern-mental repression. Under the direction of Grant-Taylor and other ex-perts, the Palmachniks drilled holes in the bases of most of the country's bridges so that if the Nazis approached, explosives could be quickly inserted and the bridges blown. There was also training in the establishment of secret radio stations. (By a twist of fortune, the Brit-ish government was later to be the victim of its own tuition when the Jewish fighters in 1946 blew up British installations in protest against Bevin's persecution.)

Even in 1942–1943 my task of liaison was not easy. Almost every day one or another of our trainees would be arrested by the British police and charged with illegal possession of firearms. Word of this was flashed to me in Jerusalem, and off I would go into action, attempt-ing to intimidate the civil police with an impressive array of docu-ments (somewhat like modern credit cards) indicating that the defen-dants might be praised for their valor rather than condemned for crime. In fact, some of the Palmachniks became so enthralled with what they were learning that they wished to put their tuition into practice at Britain's expense without even waiting for the arrival of the Nazis. The paradox was that the Palmach was both intensely il-legal and profoundly cherished in different sections of the British con-sciousness. They offered acrobatic opportunities of ingenuity to the misfortunate liaison officer. Nothing could be accomplished, neither the open use of arms nor the harmless acquisition of driving licences if the liaison officer had not enjoyed a measure of trust on both sides. Indeed, as our venture progressed, something of the self-sacrificing zeal of the Palmach trainees began to arouse the interest and admiration of their British tutors. One of them, a Cambridge pro-fessor of Greek, Nicholas Hammond, became, in his quiet way, almost as intense a Zionist zealot as the legendary British soldier Orde Win-gate, who had trained young Jews in the art of defense against Arab attacks. The Jewish Agency and Haganah leadership naturally made full use of the opportunities afforded them by their alliance with a British authority. It was stipulated that there would only be one hundred Palmach trainees in the Mishmar Ha-emek camp; and this indeed was the number at any given moment of inspection. But how could the British General Staff know that they were always the same five hundred, when the Haganah reasonably stipulated that they should all be known by name only to the liaison officer, who would promise to maintain confidentiality? To this day I have no way of estimating how many Palmach trainees were able to use the overt facilities of the Mishmar Ha-emek camp; nor did the SOE officers show great concern if, in the resistance spirit, the Jews of Palestine made the most of their opportunities.

My task was intricate, and in the nature of things, bound to engender an abrasive relationship with the representatives of the British Administration and Military Command, who were engaged in suppressing the Jewish forces whom we were training and encouraging. At the same time, I must have appeared a mysterious figure to the Jews of Jerusalem, Tel Aviv and Haifa, with whom I came in frequent contact without any possibility of discussing the nature of my task.

But all inconveniences were outweighed by the opportunity afforded me to probe the special vitality that moved Palestine Jewry and its leadership. Haganah activity came directly under Jewish Agency leaders such as Ben Gurion, Sharett, Dov Joseph and Eliahu Golomb. But my work also gave me contact with Haganah commanders in the field, principally with the leading resistance figure, Yitzhak Sadeh, whom I used to visit at Kibbutz Yagur near Haifa. A venerable countenance of gray tufty hair, but as yet no beard, contrasted with a juvenile Boy Scout costume of shirt and shorts that was considered in those days to be the mark of pioneering lineage. We would often sit late into the night drinking endless cups of coffee while he discoursed on his memories of the Russian army and spoke with a mixture of paternal criticism and ecstatic praise about the Israeli-born Jews, such as Moshe Dayan and Yigal Allon, now under his command.

The second figure among my Zionist partners was Yochanan Ratner, a professor of architecture at the Technion in Haifa. It was hard to think of a sharper contrast than between his calm, ordered, Central European temperament and the tempestuous moods and untidy improvisations of the Russian-born leaders who set the tone of our nation's political culture. Ratner drew up plans, almost esthetically beautiful in their draftsmanship, for dotting the Palestine landscape with a series of underground fortresses making full use of natural caves and crevices so that the enemy occupier would wish that he had stayed home. I had decided, in agreement with SOE and the Jewish Agency, to remain behind in the event of a Nazi invasion in order to fight from some underground position. I am now certain that I would have had an eventful but exceedingly brief resistance career.

Apart from Sadeh, Ratner and Shiloah, my experience was enriched by contact with a picturesque personality who later became the treasurer of our SOE enterprise at Mishmar Ha-emek. This was David Hacohen, then the director of the contracting firm Solel Boneh, who had already played a role in aiding the invasion of occupied Syria by Free French officers. He maintained a secret radio station at his villa in Mount Carmel. In our project, David's bizarre role as treasurer was to ensure the maximum transfer of British government funds to the coffers of the Palmach. David was what the British officials and officers called "a character." In winter he would put on a long fur coat reaching from neck to heels, which added a special grandeur to his stormy conversations. His usual discourse was a hoarse and strident scream, full of incredulous indignation and emphatic passion. Everything big and small seemed to matter to him equally, and always crescendo. His talent for expletive and a rich vocabulary of Hebrew, Arabic and English imprecations marked him off from his more puritanical Zionist colleagues. I found it hard to imagine that he was the son of a Hebrew writer, Mordechai Ben Hillel Hacohen, who had been a businessman of impeccable respectability in Russia and whose well-trimmed beard and finely garmented person adorned the pages of manuals of Hebrew literature. As time went on, it became apparent that beneath David's outer frivolity there was not only a profound Zionist passion but a serious and well-disciplined political mind. These qualities would come to expression in later years when he pioneered Israel's relations with Asia and served as chairman of Israel's Knesset Foreign Relations Committee.

As I think back on those who composed the SOE operation—General Wilson, Major Hammond, Captain Webb, Major Grant-Taylor, Captain Eban, Golomb, Sadeh, Shiloah, Hacohen, Yochanan Ratner —I find it hard to imagine a more disparate set of characters in any drama. In July 1942 the intrinsic contradiction of our operation became blatant. Much of the tension disappeared in the Middle East as a result of General Bernard Montgomery's brilliant campaign at El Alamein. Instead of living under the shadow of Nazi invasion, with its ghastly prospects of a holocaust, Palestine Jewry could now breathe freely in the knowledge that the enemy was far from the gates. But in the degree that the German peril receded, the likelihood of military and political conflict with the Arabs and British came closer. Nevertheless, the sense of mutual interest in the anti-Nazi struggle, together with Churchill's reassuring messages to Weizmann, had the effect of postponing the inevitable collision. For some months, between the summer of 1942 and the spring of 1943, I had the leisure to break out of my military compound and to become more intimately involved in the country's life.

I was kept in close touch with the political struggle, which was mainly an exercise in suspense. The Zionist task was to postpone any implementation of the White Paper in the hope that the postwar era would bring about a new consideration of Palestine's future by Britain and other powers. The social life of Jerusalem was highly fragmented, but I had an unusually free access to all its parts. I stayed very often, sometimes for weeks on end, with a relative, Annie Landau, the headmistress of the Evelina de Rothschild School. She was a sister of my aunt Elsie Sacks. The family tie brought us together across a gulf of ideological and social separation; Annie Landau had come to Jerusalem in her early youth and was now a stately spinster. Through the generosity of the Anglo-Jewish Association, which sponsored her excellent school, she was able to entertain lavishly and often, rather like a dowager queen whom nobody would lightly contradict. She was rigorously orthodox and had no patience with Zionism. Her circle included the British high commissioner, judges and leading officials, Arab notables, some Jews who belonged to the governing establishment such as Edwin Samuel, the son of the first high commissioner, or those whose views and ways of life gave them a dissident quality in her eyes, such as Dr. Judah L. Magnes, president of the Hebrew University. She lived to a great age, and I was sadly present at her deathbed. Her "anti-Zionism" was more a figure of speech than a reality, for she was passionately attached to every part of the Palestinian landscape and to all the treasures of the Jewish legacy.

I also had access to the homes of the Zionist leaders and could count on being received in the Arab cities and villages, for I was often invited to deliver Arabic lectures in Nablus, Jenin, Jerusalem and Haifa. Somebody in the British Council had discovered something of my Cambridge rhetorical background; during 1943 I gave a series of lectures under the auspices of that body, which filled the large hall of the YMCA while I discoursed on problems of democracy and postwar reconstruction. Since I was a relatively junior staff officer, the heavy attendance at these lectures reinforced my belief that I ought to seek a career in which a talent for expression was relevant.

One of my closest friendships during this period was with Nelson Glueck, head of the American School of Oriental Research. He was a brilliant archaeologist who had virtually discovered the Nabatean civilization and had excavated Solomon's seaport and copper mines in the southern Negev. He was now engaged in expeditions across the Jordan near Petra and Jerash, on which I often accompanied him. During this period I also gave Hebrew lectures in Haifa, Jerusalem,

Tel Aviv and to Palestinian troops in their camp at Sarafand. There must have been very few at that time who were able to move easily across all the varied parts of the Jerusalem tapestry.

I could have wished this period in my life to last longer, but my position in SOE was becoming untenable. When the Nazi threat of invasion receded, the British government no longer saw any purpose in maintaining a potential Jewish resistance movement. It was decided to dismantle the Mishmar Ha-emek camp and to limit the cooperation between SOE and the Jewish Agency to parachutist training, with the purpose of sending infiltrators into occupied Eastern Europe, especially Hungary and Yugoslavia. Thus, in April 1943, I received a curt operational order transferring me back to general headquarters in Cairo.

The Middle East had now become a central theater of war and politics. Accordingly, the British government had established a ministry stationed in Cairo under the direction of a Cabinet member. The Minister of State was Robert Casey, later to be Foreign Minister and Governor-General of Australia. His task was to bring together, under concerted policy direction, all the embassies, commands, supply missions and other manifestations of British power which was then still predominant in the Middle East. At the quiet headquarters of the ministry I found myself working under the orders of Brigadier Iltwyd Clayton, whose function lay more in the diplomatic than in the military field. Together with the British ambassador, Lord Killearn, and his Oriental Counsellor, Sir Walter Smart, Clayton was virtually the architect of British policy throughout the area. He had visions of contributing to a solution of the Palestine problem. Weizmann was in constant contact with him, while his main interlocutor on the Arab side was Musa Alami, a man of moderate temper and idealistic aspiration who had founded an agricultural school in Jericho and was attempting to bring the Palestine Arab leadership into a rational frame of mind. Clayton knew both of my Zionist loyalties and of my qualifications as an Orientalist, and he found the combination congenial. He used me as a kind of sounding board from which he would learn how Zionists might react to various proposals then being contemplated for a Palestine solution at the end of the war.

The rest of 1943 in Cairo was a memorable period in my life. I now came more intensively than before into contact with leaders of Arabic thought and literature. The eminent Taha Hussein presided over a lecture that I gave in the Anglo-Egyptian Union in Arabic and English on the contribution of European Orientalists to the development of Arabic studies. I met the novelist Taufiq al Hakim, a curious mixture of Arab gravity and Gallic charm. His best-known work, *Diary of a District Officer in the Provinces,* was Dickensian in its pervasive humor and in its underlying compassion for the impoverished and the dispossessed. (I thought that the English-speaking world should have some knowledge of this trend in Arabic literature, so I published a translation in London early in 1946 under the name *A Maze of Justice.* Shortly after the war I published my analysis of the modern Arab literary movement in Egypt in the form of a lecture to the Royal Institute of International Affairs at Chatham House.)

As the threat of war subsided and peace came into view, there was a growth of Jewish disquiet about what would happen when hostilities ended. While I was in Cairo during 1943 and 1944, Robert Casey was replaced by Lord Moyne as Minister of State. I was not lofty enough in the hierarchy to have any contact with him, but it was impossible to live in so restricted a framework without hearing what was going on. Thus, early in the summer of 1943 I heard that a British Cabinet Committee under Herbert Morrison was working out a proposal for a solution of the Palestine problem. The recommendation was in favor of partition, giving the Jewish state a better territorial basis than the Peel Report. One of the most constant and tenacious advocates of this solution was Lord Moyne, whose memoranda to London advocating partition were tenacious and constant. Lord Moyne had been regarded as an adversary of Zionism. But in August 1943 Sharett was invited to a talk with Moyne and his assistant, Sir Arthur Rucker, in Cairo. Moyne urged partition, which Sharett rejected, since Zionism was now committed to the Biltmore Programme. Later Lord Moyne was murdered by two Jewish resistance fighters at the orders of the Stern Group (Lechi). They were caught, tried and hanged. In their trial they displayed a heroic dignity that moved many people who did not necessarily support the orders that their commanders had given them. The murder of his friend so alienated Churchill that he froze all treatment of the Jewish-state proposal that Moyne had advocated.

It was during this period of my sojourn in Cairo that I had my only glimpse of Winston Churchill as Prime Minister. He was on his way from one of the many summit conferences with Roosevelt and Stalin, and he appeared one day in 1944 at a combined meeting of officials of the British embassy and the Minister of State's office. He was plump and pink-cheeked, and he growled, spluttered and grunted rather like a consummate actor giving an imitation of himself. He was alternately tyrannical and benign in his discourse, intolerant of any other point of view, yet confident in a relaxed kind of way that things would eventually work out as he wished. During this session he suddenly bellowed with a sonority that horrified the pro-Arab British officialdom, "I am a Zionist. Why should not the Jews who bore the brunt of the Nazi scourge bear their flag aloft when mankind celebrates its victory?" He glared around the room, and understandably, got no negative answer to the question. At that time few people used to contradict anything that he said.

Fierce battles were still raging across the Mediterranean, but it was on the world after victory that most minds were focused. It was still the assumption of the Western world that the Middle East would remain under British influence. On the other hand, it was clear that the colonial patterns were dissolving. Any Western power that wanted influence in the Middle East would have to pay greater deference to the life and culture of the Middle Eastern peoples. This principle brought Brigadier Clayton to consider the establishment of a training center in which officers, officials and business representatives who planned to make their careers in the Middle East would get a working knowledge of Arabic and a general grounding in the history of the region. I worked for some months in Cairo, drawing up the academic blueprint for what was to become the Middle East Center for Arab Studies (MECAS). To my surprise, the audacious decision was made to set it up not as anticipated in Cairo or Beirut, but in the Old City of Jerusalem. The building of the Austrian Hospice near the Damascus Gate was requisitioned for the purpose, and the Center was given a flamboyant commander, Colonel Bertram Thomas. He had made a sensational reputation two decades previously when he crossed the Rub‘ al Khali, the empty desert of the Arabian peninsula, which none had traversed before him. He set down his records in vivid prose. He had not achieved or attempted much since then and his mind seems to have stagnated through lack of evolution. It was also a shock to me to find that the handsome young man, with a Roman face portrayed in newspaper reports, had now become flaccid and alcoholic in appearance and temperament. But his fame as an Orientalist had carried him into Clayton's favor as the director of the proposed Center. The effect of this was that I could count on moving back to Jerusalem in a capacity that was both official and academic.

Before this, however, I got a far more durable benefit from my Cairo residence. One day in 1943 at a luncheon in the home of a well-known physician, Dr. Kleeberg in Jerusalem, I had met a Palestinian Jewish engineer, Simcha Ambache, who, having been born of pioneer immigrants in Neve Zedek near Jaffa, had gone to Egypt as a qualified engineer in search of employment, which was hard to find in the primitive society of Palestinian Jewry at that time. The Ambache

51

family had lived for many years at Ismailia near the Suez Canal. Simcha Ambache had prospered both in his professional and financial efforts; he now lived in Kamel Mohammed Street in Zamalek, Cairo, in a spacious mansion that had been constructed for the Mosseri family. Ambache's name struck a chord, for I had had a brief encounter with his son, Nachman, at Cambridge. When I told Mr. Ambache that I expected to be posted to Cairo on the termination of my SOE mission, he courteously invited me to call. His was one of several homes in which Palestinian and other Jewish officers would find relief from their military tedium.

When I reached Cairo later in the year, I shared an apartment with a Cambridge friend, Gershon Ellenbogen, across the street from Simcha Ambache, who was living alone in his large house. His wife and three daughters had been dispatched to South Africa when Rommel's armies were within uncomfortable proximity to Cairo. Rumor had it that the three girls in their different ways represented a broad gamut of charm and beauty. It was even alleged authoritatively that there were three pianos in the house—a convincing testimony to the emphasis on culture. The children had been educated in French-speaking schools, but a governess from Jerusalem kept their native Hebrew alive. Mrs. Ambache's parents, Mihel and Gittel Steinberg, had been among the founders of the village of Motza near Jerusalem, and it was to this solid bulwark of pioneer Zionism that the Ambache children would return from year to year.

When I went to call on Simcha Ambache he told me casually that the eldest of his daughters, Suzy, would be returning home before the others to continue her studies at the American University of Cairo. Sure enough, on my next visit, there was Suzy in all her blond and stately radiance. I had come, I saw—and was totally conquered. While her background was of Egyptian Jewry, the actual texture of her mind and loyalties was determined by the Motza background. The central ethic of the family was pioneering Zionism; and Hebrew as well as French and English were fluently on her tongue, so that there was no gap of sentiment or ideals between us. Every thought and emotion were in harmony.

I now began an implacable campaign to win her in marriage. My departure for Jerusalem to establish the Middle East Center for Arab Studies interrupted this quest, but it also gave our feelings the crucial test of separation. Whenever there was a week of leave to be won or extorted from my superiors in Jerusalem, I got a visa to Cairo from the Egyptian consul-general, Mahmoud Fawzi, later to become my adversary as Egyptian Foreign Minister. I would then take the train across the Sinai Desert, or in a more venturesome mood, fly by the one-engine Misr aircraft, which would make the journey in an hour and a half. Some of these planes had the appearance of being held together with cardboard, string and chewing gum. On some occasions my self-confidence was diminished by the spectacle of the pilot leaning back in his seat with one hand on the plane's rudder while the other held a copy of an Egyptian newspaper, which he studied with nonchalance. Once the spirit moved him to bring down the aircraft on an airstrip in the desert in order to visit his brother-in-law before pursuing the scheduled flight to Cairo.

Finally my persistence bore fruit. On the eve of the new year of 1945 Suzy and I became engaged to be married. It was typical of all our subsequent life, with its constant pull between private rights and public duties, that the very next morning I was on my way back to Jerusalem to rejoin the Middle East Center for Arab Studies.

It was not always easy in wartime to translate engagement into marriage. First, there was need of official army approval, since Suzy, though of Palestinian Jewish parentage, was herself of Egyptian birth. Therefore, in order to protect my interests, a suitably qualified British officer from the General Staff visited her at home, presumably to ascertain whether Suzy wore a black veil and a ring through her nose in the manner of Egyptian peasant women, to whose charms British officers sometimes succumbed in their "going native" moods. Overwhelmed by the extremely non-Egyptian atmosphere of the Ambache home, the officer went away without daring to ask Suzy if she could read and write.

There was still the need to synchronize the marriage with a period of leave from the Center. This, however, would only occur after Passover; and a rabbinic injunction provides that in the fifty days of the Omer, between Passover and Pentecost, there is only one day (the thirty-third) on which a marriage can be sanctified in Jewish law. Weeks of postponement stretched out before us. There was no religious bar to our marriage before Passover, but a prudent military regulation provided for a three-month delay between official approval and the wedding itself—a final opportunity for repentance. But the chaplains to the British armed forces, Rabbi Israel Brodie and Rabbi Isaac Fabricant, used their good offices to spare me the cooling-off period.

I told my surprised family in London of my engagement in a letter with explanatory photographs of Suzy. Among my Zionist friends in Jerusalem, there had been much concern. Rumor had it that Eban was going to marry an Egyptian! This alarm was only partly laid to rest when Reuven Shiloah and David Hacohen, by much careful espionage, were able to report that the mysterious bride was after all a

Jewess, since Major Eban had been a frequent visitor to the "Mosseri house." This was only partially reassuring. The assumption was that I was marrying into the assimilated aristocracy of Egyptian Jews, in whom the Zionist passion burned, if at all, on a very low flame. Finally, Sharett rescued the frayed nerves of the Zionist establishment by reporting that the Ambache parents, both born in Palestine, were well known to him from his early youth and that I was not contracting an anti-Zionist marriage.

I went through the beautiful ritual in the familiar bridegroom's attitude of ecstatic stupor. However, I remember reflecting how the guests symbolized the diversity of my attachments even at that time. Out of the corner of one eye I saw David Ben Gurion, plunged in meditation. Teddy Kollek, Ben Gurion's loyal supporter and friend, was there, as well as the Chief Rabbi of Egypt, almost blind, but splendid in blue and black vestments as he raised his hands aloft in the priestly benediction. There were the Jewish chaplains to the British armed forces, Fabricant and Cashdan. My cousin Neville Halper, a captain in the Medical Corps, whom I had fortuitously encountered in a Cairo bookshop, was best man. Nearby was Ab Kramer, an air force officer and an old colleague in the Zionist youth movement. There were tarbooshed Egyptians, friends of my father-in-law's, and Brigadier Clayton in scarlet-tabbed uniform and endless medals, at the head of the British official contingent. I wrote later to a friend: "I enjoyed it far more than any other wedding that I had ever attended. It was the first time I have been near enough to the center of the proceedings to hear and see what was going on. Suzy looked radiant. Her white *tulle* quite overshadowed my khaki barathea, and she undoubtedly looked the better of the two of us."

Our honeymoon took us by train to Upper Egypt, where we sailed the Nile and admired the antiquities of Luxor and Aswan. After a brief stop in Cairo for the Seder service, we made for Jerusalem, where we planned the continuation of our honeymoon in Galilee. But Suzy chose that moment for contracting the mumps and spent a week in Hadassah Hospital on Mount Scopus, where, with an eye on posterity, we both prayed silently—and successfully—for my immunity.

Our first home in Jerusalem was in a tiny apartment at the American School of Oriental Research, a building on its own grounds just outside Herod's Gate, near the St. George Cathedral on the east side of the Dominican Church. Nelson Glueck had become my closest friend. I was one of the few mortals that he could beat at tennis. He infected me with his archaeological fervor, introduced me to the Nabataean relics and took me to Bedouin feasts near Jerash and Petra.

I in my turn kept him in touch with Zionist developments and introduced him to Weizmann at Rehovot. I later heard that he was enrolled in the American intelligence service, the OSS, of which he told me nothing at the time.

Over twenty officers and a few civilians from oil companies had been selected for the first course at MECAS. I was in full charge of the language program which was designed to enable the students to acquire a full reading and listening knowledge of newspaper and radio Arabic within a year. An Arab teacher took charge of the colloquial instruction. History and politics were the responsibility of George Kirk, who later became an editor and research worker at the Royal Institute of International Affairs in London. His anti-Zionism was ferocious to the point of obsession until Nasser challenged Britain's position in 1956, whereupon Kirk began to think of Israel as a divine instrument of wrath against his country's foes. At MECAS much of the tuition consisted of lectures by invited dignitaries and experts. There was a procession of British Orientalists— Clayton, Glubb, Elphinstone, Kirkbride, the high commissioners and military commanders and some Arabs, including Albert Hourani and Musa Alami. And, on one unforgettable occasion I persuaded Chaim Weizmann himself to lead the discussion on Zionism.

Living in the Old City amid the strident noises and pungent smells of an Arab community, with the muezzin chanting from the minaret, the radio sets blaring away and shopkeepers screaming the quality of their wares, the students found themselves able to absorb the atmosphere as well as the structure of Arabic speech. Since they had been selected out of many dozens of applicants, the level of intellectual curiosity was high. Bertram Thomas filled the Center with social activity. His academic contributions were not ambitious, but the wines were mellow, and soon the scent of Allied victory took the tension out of what was theoretically a military unit. Beyond the busy schedules of my teaching, I commuted between the Arab Old City, the British official circle, and most of all, the Jewish life in Jerusalem and beyond. As I have mentioned, there were notably few people who had ever lived so integrally in those three divided worlds, but even for me, the divisions were growing wider and would soon compel me to an act of choice.

In the third month of our married life, the news of Germany's surrender came to us in Jerusalem. There was a special quality in the celebration of that event in that place. In historic terms, Jerusalem had triumphed over Valhalla. The most monstrous tyranny of all times had been overthrown. At the same time, it was evident that the war had been a kind of cement holding the conflicting elements of the Palestine population together in uneasy tolerance; all of us knew that nothing would be determined until hostilities came to an end. It followed that with the world conflict approaching its conclusion, the regional tensions would become more intense. "Wait until after the war" had been the slogan which kept the country in volcanic tranquillity for nearly six years. On Victory Day there was a ritual amount of dancing in the streets and hotels, but for the Arab population, the end of Hitler seemed to prove no moral point, while for the Jews there was the haunting knowledge that when the curtain went up on liberated Europe, the spectacle of Jewish disaster would be too horrendous to behold.

It also became a personal turning point for me. During the Potsdam Conference in July, a general election was announced in Britain. The Labour Party was proposing not only that Palestine become a Jewish national home but that there be an exchange of populations with the Arabs encouraged to "move out as the Jews moved in." This was the formula enunciated by Hugh Dalton, Labour's acknowledged spokesman on foreign affairs. I had not sundered all my links with the Labour Party since my university days. It now became known that the party was looking for young candidates who had distinguished themselves academically and had reached respectable military ranks. I was sitting in the King David Hotel with Francis Noel Baker, son of Philip Noel Baker, the Labour Party's most earnest supporter of international organizations, when we each simultaneously received an approach from London. Mine came from Harold Laski, who had steadily risen in the party hierarchy since I got to know him during my student days. He wished to know if I would be ready to fight for a constituency at Farnborough, a military-garrison city, largely populated by retired red-faced white-mustached colonels of fierce Tory loyalties. It was obvious to Laski that I would be crushingly defeated, but the act of self-sacrifice would entitle me to a more promising constituency in a later struggle. Anyhow, it would be a beginning, and after all, I was barely thirty years old. Francis Noel Baker was offered an equally hopeless venture at Preston in Lancashire. Since, unlike me, he had no special links tying him to Jerusalem, he used the opportunity of demobilization offered to accredited candidates and disappeared westward. A few weeks later I learned that his hopeless venture had in fact become a lucrative effort, for he was swept in with a tidal wave that brought masses of Labour MP's into what had been considered safe Tory seats. I myself courteously rejected the electoral offer. Without any clear knowledge of my specific plans, I knew that Jerusalem was my focal point and that if I abandoned it, I would be leaving home. I was able to rejoice in the circumstance that the Labour candidate for Farnborough was heavily defeated even in that golden Labour year.

The whole incident, however, reminded me that I would now have to make firm decisions about my future vocation or career. Indeed, the question whether it was going to be a career or a vocation was the essence of my predicament. In the meantime I remained with MECAS, which I could not have abandoned without damage to the academic prospects of the twenty-one officers confided to my care. In midsummer Suzy and I had moved from the American School to an apartment of our own at North Talpiot, where we lived until September 1946.

The house itself was a small cube of flaking cement, unrepaired and untended through the years of war. On the upper floor dwelt the scientist Marcus Reiner, later to become a central figure in the development of the Haifa Technion and to live into his ninetieth year. Across a small hedge dwelt Chaim Kalvarisky, one of the elder statesmen of Palestine Jewry, who had an obsessive belief in the possibility of Arab-Jewish understanding. He worked assiduously to promote contacts with Arab leaders under the overall guidance of Judah L. Magnes, president of the Hebrew University, with whom also I had conceived as much of a friendship as our gap of years and his own frigid temperament would allow. There was no telephone in our own part of the North Talpiot house, and whenever I was called, I would be summoned to the Kalvarisky residence, where, to my embarrassment, I would often hold conversations with Sharett and other Jewish Agency officials with whom Kalvarisky was not on the best of terms.

It was lonely at North Talpiot. Not more than a dozen houses were clustered in the street. One night a hand came through the window of our bedroom to abscond with my trousers and the meager contents of its pockets. But everything at North Talpiot was redeemed by a landscape so astonishing as to defy description and to put all anticipation to mockery. There was a panorama of rolling hills, some of them dotted with the buildings of new Jerusalem, others cradling the Old City with the magnificent Dome of the Rock and the ancient Wall. Far beyond on a clear day, the Moab Mountains were visible, suffused in the evening by a mauve light in which the waters of the Dead Sea could be observed. In front of us lay the Valley of Hinnom, very far in its gracious aspect from the "hell" with which "Gehinnom" was traditionally identified. Far to the right, surrounded by dark-green cyprus trees, was the white palace of the high commissioner, one of the few successful architectural enterprises of British Mandatory Palestine. I saw more clearly than before what George Adam Smith had meant when he spoke of men "looking at life under that lofty imagination." Did it seem superstitious to believe that the Judean landscape might have generated something of the reflectiveness and awe that made for prophetic experience?

*The Break
in the Clouds
1945-1947*

OUR EXPECTATIONS OF GROWING TENSIONS IN JERUSALEM AFTER THE WAR
were fulfilled more violently than we could have imagined. When the
Labour Party came into office in July 1945, Ernest Bevin was appointed as Prime Minister Clement Attlee's Foreign Secretary. He immediately subjected the Jewish people to a shock of sadistic intensity.
Instead of abrogating the 1939 White Paper, opening the gates of the
Jewish national home and offering salvation for the concentration-
camp refugees in Europe, he simply told the Jews "not to push to the
head of the queue" but rather to devote their efforts to the "reconstruction of Europe." On an unforgettable November 13, 1945, he
made a statement shattering all the hopes that Jews had invested in
the prospect of better times after the war. Bevin virtually confirmed
the White Paper, repudiated the Labour Party's conference platform
and observed piously, "We cannot accept the view that the Jews
should be driven out of Europe."

Only a few weeks before, President Truman had received a report
from his special emissary, Earl Harrison, who had visited the concentration camps, where Jewish survivors lingered on in dull despair.
"They want to be evacuated now," said Harrison. "Palestine is definitely and pre-eminently their first choice. Only in Palestine will they
be welcome and find peace and quiet and be given an opportunity to
live and work." Yet in his November 13 statement, Bevin bluntly
ascribed Truman's interest in the Jews to his hope for a great num-

59

ber of votes in New York State. (The presidential election was more than three years away!) Bevin also hinted that Truman's action was motivated by a desire to see that no more Jews got to the United States. He referred offensively to "a person named Earl Harrison" whose report he described as "having set the whole thing back." In an effort to involve the United States more deeply in his own predicaments, Bevin had announced the appointment of an Anglo-American committee of inquiry to consider the position of the Jews in Europe and to propose a solution of the Palestine problem to the two governments. It was evident from his hooligan tone that the Jewish people had come face to face with one of its cruelest adversaries.

I was in close touch with my friends in the Zionist leadership during those days and I found them almost inconsolable. In Jerusalem, Bevin's callous statements had burst the dikes of Jewish restraint. British troops and Jewish resistance groups were henceforward in almost daily conflict.

Amid such events, I found my own routine at the Middle East Center for Arab Studies irrelevant and even abrasive. Indeed, I began to give that work my minimal attention and to give as much service as I could to the embattled Zionist leadership. As an officer in a British military institution I could, of course, only work anonymously. It was thus that I drafted two memoranda for the Jewish Agency to the Anglo-American Committee on Palestine; and it was in an even stronger anonymity that I began to write editorials for Gershon Agronsky's *Palestine Post,* castigating the Mandatory government in full polemical fervor. On one occasion I wrote an article reproving the British authorities for stopping the arrival of the immigrant ship *Spezzia.* The Palestine Jewish leaders began a hunger strike. When I came into the British officers' mess in the Austrian Hospice the next morning, I found colonels and majors fuming over this editorial: "If I could just get my hands on the bastard who wrote this claptrap, I'd wring his dirty bloody neck." After listening to this denunciation, I quietly headed for the *Post* to write another blast.

But this duality could not be long or easily maintained. While my Zionist work was inhibited by cautious anonymity, the Arab office in Jerusalem was making free use of Albert Hourani and others who, in a certain sense, were my opposite numbers on the other side. I was now seeing more of Weizmann, who was beginning to be alienated from his Zionist colleagues. Ben Gurion was quite openly aiming for the leadership. Weizmann's failing health was also bringing his leadership toward its end, but he still had vast gifts to offer to Jewish statesmanship. "Today," wrote Richard Crossman in his diary on March 8, 1946, "we had Weizmann, who looks like a weary and more humane version of Lenin, very tired, very ill. He spoke for two hours with a magnificent mixture of passion and scientific detachment. He is the first witness who has frankly and openly admitted that the issue is not between right and wrong, but between the greater and lesser injustice."

Zionist leaders, especially Weizmann, Ben Gurion and Sharett, were now hinting that an "adequate partition" plan might win Jewish acquiescence. They no longer saw any hope in the continuation of British rule. But when the Anglo-American Committee reached Lausanne, it rejected partition as a "counsel of despair." It proposed that the White Paper be abolished, and 100,000 Jewish immigrants be admitted at once. Land restrictions should be removed and Palestine should be prepared for international trusteeship with no statehood for either Jews or Arabs.

Although the report had rejected Jewish proposals for a sovereign state, it was not a hostile document. Some Zionists were consoled by its immigration provisions, while others were alienated by its rejection of Jewish independence. In any case, it was hardly worthwhile for Jews to quarrel about it, since the British government had no intention of implementing it. Bevin violated his promise to the committee that he would "accept any verdict reached unanimously by its members." The report moved him to new depths of anti-Semitic invective.

Violence and sabotage in Palestine became more intense. Dark despair descended on the refugee camps in Europe. One day there was an exchange of fire in Jerusalem in which one of my MECAS students, Captain Dickie Clark, was killed in a skirmish between the British police and the resistance fighters of the Irgun Zvai Leumi (IZL). Here I saw the full paradox of colonial repression. The victim of the shooting was not an imperialist, but an intelligent young man into whose face I had looked every day for over a year. One of the victims of Bevin's callousness was a young man who, without any political interest, was simply in Jerusalem trying to learn something about Arabic and Hebrew culture. As an individual, he was not the enemy of the Jewish nation at all.

As the summer of 1946 approached, the British Foreign Office renewed its efforts to secure the prolongation of my service with MECAS. This time I refused. Instead I began to ponder Sharett's insistent request to me to join the Political Department of the Jewish Agency. Earlier, in March, Weizmann had strongly pressed me to do this, but I had not been free to give an answer while my tenure at the Center was still unexhausted.

A new phase in Jewish resistance came in June when Haganah blew up many bridges in a daring operation of wide range. The Irgun succeeded in getting the death sentence of some of its members commuted by capturing five British officers and holding them hostage. In desperation, the British authorities decided to hit back.

On June 29, a Sabbath day, Sharett was to have had lunch with Suzy and me in our North Talpiot home. I knew that this was not going to be a mere social encounter. It was to be the final conference, in which I would give Sharett my decision. When the appointed hour for the luncheon came and went without any sign of him, I knew that something must be radically wrong. Moshe Sharett was rigorously punctual. It was obvious that if he was a half-hour late without announcement, something catastrophic must have happened. At two o'clock we turned on the radio, which was announcing that British military operations had begun against the Jewish Agency and Haganah on the ground that they were responsible for "lawlessness" and violence. Jewish settlements, including Kibbutz Yagur, were being combed for arms, and Jewish Agency leaders, including Sharett, Dov Joseph and Rabbi Maimon, had been arrested for internment at Latrun. Ben Gurion and Moshe Sneh, head of the Haganah, had slipped off to Paris, where they were to live in exile for some months. Weizmann was left in the peace and dignity of his Rehovot residence. Some British officers, including the chief intelligence officer, Martin Charteris (later private secretary to Queen Elizabeth II), told me that they had hoped Weizmann would collaborate with the British high commissioner irrespective of the detention of his Zionist colleagues. But when British officials called on Weizmann, he blasted them out of the room with such violent denunciation that they concluded that maybe the "moderates" had been locked up in Latrun, while the old "extremist" had been left loose in Rehovot.

One day in July I was making my way from MECAS in the Old City to the King David Hotel, where I was going to have a haircut and meet Suzy on her way back from a piano lesson in Rehavia. I have never been particularly fanatical about punctuality and on that occasion I had no cause to regret that weakness. As I approached the hotel there was a vast explosion. The King David, which housed the British Administration and Military Command, had been blown up by combined units of Jewish resistance forces with heavy loss of British, Arab and Jewish life—more than ninety killed. When I reached the hotel I found it to be a smoking, dusty shambles. To my infinite relief, Suzy had been even less punctual than I. In the subsequent controversy, IZL leaders explained that they had intended to set off the explosive only after the building had been evacuated following a telephone warning.

A few days later on the notice board of MECAS I saw an order of the day by General Evelyn Barker, commander of British troops in the Palestine area. It was a vulgar, anti-Semitic tract urging troops to avoid Jewish shops in order to "hit the Jews in their pocket, which is the only language that the race understands." It seemed to me that the public interest demanded that the style as well as the contents of the document become widely known. It bore no classified status. But to avoid conspicuous action, I walked past the notice board six or seven times, threw a nonchalant glance at the letter, memorized a dozen words and repaired to the washroom, where I wrote them down. Then, with the text complete, I made for the Eden Hotel, where I asked to see John Kimche, who was at the height of his professional fame as correspondent of the London *Observer*, the *Economist* and the *Tribune*. Within a few minutes Kimche had cabled the letter out of Jerusalem to the international press, where it reverberated with full force.

The episode may have been small in itself, but it did much to illustrate how untenable British rule in Palestine had become. The Mandate had once been a high vision and it had known some years of radiance. But it had now declined into what Winston Churchill was to call "a squalid war" between the Mandatory government and the Jewish national home, which it had been appointed to strengthen and sustain. The national home was not to be "facilitated," but curbed and stunted and its hope of independence snuffed out in order that the number of Arab states might be increased from seven to eight— and eventually to twenty. And all this was to happen in an hour of agony for the Jewish people such as no family of the human race had ever known. It was in the chasm of this moral paradox that the British Mandate sank down and died.

The week after Sharett's internment, a letter came to me from him through the underground postal service that he had organized from the Latrun detention camp. It was communicated to me by David Horowitz, who was now a very senior Zionist official in charge of political work in Jerusalem. As I opened the envelope I saw that the letter contained one word and a signature: "Nu? M.S." I replied with similar brevity: "Certainly. A.E." Thus, with a verbal baptism of un-Zionist succinctness, I had thrown in my professional lot with the Zionist cause.

In the natural course, other influences had been brought to bear upon me. Friends in England had sought to persuade me that there was no "future" in professional Zionism and that I could probably be more "useful" if I pursued a successful political career in London. From my family, and especially my mother, I caught veiled hints that my temperament might respond better to the tranquillity of academic life than to the turbulence into which I was obviously going to move.

On the other hand, Suzy and her parents, with their deep Land of Israel roots, gave me every encouragement to choose the harder road.

Thus, on a day in September 1946, I walked out of the Middle East Center for Arab Studies in the Old City, passed through the Damascus Gate over to Rehavia, went into David Horowitz's office, signed documents enlisting me in the Jewish Agency Political Department, went to North Talpiot to pack my bags and left with Suzy for London via Cairo from the Jerusalem railway station. I was seen off by Walter Eytan, then a spokesman for the Jewish Agency in Jerusalem.

In Cairo, Suzy picked up a few articles evoking childhood memories in her parents' house, and we flew by way of Tunis, Malta and Nice to London, where I took up my duties in the Information Department of the Jewish Agency. I worked in the room which had been the abode of Nahum Sokolow until his sudden death in 1936. From that august desk I called up my mother and pointed out with filial irony that it was "all her fault" for abandoning me on November 1, 1917, in order to translate the Balfour Declaration at the Zionist office in Piccadilly. My closest colleague was Maurice Rosette, later to be Clerk of the Knesset.

Our home was in a small but charming Highgate apartment rented to us by a friend of Weizmann's, Sigmund Gestetner, whose widow is one of our closest and dearest friends to this day. In another part of West London my old collaborators Reuven Shiloah and Teddy Kollek were established at the Atheneum Court, where they were exercising their persuasive talents on British officials by a judicious mixture of careful argument and expensive cigars and alcohol. Namier was no longer on the scene, but Weizmann was still in residence at the Dorchester, exchanging letters with Ben Gurion at his place of exile in the Royal Monceau Hotel in Paris.

If I had to condemn an adversary to harsh and unusual punishment, I would sentence him to be an official of the Jewish Agency in London in the winter of 1946. In Palestine, Jewish resistance fighters were engaged in murderous combat with British soldiers. Immigrants were arriving in Palestine "illegally" and being apprehended and sent away. Exasperated British troops, longing to get home with the war at an end, were bogged down in a conflict with Jewish adversaries whom their vicious commander General Barker advised them to regard with "hatred and contempt." The expense, humiliation and sterility of the British task in Palestine was fully seized by public opinion in London, which reacted with hostility to the Zionist cause. Jewish Agency officials were being treated not as the emissaries of a legitimate national movement, but as the unwanted agents of a hostile power.

London itself was dreary, shabby, gray, its people badly fed and some-what unwashed during a winter in which food was scarce and a coal crisis generated a frigidity even more intense than usual. The debris of shattered buildings stood as a grisly reminder of recent suffering and death.

Yet, with all its defects, London was still the focus of Zionism's political struggle. Despite predictions about future American involvement, it was still the British government which decided how many immigration certificates were granted, what facilities existed for the purchase of land, and how the government of Palestine was to be fashioned. Although we had some supporters among members of Attlee's Labour Cabinet, Ernest Bevin had full control. In view of my own political background, the fact that our adversaries were members of the Labour Party added to the bitterness of my experience. My task was to capture some islands of sympathy and understanding in this wilderness of alienation. So I wrote articles, pamphlets, booklets, lunched with editors, reporters, and Members of Parliament, and occasionally accompanied an executive member, Brodetsky or Locker, to an interview with the Colonial Secretary or a Foreign Office official. At the Royal Institute of International Affairs at Chatham House, I did battle with the defenders of Arabism, Arnold Toynbee and Albert Hourani. My English translation of Taufiq al Hakim's book *A Maze of Justice* was published and favorably reviewed, but owing to postwar austerity, the paper and binding were miserably dejected.

I seemed to have committed myself to a hopeless treadmill of a life with no spark of light at the end of any visible tunnel. For Suzy, who had known nothing all her life but Mediterranean sunshine, the fog and gloom were even more overpowering. Within a few weeks of our arrival in London, I sent her with my mother in search of sun at Lugano, where it rained steadily for nine frustrating days.

As soon as I arrived at the Jewish Agency's Information Department, I made a survey of the hundred or so people who could be said to have a formative influence in British Middle Eastern policy. These were to be found in the Cabinet, in Parliament, among newspaper editors, in universities, in institutes of foreign affairs, and among those who had the closest access to the ear of policy makers. I found that the majority of these had never come within the orbit of the Zionist information effort, which had concentrated with good results on the parliamentary parties, neglecting the experts and Orientalists who formulated the strategic analyses on which the government based its policies. When I outlined my strategy to Ben Gurion during one of his early visits after the war, he commented that if a systematic approach to information had been made a few years earlier, the collapse of British support of Zionism might have been averted or at least postponed. He thought at this point it was too late. There was no likelihood that the Arab lobby in London would change its views now that Ernest Bevin gave it such exhilarating support. Moreover, Britain herself was in the last throes of her career as an imperial power. She would act henceforward out of a sense of decline and weakness, not out of confidence or strength. Nevertheless, it would be our duty to exhaust the British phase in Zionist history with a last attempt to see if a modus vivendi could be ensured.

Apart from resuming pre-war friendships, I formed some new ones. I now had frequent contact with the Family—the name given by Zionist custom to the three friends who had sustained Weizmann since Balfour Declaration days. Simon Marks and Israel Sieff, later to be ennobled as barons, combined the administration of their Marks & Spencer business empire with a touching devotion to every Zionist enterprise. The third member of the firm, the Family and the trio, was Harry Sacher. The harmony between the three was remarkable, since nobody could have devised more divergent personalities. Marks was short, dark, wiry and intense with a "no nonsense" kind of pragmatism that yielded to sentimentality in his Zionist and family relationships. Israel Sieff was more relaxed, less urgent and seemed to have been invented by the lexicographers in order to justify the existence of the word "urbane." He had an original approach to economic analysis which made him the confidant of many British statesmen in both parties. His wife, Becky, Simon Marks's sister, was a volcanic figure in her own right, erupting with singular energy as a hostess and a leader of women's Zionism. Harry Sacher outdid Sieff in the appearance of relaxation. He was an intellectual with an exquisite gift of language and a keen analytical power which he was too languid to put to maximal expression. I never found out exactly what he was doing at Marks & Spencer, since his desk was always unlittered and the telephone seldom rang. If he had any interest in the sale of clothing articles, he certainly kept his enthusiasm under strict control. His wife, Miriam, another sister of Simon Marks's, was an artist in imaginative generosity which led her to finance archaeological digs, a Jerusalem park and medical causes with great munificence. The next generation of the Family has carried on the tradition, notably through Sir Marcus Sieff and Michael Sacher. In all Zionism's vicissitudes, the Family loomed on the horizon with affluent aid and strong moral sustenance. It was a relief to escape from Great Russell Street into the world of superb wine and choice cigars at Michael House in Baker Street, for the Family was far from ascetic even in difficult times.

While I pursued my information work with more show of self-confidence than I felt, I found myself becoming more and more needed by Weizmann in the deepest personal sense. He had put a greal deal of faith in Churchill and Roosevelt. Now Roosevelt was dead, leaving behind him the equivocal effects of his promise to King Ibn Saud, from whom "he had learnt more about the Middle East in a single hour than in all the previous years." Churchill's promise of an adequate partition plan had been paralyzed by Lord Moyne's death, and was now frustrated by the change of government. Churchill himself, as he often testified, had been so alienated by the killing of his friend that he had "ceased to care" what happened to the Zionist enterprise. Weizmann saw no chance of success with the prosaic and restricted intellects of Bevin and the Colonial Secretary, George Hall. He had no hope of securing the transforming effects that he had brought about with the more rhapsodical Lloyd George and Balfour. He had also made the error of staying away from Palestine too long. His visit in November 1944 on his seventieth birthday had shown what a profound emotion he could stir in Palestine Jewry. But the effects had worn off. Indeed, they had become obliterated by the news of the Holocaust and the desperation inculcated by the policy of the Labour government. His correspondence with Ben Gurion, now "exiled" in Paris, was volatile. Sometimes it was full of temperamental political frictions. At other times it blossomed into harmony, as for instance when he received a letter from Ben Gurion in the following terms:

> *Whatever your views are on all this, you remain for me the elect of Jewish history, representing beyond compare the suffering and glory of the Jews. And wherever you go you will be attended by the love and faithful esteem of me and my colleagues.*

Despite this lyrical and deferential language, I knew that the knives were out for Weizmann. His dismissal was being seriously planned at the very time when Zionism was internationally isolated and stood in greatest need of his experience and prestige. Throughout November, I worked closely with him on his address for the forthcoming Zionist Congress. The procedure was that we would talk almost at random for two or three hours. I would then go and prepare a draft and review it with him, sometimes together with other friends such as Isaiah Berlin and Leonard Stein. His opening address to the Congress, while representing his own inner thoughts and impulses, was drafted by my hand. Its central theme was the catastrophic transformation in the Jewish condition, arising from the depletion of its numbers by the Holocaust and the betrayal by Britain of her international duty.

While Weizmann and most of the workers at Great Russell Street went to Basel for the Zionist Congress, I stayed behind to hold the fort and maintain some link of contact with the British government. From Switzerland came word of the drama of Weizmann's last Congress appearance. The draft that I had helped him write was well received. "The shadow of tragic bereavement is upon us tonight," he had said in the opening address, casting a quizzical glance over the assembly as if to ask where German, Polish, Hungarian, Dutch and Belgian Jewry had gone. The voice was choked and the eyes tense and painful behind the dark glasses. "The greatest malice in the annals of inhumanity was turned against us and found our people with no hope of defense. European Jewry had been engulfed in a tidal wave. Its centers of life and culture have been ravaged, its habitations laid waste."

He spoke of the White Paper: "Few documents in history have worse consequences for which to answer." He told of British ministerial promises which had been broken: "It seemed incredible that anybody could be playing fast and loose with us when we were so battered and exhausted. If there is antagonism directed against the British Government, its sole origin is indignation at Britain's desertion of her trust." He spoke lucidly of Arab hostility: "How can it be moderate for them to claim seven states and extreme for us to claim one?"

In a tense atmosphere he declared that he understood the motives which led many young Jews in Palestine to violence: "It is difficult in such circumstances to retain a belief in a victory of peaceful ideals, and yet I affirm without any hesitation that we have to retain it. Jews came to Palestine to build, not to destroy. Masada for all its heroism was a disaster in our history. Zionism was to mark the end of our glorious deaths and the beginning of a new path whose watchword is life."

These ideas and moods were capable of unifying the Zionist movement and the Congress. Weizmann had too much difficulty in reading the text to make much of an oratorical impression. But the tone of the speech brought him closer to the delegates. He had given deep expression to their indignation and grief.

But I had reckoned without his combative spirit. In the debate on his address, he became enraged when an American Zionist said that Palestine Jewry "should revolt against Britain while American Jews would give full political and moral support." Weizmann now uttered the rebuke which may have cost him his presidency: "Moral and political support is very little when you send other people to the barricades to face tanks and guns. The eleven new settlements just established in the Negev have a far greater weight than a hundred speeches about resistance, especially when the speeches are made in New York while the proposed resistance is to be made in Tel Aviv and Jerusalem."

As he delivered this criticism against a vicarious activism by those who intended to stay far away from the gunpowder, a delegate from New York called out "Demagogue!" Weizmann stopped his discourse and stood in stunned silence. Never had this happened to him. His age, infirmity, patient toil and sacrifice had been violated by a moment of dreadful rancor. The Congress sat in horrified tension as he pondered his reply. The *Congress Protocol* quotes him as follows: " 'Somebody has called me a demagogue. I do not know who. I hope that I never learn the man's name. I a demagogue? I who have born all the ills and travail of this movement? (*Loud applause.*) The person who flung that word in my face ought to know that in every house and stable in Nahalal, in every little workshop in Tel Aviv or Haifa, there is a drop of my blood. (*Tempestuous applause. The delegates all rise to their feet, except the Revisionists and Mizrachi.*) You know that I am telling you the truth. If you think of bringing the redemption nearer by non-Jewish methods, if you lose faith in hard work and better days, then you commit idolatory (Avodah Zara) and endanger what we have built. Would that I had a tongue of flame, the strength of prophets, to warn you against the paths of Babylon and Egypt. "Zion shall be redeemed in judgment." And not by any other means.' "

No dramatist could have conceived a more overpowering climax. He left the hall, never again to make a controversial address to a Jewish audience. Between the rows of applauding delegates standing in awe and contrition, he made his way painfully, gropingly into the street. A few days later he appeared to make a short farewell. Weizmann the Zionist had left the Congress arena for ever.

He had made his presidency dependent on freedom for the Zionist Executive, if it saw fit, to attend discussions in London in a last attempt to concert a settlement with Britain. The Congress, by a small majority, rejected a Labor Zionist resolution proposed by Golda Meir urging this. It voted categorically against attending the London conference in present circumstances. This was tantamount to a rejection of Weizmann's candidacy. On December 23, 1946, he returned to London, shorn of his office. His bitterness was sharp. He fell into an aggrieved solitude. In a letter to friends during January, he mentioned a small group of Zionists that continued to keep him in touch with the pulse and spirit of events: "Sacher, Simon Marks, Isaiah Berlin, Leonard Stein, Eban and a few others." Early in February 1947 he left for Rehovot to inaugurate the Weizmann Institute of Science.

Under the leadership of Abba Hillel Silver and David Ben Gurion, the Zionist Executive now decided to attend a conference with the British government on the future of the Mandate. In other words, they intended to do exactly what Weizmann had been dismissed for recommending. The lack of candor in this approach and my own personal fidelity to Weizmann led me to ponder the idea of resignation. Moshe Sharett, whom Weizmann had banished from his favor for not showing sufficient devotion and support, fought hard for my Zionist future: "You cannot make the end of his career a condition for the beginning of yours," he said. But above everything else, it was Weizmann's own influence that impelled me to go on. He seemed moved by the idea that a young disciple would be willing to follow him into the wilderness, but he vetoed the idea sharply. His years were passing and the shadows were growing long. His highest hopes were that the principles that he had established in his Zionist career would be actively represented by successors, not merely cherished by scholars in their libraries. In any case, he knew that the forthcoming battle of Zionism was for its very life and that if his services were needed, his successors would be unable, even if they wished, to renounce his aid and support.

Thus, in a chilly room in the Colonial Office in London, with the light repeatedly going out due to the fuel shortage, the last attempt was made to reach a settlement by consent between Britain and the Zionist leaders. The populous and unwieldy negotiations went on for many days in February 1947. The British representatives came from the Foreign Office and the Colonial Office: Bevin, Creech-Jones and their leading officials including Harold Beeley, who was regarded by Zionists as Bevin's pro-Arab Rasputin. My own feeling was that Bevin was capable of his own anti-Zionism with or without Beeley. There was a large Jewish Agency delegation: Ben Gurion, Sharett, Brodetsky, Gruenbaum, Goldmann, Neumann, Locker, Horowitz, Eban, Linton, Rosenne.

Bevin's humor was heavy. When he was told that all the lights had gone out, he said, "Except the Israelites," and then fell into a paroxysm of husky laughter in which nobody else joined. Not for a single moment did he allow a conciliatory mood to take root. The discussion ranged from partition, which Bevin professed himself unentitled to impose, to various federal schemes which he had amended ferociously to the Jewish detriment. He kept on asserting that it would be "wrong" under partition to place 300,000 Arabs under Jewish "domination."

I intervened for the only time to ask why it would be "right" to sub-ject 600,00 Jews to the domination of the Arabs. The only response I got was a glare of unlimited malevolence.

We were seeing British policy at its lowest level of expression. It had lost the old imperial dignity without adapting itself to the liberal-ism expected for the postwar age. I found it incredible that the very Cabinet which stood paralyzed before the Palestine issue was carrying out the Indian partition with such audacity and sweep.

As the talks went on into late February, Bevin sank into aggressive despair. He began to say that he would wash his hands of the whole business and send the issue to the United Nations. Most Zionists re-acted to this prospect with skepticism and distaste. They believed neither that Britain would relinquish its position, nor that the Jewish cause would triumph in the arena of multilateral diplomacy. I per-sonally felt that there might be no other way out. Churchill had for several months been advocating the end of the Mandate: "I cannot recede from the advice which I have ventured to give, namely that if we cannot fulfil our promises to the Zionists we should, without de-lay, place our Mandate for Palestine at the feet of the United Nations and give due notice of our impending evacuation of that country."

In the absence of any other solution, Bevin took a step which risked, even if it did not ensure, the end of the British Mandate. On February 18, 1947, he made a public announcement: "His Majesty's Govern-ment have of themselves no power under the terms of the Mandate to award the country either to the Arabs or to the Jews or even to par-tition it between them. We have therefore reached the conclusion that the only course open to us is to submit the problem to the judgment of the United Nations."

In preparation for a discussion in the autumn session, the United Kingdom requested a special session of the General Assembly early in the year. On April 29 the United Nations General Assembly convened in New York, with the "Palestine question" inscribed on its agenda. This, of course, was a major turning point for the Zionist movement and for all those of us who were involved in its political work. The Jewish cause had been anchored for four decades in British waters. For good or ill, it was now set loose on the international ocean.

Our first sensation was of solitude rather than of exhilaration. I remembered what a small part the League of Nations and its Man-dates Commission had played in the administration of the Mandate, of which it was theoretically the master. The United Nations seemed to be a new and seemingly more robust international organization. It was fortified by the membership of all the Great Powers, and unlike the League, it had American membership and support. But I feared that the special pathos of Zionism would be submerged in the cruder calculations of global politics. After all, the slogan of self-determination had never yet been applied to an "ingathering" of people which did not constitute a majority on its soil. And yet, along with the danger went an opportunity. The Jewish claim would now be weighed on the scales of international justice, and not made dependent on the strategic interests of a single power.

My first reaction was to go to Foyle's bookshop in Charing Cross Road and buy six books about the United Nations and its procedures.

Hastily adjusting ourselves to the new situation, we sat long into the night in Great Russell Street analyzing the possible reactions of countries, large and small, which until then had seemed remote from any operative relevance to our future. As a result of my book purchases I displayed greater learning than did any of my colleagues, who looked aggrieved when I rattled off some allusions to various articles of the Charter, of which none of them had heard. The dangers were evident. Surely the Soviet Union would express its anti-Zionist tradition. Surely the states of Latin America and some in Western Europe would be influenced by the Vatican, which had found it theologically difficult to accommodate itself to the idea of a Jewish state. Surely the wishes of their mother country would have a strong influence on the younger countries of the British Commonwealth. Surely we must understand that the Arabs had five votes in the Assembly of fifty-seven members, whereas we had none. In addition, there were countries whose attitude would be determined by their Moslem solidarities. All these "certainties" were grave, but we had to make the most of our opportunities—and the least of our dangers.

One of the difficulties in presenting our cause was ambivalence about our specific aims. In theory, Zionists were dedicated to the 1942 Biltmore Programme, which called for the transformation of an undivided Palestine into a "Jewish Commonwealth." We thus had no authorization to accept partition. But in reality we knew that a Jewish state in a part of Palestine was our maximal possibility. Ben Gurion and Weizmann had agreed on this in an exchange of letters during the winter of 1946. The Jewish Agency Executive, meeting in Paris, had authorized Dr. Nahum Goldmann to explore this idea in Washington with Assistant Secretary of State Dean Acheson. Goldmann had come back with a generally affirmative reply, based, however, on Acheson's assumption that the British government would cooperate with this solution, which, after all, had its origin in British policy before World War II. Acheson's statement meant that the United States would acquiesce in a partition solution—but not necessarily that it would crusade for it or help us overcome obstacles.

While the official Zionist line had seemed to rule out partition, Ben Gurion and Weizmann, like Goldmann, had not changed their minds since 1937. Thus, on October 28, 1946, Ben Gurion had written to Weizmann: "We should in my opinion be ready for an enlightened compromise, even if it gives us less in practice than we have a right to in theory, but only so long as what is granted to us is really in our hands. That is why I was in favour of the principle of the Peel Report in 1937 and would even now accept a Jewish State in an adequate part of the country rather than a British Mandate with the White Paper in all the country." Weizmann had replied on November 6: "I am in cordial agreement with the main lines of your policy. . . . I can't help feeling that the inexorable logic of facts will drive [America and Britain] towards partition."

It was now that I received my first independent assignment as a Zionist emissary. In advance of the April 1947 session of the General Assembly, it had been decided that Zionist envoys would divide the map of the world and go out to seek the support of governments whose votes would become crucial. For various reasons, including my command of French, I was asked to visit France, Belgium, the Netherlands and Luxembourg. Modern Israelis, pampered by nearly three decades of sovereignty, should remember that in those days we were a nongovernmental organization with no automatic right of access. Accordingly, when I arrived in Paris and Brussels, I first had to fight hard to get interviews with the prime ministers and foreign secretaries, and only then to work out a line of approach.

In Paris, aided by the Zionist socialist leader, Marc Jarblum, I obtained an interview with Prime Minister Paul Ramadier. Those were the days of volatile changes in French governments. Ramadier, like a benevolent bearded goat, sat at a desk which he had never seen until a few days before and which he had every chance of abandoning a few days hence. He offered me a cigarette, pulled a lighter from his pocket and snapped it several times. Nothing was ignited. As I took a package of matches from my own pocket, Ramadier laughed and said, "Well, that's France. Nothing works. *Mais c'est charmant, n'est-ce pas?*"

I found that Zionism had a strong public echo in France. It has always been a major French enjoyment to benefit from Britain's troubles, and we were providing this sensual satisfaction in full degree. Britain had used France's weakness to undermine the French position in Syria and Lebanon in 1945. This had rankled not only De Gaulle but all the politicians of the Third Republic. At the same time, France, because of its colonial interests, was still a Moslem power. Ramadier's offers of support to me were very carefully reserved.

Moving on to Brussels, I encountered a powerful personality in Paul Henri Spaak, who was both Prime Minister and Foreign Minister of Belgium. I found him vigorous, plump, ebullient, rhetorical and startlingly similar to Churchill. There was nobody else in the room but the two of us. Yet he spoke to me sonorously as though I were a mass audience in a vast public hall. As I listened to him I realized that I was in the presence of a sharp intellect which he delighted to bring to precise expression. Spaak said, "Partition is certainly the logical conclusion. If we see any possibility of supporting you, we will."

Some Zionist leaders received this statement with enthusiasm as though it were a hard and fast commitment. But I was beginning to learn the little "escape ladders" that sophisticated statesmen attach to their promises. Spaak's belief in the "logicality" of partition did not mean that he would support it. Logic, after all, is not everything. And the statement that support would be given "if there is a possibility" seemed to refer to the natural solidarity that linked the Belgian socialists to the British Labour Party. I reported cautiously that we had made some indentations in the West European position without having achieved anything like a breakthrough.

In any case, my mission was not destined to reach its full fruition. While I was in Amsterdam making good progress in discussions with the Dutch government, I received a cable from Moshe Sharett in New York asking me to come there as quickly as possible. It seemed that the Jewish Agency had invited a distinguished group of lawyers headed by Murray Gurfein, Abe Tulin and Simon Rifkind, to prepare a brief for the Zionist case at the United Nations. This document was scholarly, precise and authoritative; yet it seemed to Sharett to lack the tang and flavor of Palestine and the Middle East. It dealt with the region more as a "problem" than as a physical reality. Zionism was treated as a learned argument rather than as a drama. Sharett believed that the document should be supplemented by something more impassioned and polemical. Accordingly, I canceled my visit to Luxembourg and returned to London, where I closed our apartment in Highgate (never to return) and prepared to cross the Atlantic for the first time.

It was typical of the Zionist way of life at that time that if I was asked where I lived I would be unable to answer. Nor did I know, or ask, if I was being invited to New York for a week, a month, a year or a decade. I decided to take no risks and to travel with Suzy at my own expense.

Thus there opened for me an epoch which was to make America central in my consciousness. I had little preparation for this. My education in school and university had been rigidly centered on Europe.

I had probably inherited the complexes and prejudices that educated Europeans bear about a supposedly vigorous but immature America. Apart from Nelson Glueck, I could not claim a single close friendship with anybody of American origin or temperament. There was apprehension in my mood and step when I reached New York in late April after a long flight through Ireland and Newfoundland.

It was not an inspiring welcome. The housing and hotel shortage of the postwar period still affected American cities, and Zionist headquarters in New York was not disposed to be very lavish in the treatment of a young Jewish Agency officer joining it from the London branch. Suzy and I spent our first night on American soil at the Paramount Hotel near Broadway. It was a rough-and-ready kind of place surrounded by a Damon Runyon atmosphere. Indeed, in the basement of the Paramount Hotel there was an institution known as Billy Rose's Diamond Horseshoe, in which impressively tall young ladies used to parade around in what was at that time the minimal covering compatible with law. A night or two later we were in even less congenial auspices at a hotel near Sixty-seventh Street and Broadway. Thence we were shuffled from one hotel to another every few days. No reservations for long periods were feasible. Zionist service was clearly not going to be a passport to gracious living.

The discussion at the General Assembly in April 1947 was designed to end with the appointment of a special committee which would go to the Middle East to study what recommendations should be made to the Mandatory power. The committee was duly appointed; it included professional diplomats from eleven small or medium-sized states deemed to have no strategic interests in the Middle East. For us in the Jewish Agency delegation, the special assembly gave useful practice in diplomatic lobbying; and Silver, Ben Gurion and Sharett had their baptisms of fire as orators before international tribunals. But the most momentous event of the spring session was a sudden development in the attitude of the Soviet Union. Instead of making the ritual assault on Zionism as a bourgeois imperialist deviation, Andrei Gromyko referred with subtle understanding to the aspiration of the Jewish people to a state of its own. He did not yet commit the Soviet Union to the support of Jewish statehood, but he insisted on the end of the Mandate and projected two alternatives of approximately equal weight: there was the possibility of an Arab-Jewish state; and if the relations between the two communities made this impossible, there was the possibility of partition with the establishment of Arab and Jewish states.

This was a windfall. At one stroke we had to revise all our predictions about the possible outcome of a United Nations discussion. If we could obtain American consent to the partition idea, we would be celebrating the first American-Soviet agreement of the postwar era. Since partition had, after all, been a British invention, it did not seem hopeless to imagine the United Kingdom cooperating in a policy with which two Great Powers were willing to be associated.

For the first time in many months, the political darkness was lit up by a pale gleam of hope. It was no longer necessary to be romantic in order to foresee a Zionist success. On the other hand, as we listened to the Arab and Moslem delegates, it became apparent that we would have to fight hard for any advance. And there was always the possibility that Bevin, if he became unpleasantly surprised by the United Nations, would renege on his promise to accept its recommendation, as he had done with the Anglo-American Committee on Palestine.

At the end of the April 1947 Assembly, there was a procedural debate which seemed marginal at the time but whose significance was to grow more evident in later months. Both the Jewish Agency and the Palestine Arab Higher Committee were invited to attach "liaison officers" to the United Nations Special Committee on Palestine (UNSCOP). The Zionist leadership selected David Horowitz and myself for this task. It was my first approach to the international arena.

By accepting liaison officers from the Jewish Agency, the United Nations was virtually acknowledging the legitimacy of Zionism as a national liberation movement. The Palestine Arabs contemptuously refused to nominate their liaison officers. We benefited greatly from Arab errors in those day. Their doctrine was that the end of the British Mandate could be followed by nothing except the establishment of an Arab Palestine, that the UN had no jurisdiction—there was therefore nothing to talk about and no need for liaison.

Early in May, UNSCOP, with its two Jewish liaison officers, set out in an ancient York aircraft from New York to Jerusalem. There were eleven committee members and their alternates; a UN secretariat, headed by Victor Hoo, Ralph Bunche and Garcia Robles; and David Horowitz and myself, who were supposed to win the understanding and support of all of them in the next few weeks.

As we flew noisily across the Atlantic, I reflected that our national struggle had reached a decisive stage. If UNSCOP refused to recommend Jewish independence, we could hope for no remedy in the General Assembly or anywhere else. Yet, even if the committee were to make a positive recommendation, this would still not guarantee a favorable UN vote. It would at the most keep our prospect alive. The task that confronted Horowitz and myself was to eliminate the skepticism that had grown around the partition idea since 1937. There were some who thought that the Palestine area was too small and poor to contain two sovereign states in any kind of stability. Others raised the question of the effect on the Arab world of establishing a Jewish state. Would this kindle a permanent war? Or might a firm insistence of the United Nations on a Jewish sovereignty amid so many Arab lands create an atmosphere of ultimate stability and acquiescence? Could the Jews of Palestine in fact be limited to a minority status? These were the problems on which I would help to provide answers out of my knowledge and study of the Middle East.

As we analyzed the eleven members, on whose vote so much would depend, we reached the conclusion that none of the governments had sent first-rank representatives. They were men of competence rather than of inspiration. Not one of them had been involved in any decisions as momentous as that in which he would now have to participate. The chairman, Emil Sandström, was a Swedish supreme court justice, near the end of his career, slow in thought and speech, but shrewd, solid and deeply rooted in humanitarian values. Dr. Nicholas Blum of the Netherlands was a former colonial governor in the Dutch East Indies. His experienced eye would detect whether the British colonial regime in Palestine had any chance of survival. A key figure would be Justice Ivan Rand of Canada, an old-fashioned man of refinement, probity and independent temperament. John D. L. Hood of Australia was a professional diplomat whose sharp mind was concealed by an easygoing disposition and a very marked taste for conviviality.

The three Latin Americans were as different from one another as could be imagined. Salazar of Peru was like a movie stereotype of an ambassador—white-haired, taciturn, austere and charged with an air of reticent mystery that he had picked up at the Vatican, to which he was accredited. The other two were mercurial and dynamic: Rodriguez Fabregat of Uruguay, bald, passionate, loquacious, progressive and wildly sentimental; and closely associated with him was García Granados of Guatemala, short, stocky and experienced. His country had a territorial conflict with Britain about Belize, and however marginal this dispute might be to some of his colleagues in the United Nations, it played a very large role in his emotions. He was prepared to believe the worst of Britain—and the best of anybody seeking to remove British power from anywhere.

Karl Lisicky of Czechoslovakia, a friend of Jan Masaryk's, was a large, shambling, rather awkward man, caught up in the psychological torment of many Czech patriots who saw their country lurching under fragile leadership from social democracy toward Communism. The Yugoslav, Vladimir Simic, was a placid veteran diplomat, but of more consequence to us seemed to be his assistant, Josef Brilej, one of Tito's younger supporters.

Islam was represented by an Indian judge, Sir Abdul Rahman. He was about 120 percent British in his mannerisms and accent, and disarmingly candid in his Arab partisanship. More subtle was the Iranian statesman Nasrollah Entezam (he was later to be my colleague and friend for many years), who fluctuated between the positions of Iranian Foreign Minister and his country's ambassador to the United States and the United Nations.

It was a strange assortment. I wondered what most of them would have to say to one another. As we talked casually on the plane I found little evidence that any of them had studied Jewish history or the Palestine problem. They were making a voyage into undiscovered countries of thought and seemed nervous with their authority.

When we reached Malta we became aware that Bevin's animosity toward Zionists and Jews now applied to the United Nations as well. At any rate, the treatment of the committee by the British authorities in Malta fell short even of elementary courtesy. They let a distinguished international committee, including many elderly men, be housed in stark barracks and huts, fed on rough army food and offered no opportunity to see the beauties of the island. Later, on arriving in Jerusalem, the committee found a country torn by violence and unwilling to stop shooting for its benefit. Perhaps this was just as well. It was salutary for them to see the problem in its true inflammation rather than to get a euphemistic impression.

The British Administration had a large share in planning the itinerary. The committee and its liaison officers were treated to an encyclopedic sightseeing tour, carefully balanced between Jewish and Arab farms and factories. The emphasis on "balance" was so stringent that the Indian member of the committee asked me at Degania "whether we should be visiting an Arab kibbutz as well."

Between tours, conversation and hearings, the liaison officers were required to fill the minds of committee members with some ideas on a future solution. The public hearings were held in the YMCA hall, with the committee on the platform, and what were called "Arab and Jewish notables" in the auditorium.

I was charged by Sharett with the effort to make the best use of Weizmann's prestige and experience. We helped draft a careful and emotional speech which Weizmann read out to the committee in part, until his eyes failed him, whereupon he put the papers aside and went into a reverie out of which he produced a poignantly moving account of the hopes and ideals that had illuminated Zionism in the past three decades. He still saw a vision of Arab-Jewish coexistence, but only on a basis of sovereign equality. This could only be achieved by a plan for partition. Once again, he surpassed all the Jewish speakers in the depth of his impact on his hearers.

On the day that I accompanied Ben Gurion for his speech to the committee, the photographs show me sitting behind him, ostensibly in rapt attention. In fact, my mind was a few miles away, up on Mount Scopus, where Suzy was undergoing an appendectomy. Ben Gurion was resolute and emphatic in his defense of official Zionist positions, but the collective discipline of the Zionist leadership did not yet permit him to come out clearly for the partition idea, which I knew he supported strongly in the depth of his heart.

It was obvious that with their conservative frame of mind, the committee members would first want to examine whether they needed to make a drastic proposal at all. Was surgery really essential? Could the British Mandate still be pummeled and kneaded by effective international massage into a viable shape? Did Britain not wish to remain? If so, could she be trusted to do so?

It was surely providential that at the moment when the committee's mind was being torn between the maintenance of the Mandate and its cessation, Bevin decided the issue himself. An immigrant ship, *Exodus*, arrived at Haifa port, bearing forty-five hundred Jews from the displaced persons' camps of Germany. They were crowded on deck in terrible squalor, but burst into tearful rapture when the green olive groves and white houses on the slopes of Mount Carmel came into view. Horowitz and I, after consultation with Sharett, decided to try to get some of the committee to see the ship with its human cargo. It seemed to embody the whole predicament in visible form. We made the proposal to Sandström, who went to Haifa with Bunche, Granados and Brilej.

The Jewish refugees had decided not to accept banishment with docility. If any one had wanted to know what Churchill meant by a "squalid war," he would have found out by watching British soldiers using rifle butts, hose pipes and tear gas against the survivors of the death camps. Men, women and children were forcibly taken off to prison ships, locked in cages belowdecks and sent out of Palestine waters. Later Bevin decreed that they should be dispatched first to a French port and thereafter to Germany—back to the memories and scenes of their martyrdom.

While Sandström, Brilej and Granados watched this gruesome operation, I awaited their return to Jerusalem with great tension. When they came back, they were pale with shock. I could see that they were preoccupied with one point alone: if this was the only way that the British Mandate could continue, it would be better not to continue it at all.

Sandström invited Horowitz and myself to join the committee in Geneva as well as in its subsequent deliberations. The consciousness that the British Mandate was collapsing in moral ruin was strengthened in the committee members' minds as soon as they left Palestine. On July 29 the British government executed three members of the Irgun Zvai Leumi, and two days later two British sergeants held hostage by the Irgun were hanged in retaliation.

Before the committee left for Geneva, some of its members met privately with Ben Gurion and Sharett in Sharett's apartment in Jerusalem. Horowitz and I were there too. Ben Gurion, at his most authoritative, broke all reticence. He argued openly for partition, which, however, he would accept and defend only if the Jewish state included the Negev.

By the time Horowitz and I reached Geneva, Sharett was already there. Our first diplomatic test came when the committee debated whether to visit the DP camps in Europe. The representatives of India, Iran, Yugoslavia, Peru and Czechoslovakia either voted against or abstained. The other six voted in favor of the visit. It was agreed that Hood of Australia and ten deputies would go to the camps while the principal committee members remained in Geneva in consultation with Horowitz and myself.

The *Exodus* survivors were now in France, awaiting a decision from London on their subsequent voyage. The British government had threatened that unless they agreed to disembark, they would be taken to Germany. This was so monstrous that we even toyed with the idea of seeking United Nations intervention. Sandström told us that he had no power to affect a British decision, and he preferred not to give advice that was sure to be rejected.

July and August 1947 in Geneva were feverish but exhilarating. Horowitz and I spent eighteen hours a day in a campaign of intellectual attrition directed to the eleven-man committee and the influential members of the secretariat, Bunche, Robles and Vigier. We were not invited to state our case at plenary meetings, presumably lest we might observe rifts within the committee itself. We therefore carried on an endless series of meetings at offices in the Palais des Nations and in the many excellent restaurants for which Geneva was famous. Horowitz's ascetic temperament revolted against having to waste all that time on food and wine. He even reflected wistfully on a future Utopia in which men would achieve their nourishment through capsules, leaving more time for serious discussion of economic and political themes. My own epicurean strain forbade me to share this bleak aspiration, but I had no illusions about our burden, despite the luxurious setting.

Now and again we would involve Sharett in our efforts at persuasion. Sometimes we called on Weizmann, who was vacationing in a Swiss village near the Austro-Italian boundary. Sharett once visited Belgrade in an effort to win the Yugoslavs over to the support of Jewish statehood. Apart from Horowitz and myself, who had official status, the Jewish Agency maintained a large team in Geneva. This included Moshe Tov, who pioneered our contacts with the Latin-American states. This was such a closed world to us, and so crucial to our success, that Tov must be accounted by any serious historian as one of the central architects of Israel's independence; Eliahu Sasson, a shrewd expert on the Arab world; Leo Kohn, a naïve and pious scholar who followed our struggles with an almost messianic ecstasy and contributed a full dose of old-fashioned Jewish anxiety; and Gideon Rafael, a political analyst of great precision and insight, later to be our ambassador to the United Nations and Britain.

With every meeting our spirits flowed and ebbed. Almost any verdict was possible—from the unbelievably favorable to the incredibly disastrous. The eleven governments and their members were obviously affected by diverse pressures and interests. And lurking morosely in the background was Bevin, who was going to regard any decision in our favor as a massive blow to Britain, and what was more, to himself.

While UNSCOP was in session in Geneva, I spent four days in July in London trying to elicit whether the British government would take a UN partition decision seriously even if it was secured. I came back to Geneva discouraged. Talking to anti-Zionist officials such as Harold Beeley or to our friends in the Labour Party such as Richard Crossman and Harold Laski, I got the impression that the British government had written off the UN committee as a superfluous nuisance. No matter what it reported, they gave it no chance of mobilizing a two-thirds majority for a pro-Zionist solution. Beeley told me flatly that this would be the case "because of the split between the Great Powers." On this point I was more optimistic than his chilling counsel led me to be. I could not help speculating on the scope of Gromyko's remarks at the special session in April: "Both Arabs and Jews have historical roots in Palestine and it would be unjust to deny the right of the Jewish people to realize their aspirations to establish their own state." To be sure, in that speech Gromyko had advocated a Jewish state "only if relations between the Jewish and Arab populations of Palestine were so bad that it would be impossible to reconcile them and to ensure the peaceful coexistence of the Arabs and Jews." Nevertheless, the idea of Jewish independence was being discussed with a new seriousness.

My report to Sharett and my colleagues about the position in London emphasized that the British position should not be regarded as decisive. Indeed, it was during my visit to London in July 1947 that I concluded that the "British era" in our history had ended. London was growing weary of its burdens. It would not require too strong a push for Britain to decide for the evacuation of Palestine. Yet I had difficulty convincing other Zionists that the British government had any intention of relinquishing its rule. During the special session of the UN in New York in April, I had participated in sessions of the Zionist Executive. I was received with some suspicion by the American Zionist leaders, led by Abba Hillel Silver, who seemed to regard me as an agent planted there by the enemy—Weizmann and Sharett. On one occasion when I said that the British inclination would be to abandon the Mandate rather than to carry it out in a Zionist spirit, there was an explosion of skepticism and derision. Silver looked at me as though I were a cretinous pupil in an elementary school who had not learned the facts of life. One of these facts, according to American Jewish mythology, portrayed British policy as subtle, brilliant, insidious and so systematic that its reality was always in diametrical contrast to its outer expression. My own experience of the dark winter 1946–47, and of the lassitude and impotence that I had found in London, convinced me that Britain was not a clear-thinking lordly tyrant, but a confused and frightened nation looking for escape from excessive commitments.

In the meantime, there were two crucial weeks in Geneva. Horowitz and I went on explaining the dangers of continuing the Mandate, the virtues of partition, the viability of Jewish statehood, the necessity for firm international decision, the catastrophe involved in procrastination, the humane values that would be vindicated by Jewish statehood, and the moral potentiality of an imaginative act by the United Nations. We could hardly catch our breath. On and on we went, expounding, arguing, persuading, in every corridor, restaurant and hotel suite to which we could gain admission by charm or persistence or stealth. It was as much as I could do not to take the waiter aside when he brought my breakfast to get in an extra few "arguments" on behalf of our Zionist theme.

Everything, even the work of international committees, eventually comes to an end. It was fortunate that the General Assembly had imposed September 1 as a dateline for the UNSCOP report, so that the regular session might have material for its deliberations in September. Without the stimulus of that dateline, I often feel that we should still be at Geneva with UNSCOP to this very day. As it was, on August 31, 1947, everything was still in the balance. Horowitz had the triumphant feeling that Rand of Canada (who was his special preoccupation) had been won over to our cause. Sharett and he were skeptical about Sandström (who was in my sphere of responsibility). I had the intuition that behind his maddening reticence there was now a tendency to accept our cause. I had also noticed a positive change in John Hood's attitude since his traumatic contact with the displaced persons in the European camps.

The issue was not only between partition or a hostile Mandate. The size and location of the area to be allotted to a Jewish state was also a vital problem. The French member of the Secretariat, Henri Vigier, had told Sharett frankly, "The greater your sovereignty, the smaller your area. You have to choose between complete independence in a limited area, or a large area in which to work—but without independence."

In the afternoon of August 31 Bunche informed Horowitz and myself that there would be two reports. We still had no complete knowledge about the contents of either. We went to the Palais des Nations where the committee was holding its final meeting. At an earlier session, Sandström had polled the committee members as follows: "Does anyone favor an Arab state in all of Palestine?" No reply. "Does anyone favor a Jewish state in all of Palestine?" No reply. At this point the committee had clearly split between advocates of partition and those who would recommend a "democratic bi-national state with majority rule and cantonal organization."

We did not know whether partition would have a large majority. Walking the empty corridors of the Palais des Nations at midnight, I wandered into the lavish assembly hall in which Haile Selassie had pleaded with the League of Nations ten years before for help against the Italian Fascist invasion. I walked vaguely into the library and thence into the cafeteria. Shortly before midnight the doors were flung open and a committee member dashed out. Looking at Horowitz and myself, he said, "Here are the expectant fathers." Minutes later, at 12:05 A.M. on September 1, 1947, Ralph Bunche officially handed us copies of the report. The recommendations were clear. A majority of seven had advocated a partition plan with complete sovereignty in a Jewish area which included the Negev. Jerusalem was to be a *corpus separatum* under UN rule, but subject to a change of status in ten years. Three members advocated a binational federal state. The Australian member was silent.

The majority report offered the Jewish people a degree of sovereignty and territorial opportunity beyond anything proposed before. It was the first Jewish political victory for three tragic decades, and I was almost exhausted by the sheer emotion of it.

Back in our hotel, Sharett, Horowitz, Tov, Rafael and I opened a bottle of champagne and cabled our news and impressions to Jerusalem, New York, London and other Zionist centers. The next morning we took the train to Zurich, where the Zionist General Council was in session. At last we had time and spirit to admire the landscape.

Horowitz and I found Ben Gurion sitting at his desk, crouched in familiar posture with his head over his arms, rumbling with anger about the independent military actions of the IZL and the Lechi. He would speak to us of nothing except the necessity to liquidate dissident organizations so as to affirm the national discipline. I began to read out the main lines of the partition report, only to receive a grunt: "We've got to stop the dissidents [porshim]." Horowitz then explained at some length that after much hesitation the committee had included the Negev within the Jewish state, in spite of an impassioned effort by the British government to prevent this. Ben Gurion's glowering response: "We must stop the porshim." Since we were quite unable to get his attention, we started for the door, only to hear Ben Gurion's voice in our pursuit: "What was that you said? A Jewish state including the Negev? Why didn't you tell me that before?" His eyes were now agleam with the sensation of battle, and the tufts of hair seemed to stand stiffly on end.

The next morning we heard Sharett report joyfully, but in a somewhat awkward Yiddish, to the Zionist Actions Committee. Some Zionist leaders were frightened by the tortuous partition map, as well as by the painful exclusion of some areas of Jewish settlement and especially of Jerusalem. The veteran General Zionist leader, Peretz Bernstein, said, "The whole thing is a nightmare." Ben Gurion: "My greatest dream is to see this nightmare fulfilled."

The Zionist Executive expressed congratulations to Horowitz and myself for our part in influencing the UNSCOP members. It asked us to go to London to find out what the British reaction was—and then to proceed to New York for the General Assembly meeting in September 1947.

My appointment as liaison officer to UNSCOP had been made almost casually. If Sharett had not called me away from Amsterdam, I would never have had such a central place in the political struggle. Now my part in the UNSCOP report, together with that of Sharett and Horowitz, had put me in the center of the map. I had reason for some personal satisfaction as I made for London, but the national anxiety was overriding.

I found the British government seething with rage. Ernest Bevin had even refused to receive Weizmann. This was a break with tradition: constant readiness to receive Weizmann had become a kind of ritual obligation of British statesmen for thirty years—rather like attending the opening of Parliament by the sovereign. It was something that one had to do if one was a gentleman.

Bevin was out to smash the Zionist tradition in British history more drastically than any of his predecessors. On the other hand, Churchill was emerging out of his torpor. He was now reminding Weizmann how close the UNSCOP report was to the proposals that Lord Moyne's Committee would have submitted but for his assassination in November 1944. But British Middle Eastern experts, including Beeley and Martin Charteris, told me that the UNSCOP report in their view was of secondary importance; the issue would have to be decided by war, not by reports. Whether or not the General Assembly adopted the report, they said, the Arabs would fight. The Jewish state would only come into existence if it could resist the Arab assault.

Before going to New York, I had two conversations that have lived on in my memory. I went to Oxford to introduce Horowitz to Professor Reginald Coupland, who, as a member of the Peel Committee, had been the pioneer of the partition idea. Coupland told us that the UNSCOP proposals had endorsed his own ideas while adjusting them to contemporary conditions. He thought that our victory had been achieved in the nick of time. Anti-Semitism was growing in the world, now that Hitler had punctured the myth of Jewish omnipotence. Whatever the Jewish people did not achieve now, while the world's conscience was still wounded, would become unattainable in the more cynical atmosphere that would soon prevail. Coupland reminded us of what he had told Weizmann and me many times before. We should be aware of the "unitary illusion"—the illusion that two peoples who held none of the purposes of life in common could be forced by institutional compulsion to form a single statehood. In the case of Palestine, partition was even more compelling than in India. There might have to be argument about boundaries, but we should never let the partition principle drop from our minds. It was the only concept that reflected historic reality. "Palestine" as a single entity was a geographical fiction. It was the duality of national personalities that counted—not the fortuitous geographical and administrative unity in which the country had been held.

A moment of climax in this part of my political career came in a discussion in which I took part, together with Horowitz and John Kimche with Abdul Rahman Azzam Pasha, Secretary-General of the

Arab League. In those days the Arab League had a more central position in Arab diplomacy than now, and Azzam could accurately be regarded as the central figure in Arab nationalism.

After the Anglo-American Committee report in 1946, Richard Crossman had once given the keys of his London apartment to Azzam and Weizmann in the hope that they might agree to meet in secret, but Azzam had apologetically withdrawn. I have no way of knowing why he was more compliant toward us on this occasion.

We met in the Savoy Hotel with the London traffic booming a few yards away. Horowitz and I sat on each side of Azzam while Kimche, who had initiated the meeting, introduced us with full tribute to our qualities. We spoke proudly but cautiously of our success with UNSCOP, predicting that the General Assembly would ratify its conclusions and that Jewish statehood was now firmly on the international map. Horowitz and I stressed a single theme, each in his own style and voice: would it not be better for Arabs to work out a plan, instead of clinging to vain resistance, so that we might live in co-operation and compromise? Azzam's reply was courteous but firm: "The Arab world is not in a compromising temper." And then, without hesitation: "Get one thing into your heads. You will not get anything by compromise or by peaceful means. You may perhaps get something, if at all, by force of arms."

I pointed out that even if there was a war, we would not disappear. We would have to meet afterward to negotiate. "Since negotiation would have to take place after the war," I said, "why not have negotiation before and instead of the war?"

"You are too rational," Azzam replied. "The Arab world regards the Jewish as invaders. It is going to fight you. War is absolutely inevitable. If you win the war, you will get your state. If you get your state by winning a war, you have a chance that the Arabs will one day have to accept it, although that is not certain. But do not consider for a single moment that you will ever have a chance of our accepting you in advance. This is a question of historic pride. There is no shame in being compelled by force to accept an unjust and undesirable situation. It is shameful to accept such a fact without attempting to prevent it. This conflict has its roots deep in history. There will have to be a decision; and the decision will have to be by force."

His words were of grave portent for us. Azzam seemed to evoke the armies of Saladin storming the Crusader fortresses in the Middle Ages. He was appealing to the martial tradition that had given Islam its original impetus in world history. He was placid and confident, and he could afford to be personally polite. Being still young to diplomacy, I was shocked by the contradiction between atmosphere and content ("We shall try to destroy you. Won't you have another drink?").

The effect on me of this conversation was far-reaching. The Zionist movement had always attached a decisive quality to diplomacy. We had told the UN committee, as we would now tell the delegates to the General Assembly, that if only the decision was clear and firm, there was a good chance of compliance. I knew in my heart that I could say nothing else. But I realized now that the greater likelihood was that we would have to fashion our independence in the hot crucible of war. Our task that autumn and winter was to win international legitimacy for our impending struggle.

5

Present at
the Birth
1947-1948

"ONLY BY MEANS OF PARTITION CAN THESE CONFLICTING NATIONAL ASPIRA-
tions find substantial expression and qualify both peoples to take their
places as independent nations in the international community and in
the United Nations." The simple logic of this sentence in the
UNSCOP majority report was the banner around which our delegation rallied in the General Assembly. When the debate opened in
New York in September 1947, we found that the committee's report
had won more authority than skeptical British and Arab commentators had ascribed to it. The United States government, for example,
had expressed no views about partition in the special assembly in
April; it had avoided contact with UNSCOP during its deliberations.
The United States seemed reluctant to criticize British policy so actively as to become a candidate for British responsibility. The
UNSCOP report broke down this reserve. It elicited a long-awaited
American statement in the General Assembly in favor of partition.
The U.S. representative compared the positions of the Arab and Jewish peoples in the world. The former, largely owing to Allied exer-
tions, enjoyed lavish independence symbolized by the presence of six
Arab representatives in the Assembly. The Jewish aspiration for independence, first recognized in the Mandate, had not yet been fulfilled.

This declaration was followed by a Soviet admission that there was
insufficient harmony on which to base a unitary solution. Accord-

ingly, the Soviet government slid logically into its second position: support for partition. "Every people, and that includes the Jewish people, has a full right to demand that their fate should not depend on the mercy or the good will of a particular state," Ambassador Samyon Tsarapkin declared. "The members of the United Nations can help the Jewish people by acting in accordance with the principles of the Charter, which call for the guaranteeing to every people of their right to independence and self-determination." He went on, "The minority plan had its merits and advantages, since it is based on the idea of creating a single Arab-Jewish state in Palestine. However, relations between Arab and Jews have reached such a state of tension that it has become impossible to reconcile their points of view on the solution of the problem. The minority plan therefore appears impracticable. In the circumstances therefore the partition plan proposed by the majority offers more hope of realization."

There was something almost messianic in this convergence of American and Soviet ideas. The general debate had got us off to a good start, but the Arabs and Moslems were fighting a rear-guard action. After all, it only needed one third of the voting members to block a favorable recommendation. Nor had we heard the last of Bevin, who had regarded the majority UNSCOP report as a personal affront to himself. The very partition that he had derided as impractical was now being seriously advanced as the only real practicality.

The weeks between September and late November 1947 are vivid in my memory. I can still recall the daily hour-long automobile trip between the Barbizon Plaza Hotel and the temporary UN building at Lake Success, Long Island. Occasionally we would stop halfway, near La Guardia Airport, where the General Assembly held its plenary sessions at a skating rink at Flushing Meadow. Many of the recognized leaders of Palestine Jewry were in our delegation and I must frankly acknowledge that they were something of a burden to those of us who had operative tasks. Sometimes, when we should have been talking to delegates from Iceland, Luxembourg or Uruguay, we were instead soothing the venerable leaders of Palestine Jewry, or ensuring that they had tickets for the meetings, or seeing to it that their hotel accommodations were at least tolerable.

On the other hand, we took comfort from the militant and efficient way in which American Jewry was organizing itself under the somber but dynamic leadership of Abba Hillel Silver. The subterranean rivalries between him and Weizmann's followers, as well as the more overt jostling for credit between the American Zionists and the Palestine leaders led by Sharett, threatened to mar our sense of occasion. Yet it was obvious that if there were no victory there would be no spoils to argue about. So the Jewish Agency delegations under Silver and Sharett settled down into a fairly workable rhythm.

Those like myself who were employed by the Jewish Agency had no specified ranks, positions or hierarchical priorities. Looking back, I am struck by how little these things then seemed to matter. We knew vaguely that Silver and Sharett were in command, that anybody else could be argued with, that a few of us, including myself, had access to the peak of the Waldorf Towers, where Weizmann sat in dark brooding splendor. He was immensely gratified to feel that he was still indispensable in the fray. Despite his lack of office, many heads of delegation and foreign ministers were not easily accessible by anyone but him. Foreign statesmen faced him with a curious mixture of apprehension and awe. They knew that they were likely to be charmed into an unwanted commitment, or overpowered by the weight of his historic imagination. But it was worth taking the risk for the reward of an unusual experience.

The United Nations seemed to matter very much to the world in those days. It was still regarded as the central arena in which the destiny of mankind would be determined. A vast press corps, strengthened by radio and television teams, followed all its committees. Many of the utterances made from its rostrum were reported verbatim or at length in the *New York Times* and the *Herald Tribune*. It did not seem useless to develop an argument or impossible to change minds. The idea of a Jewish state was so novel that many governments had been unable to crystallize their policies; much might depend on the recommendations of their own delegates who listened to the debates.

Once again we were helped by Arab obduracy. The Arab states, spurred on by the Palestine Arab Higher Committee, urged total rejection of UNSCOP's report in both parts. The only solution which they would consider would be the establishment of an Arab state in which the existence of a separate Jewish nationality would be ignored. It should have been obvious from the start that any proposal which disregarded the existence of a Jewish nationhood was now internationally unacceptable. All the world tribunals had regarded Jewish immigration to Palestine as a matter of right and urgency. So in submitting extreme demands, the Arabs strengthened the impression that the Jews needed powerful safeguards to defend their existence and their very lives.

We had good allies. The General Assembly chairman, Brazil's Oswaldo Aranha, was religiously uplifted by the concept of Jewish statehood. At his side stood the rotund and solid figure of the Secretary-General, Trygve Lie, who had a dual interest in our success: he badly needed an achievement for the United Nations that would give it some resonance in world opinion, and as a Norwegian socialist he had seen the horrors of Nazi persecution from close at hand. The idea that the international community should represent every sovereignty and culture except that of the Jews was clearly repellent to his libertarian nature.

The Special Political Committee in which our problem was discussed was directed by a complex personality, Herbert Evatt of Australia. His self-confidence was absolute. Behind his abrasive exterior lurked an abrasive interior. He never allowed his resolution to be blunted by any confession of fallibility. The Australian people, for whom he spoke, had a traditionally chivalrous attitude to the Jewish people, as well as a close acquaintance with the Palestinian scenery in which so many Australian soldiers had found repose from the heat of desert conflict. On the other hand, Evatt was a contentious man. He did not suffer fools—or for that matter wise men—gladly. He expected deference and was seldom inclined to regard any praise of himself as excessive. There was always the danger that some injury to his vanity or sense of hierarchy might evoke vindictive reaction.

Since the majority report would have to be amended in order to reduce the number of Arabs in the Jewish state and to diminish the disparity between the areas of the two states, it was clear that detailed committee work would be needed. We were fortunate in the constitution of the subcommittee which was to discuss the partition plan. It consisted of the United States, the Soviet Union, Canada, South Africa, Poland, Czechoslovakia, Venezuela, Uruguay and Guatemala. Here were nine stalwart defenders of the partition principle; one of them, Lester Pearson of Canada, was putting his emollient diplomacy to work for the first time in a major international issue.

Our chief problem was to overcome a natural tendency to regard a unitary state as preferable to a divided one. The issue was illuminated by reference to many other experiences of national relations. Federal countries clearly understood that agreement was an essential condition of a unitary system. The Canadian representative declared, "The representative of Pakistan has said here that partition should not take place without consent. But the question arises whether it is any better to try to maintain unity without consent."

In his statement on the UNSCOP report, the Yugoslav member upheld federalism but referred to "the right of secession" as "the democratic principle which may be considered the highest achievement of human progressive thought." The Netherlands representative recalled the time after the Napoleonic Wars when Belgium and the Netherlands were brought together in one unitary state. "Although our two peoples had very close ties, relations and interests of a cultural, historical, ethnological and economic nature," he went on, "this unitary state ended rapidly and unsuccessfully. The difference between Arabs and Jews are much greater than those between Belgium and the Netherlands. Now, together with Luxembourg, our countries are reunited, not politically, but economically. And what counts now is not our political separation but our union for economic purposes. History has taught our countries this valuable lesson of independence combined with unity for certain important but limited purposes."

Much has been written about "pressure politics" in the 1947 Assembly. But the partition verdict was also based on a keen ideological analysis backed by historic experience. It was international discussion at its highest level.

My own position in the Jewish Agency team had changed since April. As a result of our success as liaison officers with UNSCOP, Horowitz and I now had a more senior position. Silver and the American Zionist leaders no longer regarded me as an exotic intruder.

I now had three major assignments. In the division of the world into what we called "spheres of influence," I was allotted four Scandinavian countries, France and the three Benelux countries. I was to work with Nahum Goldmann. In addition, the desperate nature of our struggle had induced Silver and Ben Gurion to encourage a maximal contribution by Weizmann. Very few political leaders like to have their predecessors too near, especially if they cast as formidable a shadow as Weizmann. It must therefore be recorded to the credit of Silver and Ben Gurion that they had no hesitation in harnessing Weizmann's influence in the common cause. On the other hand, their own relations with him were tense, and I was given the task of using him in the most effective way. My work was especially delicate, since Weizmann had quarreled violently with Moshe Sharett despite the affinity of their political views. Weizmann believed, I thought with little justice, that Sharett should have done more to save him from deposition at the 1946 Zionist Congress in Basel. The aged leader had never had much taste for compromise in personal relations. He was always 100 percent for or against, and Sharett was now definitely in the "against" column. Thus the hope of using Weizmann's services depended largely on me.

My third task lay in the presentation of written material. Zionism has always had a strange weakness for unreadable pamphlets. Although I enjoyed writing, I did not share the belief of my seniors in the omnipotence of logical memoranda, few of which were ever read with any great attention. I felt that more would depend on the effect of Zionist appearances before the committee and, of course, on our ability to raise echoes in the mass media.

Abba Hillel Silver and Sharett made impressive openings in addressing the Special Political Committee under Evatt's chairmanship. The trouble was that the Arabs had a numerical advantage. There were five Arab states, some of them ably represented. The most effective delegates were from Lebanon in the person of Camille Chamoun and Charles Malik. In addition, there was heavy reinforcement from Mohammed Zafarullah Khan, the Pakistani representative, an eloquent jurist, later to become a judge at the International Court in the Hague. Moreover, as full members the Arab and Moslem states could speak whenever they liked, whereas Jewish Agency representatives were invited only by special dispensation.

Weizmann's appearance was scheduled for October 24. It was now plain that American and Soviet support could be expected, but even so, the two-thirds majority was not assured. Weizmann's role was to make an impact on the uncommitted delegates who had been shaken by the strong blasts of Arab pressure. This time he wanted his address to be carefully formulated. He knew that it might be his last appearance at the bar of the nations. His eyesight was bad and the work of preparation agonizing. I find the following entry in my diary:

October 16, 1947. Saw Chief after he lunched with Henry Morgenthau. Worked on draft for four steady hours. After each sentence was written in huge letters and agreed, he would go to a lampstand and bring the text right to his glasses endeavouring to learn it by heart. By the end of the session, his eyes were watering as if in tears. Finally, he said: "We'll make this do, but how about a posuk [Biblical verse] for the ending?" We looked for a Bible and eventually found one supplied by the Waldorf-Astoria Hotel in the bedside table. Spent half an hour on Isaiah looking for a return-to-Zion passage. As I left, he said: "Well, this is it. Over the top for the last time."

The delegates of fifty-seven nations listened to him in suspense. He was more personal than usual. In describing an international assembly twenty-five years before, he said, "I came from the Council room in which the Mandate was ratified with a feeling that the most cherished ideals of our history had been sanctioned by the conscience of all mankind." He made light of Arab spokesmen's assertions that the Jews were the descendants of the Khazars of southern Russia: "It is very strange. All my life I've been a Jew, felt like a Jew, been talked about as a Jew, and I now learn in my old age that I am—what was it—oh yes, a Khazar." He spoke of the prospect that Jews might be a minority in an Arab state: "I will not discuss whether it is a good or a bad fortune to be a minority in an Arab state. I would leave the Jews of Iraq, of Yemen and of Tripoli, and the Christians, Syrians and Iraqi to pronounce on that. Here I would say that this was not the purpose for which under international auspices we were encouraged to come to Palestine. Those of us who made our homes there did not do so with the object of becoming Arab citizens of Jewish persuasion." And in conclusion, the reference to prophecy: "The Lord shall set His hand for the second time to recover the remnants of His people and He shall set up an ensign for the nations and shall assemble the outcast of Israel and gather together the dispersed of Judah from the four corners of the earth."

The effect was strong. And this was still not his last act in the drama. When it became evident that Jewish statehood in some form would be proposed by the General Assembly, our adversaries moved away from direct antipartitionism toward a policy of truncating the Jewish territory so as to make it unacceptable to us. Early in November the United States, influenced by British pressure, tried to induce us to yield the southern Negev to the Arabs. American diplomats even hinted that without this concession they would abandon support of the partition plan.

On November 19 we induced Weizmann to rise from his sickbed and go to Washington for a talk with President Truman. He decided to concentrate entirely on the importance of the southern Negev in his talk with the President. He was warmly received at the White House and plunged immediately into his theme, illustrating it with a memorandum prepared by Eliahu Elath, the Jewish Agency representative in Washington. This document pointed out that the Arab states already had an outlet to the Red Sea and the Gulf of Aqaba through Transjordan, Egypt and Saudi Arabia. For Israel, a gateway to Africa and Asia would be an indispensable part of its vision.

Weizmann managed to keep Truman's mind riveted on this point alone. The President became fascinated by his excursion into a phase of remote political geography. Grasping the simplicity and force of the argument, he gave his assent. But there was a race against time: the Jewish Agency representatives had been invited to meet the American delegate, Hershel Johnson, at three o'clock the next day in the United Nations delegates' lounge to hear the State Department's decision against retaining the Negev in the Jewish state. Ambassador Johnson faced Sharett and Horowitz and began to pronounce judgment of execution. In midsentence, he was called to the telephone. He told the messenger that he could not be disturbed and sent his deputy, General Hildring, to take the call. The general returned to whisper to him that the President himself was holding on at the Washington end of the line. Ambassador Johnson leapt to the telephone booth like a startled and portly reindeer. Twenty minutes later he returned. Seating himself opposite Sharett and Horowitz, he blurted out an embarrassed retraction: "What I really wanted to say to you was that we have no changes in the map you suggest." Horowitz has recorded the Jewish reaction with quiet understatement: "We sighed with relief. Dr. Weizmann's talk had been successful. The struggle for the frontier has ended in victory."

Eventually the Partition Committee adopted the draft of Lester Pearson of Canada, which was acceptable to both the United States and the Soviet Union. Some changes were made to the UNSCOP proposal with the object of reducing the Arab population of the Jewish state. Sharett rose to the full height of his meticulous statesmanship in the detailed evidence that he gave on each and every point of the map of the proposed Jewish state. Together with Horowitz and a water expert, Aharon Wiener, he fought hard to make everyone see that the proposed state, in spite of its tortuous boundaries, would have some economic viability.

By the third week of November we were ready for the decision. Every argument had been exhausted; all influence had been put to work. It was now a question of counting heads. For a whole week we were to live in suspense. The Political Committee adopted the majority report by a vote of 22 against 13 with about 20 abstentions—this meant that the partition proposal was alive but by no means certain of passage with a majority of two thirds. For the next few days Jews and Arabs summoned every resource of influence and persuasion to secure the victory of their cause. My own personal anxieties were great, for the abstainers in the committee included France and Belgium, whose support in the final vote would be indispensable. In particular, the prospect of French abstention threatened to disrupt the whole West European front. I went to see Weizmann and drafted a cable to Leon Blum, the socialist statesman who would have a strong influence on the French Cabinet: "Does France wish to be absent from a moment unfading in the memory of man?"

Our difficulties were compounded by the complex American position. Although President Truman had put himself firmly behind the partition proposal, many of his delegates to the United Nations, long familiar with Arab causes, were creating an atmosphere of skepticism around their own government's policy. Indeed, General Hildring had been appointed a special presidential representative acting as a kind of watchdog to ensure that the State Department's predilections did not get the better of the President's policies. This was comforting in itself. On the other hand, I reflected that if there had been no cause for disquiet, there would have been no need for such an appointment to be made. Doubts about the United States position were creating a difficult situation in Latin America and in countries such as the Philippines and Liberia, which were accustomed to follow the American lead on international issues.

At the Jewish Agency headquarters, we worked around the clock telegraphing, telephoning, writing, cajoling, pleading all over the world. Was there anybody in Manila who had access to the President? Might some friend in the United States have influence on the President of Liberia? What exactly were the motivations and impulses that could cause Haiti to vote with us? Was there some hope that Thailand would abstain? What was needed to bring France and Belgium into the yes column? How could Moshe Tov get us more Latin American votes? Here was the Jewish people at the threshold of its greatest transition, and yet there was a danger that everything would be lost through utterly marginal circumstances in countries ostensibly external to the issue.

When the General Assembly came together on November 27, we were plunged in gloom. There was every reason to fear that if the vote was taken, we would fall short of the two-thirds majority. The day before, the odds had seemed to be in our favor. But at precisely that moment the French delegate, Alexandre Parodi, had called for a postponement of the session. In the twenty-four hours since then, we had lost ground. The representative of Uruguay, Professor Rodriguez Fabregat, embarked on a long discourse that could not uncharitably be regarded as a filibuster. As the minutes ticked away, all hope seemed to be receding. It was then that the chairman, Ambassador Aranha, revived our hopes. He discovered that the hour was late, that the decision to be made was important and that the following day was an American national holiday, Thanksgiving Day. With a firm hand, oblivious of Arab protest, he adjourned the session. It was clear we would know our fate on November 29, and that November 28 would be a day of unremitting toil.

We recaptured much ground during that Thanksgiving holiday. We now had good reason to expect a favorable Philippine and Liberian vote. The news from France was reserved but more promising than before. Yet we knew that we were at the mercy of any slight parliamentary fluctuation. Nothing was assured, even if nothing had been irrevocably lost.

The die had been cast and there was very little that most of us could do, except to accompany the forthcoming verdict with our prayers. Nevertheless, last-minute efforts had to be made to avert complications and to secure the decisive vote. The Arab delegations, led by Camille Chamoun, decided on a show of moderation in order to prevent the partition judgment from being adopted. The Political Committee, in adopting the partition plan, had appointed a commission of three to see whether an "agreed solution" could be found. We knew that this was impossible. After all, if an agreed solution had been feasible, there would have been no need of an Assembly discussion at all. The members designated to explore an "agreed solution" were Australia, Thailand and Iceland. The Icelandic delegate, Ambassador Thor Thors, was to be the rapporteur. By the morning of November 29 the Thai delegate, Prince Wan, had prudently departed for Bangkok on the *Queen Mary*, ostensibly on the grounds that a revolutionary situation existed in his country, but actually in order to avoid having to cast a vote against partition. There was still some apprehension in Jewish Agency circles lest the Assembly seize on an optimistic remark by the Icelandic representative in order to defer a partition vote and explore the figment of an agreed solution. At any rate, Thor Thors would be the first speaker on that historic day, and it seemed urgent to ensure that he would set up a positive momentum. Accordingly, I began my day on November 29, 1947, with a visit to him at the Barclay Hotel.

I found my position quixotic, and I thought it best to tell him so frankly. The Jewish people was at a turning point. If we succeeded, we would realize a millennial dream. If we failed, that dream might be extinguished for generations to come. The key to this turning point in the first part of the UN meeting would lie in the hands of a small island country in the middle of the Atlantic Ocean with a population of less than 175,000. It is a quality of multilateral diplomacy that governments may sometimes determine great issues in which they themselves are only remotely involved, but which are of desperate consequence to others far away. Our future as a people depended on its most decisive day on the momentum or atmosphere which would be created by a representative of Iceland. I invited Ambassador Thors to reflect on the historic mystery involved.

He replied with disconcerting emotion. He said that Iceland was far less remote from Jewish destiny than I presumed. In its culture it was deeply impregnated with Biblical memories. Moreover, it was a stubborn and tenacious democracy, guarding its national particularity within its rain-swept island boundaries for century upon century—a people determined to be itself, sharing its language and literature with no other nation, and refusing to abandon its remote island outpost for warmer and gentler climes elsewhere. Such a people could be relied upon to understand the perseverance with which the Jewish people clung to its own specificity and to the recollections of its own patrimony. Ambassador Thors fully accepted my argument that what was needed now was "decision," not the vain pursuit of "agreement." If the decision was clear and firmly upheld, it might have a chance of securing acquiescence later on. It was only because all prospects of an agreed solution had been exhausted in the three decades of Mandatory rule that the matter had come to the United Nations Assembly. He would say that if the General Assembly made no clear recommendation, it would be failing in its duty, and with that failure some of mankind's most cherished hopes would subside.

I made for United Nations General Assembly headquarters, which was in a ferment of tension. Newspapermen, television and radio correspondents from all over the world were concentrated in the lobbies, while the delegates' seats and visitors' gallery were crowded as they had never been before. The United Nations was facing a momentous opportunity at a very early stage of its career. On the podium, pale and solemn, were the President of the Assembly, Oswaldo Aranha, Trygve Lie and the equally well nourished Assistant Secretary-General Andrew Cordier. Aranha called the meeting to order and invited the representative of Iceland to the rostrum. Thors, to my relief, was magnificent. He stated with firm conviction that despite every examination of all avenues, he and his committee were convinced that an agreement in advance was impossible. The only hope of conciliation lay in an act of judgment and decision. If the world community was firm in support of partition, then partition would come into existence and those who opposed it now would have no course but to acquiesce.

From that moment on, the debate went inexorably our way. An attempt by Chamoun to secure a postponement in order to discuss the federal proposal was firmly ruled out of order by Aranha and opposed with impressive unity by Gromyko and Hershel Johnson. By this time the United States and the Soviet Union were becoming irritated at the delaying tactics imposed on the General Assembly by the Arab and British delegations. Here, for the first time since the end of the war, two Great Powers were reaching agreement on a major international issue, and countries of lesser responsibility were preventing their accord from coming into effect. General Carlos Romulo of the Philippines, who had spoken against partition two days before, had now disappeared, and a new Filipino delegate spoke as ardently for the partition plan as Romulo had spoken against. Liberia also had swung around in our favor. To my relief, my own "clients"—the Benelux countries—now recorded their firm intention to support the partition plan. There was still the fear that a French abstention might upset this prospect.

Finally the speechmaking came to an end, and a solemn hush descended on the hall. Aranha announced his intention to call for a vote in alphabetical order. Some of us who were present still retain a memory of the tone in which Cordier recited the votes. "Argentina?" "Abstain." "Afghanistan?" "No." "Australia?" "Yes." "Belgium?" "Yes." "Bolivia?" "Yes." "Byelorussia?" "Yes." And so it went on. When France loudly said *"Oui,"* there was an outbreak of applause in the hall, which Aranha sternly suppressed. By the time we had gone halfway through the alphabet, we knew that we were safely home. Finally, after the announcement of Yugoslavia's "abstention," we heard the historic words: "Thirty-three in favor, thirteen against, ten abstentions, one absent. The resolution is adopted."

I went out into the lobby, where the Jewish delegation was caught up in the embrace of an enthusiastic throng. There were Jews in tears, and non-Jews moved by the nobility of the occasion. Nobody who lived that moment will ever lose its memory from his heart.

Suzy and I got into one of the delegation's cars with Sharett and Moshe Tov. Strangely, yet perhaps understandably, we made the journey into Manhattan in complete silence. A natural deference moved us to go to the Plaza Hotel to greet Chaim Weizmann, who had been waiting on tenterhooks. We persuaded him to go to a Labor Zionist rally in Madison Square Garden, where he was given a rapturous homage.

It was evening in Jerusalem. Crowds had gathered near the Jewish Agency building in Rehavia to hear the recitation of the vote. They burst into song and began dancing in the street. Alone in his office, Ben Gurion sat at his desk with his head buried in his hands. He understood the greatness of the moment, but he could not join the spirit of the dance. He, more than anyone, knew that the charter of Jewish freedom was also the signal for a savage war. In fact, when the partition vote was announced in the General Assembly, the Arab delegates got up and walked out of the hall, openly threatening violence. "The partition line shall be nothing but a line of fire and blood" was Azzam Pasha's ominous warning.

At midnight I went out into the New York streets to buy the next morning's papers. The headlines were strident, and for us, victorious, but they already carried the news of the first assaults on Jewish homes and shops in Jerusalem. The tide of murder was in full spate.

Few of us in New York had any illusion about the gravity of our prospect. We knew that the judgment recently given by the General

Assembly would be a mere scrap of paper unless it was ratified by sacrifice and toil. And yet, we had the intuition that the date would never lose its meaning. What a tortuous journey we had made! At the beginning of 1947 the Jewish people's hope of statehood had been nowhere recognized; it was being crushed by the convergence of British hostility and Arab violence. The displaced persons were still rotting away in their camps. Now, eleven months later, everything had changed. The Jewish people in Palestine was truly a nation, fighting for its patrimony under the momentum of international recognition. The war of independence was inevitable, but it would be fought in conditions far different from anything that could have been predicted a few months before. A splendid gleam of friendship had lit up our solitude.

Within the next few days our delegation began to disperse. Dr. Silver, with incredible serenity, went back to the prosaic business of organizing weddings and funerals in Cleveland. And Sharett, Horowitz and I made plans to return whence we had come. This meant Jerusalem for them, and London for me. Here, however, I interposed a question: Were we not acting in an absurdly routine way? What in heaven's name did London matter now? The war of survival would be fought in Jerusalem while the efforts of our adversaries to frustrate partition would be centered in New York. These were the only two places for any of us to be. Sharett immediately recognized this logic and asked Horowitz and me to remain within sight and sound of UN headquarters. Horowitz, weighed down by anxiety about his family, insisted on returning to Jerusalem, and I stayed in lonely charge.

A few days later it became clear how prudent this decision had been. No sooner had the partition resolution come to fruition than attempts were made to thwart it. The Arabs were determined to prove that it would be costly in blood. The British government, spurred by Bevin's bitterness, had announced that it would do nothing "to facilitate the fulfilment of the partition recommendation." This meant in effect that it was going to obstruct its fulfillment by allowing public order to collapse and permitting the country to fall into chaos. It must have been one of the least creditable decisions ever made by a British government, and Britain's allies in America and Europe were visibly ashamed. The nation that had taken the lead in resisting Hitler seemed determined to prevent redress for Hitler's victims. The country whose historic imagination had come to daring expression in the Balfour Declaration, the Britain that had made the idea of a Jewish national home familiar in international jurisprudence was now doing everything possible to abandon its own vision.

More serious for us, there were second thoughts in the United States. Despite Truman's lead, American policy had never been fully won over to the idea of partition. At least three hesitations were at work. First, there was a genuine fear that the Jewish population of Palestine would be massacred as a result of an action for which the United States was largely responsible. Second, there was the feeling that if immigrants poured in from Eastern and Central Europe, they would bring the Communist virus into the Middle East. Third, it was feared that America's interests in the Arab world, although not as variegated as they later became, would be subjected to threat and pressure.

The events of December 1947 seemed to confirm these fears. Although the defense of Jewish settlements by the Haganah was heroic and generally successful, the Arabs were able to sunder communications between the scattered parts of Palestine Jewry. They had cleverly decided to avoid a frontal assault and to fight a war of communications. They would cut Jerusalem off at the Latrun salient. They would interpose themselves between the northern and southern Negev. They would send volunteer armies from Lebanon and Syria into Galilee. The map of the Jewish state would be lacking in any kind of coherence so that a Jewish governmental authority could not establish its writ in any consecutive area.

Casualties multiplied at a terrifying rate. And the brunt of our sacrifice was being borne by civilians, not by soldiers. In Ben Yehuda Street in Jerusalem and in other towns, scores of Jewish men, women and children were blown to bits. From Jaffa, determined assaults were made against the civilian population of Tel Aviv. The Haganah was inflicting casualties as well as suffering them, but the more intense the fighting the more doubtful world opinion became about the possibility that the partition dream could be realized.

While making their main effort in the field of battle, the Arabs decided also to attempt a reversal of the partition resolution by appeals to the Security Council, which took the question on its agenda in mid-December. I sat helplessly among visitors and tourists while the oratorical contest was reopened. At the end of December I sent warnings to Jerusalem about the decline in our political fortunes. Around the Security Council Table, Britain, represented by Sir Alexander Cadogan, seemed to carry more weight than among fifty-seven members of the General Assembly. Of the Latin American representatives, Ambassador Alfonso Lopez of Colombia, a former President of his country, was noticeably lukewarm. So was the Belgian delegate, Ambassador Fernand Van Langenhove, who seemed to have an obsequious fixation on the British government. No comfort whatever was to be found from Dr. Tingfu Tsiang, the representative of China, which was then still under Chiang Kai-shek's regime. The Arab assault was developed intensely by a veteran Syrian statesman, Faris al-Khoury.

But it was the American attitude that was giving us most concern. I had gone with Eliahu Elath to a meeting at the State Department with senior American officials; I found them perfunctory in support of partition and deeply skeptical about the possibilities of its implementation. Our natural course would have been to seek contact with President Truman in order to transcend the hesitations of the State Department. Here, however, there was a major complication. The President had taken offense at charges made against him by Abba Silver, who was well known to be a supporter of the Republican Party. Truman developed a trauma about what he called "Zionist pressure." He gave strict orders not to allow any Zionist leaders to have access to him. In the conditions, our only direct contacts were through his Missouri friend Eddie Jacobson and his executive assistant, David K. Niles. But these friends, with all their good will, did not have an intimate knowledge of our situation, nor could they be expected to give a detailed account of the points at issue in the Security Council debates.

Meanwhile, the news from Jerusalem became more ominous. The toll of Jewish civilian life mounted tragically. The Jewish parts of Jerusalem were very nearly encircled, as well as being cut off from normal contact with the coast. Although the partition plan had given the Negev to the Jewish state, our presence there was still thin and fragile. I could sense a growing skepticism about our hope of survival if we clung to the partition plan. With Sharett and Horowitz tied down in Jerusalem and the American Zionist leaders neutralized by their alienation from the President, my own responsibilities increased. I reached out for reinforcement in the direction where I had always found it. Eddie Jacobson informed Eliahu Elath and myself that while Truman spoke with irrational rage about the official Zionist leaders, his voice became more tender when he talked of Weizmann and recalled his conversation with him about the southern Negev. It seemed evident that our only chance of access to Truman lay through the activation of Weizmann's prestige. Hence, after consulting with the Zionist leaders, I sent Weizmann a telegram on January 23:

IN VIEW WORSENING SITUATION ADVISE YOU IF POSSIBLE RECONSIDER DECISION TO GO PALESTINE JANUARY. NO CONDITIONS EXIST THERE YOUR CONSTRUCTIVE POLITICAL ACTIVITY. EVERYTHING DEPENDING ON OUTCOME CRUCIAL NEGOTIATIONS LAKE SUCCESS AND WASHINGTON. MOST CRUCIAL PHASE OF ALL NOW APPROACHES HERE IN WHICH WE SORELY MISS YOUR PRESENCE ADVICE ACTIVITY INFLUENCE. AFFECTIONATELY EBAN

Weizmann was then in London recuperating from his efforts at the General Assembly. His first reaction to my appeal was irascible; he had never fully recovered from the recollection of his deposition at the Zionist Congress in Basel, and his resentment toward his successors burned deeply in his heart. He shrewdly insisted that I obtain confirmation of my invitation from the official Zionist bodies which were subservient to Abba Silver's circle. With the aid of Arthur Lourie I was able to obtain this gesture, and a few weeks later Weizmann left London—never to return. He arrived in New York weary, old but indomitable.

Even for him it was not easy to break through Truman's ban. It was only when Eddie Jacobson in a sentimental mood compared Weizmann with President Andrew Jackson, Truman's hero, that the President relented. It would be hard to imagine a more far-fetched comparison, but it worked. The President received Weizmann on March 18 and told him that he had not changed at all in his fidelity to partition.

It therefore came as a stunning shock to Jews everywhere when on March 19 Ambassador Warren R. Austin, the American representative in the Security Council, announced what amounted to a headlong retreat from the partition plan. He proposed that a special session of the General Assembly be called to discuss the establishment of an "international trusteeship," to take effect with the end of the British Mandate. Under this protection the fighting would stop and the possibility of different solutions, including partition, would be investigated. This was only twenty-four hours after Truman had talked with Weizmann, as Truman himself wrote: "When he left my office I felt that he had reached a full understanding of my policy and that I knew what he wanted." The President had given Weizmann a specific commitment that he would work for the establishment and recognition of a Jewish state of which the Negev would be a part. The dream of Jewish statehood which had illuminated the winter months was now to be snuffed out through the inconstancy of those who had fostered it.

A frenzy of rage and disappointment rolled through the Jewish world. Not surprisingly, Truman was assailed by the armory of invective which Zionism had perforce stored up during the long years of failure and frustration. The only voice which did not join the attack was that of the man who had the most right to feel betrayed. On Monday, March 22, Weizmann had called Eddie Jacobson on the telephone to express an utterly irrational belief that Truman would still fulfill his promise. The President was never to forget this act of faith.

We reassembled our delegation in full force at the Jewish Agency headquarters and resolved to fight with every resource to ensure that the Jewish state would come into existence when the Mandate expired on May 15. Our military defenders and civilian population in Palestine no longer were fighting with the sun of international recognition on their backs. The perfidy seemed all the heavier in contrast to the joy of a few months before. It was as if we had been set on the threshold of statehood, allowed to peep within—only to be tantalizingly thrown back into the wilderness.

One of the dangers was that the British government would prolong the date that it had announced for the Mandate to end. We decided that a letter should go to President Truman expressing unconditional resistance to any extension of the British Mandate. We thought that it would be historically ironical if this letter bore the signature of Weizmann, who had cooperated for forty years with the Mandatory power:

April 19, 1948

I sound a note of solemn warning against the prolongation of British rule in Palestine. As you may know, I have cherished the British-Jewish relationship all my life. I have upheld it in difficult times. I have been grievously disappointed by its recent decline. I tremble to think of the wave of violence and repression which would sweep Palestine if the conditions of recent unhappy years were to be continued under British or indeed any foreign rule. Should your administration despite all this press for any prolongation of British tenure, it would mean a responsibility for terrible events.

In helping Weizmann draft this letter, I knew that Truman was not irrevocably lost to us. We knew now that he was in deep turmoil of spirit. In his book *Man of Independence,* Jonathan Daniels has recounted the story of Black Friday at the White House:

Truman called Clark Clifford, his administrative assistant, at 7:30 Saturday morning March 20. "Can you come right down," he said, "there is story in the papers on Palestine and I don't understand what has happened." In his office Truman was as disturbed as Clifford had ever seen him. "How could this have happened? I assured Chaim Weizmann that we were for partition and would stick to it. He must think that I am a plain liar. Find out how this could have happened."

This was all very well, but the fact remained that the United States had withdrawn its support from the partition proposal and we now had the task of working not with the United States, but against it.

When the General Assembly convened in special session in April 1948, it became evident that partition was not going to be killed as easily as Washington had hoped. In Palestine itself, partition was coming spontaneously to life. As British power receded, Jewish and Arab authority began to flow in rough approximation to the partition boundaries, except that the Negev was still empty and cut off.

Our political effort in New York now branched off into two directions. In the Jewish Agency negotiating team we mounted an assault on the trusteeship proposal. We rallied around the principle that a valid international judgment must not be overthrown by armed force. If the 1947 resolution could not be actively enforced by the United Nations, we at least wanted to prevent the annulment of its major principle, that of Jewish statehood.

There was no question that skepticism about our military prospects had played a central part in the decline of American support. David Ben Gurion now banished all other concerns to concentrate with fierce resolve on strengthening our defense forces. As April went forward, Jewish military fortunes improved. The turning point had come even earlier. One day in March, for example, I was lunching with Weizmann and Alexandre Parodi, who was full of hard-headed doubts about partition: "How can a few hundred thousand of you stand up against millions?" Weizmann replied that numbers were not decisive: "The trouble with the Egyptian army is that its soldiers are too lean and its officers too fat." If the Jews stood firm, we would win through. At that very moment a secretary put his head through the door with a copy of the New York *Post* telling of a spectacular Jewish victory at Mishmar Ha-emek.

The next few weeks were memorable for me in many respects. For one thing, the international alignment had changed and the Soviet Union was now the only major power still steadfast in its support of Jewish statehood. I thus found myself almost every night conferring conspiratorially with Soviet representatives, including Gromyko, Tsarapkin and Jacob Malik, about the possibility of frustrating the American trusteeship proposal. Soviet diplomacy has a nocturnal tendency, and most of these meetings were held very late at night in a Park Avenue mansion.

At the same time, the American Zionist movement, in its most decisive operation, led by Silver and Emanuel Neumann, mounted a vast campaign to persuade American opinion that the abandonment of partition not only would be a betrayal of a sorely tried people but would also make a mockery of international institutions and put a premium on aggression. There were other delegations at the General

Assembly who were unwilling to follow the American retreat. Australia, New Zealand and many Latin American countries were passionate in supporting the principle of resistance to aggression.

I had now been in the United States for nearly a year, apart from the few months with UNSCOP in Jerusalem and Geneva, and the New York scene was becoming more familiar to me. I had even branched out into some speaking engagements in other cities. In spite of the role that I had played in the November 23 resolution, I was still unknown to most of the Jewish public in the world. Thus, on two occasions when Sharett had to cancel speaking engagements in American cities, I almost had to be forced down the throats of the appropriate organizations as his deputy. There was one memorable objection from Philadelphia: "We know that Moshe Sharett speaks English quite fluently. How do we know that this Eban knows the language at all?"

Suzy and I moved out of our hotel into Meyer Weisgal's apartment on West End Avenue. Weisgal was Weizmann's most faithful supporter and counselor. He strengthened his chief's hands through all his political battles and was later to ensure Weizmann's legacy in the form of the Weizmann Institute of Science at Rehovot. Any meeting with him was always a drastic and unrelaxing experience. There was a shock of gray hair, a bulbous nose, a red face, a strident voice and a vocabulary so rich with unprintable imprecations as to leave the recipient shuddering with incredulity. Everything here was abrasive, rough and disconcerting. But these were only the external aspects of his character. Astonishingly, behind these habits and pretenses, there was not only a passionate Jewish loyalty but a deep esthetic sensitivity, a desire that Jewish life should not only be free but, even more improbable, become beautiful—stripped of the disharmony resulting from Diaspora experience and transmuted by science and culture into an authentic symmetry. For a few weeks I found Meyer's home a more congenial place for preparing speeches and memoranda than our tiny room in the Barbizon Plaza Hotel.

While our main task was to frustrate the American trusteeship proposal in the General Assembly, we could not absent ourselves from the Security Council which was vainly trying to get a truce. The danger was that the Arabs would be successful in making a cessation of fire dependent upon a Jewish agreement to suspend the Declaration of Independence. If we refused this suspension, we would be held responsible for the continuation of hostilities that were already costly and might well turn into a massacre.

We had now secured access to the Security Council table, as had the Arab Higher Committee, and Moshe Sharett was the vigorous exponent of our cause. But the wheels of American policy were grinding implacably. By the end of April a proposal had been put forward for what amounted to a continuation of the Mandate, with the exception that the officials would be mobilized from several United Nations member states and not from Britain. The operative result would be that we would pass from one foreign domination to another, and the moment of Jewish independence would be postponed and probably lost.

At this time I had been helping Sharett draft one of his speeches in the Security Council. I had tried to summarize the international dilemma in single sentence: "What is it that the Security Council is trying to obtain? Does it seek a solution based on justice and equity, or it is merely looking for a solution against which the Arab governments will kindly consent not to use force?"

To my pleasure but embarrassment, Sharett received many congratulations on his speech, and especially on that sentence. This fact must have been in his mind when he called me on the telephone late on April 30. I was working hard on the draft of the speech for him to make in the General Assembly, explaining why the suspension of the partition scheme would not only be unjust but unpractical. My case was that the logic of ethnic and cultural autonomy in the country, together with the creation of a vacuum by Britain's withdrawal, had, in fact, crystallized two separate areas of jurisdiction. By the time the British Mandate ended, a Jewish state would be in virtual existence. To those who had said that force would be needed to impose partition, I would reply that force would be needed to prevent or cancel it, especially since there was no likelihood that the Jewish population would accept the jurisdiction of a new trustee.

Late at night Sharett's voice came on the telephone. He said shyly that since I was writing the speech, he thought that I ought to deliver it myself. It had always been a proud tradition of Zionist leaders that they appeared in their own colors both as writers and orators. The American conception of a "speech writer" was quite foreign to our experience, unless there were, as in Weizmann's later years, compelling reasons to use such a technique. Sharett was unwilling to appear in somebody else's colors. He was also chivalrously anxious that I should have a chance of making my own mark. Thus sometime at two o'clock in the morning of May 1, I found myself for the first time writing an address that I was going to deliver to an international tribunal under the attentive scrutiny of the whole Jewish world and with a vast international audience beyond. It was nearly seven o'clock with dawn rising in the gloomy ravine of West End Avenue when I finished my task. I barely had time to send it over to Sharett for a perfunctory check before I found myself sitting at the table of the General Assembly Committee, with all fifty-seven delegations attending, and with the plaque before me announcing "Jewish Agency for Palestine." Sharett sat behind me in paternal solicitude. Others of my colleagues in the Jewish Agency delegation watched with who-knows-what kind of sentiment.

The assignment had come to me so suddenly that I had had little time to reflect on its importance for me personally. All I remember is looking around the table and feeling much younger than anybody else in sight. I also recall the curiosity of many delegates when I finally took the floor. The only Jewish spokesmen they knew were Weizmann, Abba Hillel Silver and Moshe Sharett. I was a stranger to them. I had spoken in public many times but never on a world stage with millions of listeners beyond. It was no use pretending that this was the Cambridge Union or a Zionist meeting. I knew that I wanted intensely to succeed. I tried to recall that I had been given the chance to plead for justice for our people, for its right to live like others within its own patrimony and environment without benefit of trustees or guardians. The words may have flowed easily because they were nourished by an intense conviction.

At any rate, there was not a whisper in the large hall. I could see Trygve Lie studying me intently, Gromyko smiling grimly over his spectacles, and the American delegate, Philip C. Jessup, scribbling on a pad with dejected nervousness. My speech was an attempt to demolish the American trusteeship proposal, not only by challenging its moral assumptions but also by proving that it was no longer viable in any empirical sense. Once the idea of Jewish statehood had been internationally endorsed and the Jewish community had begun to establish its autonomous structure, there was no possibility that "second thoughts" could have any effect. The movement of nations from tutelage to independence could be quick or slow, but it could only have one direction: forward. There was no such thing as a voluntary reversion from the threshold of national liberty, back to a kind of international colonialism. I described the trusteeship plan as "an attempt to appease Arab violence. . . . It is an ill-fated digression. The suffering and grief that convulse our country today can be avoided only by seeking a way back to the highway of the partition resolution."

Most people's lives have their turning point, and this was mine. One writer has said about my speech on May 1, 1948: "Had his performance that day in the General Assembly been humdrum and officialese, had he spoken without passion, without any special distinctive quality, the opportunity would have been lost and he would have remained one of the backroom boys."

I had no need to worry about a "backroom" destiny any more. I noticed that Sharett had slipped away from his seat behind me as soon as I had finished. I wondered if he had been disappointed or otherwise embarrassed. Only later did I learn that he had gone to a telegraph office from which he cabled to my family in London.

HAPPY BE ABLE CONGRATULATE ON AUBREY'S STRIKING SPEECH IN APPEARING AS OFFICIAL SPOKESMAN JEWISH PEOPLE IN INTERNATIONAL COUNCIL STOP HIS EXTRAORDINARY BRILLIANCE IN THOUGHT AND EXPRESSION POWERFUL COGENCY OF REASONING DIGNITY OF PRESENTATION DID OUTSTANDING CREDIT TO OUR CAUSE AND MADE US ALL IMMEASURABLY PROUD STOP SPEECH MADE PROFOUND IMPRESSION ON ALL STOP FRIEND AND FOE LISTENED WITH RAPT ATTENTION MANY CHARACTERIZING IT AS ONE OF THE HIGHEST WATERMARKS OF ENTIRE SESSION STOP WARMEST REGARDS STOP MOSHE

The immense generosity of his action was to abide with me across the years. I found it hard to imagine many other Zionist leaders being capable of a similar gesture.

That evening I was among the guests, together with Sharett, at Trygve Lie's home in Forest Hills. Gromyko came up to me, pumped my hand warmly and said, "You have helped to kill trusteeship." Trygve Lie was similarly ebullient. In a corner cowered Ernest Bevin and his wife, both sending out waves of venom and hostility.

There was no need to take the floor again against trusteeship. The proposal was incurring a sharp fusillade of assault from the Soviet Union for obvious reasons, and from smaller countries such as New Zealand, Australia and Latin American republics, which were affronted by the idea that the United Nations could reverse its decision in response to illicit force.

In addition to the tension of my maiden speech and the attempts to thwart the trusteeship proposal, I became involved in another enterprise. Between March and May 1948, our relations with the United States were painfully tense. Instead of being one of our main allies in support of partition, the United States had withdrawn into the trusteeship proposal which we regarded as a frustration of our dearest hopes. At the same time, President Truman's conscience was sorely tormented. Weizmann had a special capacity to arouse his remorse. Truman's subsequent writings give the impression that he had been deceived by his own officials into accepting a proposal which he regarded as preparatory to partition, and which they envisaged as a substitute for it. The evidence is not convincing; and it is doubtful whether the reversal on partition could have been made without explicit presidential acquiescence. Whatever the truth about that, however, it is clear that Truman wanted to make his way back to the partition plan.

The day after the Passover Seder, Weizmann called me to his suite in the Waldorf Towers with an exciting story to tell. He himself had planned to attend the Seder service with his friends Siegfried and Lola Kramarsky, solid and fervent Zionists who had emigrated to New York from Holland. A few hours before leaving his hotel suite, he had received a visit from Judge Samuel Rosenman, who had been Roosevelt's speech writer and was now a close and trusted adviser to Truman. The President had called Rosenman into the Oval Office and told him quite simply, "I have Dr. Weizmann on my conscience." He had not realized on March 19 that the State Department had gone so far in the abandonment of the partition plan. If the General Assembly session could be surmounted without reversing partition and if a Jewish state was declared on its own responsibility, the President would recognize it immediately. Thus, fortified by international legitimacy, the new state could fight for its survival not as an unregarded outcast, but as a member of the international family.

Truman had stipulated one absolute condition. He would deal with Weizmann, and with him alone. It was essential, therefore, for Weizmann to stay in America and be available for the unfolding of the plan.

Our fight against the American trusteeship proposal now had a new and dramatic incentive. The position must surely be recorded as bizarre. Here was a President of the United States willing to recognize a Jewish state if it was established in defiance of the trusteeship proposal that his own State Department was seeking to press on the United Nations.

Yet in the first week of May the chief obstacle to the proclamation to Jewish independence seemed to lie in Jewish hesitations. It was plain that Arab armies were mustering for invasion. The Haganah was hard pressed in resisting the assaults of Palestine Arabs and of irregular forces under Fawzi el-Kawakji from the north. On May 11 the Haganah chief of operations, Yigael Yadin, gave Zionist leaders in Jerusalem a somber and disconcerting account of the sacrifices and difficulties that would be certain to follow the invasion of Palestine by Arab armies. The chief problem was the appalling scarcity of sophisticated equipment in the Haganah, as well as the difficulty of operating freely while the remnant of British rule remained. A group of State Department officials, led by Dean Rusk, was making an earnest attempt to dissuade Moshe Sharett and Nahum Goldmann from proclaiming a state on May 15. Goldmann has explained quite candidly in his autobiography that he came to favor the postponement of the declaration. Sharett wavered; but when he saw Secretary of State George C. Marshall in Washington on May 12, he was firm as a rock. He described the impending hour of the Mandate's expiration as "a moment of opportunity for the Jewish nation, which, if missed, might be irrevocably lost." Marshall had not argued strenuously against this logic. He had simply put America in the observer's role: "If you make that decision, you will be alone. If you succeed, I will wish you well. But I warn you not to accept military advice too easily."

Our reports from Israel indicated that Ben Gurion was steadfast. He even sent Meyer Weisgal out of the country to telephone from Nice to elicit Weizmann's opinion. It was a strange role for the so-called moderate to be summoning the Jewish people to the utmost intransigence and tenacity. Weizmann told Weisgal, with some Yiddish imprecations, "Tell them to proclaim the state no matter what happens." Weizmann also pursued Sharett to the airport on his way back to Israel with an entreaty: "Don't let them weaken, Moshe; it may be now or never."

On a much humbler level, I was taking a similar line in discussions at Jewish Agency headquarters. In my first intervention, I expressed the opinion that it was vain to postpone statehood in order to avoid the Arab invasion. "The Arab invasion will happen in any case. It will be the inevitable result of British evacuation. Our problem, therefore, is not whether we can avoid invasion, but whether we shall be invaded as a state or as a hesitant, nebulous entity." I could not, of course, use the argument about the Truman-Rosenman conversation, since this was kept in the private knowledge of very few of us in Washington and New York. Yet the story was beginning to leak. On May 7, for example, Bartley Crum, who had been a member of the Anglo-American Committee, went to see Emanuel Neumann with what he called the "strange story" that President Truman would be recognizing a Jewish state within a week.

In the General Assembly we were fighting not to obtain a resolution, but to avoid one. We felt that if the United Nations declared a trusteeship, President Truman, despite his good intentions, might find it difficult to recognize a state in a way that would involve defiance of an international decision. We lobbied, pleaded and got our friends to filibuster. Everything depended now on the decision to be made by the Jewish leaders in Palestine herself. Weizmann sat down on May 13 and wrote a letter to Truman asking for recognition of the Jewish state when it was established. His secretary, Joseph Cohn, took the overnight train to Washington and brought it to the White House. On May 14, while the United Nations Political Committee was conducting a desultory debate on paragraphs of the American trusteeship proposal, there came an electric moment. On the basis of radio reports and telegrams he had received from Tel Aviv, Abba Hillel Silver, who was sitting at the Jewish Agency desk, broke in quietly with the following words:

> *This morning at ten o'clock the Jewish state was proclaimed in Palestine. Thus what was envisaged in the resolution of the General Assembly last November has been, as far as the Jewish State is concerned, implemented. Thus too there has been consummated the age old dream of Israel to be re-established as a free and independent people in its ancient homeland.*

Silver's reference to the implementation of the General Assembly resolution had great irony, since for the last few weeks the UN had been frenziedly attempting to prevent the fulfillment of its own resolution.

The Arab states were irritated but not overly alarmed by this development. They still hoped to strangle Israel in her infancy by a combination of military violence and political obstruction.

In the afternoon of May 14 the discussion was transferred to the plenary session at Flushing Meadow. Our aim was to have the meeting conclude without creating a legal fact incompatible with the establishment of a Jewish state that day. The main issue would obviously be determined by a trial of strength in the area, and not by United Nations documents. Nevertheless, the legitimacy of our state would be affected in the eyes of many governments if a United Nations regime were established, even theoretically, at the time when the British Mandate expired. Even President Truman might hesitate to recognize a state in an area in which the United Nations claimed jurisdiction.

As the hours went by, it became clear that no general trusteeship would be voted. There remained Jerusalem, to which the United Nations in November 1947 had promised "peace, order, security, well-being and constructive measure for development." None of these gifts had come from the UN. Instead, the city was abandoned to savage war. The Jewish Quarter in the Old City was under siege and doomed to fall. In the city outside the walls, the Jewish population, cut off from the coast by intervening Arab armies, was subjected not only to bombardment by Transjordanian guns, but also to the prospect of starvation and thirst. The alleged interest of the world community in the city's welfare had not been expressed in any serious effort to secure a truce. Indeed, since the absence of fighting in Jerusalem would have released Jewish forces for other sectors, the UN simply allowed the fighting to proceed rather than confer a "military advantage" on the Jews. The Arab governments were hostile to internationalization. They were sure that if the United Nations kept out of the way, the whole city would fall into their hands. The Iraqi delegate stated that the Statute for Internationalization was "illegal," that Jerusalem must take its chances with the rest of the country, and that the siege and denial of water must be maintained not only as a legitimate act of war, but even in the event of a truce.

Thus on May 14 the United Nations had its ultimate chance of taking charge in Jerusalem. The opportunity was deliberately cast away. Guatemala, Australia and the United States successively proposed resolutions which would have put a United Nations flag in Jerusalem under varying degrees of responsibility. All of them were rejected. It was not a passive default, but an active relinquishing of responsibility in a critical hour. Israel would never forget the lesson. If the United Nations would not take responsibility in time of peril, by what right could it claim authority when the danger was passed? At six o'clock, when the Mandate was ended, the representative of Iraq arose exultantly to cry "The game is up!" The General Assembly had lost its right of succession.

With supreme indifference to the flow of history, the Assembly went on to discuss the general trusteeship proposal. My own mind was fixed on Washington, where Weizmann's letter to Truman requesting recognition of a "Jewish state" had first been delivered. There was now a great deal of agitated whispering around the table where the American delegates sat. There was a rumor that the United States had recognized the new State of Israel! Ambassador Philip Jessup has since written: "We laughed it off—how could that happen without the United States delegation being informed?" The Colombian delegate, Dr. Lopez, mounted the rostrum to ask the American delegates point-blank if the rumor was true. Ambassador Francis Sayre of the American mission in the Trusteeship Council replied lamely that "for the time being he had no official information on the subject."

I went into the delegates' lounge to call Weizmann at his hotel. His wife came on the line. She told me that "all is well." I later learned that Truman had received Weizmann's letter in the morning and had used it as a lever for intensive action. He had called in his senior advisers—Secretary of State George Marshall, Undersecretary Robert Lovett, Clark Clifford and a State Department official. The meeting had dispersed several times—once in order to receive Eliahu Elath's message delivered by cab to the White House security guard, pointing out that the state for which Weizmann had sought recognition in his May 13 letter was called "Israel." This news had come from Tel Aviv in time for Elath's action and for Silver's statement to the committee at Lake Success. Truman had granted recognition by letter to Elath at six-fifteen. The announcement had been put on the air at once. Jessup had sent an aide to Trygve Lie's room to make inquiries. The Secretary-General, who rarely neglected gastronomic priorities, had naturally gone off to dine. But Jessup's aide had found Truman's statement on a ticker-tape message in Lie's wastepaper basket. Jessup smoothed it out, mounted the General Assembly rostrum and read it as best he could:

> *This Government has been informed that a Jewish State has been proclaimed in Palestine and recognition has been requested by the provisional government thereof. The United States recognizes the de facto authority of the new State of Israel.*

The United States now abandoned the trusteeship proposal and moved successfully for the appointment of a Mediator. It was now eight-thirty. In an exhausted daze I left the Assembly hall and took a cab to the Waldorf Towers, where Weizmann lay in bed triumphant but fatigued.

News came rolling in thick and fast. The Soviet Union and Guatemala had recognized Israel. Egyptian planes had bombed Tel Aviv. Ben Gurion had made his first broadcast as Prime Minister. As the tumult of Jewry's greatest day in modern history swept through the streets of New York, Weizmann lay silent in the darkened hotel room, with a few of us around him. Cables came from Tel Aviv telling of familiar Zionist leaders bearing new and glamorous ministerial titles. But there was no news or greeting for Weizmann. A sense of abandonment and ingratitude invaded his mood. Suddenly a bellboy appeared with flowers, fruit and—a telegram from the Zionist Labor leaders in Tel Aviv.

> ON THE OCCASION OF THE ESTABLISHMENT OF THE JEWISH STATE WE SEND OUR GREETINGS TO YOU WHO HAVE DONE MORE THAN ANY LIVING MAN TOWARDS ITS CREATION. YOUR HELP AND STAND HAVE STRENGTHENED ALL OF US. WE LOOK FORWARD TO THE DAY WHEN WE SHALL SEE YOU AT THE HEAD OF THE STATE ESTABLISHED IN PEACE. BEN GURION KAPLAN MYERSON REMEZ SHERTAK

I went out into Park Avenue. It was dark and late. Back in our hotel Suzy and I waited until midnight when the *New York Times* with its banner headlines gave us the news: Victory in Washington and the United Nations, but danger in the Middle East. The British High Commissioner, Sir Alan Cunningham, had sailed from Haifa on a cruiser with the last remaining units of the government. Egyptian forces had crossed the frontier and advanced into the Negev. An Iraqi column moved in strength toward the Jordan River. The Transjordanian Arab Legion was arrayed along the riverbank with its main encampment at Zerka. On the upper reaches of the Jordan a Syrian brigade was ready to attack our settlements in the hot green valley. The Arab governments had resolved to occupy the country, subjugate its Jewish population and strangle Israel's statehood at its birth. Israel was experiencing the joys of birth and the fear of death in a single taste.

How could I have dreamt a few months before that I would be anywhere near the center of this drama? It was a day that would linger and shine in the national memory forever—a moment of truth that would move Israel to its ultimate generations.

Before retiring, I sent Sharett a cabled message of congratulation. I added a personal question: "What do I do now?"

The First Flush
of Statehood
1948-1950

THE END OF BRITISH RULE; INVASION BY ARAB ARMIES; THE PROCLAMATION
of Israel's independence; the defeat of the trusteeship proposal; the
recognition of Israel by the United States. All these took place within a
single day. Could any twenty-four hours ever have been charged
with greater transformations?

The central fact in Jewish political life had always been passivity.
Jewish history had consisted of what Jews suffered, endured, resisted or
survived, not what they themselves initiated or resolved. The point of
reference had always been the attitudes and policies of others. Now,
for a change, the world had been waiting with curiosity and even
with apprehension to see what Jews would say or do. Our history had
entered a phase of autonomy.

What a long and weary journey it had been across vast space and
time since our nation had first been born under those very skies!
There had been the generations in which kings and prophets
flourished, and then the seeming end when Jerusalem crumbled before the legions of Titus Vespasianus. Across all the intervening centuries the beat of Jewish hearts had everywhere been quickened by
the prospect of return. Now the hour of choice had come, and it had
been seized. No matter what ensued, something of great moment had
been enacted of which future Jewish generations would never cease to
speak and dream.

Yet most of these contented thoughts were only to arise in our

116

minds in later weeks. On May 15 there was no disposition to ponder very deeply on what had occurred. The question was whether we had made a fleeting gesture to be followed by violent submergence—or whether we had established something which would endure. In the British and some other European newspapers our proclamation of independence was treated as a valiant but futile act of defiance that would soon be forgotten in the wrath of an Arab victory. The Etzion villages, cut off from any hinterland of Jewish defense, had been subdued and captured. Much effort, risk and sacrifice would have been saved had they been evacuated in advance; but not for the first or the last time, hard-headed security considerations had been subordinated to symbolism and morale. More ominous was the question of our prospect of survival against the new rush of Arab armies. The first stages of the war seemed to bode ill for Israel's cause. The danger came from the north, where Syrian, Lebanese, Iraqi and Jordanian armies planned to move on Haifa and capture its port and refineries. Meanwhile the Egyptians attacked along the coast while the remnants of the Arab Liberation Army harassed Jerusalem and assaulted Jewish settlements in the rest of the country. The Transjordanian Arab Legion had captured the installations of the Palestine Electric Corporation on May 14. And the ring was growing tighter around the new city of Jerusalem.

Yet between November 28, 1947, and May 14, 1948, the Jewish condition, though still fragile, had become more robust than could have been imagined before. Haifa, Safed, Tiberias and Acre had been secured. About a hundred Arab villages had fallen. Kawakji's forces had been routed in the north. All Galilee, east and west, was under Jewish control. But the Jewish position remained unstable in the Negev; and the 2,500 Jews within the walls of the Old City of Jerusalem seemed to be in danger of massacre, or at least of captivity.

Although the General Assembly had dispersed in disorder, our political battle had not ended. Our interest was, of course, to obtain a cease-fire without any diminution of our new-won sovereignty. This was also the policy of the United States and the Soviet Union. The Arab aim was to disrupt Israel's statehood by successful war, or at least to intimidate the United Nations into purchasing a cease-fire at the price of Israel's sovereignty.

The proclamation of our independence was having some curious personal effects. Zionist leaders and representatives now had to make a choice from which the lack of statehood had long shielded them. Would they take Israel's citizenship and cut themselves loose from all other allegiances? Or would they maintain their Diaspora nationalities and thus be ineligible to represent a "foreign" state? Abba Hillel

Silver and Emanuel Neumann made the latter choice. With be-
wildering rapidity they left the central arena, leaving me and a few
other colleagues in solitary vigilance at Sixty-sixth Street and at United
Nations headquarters. They had given American Zionism its most
potent and effective hour. When the Security Council convened on May
15 to consider the possibility of a cease-fire, the Jewish Agency table
was occupied by Dr. Mordechai Eliash, a gentle, venerable Jerusalem
lawyer, whom we advanced to the table with no particular instructions, simply because he seemed more "adult" than the rest of us. To
my surprise I received an indignant cable from Ben Gurion and
Sharett stating categorically that it was I who should give expression
to Israel's policies in continuation of my appearance on May 1.

Thus, on May 16, 1948, I began an almost daily vigil at the Security
Council table. On May 20 a cable from Sharett informed Trygve Lie
that the Provisional Government of Israel had appointed me as its
representative to the United Nations. I was six years younger than the
thirty-eight-year-old Gromyko, who was then the baby of the diplomats
accredited to the UN. I could not, however, deprive him of his official
juniority, since Israel only had observer status, not yet having been
elected to membership. Nevertheless, our delegates were now an
established part of the UN landscape and I proceeded to organize our
mission at 16 East Sixty-sixth Street, with Arthur Lourie, Jacob
Robinson, Moshe Tov, Michael Comay and Gideon Rafael as my chief
associates, and I. L. Kennen as our information officer. We soon moved
to our new building at 11 East Seventieth Street.

Two plaques now went up on the door. One read: CONSULATE-GEN-
ERAL OF THE STATE OF ISRAEL. The other: PERMANENT DELEGATION OF
ISRAEL TO THE UNITED NATIONS. It is hard to describe the exaltation
that radiated from this edifice to millions of Jews in New York and
countless others beyond. Whenever I came out on the steps leading
into the street, Jews would be standing there, sometimes in silence, at
other times clicking away with cameras in an effort to absorb and
perpetuate the new wonder of statehood. The consulate-general under
Arthur Lourie's leadership was now frequented by many prospective
immigrants and tourists. But we suspected that many dozens came in
and out for no purpose except to see what an Israeli passport looked
like and how an Israeli consulate functioned. The notion that there
was an Israeli delegate to the United Nations took them even further
up the ladder of ecstasy. On festive occasions the Israeli national flag
would be hoisted, whereupon the cup of Jewish contentment would
overflow.

For many months, the drama of the Jewish fight for freedom had
riveted millions of radio listeners and television watchers. The Se-

curity Council, still in its early youth, emitted an air of power and
dignity as the highest organ of the world's security, and its meetings
were newsworthy in the highest degree. The only circumstance that
marred the taste of our elevation was the fact that the plaque before
me in the Security Council still read "Jewish Agency for Palestine," although the Agency had by now become a fund-raising and propaganda
organization serving Diaspora Jews without any effect on Israeli
policies. I was not the representative or even the employee of the
Jewish Agency at all. I remarked on this anomaly to Ambassador
Warren Austin. He told me in fatherly tones that our delegations
should keep close together and watch for the first opportunity to get
the name "Israel" onto the table. He thought, however, that
there would not be the requisite seven votes for this immediately, so
that it would be wise to await a friendly president who might help us
through the procedural minefields. (The presidency rotates by alphabet each month.) In the meantime, my more important task was to
secure a cease-fire while resisting Arab and British attempts to diminish our statehood.

I intervened briefly in the May 18 discussion. It was urgent to get
the cease-fire injunction ratified. But when Arab and British representatives said that the cease-fire should avoid conferring a "military
advantage" on either party, they suggested that this should be interpreted as a ban on the immigration of able-bodied Jews to Israel, since
it would mean an accretion of fighting manpower. This, of course, was
preposterous. There was no attempt to prevent thousands of Arabs
from neighboring countries from joining the Arab armies, which had
no right to be in Palestine at all.

I decided, however, to state the Israeli case on deeper grounds of
principle. I reminded the Security Council that Israel was now a
sovereign state, that Article II (7) of the Charter forbade the United
Nations to intervene in any matters within the domestic jurisdiction
of a state, and that immigration to Israel was therefore no business of
the Arabs, the British, the Security Council, the United Nations or
anybody else.

The novelty of this observation had a startling effect on my hearers.
For the first time, we were able to explore some of the effects of
sovereignty on the style and atmosphere of the Jewish dialogue with
the outside world. The phrase "none of your business" could not
rationally have been uttered by a Jewish spokesman in all the previous
centuries.

The Arab armies were not successful in the field, but neither was
Israel's military situation unclouded. Our loss of life was heavy. The

Negev was cut off from easy communication with the rest of the country. A ring of steel enclosed us in Jerusalem. The administrative machinery of the state was moving into action under a constant shower of shrapnel and bombs. The Arab governments were determined to sell the cease-fire dearly. On May 26, with the State of Israel less than two weeks old, they brazenly proposed to the Security Council that Arab readiness to cease fire be purchased by a declaration of "the Jewish authorities" that they regarded the proclamation of Israel's statehood as null and void, and that no further Jewish immigration would be accepted.

I took the floor for five minutes that I shall never forget. My words were:

> Here is a flat and defiant rejection of the Security Council's cease-fire resolution. In its place, we have a proposal for revoking Israel's statehood and independence. The sovereignty regained by an ancient people after its long march through the dark night of exile is to be surrendered at pistol-point.
>
> It becomes my duty to make our attitude clear. If the Arab states want peace with Israel, they can have it. If they want war, they can have that too. But, whether they want peace or war, they can have it only with a sovereign State of Israel.

I went on to add that "immigration into Israel is no business of Egypt or Iraq or the Arab League and can form no part of any discussion with them."

This was dramatic stuff, with a flamboyant touch about it. It was not, however, disproportionate to the occasion. After all, Jewish states had not been proclaimed in every decade, and the idea of abolishing our sovereignty was not something to be discussed in prosaic terms. My short sentences with their monosyllabic words reverberated strongly, and I was henceforward "a television celebrity." On May 28 the New York *Post* treated its readers to a picturesque representation of me. It was good enough to describe me as having "a friendly but abrupt manner, a somewhat breathless voice, a walk reminiscent of a happy bear cub, but there is nothing vague about his mind. It has whiplash swiftness and precision. His speech is smooth, brilliant, richly ironic and marks him as a rare stylist in an organization marked chiefly by its boundless capacity for talk."

Similar things were being written elsewhere, but the most ironic impact of my sudden fame was in Israel itself. To thousands of Israelis who read their newspapers and listened to their radio endlessly in those days, I was unknown by name or face. "Who is our representative at the United Nations?" asked a leading daily journal. It was not a rhetorical question. It was asked in genuine curiosity. *Davar* had an able representative at the UN, S. N. Schneiderman, whose biographical sketch about me on June 16 was the first comprehensive attempt to tell Israelis something about the man who was trying to express their dreams and visions to the world. Opposition newspapers, faithful to the Herut Party, managed to hint darkly that I had a record in what they ominously called "British Intelligence." Since this was a reference to my role in training Palmach fighters in World War II, the irony was extreme. Israelis and Zionists are conservative in their loyalties to familiar leaders and do not admit new names into the pantheon very easily. Everybody had heard of Weizmann, Silver, Ben Gurion, Sharett. But who in heaven's name was Eban? Where had Sharett made this discovery? What had given him and Ben Gurion the courage to produce me out of obscurity with jack-in-the-box suddenness? All these themes were gravely revolved in the Israeli press and on countless Tel Aviv balconies amid the starker news of the ebb and flow of battle.

The vigor of a young Israel that had nothing to lose and was fighting with great resolution had a contagious effect on other governments. On May 28 the Security Council met to deliberate on another Arab refusal to cease fire. This time the United States came out in our support with a loud roar. Referring to Arab declarations, Ambassador Austin said:

> *Their statements are the best evidence we have of the international character of this aggression. Therefore, we have evidence of the highest type concerning the international violation of the law, namely the admission by those who commit this violation. What is it that they are trying to say? They are saying: "We are there only for the purpose of overwhelming the Government of Israel. We are going to overwhelm it by power and we're going to determine this international question ourselves." An existing independent government cannot be blotted out in that way. It cannot be blotted out by just sitting at the Security Council table and ignoring it. The Arab states are taking the only course that can be taken and that is marching in with their armies and blotting it out. This is a matter of international concern, a matter of so great importance that we cannot sit here and say "Oh, we wash our hands of it. We shall not do anything about it that will be effective. We know, of course, that this is a violation of the Charter."*

Referring to the Arab claim that their operations were aimed at the maintenance of peace, the American delegate said:

This is equivalent in its absurdity to alleging that these five armies are there to maintain peace and, at the same time, are conducting a bloody war.

The Soviet representatives tried very hard to keep pace with the United States in the vehemence of its denunciation of the Arab invasion. Never since has Israel known such rhetorical encouragement by the world's two major powers. I do not know what Andrei Gromyko thinks today of what he said in the Security Council on May 29:

What is happening in Palestine can only be described as military operations organized by a group of states against the new Jewish State. . . . The states whose forces have invaded Palestine have ignored the Security Council's resolution. This is not the first time that the Arab states, which organized the invasion of Palestine, have ignored a decision of the Security Council. The Soviet delegation deems it essential that the Council should state its opinion more clearly and more firmly with regard to this attitude of the Arab states towards the decisions of the Security Council.

On another occasion a few days later, Gromyko described Israel in memorable terms:

The Soviet delegation cannot but express surprise at the position adopted by the Arab states, and particularly the fact that those states or some of them at least have resorted to such actions as sending their troops to Palestine and carrying out military operations aimed at the suppression of the national liberation movement in Palestine! *We can only wonder at the course taken by the Arab states which have not yet achieved their own full liberation from foreign influence, and some of which have not even real national independence.*

The debate ebbed and flowed, surged and receded, for over three weeks while the clash of arms went on in the field. By early June, Israel's resistance, together with Great Power pressure at the United Nations, was beginning to take its toll of Arab ardor. It had become possible to think of a realistic cease-fire. Although Israeli forces were victorious in the stricken field, they stood in great need of rest and reinforcement. Our weapons were becoming depleted, and replacements, though obtainable in Czechoslovakia and more surreptiously in France, would take some weeks to reach our shores. On May 28 I was able to cable Jerusalem that I thought it possible that we might get a truce resolution in the Security Council's discussion the next day. To my surprise, I received a telephone call from Ben Gurion. Transatlantic conversations were not common in those days, nor was Ben Gurion the most lucid and comprehensible locutor across the wires. But he did manage to convey to me, with the utmost clarity and emphasis, that some of our military situations, and especially the one concerning supplies to Jerusalem, made it urgent to get a truce as quickly as possible. He said to me with engaging simplicity, "Why can't they have a night meeting? At the Zionist congresses we always had our most important meetings through the night."

I doubted whether the Zionist precedent would impress the Security Council, but after consultation with the Soviet and American delegates, I was able to secure an early and expedited procedure.

Sir Alexander Cadogan on behalf of the United Kingdom had proposed a truce with some very burdensome conditions. The Mediator was to impose an embargo on the export of war materials to Palestine and the Arab states. All parties were asked not to introduce able-bodied men of military age into the area. The Mediator was requested to make recommendations about an eventual settlement for Palestine—a provision which clearly put a question mark over the November 1947 resolution. The Security Council adopted this resolution on May 30. After a great deal of argument for over a week, the truce was accepted and put into operation on June 11. The cables that I received from Ben Gurion and Sharett gave me to understand that the cease-fire was nothing less than providential in saving the new city of Jerusalem from falling through lack of supplies, including water and ammunition. Although it later became fashionable to state that the United Nations had "not raised a finger" on behalf of international order or in support of Israel, the fact is that the first truce was regarded by Israeli leaders as a national success.

There was, however, no atmosphere of political truce. During June 1948 I was occupied at the Security Council in a campaign to prevent the adoption of Count Folke Bernadotte's report, which would have deprived Israel of some of its most important assets. The first sacrifice that Bernadotte asked of Israel was the virtual renunciation of its independence, for he proposed that Israel form a "union" with Transjordan. The Bernadotte plan contained the preposterous proposal that "immigration within its borders should be within the competence of each member, provided that following a period of two years from the establishment of the Union either member would be entitled to request the Council of the Union to review the immigration policy of the other member and to render a ruling thereon." If we did not agree to this ruling, the matter would be "referred to the

Economic and Social Council of the United Nations, whose decision, taking into account the principle of economic absorptive capacity, would be binding on the member whose policy was at issue."

This provision was so insulting that we had little indignation left with which to say what we thought about Bernadotte's other proposal —that all or part of the Negev, as well as Jerusalem, be included in Arab territory. There was also to be a free port at Haifa and a free airport at Lydda. Israel was to be virtually dismembered.

It would be charitable to believe that the coincidence of these proposals with Britain's strategic interests was a matter of chance. The Israeli decision was to have nothing to do with Bernadotte's plan. We would meet the Arab invaders on their chosen ground. Since they had decided to reject the 1947 delimitation in favor of a verdict by arms—so be it. We, too, would accept the judgment of the battlefield. An irritating provision of Bernadotte's report was the abandonment of the internationalization of Jerusalem in order to include it in Arab territory, with "municipal autonomy" for the Jewish community. Since Jerusalem was the only city in the Middle East, and indeed in the world, in which Jews had been a majority for three quarters of a century, the effrontery of this proposal left us breathless.

One of my preoccupations in June was created by a tragic domestic issue. On April 28, in anticipation of the end of the Mandate and an Arab invasion, the Haganah and the IZL had signed an agreement to concert all military operations. This, however, still left each force as an independent organization. The anomaly spilled over beyond the date of Israel's declaration of independence. On June 22 the Irgun sought to bring men and arms ashore at Tel Aviv from the ship *Altalena*. Ben Gurion understood that with all our need of weapons and manpower, the main issue was one of sovereignty and governmental authority; if a government does not have a monopoly of armed force, it has no way of carrying out its international obligations or maintaining its internal authority. Ben Gurion's government decided that the Irgun's action constituted civil disobedience. Orders were given to Palmach units to open fire on the *Altalena*. There were deaths and casualties. The Irgun headquarters was raided, arrests made and a curfew imposed. Ben Gurion realized that he could no longer permit the Irgun or the Lechi to fight under their own commanders. A committee was set up to reorganize the Israeli army on a unified basis. A few months later the Irgun elected to disband all its forces and come under the discipline of the Haganah. But Ben Gurion's decision on June 22 must certainly be recorded as one of his most dramatic and formative acts. Although his stand was mainly inspired by considerations of internal cohesion, the international stakes were impressive. It was clear that the Israeli government, which still bore the modest title "provisional," had concentrated an effective authority in its hands.

When the Security Council resumed its sessions in July, I developed a strong criticism of Count Bernadotte's proposals. In one speech, I said that "it was very much as though the surgeon went away with most of the patient's vital organs." The main issue, however, was whether the truce would be renewed. Here the Arab governments faced a dilemma: if the truce was prolonged, the effect would be to accept Israel's statehood as final and to pave the way for its consolidation; on the other hand, if the Arabs renewed the fighting, they stood a chance of losing even more territory than during the fighting between December and June 11. To acquiesce in the situation produced by Israel's arms was too much for their enmity to bear. The Arab governments unanimously decided to refuse the prolongation of the truce and to open fire, irrespective of the Mediator's appeal.

On July 13 I made the longest speech I had delivered at an international tribunal since my maiden speech on May 1. Having watched the General Assembly and Security Council at close hand, I decided to develop an original approach to the formulation and enunciation of my addresses. The UN was caught up in a strange semantic fog, generated very largely by a juridical and procedural emphasis. The organization was at the height of its self-importance, and something of this rubbed off on the delegates, who tended to puff out their chests with a strong premonition of universal authority. The characteristic way for a speech to begin was: "My delegation has given careful attention to document S/535 Addendum 1 as amended by S/5896/Revision 2. The question is how this proposal can be harmonized with Article 39, Paragraph 2 of the Charter which states . . ." This legalistic jargon was almost unintelligible to anybody outside the UN building and to most people within it. My decision was to seek my audience not among the few hundred people in the room, but among the hundreds of thousands, and perhaps millions, outside. To the distress of some of my diplomatic associates in our delegation, I decided to avoid being a documentary expert and to speak frankly to listening ears outside. In this spirit, I began my statement on July 13:

There is not a single person in this room or outside it who does not know in the depths of his heart that the Arab states, by resuming their attacks upon Israel, have committed an act of aggression.

After emphasizing where the responsibility for the fighting lay, I addressed myself to the Arab demand that Israel should renounce its independence:

> *Israel is the product of the most sustained historic tenacity which the ages recall. The Jewish people has not striven towards this goal for twenty centuries in order that, having once achieved it, it will now surrender it in response to an illegitimate and unsuccessful aggression. Whatever else changes, this will not. The State of Israel is an immutable part of the international landscape. To plan the future without it is to build delusions on sand.*

The tone and the spirit of this address ensured a broad resonance. By now I was not having any trouble through not being known to my fellow countrymen in Israel. Appreciative articles and comments were now rolling off the Israeli printing presses. They usually described my emergence as a "sudden apparition." This was not altogether accurate in view of my Zionist upbringing and my anonymous but effective apprenticeship in Zionist service since 1946.

Writing nearly three decades later, I can still sense the special exhilaration in which I lived during those days. I felt a complete convergence between my own political task and the triumphant feats of Israel's forces in the field. By various acts and ceremonies in May and June, the Israeli Defense Forces had been formally incorporated. Ranks had been given, and the mysterious anonymity of the Haganah broken. The Israeli public now had military leaders to adulate, but it still focused an intense interest on the United Nations arena, which had been so decisive in bringing about a transition in our fortunes.

We were able to record a diplomatic success when on July 15 the Security Council, on the joint initiative of the United States and the Soviet Union, determined that the Arab refusal to renew the truce constituted a threat to the peace and "ordered" a permanent cease-fire under penalty of sanctions.

A disastrous week in the modern history of Arab nationalism followed. The Arab states had boasted loudly of being able to inflict "a massacre as in the days of the Mongols," but now their armies were reeling back in defeat and their governments were pursued with international condemnation at United Nations headquarters, throughout the United States, the Soviet Union and much of the free world.

In the fighting during the third week in July, Israeli forces erupted beyond the November 1947 lines, captured Ramle and Lydda, and consolidated their position throughout western Galilee and in large parts of the Negev. I could not help recalling what Azzam Pasha had told me in September 1947 about the "inevitability of war" as the ultimate determinant of the birth and scope of Jewish statehood. His prediction had come to pass in the opposite sense to that which he had foreseen or desired.

Because of our successes in diplomacy and battle, I found it intolerable that Israel's name should still be forbidden in the international forum. The plaque announcing my delegation as that of "The Jewish Agency for Palestine" was becoming not only grotesque, but insulting. I decided therefore to use the month of the presidency of the Security Council of the Ukrainian representative, Dimitri Manuilski, as the occasion for correcting this anomaly. My determination was greatly sharpened by Cadogan's insistence on avoiding any reference to the forbidden word "Israel." It was still evident that we did not have seven affirmative votes for changing our appellation from the "Jewish Agency" to "Israel." But, I thought, if the chairman was calmly to call us to the table as "the representatives of Israel," there might be a chance that his ruling would be accepted, or if challenged, that the challenge would fail. I rehearsed all this with Ambassador Jessup and with the Soviet representative, Jacob Malik, who mischievously confessed to me that "the Soviet Union may have some measure of influence on the head of the Ukrainian delegation."

Thus, one day in July, Manuilski quietly opened the proceedings by saying, "I call the representative of the Provisional Government of Israel to the table." As I walked to the horseshoe desk a UN official, properly briefed by his superiors, put down in front of me a plaque reading "Israel." I do not remember ever having seen a more welcome piece of painted wood.

After a moment of silence, all hell broke loose. Led by Cadogan, the Arabs and others strongly protested the action of the Security Council's president in "forcing the issue." The Arab representatives declared that they would not sit in a room with anybody in front of whom the offensive word "Israel" was paraded on a plaque. Cadogan —a short, wizened, somewhat mummified character who gave the impression of regarding most of the human race with snobbish contempt—burst all bounds of reticence in imploring the Security Council to change its president's ruling. Since I presumed that there would only be five votes for this challenge, I suffered a strong cardiac twinge when the Argentinean delegate announced that he would support the British motion. (We were later told that since Argentina knew that Israel would carry the day, she saw no harm in winning a little Arab good will by joining the vote.) At any rate, we scraped through with one vote to spare, and thereafter the name "Israel" was never to be absent from the international concert. The representative of the

Palestine Arab Higher Committee, Jamal el-Husseini, walked out of the room, vowing to stay away as long as I was described as a representative of Israel. He has not been seen since. The effect of Jamal el-Husseini's act was that Israel superseded "Arab Palestine" at the Security Council table.

I had received Sharett's permission to come home to Israel as soon as there was a respite in the Security Council's debates. Since it seemed likely that from mid-July the arena would be quiet until the General Assembly convened in September, Suzy and I took the opportunity to go to Britain on the *Queen Elizabeth,* where we stayed for a few days and then went on to Jerusalem.

There was something triumphal in our arrival by air at the small Haifa airport in August. It turned out that the defiant tone that I had adopted in the Security Council corresponded to Israel's deepest psychological needs. Many people in Jerusalem and Tel Aviv during the siege and assault by Arab armies had listened to me on shortwave radio sets, so that my voice was better known than my face. But the constant publication of photographs had given me a high recognition factor.

Moshe Sharett went around beaming like a proud father. A meeting was convened by him in the Tel Aviv Museum, in which Israel's independence had been declared, in order to give me the chance to address a large and selective audience. The papers the next day expressed ecstatic relief at the fact that I spoke Hebrew. At a meeting of the Cabinet under Ben Gurion's kindly gaze, with David Remez and Zalman Shazar paying more attention to my Hebrew turn of phrase than to my political ideas, I analyzed the prospects of our political struggle in the coming months. My feeling was that the war might not yet be over. It would be wise to press on toward full international status while the alliance of Washington and Moscow still prevailed. I urged that we attempt to achieve membership in the United Nations; this would automatically ensure our admission to all the specialized agencies and thus bring about our integration into the expanding international fabric.

Israel in August 1948 was a wonderful place to be. There were many shortages: food was sharply rationed; many necessities were scarce; and there was, alas, a broad circle of bereavement. Yet, morale was incomparably high. The War of Independence had been a people's victory, won by countless men and women caught up in an agonizing fluctuation of courage and defeat, despair and hope. There was the sense of a new tomorrow. Israelis were frankly savoring the pride of statehood. Flags on ministerial cars were a little too large, and the proceedings in Cabinet and Parliament were enacted with solemn relish, as though by men and women who could hardly believe the titles by which they were called. Most important of all, the gates had been flung wide open to a vast onrush of immigration, first from the displaced persons' camps in Cyprus, then from the concentration-camp areas of Germany, and more unexpectedly from the communities of Jews in Yemen and Iran. There had been some 500,000 Arabs in the area proposed for the Jewish state in November 1947. As a result of their flight under the impact of war, there were now little more than 100,000 within the area of Israel's jurisdiction. The Jewish population was leaping vastly ahead of the 600,000 who had declared independence in May the previous year. Suzy and I could hardly believe that this Israel was situated in the same geographical context as the Palestine we had left in July 1947 when the "squalid war" between Palestine Jewry and the British Mandatory Government had been at its full intensity.

Ben Gurion agreed with Sharett and me that we should try to secure Israel's admission to the United Nations. He warned me, however, in an enigmatic voice that "the war is not yet over." When I asked him to expand on this prediction, he waved his hand vaguely at the Negev part of the map, as though to indicate that our tenure there was fragile, and unless consolidated, might prove to be short-lived.

Suzy and I decided to spend a few days in Geneva, where her parents were resting from the summer heat. There was also the inducement of being able to visit Chaim Weizmann, who had been prevented by the advice of the government and the army from coming home while the war was still unresolved. He was chafing indignantly at his exclusion, and becoming increasingly gloomy as it dawned on him that the presidential prerogatives in Israel were very far from those with which he was familiar in Washington. There were, in fact, some delicate moments during which he contemplated resigning from the office before he ever took it up.

I discussed our affairs with Weizmann at the Hotel Richemond. Isaiah Berlin was also there, on vacation from Oxford, and the three of us, together with Suzy, went for a walk to the place where Rhine and Rhône waters converge. Weizmann gave Isaiah Berlin some earnest advice about his future: Isaiah should write a book in four volumes with footnotes longer than the text, and in such style that no more than twenty people in the world would be able to understand it. "Once you get that out of your system, you can go on writing brilliant articles without being considered superficial," said Weizmann.

Back in my hotel, I found a message to call our Geneva office urgently. Kahany told me in his phlegmatic way that Count Bernadotte had been assassinated in Jerusalem that morning. His French driver had also been killed.

I had hardly had time to digest this news when a cable arrived from Sharett confirming the report. An hour later another telegram reached me, apparently sent some time earlier with a lower priority: PLEASE GO AHEAD WITH APPLICATION FOR OUR MEMBERSHIP IN THE UNITED NATIONS. I was to know many such moments of shock over the years, but this development had a special impact at the time. I could imagine the baleful glee on Bevin's face on hearing this news. He had been fighting a rear-guard action against the consolidation of Israel's international position, and now he could celebrate a moment of hope. Suzy and I said farewell to her parents and took the night train to Paris, where the General Assembly was to convene at the Palais Chaillot.

The first session was taken up entirely with tributes to Bernadotte's memory. I had met him in New York at an early stage of his mission. He was not a man of deep political intuitions, but he seemed to have a basic integrity. His main defect was a weakness of resolve which made him accept British and Arab pressures too uncritically, without, however, pressing them very hard on us or on anyone else. Since his first report in July he had modified his proposals, making Jerusalem an international rather than an Arab city, and abandoning his proposals for supervision or control of Jewish immigration. The territorial provisions of his plan, however, remained as they were. Indeed, the whole aim of his activity seemed to be to ensure that the Negev remain Transjordanian—in other words, British. I had said to our Cabinet that we had a good chance of defeating Bernadotte's proposals. For various and opposite reasons Israel, most Arab states, the Soviet bloc and the more zealous supporters of the 1947 partition plan would all be arrayed against Bernadotte's ideas, while the American attitude would not be hostile to us in a tight election year.

To my consternation, it was suddenly borne in upon me in Paris that I would have to go to Stockholm for Count Bernadotte's funeral. Eliahu Sasson, who had a rich experience of funerals in Arab countries after political assassinations, urged me in worried tones not to go to Stockholm, as I would surely be stoned to death by an indignant throng. Although I had never been to Sweden before, I found it hard to believe that the phlegmatic Swedes would react with Mediterranean passion against a foreign guest. I even doubted that there were many stones to be found in Stockholm's tidy streets.

In Stockholm I was received with tact and sympathy. I had a moving conversation with Countess Bernadotte, who asked me to keep contact later with her in New York. There was no disposition to personalize any of the antagonisms arising from the tragedy. Swedes were saddened by the sacrifice, but proud of their service to the international cause. Back I went to Paris, where the political battle was sharply joined.

The three months between September and the end of December 1948 were the longest consecutive period that I had ever lived in Paris. The amenities were far different from my student days, when I had stayed at the squalid Hotel de la Sorbonne on the Left Bank, with the smell of decaying cabbage and a constant noise of creaking floors as hotel guests changed their residence every hour or so with what should have struck me as suspicious speed. I had chosen it because of the (deceptive) academic name. This time the Hotel Raphael in the Avenue Kléber was my Paris destination, and it remained so for many years. Many leading UN luminaries were there, including Lester Pearson, by now Foreign Minister of Canada. Sharett had rented a villa in the area of Port St. Cloud in order to be far from the turbulence of Parisian life. I had purchased a small car in London for what then seemed to be the astronomical price of £400 and I had it brought over for use in Paris. One day I parked it somewhere near the Palais Chaillot, forgot exactly where, and spent more than two hours searching for it in growing despair.

Since Israel was not yet a member of the UN, I was not involved in any of the general discussions. Our sole task was to promote Israel's membership, and to work for the defeat of the Bernadotte plan in the difficult atmosphere created by his martyrdom.

In Israel, the pace of development was intense. Immigrants were beginning to crowd in and the economy was strained. Ben Gurion's main anxiety was that his beloved Negev was only nominally in our jurisdiction, for the Egyptians had the ability to cut off Israeli settlements in the south. Nor did we have any free approach to the port of Eilat, which had been one of the main reasons for our insistence on including the Negev in our state.

The volcano was not long in erupting. In October, Egyptian troops began to prevent passage of our road convoys. Apart from the effects on supply, it was plain that the Israeli hold on the Negev was being challenged. Our soldiers responded heavily and broke through, banishing Egyptian forces from nearly every strongpoint, except Faluja, where they were surrounded.

Our preoccupations at the UN were manifold. The Security Council was discussing the Negev on the basis of British and Arab proposals calling for Israel's withdrawal from points occupied since early October, including Beersheba. Behind the scenes, we were canvassing delegates on behalf of our membership in the United Nations. The

Political Committee of the General Assembly was due to discuss the Bernadotte report, which had been endorsed not only by Ernest Bevin on behalf of Britain but, more disconcertingly, by Secretary of State George Marshall for the United States. It was vital for us to detach the United States from the Bernadotte plan, and this involved me in heavy lobbying with the United States delegation.

Sharett and I shared this work; he sat in the Political Committee trying to frustrate the Bernadotte plan, while I held the fort in the Security Council, which, in those days, was a majestic institution, eminently manned and full of resonance in the media. There was one agonizing week in which I tried to filibuster in the Security Council to delay a cease-fire resolution until such time as Faluja would fall. I was receiving reports from our Chief of Staff, General Yigael Yadin, to say that this might take place within a few hours. Hours turned to days. The siege continued, but so did the presence of the besieged Egyptians at Faluja. News kept reaching us of General Yigal Allon's successful thrust in the south. Fighting had also broken out again in the Galilee, where Kawakji's forces were renewing their assault.

October, November and December saw many successes for Israel in the military and political arenas. The Arab governments had miscalculated by provoking hostilities without being able to absorb Israel's counteraction. Our domination of the Galilee and the Negev became complete. Indeed, our successes in the ten days after the Arab rejection of the July 1948 cease-fire were more decisive in fixing our map than our successful resistance in May before the truce. In the Political Committee I made occasional incursions to assist Sharett who was successfully building support against the Bernadotte plan. The Soviets regarded the proposal as a piece of imperialist guile. The Arab states saw it as an attempt to inflict the hated King Abdullah of Jordan upon them. And Latin American countries, together with Australia, New Zealand and Canada, took a position of fidelity to the 1947 partition, of which an Israeli Negev had been the focal point.

In the Security Council I renewed my traditional duel with the United Kingdom delegation, which the world press regarded as very good "theater." Ernest Bevin was in poor health and constantly running back to London, but Alexander Cadogan was reinforced by the Minister of State in the Foreign Office, Hector McNeil, a soft-spoken Scottish socialist. He had a talk with me in which he made an impassioned attempt to explain how easily Israel could obtain British support simply by exchanging the southern Negev for the western Galilee. At a UN committee session he took the floor to explain eloquently how useless, sterile, barren and unpromising the southern

Negev was. I replied by asking why, if the area in question was so repellent, Britain should want to deprive Israel of the horrors of its possession. I said, "I have never heard of anything so undesirable being coveted by the United Kingdom with such intensity."

It appeared to me as I watched the United Nations in session that delegates whose national interests were not acutely involved were enjoying the performance on the personal level. The diplomats who thronged into the Assembly and its committee rooms had a greater sense of self-importance than if they had been obscurely working in embassies on concrete diplomatic tasks. The spotlight was upon them. Press representatives gathered reverently around them as they took their briefcases into a committee room at nine-thirty in the morning, where they remained until one o'clock, with permission to smoke, opportunity to write letters and an occasional but spasmodic flare-up of interest around the table itself. Lunch in Paris offered countless opportunities, most of them excellent. The afternoon sessions might be a little tedious, but they would be succeeded by cocktail parties in which hard liquor flowed like water over the Niagara Falls, but without generating a similar volume of energy. One evening the French President, Vincent Auriol, held a reception to which all guests were asked to wear "decorations." This caused a wild rush on shops and jewelry stores in which various Orders of the Legion of Honor and other more exotic emblems could be obtained at gradated prices. We, in the Israeli delegation, went with our dress shirts democratically bare.

The French Jewish community, never very fervent until 1948 in its support of Zionism, was awakening to a stronger Jewish consciousness. Both Sharett and I were in heavy demand for speeches at dinners and fund-raising occasions. In our own delegation, friendships were being cemented. The leading figures were Arthur Lourie; Moshe Tov; Gideon Rafael; Eliahu Sasson; Michael Comay, even at that time eloquent, solid and level-headed; and Jacob Robinson, our legal adviser, who had been a well-known Lithuanian statesman before going to New York to pursue his researches in international law. I asked a young Harvard law student, Yosef Tekoa, to join us in a kind of apprentice role. Robinson did more than anyone else to educate us all in the potentialities and limitations of multilateral diplomacy. The only controversy between him and me was one that is familiar between diplomats and legal advisers: Should I do what he thought was legal, or should he find a legal reason for me to do what I wanted?

Our chief preoccupation was the defense of our legitimacy in the Negev. Ben Gurion was sending us worried cables about this. Sharett and I decided to try to change the American attitude. Across the Atlantic, American Jews were in an uproar, seeking to obtain assurances from President Truman in favor of our basic interests. Eventually these efforts flourished, and at Madison Square Garden late in October, President Truman virtually found his way back to the November 1947 partition plan, with a proviso that any changes in it should only be with Israel's consent.

The American delegation in Paris was of curious composition. Its titular head was Secretary of State Marshall, who had, however, gone back to America for medical treatment. His deputy as head of the American mission was an eminent Wall Street lawyer, John Foster Dulles. Dulles was carefully preparing to take over as Secretary of State under Governor Thomas E. Dewey, whose election to the presidency had already been accepted and celebrated with dogmatic certainty in the public opinion polls. Three members of the delegation—Eleanor Roosevelt, Benjamin V. Cohen and a lawyer named Charles Fahy—had been consistent supporters of the partition decision. They were alienated by the tendency of the State Department to follow Britain's lead on behalf of the Bernadotte report. Dulles, however, held the key, and with him Sharett and I began a long dialogue. We were impressed by his probing intellectual curiosity. Behind a dry manner, redolent of oak-paneled courtrooms in the United States, there was a curious strain of Protestant mysticism which led him to give the Israel question a larger importance than its geopolitical weight would indicate. His sense of logic was sharply developed. I got the impression that he revered the process of argument for its own sake, and that if a case was convincingly made, there was every possibility of changing his mind.

His predicament in those weeks came from the nemesis which follows all premature self-confidence. I was one of several representatives whom Dulles invited to a dinner party scheduled the day after the presidential election, when he would presumably lay down the broad lines of the policy to be pursued by the Dewey-Dulles administration. The only thing that went wrong with the plan was that Dewey lost the election. John Foster Dulles canceled his invitation on the grounds of "ill health," which, in a way, was an accurate description of his plight. I, with many others, had a free evening for the theater. In the ensuing weeks, however, Dulles pursued his United Nations task with impressive humility and bipartisan zeal.

The General Assembly ended successfully for Israel. A resolution was adopted containing no reference to the Bernadotte report. A Conciliation Commission was appointed, composed of the United States, France and Turkey, which was to be available to the parties for the negotiation of an overall settlement.

On November 29, 1948, the anniversary of the partition resolution, Sharett and I presented to Trygve Lie our request for admission to the United Nations. This required seven votes of the Security Council and two-thirds in the General Assembly. What with Bernadotte's death, renewed fighting in the area and the continued hostility of Britain, we were not successful in the first round in the Security Council. We did, however, obtain five out of the seven votes needed to approve our admission (the United States, the Soviet Union, the Ukraine, Argentina and Colombia). The abstentions of Canada and France disappointed us, but they seemed to have a temporary air, so I cabled Jerusalem expressing the view that if we renewed the attempt early in 1949, we would be more successful.

Of greater significance in Paris was an initiative in the Security Council in which I took an active role. The area had been governed throughout 1948 by a series of fitful truces and cease-fires. The question was whether we could seek a more stable framework of regional relations. While Sharett was busy working against the Bernadotte report in the Assembly, I canvassed Security Council delegates on this theme. My chief interlocutors were Lester Pearson of Canada, and Philip Jessup, the eminent international lawyer who had taken over the leadership of the United States delegation in the Security Council. The outcome was a Canadian proposal submitted in November 1948, calling upon Israel and the Arab states (then referred to as "the governments and authorities in the Middle East") to enter into negotiations under the auspices of the Acting Mediator, Ralph Bunche, in order to conclude armistice agreements, including the establishment of agreed "armistice demarcation lines." I spoke strongly for this proposal in the Security Council during the second and third weeks of November. Despite strong Arab opposition, a Canadian resolution in this sense was eventually adopted on November 16. I thought that this was a turning point. It virtually made the establishment of provisional boundaries dependent on the realities of the battlefield, to which, after all, the Arab governments had confided the outcome of the conflict. If we could achieve an armistice without any limitation of time, we would be liberated from a constant feeling of volcanic suspense, between one fragile truce and another.

The defeat of the Bernadotte report, the adoption of the armistice resolution, and our partial success in gaining support for UN admission seemed to me to be a fairly satisfactory conclusion to the 1948 UN campaign, which many Israelis had anticipated with hypochondriac gloom. I went back to Israel to check reactions. There was a general air of tranquillity and relief, although the military situation in the Negev was still tense. The major domestic development had been the elimination of all dissident military organizations. Ben Gurion had reacted firmly to the provocation implicit in the murder of Bernadotte. Once again an armed action with far-reaching political consequences had been taken outside the scope of constituted authority. If this kind of thing went on, the idea might well gain ground that the Jewish people was constitutionally incapable of maintaining a recognized authority. Ben Gurion felt that Israel's sovereignty was involved here as surely as it had been in the *Altalena* incident. He had called for total disbandment of all military forces outside the Israeli army. Menachem Begin, the IZL leader, had understood the implications of Israel's sovereignty and had cooperated in the merger of the dissident forces with the main body of the Israeli Defense Forces. This marked the end of the separatist actions by the IZL and the Lechi. Historians will long dispute their precise weight in the process that led to Israel's independence. It is, of course, exaggerated to claim for them the major role. If the main body of Palestine Jewry with the Haganah had not pursued a policy of resistance, the military effort of the IZL and the Lechi would have been marginal. But it is historically indisputable that these two organizations helped create the conditions of intolerability in which Britain decided to surrender her role. They certainly inculcated in their followers an authentic resistance spirit, including readiness for the ultimate sacrifice for a national cause.

Israel's international relations were still untidy, with nothing but de facto recognition from the United States, and most of Europe and Latin America still hesitant in making formal ties; nor was Israel yet a member of the specialized agencies of the UN. We were thus outside the general rhythm of international life. It was decided that I should go back to New York and pursue the campaign for Israel's admission to the United Nations. Shortly before leaving, I went with Suzy to the Share Zedek Hospital, where her grandfather, Michael Steinberg, lay dying. As a pioneer, he had been in the village of Motza since the 1880s. Twice his home and factory had been destroyed by Arab attackers and twice he had rebuilt them—the last time at the age of seventy. He typified the pious tenacity of the early pioneers. On hearing that I had been appointed Israel's representative to the United Nations, he did not seem very clear what this eminent designation signified, but he felt that a great new Jewish dignity was involved and his demeanor became utterly serene.

As I prepared to leave Jerusalem for New York, news came of a battle in the northern Sinai on January 7 during which Israel shot down six British Spitfires flying in support of Egyptian forces

in alleged fulfillment of the Anglo-Egyptian Treaty. The British reaction had been furious. In New York, Sir Alexander Cadogan had
sent his deputy, Sir Terence Shone, to Arthur Lourie with a vehement protest. The diplomatic question was how to protest against the
actions of a government which was presumed not to exist. The British
Foreign Office "solved" this problem by addressing its communication to "the Jewish Authorities in Palestine." We had long decided to
put this phrase to derision. On our crossing of the Atlantic in August
on the *Queen Elizabeth,* I had met Sir Alexander Cadogan emerging
from the ship's chapel. Our conversation was courteous, but I could
not forbear asking him if he had been "praying to the God of Abraham, Isaac and the Jewish Authorities." Now, on reading Terence
Shone's communication, Lourie quite properly returned it to him as
unacceptable for receipt. The anomaly of the Bevin policy was becoming more strident every day. There was a stormy debate in the British
House of Commons in which Churchill sent cascades of his oratory
rolling to shore in onslaught on Bevin's mulishness. The result was to
develop a clear consensus in London in favor of the recognition of
Israel, and this was to come to official expression early in 1949.

Meanwhile, pressure by the United States caused General Yigal
Allon's forces to be withdrawn, on Ben Gurion's order, from the El
Arish area, to which they had advanced across the international
boundary. On the other hand, Egypt was becoming aware of the
sterility of the conflict, and before 1948 was out, its government dra-
matically wrote a letter indicating a readiness to go to Rhodes for
armistice negotiations with Israel. These talks opened in January under the inspired leadership of Ralph Bunche, who was elected chairman of the Armistice Conference. Bunche, however, was subordinate
to Trygve Lie, who followed negotiations closely from UN headquarters in New York, where I was in vigilant contact. There was
little that we could do in New York except pray for the success of our
delegation on Rhodes under the leadership of Walter Eytan, Yigael
Yadin, Reuven Shiloah and Eliahu Sasson.

In February, a point of crisis came. Most of the armistice provisions had been agreed upon, but the question of Beersheba was still
in suspense. Would this be included in the Israeli or the Egyptian side
of the armistice line? Once again, the fate of the Negev was in the
balance. Bunche, feeling that this was a major political determination, reported it back to Trygve Lie at New York, which meant
that the matter was open to the influence of the major powers. I
visited Trygve Lie at his home in Forest Hills and secured his firm
undertaking that he would instruct Bunche to take into account the
general logic of UN policy since 1947 relating to the Negev and

therefore to side with Israel in relation to Beersheba. Lie's consultations with Moscow and Washington gave him full support in this direction. With Truman remaining in the White House, Israel's relations with the United States had recuperated since the American espousal of the Bernadotte report in September 1948.

When the news came on February 24, 1949, that an armistice had been signed with Egypt, we felt that Israel's consolidation was firm. Embassies were established between Israel and the United States, and there was recognition by Britain and by most countries of the Commonwealth, Latin America and Western Europe. It seemed on the surface that the Arab attempt to challenge Israel's legitimacy had collapsed. Yet in large parts of the Arab world, no such logic was yet accepted. Israel's nonmembership in the United Nations symbolized the unfinished nature of the enterprise. I felt that it was urgent to correct this anomaly, since it had a great bearing on our relations with a world that had difficulty in getting used to Israeli sovereignty. Above all, we had to eliminate the psychological block which prevented the Arab world from regarding Israel as an immutable part of the international landscape. Accordingly, I renewed our application to the Security Council, and on March 24, the Council voted by 8 to 1, with British abstention, to recommend Israel's admission "as a peace-loving State able and willing to carry out the obligations of the Charter." Although I knew that the distribution of votes in the General Assembly was less propitious than in the Security Council, the overwhelming verdict in the Council led me to hope for a favorable result when our membership application came up for final decision.

The General Assembly met in special session in April to take up the unfinished business left over from Paris. We hoped that our request would be ratified quickly in the plenary session as had been done in all previous membership decisions. The Arabs, however, had rallied from their defeat in the Security Council in March and were able to interpose an obstacle between the two stages of the admission process. Instead of a perfunctory and formal debate in the plenary of the Assembly, it was decided to give Israel's application a detailed scrutiny in the Ad Hoc Political Committee.

Sharett considered this a hard blow. It now seemed unlikely to him that we would succeed in our application. At best, we would be required to give such undertakings in return for membership as would seriously prejudice our sovereignty and security. He decided, despite my more optimistic protestations, to leave New York for Israel and to entrust the membership struggle to my hands. At the New York airport, when asked about Israel and the United Nations, he said irritably, "I'm quite confident about the survival of Israel. I don't know about the United Nations."

The piqued tone of his reply gave me the impression that perhaps it would be better for him to stay away at this stage. The political struggles of the past year as well as the asperities of domestic politics seemed to have taken a toll of his patience. And patience seemed to me to be our most essential attribute during the coming months. The honeymoon period in our international life was fast wearing off; henceforward we would have to fight hard for every inch of the ground. Moreover, Sharett was a political figure who could not be indifferent to issues of prestige. He was the target of virulent attack by the opposition, especially by the Herut Party at home. That party, despite Vladimir Jabotinsky's traditional reverence for the external symbols of statehood, had opposed the idea of Israel's seeking admission into the United Nations. Its newspaper wrote on April 27, 1949: "Greater, older, stronger States than we are standing outside the Organization and do not even attempt to enter it. No harm has come to them from this." The argument ignored the fact that "the greater, older, stronger States" were unchallenged in their statehood and were, with the exception of Switzerland, all striving for membership. But it was evident that if Sharett was defeated in our membership application, he would be under grave political attack.

However, I was not really thinking of defeat. It seemed to me that the task of putting a two-thirds majority together would be difficult but not insuperable. At any rate, if we did not succeed in 1949, I saw little chance that we could hope for a better result in later years. The American-Soviet convergence in our favor was not likely to be permanent and without it the statistics of the United Nations would not let any resolution be adopted in Israel's favor. This was my reaction to an unexpected expression of opposition to our UN membership from Dr. Nahum Goldmann. He thought that Israel had a better chance of maintaining a neutral posture if she was not called on to pronounce on the controversial international issues. My own feeling was that nothing could be more disastrous from the viewpoint of our hope of peace with the Arab nations than to leave a mark of interrogation over our status. I could not understand how we could claim the benefits of sovereignty without paying a price in burden and responsibilities.

I was now personally directing a political operation that had no precedent in international history. No other state had ever been called upon to secure its membership in the international community through a process of cross-examination, advocacy and rebuttals in the

General Assembly after being emphatically recommended for membership by the Security Council. The strange drama was enacted in the Ad Hoc Political Committee with all fifty-eight member states represented. The eloquent and capable Philippine statesman General Carlos Romulo presided. I was invited to the table to make a statement in support of our admission and then to reply to questions and observations by member states. Arguments had been raised against us concerning boundaries, refugees, Jerusalem and responsibility for the assassination of Count Bernadotte. There was also the question of whether Israel still regarded itself as bound by all the provisions of the 1947 partition resolution.

My opening speech on May 5 was therefore long and detailed. I pointed out that the Security Council, which had "primary responsibility for international peace and security," had given an emphatic verdict in our favor. It was therefore absurd to contend that Israel's admission would hinder the prospects of international peace. On the contrary, the pursuit of peace would be gravely impeded if Israel was to be placed in juridical and political inferiority to the Arab states:

> *The question is whether the Arab world will receive from this Committee the counsel to regard Israel as a permanent international fact with which it has to make peace; or whether by hesitating now, the Assembly will confirm the Arab peoples in their hesitations about Israel's existence and Israel's right. The General Assembly could do nothing more calculated to persuade the Arab states to maintain their strife than if it were to rise in an atmosphere of doubt about Israel's international status.*

I expressed strong resentment at the spectacle of the aggressor Arab states sitting piously in judgment on Israel's application for membership:

> *We are as one who, having been attacked in a dark street by seven men with heavy bludgeons, finds himself dragged into court only to see his assailants sitting on the bench with an air of solemn virtue, delivering homilies on the duties of a peaceful citizen.*

I added:

> *Here sit representatives of the only states which have deliberately used force against a General Assembly resolution—the only states which have ever been determined by the Security Council to have caused a threat to the peace, posing as the disinterested*

judges of their own intended victim in his efforts to secure a
modest equality in the family of nations. It is a cynical maneuver.
In the name of those who have been killed, maimed, blinded,
exiled or bereaved by that cynicism, I express our most passionate
resentment at this insincerity.

Although our membership in the United Nations was an objective
of high value, it was not worth securing by the surrender of vital
rights and interests. I therefore had to steer a careful course in defining our attitude on the final settlement. On the boundary question,
I said that Israel and the Arab states had a perfect right to agree on
such changes of the 1947 boundaries as seemed essential to them. They
should negotiate on this subject at the Lausanne Conference called
by the Palestine Conciliation Commission. In any case, the Arab states,
which had violently assaulted the 1947 resolution, could not legitimately invoke it on their own behalf. On the refugee problem, I rejected the idea that Israel had sole responsibility for a solution. I
offered Israeli compensation to the refugees and limited resettlement
in the context of a broad regional plan under which all the Middle
Eastern states would take their share of the responsibility. On this
matter I said:

> *Dr. Malik, the representative of Lebanon, informed us correctly*
> *this morning that it was not the intention of the General Assem-*
> *bly for Israel to become free of its Arab inhabitants. But, surely,*
> *it was not the intention of the General Assembly that Lebanon*
> *and six other states should make war against the General Assem-*
> *bly's resolution? Every disturbance of the 1947 plan is the plain*
> *result of the fact that a war was launched. The Arab states are*
> *thus responsible for every death, for all the bereavement and for*
> *all the panic and exile which has resulted from that futile and*
> *unnecessary conflict.*

On Jerusalem, I suggested that the international principle should be
applied not to the city as a whole, but to that which was international
and universal—namely, the Holy Places and the rights of religious
communities. I called this "functional internationalization." It was
essential to separate the secular from the spiritual aspects of Jerusalem's life. The former should be regulated by normal laws of national loyalty and political freedom. The spiritual domain justified
a measure of international supervision.

After several hours of intense rhetorical effort, I was called the next
day for questioning by members of the committee. I was apparently
so bristling and indignant in reply that most members were silent;

only the Arab delegates engaged me in a running altercation. Time and time again I questioned their moral right to be the judges of a case in which, in fact, they were the guilty defendants. Between one session and another, I lobbied for the votes needed for our admission. Fortunately, I was able to secure the agreement of both the United States and the Soviet Union to join with a number of other countries, including Australia, Canada, Norway and some Latin American republics, in sponsoring a resolution for Israel's membership. When all discussion and debate had been exhausted, I made a final plea, which was carried widely on the news media:

> At every stage of Israel's relations with the Arab world, we have felt equality of status to be the essential condition of partnership. Until the scars of conflict are healed and Israel becomes integrated with its immediate world, the United Nations may be the only forum in which Israel sits as a colleague and partner of its neighboring states in transacting international business and in the paths of social and economic cooperation.
>
> We cannot logically expect the Arabs to recognize Israel if the United Nations hesitates to recognize Israel.

And finally:

> Whatever intellectual or spiritual forces Israel evokes are at the service of the United Nations as a reinforcement of its activity and prestige. You will certainly lose nothing and you may perhaps gain some modest asset if you join our banner to your honored company. A great wheel of history comes full circle today as Israel, renewed and established, offers itself with all its imperfections but perhaps with some virtues, to the defense of the human spirit against nihilism, conflict and despair.

Despite the rules and customs of United Nations committees, this oration was greeted with applause not only from visitors but from many delegations themselves. In the voting we secured more than the two thirds needed for success. It was now important to ensure that we should not lose ground when the plenary session came to ratify the committee's decision. I therefore strongly pressed Herbert Evatt of Australia, the president of the General Assembly, to leave as little time as possible between the two occasions. The plenary meeting of the General Assembly was fixed for May 11.

Our success in the committee and the certainty of triumph in the plenary had electrified opinion in Israel. It had been feared that our refusal to reconfirm the 1947 resolution would result in many defections. There was also an apprehension that the international community, which had irritated the Arabs sufficiently in 1947, would hesitate to add to Arab injury again.

I received a cable of praise from the Cabinet, and I now decided to repay something of the gratitude that I owed Sharett for giving me my early chance. In his cable he had said nothing about coming to deliver Israel's acceptance address. His reticence flowed from a delicate instinct which told him that since I had borne the brunt of the struggle, I should not be superseded at the celebration. On the other hand, I was certain that Sharett was devoutly hoping that I would rise above this calculation and make his arrival feasible by insisting on it myself. I accordingly cabled him confidentially:

YOU MUST COME STOP YOU MUST MAKE THE SPEECH STOP WILL HOLD
UP VOTING IF NECESSARY EBAN

Back came a quick reply:

WHAT HAPPENS IF I SET OUT FROM TEL AVIV TO COME TO GENERAL
ASSEMBLY AND PLENARY SESSION DOES NOT GIVE US REQUIRED TWO-
THIRDS STOP WON'T I LOOK FOOLISH SHARETT

I replied that I could now almost guarantee a favorable vote, but if Sharett wanted to be certain, he should be ready to fly to New York as soon as he got our further signal.

Willing to take a measure of risk, Sharett embarked for New York at once. The meeting had already started with speeches from the major powers when I got word from the airport that his plane had landed and that he was on his way to Flushing Meadow in a police-escorted car.

Sharett entered the Assembly Hall to join me and my colleagues just when the voting was about to begin. It was very favorable—35 votes to 11. The UN Chief of Protocol solemnly approached us and took us from our seats in the visitors' gallery to a table on which the word "Israel" was proudly planted. There was a seething excitement in the Assembly Hall and in the visitors' gallery. Sharett had prepared an address, which he delivered in due form and with unconcealed emotion.

The next morning we went to the front of the UN building, where we raised Israel's flag aloft. I remember Eleanor Roosevelt among the spectators, standing a little distance away, obviously sharing our joy.

I felt this to be a very high moment at the time, and I have not changed my mind since. Resolutions in the United Nations have often been savagely biased against us, but the political effects of

Israel's admission to the UN were and are far-reaching. Membership in the UN is, for small states, the most visible incarnation of their equality. More than anything else, it excites their new sense of dignity. In terms of Jewish history, it was a moving symbol of a nation's return to the mainstream of world history after centuries of absence. It was no longer possible for Israel's juridical legitimacy to be denied. We were equal in law with all other members of the organized world community.

On May 12, 1949, I took Israel's seat in the plenary sessions and in the Political Committee of the General Assembly while distributing my colleagues into the other committees. By alphabetical fortune, I sat between the Iraqi and Lebanese delegates. My presence seemed to interpose a barrier of ice between them. During one committee session, I remember drawing my pipe from my pocket and lighting it. Since there was one large ashtray between each two delegates, I reached over and put the dead match in the tray that I was supposed to share with the Iraqi delegate, Dr. Fadhil Jamali. He promptly called an attendant and asked for another ashtray lest the remnant of his own cigarette ash—heaven forbid—might mingle promiscuously with the Zionist ash from an Israeli pipe.

For the first few days the Iraqi and Lebanese used to converse animatedly in Arabic across my silent back. On one occasion they agreed on engaging in some abstruse procedural gambit which would take me by surprise. To their consternation I raised my pencil, took the floor and said, "Mr. Chairman, it is quite possible that distinguished Arab delegates might soon move the adjournment on the following grounds . . ." I then cited exactly what my two neighbors were about to propose. Thereafter they took my Arabic for granted and confined their consultations to the exchange of written notes.

Within a few days we were voting on international issues, some of them delicate. The first concerned a proposal by a Latin American group led by Peru to remove the ban on the admission of Franco Spain to the United Nations. Since all the democratic socialist countries, led by Australia, Norway, Belgium and including Britain under the Labour Party, felt that the memories of the alliance with Hitler and Mussolini were too fresh, I saw no course but to join with them in solidarity. Nothing could have been more absurd than for Israel to show less concern than did other countries with the tormenting memories of the Hitler epoch. It was not logical for Israelis in later years to regret, as they did, a vote in which their representatives had no element of choice. We relented about Spain a few years later and voted for her admission to the UN.

When the General Assembly session ended in mid-May, I had every reason to feel content with the direction that my own life had taken. I was thirty-three years old, the youngest ambassador of any state at the United Nations. I had played a recognized part in Israel's political victories. I could feel a measure of personal credit in connection with the UNSCOP report, the November 29, 1947, resolution, the truce and armistice resolutions, and the defeat of the Bernadotte plan. I had carried the main burden of Israel's campaign for admission to the United Nations. In Jewish communities, especially in the United States, I was now surrounded by an atmosphere of confidence and friendship.

The Jewish world lived those months in a mood of sustained ecstasy. Back in Israel, the guns were silent and the era of mass immigration had begun. There were weeks during which 1,000 immigrants a day were arriving in the country. Indeed, more than 600,000 Jews reached us in the first three years of our statehood, while 300,000 Arabs left in the clash and peril of war.

There was now time to breathe and arrange my life in a more organized way. Social pressures were heavy. Just before the debate on our admission to membership, President Weizmann had arrived in New York to raise funds for the Weizmann Institute and make a state visit to Washington. I saw him off at the airport in New York in early May. It was destined to be his last day on American soil, and he seemed to have the sad premonition of a farewell.

The Security Council ratified the armistice agreements in August 1949 after the Syrian negotiations were concluded. The Soviet delegate thundered that they had become possible only "because Israel and the Arab states had negotiated them directly." Wise words!

After a short return to Israel for consultation, I came back to New York in September to lead Israel's delegation for the first time at a full regular session of the General Assembly.

The Israeli public was now beginning to relish the taste of international life. Despite the distance that separated me from events at home, I seemed able to articulate the national mood. One Jerusalem newspaper wrote: "The great respect which the Israeli Representative, Abba Eban, has gained at the United Nations will be enhanced by the speech which he made at the closing of the general debate."

It was known that the Arab states intended to renew their assault on our position in Jerusalem. They hoped to detach the Catholic states from our side. Toward the end of the 1949 session, the assault on Israel's rights in Jerusalem was launched in full fury. We expected to be challenged by the Arab states, but an untoward surprise came when the campaign to reaffirm the statute of internationalization suddenly obtained the support of Australia. We were never able to diagnose the cause for Herbert Evatt's strange obduracy in this matter. He had never struck me as a man of obsessive religious piety. It was known that the elections in his country would be tightly fought and that the Catholic vote was of some importance, but it was disconcerting for me to be in such embarrassed conflict with my friend and colleague John D. L. Hood. Moreover, the signal that friends of Israel could insist on the expulsion of our authority from Jerusalem communicated itself from Australia to some Latin American states. Though we achieved the support of the United States and Britain, as well as of the Protestant European countries such as Sweden, Denmark, Norway and Holland, the vote went against us.

Sharett took his defeat hard and even offered Ben Gurion his resignation. The Prime Minister reacted more robustly by deciding to ignore the UN resolution and to move the Knesset and government agencies from Tel Aviv to Jerusalem. Sharett thought that this was unnecessary defiance. This time I could not share his concern. I had cabled to the Foreign Ministry saying that the UN resolution would not be effective one way or the other since there would be no attempt to carry it out. It was not feasible to enforce a proposal opposed by such countries as the United States and Britain, who were paramount in the region. My own feeling was that Israel could do just as it liked in Jerusalem and that the new 1949 resolution would have no effect on our international position. This impression was reinforced when Dean Rusk, on behalf of Secretary of State Dean Acheson, told me that the United States intended to ignore the resolution and advised us to do the same. The fact was, however, that the Assembly resolution contained a provision under which the Trusteeship Council would work out a statute for an international regime in Jerusalem. This would involve my taking an Israeli delegation to Geneva to thwart the new political assault.

Although the Jerusalem question occupied most of our attention, we faced some complex votes in our first full session. There was a debate on the future of the Italian colonies during which a proposal was submitted for a British trusteeship in Libya. Despite the hostility of the Arab world, Sharett and I thought that it would be incongruous for Israel to impose on other nations the precise form of colonial domination from which we had freed ourselves over a year before. We voted against the British trusteeship proposal, which was narrowly rejected. We had therefore taken a measure of responsibility for expediting the independence of an Arab state. In terms of strict realpolitik, this sounded quixotic, but in the atmosphere of those times, there was a general expectation that Israel would apply some measure of vision to its international policies. The columnist I. F. Stone wrote rapturously about us on October 26. It was clear to him that Israel was making some investment in the prospect of peace.

When the session ended, I did not take kindly to the resumption of my nomadic existence. Suzy's parents, Leah and Simcha Ambache, had visited us during the early summer, and on one afternoon, Suzy had casually announced her pregnancy. We suddenly realized that in the press of public affairs we had neglected our own interests to the extent of not even having a home. For the past six months we had been staying at the Sulgrave Hotel on Park Avenue, where we had been living out of suitcases as we had been doing for more than three years since leaving Jerusalem in September 1946. Now, through the friendship of Jack Weiler, a loyal Zionist in the real-estate business, we rented a small penthouse apartment at 241 Central Park West, with a view over the reservoir and the Fifth Avenue towers beyond. This was in the seventh month of Suzy's pregnancy. We had not furnished the apartment with anything but the most primitive items when on a snowy January day our son, Eli, was born at the Harkness Pavilion in the Columbia Presbyterian Medical Center in New York. On the day of the circumcision I was engaged in urgent business at the United Nations and arrived almost too late for the operation and consequent ritual, which was supervised by the renowned and eloquent Rabbi Milton Sternberg. I had only been able to enjoy Eli's infant company for ten days when I had to leave.

I flew to Israel in January 1950 to consult about the forthcoming struggle in Geneva. There would be sessions of the Palestine Conciliation Commission. Simultaneously, the Trusteeship Council would formulate a statute for the internationalization of Jerusalem. I spent a week revolving these matters with Ben Gurion and Sharett.

On the day of my scheduled departure from Tel Aviv, there was a snowstorm such as Israel had hardly ever known. Not only the hill country, but Tel Aviv and the area near the Dead Sea were clothed in white. Just as I was leaving for the airport on my way to Geneva, I received a message that Ben Gurion urgently wanted to see me at his winter vacation residence in Haifa. I canceled my reservation and set out for the north. The roads were covered with ice, and it was only after six hours of cautious travel that I reached the Eden Hotel in Haifa. When I entered his suite, B. G. expressed surprise and pleasure at seeing me, but, he asked courteously, why had I come?

Was I not urgently needed in Geneva? After this disconcerting opening, our conversation flowed freely. He had entirely forgotten the original reason for his summons.

When I laboriously reached Tel Aviv very late at night, I learned that the plane that I would have taken but for Ben Gurion's call had taken off on the icy runway, skidded and made a forced landing which resulted in all the passengers' having to slide down the rescue chutes. A leading New York newspaper had got hold of the original passenger list and published a screaming front-page banner: EBAN IN PLANE ACCIDENT. I was very concerned about the effects of this on Suzy, twenty days after giving birth to Eli. Happily, it turned out that friends had reassured her before the newspaper came to her notice. I learned that celebrity had its inconveniences.

Geneva in winter, with the icy wind blowing across the lake, is not an attractive place. It seemed to live in a vacuum detached from any real field of gravity. The pangs of separation were strong. One of Suzy's letters to me said: "I shall never forget the lonely days and nights, just watching tenderly and sadly over little Eli. When I lecture myself and tell myself that this will probably have to happen again and again in my life, courage fails me at the mere thought." Her prediction was going to be fully borne out across the years.

The weeks in Geneva were frustrating. There was nothing for Israel to hope for. With the war over and the armistice agreements in working condition, we were more concerned to defend the achievements of the past three years than to add new ones. The Palestine Conciliation Commission floundered clumsily in the waters which Bunche had navigated so skillfully on Rhodes. It seemed to make every conceivable error. Instead of taking the armistice agreements as the basis for the next step, it chose to ignore them—and even to surround them with an atmosphere of provisionality and guilt. Instead of attempting bilateral negotiation between Israel and each Arab state, the commission assembled all the Arab delegations in a single room in which Israel was never present. It thus elicited the kind of militant unity that always develops when Arab governments seek the highest common factor of hostility. It may be that the Arab governments were not ready, so soon after their armistice signatures, to risk their lives in a new enterprise of conciliation. But insofar as the mediating techniques can have an effect, it is certain that the Palestine Conciliation Commission contributed to the deadlock. The Arab delegations made territorial demands that would have reduced Israel to a small sliver of territory along the coast. Israel was prepared to develop the armistice agreements into a final settlement, but without restoring the 1947 lines which the Arab governments had swamped with violence. The Conciliation Commission was thus reduced to dealing with subsidiary matters, such as the unblocking of bank accounts held by Arab refugees.

None of the three governments composing the Conciliation Commission extended itself in the choice of its representative. The United States had dispatched Mark Etheridge, a newspaper editor from Louisville, Kentucky, who seemed surprised to find that a peace settlement in the Middle East could not be achieved in two or three weeks. He became irascible and went home to Louisville, leaving behind a sympathetic and able career ambassador, Ely Palmer. The Turkish representative, Mr. Yalcin, was an eminent newspaperman, but so far advanced in years that his interest in the future was severely circumscribed. France was represented by a suave diplomat, Claude de Boisanger, whose status in the eyes of the Quai d'Orsay was reflected in the fact that after leaving the commission, he was assigned the directorship of the Folies-Bergère, which, for mysterious reasons reaching back into history, has its chief executive officer appointed by the Ministry of Foreign Affairs. With the best will in the world, it was hard to see Nobel Prize material in the Conciliation Commission. Both its membership and its administrative efficacy fell short both of UNSCOP and of the UN chairman of the armistice negotiations on Rhodes.

My chief associates at Geneva at this time were Gideon Rafael and Moshe Tov. There was little to do after sessions except to make a broad reconnaissance of Geneva's culinary map. When we entered some of the better-known restaurants the Iraqi delegate, Fadhil Jamali, would get up and leave in the midst of devouring a succulent steak. This gave us a sense of power over our chief adversary that we tried to use with magnanimity and restraint.

My serious business was to ensure that the life of Jerusalem and its integration into Israel were not disturbed by international shocks. We could either aim to prevent the elaboration of a statute for an international city, or if it was formulated, we could seek to prevent it from being put into effect. It was clear to me at an early stage that my only chance lay in the latter direction. I had cultivated a strong relationship with the president of the council, Roger Garreau of France. As a French government official, he was committed to internationalization, but as a Frenchman of lucid intelligence, he could not possibly believe that internationalization was anything but a fantasy. So we went through the motions of drafting a constitution for an international government of Jerusalem that would never come into existence—and of defining the powers of a high commissioner who would never be appointed. One day we found ourselves quixotically debating whether the radio and television services of the nonexistent "international government of Jerusalem" should be officially controlled or left to private enterprise.

My main effort was to influence the news media, which were focused on the Trusteeship Council's work during its earliest weeks. In February I made an address laying down the conceptual basis of Israel's approach on the Jerusalem issue. After describing the war and the siege, the callous abandonment by the United Nations of its solemn responsibilities, the ordeal of famine and thirst imposed on the stricken population, I pointed out that the citizens of Jerusalem had learned an obvious lesson: nothing except their attachment to Israel could ever ensure them the conditions of an ordered and civilized life. I attacked the trusteeship idea as a form of colonialism, the more incongruous since it was to be imposed on a developed, mature and nationally self-conscious population.

A curious feature of the talks in Geneva was that the Jordanian delegate was opposing trusteeship with even greater vehemence than Israel. Even my proposal for accepting United Nations responsibility in the Holy Places was regarded by the Jordanian delegate as an excessive concession to international interests. He pointed out that Israel was "generously" offering to internationalize the Jordanian part of Jerusalem in which all the Holy Places were located. He would accept nothing except the maintenance of full Jordanian jurisdiction in eastern Jerusalem.

In explaining Israel's attitude to the Jerusalem issue, I said:

> The spiritual ideals conceived in Jerusalem are the moral basis on which democracy rests. Would it not be incongruous if the United Nations were to advance the course of democratic liberty everywhere and yet prevent self-government from taking root in the very city where the democratic ideal was born? Our vision is of a Jerusalem wherein free people develop their reviving institutions, while a United Nations representative fulfills the universal responsibility for the safety and accessibility of the Holy Places. This is a vision worthy of the United Nations. Perhaps in this as in other critical periods of history, a free Jerusalem may proclaim redemption to mankind.

The constitution for an "international city" was eventually completed. On the last day of the Trusteeship Council's discussions, however, we achieved a tactical success. On the initiative of Roger Garreau, the Trusteeship Council agreed to leave the statute fully drafted but to refrain from appointing the governor of Jerusalem or bringing the statute into effect, pending a further decision. This meant that we had avoided a clash between our own sovereignty in Jerusalem and any new legal authority created by the international community.

This, in fact, was the last that anybody was to hear about an operative proposal for an internationalized Jerusalem. A few months later the Soviet Union took the lead in the United Nations in announcing its abandonment of the internationalization idea. It came out in favor of the situation created on the ground by the armistic agreement under which Jerusalem was divided between Israel and Jordan.

Representing the Cabinet, Sharett sent me a cable expressing appreciation of my "magnificent effort on behalf of Jerusalem." He also suggested that I come back to Israel to explain what had happened. This time I rebelled. My separation from home since the tenth day of Eli's birth had had harsh emotional effects on Suzy and me, and I insisted on going back to New York, with Sharett's full understanding. I had spent more than three months in defensive action in Geneva.

I spent most of 1950 organizing our permanent mission at the United Nations. Most members of the UN had now established relations with Israel. We were basking in a climate of international cordiality. Even Bevin had yielded after his long rear-guard action, and diplomatic relations were established between Israel and Britain. Sir Alexander Cadogan, in his attitude toward me, made a chameleon-like change of mood from frigid disdain to a correct fraternal relationship. During one week I was lunching with Jessup of the United States in Manhattan, paying a cordial visit to the Soviet Mission on Park Avenue and dining with Cadogan at Oyster Bay. It was the honeymoon period in Israel's relations with the Great Powers.

Nevertheless, I was beginning to chaff at the confinements of my UN role. I felt that the basic contribution of the UN to Israel's consolidation had already been made. Henceforward we would at best fight a defensive action to protect what we had already achieved. I felt an urge to do something more constructive than to conduct a permanent rhetorical contest with Arab representatives. Israel's main political and military aims were assured. It was time to get down to concrete business. Zionism would now have to prove itself, not in polemics and criticism, but in daily achievement. There was no doubt where the priority lay. Our task was to open the gates, to heal the wounds and to receive what remained of European Jewry. We would also have to respond to a surge of exaltation in other parts of the Jewish world. In the old communities of Yemen and Iraq where Jews had lived long before Moslem and Arab history had begun, the rise of a Jewish state was like the sound of a trumpet, calling them to change the direction of their lives and to join in the construction of a new society. Israel had become a vast workshop filled with the clatter of countless tools knocking houses, roads and schools together. But the economy had undertaken tasks far beyond its unaided power. Israel was struggling hard to keep its head above water and to become a trading partner with other nations.

I had begun to envy my colleagues in places like Washington, London and elsewhere, whose work seemed to have a direct bearing on the real problems that now faced Israeli society. The mood at home was militantly concrete and empirical. Our hands were full of work. The very air vibrated with the tumult of creation. It seemed to me that we had more important things to do than to go on arguing endlessly about ourselves in United Nations debates.

As if in answer to my thoughts—deliverance and fulfillment came. While I was at a hotel in Atlanta, Georgia, during a speaking tour for the United Jewish Appeal, I received a message from Sharett: *"Ha'im tekabel et hatafkidayim?"* (Would you accept the two-jobs-in-one?). This was Sharett's terse manner of proposing that I be ambassador both in Washington and at the United Nations; in those days there were many diplomats who combined the two functions. They even got to know each other intimately by constant meetings on planes between Washington and New York.

The explanations of Sharett's cable was that our first envoy to the Court of St. James's, Dr. Mordechai Eliash, had died suddenly of a cardiac seizure. Great Britain still had a central place in our affairs. It was our chief market; and intricate financial problems arising from the end of the Mandate still remained unsolved. Moreover, Britain had a large experience in the Middle East. Many European countries still tended to follow its political lead. It had, therefore, been decided to ask Eliahu Elath to move from Washington to London. There were, of course, other motives at work—some of them connected with Ben Gurion's vigorous likes and dislikes. He felt that he must have somebody in Washington to whom he could communicate with some political intimacy.

I called Suzy at our New York home, and on receiving assent, I cabled an affirmative reply to Sharett. It was agreed that I should be ready to take charge of the Washington embassy after a brief round of valedictory occasions for Elath in Washington and New York.

So, early in September 1950, we reluctantly liquidated our apartment on Central Park West, and I arrived in Washington as ambassador designate just before the Jewish New Year. We took up our residence at the newly acquired embassy property in Myrtle Street, in the Northwest section of the capital.

At the age of thirty-five I was the youngest member of that august diplomatic corps. As I looked forward to the vistas opening before me, and back on what had befallen me since I went obscurely to the Jewish Agency in 1946, I had reason to feel that truth is sometimes more rewarding than fiction.

7

Story of a Mission
1950-1956

OUR RESIDENCE IN MYRTLE STREET WAS MODEST BY ANY DIPLOMATIC standards. Eliahu and Zahava Elath, during their brief tenure at the embassy, had lived in a hotel, so the social tradition of the Israeli mission was still to be established. The chancery was located at first in a narrow ramshackle building on Massachusetts Avenue. It was symbolically interesting that the Luxembourg legation next door was more spacious and impressive than the rickety offices we were to occupy. Our new chancery on Columbia Avenue was in preparation. It seemed lavish at the time, but it soon became too small for our needs.

The formal framework of the American-Israeli relationship had already been set. An economic link had been established when President Weizmann secured Truman's assent to an Export-Import Bank loan of $100 million. The sum seems trivial in this age of billions, but it was astronomically high in those days. After all, Israel's export earnings in its first year amounted to only $48 million, so that the United States was providing a larger proportion of our total foreign-currency assets than it does now.

In questions of Middle Eastern security, the United States was moving cautiously. It did not wish to assume any unilateral obligations. In May 1950 it had joined Britain and France in a tripartite declaration, opposing changes of the armistice lines by force and promising to ensure that arms supplies would be regulated so as to avoid imbalances. Since the Western powers had a monopoly of the Middle

East arms market until 1955, they could virtually decide the military equilibrium by themselves.

It was obvious to me that with Arab opposition to Israel increasing, and the weight of our economic burdens growing heavy, Israel would have to broaden her relationship with the United States far beyond the scope of existing policies and agreements. And the economic problem would have the first priority. With hundreds of thousands of immigrants entering Israel in the first two or three years, there was a real danger that we would face starvation, lack of adequate housing and large-scale epidemics. If this were to occur, the exuberance of victory might well give way to disillusion and even to mass emigration.

The United States did not regard the Middle East as its central concern. The Korean War had erupted in July 1950. Large American forces were serving far from home in conditions of danger, only five years after the end of World War II. President Truman was at the height of his power and self-confidence. His sympathies with Israel had been tested under pressure, but there was no hint of effusiveness in his attitude and his friendship had to be carefully tended. The State Department, under the direction of the brilliant but frigid Dean Acheson, held Israel in very limited affection.

When I reached Washington, Supreme Court Justice Felix Frankfurter told me cheerfully and with lengthy explanation that he could not think of two people more disparate in their backgrounds, the shape of their minds and the idioms of their speech than President Truman and myself. It was therefore inconceivable that I would reach a personal harmony with the President. With this encouraging news I began my work—and a strong mutual understanding was established with Truman almost at once. It began on the day that I presented my credentials. Guided by a bland and polished Chief of Protocol and mindful of European precedents, I arrived formally attired in a black homburg, a steel-gray tie and a morning suit, carrying President Weizmann's credentials in a huge envelope. I had a carefully written oration prepared for the ceremony. I entered the White House for the first of what was to be many dozens of occasions, and was struck at once by the noisy informality that swirled along the corridors. I was shown to the Oval Office. There was the President of the United States, seated behind his desk with his jacket off and stridently red suspenders in full view. When he came from behind the desk, I saw that he was wearing shoes of two colors, brown-and-white. Nothing less majestic could have been imagined.

Before I had time to adapt myself to the sudden informality, the President whipped my speech and credentials from my hand, gave me a copy of his own response, and with a withering look at the startled Chief of Protocol, said, "Let's cut out all the crap and have a good talk." We then spent forty minutes in a detailed discussion of events in the Middle East.

Truman was utterly candid, not hesitating to say, in the presence of the perspiring protocol officer, that most of the "striped-pants boys in the State Department are against my policy of supporting Israel." But, he added darkly, they'll "soon find out who's the President of the United States." He mitigated his sweeping judgment with a few words in praise of Dean Acheson, saying, "He looks cold but he is a sensitive guy really and as loyal as they come. He'll do what he thinks I want to be done. If necessary, he'll even pretend to like it." The President then asked tenderly after Weizmann and spent five minutes telling me exactly what I already knew about the dramatic meetings which saved the southern Negev for the partition plan. Before I departed, he asked me a few cautious and somewhat apprehensive questions about Ben Gurion, whom he had never met.

I went out of the presidential presence into the street and thence to my embassy office, somewhat dazed by the force of Truman's personality. I had not expected his air of self-reliance. I had imagined more diffidence and reserve. It seemed that the experience of winning the election in his own right had transformed his demeanor. I have always been willing to accept the New Testament prediction that "the meek shall inherit the earth," but I have often wondered whether, having inherited it, they would continue to be meek. Truman seemed to be sincerely exalted and, to be frank, a little inflated by his Office. He was living in constant wonder about what fate had done to him. I noticed how, even in our short conversation, he had found it necessary to remind me several times that he really was the President of the United States, although I had been acting on that assumption all the time. He was obsessed with the suspicion that some people in high places were still not taking his leadership at its full value.

Despite its modest outer shell, the embassy over which I came to preside was impressive in the quality of its manpower. The senior member was Moshe Keren, whom the *Ha'aretz* newspaper had lent us for a brief period of diplomatic service. (He was later to serve in London and in Germany, where he met a sudden death from heart failure.) The military attaché was my brother-in-law, Chaim Herzog, whose distinguished war record had been made in the defense of the approaches to Jerusalem. In charge of information was Harry Levine, later to be our ambassador to Denmark. There was also a large economic staff. Within a few months Teddy Kollek came out to be my deputy in the embassy as minister. Even then, his movements were restless and his instincts nomadic, so that he did not remain very long. In his wake came E. David Goitein, who was to become a judge on our Supreme Court, and later Reuven Shiloah and Yaacov Herzog. I have always welcomed and sought the challenge of able associates, and the Foreign Ministry responded well.

I opened my mission intensively with the accent on economic issues. Between September and December 1950, I had to negotiate an agricultural loan of $35 million from the Export-Import Bank. Early in 1951 I initiated discussions for a Treaty of Friendship, Commerce and Navigation in order to create a juridical framework within which our relationship was to evolve. In April 1951 I sought the aid of the United States, as one of the occupying powers, for Israel's efforts to secure a compensation agreement from Germany. At the same time, I approached Secretary Acheson and congressional leaders on behalf of Israel's inclusion in the economic-aid programs of the United States. In the late summer of 1951 I requested American support for Israel's case against Egypt on the Suez Canal blockade.

The multiplicity of these tasks became symptomatic of our Washington embassy through all the years of Israel's independence. At any given moment there are always several major problems on which the understanding of the American government is urgently needed. In almost every case there is no substitute for that support. The pressure of Israel's demands on the Administration is so intense that there is always a danger of exhausting our welcome by pressing too many cases too often and too hard. I thought that the best guarantee of success lay in the creation of a public sympathy that would take Israel out of the diplomatic routine and elevate it to a special place in American confidence. This meant that I had simultaneously to pursue contacts in Washington and take a leading share in bringing Israel's cause to millions of Americans. Between one meeting and another in the State Department, at the White House or on Capitol Hill, there would be many air or train journeys to address forums of American public opinion, or to bring Israel's message to Jewish communities. When to all of this I added the leadership of Israel's delegation at the United Nations, I find it hard in retrospect to understand how, even with a strong constitution, I could possibly have survived. Indeed, on two occasions in 1951, once in the Security Council and once at a meeting in Tulsa, Oklahoma, I found myself delivering impassioned speeches after lack of sleep and on a completely empty stomach, with the result that my energy ebbed away and I briefly fainted. When this happened during a discussion in the Security Council about our contested irrigation rights, the alarm of my family and friends was shared by David Ben Gurion, who was then on his first official visit to the United States. He sent me a message suggesting that I take it easy, since, as he said blandly, "People like you are not to be found running round the streets."

Ben Gurion was triumphantly received in Washington and New York, and he established a sound relationship with Truman and other Administration leaders. He greatly preferred substantive discussions to ceremonial luncheons and dinners, which always seemed to fall short of smooth consummation. At a luncheon with Truman the first course was a pallid fish salad, of which Ben Gurion and I took small portions in order to leave room for the main course, which never came. It turned out that Truman was in an economizing mood and that in Missouri, lunch is a brief formality with the chief meal in the evening. We left Blair House famished. (The White House was undergoing repair.) I took Ben Gurion and his party to Harvey's Restaurant —renowned for its food. As we sat down, in trooped a procession of Truman's American guests, who had similar need of replenishment— Chief Justice Vinson, Secretary Acheson and the rest.

The next evening at our own embassy residence the fare was more abundant. But after the dessert I made repeated signs to Paula Ben Gurion indicating that she should rise to enable others to follow. Her response was to sink deep in her chair, and to my alarm, she seemed about to slide under the table. The Cabinet members, judges and senators coughed politely and remained seated. At last Paula surfaced like a diver reporting a rich bed of pearls and announced in triumphant Yiddish, "I've found my shoes!"

My activity was at feverish pace, and I suppose that the sustaining impulse came from the consciousness that Israel's security and development depended very greatly on the United States. Few ambassadors can feel that nearly everything they do matters. There was also a fortunate taste of early success. In the first two years of my mission, which coincided with the last period of the Truman Administration, almost everything that I attempted ended with good results. The Export-Import Bank granted its new loan, thus dissipating the fear that the first $100 million had been a one-time operation dictated by electoral motives. Secretary Acheson agreed to my request for American encouragement for the opening of our negotiations with the Federal Republic of Germany. The United States gave its support to Israel's case in the United Nations Security Council against Egypt on the Suez Canal blockade. Within a few months of my presentation of Israel's request for large-scale American aid, the Congress increased

President Truman's proposal to grant the astronomical sum of $73 million for the support of Israel's economy.

None of these tasks was easy. Much of my business was with Secretary Acheson. He was a complex and subtle figure. His outer elegance, a little too careful and refined, was the reflection of a precise intellect rather than a dandified pose. He was intolerant of excess in rhetoric or emotion. He liked everything to be in balance and in the lowest audible key. Perhaps he attached excessive weight to reason as a determining factor in the life of mankind. He sought shelter from the gusts of sentiment, passion and prejudice, by pretending that they were not blowing at all, or alternatively, that they would soon subside.

I encountered the special difficulty of communicating with him when I came with my old-time colleague David Horowitz to explain Israel's case on the duty of Germany to make some compensation for the Holocaust. In order to secure American support for this unprecedented idea, we would simply have to prove the unprecedented scope of our Jewish experience. I embarked on a short, vivid account of the Holocaust in terms of the atrocities inflicted on the victims—men, women and children. As I narrated the macabre details, I almost broke down under the weight of my own horrified emotion. There sat Acheson, his mustache bristling with defensive suspicion, draped in his chair as though in a deliberate effort to avoid creasing his perfectly tailored clothes. I felt that if I went on much longer without getting a response, the psychological atmosphere would become so explosive that I would have to get up and walk out of the room. Just when the breaking point was reached, he began to thaw. His reactions were now in tune with what his ears were absorbing, and he came as close to an expression of tenderness and grief as I ever saw from him before, or was to see again.

My problem in securing Israel's first entry into the American aid programs was more complex. At that time the main allocations of U.S. aid were closely related to America's anti-Communist alliances. The weight of commitment was to Western Europe. Israel was not a member of any of the regional or multinational organizations through which American aid generally flowed. Moreover, the dimensions of the assistance that we were seeking bore no relation to our population. President Truman, with all his sympathy, could not suggest more than $23 million for Israel's share of grant assistance. I had asked for over $100 million. Our only hope lay in the house of Congress. Truman's assistant, David K. Niles, gave me to understand that the President would not be offended if the Congress, which usually cut down his proposals, now took the exceptional step of enlarging them.

I worked closely with I. L. Kenen, whom I had brought to Wash-

ington as a lobbyist for three months; he was to stay, with excellent
results, for twenty-five years. We decided on a technique which became
traditional in Israel's work in Washington. My aim was to generate
a bipartisan proposal in each house of Congress in favor of a special
dimension of aid for Israel in view of our special role in the absorption of refugee immigrants.

One week in the hot summer of 1951 I approached two senators
who represented the most authoritative forces in American politics:
I asked Paul Douglas, a Democrat from Illinois, and the Republican
leader, Robert Taft of Ohio, to present a resolution to the Senate
in support of a very large appropriation for Israel. Senator Douglas,
tall, white-haired, professorial, kindly, sentimental, was stretched out
on a sofa, exhausted by the intensity of his own legislative efforts. As
I explained the drama of Israel's ingathering—the arrival of Jews
from the displaced persons' camps with their tattooed arms and their
obsessive memories; the ecstatic reaction of Jews in Yemen and Iraq
to the call of Israel's independence—I could see that he was moved.
He pointed out, however, that a bipartisan effort would be necessary,
and skeptically wished me "good luck with Taft."

In the office of the Senior Senator from Ohio, whose father had been
Chief Justice and President of the United States, I had a different task
to accomplish. Taft had a very stern exterior. Behind his rimless
glasses, there was rarely any glint of warmth. His prejudices were
sharp, and he was little inclined to bipartisan gestures. At a pinch
he would probably have admitted that members of the Democratic
Party could in some cases be patriotic, if misguided, Americans. But
this was about as far as he was willing to go. He represented what
remained of the isolationist, puritanical tradition in American
thought. He did not like the idea of Americans spending money at
home, much less abroad. He felt that not spending money had a high
ethical value, like patriotism or marital fidelity. He was unlikely to
react well to our hope of extracting tens of millions of dollars from
American coffers.

With him I had an experience similar to that which I had undergone with Secretary Acheson. Under persuasion, provided that it was
quiet and based on logical premises, his defensive demeanor could be
pierced. For Taft, as for many Americans, Israel was not just another
foreign country. He first explained why he was "in principle" against
foreign aid. He did this so emphatically that I had a few twinges of
despair. But, then, in sharp transition, he explained why "rules have
exceptions." He thought that the exceptions were India and Israel.
I was curious to know why we were paired with India, but I thought

it better not to probe this too far. Israel seemed to move him through the courage of its Jewish recuperation, and also because its name elicited Biblical associations familiar from his early youth. He was too realistic not to know that nearly all the Jews in the United States had voted for the Democratic Party, but this was not an obstacle to his support. He had close contacts with some American Jewish leaders, especially with Rabbi Abba Hillel Silver, his constituent in Ohio, who had obviously made a deep spiritual impression upon him. Within a week I had got Senators Taft and Douglas to sponsor a Senate resolution to which dozens of their colleagues adhered. There was probably no other cause in which such divergent partners could be brought together.

In the House of Representatives, my task was easier. The party leaders, Speaker John McCormack and Representative Joseph Martin, both from Massachusetts, had been enlisted for the Zionist cause many years before, largely through the efforts of Boston Zionists—especially of Elihu Stone, who represented the Zionist cause in the North.

When I reached Secretary Acheson to make our formal request, he said to me with resignation, "You are theoretically presenting your case to us today. But I know as well as you do that you have already seen Dave Niles, Paul Douglas and Robert Taft." The words were said without resentment but also without enthusiasm. It had become accepted that Israel's method of winning support deviated from traditional routines. It was, however, strictly legitimate in a pluralistic democratic system. An ambassador need be no more ashamed of invoking his country's assets in sympathetic opinion than of drawing attention to resources of oil, if it has any.

By the end of 1951 it was clear that Israel could rely on massive United States aid to help it on its road toward economic consolidation. The support given by Truman to our political struggle in 1948 had not been an isolated gesture. A tradition of alliance was growing up. There was no formal documentary expression of this partnership, but its stability was becoming impressive. With these successes behind us, I certainly had no reason to be disappointed with the early momentum of my mission in Washington. There was something concrete and substantial to do every day.

Most of my work was in Washington, but there were still tense occasions at the UN. Korea was the major concern of the Great Powers in those days; and to everyone's surprise, including my own, I suddenly found myself for a brief spasm of time in the center of that drama.

The *New York Times* of January 13, 1952, had a banner headline about an Israeli initiative for a cease-fire in Korea. How I became projected into this role has been vividly described by Lester Pearson, then Foreign Minister of Canada, in the second volume of his memoirs. The story is so exotic that I prefer to tell it in Pearson's words:

January 12, 1952 (Friday)

This morning [Gladwyn] Jebb telephoned me that he had been trying to arrange a sponsoring group for an endorsation resolution, but was having great difficulty. The Asians, or at least some of them, were anxious to be the exclusive sponsors, and were also anxious, he said, to amend the statement itself before it went to Peking, with a view to removing the stipulation that a cease-fire must actually take place before any negotiations begin. This, of course, is a fundamental part of the statement, and without it the Americans naturally will not support it. Apparently they, the Asians, have been influenced by [Indian Ambassador] Rau's interpretative remarks yesterday. . . .

I then telephoned [Benegal] Rau to confirm, if possible, Jebb's fears. Rau was somewhat reassuring. He said that it is true the Asians had been talking about the question of a resolution and its sponsorship, and had come to the conclusion that the sponsors should not include any country which had forces fighting in Korea, and the Chinese might use this as an excuse to state that the resolution and the statement were primarily for the purpose of extricating such forces from their present difficulties. I told Rau that this seemed to me to be not unreasonable, and I suggested to him that he use his influence to have a resolution sponsored by four or five countries, such as Mexico, Sweden, Syria, Burma, and possibly Indonesia. Rau said that he would try to do this . . .

I passed this on to Jebb and he seemed to think that sponsorship by countries not fighting in Korea would be satisfactory, and he agreed to try to get agreement on that basis. He was having a meeting for this purpose at noon.

This meeting was apparently not able to work out any satisfactory arrangement, so later in the afternoon, at Jebb's suggestion, and apparently as a last resort, Rau persuaded [Abba] Eban (then Israel's Permanent Representative to the UN) to introduce the sponsoring resolution alone. Eban did this at the end of the afternoon, and it will be discussed tomorrow.

January 13, 1952 (Saturday)

Everything should have gone smoothly today, but the contrary was the case. The difficulty arose over the fact that the resolution sponsoring the statement and referring it to Peking "for their observations" has been sponsored by Israel. This was enough to arouse the ire and opposition of the Arabs, who, one after another this morning, recanted their earlier decision of approval, and began to find fault with the resolution. This gave encouragement to other doubters, and when, by the end of the morning, amendments were submitted by El Salvador and Dr. Tsiang [Nationalist Chinese Permanent Representative to the UN], which would have completely destroyed the statement (one would have substituted Nationalist China for Communist China), things looked dreary and discouraging. Something had to be done during the lunch hour, and done quickly. As soon as we adjourned, I saw Malik of the Lebanon, who had been leading the Arab filibuster, and tried to persuade him to adopt a more reasonable course; not to allow Arab hostility to Israel to wreck a course of action which they themselves had warmly supported. Malik said that the Arabs were having a meeting during the lunch hour and he would see what he could do to straighten things out.

I then got hold of Eban, Jebb, and Padilla Nervo of Mexico, who, with Riddell and myself, went to the Hidden House (an appropriate place) for lunch and discussion. Nervo came up with an ingenious idea. He suggested that we abandon all discussion of the Israel resolution and get back to the statement of the Cease-Fire Group, which should be put to the committee by the chairman as a document on which we would vote, first for and against. After all, it was the first item on our agenda! This would do two things. It would remove the Israel-Arab difficulty, and also avoid the necessity of voting on any amendments. It was essential to do this latter, because [U.S. Ambassador] Austin had told me before lunch that he could not vote against any amendment to substitute Nationalist China for Communist China. American abstention on this issue in any vote before the committee would, of course, wreck our statement, because it would confirm Chinese suspicions that the Americans were trying to trick them.

Nervo also promised to persuade the chairman as to the rightness of this course, and Eban agreed that if the statement of principles was carried, he would withdraw all of his resolution except that paragraph which referred the statement to Peking.

At 3:00 o'clock, therefore, Nervo raised his point of order, the chairman accepted it, and, somewhat cavalierly, put the statement of principles to the vote at once without discussion and without amendment. It was carried against the protest of several members over what they considered—and not without some reason—arbitrary and unconstitutional procedure. However, the main thing is that fifty delegations voted for the statement. Then after a long wrangle . . . the Norwegians put forward a short resolution, simply asking the Secretary-General to transmit the document to Peking. Eban, therefore, withdrew his own resolution completely. The Norwegian resolution was carried and there were only one or two more hurdles to overcome. Now we can sit back and see what happens in Peking during the next few days. And I can go to Ottawa.

I had simply passed my initiative to Norway to avoid Arab trouble. A text proposed by Israel would have been opposed by the Arabs, whereas exactly the same text under the name "Norway" was accepted. The lesson of this episode is that Israel has a potential role in international conciliation, which Arab hostility is able to frustrate. In today's United Nations, statesmen like Gladwyn, Jebb, Benegal Rau and Lester Pearson, knowing this situation, would probably not even trouble to involve Israel's aid to resolve crises in the parliamentary arena.

The fact remained that a vast transition had taken place in our national status, and I did not want the exaltation to subside after three years. The theme of transition figured in most of the speeches that I made to audiences around the United States in those years. I was anxious lest amid the trappings of sovereignty we and our friends should lose a sense of wonder at Israel's sudden rebirth.

In May I spoke at a dinner in Washington in which Israel honored President Truman, who had by then announced his decision not to attempt a further period of office. I thought it appropriate to record a tribute to him:

> *We do not have orders or decorations. Our material strength is small and greatly strained. We have no tradition of formality or chivalry. One thing, however, is within the power of Israel to confer. It is the gift of immortality. Those whose names are bound up with Israel's history never become forgotten. We are, therefore, now writing the name of President Truman upon the map of our country. In a village of farmers near the airport of Lydda at the gateway to Israel, we establish a monument, not of dead stone but of living hope. Thus, when the eyes of men alight on Truman Village in Israel, they will pause in their successive generations to recall the strong chain which, at the middle of the 20th century, drew the strongest and the smallest democracies together with imperishable links.*

As I left the rostrum I saw the tough-minded President burying his face in a handkerchief without any effort to restrain his emotion. The next day he sent me a letter asking for a text of my address:

"You spoke so flatteringly about me that for a moment I had the impression that I was dead."

By now I was finding the zest of Washington more rewarding than endless debates in the United Nations. But during the autumn session of the General Assembly in 1952 I was in the center of two UN occasions. The first was to mark the death of President Weizmann after a long and agonizing illness, for the greater part of which he was totally incapacitated. It was the end of a whole era in Jewish history. The General Assembly of the United Nations, in accordance with its practice, held a session of mourning called by its president, Lester Pearson. The Arab delegates were absent. They could not show any human feeling toward an adversary even in death. When Pearson summoned me to the rostrum, I made an improvised speech of two minutes in which I said of Weizmann:

He led Israel for forty years across a wilderness of martyrdom and anguish, of savage oppression and frustrated hope, across the sharpest agony which has ever beset the life of any people, and at the end of his days, he entered in triumph upon his due inheritance of honor as the first President of Israel, the embodiment in modern times of that kingly and prophetic tradition which once flourished in Israel and became an abiding source of light and redemption for succeeding generations of men. During years of deep darkness and little hope, we looked with pride upon his erect and majestic bearing, his dignity of mind and spirit, his scientific intellect refined and ordered as a cultivated garden, and his profound moral influence in every free country on the best brains and spirits of his age.

When I came down from the rostrum Dean Acheson, Anthony Eden and Andrei Vyshinsky came from their places to shake my hand, Eden positively glowing with elegance and international authority. For a short period in the thirties he had been my boyhood hero: the lonely resister of dictators. He now took me aside for some reminiscences about his relations with Weizmann during World War II. I thought that his praise was somewhat belated, for in the dark period of Jewish catastrophe, Churchill's efforts to help our cause had received very little support from the Foreign Office under Eden's command. But in later years, after the 1956 Suez crisis, this subtle and complex British statesman was to ally himself strongly with Israel's cause. (For a time he was chairman of the Conservative Party's Israel Committee.)

A week after Weizmann's death I received an astonishing telephone call from Ben Gurion. He said that the Israeli presidency was symbolic, but our national history and faith attached great importance to symbols. Weizmann's life had conveyed a double message of statesmanship and science. The presidency could no longer express an active statesmanship, but there was an opportunity to symbolize Israel's special attachment to scientific humanism. The government wanted me to approach Albert Einstein and offer him the presidency of Israel!

I had hardly managed to digest the audacity of this idea before the wire services brought the news from Israel that Ben Gurion's idea had already been published. I doubted if this would make an impossible task any easier, and I was soon proved right. My telephone rang and an agitated voice came on the line from Princeton, New Jersey. I found myself talking to the author of the relativity theory, who was addressing me in very absolute terms. Would I please remove the idea from Ben Gurion's head? The plan was absolutely out of the question. All that Einstein asked of me was to explain how honored he was, but also how firm his refusal would be.

I realized that his shock was genuine and that his refusal was irrevocable. I added, however, that I found it hard to accept the rejection of the Israeli presidency in a telephone call; I would like to receive a written statement of his reply. A few days later Einstein sent me a letter signed in German and English. My letter and his reply follow:

November 17, 1952

Dear Professor Einstein:
The bearer of this letter is Mr. David Goitein of Jerusalem who is now serving as Minister at our Embassy in Washington. He is bringing you the question which Prime Minister Ben Gurion asked me to convey to you, namely, whether you would accept the Presidency of Israel if it were offered you by a vote of the Knesset. Acceptance would entail moving to Israel and taking its citizenship. The Prime Minister assures me that in such circumstances complete facility and freedom to pursue your great scientific work would be afforded by a government and people who are fully conscious of the supreme significance of your labors.

Whatever your inclination or decision may be, I should be deeply grateful for an opportunity to speak with you again within the next day or two at any place convenient for you. I understand the anxieties and doubts which you expressed to me this evening. On the other hand, whatever your answer, I am anxious for you to feel that the Prime Minister's question embodies the deepest respect which the Jewish people can repose in any of its sons.

Therefore, whatever your response to this question, I hope that you will think generously of those who have asked it, and will commend the high purposes and motives which prompted them to think of you at this solemn hour in our people's history.

With cordial personal wishes,

Yours respectfully,
Abba Eban

Dear Ambassador Eban:

I feel deeply moved by the offer of our State, Israel, though also sad and abashed that it is impossible for me to accept this offer. Since all my life I have been dealing with the world of objects I have neither the natural ability nor the experience necessary to deal with human beings and to carry out official functions. For these reasons I do not feel able to fulfill the requirements of this great task, even were my advanced age not to limit my strength to an increasing extent.

This situation is indeed extremely sad for me because my relation to the Jewish people has become my strongest human attachment ever since I reached complete awareness of our precarious position among the nations.

After we have lost in recent days the man who, among adverse and tragic circumstances, bore on his shoulders for many years the whole burden of leadership of our striving for independence from without, I wish from all my heart that a man be found who by his life's work and his personality may dare to assume this difficult and responsible task.

(signed) Albert Einstein

Princeton, N.J.
November 18, 1952

I have often reflected on Einstein's reference to the request of "our State, Israel" (*unseres Staates Israel*). The simplicity of this identification seemed to smash through the tormented semantics which induced so many Diaspora Jews, especially in America, to address Israel in the third person, through fear of multiple allegiance.

This was not my last contact with Einstein. A few weeks later he came to share the dais with me at the annual dinner of the Weizmann Institute of Science in the Waldorf-Astoria Ballroom. He was attired in fairly immaculate evening dress, except for the complete and conspicuous absence of socks. I assumed, wrongly, that he was fulfilling the conventional stereotype of a professor. Since he was the most eminent of all professors, he was surely entitled to set a record of absent-mindedness. In conversation he explained to me that this was not so. He knew perfectly well what he was doing. He was quite simply devoted to rationality. He did not like doing things which had no empirical or logical explanation. There was no scientific way of proving that it was necessary or useful to wear both socks and shoes. One of these acts could be justified by the need to cover the feet; two of them seemed redundant. If I could refute what he had said, he would consider changing his habitual conduct.

I decided not to attempt another unsuccessful exercise in persuasion, this time in a matter on which I had no strong feelings one way or another. A year or two later I went to Princeton to address the Student Union. It was a murderously cold and windy night. I had been warned that Princeton was attended by many Arab students, pupils of the Arab historian Phillip Hitti, who would probably heckle me mercilessly in the question period. When I approached the microphone to launch my oration, the door at the back opened and the august figure of Albert Einstein came quietly to a place near the front, where also two young Israelis on leave from a course at Harvard were sitting—Shimon Peres and Aharon Remez. Einstein's entry seemed to cast a spell of deference on the whole assembly, and the Arab students were reduced to a paralyzed silence. After my address Einstein came to shake my hand. I asked him why he had taken the trouble to honor the gathering on so cold a night. He replied, "I am interested in the ambassador of a small state. Powerful states need no ambassadors. Their force speaks for themselves. For small states it matters how they express themselves. What you are doing matters. Good night."

I duly went on "expressing myself" on matters of Israel's security. Three years after they were concluded, the armistice agreements were proving their durability. On the other hand, no real progress toward peace was being made. Israel was under constant attack on issues, the solution of which would have been feasible if the Arabs had been willing to negotiate a peace settlement. This was to be our dilemma across the years. On the one hand, they demanded that we solve problems which only a peace settlement could solve. On the other hand, they refused a peace negotiation. I therefore asked the Israel government for permission to launch a peace offensive at the General Assembly by attempting to get a majority for the principle of direct negotiations. In an address entitled "A Blueprint for Peace," delivered on December 11, 1952, I said: "If we refuse to seek new solutions of old deadlocks, we shall be living far below the level of our responsibilities and opportunities. . . . Nobody can help Israel and the Arab states to solve problems which they will not discuss freely and directly between themselves."

I then proposed a detailed agenda for a negotiation involving a transition from armistice to peace; the negotiation of final boundaries; a regional plan for the absorption and resettlement of refugees; and a system of cooperation creating an "open region" in which there would be a concerted attempt to bring about an economic renaissance in the Middle East. I called for free ports, mutual access to air and sea communications, and an intensive process of human exchange.

"Blueprint for Peace" evoked a good response. The delegations of Canada, Cuba, Denmark, Ecuador, the Netherlands, Norway, Panama and Uruguay sponsored a resolution calling for the kind of negotiated settlement for which I had argued. The United States, France and Britain indicated their support. We achieved a good majority despite Arab opposition in the Ad Hoc Political Committee. Had we been able to maintain that result in the plenary session, we would have weakened the Arab argument that peace in the future had to be based on the unfulfilled resolutions of 1947. Unhappily, within the few days between the committee and plenary stages, Ben Gurion published an interview with Cyrus Sulzberger in the *New York Times* in which he spoke contemptuously of any international interest in Jerusalem. He said simply that Jerusalem was no different than Washington, Paris and London. This was not strictly true even in Israeli jurisprudence, since we had always proposed a special status for the Holy Places. The result of the interview was that several Catholic countries, headed by the Philippines, withdrew their support from the Eight Power resolution on the grounds that they would be called upon to acquiesce in Ben Gurion's denial of Jerusalem's universal significance. Ben Gurion's interview was quite coincidental in its timing and had no relevance to our international struggle at that time. The resolutions being discussed in the General Assembly made no demands on us in relation to Jerusalem.

Another significant reason for our reduced vote in the plenary was that the Soviet Union ominously passed from abstention to opposition. This was the first time since Israel had been established that a Soviet vote on an Arab-Israel issue had been diametrically opposed to our position. Although we still had a majority for the text on direct negotiations in the plenary, we fell short of what was then regarded as the statutory two thirds. (It was to take nearly twenty years for a UN body to agree—in October 1973—that the conflict must be resolved by "negotiation.")

By this time it was clear to me that the atmosphere of my work in

Washington was going to change. The Truman Administration was in the last stages of its life. Throughout the summer all embassies in Washington had closely followed the electoral campaign. There was little else for most of them to do. Early in 1952 I had made a visit to Chicago on behalf of the Israel Bond Organization. I was to be the main speaker at a mass meeting in one of the city's largest arenas. As was now usual, the governor of the state presented me to the audience. By now I had become accustomed, and I hope immune, to the extravagent eulogy of which I was the target on occasions such as these. I had often alluded to the danger lest a public speaker come to believe what his chairmen said about him and thus become totally unfit for any future human intercourse. On this occasion my ears and heart were arrested after the first few sentences. The governor of Illinois was speaking with a felicity of phrase and spirit unusual in American political oratory. His words rang with a sensitive idealism and were held together with bonds of restraint.

The speaker was Adlai E. Stevenson; I had never seen him before. He seemed out of tune with the strident politics of the American Midwest. We met afterward for an hour and got on well together, except that I obviously had sharper passions and prejudices and a more militant partisanship than he seemed to show. I thought that he had too much understanding of opposing views to be firm about his own.

A few weeks later, when President Truman announced his refusal to run for office again, Stevenson's name burst upon the American public. I followed his dignified and rather sad demeanor as he entered the boisterous electoral arena at the Democratic National Convention in Chicago in July. Suzy and I sat up late in the night in our Washington home when his graceful and somber acceptance speech came across the television screen.

It was obvious that Stevenson's chances of victory were small against General Dwight Eisenhower. Eisenhower's contact with our cause had been superficial. Yet it included something which Ben Gurion was never to forget—a reaction of cold fury to the horrors of Nazism which unfolded before him when the forces under his command entered the concentration camps. The violence of his resentment at Hitlerist oppression was enhanced by the compassion with which he set about rehabilitating the emaciated figures stalking through the camps. But of the Zionist enterprise and Israel's resurgence, he seemed to know little.

In February 1952 Sharett and I, feeling that he might become important to our cause, had visited him at his NATO headquarters in Paris. He was buoyant, authoritative, pink-cheeked—and astonishingly fluent in speech without, however, being completely coherent. The words poured out of him without hesitation but did not always fit into sentences. I felt charitably, but I think accurately, that his mind was richer than his capacities of expression. I was also impressed by his phlegmatic temperament. While Sharett and I were explaining our problems to him, the telephone rang with the news that King George VI had died in London a few minutes before. He asked to be excused, went out of the room, supervised the removal of all the NATO countries' flags to half-mast, came back, sat down and resumed our conversation at the precise point at which it had been broken off. I found this display of normality disconcerting. After all, the dead monarch had been his close friend, associated with the most important epochs of his life.

The fear that he might lack emotional range was confirmed in our later encounters, but it was hard to be unimpressed by his air of authority. Eisenhower's lack of precision and some degree of indolence in him were counterbalanced by a dominant will. As we went out to our car I said to Sharett, "He will usually get what he wants; the question is whether he will always know what he wants."

In the November 1952 election, Eisenhower won his sweeping victory. I could not attend his somewhat imperial inauguration ceremony in January, since bereavement struck my home. Our first daughter, Meira, was born in mid-December. Three weeks later, when I was in New York for conversations with Trygve Lie after the end of the General Assembly, I came to my office at 11 East Seventieth Street, to be told by Regina Medzini, my secretary, that I should speak to my wife in Washington immediately on the telephone. I received the staggering news that Meira was dead—the victim of one of those unexplained and spontaneous crib deaths which strike so many children without known cause. Suzy and I left Washington for Florida to try to come to terms with our grief, leaving the embassy in the capable hands of David Goitein.

Returning sadly to Washington for the last week of Truman's "lame duck" period, I found that the duck was not all that lame, after all. Truman intended to act with full presidential powers up to the last minute of his tenure. On the very eve of transferring his office somewhat irascibly to his successor, he signed approval for another Export-Import Bank loan which I had negotiated the previous autumn.

But new ideas were now at work in American policy. The Egyptian monarch had been overthrown by a group of officers headed by Colonels Mohammed Naguib and Gamal Abdul Nasser. Leading members of the Democratic Administration, including Acheson and W. Averell Harriman, were considering the idea of strengthening American influence by the sale of arms to some Arab states, including Egypt.

I thought that it would be ironical for the Truman Administration to end its career in this way. I argued tenaciously with Acheson and mobilized as many influences in the White House and on Capitol Hill as I could. In the end Acheson said to me wearily, "Well, I don't see why we shouldn't bequeath some headaches to our successors."

It was sad but impressive to see Truman on the television screen getting on a train for Independence, Missouri. American democracy is at its best in its talent for the transfer of power. The little tough-spoken haberdasher looked like a simple man who had played at being a potentate and was now awakening to his modest reality. But there was nothing modest about the dimensions of his achievement. He had given democracy, peace and social equality a robust and defiant protection. In the next few years I was to see him often, vainly attempting to get him to come to be idolized in Israel. I gathered that his wife, Bess, had been reluctant about every ten miles that she had ever traveled from Missouri, and now that it was not obligatory, there was no chance of it happening. Truman went on exemplifying the simple unpretentious qualities and style of Middle America. But he had given millions of ordinary men a brief glimpse of their potentiality, and had made them proud to be ordinary.

Truman's Administration ended with the question of arms for Egypt in abeyance. But not for long. By the end of January I was visiting an unfamiliar State Department, now headed by John Foster Dulles, who was certain that he could achieve more in the Middle East than his predecessors.

The years 1953 to 1956 are a gloomy period in our national recollection. Israelis who are impressed by the intensity of our problems today would do well to recall the extraordinary gravity of our situation at that time. The Soviet Union launched the anti-Semitic trial of Jewish doctors on the preposterous grounds that they had tried to poison their patients. It was the last fling of Stalin's madness. Soviet hostility to Israel developed to the point of breaking diplomatic relations in February 1953. America, far from redressing the balance, compounded our solitude by embarking on what Dulles called a "new look." This meant a determined effort to strengthen America's influence in the Arab world and to play down its intimacy with Israel. Across our borders with Jordan, Syria and Egypt came a constant torrent of violence, with military units and marauders, organized under the name of *fedayeen,* bringing mutilation and death to our civilians in frontier areas and sometimes into the heart of the coastal plain. Israeli forces often went into action to deter and stem the violence. But there would usually be a heavy toll of Arab life, indignant Arab appeals to the Security Council, and condemnatory resolutions against Israel which encouraged Arab governments to repeat their attacks in a vicious circle of escalating tension. Sometimes, as in' a raid in Kibya in October 1953, the Israeli reaction was regarded by most Israelis as excessive. The United States opposed our retaliations without suggesting an alternative method of defending our lives. The idea that Arabs could kill Israelis without any subsequent Israeli re- action was close to becoming an international doctrine.

Israel's anguish in the nightmare years 1954–1956 was not limited to the inflamed borders alone. The conflict now lost its local character and eventually became caught up in the tangle of global rivalry. A turning point came when the Soviet Union authorized a massive arms transaction with Egypt through Czechoslovakia. Weapons of a destructive capacity hitherto unknown in the Middle East poured into Egypt at a rate beyond all previous experience. Israel saw itself faced by dangers far greater than those involved in the daily border attacks. Its long-term security was in serious question. The balance of power in the Middle East would now be a function of East-West relations. There was urgent need for the West to demonstrate to an excited Arab world that the Middle East was not going to become a uniquely Soviet preserve and that Israel would not be suffered to fall into rela- tive weakness. The new crisis could have been cheaply overcome by modest reinforcement of Israeli arms, a convincing effort to strengthen the authority of the armistice frontiers and a clarification of American support of Israel's integrity and independence. Instead of this, London and Washington kept making allusions to Israeli concessions, thus giving the armistice lines an aspect of doubtful legitimacy. Secretary of State Dulles increased Israeli nervousness by concluding regional defense treaties, such as the Baghdad Pact in 1954. This had the effect of leaving Israel as the only country not integrated into a formal defense system and lacking a contractual basis for military supplies.

This accumulation of clouds abroad was accompanied by a weak- ening of national resolution at home. The politics of purpose gave way to the politics of fatigue. Symptomatic of this trend was Ben Gurion's resignation from the premiership at the end of 1953. He had every right to be tired. While he was a buoyant, vigorous, pugnacious, defiant man who sent out sparks of energy in all directions, for over two decades he had carried heavy burdens. The first four years of independence, with their inspiring hopes and horrifying risks, must have taken a greater toll of him than most of us realized. He felt a sharp dissatisfaction with some elements in Israeli life. The intensity of parliamentary warfare, the fragmentation of the electoral system, the need to be always conciliating small groups in order to maintain a coalition—all these were repellent to his active and dominant nature.

Unfortunately, his surrender of responsibility to his successor Moshe Sharett was neither chivalrous nor wholehearted. He made it clear that his departure was temporary, and he established what was in effect an alternative government in Sdeh Boker, a Negev kibbutz to which Israeli leaders made pilgrimage in search not only of inspiration but of concrete direction. Few strong leaders are enthusiastic about their successors, and Ben Gurion's lack of regard for Sharett was not even veiled. It was stark naked. As if this were not enough to undermine Sharett's limited resources of self-confidence and authority, there came the appointment of Pinchas Lavon to head the Defense Ministry. Lavon was a man of acute intellectual power with a progressive vision of Israel's social destiny. But in the defense establishment he was largely concerned to prove his militant virility so as to live down a reputation for pacifism. The result was that he reacted almost hysterically to our global dangers, and sponsored military plans of such violence that even hard-headed soldiers like the Chief of Staff, Moshe Dayan, felt obliged to resist them. Lavon also had an original conception of Cabinet government, according to which the Prime Minister had no responsibilities at all in the domain of national security.

All in all, it is difficult for Ben Gurion's biographers, however pious, to praise either the timing of his leave of absence or his manner of carrying it into effect. Sharett, Ben Gurion and Lavon now constituted three separate centers of executive authority, and the fabric of Israel's political structure was torn apart. We had all the unsettling effects of a Prime Minister's resignation without the balancing advantage of a new, clear-cut leadership. The steep decline of immigration to a mere trickle in 1952, 1953 and 1954 added to the general disillusion. For mass immigration had given Israel's first years a special exaltation, calling forth deep impulses of solidarity, resourcefulness and self-sacrifice. Now this light was eclipsed. "When sorrows come, they come not single spies, but in battalions."

To be Israel's ambassador in Washington and to the United Nations in those days was clearly no prescription for a relaxed life. Israel's difficulties were the only possessions that nobody was trying to take away. I made a definition of my aims: in Washington to strive for a viable, if not an affectionate relationship with the Eisenhower Administration; at the United Nations to use the international platform to give some special resonance to Israel's cause; in American Jewry to create around my embassy and myself an atmosphere of solidarity and confidence; and in the general arena of American opinion to break out of diplomatic confinement so as to become a spokesman of a cause to which most Americans might be able to respond. My vocation was to develop an American-Israeli tradition based on a public sympathy that might transcend, and sometimes correct, the direction of official policy.

My main task was a dialogue with John Foster Dulles, who was clearly going to be the architect of American policy. No Secretary of State can give constant personal care to more than a few problems among the global abundance; and Dulles, unlike Acheson before him, found intellectual fascination in an issue that seemed to bore his predecessor to death. Christian fundamentalists may be attracted or repelled by Jewish history; they are very seldom indifferent to it. In general, I welcomed this upgrading of our problem. The higher the level on which our issues were discussed, the greater was our chance of at least a minimal understanding. President Truman had not erred in telling me frankly that in his experience the State Department officials found it difficult to absorb the idea of a Jewish state. Our claims fell beyond the bureaucratic routine. Civil servants, trained to think in general categories, were impatient with the particular elements of Israeli personality. Assistant Secretary of State Henry A. Byroade even suggested, grotesquely, that Israel should abandon its universal Jewish solidarities so as to become just "another Middle Eastern state." I hoped that Dulles with his larger view and his religious temperament would discern those aspects of Israel's policy that flowed from its unique history.

In my confrontation with Dulles I was aided by the fact that I had taken the trouble to keep contact with him while he was in the wilderness. The corporation lawyer, disappointed in his ambition in 1948, still hankered after a public role. I had made some visits to Wall Street in the years 1949–1953 to exchange views with him. He seemed surprised by this attention. Why should a busy ambassador bother with a man who had no power and little influence? I had the feeling that in my place he would not have risked his time with anyone who was not "in." In later years he never forgot that I had shown an interest in him when he was still "unhonored and unsung." He was a complex personality, physically shy and clumsy, but full of intellectual self-confidence. He was able to pass from moral elevation to an extraordinary deviousness and back again with little visible transition. He was marked by a thin and achromatic spirituality; but whatever was thought of him, I knew that nobody would count as much as he in determining our international position for the next decade, and I was resolved to find a way to his mind and heart.

The change in Soviet policy was hesitant. The break in diplomatic relations had come after an irresponsible bomb explosion in the Soviet embassy at Ramat Gan during a period when demonstrations were being held against the trial of Jewish doctors in Moscow. There was no objective reason for charging the Israeli government with guilt for this episode. Nothing could have served our national interest less. Assiduous efforts were made to repair the political damage, and by July 1953, with Stalin dead and embalmed, diplomatic relations had been restored on the strength of a Soviet explanation that the USSR wished "to have good relations with all states, irrespective of differences of policy and ideology." Throughout 1953 the Soviet Union took a passive attitude in all Security Council debates. After the Kibya raid the Western powers joined in a resolution of condemnation that took no account at all of previous Arab provocations. I assumed that the Soviet Union would join this criticism as a matter of course, but I dutifully lobbied the Soviet delegate Andrei Vyshinsky like other delegates to the Council. To my surprise and relief he listened impassively, and the Soviet Union alone abstained.

At the end of the year, however, the Security Council debated a complaint by Syria against Israeli water development in the demilitarized zone on the Syrian border at Bnot Yaakov Bridge. This was a frivolous complaint. There was no doubt about the legitimacy of peaceful economic development in the demilitarized zone, despite a conflict of view about sovereignty or jurisdiction. After many weeks a compromise was worked out under which the resumption of the irrigation work could be authorized by the United Nations Chief of Staff, subject to his understanding that there would be no damage to Arab water rights. I thought that I had done well to get this text accepted by the Western powers, and my own government in Jerusalem reluctantly agreed. But in February 1954 the Soviet Union vetoed this resolution. Vyshinsky explained ingeniously that no resolution deserved support unless it had the agreement both of Israel and the Arab states. This, however, turned out to be a euphemism. It was Arab and not Israeli consent that the Soviet Union regarded as a condition for allowing resolutions to pass the Security Council.

From that day on, the Security Council was closed to Israel as a court of appeal or redress. Arabs could kill Israeli citizens across the border, blockade our port of Eilat, close the Suez Canal to our shipping, send armed groups into our territory for murder and havoc, and decline to carry out stipulated clauses of the armistice agreement in the complete certainty that the Security Council would not adopt even the mildest resolution of criticism. Sometimes the veto was actually used by the Soviet Union against majority resolutions. At other times the anticipation of it prevented the majority from submitting any texts which gave support to Israel's interests. On the other hand, there was no such inhibition to resolutions criticizing Israel for retaliating against attacks. Thus, the doctrine of the United Nations came to imply that Arab governments could conduct warfare and maintain belligerency against Israel while Israel could offer no response. It was a picturesque jurisprudence and did not lack originality. What was remarkable was the apathy with which the world resigned itself to its perpetuation.

The precise reasons for the abrupt change of Soviet policy in 1953 have never been conclusively established. The most frivolous but prevalent version is that which attributes it to Israel's support of the American case against the invasion of South Korea. This is plain nonsense. The validity of the theory is destroyed by the fact that the Soviet Union took no vengeful attitude against dozens of other states that voted with the United States on this issue, including some members of the Arab group. Moreover, our vote on Korea was taken in mid-1950, and it was not until three years later that Soviet support of the Arab cause became blatant and consistent.

The truth is that Soviet policy in this as in other areas was largely determined by factors outside the Middle Eastern dispute. It arose from developments in the East-West relationship during the intensification of the Cold War. Moscow felt that it now had a good chance of winning the support of the new Arab regimes, whereas any idea that Israel could become anti-Western was inconceivable in view of the nature of our institutions and our strong links with American Jews. The new Egyptian regime had begun to make anti-Western noises: it seemed to be on the point of expelling British forces from its territory, and it strongly opposed attempts to bring Arab countries into a Western-sponsored alliance. For Moscow this marked a sudden gain in the international power balance. The Soviet Union had supported Israel in 1948 because we were the most active agent in the expulsion of British power. A similar Arab attitude toward Britain and her allies in 1954 elicited a pro-Arab attitude in Moscow. It was not accidental that the USSR chose the Bnot Yaakov project as the occasion for expressing its new attitude. Israel's work in the demilitarized zone was linked with a water development scheme sponsored by President Eisenhower through his emissary, Eric Johnston. The Soviet Union by its veto could therefore achieve a double aim: to arouse Arab sympathy, and to impede a tendency of the United States to play the leading role in political conciliation and economic development in the Middle East.

In personal terms, the effect of this darkening Soviet horizon was considerable. In the first four years of my leadership of the Israeli delegation at the UN, I had grown used to close cooperation with

Soviet representatives. Gromyko, Tsarapkin, Malik and Vyshinsky were familiar colleagues in many debates and negotiations. Contrary to the general belief, Soviet diplomats are not coldly inhuman in their diplomatic relations. Although their social occasions were formal, my discussions with them around UN tables and at their headquarters on Park Avenue were very cordial. I also learned something about the methodology of Soviet diplomacy. For example, I have mentioned the tendency for meetings in New York to be held very late at night. This meant that it was early the next morning at the Kremlin, so that our discussions with Soviet diplomats could be followed immediately by their own consultation with their capital. At that time Soviet representatives showed a great interest in the Israeli social adventure. I remember some of them coming to our own mission on East Seventieth Street to see films portraying our development, including life in the kibbutzim, which Malik and Tsarapkin constantly compared to the Russian kolkhoz. But during the months of rupture in diplomatic relations, Soviet ambassadors who had exchanged many vodka-laden dinners with me, would pass by me at the UN as though I did not exist.

When relations were resumed in July 1953, our contacts again became correct although without quite renewing the warmth of the earlier period. On one occasion Vyshinsky explained to me in detail that there was nothing subjective or emotional about the Soviet attitude. International policies were governed by "interests" and not by "sentiments." In his view, an Israeli policy of nonidentification or equilibrium was not dialectically possible, if only because Israel depended economically on the United States. It could not, in the Soviet view, take a really independent attitude. Moscow could not easily grasp the possibility of an equal relationship between a Great Power and a small country to which it gives aid. Whenever Israel seemed to be in conflict with the United States, the Soviet Union reacted with incredulity. It tended to believe that our show of independence was a well-staged pretense.

There might have been some grounds for hoping that the Soviet pressure on Israel would result in the United States giving us greater encouragement. The opposite was the case. If the USSR was out to win more support in Egypt and other Arab capitals, the American answer would be to compete for Arab affections. The United States thus collided with us head-on. When Israel defied a UN order to suspend water development at Bnot Yaakov in the north and the United States supported the Arabs, a violent furor arose in the American Jewish community. The Republican candidate for the mayoralty of New York found himself in desperate straits because of Administration policy.

Jewish leaders converged on the White House, and on a memorable day Dulles dispatched Henry Byroade to my hotel in New York to implore me to agree on an immediate statement signaling the resumption of American financial aid to Israel. It was the only occasion on which I was pressured by a foreign government to receive and not to relinquish something. Yet, we felt cold solitude, alleviated only by strong support in American public opinion. I was invited to the state legislatures of Ohio, Colorado, New Jersey and Massachusetts, where moving resolutions were adopted strengthening Israel's spirit in the face of Soviet hostility.

The year 1954 ended as bleakly as it had begun. We had made little progress in securing American understanding of our right of self-defense. After an Israeli raid at Beit Liqya in response to assaults in Jerusalem, the United States declared that while infiltration from Jordan constituted a serious problem, "Israel's apparent policy of armed retaliation had increased rather than diminished tension along the armistice lines." Whether there would really have been any less tension if Israel had fatalistically sat back and let its citizens be killed without any response is moot. Since no such experiment in national masochism has ever been tried by any country, we shall never know the answer.

After the Kibya raid in October 1953, I formally proposed a thorough review of the armistice agreement with Jordan in accordance with Article XII. This provided that if after a year from March 1949 either signatory asked the Secretary-General to convene a conference with the other party to review or revise the agreement, attendance was mandatory. Dag Hammarskjöld, who had succeeded Trygve Lie as Secretary-General, reluctantly but correctly turned to Amman, received a refusal to attend the "mandatory" conference, and there the matter ended. With the Security Council blocked by veto, with the Armistice Commissions ineffective and a review of the armistice agreement illegally refused, Israel seemed to have nothing left but deterrence by armed response. This was tried with little effect.

At home, the unfortunate Moshe Sharett, beleaguered by political intrigues, strove to achieve some international success. Yet he could not always hold out against demands for military action. He authorized an operation in Gaza in February 1955. In the previous six months there had been forty armed clashes and twenty-seven Egyptian raids into our territory, with seven Israeli deaths and twenty-seven wounded. There had been no incursions by Israel into Egyptian territory, and Egypt had been condemned by the Armistice Commission twenty-six times. The Israeli riposte in Gaza left thirty-eight Egyptian and eight Israeli dead. Sharett complained that he had "authorized" a far smaller number of Egyptian casualties. Clearly, our technique of resistance could not have controlled results.

In later years Nasser was to claim, sometimes with the support of Western observers, that his humiliation in Gaza led him to seek arms from the Soviet Union. It is difficult either to confirm or to refute this theory. In any case, it was impossible to win Israeli public support for the idea that our people should be passively killed in order to prevent Egypt from falling into the Soviet orbit. It is more likely that Gaza was the excuse rather than the cause of the Egyptian approach to Moscow for aid.

The Egyptian regime was now mounting an intensive campaign for the removal of British troops from the Suez Canal area. Iraq, then under a monarchical regime, strove together with Jordan and Lebanon to obtain American military aid. The Arab League adopted resolutions against negotiations between Israel and Jordan, against the Johnston-Eisenhower water plan, against any weakening of the Arab economic boycott of Israel, against the payment of compensation to the victims of Nazism in Austria, and against tendencies then apparent in New Delhi and Rangoon for establishing diplomatic relations with Israel. In the light of the fighting in Indochina and another failure to reach an East-West settlement at the Berlin Conference, the Western powers reinforced their pursuit of Arab favor, despite the instability of that bloc. On February 24, 1954, in a single day President Mohammed Naguib of Egypt and President Adib Shishakli of Syria were overthrown.

In Washington I made countless representations against the American intention to provide arms to Iraq. In the light of the impending British withdrawal from Egypt I went to the United Nations Security Council to seek a verdict against Egypt's continued violation of Israel's navigation rights of the Suez Canal. A majority was achieved in our favor, but the New Zealand resolution was vetoed by the Soviet Union. At home the triangle Sharett–Ben Gurion–Lavon was caught up in an alarming circle of animosities. A memorandum that reached me from Defense Minister Lavon was nothing short of apocalyptic in describing the effects on Israel's very existence of what he described as a massive concentration of hostile strength in Iraq and other Arab states.

The only relieving feature was a perceptible recovery in our economic situation. There was a rise in our foreign currency reserves to what was then the astronomic figure of $395 million with exports reaching $88 million as compared with $44 million the previous year. There was an increase both in industrial and agricultural production and a total revenue in foreign currency of $398 million of which at least 40 percent came from the United States government or American Jewry. At the end of May, five settlements were established in the Lachish area in fulfillment of an audacious plan for integrative rural settlement. The Yarkon–Negev pipeline was completed along a length of 106 kilometers. Immigration was still slender, but it rose from 10,000 to 17,000.

Nevertheless, our long-term security was visibly being eroded, and the focal point of action lay in the United States. Dulles and his associates made a determined effort to bring Arab countries into a Middle East defense organization. This was a totally unrealistic project in the light of the strong anti-Western current flowing in Egypt. The State Department preferred to believe that its troubles in the Arab world arose not from an endemic anti-Westernism in Arab capitals or a new tendency for nonidentification with either of the powers, but from what Dulles had called in his speech on June 1, 1953, "the need to allay Arab discontent arising from the establishment of the State of Israel."

Israel's decision to move the Foreign Ministry from Tel Aviv to Jerusalem caused further tension in Washington; and on April 4, 1954, Assistant Secretary of State Byroade went back to his campaign for the de-Judaization of Israel. He made a speech in which he said: "To the Israelis I say, look upon yourselves as a Middle Eastern state rather than a headquarters of world-wide groupings. Drop your attitude of conqueror and the conviction that force is the only policy that your neighbors will understand. To the Arabs I say, accept Israel. Accept at least a less dangerous modus vivendi with your neighbor." On May 1, addressing the anti-Zionist American Council for Judaism, Byroade said that unlimited Jewish immigration was a matter of grave concern. On May 5 I made an official protest against this frivolous oratory which caused a partial retraction from the State Department. When I told Byroade that the UN had asked us to establish "a Jewish state," not "another Middle Eastern state," he could hardly believe his ears.

Although the restoration of a current installment of American aid had been agreed upon during Byroade's hasty visit to me in New York late in 1953, American-Israeli relations were awkward. Not for the first or last time I found a better response in American public opinion than in the State Department. Most newspapers declared that such events as the Kibya raid stemmed from the "unwillingness of the Arab states to recognize Israel."

On July 6, Eric Johnston informed President Eisenhower that Syria, Lebanon, Jordan and Israel had accepted the principle of international sharing of the contested waters of the Jordan River and were all prepared to cooperate. Soon, however, it became apparent that the agreement of Arab specialists would not be ratified by their governments, even though Jordan and Syria received an excessively generous share of the Jordan waters.

All this time I was pursuing our economic negotiations intensely, both for their own sake and because this was in effect the only ray of light in the dark picture of American-Israeli tension. I also regarded the Johnston plan as a positive development. At the beginning of May 1954 President Eisenhower had asked the Congress to approve $160 million for that plan, and an additional project of irrigation in Sinai for the settlement of refugees. This generous initiative, however, was effectively stifled by Arab resistance.

I also moved to strengthen the instruments that could be put to the service of U.S.-Israeli relations. In January 1954 I had been able to initiate the establishment of an American-Israeli Society, which was joined by an impressive list of senators and governors of major states. It was by now becoming increasingly laborious for me to go from one Jewish organization to another in order to explain our policy. I therefore worked hard with Nahum Goldmann for the establishment in April 1954 of a permanent framework for cooperation among Jewish organizations on Israeli issues. This was the origin of the Presidents' Club. I was not yet able to persuade the influential American Jewish Committee, headed by Jacob Blaustein, to join, but that organization gave stalwart independent and effective service to the alleviation of difficulties between Washington and Jerusalem.

There still seemed to be no end to our troubles in 1954. While there was a temporary respite in border tensions from Jordan, Egypt increased its pressure. In September, Egyptian forces blew up the waterpipe at Niram in the south, and encouraged the infiltration of terrorists into villages of the northern Negev. In September the Israeli flagship *Bat Galim* attempted to pass peacefully through the Suez Canal to test our right of free passage. It was stopped by the Egyptians. While the Western powers supported our protest in the Security Council, it was obvious that they did not intend to make any effort to uphold Israel's rights.

On September 18 the Anglo-Egyptian agreement for the evacuation of the Suez Canal area was signed. I was called by Dulles to the State Department to receive what purported to be a soothing message stating that the exit of British troops would "decrease tension in the area" and that Israel "need not be concerned" at the supply of arms to Arab states. Meanwhile the *Bat Galim* discussion droned on endlessly in the Security Council. It had a dramatic end. The Egyptian representative, Mahmoud Azni, whom I had personal reason to recognize as the most moderate of Egyptian representatives, took the floor in the Security Council to answer my argument on Israel's right of free passage. In the heat of his rhetoric, he suddenly slumped in his chair, overcome by a massive heart attack. Incredibly, there was not then a doctor in the UN building, so I quickly ordered Moshe Tov, who had received full medical training without ever practicing his craft, to make an attempt at resuscitation, unfortunately in vain.

The ghastly year 1954 ended on a macabre note. On December 11 a military tribunal in Cairo began the trial of eleven Jews accused of espionage and sabotage in Cairo. It emerged that a reckless instruction had activated an espionage group which had laid explosive charges in public buildings in Cairo in the fatuous hope that the American and British governments, whose property was blown up, would attribute all this to Egyptian instigation and moderate their friendy relations with Cairo. The shadow of this "affair" was to convulse the Israeli political scene for many years to come. (Two of the accused, Dr. Marzuk and Shmuel Azar, were executed by hanging in the Cairo prison on January 31. The question whether Defense Minister Lavon was responsible for this instruction or whether he had been "framed" by his subordinates continued to agitate Israeli politics for many years.)

In face of all these dangers, we had not managed to secure action by the United States in balancing the new arms strength of the Arab countries. The new year opened in an atmosphere of emergency. Lavon's contentiousness, the suspicion about his part in the "affair," as well as concern about some of his proposals for savage security actions, led the Labor Party to advocate the return of Ben Gurion to the Defense Ministry. This was accepted both by Sharett and Ben Gurion, who returned as Defense Minister under Sharett's uneasy premiership.

It was obvious that 1955 would witness a decision for peace or war. While American officials led by Dulles continually gave me friendly assurances and reiterated their commitment to Israel's independence and economic progress, I could not take consolation from their statements as long as the central issue was unresolved: this issue was the change in the balance of armed strength and the reluctance of the United States to correct it.

The Egyptian government left us in no doubt that the main target of its new militance was Israel. On January 9 a leading member of that government, Major Salah Saleh, declared, "Egypt will strive to erase the shame of the Palestine War even if Israel should fulfill all UN resolutions. It will not sign a peace with her. Even if Israel should consist only of Tel Aviv, we should never put up with that."

It was clear that our foes were preparing for the kill. Two months later Egypt, Syria and Saudi Arabia announced that their armed forces would be placed under a unified command. The first conference of the nonaligned nations at Bandung adopted resolutions hostile to Israel in her absence. Not even the visit of Burmese Prime Minister U Nu to Israel in May could conceal the fact that the Arab and Soviet offensive was gaining momentum. The shooting down of an El Al plane over Bulgaria with heavy loss of life in July made the whole country feel like Job, too stunned to predict whence the next disaster would come.

I remember that I was in a Washington synagogue on the Jewish New Year when I heard the first definitive reports about the decision of the Soviet Union to make massive arms supplies available to Egypt through Czechoslovakia. After preparatory and noncommittal soundings in the State Department, I made a public request for American arms on October 11, 1955. In August, after many conversations with me, Dulles had attempted to give a stabilizing picture of American policy. I pointed out that the only effective way of counteracting Soviet support of Egypt was for the United States to grant a guarantee undertaking to Israel. Dulles accepted this principle, but reduced it to frustration by stating that the United States could not "guarantee temporary armistice lines"; it could only guarantee permanent agreed peace boundaries. I pointed out in public that the entire principle of a defense agreement with the United States was reduced to derision when it was made dependent on impossible conditions. All the Arabs now had to do to prevent an American guarantee to Israel was to refuse to reach "agreement" on a permanent boundary. I called this "a built-in deadlock." Moreover, Dulles' speech in August hinted broadly at the possibility that Israel might make a concession to Egypt and Jordan in a part of the Negev. Later he and his associate, Francis B. Russell, began to explore with us the possibility of creating triangles in the Negev which would enable Egyptian and Jordanian territory to meet at a certain point from east to west, while Israeli territory would pass the same point in "kissing triangles" from north to south so as to retain our access between Arab parts of the Negev.

If American policy was ominous, that of Britain was even more so. In November, Anthony Eden declared in the Guildhall that there should be a "compromise" between Israel's existing armistice boundaries and the even more meager lines proposed by the UN in 1947. Meanwhile the Baghdad Pact was becoming a reality, and on November 22 the first formal meeting of its signatories took place. Two weeks later, Arab strength in the United Nations was increased by the admission of Libya and Jordan. In December the United States and Britain rounded off another somber year for Israel by promising to give Egypt assistance in financing the High Dam at Aswan.

The State Department thesis during our many stormy discussions was that the Soviet arms transaction was "more promise than fulfillment," and that if war broke out in the Middle East, Israel would win a crushing victory. There was a total refusal to believe that there was any limit to Israel's nervous strength and that in the absence of any military aid or political commitment, desperation would come to inspire our policy. In these conditions I had a double task. The central aim was to break the resistance of the Administration to the idea of giving Israel minimal support. If this could not be achieved, the secondary duty was to create in the United States and in the United Nations an atmosphere in which Israel's action would be comprehensible if we broke forcibly out of siege.

Amid these tempests in Washington and at the UN, my daughter Gila hardly had time to be born. She arrived a little impatiently two weeks ahead of schedule while I was addressing a United Jewish Appeal meeting in New York. I told my audience that no orator ever found a better reason for cutting himself short. She was born during a Washington snowstorm in the George Washington Hospital on December 13, 1954, and I lived most of 1955 with the accompaniment of her stentorian vocal comment. The consolation of her presence was too deep for words.

Our embassy residence had now moved to Juniper Street, to a house donated by Joseph and Ruth Cherner, who were loyal supporters of Israel. It was a rambling four-story structure farther from the center of town than an embassy should be. Suzy gave it an Israeli touch, full of white colors and light, and we had no difficulty in making it a focal point for the convergence of those who fashioned United States policy and opinion. I believed that while American policy could for a time separate itself from American public opinion, it was inevitable that opinion would eventually catch up with policy. I remember 1955 as a year crowded with meetings in Dulles' office, encounters with his senior officials, a vast number of contacts with the economic officers including Harold Stassen, who presided over the Mutual Security Administration. There were constant visits to the Senate and House of Representatives to brief a Congress that was destined to play a leading role in our affairs. There were meetings of Jewish fund-raising organizations with an occasional parenthesis at an academic forum, such as the Yeshiva University, to which I brought my detailed refutation of "Toynbee's Heresy" in an address in April. (Professor Arnold Toynbee had built a formidable case against Israel on pseudoacademic grounds). Security Council and General Assembly sessions were interspersed with long introspective encounters with Secretary-General Dag Hammarskjöld. I went back and forth in airplanes between Washington and New York, had lengthy exchanges of cables with our tormented government at home, and made occasional flights back to Israel through laborious staging points at Gander in Newfoundland and Shannon in Ireland.

Although 1955 was unrewarding on the major themes of arms and American support, it was decisive in establishing a broad base for Israel in American opinion. The Israeli embassy was far more central in the political and intellectual attention of the American people than the size of our country warranted. The Israeli reality was becoming more closely understood. At grass-roots level, Americans had some early difficulty in adapting themselves to the innovation. Their Biblical background helped them to understand our general vision but prepared them very little for our concrete problems. There were even some whose religious memories made it difficult for them to grasp the prosaic aspects of Israel's modernity. At our meeting with him in Paris in 1952, Eisenhower had told Sharett and me that as a boy in Abilene, Kansas, he had believed that Jews, or more accurately the Children of Israel, were, like angels, cherubim and seraphim, the creatures of legend. He was surprised and disconcerted to find later that they existed in real life, if not in Abilene, then at least in Texas, and most unmistakably in New York. In the early fifties Suzy found herself talking to the wife of a U.S. senator at a ladies' luncheon. When the conversation lagged, the lady asked courteously, "How is your king?" Suzy explained that we had no king but a President. The response was startled and incredulous. "What? A President? No king? Isn't that terrible? First they assassinate the king of Jordan. Then they depose the king of Egypt. And now there's a revolution in your country with the monarchy deposed and a republic declared. Shall we ever know peace?" Suzy explained carefully that Israel had had no king since its establishment. "Come now," was the reply, "you don't have to be diplomatic. We all know about poor King Solomon. And now you say he has been deposed."

As the months went on, our preponderant place in the headlines must have cured many Americans of any tendency not to know everything about Israel. I plowed the Washington soil deep and wide. The President himself had suffered a heart attack, and apart from a few formal receptions, was rarely available to ambassadors. On the other hand, Vice-President Richard M. Nixon, to the reluctant surprise of American Jews, showed a sympathetic interest. At his request I visited him in his Chevy Chase home to talk of our problems. He was, after all, a member of the National Security Council and of the Cabinet, and much less remote from the levers of power than American Vice-Presidents usually are. On a memorable occasion I played golf with him at the Woodmont Country Club, defeating him by one stroke on the last hole. I had made some effort to give him the victory, since, after all, we had $50 million tied up in Senate committees. But the sheer apathy and indifference of my swing at the ball ensured a three-hundred-yard drive and an unbeatable approach shot, with eventual victory by 89 to 90. A puzzled cable from our Foreign Ministry in Jerusalem asked pedantically how, if I had scored "only" 89 and he had scored 90, it could be reported that I and not he had won. I replied that golf conformed with the rabbinical idiom *"Kol hamosif goreia"*—"The more you add the less you accomplish."

In the Senate I followed a bipartisan course, achieving some intimacy with the two party leaders, Lyndon B. Johnson of Texas and William F. Knowland of California. They were both exponents and symbols of power, tall, bulky, authoritative and plainly accustomed to getting their own way. One evening Suzy and I entertained Lyndon Johnson at dinner in our Washington home. He seemed to know nothing about Israel in the beginning, but he probed away with all the tenacity of a ruthless dentist and with about the same amount of clinical amiability. A few days later I heard that he was in the hospital; but his condition was cardiac, not gastric, so our own kitchen could not be blamed.

Johnson was no respector of persons or offices. It was common to see his anteroom piled up with ambassadors, some of whom had been waiting for more than half an hour. For all his calculated show of virile toughness there was something about Israel that stirred his pious memories. When he spoke of our cause there would be a halt in the gruffness, and an untypical tenderness would come into his eyes and voice. There were others in the Senate, such as Stuart Symington, Hubert Humphrey, Irving Ives, Leverett Saltonstall, Sherman Cooper and Clifford Chase, whose support of Israel's interests could almost be taken for granted, as could that of the Majority Leader, Hugh Scott of Pennsylvania. Senators Jacob Javits and Abraham Ribicoff formed a natural bridge between American official life at its highest level and the Jewish community, of which they were loyal members. Javits, in particular, has been a central pillar of American-Israeli relations for over two decades.

There is something evocatively Roman about the United States Senate. There is a reverence for experience, a close ésprit de corps, and the air of leisured power conferred by six-year terms of office. A senator can be a "statesman" for four years and a "politician" for the rest. At the other side of Capitol Hill the arena was commanded by Speaker Sam Rayburn of Texas, bold and suave, with southern charm, an almost unbelievable figure from American folklore, who told me that he had never been outside the United States and did not feel that he had missed much. A few months later he went on a parliamentary mission to Paris and came back regretting that he had lost his major theme of conversation without "corresponding reward."

No historian, however charitable, has ever described Eisenhower's first Cabinet as a gallery of intellectual giants, but it did contain some men of marked individuality. For example, Charles Wilson, the automobile manufacturer, was the author of the unforgettable aphorism "What's good for General Motors is good for America." It was sometimes necessary for me to see him on our defense problems, and my successive military attachés, Chaim Herzog and Aharon Yariv, trained me to pay four or five visits to the Pentagon every year. Charles Wilson surprised me once by a pointed question: "Is Turkey one of the Ayrab countries with which you don't get on very well?"

While I naturally cultivated existing depositories of power with the relentless pragmatism of ambassadors, I tried also to have some thought for the future. Thus, one day in 1954 I sent my social secretary, Ethel Ginburg, a note suggesting that she put Senator John F. Kennedy from Massachusetts and his wife on the list of invitees to our small dinner parties. Back came the reply: "Mr. Ambassador, you can do as you like, but do you realize that you only have fourteen places and shouldn't you keep them for *important* senators like Wiley, Capehart or Symington?" I was relentless, and for once, got my way. But Kennedy indicated that he didn't like crowds, so he came alone with his wife, Jacqueline, and the four of us sat around our television set watching Joe McCarthy's final expiry. I found Kennedy generally talkative and eager to listen but very reluctant to discuss the McCarthyite phenomenon. Boston Irish politics were more complicated than I had been led to believe. In June 1955 I joined Kennedy in receiving honorary degrees by Boston University. He was walking on crutches and obviously in great pain. He seemed forlorn and I had the impression that history was passing him by. He implored me to carry out the duties of response on behalf of all the other honorands, since it was beyond his physical power to withstand the ordeal.

Among Cabinet officers, my most unusual interlocutor was Ezra Benson, a Mormon from Salt Lake City, who was Secretary of Agriculture. His Biblical fundamentalism was absolute. Thus, when I came to ask for American surplus grain in view of a drought in Israel, he said that he found the drought hard to believe. Was it not written that Israel was "a land of milk and honey"? I explained that in Israel, as elsewhere, farmers knew only two conditions—too much rain or too little. I would, therefore, be seeing him every six months—either to request drought aid or to ask for flood aid.

I worked hard on the press represented in Washington by pundits who had an aura of infallible authority rather like the leading cardinals at the Vatican. One of these was Walter Lippmann, with whom it was necessary to deal on the same basis as the head of a major foreign power. The response to his invitations was mandatory, and for an ambassador to be able to invite him was a sign of relaxed prestige. I now instituted a tradition of monthly background talks in which I would say everything that was on my mind to leading press representatives in the certainty that nothing "off the record" would be divulged. I have retained some verbatim copies of those exchanges with Walter Lippmann, James Reston, the Alsops, Joseph Krock. Martin Agronsky, Marquis Childs and others. The level of discourse raises a twinge of nostalgia and envy, from this generation to that.

I would encounter Arab diplomats, mostly at cocktail parties, at which they had a habit of looking through me as nonexistent. At the United Nations, a new turn in the membership debate brought Ireland to my left and Italy to my right. I was no longer enclosed by Iraq and Lebanon as in the early days. There was a spontaneous originality in the character of the Lebanese delegate, Charles Malik, a devout Christian and an authentic scholar who, whatever his national pieties might require, seemed intellectually moved by Israel's rebirth. As he once wrote: "No civilization can be indifferent to the cradle in which it was born." His own son, Michael, was born almost simultaneously with my daughter, Gila, and we exchanged congratulations: "Dear Ambassador Eban, it was most kind of you to have sent us your personal congratulatory note, for which we sincerely thank you. We, too, wish you and Mrs. Eban the true and abiding happiness that can in truth come only from God."

Washington was beginning to awaken out of provincialism to a sense of its own centrality. America lived tensely with its own paradox. It had come into existence as an act of rebellion against the Old World, with a strong impulse for detachment. In its heart it wanted nothing more than, in Jefferson's words, "To be kindly separated by nature and a wide ocean from the exterminating havoc of one quarter of the globe"—yet here it was helplessly entangled in rivalries not only of the Old World but of the newly born nations. It was developing a sophisticated political tradition. But while its mind turned outward to the world, its heart was firmly enclosed within itself. The social mathematicians and technologists were hard at work teaching Americans that a nation must respond to its self-interest. But there was always a rhapsodic element in the American character, and it was on this part of American spiritual soil that Israel's cause could flourish.

I had come to America skeptical of its values and full of European prejudice. I had said to a Boston audience: "If your tea is always like what I drank here this morning, I'm not surprised that you threw it into the harbor." In short time I was won over to a love for the endless variety of America's scenes, and the vivid interchange of its moods. This was the greatest union of strength with freedom that had ever lived in the world of man. As the years of my service went by, I came to bear for America the kind of respect that survives occasional criticism and disappointment.

But if there was anything to admire in America in the mid-fifties, it surely lay outside its Middle Eastern policies. This was the only period in which America could be justly accused of having left Israel alone to the winds and storms. The feeling that a tragic fate was in store communicated itself to the best minds across the Continent. If Israel were to fail because it had no bargaining or nuisance value in the clash of Great Powers, would not something irrevocable happen to man's moral history?

The fear that Israel's security was being compromised to a horrifying degree was not merely a subjective "complex" of Israelis. One day in April 1955 our information officer in the consulate in New York, Reuven Dafni, called me to say that Einstein had written to express deep consternation at Israel's plight. He suggested that we meet to discuss how he might help. I made my way to Mercer Street, in Princeton, with Dafni. Einstein opened the door to us himself. He was dressed in a rumpled beige sweater and equally disheveled slacks. This time he was without tie as well as socks.

He came straight to the issue. He said that the radio and television networks were always asking him for interviews, which he always refused. He now thought that if he had some "publicity interest" he might as well use it. Did I think that the media would be interested to record a talk by him to the American people and the world? I exchanged glances with Dafni, as if to say that this was the newspaperman's dream. Einstein took out a pen, dipped it in an old-fashioned inkwell and began to scratch some sentences on a writing block. We soon decided that he needed more time and arranged for Dafni and me to come and help him with the formulation of the text another day. Einstein courteously asked if we would like some coffee. Assuming that he would get a housekeeper or maid to produce the beverage, I politely accepted. To my horror Einstein trotted into the kitchen from which we soon heard the clatter of cups and pots, with an occasional piece of crockery falling to earth, as if to honor the gravity theory of our host's great predecessor, Newton.

That night I spoke by telephone to Suzy, who was on a visit to her parents in Haifa, leaving the recently born Gila with me and my mother, who had agreed to fulfill her grandmotherly function in Washington. Suzy asked me if I had an interesting day at the office. I said that nothing particular had happened, and then added with calculated nonchalance, "Oh yes, I forgot. Einstein made coffee for me today." I was celebrating a splendid moment in my career of marital conversation.

Arrangements went forward in Dafni's energetic hands for Einstein's planned television address, which was to be nationwide. But when Dafni and I were to meet him we were told that the professor had been taken to the hospital with an affliction of the aorta. A few days later he died. Among his papers were found the hand-written pages that he had prepared for the opening of his address. It began: "I speak to you tonight as an American citizen and also as a Jew and as a human being who has always striven to consider matters objectively." His unspoken text went on:

> *What I am trying to do is simply to serve truth and justice with my modest strength.*
>
> *You may think that the conflict between Israel and Egypt is a small and unimportant problem. "We have more important concerns" you might say. That is not the case. When it comes to truth and justice there is no difference between small and great problems. Whosoever fails to take small matters seriously in a spirit of truth, cannot be trusted in greater affairs. . . .*

The extract breaks off after a few reflections on the Cold War. We shall never know how Einstein proposed to end his appeal on Israel's behalf.

At a crowded memorial to Einstein in Carnegie Hall on May 14, 1955, the seventh anniversary of Israel's independence, I said:

> *He saw the rebirth of Israel as one of the few political acts in his lifetime which was of an essentially moral quality . . . When he felt the cold wind of Israel's insecurity, he apprehended that something very precious was being endangered; and at that moment he fell into a deep, responsible and active preoccupation with Israel's future, which brought me to him in the final days of his life, in encounters which I shall everlastingly cherish, recalling the warm and proud Jewish solidarity which enriched his discourse and endowed it with undying grace.*

I made many new acquaintanceships at the San Francisco ceremonies honoring the tenth anniversary of the UN. One was British
Foreign Secretary Harold Macmillan, who invited me for a drink—
or more precisely, for a number of drinks on his part and one
tepid whisky and soda on mine. He discoursed in a rich Edwardian
Oxford accent as though he were doing an exaggerated imitation of
himself. Everything about him was easy, languid, without tears. But
when I left him I realized to my surprise that everything that he had
said so lazily seemed to hang together in rigorous intellectual coherence.

More exacting was a luncheon party Foreign Minister Vyacheslav
Molotov of the Soviet Union gave in honor of our delegation. Before
the convivial part of our meeting, I had a talk with him for an hour
and a half. There was a legend that nobody had ever seen him smile,
and I was curious to know if this was true. I left him a few hours
later with the legend intact. He had given notice to me that he did
not speak or understand English and that I should bring an interpreter. I decided that if I was to talk a language that he did not
understand, it might just as well be Hebrew. Accompanied by our
erudite legal counseler, Dr. Jacob Robinson, I arrived at Molotov's
headquarters and began my Hebrew remarks. I had not gone very far
when he interrupted me: "What exactly is the language you are
talking? I've listened carefully and it sounds nothing like Yiddish.
I know, because my wife speaks Yiddish."

After the necessary philological clarification we went on to our
business. He was plain and blunt. His information was that the
United States was going to get Israel to sign a defense treaty. This
would be a tragic development; the central aim of Soviet policy was
to avoid being encircled by American and other imperialist bases.
The Soviet Union had helped Israel come into existence in the hope
that it would never lend itself as a base for the hostile actions of one
power against the other.

The idea that Eisenhower and Dulles were ardently pursuing Israel
as a partner for their defense pacts was too painful an irony for me to
sustain. I could see, however, that Soviet policy makers were in
earnest. They cared little how Israel voted and not much about what
Israel would do in the UN. They would maintain a correct, if not a
cordial official relationship. They believed at least that Israel's statehood was immutable. They had a quarrel with her policies, not with
her existence. The only serious thing they asked of us was that we
should resist the blandishments of American policy makers, who
were trying hard to conclude military alliance with us.

When we sat down to the table, Molotov and the other Soviet

diplomats with him seemed to be concentrating their most suspicious gaze upon me, as if to probe whether I had been negotiating defense alliances with the United States between drinks and first course. It was decided that at the dinner there would only be toasts, no speeches and no political remarks. Molotov's toast was "to the government and people and delegation of Israel, health and prosperity—and please do *not* sign defense pacts with the United States."

In our conversation I had referred mainly to the nervousness created in Israel by the Soviet arms transactions in Egypt. His response was brisk: Soviet arms were being supplied to Egypt to help defend her against imperialist belligerent threats and not in order to enable Egypt to make war with Israel. I pointed out that I had no doubt that this was the motivation of the arms supply, but "might the recipient not have motives not shared by the donor?" Molotov replied that the question sounded logical but in fact it had a clear answer: the Soviet Union was supplying military and other aid to Egypt not for the purpose that Egypt should make war against Israel. It "followed" therefore that the arms would not be used for that purpose.

In a year in which there were few consolations, we had to draw some comfort from the fact that we had access to all the Great Powers and could hold discourse with them. France had spent two years almost totally concentrated on its predicaments in Tunisia and Morocco. This created both a sense of detachment and an atmosphere of sympathy. Twice French prime ministers had come to Washington and stayed at Blair House. Twice they had received me. By strange coincidence, they were both Jews; Pierre Mendès-France at the height of his prestige after the Indochina conference and the Tunisian settlements, and later René Mayer.

Since our ability to seize the ear of all governments was one of our few weapons, the idea arose toward the end of 1955 that we should make a dramatic attempt to project Israel's plight into the dialogue of the Great Powers that had begun at the Geneva summit meeting in July and would be resumed by the foreign ministers in October. If my memory serves me right, the idea was first projected by Gideon Rafael to Sharett and myself. Our Prime Minister accepted it, perhaps with too much haste. On the other hand, Sharett had very little to lose. While the United States and Britain should, in theory, have had an interest in strengthening his position, they had behaved as though it was their deliberate purpose to inflict political death on him by sheer frustration. They stubbornly ensured that he should have nothing to show for his patient reliance on diplomacy and international opinion. Sharett was too realistic to expect success from his visit to Geneva, but he believed in historic duty. Even if we did not achieve anything by talking to the Great Powers at Geneva, it was our duty to try. Thus, he and I met in Paris for conversations with John Foster Dulles, with the intention to continue at Geneva with Macmillan, Antoine Pinay and Molotov.

It was a strange gamble. The summit meeting had not been called with any particular reference to the Middle East. Sharett's idea, which I supported, was to make a frank and uninvited invasion; to seize the news media and world opinion by illustrating that talk of world security was futile if Israel's security were excluded.

In Paris, we began with a protocolar debate. Sharett was Prime Minister as well as Foreign Minister; Dulles was "only" Secretary of State. Dulles ought, therefore, to visit Sharett. On the other hand, Dulles suffered from sinus trouble and the "flu" and "would therefore appreciate it if . . ."

We duly met in the gloomy ambassador's residence at the Rue d'Iena and found Dulles genial in tone but unyielding in content. His refusal of arms was no longer stated as a theological principle. It was pragmatic and conditional. In his view, the balance had not changed in Israel's disfavor. If it were to change, the United States would, of course, think again. Moreover, the European powers, and not America, had been the traditional suppliers of arms to the Arab-Israeli area. The United States had entered the supply picture with Pakistan, Iraq and Saudi Arabia, but these were on the outer circle of Middle Eastern tension. It was not advisable for America to get into the inner circle. I asked innocently why there was any greater moral imperative in supplying arms to an external than to an internal ring of countries if there was a danger of imbalance. No reply. Dulles chewed a pencil, wrote and doodled on a yellow pad, and to his credit, looked infinitely uncomfortable under the pathos of Sharett's exposition. I thought at one point that it might be advisable for Sharett to give some time for Dulles to respond to what he was saying. I passed a few tactful notes across the table with no effect. In the end Dulles, having listened with care, said, "We can't finish our conversation here. Let's continue it in Geneva."

He was already famous for his nomadic impulse. He founded the tradition according to which diplomatic eminence is measured by air mileage. We duly went to Paris where Israel's ambassadors to all the Great Powers were assembled, together with Eliahu Sasson, our Arab expert, with Reuven Shiloah and Gideon Rafael. While I cultivated Dulles and his entourage, Sharett's meeting with Macmillan, Pinay and Molotov were held with the accompaniment of Ambassadors

Elath, Yaacov Tsur and Yosef Avidar. Macmillan was bland, amiable and totally noncommittal. Molotov was unresponsive to the point of rudeness and with none of the conviviality that he had shown me in San Francisco. He obviously regarded Israel's intrusion in Geneva as irrelevant. The issue was not Israel and the Arab states, but America and Russia. The United States was trying to build a ring of bases around the Soviet Union, in the course of which it would make "so-called defense treaties" with Middle Eastern states. The central imperative of Soviet security was to frustrate this design. This meant that the Soviet Union had to have influence in Arab states which had hitherto been under "the monopolistic influence of Western powers." This was the reason for the supply of arms to Arab states. Since the arms were "not intended for use against Israel," they would not be used against Israel. From this he would not budge.

While Sharett was in Geneva, Ben Gurion was constructing a new Cabinet to be formed on the basis of the 1955 elections, in which Ben Gurion had again appeared at the head of the Labor Party list. It was while we were at Geneva that Sharett reverted from prime-ministerial to foreign-ministerial role, so that no further protocolar problems arose. Sharett was plainly agitated by a struggle within himself. He felt that it was going to be disastrous for him to be Foreign Minister under Ben Gurion, with whom his temperamental conflicts were becoming sharper. On the other hand, the Labor Party, without having given Sharett any conspicuous support as Prime Minister, was not willing to have him jettisoned.

His premiership, though marred by internecine conflicts, had introduced a sense of order and conciliation to the nation's life. Sharett's methodical approach had had a good effect on the tone and texture of the Administration. All in all, the Israeli people was growing accustomed to his tutelage.

It may not be ungenerous to think that this very fact contributed to Ben Gurion's hasty decision to curtail his retirement. On resigning his office, Ben Gurion had told me that "nobody was indispensable." But I had the impression that he would not be too disappointed if that generalization proved to have one particular exception.

While we drew no comfort from Molotov, Dulles or Macmillan, Sharett's talks with the French authorities were more fruitful. Indeed, it was in Paris during his meeting with Edgar Faure, the Prime Minister, that Israel received the first concrete promise for the supply of Mystère aircraft. We would now celebrate our transition from the propeller to the jet age, and eliminate the most serious imbalance in relation to the Arab states. But this opening had come in the framework of our direct relations with Paris. It does not refute the fact that Sharett's visit to the Geneva summit did nothing to lessen Israel's vulnerability.

Yet I do not think that the visit itself was a mistake. Israel must always exhaust every remedy and learn exactly what her position is. Whatever the prospect of failure, and irrespective of his own political fortune, it was Sharett's moral duty to do what he did. The best way to put this to the test is to imagine what would have happened if he had stayed at home. Would we not have heard resounding statements about "lost opportunities," and a failure to make the ultimate effort to awaken the powers to our growing fragility? After war erupted in 1956, how many historians would have received doctorates for analyzing how the 1956 war might have been averted by a special Israeli effort at the Geneva summit in 1955? The tragic contingency in Israeli history is always so probable that there is a strong case for exhausting every recourse or alleviation, sometimes beyond the rational point of hope.

From Geneva I went back to my post in Washington and reflected long and hard on the national situation. After consultation with my principal colleagues—Reuven Shiloah in Washington, Reggie Kidron and Gideon Rafael in New York—I sent a cable to Sharett in January 1956 with a conclusion that surprised him. I pointed out that in spite of constant and maximal efforts we had not elicited any substantive response by the United States to the new balance of power created by the Soviet-Egyptian alliance and the rearmament of Arab states by East and West alike. Although the United States basically wished us well and was not doing anything actively to prejudice our position on boundaries, Jerusalem or the refugees, its failure to support us on the balance of power would expose us to weakness when it came to defending our vital interests, either at the negotiating table or on the battlefield. American official rhetoric was giving currency to the idea that Israel was not the victim of Arab hostility, but the successful victor, endowed with spoils some of which it could part from without any loss of vital interest. If this process went on, we would find ourselves virtually defenseless against an increasingly arrogant and cohesive Arab power. I went on to say that unless the United States did something serious, both in the supplying of arms and in the increase of our political weight, we would have to ask ourselves if there was any way of avoiding a military clash. This would be forced on us by the intensity of frontier raids. But I asked Sharett seriously to consider his duty to prepare the nation for the inevitability of large-scale Israeli military response unless the powers moved out of their apathy.

Since I was expected always to reflect the diplomatic nonmilitary emphasis in Israeli thought, this cable aroused surprise in Jerusalem. Sharett was far from pleased. I was giving inadvertent reinforcement to currents of thought that were already awake in Israel, and of which I was not fully aware. It was not my intention to strengthen the activist element in Israeli policy making. But it was my intellectual conviction that we were being slowly strangled, that our strength and spirit were ebbing away and that there might soon be no alternative to armed resistance if Egyptian pressure increased. I knew that the equilibrium could be restored if the United States made available twenty-four jet planes and auxiliary weapons. This thought aroused my fury against an Administration which obtusely refused to achieve so much stability at so small a price. I was still convinced that Washington would finally take a hand on Israel's side in the arms balance, but the pace of its movement bore no relationship to the rhythm of Arab rearmament.

The paradox of Dulles' position was reinforced by the fact that he had no objection to other countries giving Israel arms. Actually, he would rather have liked this to happen. Thus, when it appeared that the only jet aircraft that France could make available would be those contracted for manufacture for the U.S. Air Force, I was authorized to tell Paris that if France wished to make these available to Israel instead of to the United States, America would see no objection. I duly conveyed this, as was my duty, to the French ambassador in Washington, Maurice Couve de Murville, who thanked me in a personal note, but added in conversation that if there were to be a Western policy for maintaining the balance of power, the United States could not put all the odium for arming Israel on its allies, while keeping its own hands formally clean.

In my cable to Jerusalem I had said that there was little chance of 1956 passing without war unless there were a substantive change in the American attitude toward Israel's defense needs. Ben Gurion, back at the helm, now found ways of expressing his agreement with this analysis. He still hoped, however, that the United States would move to a deeper understanding of our plight.

Secretary of State Dulles had told me that he and his advisers would not feel that the balance of power could be defined as having changed unless they heard that the first Russian MIG-15s had actually arrived in Egypt. In early December 1955, this intelligence was received. For the first time we heard of discussions between the White House, the State Department and the Pentagon in which Israel's military position was seriously appraised. Sharett had come to Washington for talks with the Administration and he was told that by December 12 he would receive a carefully formulated reply to our requests. From well-informed newspapermen, including James Reston, I heard that the reply would not be completely negative. It later appeared that the United States intended to offer Israel a "package deal" under which we would receive limited supplies of arms, including jet aircraft, from Britain, France and the United States, with America using its diplomatic good offices to put much of this traffic as possible on the shoulders of its allies. We would not have regarded this as a victory. On the other hand, it would have done something to relieve Israel's sense of isolation and to establish the principle of a balance of strength as an element of American and Western policy. Since Dulles and his associates had advised me specifically to get Sharett to wait in Washington for the answer, it is inconceivable that they could have planned a totally negative reply.

The inherent complexity of our situation came to expression in what happened next. On December 10 Syrian guns fired on Israeli fishing vessels on Lake Tiberias (Sea of Galilee) in an effort to deny us the use of the lake and of the ten-meter strip on the northeastern shore which the armistice agreement had put under Israeli control. We had worked hard for those ten meters, not for their own sake, but because they created a juridical situation in which no part of the shore of Lake Tiberias was contiguous to Syrian territory. Thus Syria could not justly claim to be a riparian state in relation to Lake Tiberias.

It was right for the Israeli government to react sensitively to an encroachment on its sovereignty over the only body of fresh water in our complete possession. I knew from my reading how Lloyd George had told Clemenceau at the Paris Peace Conference in 1919 that without the northern water resources, "Palestine could be reduced to a parched wilderness by anybody to the north." We could hardly be less concerned ourselves than Lloyd George had been.

In all military reaction, there is some need for "proportion." The Syrians had not caused any Israeli casualties in their December 10 attack, but when Israeli forces crossed into Syria the next night, they left behind seventy-three dead Syrians, six Israeli dead and many others wounded or missing. It was a shocking spectacle of carnage with very little attempt to give world opinion any warning of its necessity or dimensions. This action at Kinneret naturally killed any chance of a favorable reply to our arms request from the United States, even if such a reply was in the offing.

The international community was in furor and Sharett was plunged into depression. Golda Meir, the Minister of Labor, reached New York that night for a speaking tour and confirmed that there had not been any consultation either with the Foreign Ministry or with other ministers. Ben Gurion had merely conducted a consultation with himself. Sharett thought that, at best, Ben Gurion's timing had shown indifference to his own diplomatic efforts, which, after all, had been ordered by the Cabinet. At worst Sharett seemed to believe that there was something subconsciously deliberate in an action which deprived him of a slender hope of a personal diplomatic triumph. Back in Israel he was to say with some hyperbole, "Not even the devil could have chosen a worse time or a worse context for such an action."

My own feeling is that whatever remnants existed of Sharett's ability to work with Ben Gurion went up in flames in Galilee that night. I, too, found it impossible to understand how Ben Gurion could reconcile two such lines of action. On the one hand he had asked Sharett to make a big effort to secure a breakthrough on our arms request. On the other hand, he had authorized a military operation of such strong repercussion as to make an affirmative answer inconceivable. I thought that an error of judgment had been made. I said so frankly in a long letter to Ben Gurion in January 1956 after we had gone through the routine of discussion and condemnation in the Security Council. I got an immediate reply through his secretary saying: "I fully understand your, concern about the Kinneret operation. I must confess that I, too, began to have my doubts about the wisdom of it. But when I read the full text of your brilliant defense of our action in the Security Council, all my doubts were set at rest. You have convinced me that we were right, after all."

I regarded this somewhat mischievous reply as being as close to repentance as I was likely to secure from Ben Gurion. My discussion with Jerusalem was not a defense of diplomacy against military needs. There was a clash between two military needs—the need for retaliation and the long-term need for defensive arms. It seemed to me that the short-term objective had triumphed unduly over our long-term aims.

In the first months of 1956, the dispatch of arms to Arab states from all parts of the world went on without Israel having received any response to its arms requests. All I could do was stimulate the growth of public opinion in our favor. I went on the CBS program *Face the Nation* at the end of February and tried to put the matter as simply as I could to the American public:

"British tanks to Egypt; American tanks to Saudi Arabia; British planes and tanks to Iraq; British planes and tanks to Jordan; American arms to Iraq; Soviet bombers, fighters, tanks and submarines to Egypt; and no arms for Israel. Bombers to Egypt to terrorize our cities? Yes. Fighters to Israel to help ward off those perils? **No.**"

By this time the pressure on Eisenhower and Dulles to do something effective about Israel's declining balance of power was coming loudly from the American public, and not only from the Israeli embassy. American Jewry was skilled in organizing mass assemblies on our behalf. In April, Israel's eighth birthday was celebrated with a mass meeting in Yankee Stadium in New York. My colleague on the rostrum was Senator John F. Kennedy of Massachusetts. When I finished speaking he said, "That was the first time that Macaulay's English has been heard in Yankee Stadium." My recollection of that occasion becomes even more surrealistic when I remember that one of the other star attractions was Marilyn Monroe. John F. Kennedy, Marilyn Monroe and Abba Eban riding around Yankee Stadium in an open car receiving the plaudits of the masses is something to remember. Miss Monroe seemed to make a stronger physical impression on most of the audience than did Kennedy or I, but we could claim to have a somewhat broader conceptual range. The sporting occasion was a soccer match between Israel and the United States. The game is not highly regarded in America, so that our team had some chance of victory. I said at the beginning of my address that I was quite impartial. I didn't care who won, as long as it was Israel's soccer team. It was.

By now Dulles' resistance to our arms request was beginning slowly to erode. At a B'nai B'rith dinner in Washington he said cautiously that the United States had an obligation to prevent Israel suffering from "an imbalance" of arms. Later that month he confessed his dilemma to me with candor. He said that he was now convinced that the needs of equilibrium required Israel to receive some modern jet fighters and other arms. On the other hand, if the United States supplied them directly, it would be under irresistible pressure to open a supply relationship with Arab states. The question was whether Israel could get what she wanted from somewhere else.

I replied that what we needed were F-86 jet fighters, and these were, as far as I knew, manufactured only in the United States and Canada. On hearing the word "Canada," Dulles pricked up his ears and told me that Lester Pearson would be visiting him that very day, and that some American F-86s were manufactured on license in Canada but were nevertheless at the disposition of the United States. A few hours later I called the Canadian embassy, where Ambassador Arnold Heeney informed me that in a talk with Lester Pearson, Dulles had requested him to make twenty-four F-86 jet fighters available to Israel out of the American quota production line!

There now began an extraordinary period of equivocation in which the United States pressed Canada and France to do that which it wanted to avoid doing itself, namely to appear in the eyes of the Arab world as the architects of a modest Israeli armament. From my point of view, this was better than nothing at all, but I could well understand the resentment in Paris and Ottawa which bred a spontaneous resistance to Dulles' importunities. I also thought there was something rather childish in the exercise. It would not be beyond the wit or resource of the Arab governments to learn the active role of the United States in producing this equipment for Israel. In fact, as we expected, the Canadian government, when it decided to give its authorization in September, stipulated that the United States should let it be known publicly that this was being done with American approval.

By that time, however, the whole question of arming Israel had passed out of the orbit of the United States and into the realm of a special French connection. All that can be said for Dulles, therefore, is that he accepted the principle of the balance of arms after much belated obduracy, and that having accepted the doctrine, he tried, albeit clumsily and indirectly, to put it into practice.

Most of these discussions went on through the hot summer, during which I made a vain effort to take some leave. Suzy and I had been introduced by Dave Niles to the charm of Martha's Vineyard, where we used to find a tranquillity far from the tumult and noise of the mainland. Martha's Vineyard had kept its Colonial and whaling association more effectively than it could ever have done without the advantage of insularity. My own enjoyment of the beaches and golf courses was sporadic; I would constantly be called by telephone to Washington, whither I would fly in a somewhat dilapidated Dakota of Northeast Airlines, either through New York or directly. In fact, I was on and off the island airport so often that it might have been better not to have attempted a vacation at all.

The summer months were explosive with drama both in our domestic politics and in the regional context. With our civilians constantly harried by *fedayeen* attacks from Egyptian, Jordanian and Syrian territory, and with the government unable to show concrete results from its request for Western arms, the nation was plunged into an embattled mood. Ben Gurion encouraged his Defense Ministry aides to go full speed ahead with their efforts to get as much out of our French military connections as possible. In doing this he was clearly undermining the jurisdictional authority of Foreign Minister

Sharett. But there were other difficulties between the two men. In theory, they should have constituted a balanced harmony. Each possessed some virtues and had some faults that the other lacked: Ben Gurion was impulsive, imaginative, daring, dynamic; Sharett was prudent, rational, analytical, realistic. Had they been able to work in close harness, an ideal equilibrium might have been achieved. Unfortunately, the very contradictions that divided their characters also created an incompatibility of emotion. They had gone together through many of the most testing ordeals of Jewish history, each presumably adding emphasis to the particular contours of his own character. So, far from having grown together like partners in a marriage, they had become almost physically unable to bear the sight of each other. Ben Gurion thought that Sharett was verbose, pedantic, finicky and inclined to confuse the vital with the incidental, the primary with the secondary. Sharett, with all his admiration for Ben Gurion, considered him demagogic, tyrannical, opinionated, devious, and on some occasions, not quite rational. Israel's foreign and security policies faced heavy days. Without some personal harmony, the two of them would be unable to guide our course.

By this time Ben Gurion must also have known that he would have to make decisions in 1956 that Sharett would be certain to contest, if not obstruct. Each had his loyal adherents within the Labor Party, but this very fact created the danger that in the absence of a clear-cut adjudication between them, the party itself would become split into rival camps. In June 1956, after many relatively polite maneuvers, Ben Gurion had directly requested Sharett's resignation. Despite the opposition of 40 percent of the party's Central Committee—an unusual scale of revolt against Ben Gurion—Sharett made his resignation effective in June. He sent me a touching letter, full of gratitude for the support that I had been able to give him, but also charged with bitter reflections on the circumstances that had brought about his resignation.

This was to be Sharett's last appearance at the center of Israel's stage. Although he was not advanced in years by the standards of Israeli leadership, he never managed to overcome his rancor sufficiently to assume a place in the national leadership under Ben Gurion's authority. By the time Ben Gurion left the scene in 1963, Sharett had already been sidetracked into the motionless waters of the Zionist Organization, with Levi Eshkol filling Ben Gurion's place.

Sharett impressed his personality deeply on the first decades of our political struggle. He had the same zeal and single-mindedness as the rest of his colleagues in the Labor leadership and the Israeli government. But what separated him from them was the precision of his thinking, his reverence for correctness and symmetry of form, his deep roots in the Hebrew and Arabic cultural traditions, his disrespect for anything that was shoddy, careless, untidy, imprecise, or still worse, morally questionable. Not all his colleagues welcomed his habit of correcting their Hebrew or pointing out faults in their logic. He was a man of sharp colors and straight lines, and the very probity of his character and the constancy of his values made it difficult for him to accept the compromises that are needed for cooperative work in a national team. He seemed unable to give some of Ben Gurion's foibles the particular indulgence to which Ben Gurion was entitled by the compensating weight of his virtues. Sharett spent the next decade brooding unfruitfully on his fall with no serious effort at political recuperation. In one quality he surpassed all the leaders of Zionism and Israel—in his warm human spirit and his proud and unselfish cultivation of younger talents.

Ben Gurion was aware that with Sharett's departure he was losing specialized skills that might be hard to replace. He asked me to come home to Jerusalem for consultation and suggested that I leave my Washington embassy to become chief adviser on foreign affairs to himself. I would thus be a kind of watchdog over the new Foreign Minister, Golda Meir, with a direct line of command to Ben Gurion. It seemed clear to me—and even clearer to Golda Meir—that this was a sure prescription for antagonistic explosions in which Mrs. Meir and I and, perhaps, even Ben Gurion would be injured every day by flying splinters of jurisdictional discord. At lunch in her house, Mrs. Meir and I agreed that we could best cooperate across the ocean, with me pursuing my mission in Washington, which, in any case, had reached such a point of cruciality that it would have been irresponsible to abandon it. Whatever status and resonance I had been able to develop in Washington and throughout America in the past six years would now have to prove their value in great ordeals.

Sure enough, barely a few weeks had passed when we were confirmed in our impression that 1956 was going to be a pyrotechnic year. It began with an imaginative American initiative. One day I was called to Dulles' office in Washington to receive a message for Ben Gurion. Eisenhower and Dulles wanted to exhaust every possibility of a peace settlement. They would not recoil from the idea of a continuing armistice resting on a balance of arms, but this would involve permanent tension both regionally and in the global context. They therefore proposed to test the Arab and Israeli attitudes to a peace negotiation. Since Nasser claimed to be the leader of the Arab world, it was natural for him to be the testing ground. The proposal was that a close personal friend of the President, Robert Anderson, who had been Secretary of the Navy and was now in private business in New York and Texas, should go secretly to the Middle East, meet Nasser and Ben Gurion, and explore the idea of an encounter between them at an agreed place in or outside the area.

Ben Gurion reacted enthusiastically to this idea, and I was authorized to brief Anderson on our basic positions. He set out in strong hope and returned a few weeks later in despondency. It was clear that Ben Gurion had succeeded in conveying a strong and sincere impression of Israel's desire for peace, whereas Nasser, already inhibited by his closer relationship with the Soviet Union, found ways of evading any encounter with Ben Gurion. I even had the impression that he showed a marked reserve toward the United States. It may not be accidental that from that point onward, the Eisenhower Administration drew closer to Israel and even began to be less tight on the matter of the arms balance. I could detect a growing intimacy and confidence between Washington and Jerusalem. It is possible that Nasser's lack of cooperation with the Anderson mission played a part in the dramatic change of heart by the United States on the issue of the Aswan High Dam.

Throughout the summer months Egypt had been pursuing her negotiations with the World Bank for the financing of the Aswan High Dam. Late in 1955 the United States and Britain had favored this project, but as the months went on, they became increasingly disenchanted with Nasser. He seemed to be in collision with Western policy everywhere in the world. He had brought Soviet influence into the very heart of the Middle East. He was flirting intensely with Communist China. He was attempting to bring about the overthrow through violence and assassination of every Arab regime that refused to accept his authority. He plotted against President Camille Chamoun in Lebanon, against King Hussein in Jordan, against the monarchical regime in Iraq, against the conservative forces that controlled the Arabian peninsula, and against the Tunisian regime newly established under Habib Bourguiba. Not only did this involve him in the hostility of Arab regimes, it also won him the distrust of Britain and the United States, who had a stake in the stability of all Middle Eastern governments. When to this was added his blockade of the Suez Canal, his seizure of the *Bat Galim,* his refusal to help the United States implement the Johnston water plan, and the constant pressure of his armed raids on Israel's boundaries, it becomes clear why the Western powers, and especially Britain and France, should have dreamed nostalgically of "living without Nasser."

On instructions from Jerusalem we joined in helping to frustrate Egypt's ambitions for American aid in the Aswan Dam project. In different conditions I personally would have welcomed the preoccupation of Egypt with large-scale economic projects. It was clear, however, that Nasser regarded his new economic strength not as an aim in itself, but as the handmaiden of an aggressive military and diplomatic policy. If he could receive arms from the Soviet Union as well as vast financial aid from the West without any modification of his policies toward the West or Israel, he would become the arrogant lord of the Arab world. Nothing could be more disastrous for us than to let Nasser celebrate a victory of pride that he would certainly use for aggravated pressure upon us. So Israel's friends in the Congress joined their colleagues who, for other American reasons, opposed the idea of giving Nasser a windfall without any reciprocal gesture on his part.

The Egyptian ambassador in Washington, Ahmed Hussein, had apparently not been following these tendencies when he arrived blithely from Cairo to see Dulles in the expectation of receiving American confirmation of the Aswan Dam project. He crossed me in the lobby of Dulles' office as I went out and he went in.

To his consternation, Dulles brutally informed him of the American refusal to finance the Aswan Dam project. Without the American contribution, the World Bank under the direction of Eugene Black had no way of executing it. The British contribution also lapsed automatically. Eden was later to claim that Britain and France were drastically affected by an American action on which they had not been informed or consulted.

Nasser, in cold, fierce resentment, looked around for a sensitive Western nerve against which he could hit back. He found it on July 27, the anniversary of the revolution, when to hysterically cheering crowds in Alexandria he proclaimed that he had decided to take over the Suez Canal and make it a nationalized Egyptian property. The die was cast for war.

Explosion at Suez
1956-1957

FRANCE AND BRITAIN HAD COME TO REGARD THE SUEZ CANAL ALMOST AS A
part of their metropolitan territory. They believed, with exaggeration,
that it was their jugular vein. How could they maintain their strength
or prosperity without it? In Egyptian hands it would be a weapon of
extortion; it would also be beyond Egyptian capacity to operate it.
The atavistic habit of regarding the Canal as an extension of their
own national territory, as integral to them as Normandy, Kent and
Sussex, was hard to break. In Britain, especially, it was recalled that
in 1940 when the Nazi-Fascist axis threatened the Western Desert of
Egypt as well as the British Isles, Churchill had allocated priority
of weapons to the Western Desert at the expense of greater vulnerability for the British homeland. Eden in Britain and Premier Guy
Mollet in France, enraged by Nasser's subversions in Jordan, Iraq,
Algeria and elsewhere, found the insult of nationalization too great
to bear. They decided to resist Nasser's provocation. Eden, thinking
back to his golden years in the thirties, identified Nasser with Hitler,
and himself with the forces of light and salvation that would break
the tyrant's power before it was too late. He had been prevented by
Chamberlain from playing this role in his youth. He was not going
to let it desert him now that he had reached the peak. On July 29,
he wrote to President Eisenhower:

My colleagues and I are convinced that we must be ready in the last resort to use force to bring Nasser to his senses. For our part we are prepared to do so. I have this morning instructed our Chiefs of Staff to prepare a military plan accordingly.

Similar communications went from Guy Mollet to Eisenhower and Eden. It should have been clear everywhere that the two Western powers were bent on a forcible solution. Eisenhower's response was ambivalent. His main reaction was to send an experienced diplomat, Robert Murphy, to represent the United States in talks with the British and French in London. Eden was to write: ". . . we assumed that the American attitude was one of prudence rather than divergence." The French Foreign Minister, Christian Pineau, was quick to tell Murphy "that since the United States was responsible for the Aswan decision, it should not disinterest itself from the consequences."

My own reading of Eisenhower's character led me to believe that he would not support an Anglo-French military expedition. I said this to some British diplomats who wanted to believe in "English-speaking solidarity." On July 31 Eisenhower wrote to Eden expressing his "personal conviction as to the unwisdom of even contemplating the use of force at this moment. I realize that the messages from both you and Harold [Macmillan] stress that the decision was firm and irrevocable. I hope you will consent to reviewing this matter once more in its broadest aspects. I have asked Foster Dulles to leave this afternoon to meet with your people in London."

Dulles' tactic for the next crucial months was to satisfy his European allies by words—and to prolong negotiations so as to let the steam out of their bellicose instincts. He even gave Eden the impression that he might support a forceful solution. This, at any rate, is how Eden interpreted Dulles' phrase "A way has to be found to make Nasser disgorge what he is attempting to swallow." On this foundation Eden was later to build a whole edifice of conviction that Dulles had deceived him. Pineau, less passionate, has written: "Dulles' policy was always clear enough."

In the meantime the British determination for military action grew more fervid. It was nourished by an assumption, which proved to be illusory, that the Labour Party would give support. Had not Herbert Morrison said in the House of Commons: "If the United States will not stand with us we may have to stand without them"?

From my vantage point in Washington and the United Nations, it was obvious that although Israel was not in the center of the crisis, we would be affected by its course. The first consequence was irritating. It had been planned that on July 28 the United States and Canada would make a joint statement assuring us that we would receive two squadrons of F-86s in accordance with agreements between the two governments. Dulles, leaning back in his familiar leather armchair, biting the top of a pencil before scribbling with it on a yellow pad, never looking me straight in the face, twitching nervously at the corner of his mouth, told me that this would "of course" now have to be postponed. Relations between Egypt and the Western world were tense enough without adding a new explosive element.

I now heard from Jerusalem that French leaders were speaking openly to Israelis, especially in our Defense Ministry, about the inevitability of a military showdown. Moreover, Eden had committed himself to prevent a situation "which would leave the Canal in the unfettered control of a single power which could, as recent events have shown, exploit it purely for purposes of national policy." By early August a joint team of Anglo-French military planners went to work. Bourgès Maunoury, the French Defense Minister, and his *chef de cabinet*, Abel Thomas, were flying across the Channel several times a day. Britain would provide a supreme commander, General Sir Charles Keightley, with a French deputy, Vice-Admiral Barjot. Keightley was—irrelevantly—a cavalry officer, but would presumably leave his horses behind. Cyprus would be the place at which the Expeditionary Force would be put together.

At a UN Security Council meeting held at foreign-minister level in October, it became apparent that Britain and France were merely going through the motions of diplomatic remedy. They were convinced that nothing but force would induce Nasser to "disgorge" the Suez Canal. I held meetings with Dulles in New York at his United Nations headquarters, where I pointed to the anomaly of Israel's exclusion from the debate. If there was any real evidence that Egypt would use the Canal as an "instrument of unilateral national policy," it lay in the prolonged Egyptian blockade of Israeli shipping after the Security Council's resolution of 1951 had ruled the restrictions to be illegal. Dulles and British Foreign Secretary Selwyn Lloyd told me, as did Pineau later on, that it would be unwise to transform the conflict from a confrontation between Egypt and maritime powers into a new episode of Arab-Israeli conflict.

There was some point in this logic and I was content at that stage to submit a detailed memorandum to the Security Council on Egypt's abuse of its geographical position to block international waterways. This was useful evidence for the Western powers, who did not, however, want me to bring Israel's full case to the Security Council. In any event, I felt that our cause was not logically bound up with theirs. After all, the Canal had been closed to Israeli shipping and cargoes even while the alleged "international system" was in force. I had no great hopes that we would have use of the Suez Canal even if Britain and France managed to renew their possession of it. For me, the Egyptian blockade of the Canal was important, not for any intrinsic economic reason, but as a conspicuous symptom of the illicit belligerency which governed the Egyptian attitude toward Israel.

The Security Council was in session under the chairmanship of the French Foreign Minister, Christian Pineau, when General Yehoshafat Harkavi, the Israeli chief of military intelligence, arrived in New York. He went to talk with Pineau and General Maurice Challe at the French delegation headquarters. I myself conducted my business with Pineau on Security Council procedures by a separate channel. Israel had achieved a greater intimacy and confidence with France than with any other country since our establishment. A closed and secret meeting of the Knesset in October had heard Ben Gurion lyrically describe the arrival of the first French arms. The poet Nathan Alterman celebrated this event in rhapsodic verse.

On October 16 I flew to Tel Aviv, where Ben Gurion had called for a meeting of Israeli ambassadors in the major capitals. My plane stopped over in London. As I went into the transit section at the airport I observed a busy scene a few yards away. Prime Minister Anthony Eden was arriving at the airport to join Selwyn Lloyd, who had flown in from the United Nations in New York. Both of them went on board a plane, which, I learned later, was bound for Paris. This was to be the encounter during which the British and French government would make their decision for action against Nasser.

In Jerusalem I joined the ambassadors' conference, at which Ben Gurion put the accent on the Jordan front, where we were threatened by daily incursions. There was also a prospect of Iraqi troops moving in to reinforce the Jordanian battle order. Some of us suspected that Ben Gurion's objective was diversionary and that his main concern was with Nasser. Before leaving Israel on October 20, I had a private talk with Ben Gurion. He told me that our security situation was becoming increasingly grave. He described a visit to Paris of an Israeli mission headed by Golda Meir on September 28. He himself had now been asked to meet Premier Mollet in France later that day. He was skeptical about any outcome of the meeting; he doubted that France would join Israel in operational security measures. If, to his surprise, agreements were reached, he said, "you will be feeling certain consequences in Washington."

I returned to America, where, during the next week, my preoccupation was not with Egypt at all. Raids from the Jordan frontier were increasing, and there were reports about a decision of the Iraqi government to station large contingents of troops in Jordan. It had always been Israel's position that the armistice agreement depended on a military balance and that the signatory governments had an obligation not to allow the troops of foreign powers on their soil. Israel's repeated warnings that she would not be bound by the armistice agreement if a part of Jordanian territory was occupied by other Arab armies had paradoxically helped to preserve Jordan's independence over the years: without the interposition of Israel, Egypt's demographic strength and regional leadership would have led to the inundation of Jordan by Egyptian forces long before.

A meeting of the Security Council on this matter was held in October. I had acrimonious exchanges with the British delegate, who hinted that if there was an Israeli move, the British guarantee of Jordan's integrity would come into play. Yet while the conflict on the open level of diplomacy was between Israel and Jordan, a different alignment was at work beneath the surface. At a meeting in Sèvres between Ben Gurion, Selwyn Lloyd and Mollet, Britain was brought into a plan for a concerted "stop Nasser" operation. While I had been in touch with the movement of French-Israeli relations, I had not been informed at all of this British development.

Indeed, I was puzzled by directives from Jerusalem in late October urging me to sharpen the conflict with Jordan and, indirectly, with Britain about the position on our eastern frontier. I innocently assumed at first that Ben Gurion had failed to win support from France against Egypt and was working off steam against Jordan. Moshe Dayan has since revealed that the decision to go ahead with a joint Anglo-French-Israeli operation in Sinai was made in Sèvres on October 23. He had exultantly cabled from Paris ordering the General Staff to get ready and to undertake camouflage maneuvers for diverting attention to Jordan.

On October 27 I was playing golf at the Woodmont Country Club near Washington with Martin Agronsky, a leading television commentator, and Sidney Yates, a congressman from Illinois. They had often been my partners. Martin's game was erratic and volatile, thus comforting me in my own irregularities, while Sidney reduced us both to despair by his professional talent. I had taken up the game in the early fifties when I received medical advice to find at least minimal opportunities for exercise. The most specific suggestion to translate this advice into golf came to me from the Labor leader, George Meany, who, in his mid-eighties, is still a zealot of the game.

Early in the game a messenger came to me, asking me to call Secretary Dulles at the State Department immediately. Dulles' need to be in constant touch with President Eisenhower had made him something of an authority on the location of Washington's golf courses. Dulles spoke to me excitedly about Israeli troop concentrations. I said that I could not effectively deal with this matter from a golf-course telephone and would come over at once. I got in touch with my deputy, Reuven Shiloah, asking him to meet me in the Department of State. When we arrived, Dulles, surrounded by an anxious retinue of advisers, was looking hard at a map in the middle of the room. But I noticed that the map portrayed the Israeli-Jordan armistice boundary, and nowhere touched Sinai. The Secretary's mood was somber. From U.S. ambassadors in the Middle East, including Edward B. Lawson in Israel, reports had come of great Israeli troop concentrations amounting to virtual mobilization. Dulles replied with frank skepticism to my argument that Israel was, after all, faced by grave danger. "What have you to worry about?" he said. "Egypt is living in constant fear of a British and French attack. Jordan is weak. It is now clear that the Iraqis are not going to enter Jordan. On the other hand, if it is Israel that is planning to attack, it is perhaps because your government regards the present time as suitable." I promised to convey what he had said, but added an expression of regret that "the United States government has not shown a greater degree of faith in Israel's basic intentions."

On the morning of October 29 the atmosphere of emergency was aggravated. The U.S. embassy in Tel Aviv reiterated its advice to American citizens to leave the country. I felt that it was almost impossible to react to American pressures without myself knowing more of what was going on. I sent a cable to Ben Gurion and Golda Meir explaining that we were living in an emergency atmosphere and that Arab responsibility for the situation should be emphasized more. It was not clear to public opinion that Israel had been the victim, not the author, of the situation which had erupted in war.

In reply I received a laconic message urging me to describe the situation as arising from "security measures" and to stress that there was no connection between what we were doing and the conflict of other powers with Egypt. Shiloah and I were in the office of William Rountree, Assistant Secretary of State for Middle Eastern Affairs, emphasizing our defensive posture, when Donald Bergus, head of the Palestine desk, came in with a note that he passed to Rountree, who read it out loud. It spoke of a massive eruption of Israeli forces across the Egyptian frontier, and a subsequent forking movement and parachute drop deep into Sinai. Rountree said with sarcasm, "I'm certain, Mr. Ambassador, that you will wish to get back to your embassy to find out exactly what is happening in your country."

Our contact with the State Department was now virtually sundered. On October 30, when my counselor, Yochanan Meroz, made some representation to Bergus, he received the cold reply that "the only matter to be discussed between the State Department and the embassy of Israel is the evacuation of American citizens from Israel."

The news of the Israeli operation had reached President Eisenhower when he was en route by plane to Florida in the course of his electoral campaign. At the Miami airport he promised to put the full weight of the United States to work in an effort to prevent a clash between Israel and the Arab states. He promised that "the United States would not do anything simply to win cheers." On hearing how deep the penetration of Sinai had been, he interrupted his tour and returned to Washington. That afternoon Dulles called the members of the Senate Foreign Relations Committee for emergency consultation. In the evening he summoned the British and French ambassadors and requested their governments to activate the Tripartite Declaration of 1950. I understood that the replies of Paris and London were evasive. That night Eisenhower convened a meeting with Dulles; the Chief of Staff, Admiral William Radford; the Secretary of Defense, Charles Wilson; and Allen Dulles, head of the CIA; together with other high officials of the State Department, the White House and the Pentagon.

The President expressed "disappointment" with the Israeli government. He said that until that day he had been sincerely convinced that Prime Minister Ben Gurion's opposition to a deliberate war was genuine. Now his faith was shattered. Dulles referred to his own statement of April 9 about the support of the United States "for any country that was attacked." That declaration had been drafted in the National Security Council as a promise of protection for Israel in an effort to reassure us in the face of Arab rearmament. It was now decided to use the declaration against Israel.

Official Washington was in an angry mood. It had no doubt that we had deliberately chosen the election week as the occasion for our operation. This suspicion increased the President's rage. He felt that his personal prestige was at stake. He also told all who spoke to him that day that Israel was "doing a great service to the Soviet Union by diverting world opinion from resistance to the Soviet repression in Poland and Hungary." That evening a statement was published in the White House:

> The President recalled that the United States under this and prior Administrations had pledged itself to assist the victim of any aggression in the Middle East. We shall honor our pledge.

ALEXANDER ARCHER

My grandfather Eliahu Sacks

Alida Eban

My father, A. M. Solomon (third from left) , *at Zionist meeting in Capetown, 1902.*

Cambridge Don, 1938

With Suzy's parents and Eli and Gila.

A meeting in Cairo, 1943, with Moshe Sharett and Rabbi Israel Brodie (later Chief Rabbi of Britain). In foreground: *Reuven Shiloah.*

Escorting Dr. and Mrs. Chaim Weizmann at UN committee hearings, Jerusalem, July 1947.

Meeting at White House, January 8, 1953, with President Truman and Mrs. Vera Weizmann.

The first Israel Bonds are sold—Madison Square Garden 1954. David Ben Gurion and Finance Minister Eliezer Kaplan.

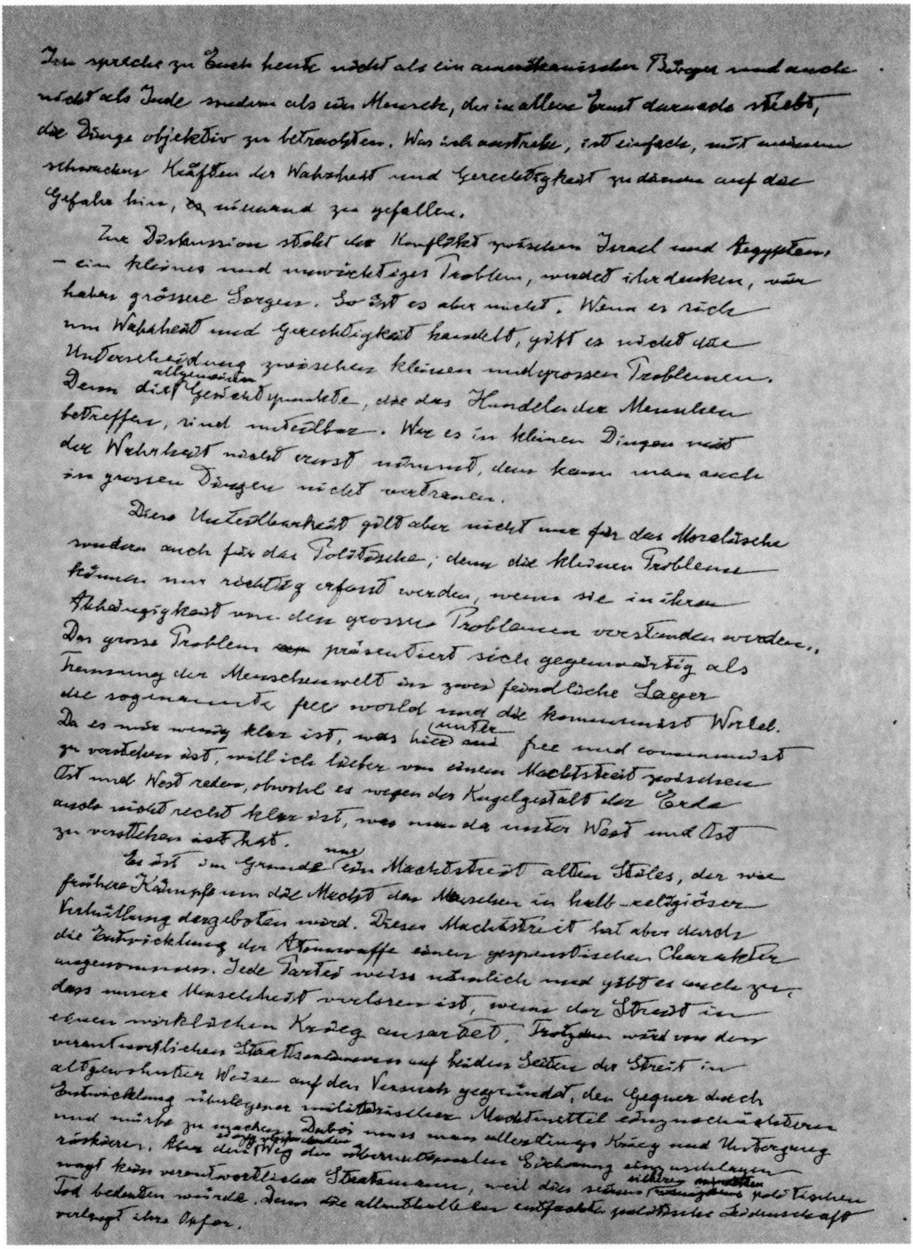
Ich spreche zu Euch heute nicht als ein amerikanischer Bürger und auch nicht als Jude, sondern als ein Mensch, der in allem Ernst danach strebt, die Dinge objektiv zu betrachten. Was ich anstrebe, ist einfach, mit meinen schwachen Kräften der Wahrheit und Gerechtigkeit zu dienen auf die Gefahr hin, niemand zu gefallen.

Zur Diskussion steht der Konflikt zwischen Israel und Aegypten. – ein kleines und unwichtiges Problem, werdet ihr denken, wir haben grössere Sorgen. So ist es aber nicht. Wenn es sich um Wahrheit und Gerechtigkeit handelt, gibt es nicht die Unterscheidung zwischen kleinen und grossen Problemen. Denn die allgemeinen Gesichtspunkte, die das Handeln der Menschen betreffen, sind unteilbar. Wer es in kleinen Dingen mit der Wahrheit nicht ernst nimmt, dem kann man auch in grossen Dingen nicht vertrauen.

Diese Unteilbarkeit gilt aber nicht nur für das Moralische sondern auch für das Politische; denn die kleinen Probleme können nur richtig erfasst werden, wenn sie in ihrer Abhängigkeit von den grossen Problemen verstanden werden. Das grosse Problem präsentiert sich gegenwärtig als Trennung der Menschenwelt in zwei feindliche Lager die sogenannte free world und die kommunist world. Da es mir wenig klar ist, was hier unter free und communist zu verstehen ist, will ich lieber von einem Machtstreit zwischen Ost und West reden, obwohl es wegen der Kugelgestalt der Erde auch nicht recht klar ist, was man da unter West und Ost zu verstehen hat.

Es ist im Grunde nur ein Machtstreit alten Stiles, der wie frühere Kämpfe um die Macht den Menschen in halb-religiöser Verhüllung dargeboten wird. Dieser Machtstreit hat aber durch die Entwicklung der Atomwaffe einen gespenstischen Charakter angenommen. Jede Partei weiss nämlich und gibt es auch zu, dass unsere Menschheit verloren ist, wenn der Streit in einen wirklichen Krieg ausartet. Trotzdem wird von den verantwortlichen Staatsmännern auf beiden Seiten der Streit in altgewohnter Weise auf den Versuch gegründet, den Gegner durch Entwicklung überlegener militärischer Machtmittel einzuschüchtern und mürbe zu machen. Dabei muss man allerdings Krieg und Untergang riskieren. Aber den Weg der übernationalen Sicherung einzuschlagen wagt kein verantwortlicher Staatsmann, weil dies seinen sicheren politischen Tod bedeuten würde. Denn die allenthalben entfachte politische Leidenschaft verlangt ihre Opfer.

The undelivered speech. Einstein's last draft, April 1955.

Two new members of the Knesset, 1960.

Wooing the electorate in Haifa Bay, 1965.

With Israeli ambassadors to Eastern Europe outside the gas chamber, Auschwitz, May 1966.

That night I called on the French ambassador, Hervé Alphand. He himself did not yet know what was later to develop in the Security Council or that France was involved at least as much as Israel in the current operation.

The first reactions of American opinion were hostile. Typical was the Washington *Post* editorial:

> *No amount of provocation can justify Israeli aggression against Egypt. In either case, it involves the most frightful risk of larger war, and it may well lose for Israel the sympathy of the free world.*

A wave of high tension ran through the city. Senators, congressmen and newspapermen friendly to Israel expressed the apprehension that the conflict would spread. They strongly urged us to do everything possible to bring military operations to an end.

Among American Jews the confusion was great. The Zionist leader, Abba Hillel Silver, telephoned me from Cleveland and promised to give his full assistance. He thought there had been "an error in judgment even more serious than in the case of the Kinneret operation." Other Jewish leaders told me that no ground had been prepared and that a military operation a week before the presidential election increased their embarrassment and threatened their position. But I also received expressions of pride about the efficiency with which the Israeli forces were carrying out their tasks. The Zionist leaders, meeting on Tuesday, October 30, in New York, recommended full solidarity with Israel. They also wanted to criticize President Eisenhower, his party and his Administration. Since I had been called to the Security Council, I dispatched Shiloah to a meeting of the Presidents' Club. From his report I gathered that he had a difficult hour. For the first time in our memory there was reluctance to justify Israel's action without reserve. Jewish leaders had been impressed by Israeli statements in previous weeks that we would not start a war. They found it hard to make a swift change in what they were telling their followers. Some suggested that Jewish reservations about Israel's step be openly published. In the end, however, more normal counsels prevailed, and the Jewish leaders rose with an expression of solidarity for Israel and an appeal to the United States to strengthen Israel's security and Middle Eastern peace.

There had been an immense tumult in the Security Council on the morning of October 30. The French representative, Bernard Cornut-Gentille, presided with manifest discomfort. The agenda item was the U.S. proposal for "steps for immediate termination of Israeli military activity in Egypt." The Egyptian delegate and I were called to the table. The U.S. representative, Henry Cabot Lodge, expressed his government's shock at the Israeli action which had been taken "twenty-four hours after the personal appeal of Eisenhower to the Israeli Prime Minister." He called on the Council to take immediate measures for Israeli withdrawal to the armistice line. He asked all members of the United Nations to abstain from extending any aid which might prolong the hostilities.

Secretary-General Hammarskjöld now conveyed the information that he had received from his representative in the area, Canadian General E. M. Burns. There were speeches by Yugoslavia, Iran, the Soviet Union, Australia, China, Cuba, Peru and Egypt. The Soviet delegate, Arkady Sobolev, quoted a news item from London about the intention of Britain and France to intervene in Egypt. This was received in tense silence. There was a growing conviction that we were not discussing a mere Israeli-Egyptian clash. Newspapermen scurried to and fro, preparing for surprises.

The debate had gone on for a long time without a single word from the French or British representative. Tension became immense when the British delegate, Sir Pierson Dixon, announced that he was expecting an important declaration which was now being put out by the British Prime Minister, and that as soon as it reached him, he would communicate it to the Council. It seemed that the French delegate already knew more than his British colleague. Cornut-Gentille took me aside while the session was in progress and whispered, "Don't worry, there will be a veto." This was the first hint that reached me that we were not alone.

The session was resumed at four o'clock. It opened with a bombshell. The British delegate read a declaration by his Prime Minister about an Anglo-French ultimatum that been handed to Egypt and Israel calling on them "to remove their troops to a distance of ten miles from the Suez Canal." The French representative made an identical speech. Since we were nowhere near the Canal, we would have to "remove ourselves" forward in order to obey the ultimatum.

The sudden revelation that Britain and France were taking an active part in the Israeli operation acted like oil on fire. Lodge made a passionate address calling for the immediate approval of the American resolution before a dangerous complication caused the peace of the area to go up in flames. His resolution called for withdrawal to the armistice lines, the strict observance of the armistice agreement, and the duty of all member states to withhold all military, economic or financial aid for Israel until she complied with the resolution. The Soviet representative now asked for strong condemnation of Israel—but he was willing, if necessary, to accept the more "moderate" American text. In the debate that now followed, Israel found itself with unusually strong support. France, Britain and, somewhat less heatedly, Australia and Belgium were trying to save time and to delay the Security Council's action. On the other hand, the United States and the Soviet Union were arrayed in an unusual alliance against us.

I took the floor to describe the *fedayeen* raids, the threats to Israel's existence, the impotence of the United Nations and the Egyptian "paradox of unilateral belligerency." Relying on a communication that I had received from our Foreign Ministry, I stated categorically that we did not intend to acquire new territories, but merely to eliminate threats to our security arising from the murder gangs and hostile armies.

Eventually the American resolution was put to the vote. There were seven in favor. Australia and Belgium abstained, and Britain and France registered negative votes that amounted to a double veto. The chairman announced that the resolution had not been adopted.

It was now clear that there could not be any decisive action in the Security Council. Any continuation of its discussions would be mere propaganda. A spectacular split had taken place between the United States and its traditional allies. We found ourselves in stronger company than usual. Two permanent members of the Security Council were on our side. After the vote Sobolev, the Soviet representative, called for a shorter resolution, shorn of all criticism or condemnation or threat of sanctions, calling for an immediate cease-fire. The majority voted to suspend discussions for an hour and a quarter. When the Security Council reassembled at nine in the evening, the Soviet resolutions received seven votes, with Belgium and Australia abstaining and Britain and France again voting against. This resolution, too, had failed. Various suggestions for adopting a cease-fire resolution under diverse texts were defeated by negative British and French votes.

When Lodge saw that he was having no effect against British and French opposition, he asked the Security Council to stop further voting.

The British and French positions had an electric effect on public opinion. Many Americans began to ask whether U.S. policy might have driven America's allies to desperation. Israel was now relieved of the brunt of hostile opinion, which fell mainly on Britain and France.

The next day, October 31, the Security Council convened again. It was reported that the Israeli government had accepted the Anglo-French "ultimatum," whereas Egypt had rejected it, whereupon British and French planes had begun to bomb Egypt as a preliminary to military landings. In the Council's discussions the British delegate strongly denied that Britain and France had acted in common cause with Israel. He asserted that his government "did not support Israeli intentions to capture Egyptian territories." In fact, he thought that Israel should remove its forces as soon as suitable arrangements could be made. Britain "had no doubt that in crossing the Egyptian boundary Israel had violated the armistice agreement"!

In the light of what we subsequently heard about the Sèvres meeting and Eden's dynamic role in the whole operation, the sanctimonious tone of this statement was very hard to take. At the same time the Security Council was paralyzed. The United Nations aspect of the Suez operation had been planned by London, Paris and Jerusalem on the assumption that the British and French vetoes would remove the United Nations from the arena. This action took astonishingly little account of the constitutional change in the UN system under the Uniting for Peace resolution of 1951, which enabled the General Assembly to act if the Security Council was deadlocked by veto.

An emergency meeting of the General Assembly was fixed for November 1, at five-thirty, but by now we had another adversary who strongly reinforced the American and Soviet positions. Secretary-General Hammarskjöld, in a voice shaking with emotion, read out "a personal declaration" which was interpreted as a threat to resign in protest against British and French violations of their Charter obligations. He began with a statement of his beliefs about the role of the UN and its Secretary-General. He said that the principles of the Charter were infinitely more important than the organization that embodied them. The aims which those principles were designed to fulfill had a greater sanctity than the policy of any state or people. In order to preserve the efficacy of the organization, its Secretary-General must abstain from taking a public position in relation to a conflict between member states unless taking such a position would assist to remove the conflict. It was inadmissible to maneuver the organization into a policy of expediency. A Secretary-General could not fulfill his function except on the assumption that all members of the UN, especially the permanent members of the Security Council, would carry out their obligations. If there were members who believed that the welfare of the organization required a different conception of the Secretary-General's function, it was their right to act accordingly.

Hammarskjöld had a refined sense of drama, and his passionate speech had a sharp effect on the news media. It was obvious that his position would be based not on geopolitical realities or general equities, but on a legalistic interpretation of what the Charter allowed or forbade. World opinion, shattered by the impotence of the Security Council and the suddenness with which the conflict had erupted, was looking for an international hero. Hammarskjöld rose toward that vocation. There was an air of deliberate martyrdom in his bearing. A chorus of loyalty and almost of worship went up loudly around the table.

There was total confusion in the White House. The breakdown of the Western alliance was a more crushing event than an eruption of familiar violence between Egypt and Israel. The fact that the United States found itself arrayed with the Soviet Union against its allies, England and France, could only be interpreted as a sad failure of American foreign policy. The election atmosphere added fuel to the fire. Adlai Stevenson, in a speech delivered on the evening of October 29, condemned the failure of American policy in the Middle East, and accused the Administration of having deceived the nation. He was referring to statements made by Republican spokesmen only a few days before to the effect that American policy in the Middle East "was developing well." The tension was especially heavy in New York. The Democratic candidate for the Senate, Robert Wagner, a Catholic, was running against the Republican candidate Jacob Javits, a stalwart member of the Jewish community. There was a possibility that if Javits was elected, a Republican majority would be ensured in the Senate. I knew both candidates personally. While Wagner was free to criticize the Administration's foreign policy, the unfortunate Javits, not for the first or last time, was inhibited by his loyalty to the Administration policy.

On October 30 Sherman Adams, President Eisenhower's chief of staff at the White House, got in touch with Abba Hillel Silver and requested him to convey to Ben Gurion that the President intended to broadcast to the nation the next day and would like to abstain from any condemnation of Israel. Therefore, he wished to receive a promise that Israel would not retain her forces in the area that she had occupied. He wanted Ben Gurion to announce that since the Israeli forces had now completed their mission, namely the liquidation of the *fedayeen* bases, they would return to the previous boundary. If we were to do this, the President would include in his broadcast a statement of deep appreciation and of friendship toward Israel. Eisenhower added that even though it seemed that there was a convergence of interests between Israel and those of Britain and France, "the fact is that Israel's power and future are in fact bound up with the United States." Silver gave me this message and at my suggestion telephoned it personally to Ben Gurion. The Prime Minister said, "The enemy is listening and I cannot possibly tell you now if we will withdraw or not." I had a similar conversation with Ben Gurion that evening.

On the morning of October 31 I met leaders of the American Jewish Committee led by Jacob Blaustein and Joseph Proskauer. They did not criticize but gave friendly advice that we should regard time as an important factor. We should do everything we could to bring the operation to a speedy conclusion before the danger of a world war arose. Judge Proskauer was impressed by my exposition of our situation. He therefore suggested that I bring it to the attention of Governor Thomas Dewey, the titular head of the Republican Party who had run unsuccessfully against Roosevelt and Truman in the last election campaigns and who had Eisenhower's ear.

I immediately went down to Wall Street and had a long talk with Dewey. According to him, Eisenhower's chief apprehension lay in the suspicion that we intended a permanent occupation. Dewey added that there was a view in the Pentagon that if the hostilities did not come to an early end, there would be a danger of Soviet intervention, and therefore of a world conflagration. I immediately conveyed this to Ben Gurion and suggested that whatever his policy was, he should make some statement of it to President Eisenhower. I added, on the basis of my contacts, that one school of thought in the Pentagon considered that it might be better to bring down Nasser and thereby reduce Soviet influence in the Middle East. But even those who took that view emphasized the need for a speedy end of hostilities.

On October 31 Ben Gurion sent me his reply to the message from Eisenhower through Sherman Adams to Silver. I passed it on to Silver in Cleveland so that he could telephone it to the White House. At Proskauer's suggestion I also made the text available to Governor Dewey. In his reply Ben Gurion stated that he would be prepared to suggest the withdrawal of our forces if Nasser would sign a peace treaty including clear assurances to abstain from hostile acts against Israel. This would have to include the dispersion of the *fedayeen* units, the abolition of the economic boycott, the stoppage of the blockade in the Red Sea and the Suez Canal and abstention from any military alliance against Israel. On the other hand, the withdrawal of our forces from the area before a peace agreement was signed by Nasser would be suicidal. Ben Gurion expressed the hope that the President would not regard the present action of Israel as a disruption of the Israeli-American friendship. That friendship was one of the most cherished assets of the Israeli government and people. "Israel would always attach priority to its relations with the United States." But he feared that if Israeli forces left the area before peace was concluded, Nasser would strengthen the maritime blockade in the Suez Canal and the Red Sea, would reinforce his army and develop his cooperation with other Arab armies with the aim of bringing about our destruction. He added—not very diplomatically—that Israel's action had now flowed into the same channel as that of two friendly nations, France and Britain, who, like us, understood the danger to peace in our area arising from the Nasser regime's expansionist appetite. While he would bring President Eisenhower's appeal to the attention of the Israeli government, the Prime Minister, "in accordance with the dictates of decency and common interest," would have to consult with the governments of Britain and France.

In transmitting this message, I pointed out to the White House that for the first time there was now an authoritative description of our war aims. The aim was not territorial expansion, but the assurance of stability, peace and the elimination of active hostilities.

Ben Gurion's message reached the White House at four in the afternoon on November 1; it appears to have had some influence on Eisenhower's speech. In sending it to Ben Gurion, I said that if he read the text carefully he would see that despite the present crisis, the prospects for our political struggle in the United States were improving. Instead of the savage reactions of the first twenty-four hours, we now had a measured statement in which responsibility was put on Egypt and not only on Israel, Britain and France. The three of us were described as allies and friends who had a right to act in their own interest, even if they evoked American dissent. There was an implication of willingness to repair the relations between the United States and the three "allies and friends."

On the morning of November 1 I had telephone conversations with Golda Meir and Shimon Peres in Tel Aviv. They told me about the brilliant success of our military operations: our forces had come within ten miles of the Suez Canal; most of Sinai and the Gaza Strip were in our hands. The crew of an Egyptian warship that had tried to bomb Haifa had surrendered and been taken prisoner together with its ship; the Egyptian armies in Sinai had collapsed and were completely broken. Thousands of prisoners had been taken; enormous quantities of arms and equipment had come into our hands.

Encouraged by this news, I flew to Washington for my talk with Dulles. Since my plane from New York was delayed that night, the meeting was put off to the following day. I expected that Dulles would threaten us with economic sanctions. We already had indications of this in the State Department. Everything had been frozen. The journey of a team of the Export-Import Bank which was supposed to recommend a new loan of $75 million had been held up. So, too, had negotiations on the utilization of the residue of the grant-in-aid and the Food Surplus Agreement. Even the small technical-assistance program had been held in abeyance.

My talk with Dulles was brief but significant. Shiloah and Frazer Wilkins took part. Dulles said that the U.S. government was naturally looking at its aid programs, but he would first like to hear about our intentions. Did we intend to remain in Sinai or go back to the previous boundary after carrying out the mission that we had assumed?

The news I had received that morning about our military victory changed my approach to this conversation. I decided to go on the offensive. I said rather grandly, with an opulent sweep of my hand, that with all the importance of the money which we appreciated very deeply, my own mind was occupied by fundamental thoughts about the future of our region. "The military power of Nasser is in collapse," I added. "His prestige is sinking. It is possible to bring him down and thereby to deal a heavy blow to Soviet influence in the Middle East, simultaneously with Soviet troubles in Europe. In this revolutionary situation a crucial hour has been reached. The aim should be not to restore a situation charged with explosiveness, but rather to make a dramatic leap forward to peace. I am convinced that if a regime like that of Nasser had managed to consolidate itself in the Western hemisphere under Soviet influence, the United States would have intervened strongly, even if distant countries took a dissenting attitude. I ended my short remarks by suggesting that he should try to digest what I had said and to think in broad strategic terms of a durable solution.

When the talk began, Dulles had been tense and angry, but when I launched into a description of the global implications I could see that he understood the complexities. The question of economic aid which had been the reason for our meeting was completely forgotten. In his book *Dulles Over Suez*, Professor Herman Finer describes the scene:

> *Dulles thrust his hands deeper into his trouser pockets and wrinkled his brow, as he strode around the office. Eban's conceptions were big and he liked them. "Look," he said, "I'm terribly torn. No-one can be happier than I am that Nasser has been defeated. Since spring I've only had cause to detest him.*
>
> *"Yet can we accept a good end when it is achieved by means that violate the Charter? Look here, we could improve our position in the world if we used force, say, in Korea or Quemoy or in Germany. But if we did that the UN would collapse. So I am forced to turn back to the Charter. I have to work on the basis that the long-term interests of the United States and the world are superior to these considerations of self-benefit."*

Dulles seemed to be saying that even if conflicts could be satisfactorily resolved, it would be better not to resolve them if the consequence would be to weaken the United Nations system! He asked, "Do you think we should have one standard of reaction to our adversaries and another standard for our friends?" To his dismay I replied, "Yes, Mr. Secretary, I do. That is what friendship is about."

At any rate, there was a more relaxed atmosphere. As I rose to leave, Dulles said with a vestige of a smile, "You must admit I was right when I told you that your military position was not all that bad and you didn't have to be so alarmed about Egypt receiving Soviet arms." This seemed to amuse him inordinately, and his unaccustomed laughter followed me down the corridor.

The General Assembly meeting opened at five o'clock on October 31. The General Assembly Hall had never been so crowded, nor had there ever been a debate charged with such tension since the UN was established. It was estimated that some 70 million people were watching the proceedings on the television.

All the early speakers called for a cease-fire. The Arabs also requested a strong condemnation and sanctions. A resolution was introduced by Dulles, who opened on a personal note, expressing doubt that anybody had ever addressed the United Nations with such a heavy heart. The United States found itself in conflict with three countries to which it was bound by deep ties of friendship, admiration and respect. Two of them were its oldest and most faithful allies. He admitted that there were "provocations" and that there had been a certain measure of "neglect by the United States" in dealing with Middle Eastern problems. But all that could not justify recourse to force. He argued that even though Israel had a just grievance, since Egypt had never conformed with the Security Council resolution of 1951 recognizing Israel's right to use the Canal, there was surely a better prospect to satisfy this interest by peaceful means.

My own turn to speak was to come late that night. The feverish pace of events had given me no possibility to prepare a set speech. Yet a major challenge now lay ahead. I would be able to address tens of millions of television viewers, radio listeners and newspaper readers across the globe. There had never been such an opportunity to tell the world what the Israeli enterprise meant and implied. Having made certain that some of our friends, especially from Latin America, would keep the debate going for a couple of hours, I adjourned to the Westbury Hotel Restaurant on East Seventieth Street, just opposite our delegation building. I took with me a faithful friend, Dr. Jacob Robinson, our legal adviser, with whom I explored the idea of defending our action in terms of Article 51 of the United Nations Charter. This provides for the exercise of the "inherent right of self-defense." This meant, of course, that I would totally separate the Israeli action from the more dubious motives that had inspired the British and French interventions. When Robinson left, I borrowed a pencil and a few pieces of paper from the waiter and hurriedly wrote out a few main headings for my speech. There would certainly not be time to prepare a formulated and mimeographed text.

When I got back to the Assembly Hall at ten-thirty, a telephone call came from David Sarnoff, president of the Radio Corporation of America, who may well be regarded as the founder of modern telecommunications in the United States. Sarnoff said that if I could arrange to come on the air at eleven-thirty or later, I would get complete national coverage, since all the regular television programs would be over. It was nearly midnight when I rose to make my address. The French and British delegates had been brief and apologetic; in the case of Pierson Dixon, his brevity probably reflected his lack of personal enthusiasm for the cause that he was defending. Cornut-Gentille was very close to a nervous collapse and had handed over to his deputy, Louis de Guiringaud (now Foreign Minister).

In my first sentence I plunged straight to the heart of our decision and action:

> On Monday, 29 October, the Israel Defense Forces took security measures in the Sinai Peninsula in the exercise of our country's inherent right of self-defense. The object of these operations is to eliminate the bases from which armed Egyptian units, under the special care and authority of Colonel Nasser, invade Israel's territory for murder, sabotage and the creation of permanent insecurity to peaceful life.

But it was my determination that evening to transcend the immediate hostilities, which were nothing but the symptom of a deeper reality:

> Stretching far back behind the events of this week lies the unique and somber story of a small people, subjected throughout all the years of its national existence to a furious, implacable, comprehensive campaign of hatred and siege for which there is no parallel or precedent in the modern history of nations. Not for one single moment throughout the entire period of its modern national existence has Israel enjoyed that minimal physical security which the United Nations Charter confers on all member states, and which all other member states have been able to command.
> Whatever rights are enjoyed by other members of this Organiza-

tion belong to Israel without addition or diminution. Whatever obligation any member state owes to another, Egypt owes to Israel and Israel to Egypt.

Then, looking straight at my audience, I delivered what the newspapers the next day called the "punchline," in words which have often been quoted since:

Surrounded by hostile armies on all its land frontiers; subjected to savage and relentless hostility; exposed to penetration, raids and assaults by day and by night; suffering constant toll of life among its citizenry; bombarded by threats of neighboring governments to accomplish its extinction by armed force; overshadowed by a new menace of irresponsible rearmament—embattled, blockaded, besieged, Israel alone amongst the nations faces a battle for its security anew with every approaching nightfall and every rising dawn. . . .

In recent days, the government of Israel had to face a tormenting question. Do its obligations under the United Nations Charter require it to resign itself to uninterrupted activity to the south and north and east of armed units practicing open warfare against it, and working from their bases in the Sinai Peninsula and elsewhere for the invasion of our homes, our land and our very lives? Or on the other hand, are we acting legitimately within our inherent right of self-defense when, having found no other remedy for two years, we cross the frontier against those who have no scruples in crossing the frontier against us?

. . . There is aggression. There is belligerency in the Middle East, but we for eight years have been its victims and not its authors. That is what I mean when I say that world opinion should decide whom to trust. Should it be the small, free people establishing its homeland in peace and constructive progress? Or shall it be the dictatorship which has bullied and blustered and blackmailed its way across the international life of our times, threatening peace in many continents, openly avowing belligerency, placing its fist upon the jugular vein of the world's communications, bringing the Middle East and the world ever nearer to the threshold of conflict, intimidating all those who stand in its path; all except one people, at least, that will not be intimidated; one people whom no dictator has ever intimidated. The people that has risen up against all the tyrants of history. The people that knows that the appeasement of despots yields nothing but an uneasy respite, and that a Government that allowed its own citizens to be murdered daily in their homes would lose the dignity and justification for which governments are instituted amongst men.

Israel has no desire or intention to wield arms beyond the limit of its legitimate defensive mission. But whatever is demanded of us by way of restoring Egypt's rights and respecting Egypt's security must surely be accompanied by equally binding Egyptian undertakings to respect Israel's security and Israel's rights.

Our signpost is not backward to belligerency, but forward to peace.

As I went down from the rostrum and walked across the aisle back to my seat, a cascade of applause arose all around me, growing in intensity, sometimes accompanied by emotional stamping of feet. It was a moment both of exhaustion and of relief. The exhaustion belonged to the tension of recent days and the knowledge that I had been afforded a unique opportunity to affect the direction of world opinion. The relief came from the feeling that I had got something off Israel's chest that had badly needed saying. No matter what the political outcome might be, the cathartic liberation from a pent-up grievance would have a healing effect, not only on me, but more important, on the besieged, tormented people for whom I had spoken.

The General Assembly, as expected, adopted the American resolution on cease-fire and the withdrawal of forces. It was past two o'clock in the morning when the vote came. There were 64 in favor of the American resolution, 5 against—Britain, France, Israel, Australia and New Zealand—with 6 abstentions. I went down into the lobby. Dulles was waiting for his car, together with Herman Phleger, the legal adviser to the State Department. I thought that Dulles looked haggard and yellow. Advancing toward me for what became a much photographed handshake, he chewed and swallowed nervously, as was his habit. Then, with typically forensic professionalism, he began to ask me about technicalities: "Listen, you didn't seem to be reading. Did you have a manuscript?" I told him that owing to pressure of time I had not prepared my speech at all but had formulated it on the basis of a few notes. I took out the pieces of paper on which I had written about twenty lines at the Westbury Hotel. He looked hard at me and made a memorable reply, "Jesus Christ," as he strolled away. I was told that this was the only occasion on which this austere churchman had been heard to utter the familiar but irreverent expletive.

On November 2 I had satisfying echoes from my address the previous night. The radio and television stations kept repeating a full transmission of it. Our delegation, with miraculous speed, produced a verbatim copy. About six hundred telegrams reached me on that day, and by the end of a week the number had gone into the thousands. An enterprising company put a record into the stores within a few days.

One of the countries that had abstained in the vote in the early hours of November 2 was Canada, which was obviously caught up in a clash of loyalties between her British and French origins and her American proximity. In my talk with Pearson that night, I had found him divided within himself. He obviously thought that Nasser had been provocative; on the other hand, Pearson was a zealot of the United Nations idea and a firm supporter of its law. I got the impression that he would have been happier if Israel had acted alone, in self-defense, rather than within the framework of a joint operation with Britain and France. In a memorable address explaining his abstention, he suggested that the General Assembly should use the cease-fire not simply for deadlock, but for advancing a political solution of the problems of the Suez Canal and the Arab-Israeli relationship. He threw an idea into the air that was to play a central role in future events: the United Nations should establish an international force that would ensure the maintenance of peace on the boundaries.

In later months and years the UN peacekeeping role developed quickly, and Pearson was awarded the Nobel Prize. There is, however, a view that the concept was born in the United States, and that its authors included Dulles, Herman Phleger and David Wainhouse, an able American Jew who worked in the State Department's Office of UN Affairs. It was clear that the United States could not propose a UN force without evoking a suspicious reaction from the Soviet Union, which would never agree to an American presence, even under the UN flag, without a concurrent Soviet presence. The United States, therefore, decided to find a respectable neutral country that would make the proposal. Henry Cabot Lodge decided that he would "sell" the idea either to Brazil or to Canada. When he got into the elevator at United Nations headquarters, Lester Pearson happened to be there, while the Brazilian delegate was nowhere to be seen.

Whether or not we accept Lodge's anecdote, the fact remains that it was Lester Pearson's eloquence and prestige that caused the UN General Assembly to adopt his proposal in a few days.

In cabling home to Ben Gurion and Golda Meir, I pointed out that the United States resolution contained a few loopholes within which we could maneuver. The references in the Security Council text to withholding aid from Israel had been omitted. The General Assembly had determined that our neighbors had often violated the armistice agreement. Most important of all, there was a gap of time between the cease-fire and the withdrawal of forces. The cease-fire was to be "immediate," while the withdrawal of forces was to take place "as soon as possible."

The paradox was that Israel was now closer to a readiness for cease-fire than Britain and France. We had almost accomplished our military aim while they had not seriously begun theirs. Indeed, on November 3, when the cease-fire was to go into effect, we had nearly all of Sinai, except Sharm el-Sheikh, in our hands. The Anglo-French landing in the Canal Zone had not begun at all. Britain and France therefore rejected the call for a cease-fire. I continued to say that while we accepted the cease-fire "in principle," it must be accompanied by an assurance about Egypt's peaceful intention. I made this clear in a memorandum I gave Secretary-General Hammarskjöld in November.

When I had let it be known that we saw no objection to a cease-fire, I received an agitated telephone call from the Foreign Ministry in Tel Aviv. I was told that while we had very little more to do in the field, the French and the British were embarrassed by the idea that we would cease fire before they had begun. This was the only occasion in my experience on which other powers ever have objected to Israel ceasing fire too soon.

On November 3 and 4 I became reinforced in my conviction that our efforts in Washington and the UN had not been in vain. The American position seemed to be emerging out of rage into lucidity. Lodge now proposed two resolutions. The first called for the Palestine Conciliation Commission to conclude its work and be succeeded by a committee of five which would investigate the problem and bring recommendations to the United Nations. The second resolution concerned the Suez Canal. It called for the establishment of a committee of three—Egypt, Britain and France—to work out a procedure for activating the Canal for free navigation.

The American attitude had clearly moved far in our direction. Anxious Asian and pro-Arab states came to the forum attempting to drown Lodge's "revisionist" ideas with heated affirmations of the need to concentrate exclusively on a cease-fire and withdrawal of forces. Lodge had no course but to accept priority for the Canadian resolution asking the Secretary-General to establish an international force in the next forty-eight hours. He announced that the United States would not press for action on its two resolutions at that stage.

Remarkable staff work by Hammarskjöld, Bunche and the UN Secretariat made it possible for a United Nations Emergency Force to be proposed in the General Assembly on November 5. In Israel we had not given much consideration to this concept, and my own speech on the motion was noncommittal. I could only promise to clarify the Israeli policy after consultation with my government.

At three-thirty on the morning of November 5 the General Assembly adopted the Canadian resolution, with 16 abstentions, including the Soviet bloc, France, Britain, Australia, New Zealand, South Africa, Israel and Egypt. It also adopted a repeated call for withdrawal to which, again, there were 5 opposing votes—Israel, France, Britain, New Zealand and Australia.

Soviet opposition to the plan for a UN force was instructive. It indicated Moscow's sensitivity about a force which would probably be confined to Western and neutral countries and which would reflect the power of the pro-American majority in the General Assembly. The Soviet Union was also traumatically affected by the memory of a previous "United Nations force" which had in fact been a cover for an American operation under General Douglas MacArthur in Korea. On the other hand, Egypt, despite her discreet abstention, was very interested in the UNEF proposal. Obviously there was no hope of ensuring a complete evacuation of troops from her territory unless the initial recipient of the occupied areas was an authority other than the Egyptian government itself.

At dawn on November 5, the airborne assault by Britain and France on the Canal Zone began at last. Having been late in its commencement, it was now to be ineffective in its execution. The attack naturally brought about a vast intensification of international pressures. This time the Soviet resolution in the Security Council calling for a cease-fire stipulated that it must come into effect "within twelve hours." The Soviet proposal went on to say that if this did not happen, the United States and the Soviet Union as two countries with air and sea power should help Egypt with weapons, volunteers and other military means. This proposal was supported only by Yugoslavia and Iran. Four countries, including the United States, voted against. Lodge said that any idea of joint Soviet and American forces in the area was "unthinkable."

We were now to come under the cruelest international pressure that we, or perhaps any small nation, had known in the postwar era. On the evening of November 5 Ben Gurion received a letter from Soviet Premier Nikolai Bulganin. Israel was accused of "criminal acts and of acting as an instrument of external imperialistic forces." Then came the menace:

The Government of Israel is criminally and irresponsibly playing with the fate of the world, with the fate of its own people. It is sowing hatred of the State of Israel amongst the Eastern peoples, such as cannot but leave its mark on the future of Israel and places in question the very existence of Israel as a state. *The Soviet Government is at this moment taking steps to put an end to the war and to restrain the aggressors. The Government of Israel should consider before it is too late. We hope that the Government of Israel will fully understand and appreciate this warning of ours.*

This brutal letter, together with a more friendly but very exigent note from Eisenhower, created something close to panic in Israel. Our first task was to find out how other countries reacted, and for this purpose Ben Gurion asked Foreign Minister Golda Meir, together with Shimon Peres, to go to Paris for advice. In conversations with French Foreign Minister Christian Pineau, it appeared that France took the Soviet threat very literally. He said to his Israeli interlocutors, "We have no means of defense against missiles. I suggest that you do not belittle Bulganin's warning." On the other hand, the French Defense Minister, Maurice Bourgès-Maunoury, telephoned Peres to say, "In truth, I have no precise documentary evidence, but in my view the Soviet threat is nothing but a bluff. They will not create the danger of a third world war. This is only a personal opinion, but it is well that you should take this too into account."

But from Israel came a picture of a people in the full flush of victory. All of a sudden the hands clutching at our throat had been torn away. We could breathe freely again. The consequent exuberance was understandable, but it may well have passed the limits of rationality. In a "victory speech" to the Knesset on the evening of November 7, Ben Gurion said with some hyperbole, "This was the greatest and most glorious military operation in the annals of our people, and one of the most remarkable operations in world history."

Ben Gurion now went far beyond any of the positions that I had been empowered to take up in the Security Council and the General Assembly. In all my speeches I had stated clearly that the people of Israel had "no desire to wield arms beyond their legitimate defensive mission." I also strongly implied, at Ben Gurion's behest, that we did not regard ourselves as having a need of permanent presence in Sinai or Gaza. Indeed, I already knew from Jerusalem that before launching our military operation, Ben Gurion had told Mapam ministers and others that there was no prospect whatever of Israel being allowed to remain in Sinai, and that our real aims were the opening of the straits and the creation of tranquillity on our border facing the Gaza Strip. All this, however, had been forgotten on November 7. Ben Gurion now stated "with full force and unflinching determination:

· The armistice agreement with Egypt is dead and buried and cannot be restored to life.

· In consequence, the armistice lines between Israel and Egypt have no more validity.

· We are ready to enter into negotiations for a stable peace, cooperation and good neighborly relations with Egypt on condition that they are direct negotiations, without prior conditions on either side and not under duress from any quarter whatsoever.

· On no account will Israel agree to the stationing of a foreign force, no matter how called, in her territory or in any of the areas occupied by her.

From the moment that I heard this address, I saw it as a political error. There was no chance whatever that Ben Gurion could maintain those positions, and to retreat from them would affect our credibility. He was alienating not only Israel's adversaries but also her friends. Lester Pearson said to me that day that whatever sympathy for Israel had existed in the United Nations and elsewhere had been unaccountably thrown away by Ben Gurion. "That speech must have been as offensive to the British, the French, the Americans and to us Canadians as it was to the Arabs," Pearson went on. "If you people persist with this, you run the risk of losing all your friends."

The general reaction to Ben Gurion's speech was confusion and consternation. The pressure for our withdrawal increased. Much of the understanding that we had acquired after October 29 was now dissipated. One indication was the total isolation of Israel in the General Assembly on the night of November 7. The vote for an immediate cease-fire and withdrawal was now 65 to 1—Israel. Britain, France, their NATO allies and Australia and New Zealand abstained. I had to leave the General Assembly to meet the Jewish leaders, leaving my able deputy, Reggie Kidron, behind. He told me later that to cast a sole negative vote had given him a macabre feeling of Jewish solitude.

Finding us isolated even from our closest friends, Hammarskjöld swooped down for the political kill. In remarks to newspapermen he blamed Israel for endangering world peace and raised doubts about her future "existence." He also refused to discuss any claims or grievances until we agreed to withdraw.

Many explanations have been given for Ben Gurion's unexpected speech of November 7. Ben Gurion's principal adviser at that time, Yaacov Herzog, said, "One must place it in the atmosphere of the time. Ben Gurion and all Israelis felt that we must terminate the nightmare once and for all, *fedayeen* raids, threats of annihilation. We were playing for big stakes—peace." Shimon Peres, however, held the view that Ben Gurion gave a calculated impression of a plan to annex Sinai merely as a bargaining device to secure free passage through the Gulf. Mrs. Meir's view was: "I think Ben Gurion believed that we could stay in Sinai and Gaza. He did not take into consideration, nor did any of us, that the Soviet Union would respond as it did." Ben Gurion, however, gave a simpler and more innocent explanation: "I made a few mistakes in that speech, saying that the armistice agreement was dead and buried, that Egypt would not be allowed to return to Sinai. I went too far and it was against the views I had expressed in the Government on October 28, that they would not let us stay in Sinai—Russia, America, the UN, Africa and Asia." And then, after a thoughtful pause, the essential truth was stated with almost childlike innocence and veracity: "But you see, the victory was too quick. *I was too drunk with victory.*" *

Ben Gurion's speech on November 7 was made in full knowledge that the Soviets were threatening Israel in the most drastic terms. On that day, however, the clouds gathered thick and strong. A report was going around Paris that the Soviets intended to "flatten" Israel the next day. The French passed the grim news on to Israel. Our ambassador in Rome, Eliahu Sasson, cabled Jerusalem for transmission to me that the Soviet ambassador in Italy was making similar threats. Another source of worry was the knowledge that the U.S. ambassador in Paris had assured Guy Mollet that a Soviet missile attack on Britain or France would lead to American retaliation. Israel was conspicuously absent from this reassurance.

To the Soviet threat was now added American pressure. In the late afternoon of November 7 while I was at the United Nations, Shiloah called me from Washington to say that the reaction to Ben Gurion's Knesset speech was "terrible." Eisenhower had sent Ben Gurion an angry message through our embassy: Shiloah had been called to the State Department for a conversation with the Under-Secretary, Herbert Hoover Jr., who was acting for Dulles, now in the hospital with diagnosed cancer. Hoover had said, "I consider this to be the most important meeting ever held with Israeli representatives. Israel will be the first to be swallowed up by Soviet penetration. In these circumstances, Israel's attitude will inevitably lead to most serious measures such as the termination of all United States governmental and private

---

* Michael Brecher, *Decisions in Israel's Foreign Policy* (Yale University Press, 1974), p. 283.

aid, United Nations sanctions and eventual expulsion from the United Nations. I speak with the utmost seriousness and gravity."

Rountree, who was present, added, "We have been profoundly shocked at the report of the Prime Minister's latest speech." I telephoned these messages to Ben Gurion via Yaacov Herzog at eight-thirty on November 8.

I now decided that I had to take responsibility by myself. Ben Gurion was clearly acting in the intoxicating atmosphere of Israel's victory and under strong militant pressure at home. I wanted to propose a formula which would enable us to satisfy the United States, if not the Soviet Union, while leaving the door open for us to resume our struggle in pursuit of our war aims. I cabled Ben Gurion reminding him that the world was waiting in great tension for his reply to Eisenhower's letter. I told him frankly that our friends in the Jewish community and throughout America and the United Nations wanted him to withdraw from his refusal to allow an international force into Sinai. My recommendation was that Israel should declare her willingness to withdraw from Sinai when satisfactory arrangements were made with the international force about to enter the Canal Zone. I added that we should make the announcement within twenty-four hours because of "growing evidence of Soviet plans to intervene."

Ben Gurion's first reaction was to ask me whether an immediate meeting between him and Eisenhower could be arranged, if necessary in secret. Eisenhower's mood at that moment was punitive. He was certainly not concerned to give Ben Gurion the prestige victory of a summit meeting. In fact, he asked Silver by telephone that night whether Ben Gurion's reputation for balance and rationality was really well founded.

Throughout November 7 the Soviet Union went on multiplying its threats that if the invading forces did not depart, the USSR would intervene. The United States took this threat seriously. It acted as though there was at least a contingency of world conflagration. The ships of the Sixth Fleet were ordered to sail onto the high seas to avoid a Pearl Harbor attack. I cabled Ben Gurion to say that whether the American appreciation of the situation was right or wrong, we had to take it as a fact. Washington would not be influenced either by our own representations or by Jewish pressures because, in its view, the peace of the world and the avoidance of an atomic war were now in the balance. My appraisal was that the United States would not use armed force to remove us from Sinai, at least at that stage, but that it would exercise its maximum influence to bring about our agreement for our withdrawal and the entry of the international force. I added that although what I was saying should be taken in full gravity, I still thought that I could get international agreement for the nonentry of Egyptian forces into Gaza and Sinai, including Sharm el-Sheikh.

The Israeli Cabinet now went into uninterrupted session on November 7 from five o'clock until after midnight. Aranne and Sapir, in the most vehement tones, said that the nation was in danger. The peril of destruction was real. History would never forgive the Israeli government if another holocaust ensued. With the Cabinet in a mood of intense alarm, it was agreed to put the responsibility on Ben Gurion.

I was now to be faced by one of the most extraordinary situations in which an ambassador has ever found himself. Ben Gurion did no more or less than transfer the crucial decision to me! His question was: Could we afford to accept my formula, making withdrawal conditional on "satisfactory arrangements with UN forces"? If this could be done, then our agreement could be given at once. We could continue for some days, weeks or even months to bargain about what was meant by "satisfactory arrangements with UN forces." On the other hand, if the result of this equivocation would be to bring about Soviet military intervention, we could not afford to hold our ground. Ben Gurion prepared two alternative texts of a speech to be broadcast to the nation: one accepting my formula of conditional and gradual withdrawal enabling us to fight for our major aims; the other announcing a readiness for "immediate and unconditional" withdrawal. Which of these texts would be used depended on how I would reply.

Yaacov Herzog, trembling with excitement, asked me to give my judgment. This was at nine o'clock in the evening. By eleven-thirty I had made soundings with John Foster Dulles, Allen Dulles, Walter Bedell Smith and others and had reached the conclusion that the acceptance of my formula would be satisfactory to the United States. In that case the Soviet attitude would become irrelevant, for the United States would deter the fulfillment or even the reiteration of Soviet threats. Yaacov Herzog and Gideon Rafael have recorded since then that Ben Gurion's reaction was: "If Eban really takes responsibility that it is feasible, then I agree." Shiloah and Kidron participated in the fateful consultation with me.

Three reasons inspired me to make my recommendation. First, the conditional sentence was important to gain time to continue our political struggle, and to ensure that evacuated areas would not be handed over to the Egyptian army. Second, a reply satisfactory to the

United States was essential to remove the danger of Soviet intervention. Third, if the Soviets abstained from intimidation because of possible United States reaction, then my formula of conditional withdrawal could be enough to dispel the crisis. Why concede everything? Professor Brecher has written:

> *This summation by Eban reflects the important role of a diplomat in the decision-making process. The strategic decision to withdraw was taken by Ben Gurion before consulting Israel's envoy in America. Eban's recommendation to retain the formula followed approval by the US Secretary of State. At the same time, his role was innovative and the burden of responsibility placed upon him on November 8 was very heavy. He reacted decisively. Finally, the formula permitted phased withdrawal and therefore ample time to secure concessions, the raison d'être of the political struggle to follow.*

I gave our compromise reply to Dulles, and Ben Gurion went ahead with his speech to the nation, which most listeners described as weary and dejected. But he told Israelis that we had three goals, none of which had yet been lost—the defeat of Egyptian armed forces; liberation of the territory of the homeland; and safeguarding of free navigation through the Gulf and the Canal.

The next morning I gave Hammarskjöld a reply identical to that which we had sent to Eisenhower. He expressed tremendous relief. The possibility that Ben Gurion's recalcitrance would lead to a world conflagration had been taken seriously in international quarters. As Yaacov Herzog has written: "There was a genuine fear of world war that day."

By now the Anglo-French landings and air bombings had subsided in ignominious sterility and our two European partners had fallen by the way. In their history, the Suez adventure was a turning point. In France it led to the rise of Gaullism and the virtual crumbling of the Atlantic orientation. In Britain it brought the imperial dream to an end, reminding Britain that she no longer had the power to sustain difficult international enterprises without American backing. Henceforward U.S.-Soviet hegemony was virtually ensured. Israeli policy makers were harshly reminded that no country except the United States could help us redress the adverse balance arising from the geopolitical predominance of the Arabs and their alliance with Soviet power. This is still the central truth of Israel's foreign policy today.

From November 7 onward I felt, paradoxically, that we were aided by our solitude. We no longer bore the stigma of collusion with Western imperialist interests. We were now struggling for the kind of Israeli aims that simple people all over the world could understand. We did not seek territorial aggrandizement. We sought free use of our maritime channels and freedom to live in peace in our homes.

During the next four months a political struggle developed which I look back on as one of the most satisfactory episodes in my public service. At the beginning the international position was that Israel should simply return to the previously held lines without any reward or compensation for her military sacrifice. Hammarskjöld upheld this doctrine with theological dogmatism, but it also had wide currency in the United States. I had said in my speech on November 1: "Least of all can we be satisfied to return to an imperfect armistice distorted by unilateral belligerency, to a system designed seven years ago as a transition to peace—and interpreted for seven years by one of the parties as a continuing state of war."

In a detailed cable from Jerusalem, Yaacov Herzog gave me clear directives to this effect from Ben Gurion: We should use the favorable atmosphere created by our offer of withdrawal and by the consequent American relief to secure "guarantees" that would effectively keep the Gulf of Aqaba (Eilat) open after our withdrawal and would prevent Gaza from reverting to *fedayeen* control. Ben Gurion also made it quite clear that he distinguished very sharply between "UN guarantees" that were worthless and probably unobtainable, and American guarantees that might satisfy our basic interests. I now set to work, together with Shiloah at the embassy and Kidron in our UN delegation, to ensure that our withdrawal would be exchanged for new situations in the Gulf and in the Gaza Strip.

I decided to make the focus of our effort the situation in the Straits of Tiran. Here, after all, was the possibility of a major change in Israel's geopolitical dimensions. If we could keep that artery open in the ensuing years, we would be saved from our exclusive dependence on the West across the Mediterranean. It would be possible to open an oil route to the Persian Gulf and to weave a network of connections and relationships with East Africa and Asia. This was one of the central visions that had inspired us in accepting the UN partition idea. It had been virtually frustrated by our exclusion from the Indian Ocean through the dual blockade in the Suez Canal and in the Gulf of Aqaba. I thought I could play on the inherent absurdity of returning to a status quo that meant the restoration of an illicit blockade. The idea of the United Nations exchanging an open international waterway for a blockaded one seemed to me to hold enough absurdity to make our persuasion feasible.

I therefore laid down a heavy bombardment of speeches, memoranda, meetings, pressures, influences all over the United States, with a special concentration on Dulles himself and on leaders in the Congress. I developed a close relationship with Dulles' legal adviser, Herman Phleger, because I had noticed the juridical emphasis in Dulles' way of thought. International law was once described as "the law that the righteous do not need and the wicked do not obey." I knew well that it is more frequent for legal advisers in Foreign Offices to give juridical sanction to what their ministers want than for ministers to change their policies as a result of legal advice. Nevertheless, if Dulles could be persuaded that there was a strong legality in our demand for an open waterway, I thought it unlikely that he would stubbornly insist on a return to belligerency and blockade.

In addition to Phleger, another ally was the senior American diplomat Robert Murphy, who had won fame as Roosevelt's representative during Eisenhower's military rule in North Africa. His experience had given him a special prestige with the President.

At the United Nations, Henry Cabot Lodge was less vehement and abrasive toward us now that we had offered to withdraw, but I feared that he was more closely influenced by Hammarskjöld's legalism than by the currents of thought in his own capital. Moreover, he was attracted by the idea projected by Vice-President Richard Nixon in a speech in December 1956, according to which the United States should take pride in having cut loose from its "colonialist allies" in order to adopt an independent attitude of friendship to the "developing world."

It had been agreed in my exchanges with Ben Gurion, through Yaacov Herzog, that I would fight to get American support on our case on Eilat and Gaza while, at home, we would take delaying action. We would withdraw in installments, quickly enough to avoid a political showdown with the UN and the United States, but not so quickly as to bring our forces out of Sinai and Gaza before achieving our minimal demands. When Hammarskjöld asked me, "Do you mean that your withdrawal is to be conditional on your getting your way?," I replied that words were of no importance to me at this stage. I was willing to abandon the principle of "conditionality" and to say that we insisted that our "unconditional" withdrawal should have "accompanying circumstances" including the abolition of the blockade and the establishment of peaceful conditions on the Gaza border.

In early February we went through a period of anxiety when King Saud of Saudi Arabia visited the United States and insisted fanatically that Israeli forces leave Sinai and Gaza that very week if the United States wanted oil supplies and bases. On this occasion, to my relief, Eisenhower and Dulles stood firm. The United States believed that Israel would withdraw, but it insisted on being given time to create suitable "circumstances" for the withdrawal.

In addition to the mobilization of congressional leaders and Administration figures, I was able to enlist the help of many elder statesmen who were close to the levers of power. I have always been impressed by the ability of U.S. Presidents and Secretaries of State to have recourse to distinguished people who hold no official position, but whose disinterested advice is warmly received. I had a close relationship with Arthur Dean, who was John Foster Dulles' law partner in Wall Street; with General Lucius Clay, the hero of Berlin, later a corporation president in New York; with John J. McCloy, who had been High Commissioner of the United States in Germany; with General Walter Bedell Smith, who had been Under-Secretary of State with Dulles, and even after retirement, had a closer relationship with President Eisenhower than Secretary Dulles was ever able to obtain; and with Robert Anderson, later to be Secretary of Defense, whose traumatic experience in Cairo in early 1956 had given him a warm understanding of our cause.

At last, in early February, the ice began to melt. Robert Murphy came to have breakfast with me in my home on Juniper Street. He told me that my latest memorandum on the illegality of the blockade in the Gulf of Eilat (Aqaba) had made a strong impression on Dulles and Phleger. He now wanted to ask me a straight question. "Which of your two demands is the most important? Free passage in the Gulf of Eilat or an international regime in Gaza?"

I told him that it was like asking a man whether he gave greater affection to his mother or his father, but that if I had to give a personal estimate, I would say that the maintenance of an open waterway at Eilat was a more stable and profound geopolitical interest than a situation in Gaza that could at best be temporary. On the other hand, I refused to believe that it was impossible to give substantive satisfaction to each of our demands. Even if we got full satisfaction about the Gulf of Eilat, we would not be able to withdraw unless we had a reasonable, if not watertight, assurance that Gaza would not again become a *fedayeen* nest.

Murphy said that he understood my reply perfectly. The point was that the United States had a greater capacity to satisfy our claims of free passage in the Gulf than to change the situation in Gaza, where Egypt had a contractual position under the armistice agreement. On the other hand, he felt that world opinion might be less opposed to a prolongation of Israel's tenure in Gaza if it thought that Israel would fully absorb into its own economy and society the 300,000 Arab refugees who were languishing in camps in that zone.

From this conversation onward, I felt that we were on a favorable road. I could afford to listen with patient skepticism to Nahum Goldmann, who, under Hammarskjöld's influence, was telling me that the United States would never offer Israel anything in the Gulf of Eilat or in Gaza in return for our withdrawal, which would have to be unconditional. Israel, said Goldmann, according to Hammarskjöld, would not be allowed to gain anything from its military initiative. It was, therefore, a waste of time to prolong the withdrawal.

One of my major assets was that the two party leaders in the Senate, Lyndon B. Johnson and William K. Knowland, were in close personal touch with me. They were in a mood to make the Eisenhower Administration's response to Israel's requests a condition for their support of the Administration's other proposals in the Middle East. Knowland announced that he had been affronted by the fact that the United Nations had surrendered to Soviet force in Hungary. If it now applied to Israel the kind of pressures that it refused to apply to the Soviet Union, he would regard the United Nations as a mischievous organization and would symbolize this by resigning from the United States delegation. Lyndon Johnson was no less emphatic. One day he called me at my embassy office and said, "Are they negotiating seriously with you [about Gaza and Aqaba]?" I asked him why he wanted to know. He replied that there was legislation in the Senate which he had the power to speed up or to slow down, and that he would be influenced by whether or not the Administration was "honestly trying" to come to terms with Israel. In his view the problems of Aqaba and Gaza were not so insoluble as to make it justifiable for the United States to apply punitive measures. If time is needed, then—hell—let time be given. By the second week of February I was able to cable to Herzog for Ben Gurion and Golda Meir that I saw "a breakthrough on the early horizon."

I had given Dulles a detailed memorandum on the Straits of Tiran on January 2. My theme was that Israel had endured a serious deprivation for eight years during which the straits had been closed to its shipping. My memorandum went beyond the juridical aspect to touch on a larger vision; a new artery of maritime communication linking the continents of the old world, depriving Suez of its monopoly and reducing Europe's explosive dependence on a single oil route which Egypt could open and close at will. By early February I had received encouraging comments on this memorandum from diplomats, jurists and political scientists. I had been told that Herman Phleger had recommended it to Dulles' favorable study.

Thus, when Dulles invited me to see him on February 11, I already knew that we had passed from confrontation to negotiation with the United States. In a memorandum to UN members on January 24, Hammarskjöld had come very close to the idea that even a sinful and illegal status quo must be restored if it had been changed by illicit force. He stressed that the status-quo principle forbade any Israeli presence, military or civilian, in Gaza; and that although the question of the Gulf of Eilat had a special character, it was important that the Israeli military action should "have no effect on its solution"! Hammarskjöld was thus becoming a blind defender of all pre–October 1956 situations. Everything had to be put back where it was, including the gasoline-soaked bonfire as close as possible to the box of matches. Not a single spark of political imagination illuminated the arid wastes of his legalism. Even his juridical doctrine was subjective. Hammarskjöld had some high and low moments in his extraordinary career. His reaction to the Middle Eastern security balance in the fifties was surely his lowest ebb. Even State Department officials, who had usually been rather worshipful of the Secretary-General, were now finding him hard to take. Ralph Bunche, normally a model of hierarchical loyalty, took me into his confidence one day for sad complaints about his chief, who, in his words, "sometimes tends to go berserk."

Robert Murphy had been correct in advising me to seek a settlement in the American context rather than at the UN. He also continued to emphasize that we should attach more importance to the Straits of Tiran issue than to the question of Gaza. These constructive thoughts were now having their effects on Lodge at the UN. On January 29 he had said, "It is important that units of the UNEF should be stationed in the Straits of Tiran to separate the forces of Israel and Egypt by land and sea, wherever such separation is essential until it becomes evident that there is no exercise of belligerent rights, and that passage in those waters which are of international significance goes forward peacefully." Lodge went on to say that the Assembly could not be satisfied "with a return to the disquieting situation which has brought about recent hostilities."

Our information campaign during January had spectacular success on the Eilat issue. Nearly all the reputable newspapers ridiculed the idea that the UN should restore a condition of belligerent blockade. On the other hand, I had to tell Jerusalem in all frankness that the same intense efforts devoted to a defense of our Gaza position were not having a similar result. With King Saud back home after his embarrassing Washington visit, the United States, despairing of any salvation from Hammarskjöld, decided to take the matter into its own hands.

In my meeting with Dulles on February 11, I was accompanied by Shiloah. The Secretary was attended by Murphy and Fraser Wilkins. Dulles began by reading the text of an *aide-mémoire*. The main points were that if Israel withdrew from Sinai and Gaza, the United States would announce its intention to exercise free passage in the Straits of Tiran and to encourage others to exercise that right. It would support the presence of the UN force in Sharm el-Sheikh and Gaza for as long as necessary to avoid a recrudescence of belligerency.

Before I could respond, Dulles went on to say that the memorandum should be regarded as giving substantial satisfaction to Israel's positions. I said that it was clearly an important document and I would pass it to my government without delay. The question in our mind would be: To what degree does the memorandum guarantee that there will be no return to the vulnerabilities and illegalities out of which the October war erupted? Dulles replied that the United States had been sympathetic to Israeli aims before the war, and had only considered that the methods which Israel, Britain and France had used were erroneous and dangerous. The United States still believed that Israel's legitimate aims could be achieved by political means. He therefore wanted us to take a serious look at the American commitment on free passage in the paper that he had handed to me. Was not an American engagement far more valuable than a dubious declaration by Egypt on abstention from belligerency? He referred to what I had told him in previous talks about our plans for an oil pipeline from Eilat to the coast. He said that if Israel remained with its forces at Sharm el-Sheikh, there might well be a pipeline, but it was doubtful that anybody would put any oil into it.

I now asked him to clarify the American position on Gaza. Would the Israeli withdrawal be only of military forces or also of civilian personnel? Dulles was evasive. He said that he was not "well versed" in that problem and that the United States had not taken a definite position.

There was a sound of deep urgency in his voice. He said that the United States wanted to get into a posture of cooperation with Israel on the serious matters common to the two countries. There was a lot of talk of sanctions in the air, but such talk was not serious. "What are sanctions?" he said. "Surely the most serious sanction that could be inflicted on America and Israel would be a position in which these two enlightened governments would be shown incapable of cooperating in a pragmatic attempt to allay tension in the area. It would be disastrous if we are forced to confess failure."

Since I did not want to prejudice our bargaining position, I avoided further comment and broke off the conversation. Shiloah and I went to lunch with Murphy, who asked us to regard the memorandum as a sensational development. The United States would get the other maritime powers to join the doctrine of free and innocent passage in the Gulf of Eilat. The essence of the guarantee lay in the clear recognition that each maritime power would have a right to protect its own shipping. This would apply to Israel as well. The UN force would symbolize this freedom and ensure the absence of Egyptian soldiers. Murphy pressed me hard to get at least a preliminary favorable reply by February 14, that is, within three days. Our Foreign Minister, Golda Meir, had now reached UN headquarters, where she was leading our delegation, while I concentrated on the Washington scene. She recommended to Jerusalem that we regard the memorandum as "a basis for discussion," subject to working out more solid arrangements, especially in Gaza.

In the evening Dulles assembled press representatives and gave a detailed lecture on free passage in the Straits of Tiran. The American and world press wrote frankly of "a major Israeli success." Yet our tactical situation was more difficult. All friendly newspapers now released Dulles from their pressure and turned on us with an exigent hope that Israel would utilize the opening that had now been offered. The Washington *Post,* which had given us ardent support, wrote on February 13 that "it is now Israel's turn to be reasonable." The *New York Times* and the New York *Herald Tribune* spoke in a similar vein. James Reston called me three times that day to emphasize, with some emotion, that Israel would make a grave error if she neglected a historic opportunity to transform her status in the Red Sea and the Gulf of Eilat and—no less important—to achieve a new atmosphere of understanding with the United States.

Twelve maritime powers were approached by the United States with a request to join in elaborating the doctrine of free and innocent passage. At the United Nations the Arab delegates were in some confusion. Many of them were hoping that Israel would turn down the American proposition and that the punitive anti-Israeli atmosphere could be reconstructed.

I sent Ben Gurion a long cable explaining why I thought a propitious turning point had come. While we should bargain meticulously on specific issues, I thought that it would be an error to reject the February 11 memorandum. We should do everything to keep the UN General Assembly out of the picture, and in order to achieve this, we should give our assent to Dulles in principle and pursue a detailed discussion in greater leisure. Ben Gurion sent me his reactions on February 12. In effect his main conclusions were:

1. The memorandum showed a desire to achieve a positive solution, but the suggested solution was not positive, and we could not accept it.
2. There was no specific guarantee to protect Israeli shipping and the concept of free passage was limited to "innocent passage."
3. We could not possibly go back to the armistice agreement.
4. We could not agree to the stationing of UN forces at Nitsana (El Auja).
5. In Gaza there was room for compromise. We would agree to evacuate it on condition that the Egyptians did not come back; and that an Israeli civilian authority would cooperate with the UN for the benefit of the inhabitants of the area.

Ben Gurion added that we could not change the positions that he had outlined even if sanctions were threatened.

I could see that Ben Gurion had either failed in his usual perspicacity or, more probably, was under domestic pressures. The complaint about passage being "only innocent" seemed bizarre. "Innocent passage" only excluded trade in illicit traffic such as narcotics and white slaves. I did not imagine that our Zionist vision of the southern Negev had anything so picturesque or exotic in mind. I pointed out that even the passage of warships was not excluded by the term "innocent passage." I could not for the life of me understand what Ben Gurion's reference to Nitsana was about, since the Dulles memorandum contained no indication of stationing UN forces anywhere except in Gaza and in the Straits. In my cable home I said that the chief value of the memorandum lay in its treatment of the Straits of Tiran problem, rather than Gaza. I concluded by saying that a frontal rejection of the American memorandum would not bring us any serious support from our friends.

On February 15 I gave Dulles a new memorandum from Ben Gurion which expressed reluctant satisfaction over some elements in the February 11 *aide-mémoire,* but which still argued suspiciously about the text. I told Dulles that we were all impressed by his statement that "the United States would take a heavy responsibility if Israel were to withdraw and the blockade were to be renewed." Nevertheless, we were worried by the prospect that this was exactly what would happen if we withdrew before a peace agreement was concluded.

When Dulles read the Ben Gurion memorandum, his disappointment was vast. He said that in his opinion the government of Israel had failed to understand the spirit of the American initiative. The United States was not strictly making "proposals to Israel." As a member of the United Nations it could use its influence, and as a maritime power it could unilaterally carry out a certain policy toward the Gulf and the Straits which would, in fact, create a new international law. If Israel was not interested in taking up the American initiative, the matter would have to go back to the United Nations, where he doubted that Israel could get any worthwhile guarantees at all.

I told Dulles that I thought he was exaggerating the gap between our positions and that we should both strive to give time for mature and detailed consideration.

In a cable to Jerusalem on February 16 I pointed out that in my appraisal the Dulles *aide-mémoire* was the optimal American position, apart from improvements that might arise in a detailed negotiation. I was certain that the President had given his assent to this approach. Friendly newspapers, congressmen and others were beginning to think that Israel was unreasonable. The only way to avoid a crisis was to accept the document as a basis for detailed negotiation and to avoid generalized rejection.

The Israeli government's vacillation was beginning to irritate the United States. On February 16 Dulles came back to Washington from Georgia and invited me to his home, where I found Phleger; Francis Wilcox, the head of the UN department; and Rountree. Dulles was irascible and impatient. If we did not see any value in the American initiative, the best thing that we could do would be "to try our luck elsewhere." "The President and I know that Israel faces a grave choice," he added, "but we believe that our proposals offer desirable results. The policy of the United States does not flow from transitory considerations. There is a real attempt to create a new pattern of stability in the area. This is a matter of supreme importance. If Israel accepts the American proposal and withdraws from Gaza and Sinai, America and all mankind will owe a great debt to Israel. I believe that the debt will be paid." I asked what the United States would do if, despite everything, Egyptian illegalities were renewed. Dulles replied that he was not a pacifist and that the United States understood the heavy responsibility that it would incur if, after Israel's withdrawal, we were the victims of renewed aggression or blockade.

We were not getting anywhere and the room was thick with tension. I promised to report to Ben Gurion and Golda Meir and added that I expected that my government would invite me home to hear a more detailed description of what had occurred. However, if the

General Assembly were to start talking about sanctions, this would prevent any favorable consideration of the American proposals. I therefore suggested that the United States should postpone the UN session.

I had invented the idea of my return to Israel as a desperate way to postpone the crisis and to rescue the accumulated results of our work over the past four months. I was also convinced that long argumentative cables would not bring about the necessary harmony between Ben Gurion and myself about our attitude to the Dulles proposals.

That evening the State Department published the February 11 memorandum. We were told of a consultation between Eisenhower and Dulles in which the President had shown impatience with Ben Gurion's attitude. The newspaper friendliest to Israel, the New York *Journal-American,* published by the Hearst press, wrote on February 19: "President Eisenhower has placed his tremendous influence and this nation's prestige behind his assurances to Israel. Further than that, he does not feel he should go. Further than that, we do not think he should go."

When I assembled the staffs of the embassy and the UN delegation on February 16, I summed up the position by saying, "I am afraid that our government will not take yes for an answer." It was a peculiarly frustrating moment. It appeared to me that in the zest of waging the conflict, some of our leaders had forgotten what the conflict had been about. Unlike the British and French expeditions, which were imprecise in their goals, the Israeli war aims had been carefully formulated by Ben Gurion before the October 29 operations began. He had two direct objectives: to open a sea route from Eilat to the east and to expel the Egyptian army from Gaza. Corollary objectives included the aim of making the United States react more seriously to the provocations under which we had lived.

It was obvious to me since the February 11 memorandum that all these aims were attainable. We had made a major breakthrough. If we rejected the opportunity of an agreement with the United States, the question would be thrown back into the chaotic and sterile maelstrom of the United Nations. I told Ben Gurion that for Israel, the United Nations was "a beehive without honey." We got all the stings with no compensating advantage. Ben Gurion was refusing to recognize the immensity of his own victory.

Ben Gurion now formally asked me to come home. I went to say farewell to Dulles before my departure on the afternoon of February 17. He was again accompanied by Phleger, Wilcox and Rountree. This meeting was downright unpleasant. I gave Dulles an account of

Ben Gurion's comments on the February 11 memorandum. Dulles interrupted me while he talked to President Eisenhower. When I resumed my analysis, Dulles cut me short by saying that what I had to say was very interesting but "was not of much use since the government of Israel had apparently decided not to accept the American proposal, even in principle." He said that he had done everything possible to put off the UN debate which would spoil every prospect of a solution, but he doubted if he could do any more. He said that he felt we were on "the verge of a catastrophe." The most serious possibility ever achieved of cooperation between Israel and the United States was going to be wasted, and we were going to enter a period of tension between our two countries. He presumed that Ben Gurion had carefully weighed all the dangers inherent in this course, against the bright prospects available from negotiating on the basis of the American memorandum. If so, he was unable to understand how Israel had reached such an eccentric conclusion.

While I was in the air on the way home, Eisenhower made a broadcast to the American people. He took credit for a major effort to allay Israel's concerns. He expressed the fear that if Israel was unreasonable, the United States would "have to adopt measures which might have far-reaching effects on Israel's relations throughout the world." Despite the vigorous nature of this speech, Silver called Shiloah to say that the object of Eisenhower's address was not to close the door but to leave it open, and above all, to gain time for my mission home.

The Administration was now making an interesting attempt to soften the Israeli position by influencing Jewish leaders. Through the Secretary of the Treasury, George Humphrey, a meeting was arranged with a number of Jewish leaders, most of whom would normally be described as "non-Zionist." These included Jacob Blaustein, Irving Engel, Philip Klutznik, Barney Balaban, Bill Rosenwald, Sam Leidersdorf, Mendel Silberberg. The meeting took place on February 21, and to the Administration's astonishment, the leaders of what was regarded as the "assimilated" part of American Jewry spoke defiantly in defense of all Israel's positions.

After a tiring journey I reached Jerusalem and took part in Cabinet sessions throughout February 21 and 22. In talks with me Ben Gurion paid generous tribute to the results of my diplomatic and information efforts over the past four months, and especially to my speech on November 1. I reported my own conclusions to the Cabinet: we had reached the optimal results of our pressure and should now turn from polemics to negotiation. There was at least the prospect of a settlement which would ensure free passage in the Straits of Tiran, prevent a return of the Egyptian army to Gaza, and obligate the United States to make a supreme effort to avoid dangers to Israel's security.

While I was in Jerusalem, Ben Gurion received a personal letter from General Bedell Smith, whom he regarded as Israel's staunchest friend. Bedell Smith, a rough-hewn soldier, with a no-nonsense type of mentality, thin, scholarly and bespectacled, looked less like a general than any general that had ever lived. He now drew fully on the confidence that he enjoyed with Israel's leaders. He wrote to Ben Gurion bluntly that he ought to give "some flexibility to Eban," who was "perfectly capable of reaching a negotiation which would ensure stability for many years."

I found that my presence in Jerusalem had a marked effect on Ben Gurion. The instructions that he gave me now were to aim at a detailed clarification of what each sentence of the February 11 memorandum meant. On February 22 Ben Gurion cabled Eisenhower in reply to the message he had received from Eisenhower late the night before. Ben Gurion stated that the Israeli government had been holding discussions all day with me, and had examined the report that I gave of the views of the American government. He informed Eisenhower that I would leave the next morning with new instructions expressing the considered position of Ben Gurion himself and his colleagues. He concluded by saying that he hoped the United Nations discussions could be put off until Monday in order to enable me to see Dulles before the Assembly convened.

Owing to weather delays, my plane from Israel to New York reached London at an hour when there was no further service to the United States. Since I had to stay in London overnight, I had long conversations with Ambassador Elath and his minister, Shmuel Bendor, but avoided any meeting with British officials. Obsessed by the collusion trauma of the previous October, Secretary Dulles was apparently in a suspicious mood. He instructed the American chargé d'affaires, Walworth Barbour, to keep a close watch and report if I made contact with the British authorities before resuming my onward journey. The British newspapers were giving enormous coverage to my journey, and the atmosphere of tension was thick.

On February 24, in the early morning, I touched down in New York. I reported on my discussion in Jerusalem to Golda Meir and met Arthur Dean in the hope that he would "soften up" Dulles before I reached Washington. In my talks with Golda I was able to solve a mystery that had worried both of us. What exactly was Ben Gurion's long-term position about Israel and the Gaza Strip? When I had discussed this with him in Jerusalem, he reacted with sharp and vocal alarm: "Gaza as a part of Israel could be like a cancer.

In return for a small sliver of territory we would take responsibility for some two hundred and fifty to three hundred thousand Arabs. How can we absorb three hundred thousand Arabs against the will of mankind, while also hoping to receive hundreds of thousands of our own immigrants? Our interest in Gaza is security. To take a small territory with a vast Arab population would be the worst possible exchange." He added that my purpose should be "to find an elegant way for us to avoid any permanent responsibility for the entire population of Gaza." In no circumstances should we accept a proposal that would commit Israel to the absorption of an enormous Arab population that would prejudice the internal cohesion of the state.

When I reached Dulles' home on February 24, weary but full of the zest of challenge, I found the street thronged with newspapermen. I was accompanied by Shiloah. On the American side were Dulles, Under-Secretary Christian Herter, Phleger, Wilcox and Rountree. Dulles said that in response to the Prime Minister's request, the United States had managed to put off any detrimental action in the General Assembly.

I told Dulles that I found the Prime Minister unwilling to get into conflict with the United States. He had been impressed by the American attitude since February 11, and wanted me to reach a conclusion. I would ask for clarification of the American commitment on the Straits of Tiran. We would propose that recognition of our right to free navigation in the Straits of Tiran and the Gulf of Eilat should not be made conditional on the removal of our civilian administration from Gaza. I would suggest a separation of the two issues. We proposed that as soon as we left Sharm el-Sheikh, the American commitment on free passage should go into effect, leaving the problem of Gaza for later solution.

When I finished my exposition, there was a tense silence which Dulles broke with a statement of relief: "Your attitude is constructive." He asked for a short interval to consult his colleagues. When we resumed twenty minutes later, Dulles repeated that having studied my reply, he felt that the Israeli government had made a sincere effort to find a solution. Several details still remained for clarification, but he was now convinced that when an agreement was reached, we would have no reason to regret our attitude. We then conducted a kind of Socratic inquiry by question and answer so that I could send Ben Gurion a precise account of the assurances that I had obtained. First I asked if U.S. shipping would regularly use the Straits of Tiran for actual trade, including the conveyance of oil to Eilat, when appropriate facilities were constructed. Dulles said yes. I asked if the United States understood "free and innocent passage" to mean passage of all ships of commerce and war, provided their conduct did no injury. Dulles accepted this definition. I asked if the UN Force in the Straits could include naval units. Dulles said that this was reasonable and the UN Secretary-General had the necessary authority. I asked if the United States would recognize an Israeli declaration announcing our intention to protect Israeli ships and their rights against attack. Dulles said that the United States would recognize the right under Article 51 of the UN Charter as an exercise of the "inherent right of self-defense."

In response to other questions Dulles promised to secure the association of other maritime countries with the American policy of free passage in the Straits. He said that if there was an attempt to remove the UN Force, the United States would expect the General Assembly to consider the request before such withdrawal was made. He agreed to my request for a restatement of the U.S. position according to which the UN Force would remain as long as necessary to prevent a blockade. He also consented to my request for a letter by the President to Prime Minister Ben Gurion reiterating American commitments. I reaffirmed the Israeli position on Gaza. Dulles replied that it was hard to imagine Egypt abrogating her rights in Gaza under the 1949 Armistice Agreement, but it was possible for Egypt to acquiesce in the nonexercise of those rights and in their exercise by the UN.

Dulles said that the answers he had given me would be embodied or reflected in the United States speech in the General Assembly.

It had been an exhausting day, and I came out of Dulles' residence with a feeling that we had broken through. I cabled the exchange to Jerusalem.

I noted that two or three items in Dulles' assurances needed the endorsement of Secretary-General Hammarskjöld. Accordingly, I flew to New York for a meeting with him. We conferred for three hours, during which the hopes of an early solution faded minute by minute. Hammarskjöld refused to endorse Dulles' readiness to have a UN navy patrol in the Straits of Tiran. Far more serious was his utter refusal to recognize any legitimate Israeli interest in the future of Gaza, and he handed me a memorandum to this effect. At the end of our discussion Hammarskjöld said that he had no way of holding up the General Assembly meeting beyond February 26.

After my talk with Hammarskjöld I called Dulles urgently on the telephone from New York. I told him that Hammarskjöld was frustrating our agreement. He was not only unhelpful in the Straits of Tiran; he seemed to envisage nothing better for Gaza than a return to the status quo, leaving Israel with no assurance of security. I felt that unless we could separate Gaza from the Straits of Tiran, we might end up with a sterile result on both of them. Dulles replied that he would still like to reach an integral solution of all the problems together.

The next day, February 25, I was back in Washington talking with Dulles, Phleger, Wilcox and Rountree in the early afternoon. Dulles reiterated that it was impossible to separate the Gaza problem from that of the Straits of Tiran. The legal basis for the American commitment on free passage in the Straits was the absence of belligerency in accordance with the Security Council's resolution of September 1, 1951. But if Israel remained in the "illicit" possession of Egyptian territory in Gaza, it could not be said that belligerency had ended. Thus the legal consequences of our military presence in Gaza would spill over into the Straits of Tiran and frustrate the application of the American commitment.

We seemed to be in a deadlock. It was here that Dulles made an unexpected approach. He informed us that the Prime Minister and Foreign Minister of France, Guy Mollet and Christian Pineau, were in Washington on an official visit. The French leaders had made a proposal which Eisenhower and Dulles thought might help to solve the deadlock. Dulles suggested that I see Pineau right away; he himself did not feel competent to reveal the content of the proposal, since it was French and not American. But if Israel found the French suggestion "interesting," Eisenhower and Dulles would give it their support.

This was the first time that we had heard of a French initiative to solve the Gaza problem. I immediately went to the French embassy with Shiloah, to be cordially greeted by Pineau, who was accompanied by Ambassador Hervé Alphand. Pineau said that instead of a discursive verbal discussion, he would give me a memorandum in the original French, together with a translation that he had made for Eisenhower. The French memorandum suggested that Israel announce complete withdrawal in accordance with UN resolutions, on the understanding that the initial takeover of Gaza from Israeli military and civilian control would be exclusively by the UN Emergency Force; that the United Nations would be the agency used for civilian administration; that UN administration would continue until a peace settlement; and that if Egypt created conditions of deterioration such as existed previously, "Israel would reserve its freedom to act to defend its rights." The memo went on to suggest that the United States and other states that so decided would approve Israel's declaration.

The new element in Pineau's proposal was the idea that Israel, with American assent, should specifically reserve her right to return to Gaza if her withdrawal was followed by renewed *fedayeen* activities.

Just as the United States had recognized our right of self-defense in relation to the Straits of Tiran, so France was proposing a similar recognition of Israel's right of self-defense in the event that our security in the vicinity of Gaza was violated after withdrawal. Pineau pointed out that another objective that France had in mind was to circumvent the awkward fact that we had no majority in the United Nations. Instead of asking for UN endorsement of our positions, the United States, France and Israel would state their view of the international and legal situation and get the General Assembly to acquiesce passively. Pineau was certain that there would not be a majority to vote against what we were saying. There was even a chance that Egypt, which was getting impatient at Israeli occupation, might keep silent in order to secure our withdrawal.

In my cable to Jerusalem I wrote that there were still some problems of formulation, procedure and law that were obscure but that our government should decide in principle if we were prepared to make common cause with the United States and France to establish a special regime in Gaza based on UN control and without Egyptian forces. I recommended a positive answer.

Most of the literature on the end of the Sinai-Suez campaigns does inadequate justice to the French role in breaking the deadlock. In September 1976 Christian Pineau published his version of this episode with a measure of pride.

As I expected, the French initiative had a decisive effect on the Israeli government's attitude. The instructions that I got back from Ben Gurion enabled me to go forward with the formulation of a settlement based on the U.S. memorandum of February 11 and the new French suggestions. The idea was that the United States, France and others should endorse the Israeli Foreign Minister's speech in the General Assembly in which Mrs. Meir would base our withdrawal on the "assumption" of free passage in the Straits of Tiran; the expectation of the maintenance of a UN force until such time as belligerency ended; and the establishment of UN, not Egyptian, control in the Gaza Strip. Israel would announce that if these "expectations and assumptions" were wrecked by Egyptian aggression, Israel would exercise its right of self-defense and would be supported by the United States, France and other countries.

After my talks with Pineau in the French embassy I worked for many hours with State Department officials to formulate our common understanding. Then an unusual episode in modern diplomacy took place. The speech to be made by the Israeli Foreign Minister in the General Assembly was to be not only concerted but actually drafted in advance with the United States. It was arranged that when we were close to an agreed text, Mrs. Meir would come from New York to join us at a meeting with Dulles.

By the afternoon of February 28 Dulles, Pineau and I had agreed to the text which would be endorsed by Washington and Paris and proclaimed by Israel in the General Assembly.

With regard to the Straits of Tiran, the Israeli speech would reiterate the doctrine of free passage laid down in the February 11 memorandum and would announce "Israel's intention to protect ships of its flag exercising the right of free and innocent passage on the high seas and in international waters." We would go on to state that interference by the use or threat of force with ships under Israeli flag exercising free passage of the Gulf of Aqaba and through the Straits of Tiran "will be regarded by Israel as an attack, entitling her to exercise her inherent right of self-defense under Article 51 of the Charter, and to take all such measures as are necessary to ensure the free passage of her ships in the Gulf and in the Straits." On the Gaza problem Mrs. Meir's speech would be a detailed recital of Pineau's proposal, including the idea that Israel would have a recognized right to defend itself if raids were renewed.

While our discussions were going forward with State Department officials, a message came saying that the Secretary himself would like to join our deliberations. We went down to his room and proceeded with the drafting process. Dulles himself suggested certain changes:

1. Whereas our text spoke of "complete withdrawal" from Sharm el-Sheikh and Gaza, the Secretary suggested "complete and prompt withdrawal."
2. Whereas I had written that interference "by the use or threat of force" would justify Israeli reaction, Dulles insisted on a more cautious phrase. He would agree to say that we should be entitled to react only if there was actual "interference by armed force," and not merely a "threat."
3. Instead of saying that the UN force would remain in position in Gaza "until a peace agreement was reached," Dulles insisted on adding the phrase "or a definitive arrangement on the future of the Gaza Strip."

At this stage Dulles told us that Lodge would be instructed to give American endorsement to the agreed text of Mrs. Meir's speech. I asked if we could see or hear exactly what Lodge would say. According to Dulles, they were only now beginning to draft Lodge's declaration, but he assured us that it would include all the agreements that we had reached with him. When Mrs. Meir joined us to work on the final draft of her impending speech, the understandings we reached became an American-Israeli contract in every real sense.

Before February 28 was out, Dulles and Wilcox had met with the ambassadors of Britain and Canada, as well as representatives of the French embassy. Dulles read out the Israeli declaration and received assurances that France, Canada and Britain would almost certainly give their support.

We had now completed the negotiations. Mrs. Meir had given her assent to the text and gone back to New York. Before leaving for the United Nations meeting on March 1, I asked Dulles for a private meeting. I wanted to stress the importance of making sure that there would be no Egyptian return to Gaza. I still felt uneasy that there was some ambivalence on this point. Dulles invited me to his home that night and we spoke for forty minutes, alone.

I said that our decision to cooperate with Pineau's plan was based on the assumption that there would be no Egyptian return to Gaza in any form, directly or indirectly. For us this was a fundamental and central consideration. It was, therefore, disquieting that the implementation would depend on Hammarskjöld. It was important that I should hear that very evening what exactly the American attitude was on this problem.

Dulles got up from his chair and spoke without interruption for twenty minutes. As he walked up and down the room he said that he welcomed this unofficial opportunity to talk to me frankly. "I assume that you know what a big political victory Israel is getting today," he went on. "The opening of the Gulf of Eilat as an international waterway is ensured with almost a hundred percent of certainty. In Gaza, the era of exclusive Egyptian control is over, and from now on the effective control will be with the United Nations. This also is an important gain for you. In addition, you are gaining something no less important—the strengthening of friendship between America and Israel. The Arabs have a completely accurate appraisal of the situation and they are not attempting to disguise their disappointment. They don't really want you to evacuate Sharm el-Sheikh and Gaza at all. Their real desire is that you continue to occupy those places and become weakened and isolated, and especially that you lose your support in the United States. Your cooperation with the United States and France will strengthen Israel's international position beyond recognition. As for Gaza, the American attitude is clear. We want an international regime without Egypt there at all. Egypt has no good reason to return to Gaza which was never a part of sovereign Egyptian territory. The scheme which we have worked out with Mollet and Pineau is designed to prevent Egyptian return to Gaza, both military or political. But the United States is not omnipotent, even though there is an illusion in the world that it is enough for us to want something for that thing to happen. We are, however, not without influence. You can tell your government that the United States will do its utmost to ensure that Egypt does not come back to Gaza." He paused and went on, "I cannot guarantee full success. I can only guarantee a supreme effort to ensure this objective." He added, "What I am telling you is also the view of the French ministers. You don't have better friends than them and us." Then, with some emotion: "I have never concealed from you that your choice is difficult, but when I compare the arrangement that we've agreed upon today with the position that you would find yourself in by remaining in those two places against world opinion, I'm quite unable to imagine how the balance could be portrayed as anything but favorable." He ended by promising to talk to Hammarskjöld and Pineau.

On the morning of March 1, in an atmosphere of tension, Mrs. Meir went up to the UN rostrum to make an address containing the following passages:

> *Israel is resolved on behalf of vessels of Israel registry to·exercise the right of free and innocent passage and is prepared to join with others to secure universal respect of this right.*
>
> *Israel will protect ships of its own flag exercising the right of free and innocent passage on the high seas and in international waters. Interference, by armed force, with ships of Israel flag exercising free and innocent passage in the Gulf of Aqaba and through the Straits of Tiran, will be regarded by Israel as an attack entitling it to exercise its inherent right of self-defence under Article 51 of the Charter and to take all such measures as are necessary to ensure the free and innocent passage of its ships in the Gulf and in the Straits . . .*
>
> *. . . It is the position of Israel that if conditions are created in the Gaza Strip which indicate a return to the conditions of deterioration which existed previously, Israel would reserve its freedom to act to defend its rights.*

Mrs. Meir was succeeded at the rostrum by Henry Cabot Lodge. Throughout the morning we had made vain efforts to get a copy of the speech that Lodge intended to make. He had replied that the formulation was still not complete. When he made his speech it became apparent that this evasion had not been accidental. In discussing the issue of the Gulf of Aqaba, his statements were entirely satisfactory. But when he came to Gaza, there were serious deviations from the original Pineau-Dulles text. In the first place, he made a specific reference to the armistice agreement, which gave Egypt jurisdiction in Gaza. Our understanding with Dulles was that nothing would be said about the armistice agreement. The effect of this was to emphasize Egypt's juridical position in the Gaza area instead of leaving the question unresolved.

The speech by the French delegate, Georges Picot, was very strong. France made it plain that if Israel were to suffer Egyptian encroachments at Gaza or the Straits of Tiran, it would be fully entitled to use its right of self-defense. The British speech was satisfactory, as were those of other maritime countries. The Egyptian delegates sat silent.

On leaving the Assembly Hall, I called Dulles on the phone to complain bitterly about Lodge's references to Gaza. When I reached the hotel, I found an urgent invitation from Dulles to come and see him the next day, March 2, at home. I called him again and continued to express my surprise and indignation. Dulles said that he thought things had gone well during the day, but that if I was anxious, he was anxious because of my anxiety. He added that I ought to know that the Arab world was up in arms about the American-French-Israeli agreement. He implored me to ascertain that we would carry out our undertaking on withdrawal and get into immediate talk with General Burns, if possible by Sunday. The United States would be vigilant to ensure that what we had agreed upon would be carried out.

That afternoon Golda Meir, Emile Najar and I had a talk with Mollet and Pineau, who were accompanied by Alphand and Picot. Pineau thought that things had gone rather well in the General Assembly. On the Straits of Tiran, Lodge's speech was perfectly in order, and Pineau thought that the deviations about Gaza were merely "nuances." But he agreed that Alphand should go back to Washington the next day and strengthen my efforts to get Dulles to make a statement which would restore the situation to what it had been before Lodge's speech.

Later that day Pineau asked me for a personal talk. He said with great emotion that he hoped that we would continue on the path that we had begun. The important things were not parliamentary formulations or United Nations texts, but "reality." The reality was that France and the United States had agreed to ensure free passage in the Straits and to attempt to establish international control in Gaza. As a professional politician, he understood that we had internal problems. His advice was that we should present the situation in its true light as an important political victory. He urged us to announce by

Monday that we had begun to withdraw and that there should be common efforts by France and Israel in Washington to make certain that the United States kept its word.

The next morning, March 2, I was awakened by a telephone call from Jerusalem. Ben Gurion was on the line in great agitation. He asked me to make it clear that the changes that Lodge had introduced had caused confusion in Israel. The Cabinet would meet the next day to decide its attitude to withdrawal. I was asked to demand:

1. A clear American statement on UN control in Gaza with no Egyptian presence.
2. Recognition of Israel's right of self-defense in relation to the Straits and Gaza Strip.
3. An American undertaking not to press us to accept Hammarskjöld's proposal that in order for the UN force to be stationed in Gaza, there should be a symbolic UN presence on the Israeli side of the armistice line.

I was asked to lay special stress on the first two points. In an addendum from Yaacov Herzog, it was stated that if there was no response from the Secretary, I ought to hint to him or somebody else in the State Department that if the whole withdrawal plan exploded, we would have no choice but to publish the fact that we had been led astray by the American speech at the UN.

On that Sabbath afternoon, Shiloah and I spoke with Dulles and his advisers at his home. Dulles made no attempt to explain Lodge's speech, but he stated that American endorsement of Mrs. Meir's address was intact and complete. Dulles said that he was prepared to write a letter to Ben Gurion, giving strong assurances of American support of Israel's position in relation to the Straits of Tiran and the Gaza Strip. If I liked, he would publish the letter that very night. I replied, with as much delicacy as possible, that if it was intended to make an impression on Ben Gurion and the Israeli Cabinet, might it not be better for the President's authority to be invoked? Dulles and his advisers went out of the room for thirty minutes, leaving Shiloah and myself in exclusive possession of an excellent bottle of French cognac that had been presented to Dulles by Guy Mollet. I do no offense to Reuven Shiloah's memory if I record that his depredations on that bottle were more far-reaching than mine. When Dulles came back, he showed me the draft of a letter to be written by Eisenhower to Ben Gurion, strongly committing the United States to support Israel's rights in the Strait of Tiran and to be free from attack from Gaza.

At that moment the President did not know what we had "decided" that he should say. Dulles picked up the telephone in our presence and spoke to James Hagerty, the President's press secretary, who was with Eisenhower on his yacht on the Potomac. We had a bad connection, and I could hear the lapping waves through the receiver. Dulles said that it was essential to help Prime Minister Ben Gurion, who had made a difficult decision. It was vital that the President give him a letter in full support. Hagerty apparently said that he would get Eisenhower's assent as soon as possible.

Meanwhile, news came from Israel about our hesitations concerning withdrawal. This set off a spate of articles in the American press, urging Israel to carry out its undertaking. Most newspapers thought that the engagements of the American and French governments at the highest level were far more important than the precise text of Lodge's speech. Silver called me to praise Mrs. Meir's speech and to urge us not to reach any extreme conclusions as a result of Lodge's formulation.

The two French leaders had now reached Canada on an official visit. Alphand called me from his embassy to say on behalf of Pineau that with all the difficulties involved, the French leaders nevertheless strongly urged us not to create a crisis or to hold up our withdrawal because of Lodge's speech. "France is not going to press you in any way and the decision must remain in your hands."

When I told him about Eisenhower's letter to Ben Gurion, Alphand said that the French would be surprised. They never believed that it was possible to obtain such a declaration with the President's full authority. He then gave me the copy of a message that Pineau had sent to Dulles from Ottawa on March 3. This message outlined the French understanding of the situation resulting from the deliberations in the UN. The result, in the French view, would be that the UN would assume "the exclusive responsibility of the civil and military administration of Gaza until the conclusion of a peace treaty or of a definitive settlement of that area." In the event that the UN abandoned its responsibility in whole or part to Egypt, Israel would have the right to apply the safeguard clauses under Mrs. Meir's declaration.

The next day, March 4, Pineau sent a message to Ben Gurion through the French embassy in Washington with a copy to me describing the message that he had sent to Dulles.

When I added these French assurances on Gaza to the undertaking given by Eisenhower about the Straits of Tiran, the picture was clear. The two friendliest powers to Israel had not promised to fight for us if we were again blockaded or threatened by violence and terrorism, but they had certainly undertaken to support Israel if we took our own armed action to prevent a return to belligerent policies against us in Gaza or the Straits. We shall see in a later chapter what happened to these promises ten years later.

I attached importance to Eisenhower's letter and to the French assurances. In a long cable to Ben Gurion I advised him to make the most of these commitments. To my relief, I received a reply stating that in the light of my talk with Dulles, and especially Eisenhower's letter, the Prime Minister intended to accept the arrangement. Ben Gurion hoped that I might still try to get Dulles to make clearer undertakings of American support for Israel if I used our right of self-defense against provocations from Gaza. I sought out Dulles again. As I had expected, he was unwilling to go beyond the President's letter in writing. He felt quite certain that we had reduced our risks to the minimum. All he could suggest was that we meet a year from now and see who was right and who was wrong. Would there be free passage in the Gulf of Aqaba and the Straits of Tiran? Would there be a full year of peace behind us on the Gaza boundary? He was absolutely convinced that the answer would be yes, and that this would be the case for the following years as well.

Later that day the news came from Israel that we were carrying out our undertaking of withdrawal on the basis of Mrs. Meir's speech, which had been endorsed by the United States, France and others.

Seldom if ever have I spent weeks as exhausting as those which I lived between the end of October and the conclusion of our agreements with the United States and France. Taking advantage of the hospitality of friends in Florida, I went with Suzy and our two children to Palm Beach. After a couple of days of repose and diversion, I was awakened on March 11 with the news that the Egyptian government had announced its intention to resume its administration of the Gaza Strip. This was a violation not only of what we had been led to expect from the United States and France, but even of Hammarskjöld's statement that any attempt to interfere with the UN forces would first be discussed with the Advisory Committee, made up of states contributing contingents to the UN force. I went back to Washington for talks on March 13. I handed Acting Secretary of State Christian Herter a letter of protest from Ben Gurion that hinted at the possibility of Israeli action to prevent the Egyptian army from following the Egyptian administrators back to Gaza.

The return of the Egyptian administration to the Gaza Strip even without the Egyptian army shook Israel's faith in the stability of the settlement we had so laboriously reached. While the United States shared our disappointment, it still did not believe that the agreed arrangements had totally collapsed. When Mrs. Meir came to Washington on March 17 to express our concern to Secretary Dulles, he received her with courtesy. His attitude was that Nasser's reputation for unreliability was further enhanced. On the other hand, Dulles advised Mrs. Meir and me to regard the absence of the Egyptian army and the presence of the UN forces in Gaza as a radical change in our security situation. Similar advice came from the French government, which had taken the major responsibility for the Gaza paragraph of the settlement. Washington and Paris both predicted that Israel had achieved her major aim. After all, what did it matter if a UN or an Egyptian governor was in Gaza so long as the Egyptian army was removed from our throat and *fedayeen* operations were arrested through the presence of a UN force?

The optimistic prediction was, for once, destined to be fulfilled. Between March 1957 and May 1967, not a single episode of armed attack took place against Israel from the Gaza Strip.

With the final withdrawal of Israeli forces on March 19, the Sinai Campaign had come to an end. In a comprehensive article summarizing the campaign in his book *Netzach Yisrael,* Ben Gurion paid generous tribute to the work of the two missions over which I presided:

> *The great work accomplished by our Embassy in Washington and our delegation in the United Nations made a strong impression on American public opinion. The press, Congressional circles and intellectuals showed deep understanding of Israel's attitude and of the justice of her struggle. It was the result of pressure of public opinion that brought about a change in American opinion, leading to the final stage of our struggle on February 11, 1957 and thereafter.*

The next three years, 1956 to 1959, were to be as rewarding as the two years before the Sinai Campaign had been frustrating. The Eisenhower Administration made every effort to honor the President's prediction that Israel would not regret its action. During April 1957 I worked with Dulles and Herter to bring about a symbolic expression of our political victory. I wanted the first flag to pass through the Straits of Tiran to be that of the United States, both in order to commit the United States concretely to its doctrine of free passage, and also because I thought it less likely that Egypt would obstruct an American vessel than any other. On April 24 when the S.S. *Kernhills,* with many thousands of tons of crude oil, docked in Eilat, having passed under the gaze of the UN forces, the celebration in Israel was heartfelt and sincere.

All the aims that Ben Gurion had formulated for the Sinai Campaign on October 28 had been fulfilled. We had broken the blockade of our southern approaches. We had achieved peace in the areas surrounding the Gaza Strip. We had made the United States more careful and vigilant about Israel's moods and fears, and despite dark forebodings about "isolation," Israel's international relations were to flourish and expand.

End of a Mission:
First Steps in Politics
1957-1960

THE POLITICAL STRUGGLE SINCE OCTOBER 1956 HAD BEEN GLADIATORIAL AND
dramatic, and it had been conducted in full public view. My face and
voice were now known to cabdrivers, bellhops, shopkeepers and passers-by, as well as to the diplomatic community in which I worked.
This was not the usual fate of ambassadors, most of whom passed
without notice in the streets of Washington and New York. The inconvenient loss of privacy was offset by the advantage of wide resonance. I was also able, unexpectedly, to begin my publishing career.
Sam Raeburn of Horizon Press came to see me on the morrow of my
General Assembly address on November 1, 1956, to propose that I
publish my principal speeches. I was doubtful about this, since few
volumes of speeches have ever achieved much success. The spoken
and the written words are not usually of the same idiom and cadence.
But I acceded to Raeburn's plea, and was rewarded by a sale of many
tens of thousands of copies.

One day I received a telephone call from a friend in a New York
publishing office recommending that I swear never to publish a book
again. I was taken aback by what seemed churlish counsel, but my
friend pointed out that he had just read two reviews of *Voice of Israel*
which were so rhapsodic that I ought to leave the record as it stood
in case the critics changed their mind. Henry Steele Commager, the
Columbia University historian, had written: "As Ben Gurion has been
the spirit of Israel, so Abba Eban has been its voice. It is a

voice of rare eloquence: indeed now that Churchill and De Gaulle are off the stage, Eban's voice is the most eloquent of all the leading actors." A few weeks later, the *Times Literary Supplement* in London, usually sparing in praise, compared me to Cicero and Burke! It was not necessary to take all these eulogies at full value in order to be humanly encouraged. They certainly did no harm to my capacity to fulfill my diplomatic functions.

The pace of my work now became less hectic. There was room for occasional periods of repose in the company of friends. We would sometimes go for long weekends to the home of Rebecca Shulman in Stamford, Connecticut. She is the widow of an eminent corporation lawyer, Herman Shulman, who had built an exquisite collection of modern art. The combination of warm friendship, rural peace, esthetic beauty and a burning devotion to Israel made Rebecca Shulman's environment magnetic for us. In the heat of summer we found seclusion in Martha's Vineyard. Throughout the year we were sustained by the friendship of Dewey and Anne Stone of Brockton, Massachusetts. Dewey's fierce energies were at work on behalf of the Weizmann Institute, the United Jewish Appeal and every cause that had anything to do with Israel's security and Jewish honor. Standing with him in loyalty to the same causes were Harry and Lee Levine of Cambridge, Massachusetts, who were also among the heirs of Weizmann's legacy.

Washington had its particular social round, in which some degree of participation was ritually necessary. I fear that I sometimes carried out this part of my duties with minimal grace. I have no taste whatever for cocktail parties, which I regard as an advanced form of man's inhumanity to man. At dinner parties I was often handicapped by a distaste for conventional small talk with Cabinet and Congress wives, some of whom may have found me too direct. When a hostess said gushingly and at enormous length that she liked the flowers I had sent her but "I really should not have troubled," I replied after the fourth repetition, "Yes, I agree. I suppose it was not really necessary."

I enjoyed the intellectual and fraternal challenge of my speeches to Jewish audiences, but am unable to this day to endure the accompanying "ritual" without symptoms of impatience. The reception at five-thirty, the laborious arrangement of dais speakers, the invocations and benedictions in which rabbis carry out an emotional campaign of attrition against the Creator, the soggy chicken, and the panegyrics extolling preceding speakers—all this used to leave me exhausted and drained before I could get near the podium to make my address. I have often wondered if there is not a less tormenting method of mobilizing sympathy and resources for Israel. But the ardor of Jews in support of Israel is so profound that any effort to nourish it is worthwhile.

By the end of March 1957 Eisenhower had persuaded the Congress to ratify his "doctrine" under which the United States would aid any country in the Middle East threatened by "international Communism." This was not a relevant security guarantee to Israel. The threat to us came not from "international Communism" but from Arab states of varying orientation. Yet we could not forget that the Soviet Union had recently intimidated us with violent menace; this might happen again. And it was not inconceivable that an Arab state contiguous to Israel might one day qualify for description as part of the "international Communist system." Thus, while official Israeli opinion was divided on the question whether Israel should seek inclusion in the Eisenhower Doctrine, I had no doubt that our course was clear. It would be politically and psychologically quixotic for the United States to have a more intimate commitment to other Middle Eastern states than to Israel. Had we not spent many years complaining about the discrimination by which the West excluded us from their arms treaties and their plans for defense organization? It would be absurd for us to be willingly left out even of a demonstrative American policy that might never come to fruition.

Therefore, when the Eisenhower Administration empowered James P. Richards, a former chairman of the Foreign Affairs Committee of the House of Representatives, to tour Middle Eastern countries and obtain statements of adherence to the Eisenhower Doctrine, I supported Ben Gurion against those of his colleagues who suggested that we reject the invitation. I thought it particularly inconsistent that ministers who had shown alarm at the prospect of a Soviet attack should now be so cavalier in rejecting American deterrence of such an assault.

Indeed, we were soon to be reminded that the Middle Eastern conflict had a global dimension. In August 1957 Syria took a sharp turn toward the left. An officer of Communist sympathies was appointed as Chief of Staff, and American diplomats were expelled from Damascus. The United States responded by sending arms to Lebanon and Jordan, which were Syria's rivals and potential victims. Washington also encouraged Turkey to concentrate her troops on the Syrian border. The Soviet Union announced that it would "not be indifferent to what goes on in the Middle East," and began to treat Turkey to the kind of intimidatory notes that London, Paris and Jerusalem had received in 1956. The crisis petered out by the end of 1957, but one of its results was to strengthen the solidarity between Egypt and Syria, and to confirm the Syrian government in its view that it had something to fear from Western hostility. Thus, in February 1958, Egypt and Syria announced their merger in the framework of the "United Arab Republic." Nasser's prestige had reached its climax. The Syrian-Egyptian coalition set off protective reactions in the conservative Arab states. Jordan and Iraq announced a "federation," and when Nasserist elements attempted to overthrow the pro-Western Lebanese government headed by Camille Chamoun, the United States took measures that seemed quixotically in contradiction to its posture of supporting Nasser in 1956. It strengthened Lebanon with arms and ordered naval concentrations off Beirut.

When a revolution broke out in Iraq on July 14, 1958, sweeping away the Hashemite monarchy and the pro-Western Prime Minister Nuri Said, the United States decided on a drastic revision of its Middle Eastern policy. First, Washington and London agreed to diagnose the revolution in Iraq as a success for Nasser. It was soon to emerge that the new Iraqi rulers, led by Brigadier General Abdul Karim Kassem, were as hostile to Nasser as it was possible to be. When the Lebanese government, through Camille Chamoun and Charles Malik, requested American military intervention, the United States acceded. Marines landed in Beirut while British paratroops arrived simultaneously in Jordan in response to an appeal from King Hussein.

Throughout this crisis the United States kept in close and intimate touch with us. Together with Yaacov Herzog, my new minister at the embassy, I was closeted with Dulles several times a week. Israeli acquiescence was needed for British paratroopers to overfly our territory on their way to Jordan. Beyond this, the United States required Israel's influence on Capitol Hill in support of its intervention. A special session of the UN General Assembly was called in which we witnessed the unique spectacle of Arab regimes attacking one another, while their common hostility to Israel was relegated to a minor place. In the end the Arab League pretended to achieve a reconciliation which enabled the General Assembly to disperse and American and British troops to leave Lebanon and Jordan after a stay of less than six months.

In talks with me, Dulles made tormented attempts to prove that there was no contradiction between American support of Nasser in 1956 and American military action against him in 1958. The rationalization was that in 1956 Nasser had been the victim of armed assault, whereas in 1958 he was the architect of threats, intimidations and acts of violence. In August 1958 Dulles sent me a memorandum pointing out that it was one thing to support "Arab nationalism," but quite another to endorse "radical Arab nationalism," which took the form of an attempt by one Arab country to impose its system of government and ideology by force or subversion on others. In the United Nations General Assembly, Eisenhower and Dulles attempted without much success to secure condemnation of what they called "indirect aggression," by which they meant attempts to achieve changes by subversion and infiltration rather than through the overt crossing of boundaries by armed forces.

Together with the crucial opening of the oil route through Eilat by an American tanker, the United States symbolized its new benevolence by economic aid and by support of our water development. There was also a habit of a close consultation, the intimacy of which had deepened as a result of my contacts with Dulles in the months of 1956 and 1957. The United States was obviously coming to regard Israel not as a burden to be chivalrously sustained, but as an asset in the global and ideological balance.

One day in August 1958 I went to see Dulles with a letter from Ben Gurion inviting American attention to our efforts to strengthen Israel's links with the developing countries of Asia and Africa. Ben Gurion reached a high level of eloquence in describing Israel's role in this human drama. Dulles told me that the President and he were astonished by the scope of this Israeli effort. The newly emerging societies were in desperate need of training in various aspects of the development process. On the other hand, they were suspicious both of the European countries with their colonial tradition, and of the United States, whose immense power gave small states a sense of inferiority. Israel had no history in Africa or East Asia, and was not suspected of imperialist capacity or intention. It might, therefore, be able to fill a gap. We did not seek any direct American assistance for our work in the developing countries, but I invoked it as an additional argument in favor of strengthening Israel's economy. After all, we would not be very effective as a teacher of accelerated development to other nations if our own economy and society did not show signs of progress.

A sense of common purpose now caused the Eisenhower Administration to seek other ways of emphasizing its harmony with Israel. There was also a desire to block Soviet penetration with the support of the Nasser regime. Together with his memorandum against "Arab radicalism" Dulles sent me a note pointing out that the action taken by President Eisenhower to defend Lebanon's independence should be taken as an example of what the United States would do if Israel's survival were really threatened. I myself had some reservations about the parallelism between the two cases; Lebanon had, after all, not been the victim of an external international aggression. I nevertheless hinted that if there was to be an attempt to build a stronger American commitment to Israel, a presidential signature would be valuable. The result was a note from Eisenhower to Ben Gurion asking him to regard the defense of Lebanese independence as symbolic of the seriousness with which the United States took its international obligations.

John Foster Dulles was now pursuing the last stages of his unusual career in the throes of cancer, against which he was battling bravely, but in vain. Early in 1959 it became obvious that the illness was terminal. Toward the end of his stewardship at the State Department, he was recommending heavy economic aid for Israel, encouraging the strengthening of our forces with a modest but symbolically important American component, and praising our role in the developing countries. He was also taking counsel with us in militant resistance to the hegemonistic policies of Nasser. In May 1958, on the tenth anniversary of our independence, he came to my residence at Juniper Street for a dinner celebration, attended also by Senators Stuart Symington and Jacob Javits, and George Meany, the labor leader, as well as Senator William Knowland, the Republican Senate Leader, and Justice Felix Frankfurter. One of the guests remarked that Israel had a special capacity for bringing political and personal rivals around a friendly table. Though this was an exaggeration, it is true that, at that time, the tension between Knowland and Meany was especially virulent. Dulles made a graceful and moving after-dinner speech in which he managed to describe Israel's spiritual origins and explain the special place that Israel occupied in the hearts of the American people.

Dulles had been somewhat of an ogre for Israelis during most of his six years in office. By the time he retired he was regarded by Ben Gurion and others as a friend. Golda Meir has recorded that "at the end he was very helpful. As time went on he saw that Israel's case had merit. This was due mainly to Eban's influence."

The truth is that I tried to help Dulles not only toward an understanding of Israel but also toward a deeper conception of the Arab world. Nasserism had become something more than a doctrine of Egyptian revolution. Its central theme was hegemonistic. Cairo saw itself not only as the capital of Egypt but also as the center in which all Arab policies should be determined. Nasser's policy was "One empire, one nation, one leader," and there was no difficulty in diagnosing who he thought the leader should be. Whenever there was a government in the Arab world dedicated to traditional Moslem values or to cordial relations to the West, Nasser and his agents would move for its overthrow. In a strictly political sense, Nasser was the foe of all the aims that the United States and Israel upheld. Many Arab countries at different times saw his domination as a violation of their own sovereign rights.

In 1959 I published a book called *The Tide of Nationalism,* in which I portrayed the tension in Arab history between pan-Arabism and particularism. In this book I pointed out that there is a trend toward community of purpose among all peoples of Arab speech, but there is also a desire of separate Arab regions to avoid being dominated by a single Arab capital or to break away from that domination once it is imposed.

By the end of 1958 I had spent the best part of a decade in Israel's service abroad. I had at least three reasons for wanting to end my mission. First, I was afraid that despite my frequent journeys home, I would soon lack an intimate relationship with the reality that I was supposed to represent. On the personal level, it was important that Eli and Gila, now aged eight and four, should be immersed in a Hebrew atmosphere and integrated into the Israeli educational system. Finally, I was growing tired of being Israel's "voice," charged to give utterance to policies determined by others. I had strong views of what our policies should be, and not only about how they should be formulated. I thought that this was the time to enter the parliamentary arena back home.

News was coming of rumblings and tensions within the Labor Party (Mapai). The veteran leaders under Ben Gurion—Eshkol, Sapir, Golda Meir, as well as Pinchas Lavon, now eminently installed as Secretary-General of the Histadrut—felt threatened by Ben Gurion's determination to introduce new blood into the party and national leadership. At a party gathering at Kfar Hayarok, Golda had even spoken of resigning. Ben Gurion's main intention was to bring Chief of Staff Moshe Dayan and Shimon Peres, Director of the Defense Ministry, into the governmental structure at high levels. Yet there was also concern at what seemed to be the rising support for the conservative Likud Party under Menachem Begin, who was developing expansionist concepts together with a populist image. He was benefiting from the social protest in the slum quarters of large towns such as the Hatikvah Quarter in Tel Aviv and Wadi Salib in Haifa. Ben Gurion felt that his present team lacked drawing power. If the Mapai Party wanted to maintain its leading position, it had to open its leadership ranks. At that time the other labor parties, Achdut Ha'avodah and Mapam, were in opposition to Mapai, and could not even be counted upon for loyal cooperation in a coalition. It was essential that Mapai's strength be not only maintained but, if possible, enhanced.

Ben Gurion proposed that sometime before the election in 1959 I come back to Israel to campaign for membership in the Knesset. He said that he would advocate my having a high place on our party list, and that if he formed the next government, I would be a member of it. He was vague about what he expected me to do in his Cabinet but he did say, "You have an unexampled experience in international affairs. That is the subject with which you should be dealing in the government." Giora Josephtal, who was then the secretary-general of our party, made the point of coming to see me at my father-in-law's home in Herzliya to confirm this understanding.

The decision was made easier for me as a result of an episode that had taken place in April of that year. I had been the main speaker, together with UN Ambassador Henry Cabot Lodge, at the annual dinner of the American-Israel Cultural Foundation. Avoiding the familiar political themes, I had reflected on the challenges facing Israel in the realm of the mind and the spirit. I have always found it hard to build a convincing picture of Israel without a degree of intellectual romanticism. When it comes to territories, populations, oil resources, money, multiplicity of state and all the other ingredients of geopolitical strength, Israel looks puny compared to its neighbors. The question is whether by intellectual vitality and scientific dynamism she can build a compensating strength. Throughout the generations, the Jews have taken with them a great deal of history but very little geography—a vast amount of intellectual and spiritual effort with very few material assets.

When I left the platform after expounding this theme Meyer Weisgal, who was sitting up front, every hair on his head bristling with aggressive expectation, took me in head-on assault. He said in a voice that managed to combine a whisper and a scream, "Magnificent! You've got to be president of the Weizmann Institute." It was unexpected to hear this accolade conferred suddenly at eleven o'clock at night. But Meyer Weisgal, like other hurricanes, does not act in precise accordance with forecasts. We went on to our hotel suite and pursued the matter further. At first the idea seemed far-fetched, but as we explored its implications, it became increasingly attractive. Since Weizmann's death at the end of 1952, no president of the Institute had been appointed. The time had come when this deference would have to be put aside in the Institute's interest. The next president, whether a scientist or not, should try to give enlargement to Weizmann's legacy, to arrange the Institute's relations with the outside world, and of course, to let his name and efforts be used on behalf of the budget.

I made it clear to Weisgal that while I cherished the idea that I would contribute to the Weizmann cause, I was innocent and young enough to aspire to an active political role, and I told him of my discussions with Ben Gurion and Josephtal. He made it clear that he would not expect me to act in an executive capacity. (I reflected silently that anyone who tried to do this would become shriveled up in Weisgal's own magnetic field.)

Thus in November 1958 I went to Rehovot as the president designate of the Weizmann Institute to address the annual Weizmann memorial meeting held in the Plaza. In my audience, comprising many thousands in the fragrant coolness of a Rehovot evening, were Ben Gurion, Eshkol, Golda Meir, Yigael Yadin, most members of the Israeli government, and almost the entire intellectual community. It was one of the occasions on which it seemed important for a speaker to succeed. Since no Israeli mind can work for more than five minutes without a politial thought, the tongues were soon wagging about what my impending return to Israel meant. The press speculated on whether the oratorical qualities that I had displayed that night were really meant to be confined to the campus alone.

The guiding spirit of the Weizmann Institute, after Meyer Weisgal, was my closest friend, Dewey D. Stone. With Dewey, his wife, Anne, and Meyer, Suzy and I inspected the modest but comfortable house on the Institute's grounds, to which we would come to live on the conclusion of my mission in May 1959. A deep serenity seemed to await me here compared with the hectic pace at which we had lived for the past decade and more.

On February 2, 1959, back in Washington, I authorized an announcement on my decision to resign from the posts of ambassador to the United States and the United Nations. Although I had been in office for over a decade in the United Nations and for over eight years in Washington, this declaration was treated as a revolutionary surprise. The Jewish organizations, the Washington diplomatic corps, the American-Israeli Society and delegations at the United Nations prepared a festive farewell. What followed was all very much like an electoral campaign, crisscrossing the country in a constant surge of celebration. A National Testimonial Committee was established, headed by Vice-President Richard Nixon, Chief Justice Earl Warren, ex-Presidents Harry Truman and Herbert Hoover, the future Presidents Senators John F. Kennedy and Lyndon B. Johnson, Adlai Stevenson and a host of governors, senators, congressmen, judges and leaders of the intellectual community. It had been an eventful decade in my life and I was humanly pleased that I may have left some "footprints on the sands of time."

The *New York Times* and the Washington *Post* published editorials of appreciation. But what moved me even more deeply was to receive press clippings of similar tribute from newspapers across the country such as the *Daily Tribune* of Royal Oak, Michigan; the *Mining Journal* of Marquette, Michigan; the *Press* of Middletown, Connecticut; and the *Press* of Sheboygan, Wisconsin. I doubt that the mayor of San Antonio, Texas, knew the name of any other ambassador in Washington, and yet the *Light of San Antonio* published a moving editorial bidding me farewell. In the Chicago Opera House an audience of six thousand heard Senator Paul Douglas and other Illinoisans express their friendship. Douglas said that he wished I were the Democratic presidential candidate. (The next morning Adlai Stevenson called on me and expressed surprise that an "ostensibly intelligent person would want to resign as an ambassador to become a politician and enter an electoral combat." He seemed to be speaking out of the pain and grief of his own experience.) And so on to Louisville, Philadelphia, Rochester, New York, St. Louis, Tuscon, Los Angeles, San Francisco, Miami and finally to New York, where the ambassadors of fifty nations bade me farewell with Governor Thomas Dewey, Secretary-General U Thant and Eleanor Roosevelt among the speakers. It was, of course, Mrs. Roosevelt who said what was in my heart when she ended her tribute: "It must be wonderful to be young today and to have your ability and already so much experience and now to have a new opportunity to serve a country which, so small, has had an impact on so many nations."

The next evening I said goodbye to American Jewry officially at a mass meeting with eighteen thousand people in Madison Square Garden under the chairmanship of Rabbi Hillel Silver. Yigael Yadin, who was on a visit to the United States, had been asked by Ben Gurion to read his letter to me:

As the Representative of a young and small country, you were sent to the capital of the greatest power in the new world. You immediately evoked a rare degree of attention and respect from the leaders, representatives and thinkers of that country. With skill and a unique grace of exposition you won the hearts of your listeners in all regions and among all groups in America. Your appearances in the General Assembly and Security Council of the United Nations brought honor to your country and pride to all your people. Our international situation continues to improve and you have no small part in that achievement. I am, however, confident that the destiny of Israel with which the historic mission of the Jewish people is intertwined will be determined primarily by what is done in Israel. It is in that spirit that I welcome you home.

In the meantime I was packing my belongings, books, souvenirs and mementos. Somebody in the embassy figured out that during my decade I had visited forty-two of the forty-eight states, had traveled two million miles and had fulfilled more than a thousand engagements at radio and television stations, luncheons, banquets and rallies, as well as hundreds of meetings of the United Nations Security Council and General Assembly. In one of my farewell speeches I said that I had found it easier to live my decade in the United States than to celebrate it.

When all the celebrations came to an end, Suzy and I suddenly found ourselves at Washington's International Airport, with Yaacov Herzog and the embassy staff seeing us off. We had every reason to be exhilarated by what had gone before and what awaited us in the future. Yet, the methodical liquidation of ten years of our life suddenly struck a sharp blow to our consciousness—and Suzy was very close to tears.

There is a conventional envy of diplomats for the intensity of their experience and the amenities by which they are surrounded. There would be less jealousy if more account were taken of the sacrifice inherent in the constant rootlessness. It is a nomadic destiny with countless reunions and partings and abrupt sunderings of relationships that stretch deep into the habit and the affections. I have known many foreign service officers in Israel and other countries who have never managed to restore emotional stability when, after being "in orbit" through so many different planets of experience, they suddenly return to the hard earth of normality. Their wives and children suffer even more intensely, without the compensation that comes from the work itself.

I felt that I had been totally saturated with the dilemmas of an emissary and advocate. My decision not to go on with diplomacy was firm. Although I had only served one period in two diplomatic posts, I knew that I was past all possibility of starting a new mission somewhere else. In the future, such expeditions as I would make in the outside world would be from a home base to which, after spasms of external activity, I would gratefully return.

On May 22, 1959, Suzy, Eli, Gila and I, with sixteen hundred other passengers, sailed from New York on S.S. *United States* for Southampton. We had planned a short vacation in London and Switzerland before arriving in Israel. In London I performed my first duty as president of the Weizmann Institute by addressing a large dinner in the Dorchester Hotel. Suzy and I then proceeded to Crans-sur-Sierre for a brief stay in the mountains, with sporadic golf between intense rain showers. I was undergoing what many politicians call "withdrawal symptoms." After nearly a dozen years of constant responsibility, with confidential papers flowing in and out of my desk in an atmosphere of urgency, I suddenly found myself in a kind of vacuum. Nothing flowed to or from me.

After ten days of repose, the sense of being outside the official communication system became frustrating. I do not think that there was any element of hurt prestige. The injury was rather in the intellectual domain. The muscles of my mind had been trained over long years to expand and contract with practiced speed in face of problems that could assault me at any hour. I now learned with humility that my previous worlds continued to revolve without me, for better or for worse, but in any case with inexorable continuity. There is a curious sense of hurt that goes along with the relief. Some of my worst golf shots at Crans-sur-Sierre came at moments when my mind was wandering back to Washington and the United Nations. My sense of being in a vacuum was enhanced by the knowledge that no successor had been appointed to either post.

I was confident of the stewardship of Yaacov Herzog in Washington and Mordecai Kidron in New York. Herzog's life is a unique drama in the story of our foreign service. The son of the Chief Rabbi of Israel, Rabbi Isaac Halevi Herzog, Yaacov was brought up in scholarly and pious seclusion, close to his father's spiritual world while creating a special mental universe of his own. His mercurial mind transferred itself fitfully from learning to politics. He was an original figure, orthodox without being sanctimonious, intellectually ambitious yet curiously reluctant to assume a central responsibility. He always worked in the shelter of someone else, first Ben Gurion, then Golda Meir, and later Eshkol and Golda again. He served us all with precision and a somewhat courtly deference out of tune with Israeli habit. When he came to me in Washington I had the sense of promoting his emancipation from a parental custody that must have been restrictive as well as warm. He brought to diplomacy a long sense of history as well as a subtle imagination. He had no time or thought for anything that did not bear directly on the interests of the Jewish people.

Everything about him was abrupt; his style and manner of speech and even his physical habits. He would come and speak to me at length and in detail and then, before I had time to look up, he would have risen from his chair and rushed out of the room. There was a constant hurry about him, as though he knew that some destiny was treading on his heels. In sad fact, he was in fragile health and was to die before the age of fifty. I had the superstition that his habit of departing without small talk after each conversation expressed a premonition that his time was circumscribed, that none of it should be wasted and that whatever could not be done today had no sure chance of being accomplished tomorrow. When he died in the prime of his life, I thought of Milton: "For Lycidas is dead, dead ere his prime, young Lycidas and hath not left his peer."

At Crans-sur-Sierre, telegrams were reaching me from our party headquarters, urging me to expedite my return to join an election campaign which might be started earlier than expected. Our last day in Europe was spent in search of the best available meal in a Zurich restaurant, and on July 2, we landed at Lod Airport in Tel Aviv, no longer as an ambassador and his wife on leave, but as private citizens returning home.

To my surprise, the airport lounge was filled not only with Weizmann Institute dignitaries, led by Meyer Weisgal, but by a whole panoply of Labor Party leaders, including Zalman Shazar, Beba Idelson, Mordecai Namir, Shraga Netzer and many others of the party faithful. There was evidently some scare about the possibility of a Herut victory. Although Dayan and Peres, like myself, had been harnessed to Mapai's electoral campaign, they were giving the party some trouble as well as much reinforcement. Dayan had made abrasive references to the "fifth floor of the Histadrut," where the Secretary-General dwelled. He had also said that if he could not join the Cabinet, nothing would interest him less than sitting around in the Knesset, where members have nothing to do but "drink tea in the cafeteria."

The old guard in the party was resentful of Ben Gurion's attempt to introduce new blood. But the Hebrew press was writing appreciatively of my mission, pointing out that I had been correct in my stable view of American-Israeli relations. The catastrophe that had been predicted for Israel under the Eisenhower regime had come to nothing. Israel was enjoying the fruits of the Sinai Campaign and was under no pressure on boundaries, refugees or Jerusalem. We had become the subject of sympathetic emotion on the part of Secretary Dulles, who had died while I was crossing the Atlantic. There was even a glimmer of rationality in the American attitude to the arms problem. A few items of U.S. equipment were being supplied, and an initially favorable response had been given by Secretary Herter to Israel's application for ground-to-air missiles. The fact that we had now gone through two Administrations, those of Truman and Eisenhower, with the basic elements of the American-Israeli partnership unimpaired, seemed to be of great importance. It proved that there were durable elements in the relationship that were not dependent on Truman's favorable attitude or on the special place that the American Jews occupied in the Democratic Party.

On July 5 I delivered my inaugural address on assuming the presidency of the Weizmann Institute. I dealt not only with the role of the Weizmann Institute and of Israeli science in the construction of a new community but also with a specific project that I had revolved for several weeks in New York before my departure: my intention to convene an international conference the following year, bringing some of the world's leading scientists together with leaders of government from developing states in Africa, Asia and Latin America. I felt that the two dominant movements in twentieth-century life were the movement of national liberation and the movement of scientific progress. One of them had changed the political map; the other had transformed every prospect of human welfare or disaster. These two movements, however, were living in separation from each other. Science was having little effect on the economic, social and cultural levels of the new states, while the leaders of emerging countries had little consciousness of what science and technology could do to accelerate their development and save them the long periods of transition that the industrialized states had been forced to undergo. I felt that if I could bring the leaders of these two movements together in creative encounter, and in some mutuality of human concern, I might help create a new dimension in international relations of which Israel and the Weizmann Institute would be both the arena and the beneficiary. I had discussed this in New York with Meyer Weisgal and the dynamic adviser to the Institute, Lily Shultz, who had prepared a memorandum on how the proposed conference could be organized and composed. I had now developed this theme into a broader conceptual argument and sought to relate it to one of the problems of Israel's foreign relations, namely the need to consolidate our position among developing nations.

The Weizmann Institute is the culmination of Israel's quest for quality. Science is one of the few domains in which our small, poor country can transcend its material limitations and stand on a level of equality with the advanced nations of the world. The existence of a family of research workers probing the mysteries of nature gives Israeli society a quality quite different from what it would have possessed without such an asset. I hoped that the atmosphere of rationality, balance and universal solidarity which distinguished the scientific community would diffuse its influence over other sectors of Israeli life. As I walked through the grounds, sensing the orange blossom still in the air and contemplating the rich landscape climbing from the green valley toward the pale Judean hills, I was often tempted to devote myself exclusively to the guardianship of Weizmann's legacy. And yet, I was pulled by the urgent compulsions of Israel's need into the pursuit of a political vocation. With a full decade of service in the United States and the United Nations behind me, I was still only in my early forties. I felt that my energies were too restless to be satisfied with the limited concerns of a university president fighting for his budget and entertaining his faculty and graduates. I decided, therefore, to remain faithful to the understanding that I had reached with Weisgal in New York. The executive tasks would continue to fall upon him, while I would give the Institute such service and reinforcement as my name and energies could offer.

Not that it was easy to abandon the tranquillities of the campus for the din and turmoil of the electoral battlefield. Something of my relief on returning to Israel was expressed by Suzy in a letter to my mother:

> At last we are in our own country and our own home. The house is beautiful beyond all expectations. Especially both the children love their charming and comfortable rooms. I can hardly wait to hear their voices and see them in the delightful garden and all the little neighbors waiting for them. We are happy and excited. It all seems so logical. We had a terrific welcome at the airport with speeches and cameras and flowers. The Institute and Meyer [Weisgal] have put themselves out most warmly and generously. I feel that for the first time we can live like a family and it moves me very deeply.

Many visitors came to the Weizmann Institute, some seeking an outlet for their generosity, others arriving from distant countries, especially from Africa and Asia, where it had been commonly believed that the scientific revolution was the inheritance of rich countries in the North and West alone. A small nation with a scientific research system was—and remains—a rarity. I was available for consultation, entertainment and the persuasion of the Jewish visitors to channel their support of Israel through the reinforcement of its scientific tradition. It was in those days that a visitor from New York, Siegfried Ullman, called on me by chance at home and began a connection with Rehovot that led to the establishment of its Institute of Life Sciences. The preparation for the first Rehovot conference went on under my active guidance and supervision. But many hours during the summer and early autumn were spent in the domestic political arena.

The political outlook seemed bright. At my inauguration ceremony on July 5, Ben Gurion had surprised the two thousand participants by calling me "the most distinguished emissary of the Jewish people in our generation." A few days later, at a party rally at the Habima Theatre, he referred to me as "the greatest spokesman for our nation's cause since Weizmann." Nobody could say this was not a generous eulogy, but the "Ben Gurionologists" knew what to look for beneath the latent surface of the words. They told me darkly that it was not all that simple. According to them, I was being put in a special place in Ben Gurion's consciousness. The notions of "emissary" and "spokesman" did not belong to the language of leadership. Ben Gurion was hinting that it was for him and others to make the policy, and for me to be its advocate. There was also a diminution of Weizmann's image in the idea that he had merely been the "spokesman" rather than a leader and decision maker. Ben Gurion was tenacious in the stereotypes of thought that he fixed in his own mind. He was also less afraid of constant repetition than any human being could be. When the election campaign was successfully over, he sent me a portrait of himself with a dedication: "To Abba Eban, *spokesman* of the Jewish people." I had now begun to regret the emphasis that the public placed on my forensic experience. I even wished that I had not called my book *The Voice of Israel*, as though I were eternally destined to articulate policies made by others.

After crowding my institute duties into the first two days of the week, I would go out of the main gate of Yad Weizmann with a sharp sense of transition. It was like moving to a foreign land. The hard world began with the noisy main street of Rehovot and its strident chaos of trucks, bicycles, buses and the odd donkey cart urged on its way by a patient, bearded, sad-eyed Jew in a cloth cap who seemed to represent the special tone of Israeli rural life. A few minutes later I would be in Tel Aviv, where I would plunge into the struggle of Mapai for a renewal of its mandate.

My transition from diplomacy to party politics raised eyebrows among friends and adversaries alike. It took some time before they could tear themselves away from the metaphors of incongruity. The tension was real, and an American writer has described it well:

> One of Eban's great problems was that he was entering a struggle for political power with the ruling clique of Mapai composed largely of men who were not distinguished by either intellectual prowess or academic distinction. Many were actually antiintellectual. In the early days they had dug ditches, worked in the vineyards and wine cellars, ploughed the earth, spread manure,

drained swamps, pioneered. Later they had helped establish Kib-
butzim and Moshavim. They had formed a closely-knit group,
almost all from Central or Eastern Europe. They were rough-hewn,
blunt-speaking, short of formality,. suspicious of rhetoric, given
more to emotionalism than intellectuality and defiant of propriety
and conventionality, especially in matters of dress and social
niceties. . . . Eban, the scholar, who retained his high position by
force of intellect, seemed strangely out of place amongst them. All
these Party stalwarts acknowledged his great contribution to
Israel, respected his talents, recognised his vote-getting potentiality
and gave him provisional approval. Yet, at the same time, he did
not fit their pattern and they made no secret of their feeling that
"he is not really one of us."

"Provisional approval" was perhaps all that I needed. It was certainly as much as I was going to get. The party veterans were not
particularly pleased about myself and Dayan occupying the twelfth
and thirteenth places on the party list, with the clear implication
of instant ministerial rank ahead. Some of the political figures, organized in what was called the Gush, probably felt that both of us
were newcomers to politics and should have been required to "take
our place in the line." But the Israeli electors came en masse to hear
and see the new candidates, not the veterans. I drew a crowd of
twelve thousand one day in Tel Aviv, ten thousand in Ramat Gan,
fifteen thousand in a stadium in Haifa, seven thousand in Bat Yam,
fifteen thousand in Rehovot, five thousand in Bnei Brak. In the
squalid but vibrant Tel Aviv quarter of Hatikvah, I spoke from a
balcony in Hebrew and Arabic to twelve thousand. I looked down on
the mass of swarthy faces, and throwing away my learned speech about
electoral reforms, I talked to them more from the heart. I found a
special access to Sephardic Jews. It may have had something to do with
their respect for words, their dedication to form and their courtly response to the big world in which I had served them abroad.

The fact that I was having some success now began to be reflected
in opposition and criticism. Little of this caused me any sharp hurt.
The Herut press argued hopefully that what I was saying was beyond
the grasp of my listeners. This, however, appeared to be more of an
insult to my listeners than to me, and many of them responded in
kind. In general, while much is talked about "the average man," I have
never met anybody in Israel who agrees to accept that phrase as a
definition of himself.

Whether my audiences agreed with me or not, they followed me
with much curiosity. The press was respectably fair, although one
enterprising journalist, who should have known better, did try to

create a sensation by photographing my somewhat modest home in Rehovot with a trick lens so as to make it appear like the gigantic central palace in the Versailles complex. The implication was that a feudal lord like Eban should be suspiciously received in the Hatikvah Quarter.

By the time it had all ended, I had spoken to a quarter of a million people in a country of less than three million. Apart from Ben Gurion and Begin, I seemed to have drawn the largest crowds of any candidate of any party. It was an encouraging encounter. I felt that most of our citizens were looking for an idealistic backdrop to their material concerns.

When the votes were counted on a stifling, hot day in early November, our party had received the greatest vote in its history. Ben Gurion and his mixed team of veterans and newcomers were in possession of the field.

I was sworn in as a member of the Knesset on November 30, 1959. Two weeks later Ben Gurion made the formal announcement of his Cabinet. He himself would continue as Defense Minister, and Golda Meir as Foreign Minister. Dayan would be Minister of Agriculture; Peres, Deputy Defense Minister; and I would be Minister without Portfolio.

In several conversations Ben Gurion had given me the impression that my roving commission in the Cabinet would take me into the area of international affairs. He had spoken of the British precedent, under which there were Cabinet ministers without portfolio dealing with some sectors of foreign affairs under the general authority of the Foreign Minister. The expanding range of Israel's international interests made all this theoretically tenable. It took no account, however, of temperamental realities. Mrs. Meir told me frankly that while I was competent to be a Foreign Minister one day, I had qualities beyond those that were feasible for a mere deputy. The best thing, therefore, would be for me to wait my turn, and in the meantime, to deal with "other matters." This was fair enough, but when I asked Ben Gurion what the "other matters" were, he was engagingly vague. The truth is that behind his somewhat childlike innocence, there was a very pragmatic cunning. He knew that Mapai had used me as it had used Dayan and Peres in the electoral struggle. This did not, however, mean that we were to be rewarded too fulsomely once the wedding was over. He had created an illusion—that more than one minister could work on foreign affairs in Israel—and had not seriously explored whether this was true or not. He was not prepared to push his commitment very far. He wanted to live in some kind of peace with his contemporaries, not only with his juniors.

The first result for me was frustration. The Cabinet post was nebulous and empty. In the Israeli system, a minister without portfolio means exactly what it says—it is a function without duties. I had little to do except pursue my plan for the international conference under the auspices of the Weizmann Institute and to take part in the many ministerial committees which transacted the more concrete parts of the Cabinet's work. Although the Cabinet meetings and ministerial consultations were interesting, I felt myself to be a spectator of the national drama. I contributed my advice, but had no part in the execution.

The fact remained that within a year I had gone from my embassy to Cabinet status, and foreign opinion was more impressed with the rank than conscious of its emptiness. Thus, the mayor of New York, Robert Wagner, wrote: "New York is proud of you. Do not forget that you are only one of the six men ever to have been awarded the freedom of the city." In a letter to a friend Suzy wrote: "We are marking time as gracefully as we can and waiting for his time and his proper place. So far, the appearance of things is excellent, but the substance is lacking. It lacks completeness, sweep, authority and, above all, a chance to do a creative job for the country and its people."

One day in early May 1960, the Cabinet asked me to represent it at the celebration in Buenos Aires of the 150th year of Argentinean independence. My delegation was to include Brigadier Meir Zorea of the Northern Command and three civilian officials. We would fly in an El Al Britannia on flight #601, leaving Lod Airport on May 18. This was the first and only El Al flight scheduled for Argentina, where we had not yet secured regular landing rights. Twenty-four hours after its arrival at the Buenos Aires airport, the plane took off again at midnight on Friday, May 20, with Adolf Eichmann aboard. He had been forcibly, but gently, spirited onto the plane in drugged condition in an El Al uniform, and the Argentinean authorities knew nothing of it. Eichmann was the Nazi officer in charge of the extermination of Jews in Europe. His capture by Israeli intelligence agents was a brilliant enterprise.

During the hot summer of 1960, I threw myself into the organization of the Rehovot Conference. It was a splendid success. The participants came from forty nations. They included the President of the Congo Republic, the Prime Minister of Nepal, Vice-Presidents, finance ministers, ministers of commerce, housing and labor, bank presidents, ministers of education and heads of atomic centers; the director-general of the World Health Organization; Paul Hoffmann, managing director of the UN Special Fund; and a brilliant corps of scientists headed by the great nuclear physicist Sir John Cockroft; his fellow Nobel laureate, Professor Patrick Blackett; Alvin Weinberg, director of the Oak Ridge National Laboratory; Jerrold Zacharias of the Massachusetts Institute of Technology; Arthur Lewis, the principal of University College in Jamaica; and the director-general of Euratom. Apart from the visit of Prime Minister U Nu of Burma in 1954, no head of state or head of government had ever visited Israel before. Now there were some thirty ministerial guests helping to take Israel out of diplomatic isolation. In my opening address I described the speed with which African and Asian countries had broken out of tutelage to liberation:

> If institutional freedom could itself guarantee peace and welfare we should now be celebrating mankind's golden age. But, alas, the flags are not enough. In the awakening continents freedom has not been attended by a parallel liberation of peoples from their social and economic ills. Behind the new emblems of institutional freedom millions continue to languish in squalor, exploitation and disease. Men awaken to learn that they may be free in every constitutional sense and yet lose the essence of their freedom in the throes of famine and want.

I called on the scientists to give a greater proportion of their care and compassion to the problems of the developing countries, and I advised the leaders of new nations to establish an indigenous scientific tradition in their countries as an instrument of intellectual freedom and expanding welfare.

The Israeli public reacted with pride to the convergence of so many eminent visitors. After the first awkward silences were broken, the scientists and statesmen of new countries found a common language born of their human solidarity. I pointed out that "the business of science is the investigation of nature, but science has a human origin and a human destination."

In her recently published memoirs, Golda Meir has paid tribute to the first Rehovot Conference as something of a breakthrough in Israel's international relations. One of the most sensitive participants was the head of Victoria College in Sierra Leone, Dr. Solomon Caulker. He rose with tears in his eyes to say, "I came in darkness, but I leave in light." A few hours later on his way back home, his plane crashed at Dakar, leaving the only sad repercussion of the conference.

In personal terms, the conference was significant for me. While most of my political and diplomatic experience had been in the West, I had now established links with leading statesmen in dozens of developing Third World countries, especially in Africa. I had also achieved another result. There is always the danger of claustrophobia in Israel's intellectual climate: the peril of intense preoccupation with our own affairs; the assumption that others owe attention to our problems while we have no particular obligations toward theirs. I felt during that glittering week that I may have helped focus Israel's interest on something less provincial than her own concerns. We were able to make a contribution beyond our own immediate necessities to the exploration of one of the world's most tragic and fateful predicaments.

A few weeks before the conference opened, Ben Gurion had appointed me Minister of Education and Culture in place of Zalman Aranne, who had resigned in protest against a lack of support of his position on teachers' strikes. Ben Gurion had toyed with the idea of appointing Yigael Yadin; and a few days before the decision on the Education Ministry was made, Teddy Kollek, his director-general, asked me innocently if I would like to take the vacant portfolio of Minister of Posts. I replied with some heat. It was quite clear that an attempt was being made to cut my international stature down to size, and to make me somewhat ridiculous. Education and Culture was quite another matter. After Defense, it was the most far-flung of all the Israeli ministries. It had more importance than corresponding ministries in most countries. The Israeli school network is highly centralized, certainly no less so than the Napoleonic system under which a Minister of Education in Paris could tell you from his files exactly what subjects were being taught at any given hour in any of the thousands of schools throughout the Republic. In Israel the Ministry had total control of the elementary-school system, and was beginning to participate more actively in the secondary-school system, which, however, was then somewhat slender in its development. Higher education then consisted entirely of the three veteran institutions: the Hebrew University of Jerusalem, the Haifa Technion and the Weizmann Institute of Science. But it was clear that there would be a chance for expansion, and Tel Aviv and Bar Ilan universities were waiting at the gate.

10

Seven
Ministerial Years
1960-1966

THE ISRAELI PRESS AND THE INTELLECTUAL COMMUNITY WELCOMED MY appointment as Minister of Education and Culture on the basis of my academic background and qualifications. But my main concern in the first stages of my ministry was not so much with academic levels as with the social responsibility of our educational system. I appointed a new director-general, Hanoch Rinot, who compassionately administered the educational institutions of Youth Aliyah which were concerned with children who had been saved from Europe before and after the Holocaust.

On my desk I found a research study by Aryeh Simon, the Inspector of Education in the southern region, in which he analyzed the educational attainments of children whose parents had immigrated from Oriental communities. The picture was horrifying. The rate of illiteracy was high. There was little chance for them to qualify for post-elementary education. The university was a distant and unattainable world. It was unlikely that many of them could ever be productively employed. The defect did not arise from any lack of innate intelligence, but from the environmental conditions in which their schooling took place. They lived in squalid, crowded homes with no possibility of orderly study and little intellectual inspiration from their surroundings. They could not digest even the modest range of conceptual ideas that the elementary school tried to inculcate. As I projected this picture across the country as a whole, I could only arrive at a dark forecast. Israel was becoming a country of two nations, one with a high capacity of "takeoff" into a swift orbit of intellectual progress, the other hopelessly tied down in a vicious circle of handicap. What made this condition particularly explosive was the fact that educational backwardness coincided with recognizable ethnic criteria. Israelis of European origin would occupy the top half of the social pyramid, while the broad base of the unskilled and underprivileged would be occupied by citizens whose origins lay in Moslem countries.

I took an early opportunity to bring this situation to a Cabinet meeting at the end of 1960 and I could see that my colleagues, and especially Ben Gurion, were fascinated and surprised. It was unusual to hear a report on education at the Cabinet table, which usually occupied most of its time with international and security problems. Ministers were shocked by the evidence that a hard core of misery, resentment, bitterness and ultimate social revolt was deeply embedded in our society and yet had been so remote from the horizon of ministers and high officials that my lecture had some element of innovation. I told the Cabinet that there was no room for "equal" educational treatment of all segments of the population, since the point of departure was not equal. A special allocation of resources and effort on a basis of favoritism would have to be made in order to keep the gap under control and eventually to make it narrower.

For some weeks thereafter, the problem of the educational gap seized the headlines in the national press and became a central theme in the public dialogue. I regarded this with satisfaction. It has always seemed to me that one of the main functions of a minister is to make his departmental concerns a theme of public interest and attention. I spent many hours with my associates in the ministry devising an acceptable semantic definition for the condition that we were trying to change.

We established schools called *te'unei tapuach,* schools for children in "need of development." The emphasis was not on past failure, but on what could be done to redeem it. We devoted extra budgetary resources, special textbooks, a particular effort to keep classes to a minimal number of participants with specially trained teachers. I officially inaugurated the long school day in 1962 to ensure that children would spend more time in the atmosphere of school and, more important, less time at home. In later years, under the leadership of my successor, Zalman Aranne, the "special education" sector became the main preoccupation of the ministry. In a report published on the tenth anniversary of the selective educational process, the leading pedagogical authorities were able to report significant progress. Children of

Oriental communities were pouring into the secondary-school system in larger numbers, while their percentage in the higher-education network, though still lower than it should have been, had gone beyond the original 6 percent to something. approaching 20 percent. The tunnel was still long, but there was light at the end.

From this problem I turned to post-elementary education. I was surprised to find how little emphasis had been given to this sector of the educational system. Historically, secondary education had grown up outside the governmental framework, under the initiative of private institutions such as the Herzliya Gymnasium and the Reali School in Haifa, or under municipal control. I wanted to ensure that a larger proportion of children who completed elementary school would continue up to and beyond the secondary stage.

My advisers were strongly polarized in their affections between the elementary- and the secondary-education systems. I fear that I soon got the reputation of belonging to the latter. I had no reason to regret this. I thought that the grievances of academically trained teachers were genuine. Their desire was to have their wages and status equalized with those of other academicians such as engineers and lawyers, rather than to be in the same category as elementary-school teachers, who, unfortunately, were for the most part seminar-trained without university qualification.

One of the problems in the secondary sector was the existence of a somewhat snobbish division between humanistic education, which was fashionable, and technical or professional education, which was thought to be the preserve of lesser-endowed pupils. I felt that the Israeli pioneer economy, with its accent on industrialization and technology, would have more need of mechanics and engineers than of more lawyers and journalists. Here I was working against the prejudice of my own classical and literary background, and trying to see the Israeli reality in its own perspective.

I therefore thought it wise to look abroad, and especially to Britain, so as to emulate the "comprehensive school," in which the traditional curricular uniformity was broken up into a broad diversity of specializations within a heavily populated school. Since the new-development towns were showing signs of cultural degeneration, I thought that comprehensive schools should be in such places as Kiryat Shmona, Beit Shemesh, Hazor, Dimona, Eilat and similar localities. This would decrease the prospect of parents' leaving for the big cities in search of secondary education, thus weakening the human structure of the new townships. The comprehensive school might also become the center of culture and communal leadership in these areas.

In higher education the chief question was whether the virtual monopoly of the Hebrew University of Jerusalem could any longer be maintained. Some university facilities existed in Tel Aviv, as branches of the Jerusalem university, but I thought that there was now a need for an authentic Tel Aviv University, independently administered and sustained by civic pride. It should not simply fill gaps in the Hebrew University's facilities; it should constitute a full university community. Meanwhile, the religious Zionist movement had established the base of a higher-education development near Ramat Gan, called Bar Ilan University. In my capacity as chairman of the Council on Higher Education, I would obviously have an influence on whether this pluralism was checked or developed.

I found vehement resistance from many leaders of the Hebrew University. It is clear that the outlook of some of them was monopolistic. Jerusalem was to be the intellectual center of the country, Haifa its industrial center, and Tel Aviv its main arena of commercial activity. Students from all over the country should, therefore, see Jerusalem as their university destination. To my surprise, I found that Ben Gurion was sympathetic to this categorization. He found it hard to believe that there should be a university anywhere but in Jerusalem. My own experience led me to believe that any urban community that reached a certain demographic size would be incomplete without a university. With Mayor Mordecai Namir I was affronted by the idea that Tel Aviv, in 1960, was a city with no university, no public library, and no museum. I also thought that once the religious Zionists had established their institution at Bar Ilan, we should be concerned to promote its development. The religious school system in Israel occupied some 30 percent of the educational sector at elementary and secondary levels. The academic levels were variable, but there was no crisis of values, no inner doubts about the meaning and purpose of Jewish existence. Indeed, the certitudes of Jewish tradition gave the educational process a solidity that was painfully lacking in the general state system. I have always regretted the absence of the special "labor section" within the educational system, abolished by Ben Gurion in his desire to avoid a political division of the educational system.

The discussions of the Council on Higher Education for and against recognition of the Tel Aviv and Bar Ilan universities were as rancorous as any that I had known around the tables of the United Nations organization. I soon threw my full weight as chairman on the side of pluralism. There was a tendency by the Hebrew University leaders to be rigorous about the right to confer degrees in institutions that did not reach a very high level. My own feeling was that it was better to have some initial diversity in levels of academic degrees than to maintain Jerusalem's monopoly and impede the early development of Tel Aviv and Bar Ilan. I had also in mind the problem of our university teachers. If a lecturer or a professor could not make good in our only university at Jerusalem, either for academic reasons or through tense relations with his colleagues, he had no course but to emigrate. Certainly the absorption of an increasing number of academically trained people in Israel required a broader academic employment market in the form of more universities. I thus worked actively toward granting Tel Aviv and Bar Ilan the necessary recognition, even at the expense of a certain leniency and lack of academic rigor in the early stages. I hope that the university fathers in Jerusalem have forgiven me by now.

As I look at the campuses of the Tel Aviv and Bar Ilan universities today and of the subsequent developments in Haifa University and Ben Gurion University at Beersheba, I feel a twinge of pride at the stand that I then took in favor of controlled proliferation. Today, any young Israeli can find a university in some proximity to his home.

Since I had not been closely involved in the early history of the educational system in Israel, I was disposed to take a comparative approach and to see what could be learned from education movements outside our country. I found the Israeli school a very conservative place. It was simple and even primitive in its physical facilities. The strong Hebrew and Biblical emphasis could, of course, be understood in terms of our need to create a national consciousness, but I was less pleased with traditionalism in other domains, such as the teaching of English. Here the emphasis seemed to be on understanding and analyzing Shakespeare rather than on acquiring a tongue for use. I pointed out to the appropriate pedagogic committee that the object of language was to be spoken. If a child spoke and read a modern language, he would seek his own access to its treasures.

As I looked around the world, I found new techniques at work. I was, and remain, somewhat skeptical about language machines and other electronic devices. On the other hand, I was impressed by the potential of television as an educational tool. I felt that Israel had a special need for this device. In addition to the inequalities arising from diverse backgrounds, origins and experiences, there was an educational gap between the cities and the countryside. The schools in development villages and small agricultural communities were not able to attract skilled teachers. A television studio would be able to produce the highest quality of instruction and diffuse it throughout the whole country, giving rural populations a glimpse of teaching at its highest level. When Mrs. Dorothy de Rothschild and Lord Rothschild in England indicated a readiness to assume the expense of establishing an educational television system in Israel, I responded at once.

On the surface this seemed a simple matter, within the competence of the responsible minister. But I had reckoned without another paradox of Israeli life. On the one hand, there is a great worship of science, technology and modernism; on the other, Israelis do not easily change established systems, whether in farming, educational methods or anything else. Opposition to the plan for educational television arose from varied quarters. The religious Zionists thought it had some element of infidelity—the Jewish religion is suspicious of visual representation or photography. There was also the fear that television would take orthodox viewers outside their Jewish world into a wider realm of secular ideas. It was also pointed out that an educational television network would expedite the introduction of general television in Israel. I myself saw no danger in this. I could not forget André Malraux's reminder that through television more Frenchmen had seen the plays of Molière and Racine in a single year than in all the centuries since they created their masterpieces. The popularization of science and language and a greater involvement in public issues were other results of television that I thought salutary for Israel.

Here again, I was in for a surprise from Ben Gurion. Realizing that educational television would lead to a general television system, the Prime Minister dug his heels in and expressed opposition. He had inadvertently turned on his television sets in London and New York and had seen people shooting one another for no easily perceptible reason. He tended to believe that this was the main theme of the television medium, and that, in his words, "Israel can do without this for some years." I tried to point out that nothing came out of a television set that had not previously been put into it. To invalidate television because of poor programs was rather like attacking literature because some books are frivolous or degrading. Happily, Ben Gurion's chief lieutenant, Teddy Kollek, shared my view and worked hard to ensure that Ben Gurion's reservations would not take the form of a veto.

To make things more complicated, there was a segment of opposition to educational television on the grounds that it was being provided by the Rothschilds: some Zionist parties, especially on the left, saw a repetition of the old days when Baron Edmond de Rothschild ruled over our first agricultural settlements with his Parisian officials. The implication was that to accept this gift from the Rothschild Foundation was to surrender sovereignty to plutocracy. I found it shocking that the generosity of the Rothschild family could be so distorted.

Some of the opponents of educational television in the religious camp were worried by the prospect that teachers not wearing skull-caps might appear on the screen. There were even some concerned about the teachings of Darwinian biology, which were not compatible with statements that the world is exactly five thousand seven hundred odd years old. The skullcap matter was easily solved. I was able to adduce that most of the teachers were women, and only the sharpest eye would be able to discern whether the learned ladies had the head crowned with a *sheitel* or with their own hair! One humorist in my ministry suggested that in religious schools a yarmulke could be placed on the television set in order to conceal the bare-headedness of a secular teacher. His only reward was a stern ministerial glare.

After an unbelievably difficult parliamentary battle I managed to put the legislation through. Israel's instructional television is now one of the major assets of our educational system and has won broad renown.

It was the cultural aspect of my ministerial responsibility that involved me in the sharpest controversies. There is a remarkable public docility in Israel, side by side with a natural Jewish skepticism. The result is that any controversial problem is referred to ministerial responsibility. When I acquiesced in a chamber-music quartet going on a visit to Germany, there was an uproar from the anti-German groups, who wanted us never to acknowledge the rise of a liberal democracy in the German Federal Republic. When a German pastor, with an impeccable anti-Nazi record, was allowed by a headmaster to visit a school, all the parliamentary bombardment fell upon me. When the Israeli national soccer team rashly played a match against Italy on a Sabbath, it was I who received the stern denunciation of the religious parties as though I, personally, were the enemy of the traditional fidelities.

I gave much attention to the Arab educational sector, since this was one of the few areas in which accelerated expansion of amenities was possible. The Israeli policy is one of cultural autonomy. There is no attempt to make the Arabs into Jews or Zionists. On the contrary, they are encouraged to revere Arab traditions, Arab poets and Arab heroes. Our only reservation is the rejection of textbooks full of anti-Jewish and anti-Israeli incitement that are published in the Arab capitals and used, shamefully, by the United Nations Refugee Agency in its schools.

I could not avoid the rougher and more prosaic aspects of my task. There was a constant struggle between the Finance Ministry, trying to guard the national revenue, and the powerful Teachers' Unions, convinced that their members were victimized by a government that refused to acknowledge the primacy of intellectual values. It is hard to imagine any trade unions as tenacious, exacting and vehement as those of the elementary- and secondary-school teachers. To make things more complicated, they lived in a reciprocal distrust of one another. Even their common hostility to the Education Ministry was unable to transcend this conflict.

I was basically on the side of the teachers. In spite of all the rhetoric about the primacy of education in Israel's destiny, the status of the teacher in the community was often several levels below that of dignity. It is a paradox that the nations that have attached the greatest importance to intellectual effort seem to have held their teachers in the least regard. Thus, the ancient Athenians used slaves as "pedagogues," while in the Jewish Pale of Settlement, a reverence for learning went hand in hand with a tendency to use the word *melamed* as an epithet of contempt. Having been accustomed to British schools with academically university-trained and -gowned teachers who emitted an atmosphere of authority and dignity, I found the informally dressed young women teaching in Israel somewhat disconcerting. It was the pupils who seemed to hold the upper hand in the classrooms. The Israeli community from its earliest days has been "paideiocentric," cherishing its children like precious plants whose very growth was a miracle beyond expectation. The "progressive" and permissive educational theories took root in Israel's educational system at a very early stage. They have yet to prove their value.

While it is fashionable in Israeli gossip to denigrate the school system and to compare it adversely with the army and the agricultural settlements, the truth is that most of Israel's soldiers and farmers, as well as her scientists, are now the product of Israeli schools. As Minister of Education and Culture, I realized that I had official responsibilities affecting more than one third of the total population of the country. There is no precedent in educational history for the expansion of a student population between kindergarten and university from the 120,000 in 1948 to over a million less than three decades later. To have maintained a viable level at so steep a rate of growth is one of Israel's major achievements.

It was in the educational system that the problems of social integration in Israel came to acute expression. Toward the end of my tenure a situation arose similar to that which had agitated American society in the Little Rock case. The parents of children in a school in Kiryat Gat, most of them of sabra or European origin, objected to the attempts of our ministry to ensure social integration by introducing pupils from a poorer district. The proposal was to use public transportation to bring children from Oriental communities into the school in order to promote coexistence. In spite of intimidatory protest, I was prepared to use the compulsion of law to oblige parents to accept the judgment of the ministry's inspectors on the distribution of children in the state schools.

My three years in the Ministry of Education brought me into contact with every part of the population in homes and schools, at teachers' meetings and parents' associations. There is probably no other ministry which gives its leaders such a constant relationship with the concrete realities of Israeli life. In the early stages many pupils, students, teachers and even professors reacted to me with something of the remoteness arising from my association with international diplomacy. I remember visiting a classroom in which English was taught with a Central European accent by a recent immigrant. The teacher, a young woman in her thirties, was petrified when she heard that I was going to enter her classroom. She made a point of occupying the class for twenty minutes with general questions. She was determined to avoid proceeding with the English lesson until I was able, somehow, to put her at relative ease.

Education in Israel is surrounded by an atmosphere of challenge. Some of the stimulating forces at work in Jewish intellectual history do not operate in the safer but narrower context of statehood. The Jews alone of all historic nations have lived intimately with all the intellectual currents in recorded history, from ancient prophecy to modern science, from the dim roots of man's past to the shining possibilities of his future. It is not easy to keep the targets high and the vision broad. My view on the priority of education was not everywhere accepted. It cannot be denied that there is an anti-intellectual theme in the early history of pioneering Zionism. The object was to convert an excessively academized people into a nation distributed into normal categories. Thus, the hero of the Zionist saga was the mathematician or scholar who had left his research to milk a cow on a Zionist farm. There was reason and method in this process some decades ago. But such a waste of intellectual power would spell weakness for Israel's security and economy in the conditions of today.

In speaking of Israeli science, my eyes were focused on the future. But Israel is not a new synthetic nation, writing its history on a clean slate. The past follows it wherever it goes. The revival of the Hebrew language in daily speech, its steady growth in conceptual precision, the spectacular results in archaelogical discovery, the role of the Bible in secular as well as in religious education, the privileged status of religious tradition in some domains of personal law, are all symptoms of the yearning for continuity. The Shrine of the Book housing the Dead Sea Scrolls and the Yad Vashem memorial to the Holocaust a few kilometers away are two institutions which could not exist anywhere but in Israel. They stand out on Jerusalem's skyline, the one in testimony to Israel's origins, the other in mute and painful witness to her people's recent martyrdom. With all its outward signs of modernity, Israel is still a nation haunted by memories too powerful to fade.

During my three years of service as Minister of Education, I was almost totally cut off from my familiar concerns with international relations. But in 1962, when Mrs. Meir went to the General Assembly of the United Nations, she asked me to act as Foreign Minister during her absence. This is a necessity of Israeli law but has rarely any significance beyond the availability of a minister to sign documents or to be consulted in emergencies. On one occasion, however, a debate arose in the Knesset on Israel's attitude to Communist China. I was able to speak on this subject with greater familiarity than a stopgap minister might have been expected to display. When Dag Hammarskjöld died early in 1961, I went to Stockholm for his funeral, renewing my contact with people with whom I had been in close partnership during my United Nations years. I particularly remember encountering Lyndon B. Johnson, then Vice-President of the United States. I said to him: "Mr. Vice-President, how do you like your new job?" He gave me a withering glare, pointed at his frock coat, striped trousers and top hat, and said in his broad Southern accent: "Do you see this monkey suit? Ah never wore one of these before. Now Ah sleep in the damn things." His volcanic energy was clearly being suppressed to the point of acute pain.

My service in the Ministry of Education coincided with a stormy period in Israel's domestic politics. In December 1960 Ben Gurion resigned, and for eight months the nation lived in the expectation of an election that was eventually held in August 1961. There was no objective necessity for this sudden disturbance. Our parliamentary majority was strong and the general trend was toward consolidation. It is true that the nation was less cohesive than it had been in its first decade. Israelis stood together for life and death, but in less extreme ordeals they were very conscious of the things that divided them. The word "gap" began to figure endlessly in Israel's constant exploration of herself. There was the gap between the new urban middle class and the old rural élite. There was the gap between both of these and the struggling disinherited proletariat in the slum areas and shantytowns. There was the gap between the European-educated population and the immigrants from Arab countries with their special pieties, loyalties and family traditions. There was also a generation gap. The young Israeli generation born in the sun and under the open skies was given to a simpler, less tormented but more superficial intellectual outlook than that which had been common to the pioneering generation. There was also a gap of alienation growing up between young, matter-of-fact Israelis and the more sentimental, complicated, introspective but creative Diaspora Jews. All this gave our politics an additional dimension of turbulence.

And yet, there were common memories which reminded Israelis that history had dealt with the whole of the Jewish people in a special way, so that in the last resort they were indivisible in their fate. One such moment came with the Eichmann judgment. The trial was exemplary in its dignity and precision. The court of three judges under the presidency of Justice Moshe Landau heard hundreds of witnesses who unfolded stories so macabre that the whole nation was stunned by a new flow of grief. It lived its trauma all over again. The Israeli Attorney General, Gideon Hausner, rose to lofty heights in bringing the indictment in the name of six million accusers "whose blood cries out, but whose voice is stilled." The sentence of death was passed and upheld in the Court of Appeal, and for the only time in Israel's history, presidential clemency was withheld. But of far greater significance than the justice meted out to a single odious monster was the electrifying effect of the trial on the younger generation. One could feel Israelis, born since the Holocaust, shuddering in a paroxysm of horror. The Eichmann trial had risen above the level of retribution, vengeance and even formal justice. It had achieved a transforming effect on a people's consciousness.

The hope of a stable period in Israel's domestic life was shattered by the "Lavon affair" or, more accurately, by the intensity of Ben Gurion's reaction to it. The "affair" erupted in the autumn of 1960 but its roots went back to 1954, when Pinchas Lavon was Minister of Defense in Sharett's Cabinet. The central event was what was called "a security mishap." An intelligence unit consisting of Egyptian Jews had been working in Cairo under Israeli control since 1951. In 1954 Britain agreed to evacuate its forces from the Canal Zone. While the British military presence there had served as a buffer between Israeli and Egyptian military forces, there would now be proximity instead of separation. The Anglo-Egyptian treaty was regarded by some Israelis, including Lavon, as a drastic change in the regional balance of power. It came at a time when Israel was reminded of her vulnerability by the refusal of the United States to supply balancing arms. In an apparent effort to complicate relations between

Nasser's regime and the West, the intelligence unit set off explosions in Cairo and Alexandria, in circumstances tending to give the impression that Egypt was endangering Western interests. The question in Israel was who had given the reckless and fatal instructions. Neither Prime Minister Sharett nor the Cabinet had been informed or consulted. Inquiries instituted during Sharett's premiership neither convicted nor completely exonerated Lavon. The fact that two of the Israeli agents were sentenced to death and executed on January 31, 1955, gave the affair a somber aspect. On February 2 Lavon resigned. His career seemed to have ended, but his dynamism and talent elevated him within a year to the position of secretary-general of the Histadrut. The "affair" seemed to have been left far behind.

It was not to be. In 1959 the Israeli officer who had commanded the operation known as the "security mishap" managed to escape from Egypt, was brought to trial in Israel on charges unrelated to the "security mishap" and sentenced to long imprisonment. Some new facts concerning the operation of 1954 were revealed during the trial. Lavon considered that he had new evidence which would remove the question mark left behind by Sharett's inquiry. On September 26, 1960, he asked the Prime Minister for a statement clearing him of responsibility. Ben Gurion refused to make a judgment, pointing out that he had no judicial capacity and had not even studied the affair. Lavon placed the issue before the Knesset Security and Foreign Affairs Committee. Most of the press supported Lavon, claiming that he had been wrongly accused, and implying that there had been a conspiracy against him. Ben Gurion's response was consistent: the only way to establish the facts was by a formal judicial inquiry. The majority of the Cabinet thought that the matter should be investigated by a Cabinet committee, including the Minister of Justice. The committee, composed of seven members, presented its findings to the Cabinet on December 25, 1960. Its report completely exonerated Lavon from any responsibility for the mishap, and its verdict was endorsed by the Cabinet with three abstentions, including myself, and without Ben Gurion's participation in the vote. Ben Gurion was resentful of this result and resigned a few weeks later. I shared Ben Gurion's doubts about the propriety of the Cabinet committee's report, and I therefore supported him in my abstention, to the vast indignation of Pinhas Sapir, who was then sharply hostile to Ben Gurion. But I could not agree that the incident was important enough to justify Ben Gurion's prolonged obsession with it so many years after the event.

This controversy agitated Israeli opinion for months on end. Ben Gurion's principle was that a political body such as a Cabinet committee could not exonerate anybody, since this was a judicial function. He therefore believed that the balance of Israel's democratic structure had been violated. He argued somewhat excessively that if Lavon was exonerated, it followed that the officer subordinate to him had been virtually convicted for having given a fatal order without authority. To convict by a Cabinet decision without judicial authority was even worse than to exonerate by such means. Ben Gurion thus presented the action of the Cabinet as a major corruption of the democratic process and of juridical integrity. He pursued this theme in writings of unbelievable vehemence and profusion and began to express disparaging sentiments about the Cabinet committee, especially his Finance Minister, Levi Eshkol, and the Minister of Justice, Pinchas Rosen.

Ben Gurion's critics had a more varied indictment to make. He was exaggerating the importance of a formalistic and debatable issue, upsetting the national priorities and preventing the nation from getting on with its vital work. By creating a choice between dismissing Lavon or doing without his own leadership, he was forcing his party to vote against its objective judgment, for in its heart it wanted both Ben Gurion and Lavon to continue their tasks. Leading academic figures entered the fray to allege charismatic and authoritarian elements in Ben Gurion's leadership. They raised the question whether any leader should refuse to accept a collective Cabinet, parliamentary and party decision, for the Knesset had endorsed the exoneration of Lavon by the committee. Ben Gurion found himself abandoned by public opinion after many years of general adulation.

So the argument flowed on. Its major consequence was that it expedited Ben Gurion's departure from the national leadership. There were other points of tension between him and the party, but it was the controversy over the "affair" that tore his mind away from the central national issues to brood darkly on something in which most Israelis wanted to lose interest. In the election which he forced in 1961, our party retained power but lost seven seats. There was an ardent resolve to have done with the whole issue. The public had the feeling that the nation would lose its sanity unless it learned to abandon the "affair" which was eating away at its heart and mind, like some curse in medieval demonology.

Ben Gurion initially weathered this storm, but he was now estranged from many of his contemporaries, apathetic about many of Israel's parliamentary conflicts, wounded by the rejection of his position on the "affair" and full of dark fears about the future. In April 1963, when Egypt, Syria and Iraq announced one of their periodic paper federations, with the usual dire threats of Israel's destruction,

Ben Gurion reacted in an apocalyptic spirit that contrasted with his usual confidence. He sent letters to over a hundred heads of government, including Kennedy, De Gaulle and Macmillan, expressing doubt about Israel's ability to survive in the future. One morning in June 1963 he opened a Cabinet meeting with the casual remark that he would resign as soon as the meeting was over. An era of large and vivid leadership had come to an end.

Ben Gurion had a profound impact on his nation's formative years. He occupied a larger area of the national consciousness than the premiership strictly required. His squat figure, beetle brows, white tufts of hair, staccato speech, his quick, jerky manner of moving about, gave an infectious impression of clarity and purpose. He had a talent for animating the national will. He created a permanent sense of excitement about those objectives he deemed central and decisive at any given time. His was a broad, simple vision of Israel's destiny: we were the descendants of the ancient prophetic Israel, harbinger to the world of the messianic dream. By developing her intellectual and moral resources, Israel could again become a nation of special vitality.

Ben Gurion was ubiquitous and all-pervasive in Israeli life. He had something to say about Biblical research, science, history, education, religion, and of course, military strategy and organization. His intellect was vigilant and lively, though not formally disciplined. He was permanently open to new interests and enthusiasms but tended to sharpen his judgments so as to exclude subtleties or ambivalence. For example, he felt that not much could be done about peace with the Arabs until Israel was unbreakably strong. He therefore banished this problem from his active concern and gave an impression of being unconciliatory. The impression was inaccurate. His international policy, though sometimes expressed in barks of defiance, was essentially moderate. His immense domestic prestige gave him a wide discretion, which he often used to withdraw from untenable situations, as when he put this power to work in the courageous decision to withdraw from Sinai in March 1957, inaugurating a period of progress and dynamism in Israel's life.

He sometimes disconcerted us by declarations of autarchy ("What matters is not what the nations of the world [goyim] say, but what the Jews do"). This was probably more extreme than he seriously intended. He knew in his heart that Israel had been more dependent on outside support, and more successful in obtaining it, than any other state faced with similar hazards. His aim was didactic. He was trying to get Israelis to understand the need for self-reliance and autonomous decision. His method was to concentrate a powerful searchlight on one aspect of a problem even if it meant creating darkness in the surrounding areas. The issues selected for illumination were usually the right ones—military strength, mass immigration, social integration, educational progress. Ben Gurion was, however, less fortunate in his domestic political relations. He fully understood the mechanics of power, but he was limited in his talent for personal contact. He was lonely, introspective, uninterested in outward forms, impatient of small talk. In the end he placed himself on roads where none but the most uncritical of his devotees were willing to follow him. The public simply refused to understand his excessive concern with the Lavon affair. Israeli society was emerging from innocence to sophistication, and was finding Ben Gurion's paternalism too stringent and authoritative. It admired his leadership but secretly longed for the experience of breathing for itself. His attacks on Eshkol were ascribed by most Israelis to the human failings that afflict many strong men in their relations with successors.

Ben Gurion had subconsciously come to identify himself with Israel's rebirth to the point where he could not easily admit that the national history would one day have to flow without him. His final months in office, and his first few years outside it, were unhappy and contentious, but long after they were over, his brilliant leadership was to live on in Israel's memory and gratitude. He was a leader cast in large dimensions and he endowed Israel's early years with originality and vital power.

Ben Gurion's resignation in June 1963, followed by his movingly simple retirement to Sdeh Boker in the Negev, made a Cabinet reshuffle necessary. Levi Eshkol, who had been Finance Minister for a decade, stepped into the vacant place with an air of assurance. Eshkol had been the choice of everyone, including Ben Gurion, who had indeed preferred him to Moshe Sharett as the Prime Minister in 1953. He had been Ben Gurion's loyal disciple and carried many burdens for his chief, including the distasteful task of settling the Lavon affair. His mannerisms were so different from those of his predecessor that there was no danger of imitation. Eshkol was in his late sixties when he took office. His place in Israel's history had been won not in the heady atmosphere of international politics and strategy, but in the dust and heat of pioneering and economic construction. He was the first authentic kibbutznik to take the supreme office, and the agricultural community sustained him with fraternal pride. His warm humanism was derived from the traditions first of Yiddish-speaking Russian Jewry and later of the Hebrew Labor movement. He had no charismatic pretensions. He sought not to dominate, but to persuade. He could rightly feel that every mile of water pipe, every village, every bungalow in Lachish, every factory owed something to his cumulative and constructive zeal. He knew exactly what he was and what he was not, and he wielded his responsibilities in strict proportion to his gifts. He had been happiest when his gnarled fingers could dig deep into the soil of practical affairs. Now he would have to test his capacities of supervision and command. That he had few gifts of expression was a grave handicap which proved fatal at moments when the nation expected a trumpet call to action in the service of clearly defined aims. (In fact, his lack of eloquence nearly brought about his downfall in 1967.) But he believed that solid facts had an intrinsic power which would make itself heard where it mattered most.

With all Cabinet posts now up for allocation, the question of Zalman Aranne's return to the government arose with great acuteness. One of the Israeli Labor movement's most original characters, his roots lay in the revolutionary atmosphere of Russia and in its tormented but fertile Jewish life. He was a man of extreme moods, untidy, unorganized, full of passion, ecstasy, morbid depressions and deep introspection. Although an autodidact himself, he had a profound respect for the intellectual process. Indeed, this theme was so strong in his mind that he could not bear to think of himself in any official function except that of Minister of Education. To oppose his return to that office would be tantamount to ending his political career.

One day Eshkol called me in for a conversation and suggested that I leave the Ministry of Education in order to become Deputy Prime Minister in his new Cabinet, thus paving the way for Aranne's return. He made it clear that he would accept my negative answer and that I had the option of remaining Minister of Education if I wanted. I would, however, then have to understand that the party would regard me as responsible for a prolonged and probably final eclipse of Aranne, who had a very broad support within our movement.

I had only twenty-four hours to weigh my decision. It was not an easy one. I had every reason to regard my tenure of the Ministry of Education as fruitful. After all, I had helped to heal the savage labor disputes that had paralyzed the teaching community, and there were no strikes on the horizon any more. Some innovations in the school system had been able to grow, but not less important was the fact that I had managed to make education a headline issue in Israel's national consciousness; I had also given more emphasis than my predecessors to the growing role of the natural sciences and technology in Israel's intellectual vocation. There was nothing to be ashamed of in any of this. Moreover, the ministry was a basis for domestic political power, bringing the minister into daily connection with masses of citizens at grass-roots level, something of which I had stood in greater need than many of my colleagues with longer records in the leadership of Israel's society. I would now have to give up all of this for an elevated title without departmental control or authority.

I consulted some friends, including Moshe Sharett, and of course, all members of my family. The consensus was that I would make a mistake in turning down Eshkol's offer. I would not only be delaying my own promotion, but would be leaving a scar in my relations with the party circles grouped around Zalman Aranne. If I accepted Eshkol's proposal, the party would have the services both of Aranne and myself at Cabinet level. If I refused it, Aranne would be excluded. I therefore said a regretful farewell to the Education Ministry at its ramshackle, rambling headquarters in the Street of the Prophets. I felt that the disappointment of the teachers' organizations was especially authentic. To be frank, however, my popularity with them was inspired as much by their apprehensions about their relations with Aranne as by their affection for me.

At the end of June 1963 I moved into a few small rooms in the Prime Minister's office, close to the Cabinet room and next door to Eshkol himself. I found myself immediately at work in helping to draft the speech in which he would present his Cabinet to the Knesset.

My transition to my new post was well received in the Jewish world and in the international press. I had already made some kind of return to the international field a few months before my change of post. Earlier in the year I had gone to Geneva to take part in the United Nations Conference on the Application of Science and Technology for the Benefit of Less Developed Areas. This was the largest conference with the longest title in international history. It had sprung, as Hammarskjöld himself generously admitted, out of my own Rehovot conferences. I had often discussed with Hammarskjöld the need for the United Nations to branch out into a specific dimension of scientific cooperation. It was therefore a graceful but not an abnormal gesture when his successor, U Thant, recommended me for one of the vice-presidency's of the conference. There were 2,500 delegates, including thirty Nobel Prize laureates. I headed a twenty-three-man Israeli delegation, including many of our leading scientific figures. I managed to stir some signs of enthusiasm in the closing address, in which I called for a rearrangement of international scientific priorities. Pointing to the large sums devoted on exploration of outer space, I asked, "What is our purpose? To conquer the moon—or to save this planet for human peace and welfare?"

In the international field, the main Israeli task was the establishment of close cooperation with the new President of the United States, John F. Kennedy. Ben Gurion had met him late in 1960 and came away shaking his head: "He is a mere boy. How can such a young man be President?" When Kennedy took the world to the brink by resisting Soviet intimidation in the Cuban crisis, I detected a skeptical note in Ben Gurion's attitude: "Was it not a huge gamble and was it really for something vital and important?" In a memorable meeting with him in Florida, Mrs. Meir heard Kennedy speak enthusiastically of Israel as "America's ally." What kind of rapport Ben Gurion would have established with him remains an academic question, for he resigned before Kennedy's Middle Eastern policy had come to full expression. Kennedy, however, had helped us on our way by endorsing the sale of Hawk anti-aircraft missiles and giving full support in our water development program. There was some evidence, however, that he would have liked Ben Gurion to show a more affirmative attitude in contributing to a solution of the Arab refugee problem.

I was Acting Foreign Minister (with Golda Meir at the United Nations) when a telephone call came to me from Walworth Barbour, the corpulent, good-natured and brilliantly incisive American ambassador to Israel. Barbour advised me to listen carefully to the next news bulletin which would announce Kennedy's death. I was in my Rehovot home at the time and had not turned on the radio for one of the hourly news bulletins. The shock hit me hard and strong. A few days later, in an address to the official Israeli memorial meeting, I said: "Tragedy is the difference between what is and what might have been. There will, of course, be other eras of zest and vitality when men feel that it is morning and it is good to be alive. This, however, belongs to the future. In the meantime, let us be frank with each other. The world is darker than it was a week ago."

The task was now to create a relationship not between Ben Gurion and Kennedy, but between Eshkol and Lyndon B. Johnson. While that was going on, during the following year, I took my share of the general diplomatic burden. I went to France, Britain, Mexico, Colombia, Venezuela and Canada and four times to the United States. In Mexico I was honored by an invitation to address a session of the Congress, and my fluency in Spanish came to good use. Latin Americans are sensitive on many things, including the attitude of foreigners to their language and culture.

But perhaps the most sensational thing that I did in August 1964, was to go on a normal vacation. I sailed with Suzy, Eli and Gila on the Israeli passenger ship S.S. *Shalom*. We landed at Marseilles, went in leisure by train to Paris, showed the children the Eiffel Tower, the Louvre, Versailles, went boat-riding on the Seine and showed them the wonders of London and Cambridge. In one of her letters to a friend, Suzy expressed the novelty of this situation:

> *Aubrey is simply marvellous. He orders the children's breakfast and tells them when to go to bed. I can't believe my eyes or ears it is so good. I shall always remember these precious moments. We are so relaxed, so human and familial. It is amazing what tensions must do to us, because really we are quite normal when not under pressure. Aubrey right through has been in charge of all of us. He even took care of the tipping and little arrangements which I have done for him for years.*

Nothing so leisured or normal was to happen to me again for many years. It may well be that this vacation signified the relative lack of centrality in a Deputy Prime Minister's job. There was a fireman's atmosphere about it, with long periods of waiting, but always with the possibility of being called to meaningful action. Thus, during 1964, I substituted for Golda Meir in receiving the visit of Pope Paul VI. Although the Vatican was unnecessarily finicky in depriving the trip of its full diplomatic scope, I told the Cabinet that, on the whole, the visit had increased the Vatican's perception of Israeli statehood. On the eve of the annual meeting of the General Assembly, Mrs. Meir was taken ill and I led our delegation in the early stages, making a statement of Israeli policy in the general debate. I was welcomed in the United Nations like a prodigal son, returning so unexpectedly that there was no time to fatten any calf.

I delivered the ritual review of the Israeli foreign policy to the General Assembly. The session, however, soon expired owing to the financial crisis arising out of a refusal by the Soviet Union and France to pay their share of the expenses for the United Nations Forces in Cyprus and Sinai. According to the strict letter of the Charter, this deprived them of their voting rights. On the other hand, it was felt that to take votes in which they were disqualified would have such effects, both on the Soviet leaders and on General de Gaulle, as to put the existence of the United Nations in jeopardy. It was thought better, therefore, to avoid all committee meetings in which votes would have to be held and to limit the session to the general debate.

Yet, during those few weeks in New York, I recaptured the taste of international life. The chalky smell of the classrooms was behind me, and the teachers' strikes a faint memory. I had long and intimate conversations with old friends, including Adlai Stevenson, who then presided in some frustration over the United States delegation. In my breakfast with him, he was surprisingly frank in expressing a lack of enthusiasm for the late President Kennedy and his Administration. I thought that a man with such an independent shape of mind and large following had made a mistake in putting himself back into a subordinate position in which his own intellectual profile would be obscured by the need to defend policies he could not help to fashion. A year later in Tel Aviv, I was to receive the shock of his sudden death in London. A destiny of failure was written into the very mold of his character. Yet, for a decade, he ennobled the American political discourse, and gave many across the world the sentiment that politics has its nobility along with its more familiar quota of sordidness.

Back home in the Deputy Prime Minister's office, my main task was to help Eshkol in his international role. I believe that we succeeded in this. After a difficult beginning, he won the intimate confidence of Lyndon Johnson, to whom the roughness of his character and speech was by no means a disadvantage. Johnson seemed to feel that if only Israel had a Texas, Eshkol would have belonged to it rather than to some "Eastern establishment" with its nose in the air and its mind in the clouds.

I took part with Eshkol and Golda Meir in a meeting in Jerusalem to discuss the prospect of arms from the United States. Although relations with France still seemed cordial and the supply belt was moving smoothly, we had reached the stage where we could not maintain a balance of power without an American component in armor and aircraft. There were some in Israel, especially in the Defense Ministry, who were reluctant to diversify our supply policy, fearing that by introducing American planes, we might alienate the French aircraft industry and perhaps the French government itself. This tactical difference was exaggeratedly described in the Israeli press as a struggle between the "European" and "American" schools of Israeli security, with myself placed firmly in the American school and Shimon Peres and others in the French school. In point of fact, there was no ideology involved at all. It was a matter of availability: I felt that our defense establishment had become so enchanted with the French connection that they tended to look with jaundiced eye on alternative links.

In my capacity as the senior member of the Cabinet's "reserve bench," I never did know at what stage of the game I would be thrown into action. It very often depended on chance. Thus, I was Acting Prime Minister in Eshkol's absence on a memorable day when we went up north to inaugurate the National Water Carrier. It is a curious fact that Israel has had to fight politically even for the right to use a modest part of her own water supply. The day that we

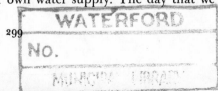

pulled the switch to send water cascading from Galilee through pipes into the Negev was memorable not only for our agriculture but also for our policy. It represented the collapse of the Arab deterrent. The Arab states had mounted a vehement campaign, full of dark threats, to prevent us from doing what we had done. They had failed to win international support for a purely negative policy. Once they had threatened "war to the death" to prevent us from bringing water to the Negev and had failed to deliver on their threats, the erosion of their credibility gave a boost to Israel's international position.

Then it happened that both Eshkol and Meir were indisposed on the day that we had to present a motion to the Knesset for establishing diplomatic relations with the Federal Republic of West Germany. I had been centrally involved in the negotiations with Chancellor Ludwig Erhard's representative, Dr. Kurt Birenbach, who came to Jerusalem at a tempestuous moment in the development of our relations. Israel had maintained a clandestine military supply relationship with the Federal Republic for some time. When this came to public view in 1965, there was an immense Arab uproar which led Bonn to suspend its sale of arms to Israel. This, in turn, brought a torrent of condemnation on Germany's head from Israel, the Jewish world and many in the West who thought that Germany was the last country that had a right to refuse assistance to Israel, which was defending what remained of Jewish security. Erhard played a shrewd game of balance to offset the decline of our military relations. He was ready to move forward on the diplomatic plane, in which, curiously, Konrad Adenauer had shown remarkable timidity. What prevented Adenauer from ever establishing diplomatic relations with Israel remains mysterious to this very day.

Erhard's approach to us aroused mixed feelings within the context of passion and memory that controls Israel's reaction to anything concerning Germany. My own feeling was that we would do ourselves no harm if we transferred the brunt of our German relationship from underground military supplies to overt diplomatic recognition—and to economic agreements which would enable us to purchase arms elsewhere in Europe. Together with Shinnar, Zeev Shek and Yochanan Meroz of the Foreign Ministry, and Yaacov Herzog representing the Prime Minister, I worked many long hours to bring this arrangement to fruition before its presentation to the Knesset.

It had been anticipated that this would be a stormy session. Had not the supporters of the Herut Party besieged the Knesset with hostile crowds and throwing of stones in 1952, when the first decision was made to accept German compensation? To my relief, the Knesset session went off smoothly. I made no attempt to underestimate the depth of the emotion which moved my opponents. My theme was that the Holocaust had left behind a legacy of grief and loss for which there was no consolation. All we could do to honor the memory of our dead was to give the Jewish people the assurance of its own future life. Israel's statehood was the decisive refutation of Hitler. He had wanted the Jewish people to disappear from history. Instead, the Jewish people had made a forward leap to sovereign status, giving security and enlargement to the Jewish future. To strengthen Israel at the expense of the Federal Republic of Germany thus had an intrinsic historic dignity, as well as a concrete measure of reinforcement. The Knesset accepted the recommendation and official relations were established with Germany.

Since my appointment as Deputy Prime Minister, the prospect of my eventual succession to the Foreign Ministry had never been in serious doubt. But the fact that I was able to appear convincingly both in the international domain and in our Parliament on these issues probably clinched the matter more firmly. Sometime before the 1965 election, Eshkol told me confidentially that he would expect me to take this post when it became vacant at Golda Meir's desire.

I played a large part in the rancorous 1965 Knesset elections. Ben Gurion had resigned voluntarily, but by no means in good spirit and, after a few months of quiescence, he began to chaff at his solitude and inaction. He also directed a fantastically bitter vendetta toward his successor. He stated that Eshkol had qualities that were not appropriate for a Prime Minister, and lacked the qualities that a Prime Minister ought to have. He was resentful when the Israeli public failed to share this view, and especially when Eshkol was taken quite seriously as a spokesman for Israel in the international arena. I had always felt that Ben Gurion's notes to Kennedy, De Gaulle and others in May 1963 expressing doubt that Israel would survive after him represented a subconscious identification of Israeli history with his own autobiography. This conclusion was borne out by his refusal to admit that anything good or normal could even happen under Eshkol's guidance. He accused the Eshkol government of unspecified security failures, presumably relating to our scientific development, and brought his bitterness to a point of culmination in breaking away from the Mapai Party and forming his own independent party under the name "Rafi." He was followed with some reluctance into the wilderness by Moshe Dayan, Shimon Peres, Yosef Almogi and other vigorous members of our party leadership. They were joined by some intellectuals, generals and public figures who had never been associated with the Labor movement at all, and who found Rafi's reformist zeal and nonideological outlook congenial to their temperament.

Before making the break, Ben Gurion had tried to unseat Eshkol by a head-on confrontation at the party's conference. He won 40 percent of the votes in his effort to replace Eshkol with himself—no mean achievement for a man nearing his eightieth year who had given every impression of having resigned for good. Most of our party not only felt that it would be putting the clock backward to restore Ben Gurion at so advanced an age, but also that his wholesale condemnation of Eshkol was not justified.

The Rafi Party was skillful in its propaganda and had a stronger position in the press than it turned out to possess in the general public sentiment. The defection had certainly weakened our electoral mechanism. After all, in our previous elections since 1959, Ben Gurion, Dayan, Peres and Yosef Almogi had each been a considerable force. Now they were on the opposite side. The number of leaders in the Labor Alignment who could be expected to draw crowds and to excite the public was correspondingly reduced. Eshkol himself did not have Ben Gurion's genius for communication. Pinhas Sapir was a superb organizer, but deficient in public appeal. I was, therefore, one of the very few who had to carry the weight of the party's information campaign over which I presided together with Moshe Carmel of Achdut Ha'avodah, which had now joined Mapai in the Labor Alignment (Ma'arach), on which Ben Gurion poured seething contempt ("Ma'arach Shma'arach").

On the day before the election itself, I was lunching in the Yarden Restaurant at a table near which sat John Kimche, then editor of the *Jewish Observer* and *Middle East Review*, Aryeh Disenchik, the publisher of *Ma'ariv*, and some Israeli guests. They were making estimates about the electoral result. Some of them were predicting that Rafi would secure thirty seats in the Knesset, which would of course involve the complete mutilation of our own Labor Alignment. I defiantly predicted only ten or eleven seats for Rafi. On election night I listened in my home in Herzliya as the results came in. Eshkol and his followers had won a dramatic victory. Ben Gurion, Dayan, Peres, Almogi and the rest of the Rafi list had won no more than 8 percent of the vote with ten Knesset seats, while Eshkol's Alignment reached the figure of forty-nine and became the largest single parliamentary party ever to be elected in Israel. Eshkol was no longer the designated heir, but a national leader in his own right. He could move into the future with confident step.

Shortly after the electoral result was known, Eshkol began the formation of his new Cabinet. This was complicated by his own first heart attack and by the inherent difficulties of coalition-making. Mrs. Meir fulfilled her long-expressed desire to retire from public service, little knowing the new lease of leadership that still lay ahead of her. Early in February 1966 my appointment as Minister of Foreign Affairs was announced. I drove to Beit Elisheva in Jerusalem, where Golda cordially introduced me to the Foreign Ministry staff, with so many of whom I had cooperated throughout my international decade. Suzy and I went to our small apartment in Jabotinsky Street, where we opened a bottle of remarkably noneffervescent Israeli champagne and drank to the future, together with our small and faithful group of workers: my personal secretary, Rachel Carmel, since married to a talented labor leader, Uri Gordon; her assistant, Nitza Pines; my Head of Bureau, Emanuel Shimoni; and my driver, Yankele Markovitch, a steadfast counselor and a friend of intense fidelity.

Seven years had passed since I took office under Ben Gurion, and I had now reached the opportunity that I sought. I had absorbed an Israeli reality deeper and wider than the diplomatic environment in which I had lived before. I no longer felt myself to be an amateur in the hard world of Israeli politics. My part in the election campaign gave me the knowledge that the party chiefs could hardly ignore me, even if they were still perplexed by my presence in the domestic political scene. When I entered the Foreign Ministry as its head I had made my way, by the hard road, back to familiar ground.

11

The Foreign Ministry 1966-1967

I FELT AT HOME IN THE MINISTRY OF FOREIGN AFFAIRS FROM THE VERY FIRST day. My embassies at Washington and the United Nations had been something like a Foreign Office on their own. I had worked with many dozens of senior diplomats whom I was to encounter at later stages of my work. Like all foreign ministries, ours faced a predicament in its relationship with the rest of the country. In most nations public opinion is in revolt against foreign policy. Here is a realm in which the national will is not sovereign. The coercions and frustrations imposed by the international systems are blamed on the ministry that mediates between the nation and its external field. And even in their home capitals, Foreign Ministry officials are in danger of living outside their own social reality in a special, closed diplomatic world.

I now came back to service with former colleagues in the foreign service, equipped with a dimension beyond their reach: seven years of immersion in the harder realities of Israeli life. I was the constitutional chief of those who had long been my equal colleagues. This turned out to be less embarrassing than I had expected. No previous first-name habits were suspended, and the team spirit prevailed over hierarchy. In her memoirs, Golda Meir has described a constant tension between herself and the Foreign Ministry officials. For me, on the other hand, the harmony was deep and broad.

Our residence was a large house in Balfour Street, constructed by an Egyptian Jewish merchant whose soaring ambitions extended to a swimming pool on the roof which, as far as anyone could remember, had been permanently without water. We moved out of our Rehovot home, to the dismay of both our children, who had put down their roots there for six years, then a majority of their conscious lives.

As I gathered my staff about me and brought in leading ambassadors for consultation, I made a quick survey of our international condition. In general, the barometer was set fair. The decade which opened in 1957 with the end of the Sinai Campaign held a richer promise than any in Israel's history. The population grew by immigration from 1,800,000 to 2,700,000. Across the Gulf of Aqaba from Eilat a bridge of commerce and friendship was patiently constructed toward the eastern half of the globe. The National Water Carrier was impressively completed. The country was bountifully visited, inspected, explored, praised and often flattered by countless heads of states and governments, and by spokesmen of the world's international community. The advanced countries admired Israel for her pioneering vitality, while new nations probed the secret of her accelerated development. Thus, some envied us for what we had already accomplished, others for what we still had to do. The harmony that we had patiently restored with the United States after the 1956 war was still in full depth. The kinship of France was touched by a sentiment close to alliance. Some had feared that our cooperation with France was due to the unifying influence of a common foe, but the Algerian war had been over for some years when President de Gaulle reaffirmed to Prime Minister Eshkol in June 1964 that Israel was a "friend and ally of France." De Gaulle then saw no contradiction between traditional French interests in the Arab world and the maintenance of strong relations with Israel.

We were celebrating the florescence of our relations with the newly developing states. What had begun as isolated ventures in economic cooperation with Burma and Ghana evolved during the sixties into a recognized international vocation. Here we were, a state with a population of little over two million, beset by acute scarcity of resources, caught up in a regional conflict, yet actively promoting the development of sixty other countries in three continents of the world. It was clear, as the years went by, that the Arab view of Israel as a dark conspiracy, a rapacious colonial adventure, or a regrettable but temporary crusade, had been rejected by the opinion and emotion of mankind.

Our security doctrine was rooted in the idea of an independent deterrent power. By 1966 the armed strength of Israel in relation to any Arab force likely to be pitted against us was no less formidable than it had been ten years before. The Yemen War, which had raged since 1961, found the Arab family deeply divided. Frustrated by their failure to prevent the fulfillment of our national water plan, the Arab states had created their summit conferences, established a Palestine Liberation Organization and appointed a Joint Arab Command. But none of the instruments created at the summit was as formidable as it tried to appear. The PLO was ferocious enough in pamphleteering and broadcast, but its martial qualities were dubious. It was led by my old acquaintance from United Nations debates, Ahmed Shukairy, whose pompous demeanor and blatant concern for his own vanity and comfort were reassuring to his prospective Israeli victims. I felt that if Shukairy was our chief danger, then we were tolerably safe.

My first visit abroad as Foreign Minister took me to Paris in February 1966, where French ministers assured me of uninterrupted support of Israel's defense. Their only criticism was directed to what they called an "excessive Israeli nervousness" about the durability of the French alliance. My exchange of views with Couve de Murville revealed no major divergence in our policies. From Paris I went on to fulfill a previously arranged visit to Ottawa. I was in friendly conversation with an old acquaintance, Prime Minister Lester Pearson, and his Foreign Minister, Paul Martin, when I got a sudden call from Washington. Last-minute difficulties had arisen in our negotiations for the supply of the Skyhawk aircraft. It would have been a great disappointment at the beginning of my ministry for this vital prospect to subside. Lester Pearson offered me his private plane to make my way to Washington for talks with President Lyndon Johnson and Secretary Robert McNamara. Within a few days the crisis was disentangled and our delighted air force began to prepare for a new stage in its technological and operative progress.

While our international relations appeared stable, I thought it useful to look hard at the weaker points. Since 1956 there had been very little development of contacts with the Arab world. Ben Gurion had concluded that there was no chance of reconciliation until Israel's strength and stability became so manifest that the Arab states would reconcile themselves to our permanence. In the meantime, he had not thought it wise to invest very deeply in contacts throughout the Arab world. There was also the cloud on our relations with the Soviet Union. We had diplomatic relations with six Communist countries, but beyond the formalities of mutual recognition, there was little human or economic encounter. I, therefore, took two initiatives. I appointed a new envoy to Bucharest, Eliezer Doron, and instructed him to formulate a program of cooperation with Rumania, going beyond the normal diplomatic and commercial ties. As I checked the records I discovered that no Israeli Cabinet minister had ever been to Eastern Europe in his official capacity. So with the aid and initiative of my assistant, Moshe Raviv, I decided to convene a regional conference of all Israeli ambassadors to East European countries in Warsaw instead of at the usual venues in Vienna or Paris.

I instructed our ambassador in Warsaw to sound out the Polish government. A reply came that the Polish government would permit such a conference, and I set out for my first contact with Communist Europe in May 1966. The Israeli ambassadors from Bucharest, Budapest, Prague, Belgrade, Moscow and Warsaw were assembled. In general, the Polish authorities were no more than stiffly correct, but the Foreign Minister, Adam Rapacki, had a gentler, old-world style remote from the Communist diplomatic routine. In proposing a toast at a dinner, he told me that the Polish government would continue to maintain steadfast links with Israel based on "memories of a common struggle and a common agony."

As I walked through the streets of Warsaw, gazing into the faces of its inhabitants, I was afflicted by sharp grief. After all, less than two decades before, almost every third face in the Polish capital would have been Jewish. The tragedy of our people had struck us with special violence on Polish soil.

I asked my hosts for permission to visit Auschwitz. With the six Israeli ambassadors and Raviv, we flew to Cracow and thence thirty miles by bus to the spot where two and a half million Jews had been executed by gas and cremation, and another half million starved to death. The most terrible moment was when our bus stopped at a railway crossing for a train to go by. As I looked at the glint of the steel rails, there came to mind the ghastly vision of the railway trucks that had transported millions of our people to their final doom.

The Polish government had sent its representatives to serve as our guides. The buildings at Auschwitz were preserved as if its inhabitants had moved out only yesterday. Everything remained as it had been on the day of liberation. The hideous apparatus of torture, the cells, the furnaces, the gas chambers, all stood as if they were the normal accouterments of daily life.

The Polish authorities were diffident about letting it be known that nearly all the victims at Auschwitz had been Jews. There were signs explaining that the deportees came from "Norway, Belgium, Holland, Greece." There was only one sign which mentioned that two and a half million of the three million killed had been Jews. I looked in stunned horror at the mountain of hair shaved from the heads of victims. Even more horrifying was the sight of a vast pile of childrens' shoes reaching almost to the ceiling. They had been taken from their little owners before cremation. I could not tear my eyes away. In silence I walked with my fellow countrymen through the Auschwitz fields. Behind me, at a crawling pace, came our official limousine bearing the Israeli flag. For all the millions who lay buried there, that flag would have been not only a symbol of pride, but a key to deliverance. It now seemed to whisper a consolation so belated as to be unbearable in its poignancy. I was oppressed by a sense of desolation. Everything, everything was too late.

We stood by the mass grave where I said *Kaddish,* the prayer of mourning. It was too hard to endure, and yet it was harder still to take ourselves away. On returning to Warsaw, our party went with Rapacki to the Yiddish theater and the next morning to a Jewish museum—preserved by the Polish state, a dim memory of a ravaged people.

The efforts that I had initiated with Ambassador Doron in Bucharest were bearing fruit. Relations were so solid that they were later to stand the shock of rupture with all other East European socialist stages. In Warsaw, however, while my contact with Poland had been popular with Israeli opinion, I had a sense that we were already being overtaken by events. Reports were coming in of recent discussions in the Kremlin of which the outcome was a more intense Soviet partnership with the Arab states for the better pursuit of the Cold War.

I took a hard look at our situation in Western Europe. My belief was that the United Nations had lost its importance, and that the Arab preponderance against Israel had made it impossible for us to avoid hostile decisions there. The real weight of international relations was moving into regional channels. The Latin American countries, whose supremacy was threatened by incoming African governments, were putting their trust more and more in the Organization of American States. Europe, now reduced to inferiority in the United Nations, was seeking its security in the North Atlantic Treaty Organization, and its economic welfare in the European Economic Community. I decided to attempt closer links with these regional bodies. In Washington I signed a cooperation agreement with the OAS, and in October 1966 I formally submitted Israel's request for a preferential agreement designed to lead to association with the EEC.

The success of Golda Meir's efforts to build a network of friendship and cooperation agreements in Africa naturally drew my attention to Southeast Asia, where there was no similar impress of the Israeli presence. Even in Burma, the replacement of U Nu by Ne Win had been followed by an almost complete disruption of our aid programs.

In March 1967 Suzy and I went on an extended series of official visits to Thailand, Burma, Singapore, Cambodia, the Philippines, Japan, Australia and New Zealand. In many of these countries we laid the foundations of increased cooperation programs. In Tokyo, Takeyo Miki explained to me both the possibilities and the limitations of Japanese-Israeli cooperation. Everything was possible so long as it was unobtrusive. When it came to the caution of the large electronic corporations, the government seemed unable to help. In Kyoto we tasted the special charm and authenticity of old-world Japanese life. In Bangkok old diplomatic friends, such as Prince Wan and Pote Sarasin, former Washington ambassadors, entertained me profusely, as did the able Foreign Minister, Thanat Khoman, who diplomatically allowed me to defeat him narrowly at golf. I doubt that this was the trauma that led him eventually to abandon diplomacy in favor of the asceticism of a Buddhist monk. King Bhumibol and his beautiful Queen Sirikit explained to us the paradox of Southeast Asian life. Just because nature was so bountiful, said His Majesty, there was not the desperate incentive to intense labor that existed in the cold, ungenerous lands of the North and the West. Even those who did not work in Southeast Asia simply had to extend a hand to find a banana or to throw a string into a pond to catch a fish. The result was that the stimulus to accelerated development was less sharp than in Europe. The abundance of Asia was, in a sense, its major difficulty.

In Singapore, where I was received by Foreign Minister Rajaratnam, my only problem was with the local press. The brilliant Prime Minister, Lee Kuan Yew, had won a Double First at Cambridge. Most of his countrymen had the impression that this was the highest academic honor possible. When our press officers distributed my biography, innocently mentioning my Triple First at Cambridge, there was a crisis about whether it would be tactful to release the dark secret. Singapore stood out by the intensity of its commercial energies, as if it were searching beyond its limited space toward sources of power and stability that transcended its smallness.

In Cambodia I had a most unusual experience in hours of conversation with the head of state, Prince Norodom Sihanouk, at his palace in Phnom Penh. He addressed me in immaculate French with the kind of reverberation that most people reserved for mass meetings. There was a Gaullist note both in his manner and in his literary style. He, more than any other statesman in the area, felt the torment of small nations caught up in the global struggle, trying to find a central path of safety between the allurements of Western aid and the need to conciliate the growing power of China. He spoke to me so sincerely about Israel that I was correspondingly saddened by his later decision to turn his back on us. But I managed to spend a day with Suzy amid the glories of Angkor Wat and to see an Israeli mission at work teaching Cambodian farmers to increase rice production.

In the Philippines, where my opposite number was my old friend Carlos Romulo, everything was easygoing and benign. President Ferdinand Marcos and his talented wife presided over an American-style democracy which certainly had its own features of permissiveness, but which gave no signs in 1967 of becoming so intolerable as to augur the rigorous changes which were later introduced. In Australia the Governor-General was none other than Robert Casey, who had been my chief as Minister of State in Cairo during World War II. In Melbourne and Sydney I found the warm welcome of distant Jewish communities linked to Israel by strong family ties. In New Zealand I had a nostalgic encounter with Sir Carl Berensen, who, in the United Nations debates in 1947, had thunderously denounced all attempts to abandon the partition scheme. Here, too, was Leslie Munroe, who had been the New Zealand representative during the stormy discussions about Suez and the Gulf of Aqaba in 1954 to 1957. I had a sense of remoteness from the central core of the world. I felt that if I went a few more miles, I would fall off the globe entirely. I began to understand something of the desperate search for intimacy that had led New Zealanders to cherish their relations with England and Scotland, thousands of miles away.

Back home in Jerusalem, I began to build a series of informal Arab connections. The time has not yet come to talk specifically of these, but in various European capitals I was able to learn from Jordanian, Lebanese or Tunisian citizens something of the inner workings of moderate Arab minds.

In general, opportunities beckoned us wherever we looked. Every seed of new effort seemed to bear some fruit. President Habib Bourgiba of Tunisia had shattered the conventional Arab ideology by appealing for "moderation and logic instead of passion" and urging a negotiated settlement with Israel. At the United Nations in October 1966 Gromyko reminded me nostalgically of the Soviet role in the establishment of Israel. During that year, two thousand Jews reached us from the USSR. The trickle was small, but it had come after decades of absolute drought. If it could be gradually pumped to a greater profusion, would not a new vision of growth come into Israel's view?

Despite occasional setbacks, the mood at home was receptive to a broad consolidation of Israel's international links. Criticism came only from a few predictable sources. The Herut Party traditionally advocated violent retaliation against every act of Arab provocation. From the Rafi group we heard advice to rely more exclusively on France for our air strength; to be hesitant about expanding security ties with the United States; and to look with skepticism on any attempt to achieve a thaw in relations with Eastern Europe. Setting my face against any restrictive orientation, I worked with Eshkol for a foreign policy based on a universal quest for friendship and understanding wherever they could be found. Our strategy was plain. Instead of allowing Arab hostility to isolate Israel, we would try to isolate Arab hostility until it choked for lack of sympathetic air.

There was nothing in the early months of 1967 which seemed to contradict this prospect. The argument among our intelligence and planning groups was simply about whether we could count on a continuing respite for five years or for ten.

My visit to Western Europe encouraged me to ensure that more foreign ministers and prime ministers of European countries should obtain an impression of the Israeli reality. The countries with whom foreign-ministerial or prime-ministerial visits were exchanged during this period included all the Scandinavian and Benelux countries, West Germany, Italy, Britain, Austria and later Rumania. I noticed that France did not yet figure on the list of countries with whom such courtesies were exchanged.

I have no firm opinion on the value of official ministerial trips. They certainly provide enjoyment for the participants. There is always interesting talk. More important—a chance to make contact with masses of people through the media. During the three or four days of an Israeli Foreign Minister's stay in a European capital, the local press gives more attention to our country's problems than at other times. The arrival of ministers in Israel from abroad helps to take Israelis out of their choking sense of isolation. Now and again some outstanding business is abbreviated by agreements which cut through the protracted bureaucratic process. I emphasized the need for more exchanges of visits with Latin American countries so as to overcome the immensity of the separating distances.

The trouble is that when reciprocal ministerial visits are followed by annual sojourns at United Nations meetings, the rhythm of a Foreign Minister's life becomes fragmented. There is a loss of contact with the domestic political scene, and it becomes intellectually difficult to achieve a "settled-down" condition. My conclusion is that frequent exchanges of ministerial visits would be useful if they were taken in more modest doses than is the habit today.

There was no reason to doubt the official appraisals in 1967 that predicted a prolonged stability. To explain why this hope came to nothing, we must refer to Damascus and Moscow.

Across three of our armistice borders, there were Arab governments which, for divergent reasons, seemed reconciled to a continuing stability. In the south, Nasser managed to combine verbal extremism with tactical prudence. Israel in his view must eventually "be destroyed," but the battle would be joined only when the Arab armies were ready and "Arab unity" was complete. The second condition was so remote that it seemed to convert the threat of Israel's annihilation into an abstract theological idea.

To the east, the King of Jordan was being described by Nasser as "the Hashemite harlot," "imperialist lackey" and "the treacherous dwarf." This seemed to give no incentive to Hussein to join a Nasserist enterprise against Israel. He understood well that the terrorist bands of El Fatah were a much sharper threat to his kingdom than was Israel. He generally managed to hold his ground with an independent policy against Cairo, Damascus and the terrorist groups, but sometimes the Jordan authorities lost control of areas in which terrorists operated against Israel. In November 1966 the village of Samua, near Hebron, suffered havoc when Israeli forces moved to clean out terrorist bases. Many uncomfortable questions were asked in Israel about the unanticipated severity of our raid.

There had long been a paradox in our relations with Jordan. Israel had an interest in Jordanian stability. Yet Jordanian territory until 1970 was to be the main source of danger to Israeli security. There was never any Israeli intention to go beyond isolated reactions into a sustained invasion of Jordanian territory west or east of the river. Furthermore, during this time Lebanon was occupied with its own mercantile success and gave no attention to military assaults against Israel. Alone among our neighbors, she maintained a policy commensurate with her resources. Thus, from three directions—Egypt, Jordan and Lebanon—the Arab war against Israel was purely verbal. If Syria had been content with a similar sensible policy, 1967 and the succeeding years would have rolled on, tense and rancorous, but without war.

But there was no such contentment in Syria. The Baath Party, in an effort to wrest leadership from Cairo, was openly sponsoring "revolutionary activism." This meant that Israel should not be left alone in peace, even for a single week. At the Arab summit conferences of 1964 and 1965, Syria was almost alone in calling for immediate confrontation. In February 1966 an even more militant Syrian government came into power. The new leaders, with Atassi at their head, urged that the war against Israel be given reality and substance all the time. If the balance of regular armies made the clash of forces unrewarding, then it must be transcended by guerrilla techniques.

It was, of course, absurd to imagine that terrorist infiltration and attacks could by themselves "destroy" anything as solid as the State of Israel. On the other hand, Israeli acquiescence was inconceivable. The raids reminded us deeply of our unique vulnerability. If our borders could be breached at any point convenient to the guerrilla command, the whole nation would be obsessed by insecurity.

In the last months of 1966, terrorist units of a few dozen men, operating mainly from Syria, had achieved several results. The railway between our capital, Jerusalem, and the largest town, Tel Aviv, had been made unsafe for regular travel. Residences had been blown up within a few hundred yards of the Knesset. Several roads in the north could only be traversed after initial probing by mine-detecting vehicles. A youth was blown to pieces while playing football near the Lebanese boundary. Four soldiers were blasted to death in the Upper Galilee, and six others killed or wounded in the area opposite the Hebron hills. If such results could be achieved by a few dozen infiltrators, what would remain of our tranquillity if the terrorist movement were allowed to deploy its activities over a broader field? No country in the world was more exposed to a form of aggression so cheap in risk and requiring such small investment of valor and skill.

Apart from the sabotage techniques, there was another area of confrontation in which Syria had a great advantage. The collective farming villages in the Upper Galilee and the Jordan Valley are the jewel in Israel's crown. Set in a frame of serene physical beauty, they represent the pioneering values which have given our society so much of its originality. On the hills looking down upon them with rancorous vigilance, were the Syrian gun emplacements and fortified positions on the Golan Heights. When Syrian bombardments of our northern settlements were added to terrorist raids, our security predicament became acute.

Israeli reactions naturally escalated to keep pace with the mounting intensity of Syrian and Palestinian provocation. On July 14, 1966, a Syrian MIG-21 was shot down by an Israeli Mirage. On August 15 Syrian aircraft attacked a disabled Israeli motor launch on the Sea of Galilee. Two more Syrian planes were brought down. The Syrians at that time were unvarying in the constancy of their assaults as well as in their inefficiency. But their political logic was sound. The aim was to prevent any stabilization of our frontier, and this was certainly achieved.

Since the contingencies were very grave, we decided to exhaust other remedies. On October 14 I appeared in the Security Council to discuss the murderous Syrian attacks. After many laborious weeks, a resolution was drafted expressing criticism of Syria in terms so mild as to be almost deferential. It was sponsored by nations from five continents—Argentina, Japan, the Netherlands, New Zealand and Nigeria. It expressed "regret at infiltration from Syria and loss of human life caused by the incidents in October and November 1966." The adoption of this text would have consoled no widows or orphans in Israel. It would have saved no lives. At the most, it would have given a harassed nation the minimal comfort which comes from an enlightened human solidarity. But even this was denied. The Soviet Union vetoed the resolution on the grounds that it dared to imply an absence of total virtue among the colonels in Damascus.

The alignment between the Soviet Union and Syria had now become one of our main preoccupations. I had no trouble in maintaining correct personal relations with the Soviet ambassador, Dmitri Chuvakhin, or more occasionally, with Foreign Minister Gromyko. With some of the smaller Communist countries our relations were even more cordial, although Yugoslavia was developing a virulent bias against our policies. The heart of the matter was that Soviet-Israeli relations did not depend on what Israel did or said. It was a coldly calculated function of the Soviet policy in the Cold War. There was more chance of enlisting the Arabs against the West than of utilizing Israel in that cause.

At home, Eshkol, assailed both by the official opposition on the right and by the Rafi Party, was under hard pressure. He had taken over Ben Gurion's team with minimal adjustments. Eshkol began with an effort at domestic conciliation, since he saw no reason to inherit all Ben Gurion's quarrels. I supported his decision to accept the official interment of the remains of Zeev Jabotinsky, the Revisionist Zionist leader, who had been venerated by the Herut Party and respected by countless others. Jabotinsky had died and been buried in New York, leaving an injunction that he was only to be reinterred in Israel at the behest of a sovereign Jewish government. Ben Gurion had refused to give this authorization. Eshkol did not hesitate. He also showed more sensitivity than Ben Gurion for the sentiments and complexes of Zionists in the Diaspora. In the same harmonizing spirit he brought about a union between Mapai and Achdut Ha'avodah in a new "Labor Party," an objective for which Ben Gurion had worked hard in vain. Eshkol was setting his own style and not merely following his predecessor's steps.

There had been fears that Ben Gurion's departure would weaken the state in its international relations, by removing the special awe which had accompanied him across the world. That danger, too, was surmounted. Eshkol became, surprisingly, the first Israeli Prime Minister to be officially invited by a President of the United States to visit Washington. He was also the first of our prime ministers to make a tour of African capitals. In 1965, when Germany ceased arms supplies to Israel as a result of Arab protests, the Eshkol government had secured an impressive compensation by establishing diplomatic relations with the Federal Republic. But for some sections of the Labor movement, the idea of living without Ben Gurion at the helm was hard to bear. Exaggerated versions of our economic and social distress were spread throughout the country, and certainly reached Arab ears. The question whether the new Israeli government would react to provocation with Ben Gurion's familiar ferocity must have been planted in many Arab minds.

Yet at the beginning of May 1967, there was no premonition of crisis. I had come back from my tour of Southeast Asia and Australasia in March to find the country in a tranquil mood. Israelis realized, of course, that there would always be a quota of murderous infiltrations. Now and then a flame of aggression would erupt and then subside, leaving some death and wreckage in its wake. This was the familiar rhythm. The special dignity of Israeli life comes from the large place that it gives to sacrifice. Israel lives intimately with danger, so that the very permanence of it dulls its edge and breeds a special adaptability to assault. But it became clear in the third week of May 1967, that we were going to face something radically different from the usual ebb and flow of intermittent violence. All possibilities, including the most unthinkable, suddenly came into view.

12

Nasser toward the Brink 1967

INDEPENDENCE DAY IN 1967 OPENED WITH A MILITARY REVIEW IN JERU-salem and ended with a public competition in Biblical knowledge among pupils of secondary schools. This is the duality of Israel's experience; it swerves between physical danger and the symbolism of normality and peace. The Biblical competition was followed on radio with a kind of partisan tension that most other nations reserve for major sports events. When it ended, the holiday was over. The road became dense with the traffic of citizens scattering to their homes and Jerusalem went back to its placid sobriety. It was thus that on May 15, 1967, the last year of Israel's second decade began its course.

The early part of 1967 had been turbulent, but no more than during many other years. There seemed no reason to expect that the usual raids and reprisals would set off a total clash of arms. This time, however, there was a chain of mutual commitment between Syria, the Soviet Union and Egypt to keep Israel under murderous harassment while protecting Syria from reprisals. It was out of this tangled relationship that war was to grow.

Syria had been brooding in diminished pride over the debacle of its air force on April 7, 1967. After several terrorist raids, the Syrians had attacked Israeli farmers in the Galilee area. The exchange of fire escalated. In air engagements, six Syrian MIGs were brought down, two of them in the territory of Jordan, whose government made no attempt to hide its satisfaction. The extent of the Syrian defeat was

unexpected even in Israel. Elsewhere in the Arab world, the response
to Syria's discomfiture ranged all the way from open derision in
Amman to embarrassed silence in Cairo. Egypt made an awkward attempt to point out that her commitment to aid Syria if attacked referred only to sustained warfare and not to "spasmodic incidents."

The April 7 air encounter had not been expensive in lives to either
side. No civilian suffering was involved and Israeli representatives
reported a satisfied reaction in most capitals. There were overt congratulations in Paris, where the victory of Mirage over MIGs had
kindled technological pride.

But there was deep irritation in Moscow. The Soviet leadership
at that time was disturbed by the tendency of its "progressive" friends
to get into trouble. In Algeria, Ghana and Indonesia, the radical
leaders Ben Bella, Nkrumah and Sukarno had been driven from
power. If anything of this sort happened to the Syrian regime, would
not the developing countries begin to ask whether Russian sponsorship was bringing them any real advantage or security? The Soviet
Union, therefore, decided to make the preservation of the Syrian
regime a principle of its wider strategy. But since direct Soviet intervention would have invited a confrontation with the United States,
it was better for pressure to be exercised on Israel by someone else.
Moscow called on Cairo to rescue Damascus from its self-inflicted humiliation. In mid-April 1967, prodded by Soviet leaders, Egyptian missions went to Damascus, where they reinforced their commitment to
protect Syria from Israeli reaction. The war alignment was taking
shape. It was not for nothing that Soviet Ambassador Chuvakhin
told me in icy words that although Israel seemed to be celebrating
a victory by its air exploits on April 7, before long it would regret
its alleged success.

Terrorist raids from Syrian territory multiplied. At no time did they
affect thousands of lives or bring about a collapse of public order.
But Israel is a close-knit society; personal grief afflicting a kibbutz
or a suburb invades the whole public mood. We had every cause to
regard this Syrian terrorism as an early stage of malignancy. It could
not be left alone. Our policy was to make an attempt, however despairing, to dissuade the Soviet Union from supporting the inflammatory policies of Damascus. If we failed, we would reinforce defensive
remedies on our own soil by minefields and barbed wire. We would
then interpose a stage of verbal warnings to Syria before any military
reaction was approved. Only if all this failed and violence had to be
met by force would our response come into effect. Even then, it would
be swift and of local scope, leaving the existing borders intact.

All my efforts to enlist Soviet influence against terrorism were in vain. At first Ambassador Chuvakhin hinted to me that the Israeli victims of terrorism might have blown themselves up in a cunning attempt to create an atmosphere of Syrian-Israeli hostility. Later he asked me to "give serious consideration" to the possibility that agents of American oil interests and the CIA, disguised as El Fatah infiltrators were laying mines on Israeli roads in order to provoke Israel into retaliation which would, in turn, weaken the regime of Damascus! In reply I asked the ambassador that his government "give serious consideration" to a less sophisticated idea, namely that when the Syrians and the terrorists said that they were laying the mines, they really were. I added that "if it were made clear to the Syrians that the USSR opposes terrorist acts, it is probable that these would be stopped."

Nothing of the kind was "made clear." Instead, the Soviet Union began to incite Egypt against Israel so as to involve Egypt in the burden of protecting Syria. In Moscow on May 12 and 13, an Egyptian parliamentary delegation headed by the president of the National Council, Anwar Sadat, had been told to expect "an Israeli invasion of Syria immediately after Independence Day, with the aim of overthrowing the Damascus regime."

After the 1967 war, Nasser never concealed that Soviet informants had spurred him to the course on which he had embarked. At midnight on May 22, when he announced the blockade of the Straits of Tiran, he said:

> On May 13, we received accurate information that Israel was concentrating on the Syrian border huge armed forces of about eleven to thirteen brigades. These forces were divided into two fronts, one south of the Sea of Galilee and one north of the Lake. The decision made by Israel at the time was to carry out an attack on Syria starting on May 17. On May 14, we took action, discussed the matter and contacted our Syrian brothers. The Syrians also had this information.

On May 11 Suzy and I had gone on a tour of our northern boundary. The green landscape lay beneath the warm Israeli sun, bathed in total repose. The officer commanding the north, General David Elazar, took us around his area of jurisdiction. I remember being concerned by the absence of any kind of military preparation. On that same day Eshkol invited the Soviet ambassador to take his military attaché on an unannounced tour of the northern border in search of the "eleven to thirteen brigades" which Moscow had declared to be concentrated there. Chuvakhin's response was that his function was to communicate Soviet truths, not to put them to a test.

In the meantime we had got news of intensified terrorist training at the Syrian camp near Kuneitra, and of plans to multiply incursions through Jordan and Lebanon in the summer. The Prime Minister and the Chief of Staff, Yitzhak Rabin, sought to dissuade the Syrians by warning them that Israel's capacity to endure the murder of her citizens had its limits.

On May 14 three of our newspapers simultaneously carried interviews with General Rabin, warning Damascus of the consequences likely to arise from continued terrorism. At Independence Day meetings, Israeli public figures made the conventional speeches of embattled defiance. If there had been a little more silence, the sum of human wisdom would probably have remained intact. The same is true of the briefing of foreign military attachés on May 11, in terms which they understood to augur a major assault by Israel in the coming days. But all these Israeli statements, separately and together, were models of temperance in comparison with the threats of total annihilation by which Israel was being assailed. While Rabin had stated that the key to a tranquil frontier lay "in Damascus," there was no intention to indicate that Israel meant to capture an Arab capital. Since some Western writers have made much of Israel's belligerent rhetoric, it might be relevant to quote Mr. Eshkol's May 12 speech:

> In view of the fourteen incidents of sabotage and infiltration perpetrated in the past month alone, Israel may have no other choice but to adopt suitable countermeasures against the focal points of sabotage. Israel will continue to take action to prevent any and all attempts to perpetrate sabotage within her territory. There will be no immunity for any state which aids or abets such acts.

Nevertheless, Israel's warnings seemed to have been received in Syria with something close to panic. Damascus and Moscow sent out an appeal to Cairo for a military demonstration that would take the pressure off Syria.

We tried to hold the fever down. On May 15 I instructed our UN representative, Ambassador Rafael, to assure the Arab states through U Thant that Israel had no thought of initiating conflict in any sector. At the same time, a unanimous Cabinet decision was made to keep the 1967 Independence Day parade in Jerusalem strictly within the limits prescribed by the armistice agreement with Jordan. This prudence was well received in most of the country except, strangely, by Ben Gurion, who called it "deceit." In the Cabinet we unanimously believed in the need for combining respect for an existing contract with a sense of Israel's need to shorten her political front.

The moderation of our decision on the Independence Day parade had a strange sequel. Instead of interpreting this restraint at its face value, the Soviet and Arab governments gave it a sinister meaning. If there were so few Israeli troops in Jerusalem for the parade, the argument ran, surely this was proof that Israel had concentrated most of her army on the Syrian frontier! (Nasser actually repeated this falsehood on May 26.)

Great events seldom have a single cause. But I have never had any doubt that the decisive link in the chain of events which unfolded during 1967 was forged, in both senses of the word, by the Soviet Union. It is undeniable that Soviet warnings about imaginary Israeli "troop concentrations" on the Syrian boundary prodded Nasser to action. And it is quite impossible that Moscow could have believed what it was saying. The mobilization of "eleven to thirteen" Israeli brigades, to say nothing of their concentration in the north, would have had a conspicuous effect on our national life. The disruption of normality in so many families would have resounded across the chanceries and newspapers of the world. Nine months after the 1967 war, at his trial in Cairo, the former Minister of Defense Shamseddin Badran confirmed that "false Soviet reports" of an imminent Israeli drive for Damascus had caused Egypt to undertake a policy of confrontation in Sinai. United only by a common rancor, Moscow, Damascus and Cairo had laid an explosive charge of falsehood at the foundations of Middle Eastern peace. The wick was to be three weeks long.

However, by the time Independence Day dawned on May 15, few of us felt much concern. It was only toward evening that I found anxious messages on my desk. Infantry and armored units of the Egyptian army had moved to the Suez Canal and were crossing into Sinai with ostentatious publicity. Large convoys were deliberately routed through Cairo's busiest streets on their way to Ismailia. The day before, the Egyptian Chief of Staff, General Mohamed Fawzi, had flown to Damascus. The Egyptian parliamentary delegation had returned to Cairo with Soviet information about Israel's imminent plan "to conquer Damascus." Egyptian armed forces had been alerted to a state of emergency because of what they described as "the tense situation on the Syrian-Israeli armistice lines."

The scale of these movements created no immediate military threat, but their political consequences were inflammatory. A torrent of passionate invective against Israel poured from all the radio stations in the Arab world. From Eshkol and Rabin I learned of our own plan to reinforce our dispositions in the Negev, where only a single battalion was keeping watch. At a special Cabinet meeting we decided to act without fanfare. In Washington and London, high officials told us with excessive confidence that the Egyptian troop movements were "demonstrative" and without military intent.

On the morning of May 17, graver contingencies came into view. The Egyptian press and radio announced that the commander of the UN Emergency Force, General Rikieh, had received a request from General Mohamed Fawzi to withdraw his troops from their positions. Within a few hours, U Thant had acceded.

However great his juridical compulsions, U Thant was destroying, in a single stroke, the most central "hopes and expectations" on which we had relied on withdrawing from Sinai in 1957. At that time, when I asked Secretary Dulles if there was no danger of precipitate withdrawal by the UN, he argued with emphatic conviction that nothing of the sort was conceivable. On February 25, 1957, I asked Secretary-General Hammarskjöld if I could assume that the task of UN Emergency Force in the Straits of Tiran would be "to prevent belligerency." He replied to me in writing: "With regard to the function of UNEF in the prevention of belligerency, the answer is affirmative." I then asked him whether there was no danger of the force's being withdrawn overnight without giving time for Israel to correct any consequent disturbance of the local military balance. Hammarskjöld emphatically rejected this apprehension. His assurance had an important effect on our decision to withdraw from the Sinai in 1957.

All of this came to my memory as I speculated with my colleagues on U Thant's reaction to the Egyptian request. Here was the international peace organization being specifically invited to act as to enable "Egyptian armed forces to go into action against Israel." In other words, the UN was being asked to cooperate in making room for war! At the very least, we had assumed in 1957 that a broad international consultation would be held in the event that a request for the removal of UNEF was made.

On May 17, shocked by U Thant's precipitate reaction, I instructed Ambassador Rafael to bring our views urgently to the Secretary-General. I asked him to remind U Thant of a specific commitment that his predecessor had given us in 1957 in order to secure our withdrawal from Sharm el-Sheikh and Gaza. Hammarskjöld had acknowledged that since the stationing of UNEF had been a factor in inducing Israel to withdraw, there was "in the moral sense a kind of bilateral agreement between Egypt and Israel." In a document published after his death but written on August 5, 1957, he had discussed the very contingency which arose in May 1967:

> "It would be obvious that the procedure in case of a request from Egypt for the withdrawal of UNEF would be as follows: the matter would at once be brought before the General Assembly. If the General Assembly found that the task [of UNEF] was completed, everything would be alright. If they found that the task was not completed, and Egypt all the same maintained its position and enforced the withdrawal, Egypt would be breaking the agreement with the United Nations." I showed this text to Fawzi at our first talk on 16 November, and I discussed this issue with Nasser for seven hours on the evening and night of 17 November [1956].

Hammarskjöld had added that "if a difference should develop, the matter would be brought up for negotiation with the United Nations."

In the event, nothing of the sort was done or attempted. When Ambassador Rafael reported to me on his conversations of May 17 and 18, it became clear that the die had already been cast. In his first letter on May 16, U Thant had conveyed a decisive reply to Cairo through the Egyptian permanent representative. His language was clear:

> A request by the UAR authorities for a temporary withdrawal of UNEF from the armistice demarcation line in the international frontier or from any parts of them, would be considered by the Secretary-General as tantamount to a request for the complete withdrawal of UNEF from Gaza and Sinai, since this would reduce UNEF to ineffectiveness.

This was "all or nothing" language. Bunche told us that if the UAR faced the choice, he was sure that it would retreat from the attempt to change UNEF's deployment. How wrong he was! Cairo simply reacted to the challenge by asking for "complete withdrawal" even more clearly than before.

On April 15, 1957, Foster Dulles had said, "I think that consent given by Egypt cannot be arbitrarily withdrawn. I don't say that it can't ever be withdrawn, but I say it can't be arbitrarily withdrawn without giving countries who have relief upon it an opportunity to turn around and re-appraise their position in the light of the new situation." The prediction sounded reasonable at the time. It now proved wrong. Nobody was to be given "an opportunity to turn around."

No action by the United Nations has ever been more contentiously discussed by governments, the world press and public opinion. In a heated response on June 27, 1967, U Thant ascribed all the criticism to "distortions of the record which in some places apparently have emanated from panic, emotion and political bias." In the more tranquil parts of his memorandum the Secretary-General gave a moving account of the pressures which compelled his action: he had no alternative in law but to accede to a request rooted in Egypt's sovereign rights; the countries which supplied contingents would obey the Egyptian request whatever the Secretary-General said or did; Egyptian troops were, in any case, physically expelling United Nations units from their main observation posts in Sinai; the assumption that there would be time for international consultation after a request for withdrawal had always been vague and elusive. But the most convincing sentence in U Thant's report was that which referred to "the essentially fragile nature of the basis for UNEF's operation throughout its existence." All this is beyond challenge. But it is precisely the lesson of "fragility" which thereafter inspired Israel's refusal to place her vital interests again in United Nations hands. What had for ten years appeared to be a stable international reality turned out, within two hours, to be as unsubstantial as a spider's web.

For Israel the week between May 16 and May 22 brought a full and serious understanding of Nasser's design. Every few hours the wave of concern mounted higher. On May 17 our military advisers were still reporting in a relatively sanguine mood. Only a single infantry division with armored support in the rear had taken up its position against the Negev border. There was nothing here to show that Egypt was planning an immediate assault or was prepared to absorb a strong Israeli reaction. Indeed, the day before, military correspondents had been briefed by our military spokesmen about the precedent of 1960, when Egyptian troops had advanced across Sinai to the Israeli border in demonstrative solidarity with Syria, only to be withdrawn a few weeks later.

The prevalent view of military men everywhere seemed to be that Egypt hoped the presence of her forces would give Syria a greater sense of security for the dispatch of guerrilla raiders into Israel. We had no solid reason to question this appraisal, but the excited tone of Arab broadcasts throughout the whole Middle East caused me to take graver possibilities into account. There was thunder in the air. On Tuesday, May 16, I had advised political correspondents in my office in Jerusalem to avoid the theory that Egypt's motives were purely "demonstrative" or "psychological." "The theory," I said, "might be true, but the practice could be different."

May 18 was the day on which all lenient predictions collapsed. U Thant had now acceded without reservation to the withdrawal of UNEF. News came of operational activity at air bases in northern and central Sinai. An Egyptian MIG-21 made extensive photographic reconnaissance of possible targets in the central Negev. The Fourth Armored Division, Egypt's most effective striking force, was still lurking to the west of the Suez Canal. But the pressure against Israel was being piled up in a methodical progression which boded ill. There had been a whole decade of peace on the Egyptian-Israeli border, while constant harassment came from Syria and Jordan. Accordingly, our military dispositions took relatively little account of danger from the south. I was told that a period "not to be measured in a few days" would be required before Israel could develop a serious deterrent posture in the Negev. Our senior officers emphasized the need for political action, during which defensive preparations could go forward; at one meeting General Rabin discussed the possibility that Israel convene a meeting of the Security Council.

Those whom I consulted, especially among our delegation at the United Nations, argued against this idea. Israel's cause, even if considered righteous by a majority, could never be vindicated in that forum. A Soviet veto was available at Arab request. Such a political rebuff for Israel would give vast encouragement to Nasser and generate a desperate mood in Israel. Moreover, a call to the Security Council would be interpreted as a renunciation, however temporary, of any Israeli intention to resist. A member state which asked for a discussion would be in a poor position to take other measures before the debate came to an end. I knew from long experience that it was easier to turn on the tap of United Nations debate than to turn it off.

As an alternative step I suggested to leading members of the Security Council through Ambassador Rafael, that U Thant be induced to make a visit to Cairo and Jerusalem. If he could set out immediately before withdrawal of UNEF on the ground and at a time when the Expeditionary Force was still in its positions at Sharm el-Sheikh, his journey might freeze the situation and give Nasser an opportunity to stay his hand. The seed of this idea was duly planted among western delegations in New York. My thought was that the Secretary-General would announce his visit, take to the air and reach Cairo before the blockade was decided. It was hard to believe that a member state would refuse to receive the Secretary-General even if he arrived unannounced.

Cairo's brutal advice to U Thant on May 18 not to move until he was invited gave ominous indication that Nasser's course was set. The United Nations was being told, at all levels, to keep out of Nasser's war plans; he must have found its compliance entirely satisfactory. Not only could he prevent the UN from acting; he could even prevent it from expressing its views.

While awaiting replies from their capitals, we kept frequent contact with the ambassadors of the leading powers. We decided on a last attempt to enlist Soviet support for a policy of restraint. On May 19 I invited Ambassador Chuvakhin to come to my office, where he informed me that the cause of the situation lay in the aggressive propaganda of the government of Israel and especially the speeches of its leaders against Arab states, notably Syria. Israel was "now tasting the fruits of its policy." The Soviet government had often warned Israel that her policy would bring grave results. The development of the position proved that the Soviet government was correct in its appraisal. Here the ambassador recalled the statements that were conveyed to Israel in Moscow in November 1966 and April 1967. He repeated the warning that the entire responsibility for the position now created rested on Israel. "History will pass judgment on Israel for having played with fire." The ambassador went on to say that he did not want to discuss the specific points which I had raised, such as the acts of sabotage and the troop concentrations, because this was not within his competence. As for UNEF, its presence on the territory of any state depended on the free consent of that state, which had full power to demand its removal.

The ambassador said that very little was required in order to bring about a relaxation of the tension. All that was needed was to take into account the declarations which had been transmitted to Israel in Moscow and to put an end to the aggressive declarations by Israeli leaders.

I asked if this was really sufficient. Should there not be abstention from violent actions, as well as bellicose declarations by Arab leaders? I emphasized that facts are more important than rhetorical declarations. The bombardment of Manara, the mining of the road to Rosh Pina, the vast concentrations of Egyptian troops in Sinai were facts which must be considered to be far more serious than any speeches. If our neighbors would only make speeches without accompanying them by such acts, the position would be less dangerous. At this point Ambassador Chuvakhin said, unforgettably, "We keep hearing about mining and sabotage and infiltrations, but we have not seen any proof so far that those responsible are Syrians rather than agents of the American Central Intelligence Agency."

The decisive question, of course, was whether Nasser would actually blockade the Straits of Tiran. Everything came together to make this question fateful for Israel and the world. If the blockade was imposed, Israel would be challenged to defend or abandon a vital national interest. The juridical implication was that Nasser would not recoil from proclaiming an overt state of war. And a blockade in the Straits and in the Gulf of Aqaba, unlike the troop concentrations, would take us to a point of no return. Troop movements, after all, could be ordered and later dispersed without loss of face or implication of retreat. But if a blockade was imposed, its cancellation was inconceivable except under pressure or threat of physical force.

As long as Nasser was not publicly committed and shipping passed normally through the Straits, Mr. Eshkol and I saw no reason to force his hand by rhetorical defiance. On May 20 a cargo ship passed the Straits bound for Eilat without interference. On the other hand, we could not leave the principal powers in any illusion about our resolve to resist if the Straits were closed. When it became clear that Egyptian forces would move into Sharm el-Sheikh, the United States suggested to us that Israel should not use force "*until or unless* Egyptian forces attempt to close the Straits to Israel-bound shipping." This phraseology interested me both for what it said and for what it implied. We decided to make it our own. The signal for resistance would be not the occupation of Sharm el-Sheikh, but the imposition of blockade. Between May 18 and 20 we informed the leading maritime powers that if the Straits of Tiran were closed, Israel would stop short of nothing to cancel the blockade.

On May 19 U Thant told members of the Security Council: "I do not want to cause alarm, but it is difficult for me not to warn the Council that, as I see it, the position in the Middle East is more disquieting than at any time since the end of 1956." This was now the universal sentiment. U Thant went on to single out the increase of El Fatah activity as the first cause of the crisis:

El Fatah activities, consisting of terrorism and sabotage are a major factor in that they provoke strong reactions in Israel by the Government and population alike. Some recent incidents of this type have seemed to indicate a new level of organization and training of those who participate in these actions. Although allegations are often made, to the best of my knowledge, there is no verified information [*emphasis added*] *about the organization's central direction and originating source for these acts and those who perpetrate them.*

In the Middle East there was much less mystery than in New York about who organized, directed and perpetrated El Fatah activities. The Syrian government, in particular, was officially declaring the training camps open for recruits. But on May 19 we had little time or mood for polemics; our business was to exhaust the dwindling possibilities of restraining Nasser in his headlong rush to the brink. The Secretary-General's report went on to say: "The timing of the withdrawal of UNEF leaves much to be desired." I still recall that amid all my worries, I found time to admire the immensity of this understatement.

Later that day Prime Minister Eshkol cabled to General de Gaulle: "Israel on her part will not initiate hostile acts, but she is firmly resolved to defend her territory and her international rights. Our decision is that if Egypt will not attack us, we will not take action against Egyptian forces at Sharm el-Sheikh—until or unless they close the Straits of Tiran to free navigation by Israel."

I developed the same theme further in notes to French Foreign Minister Maurice Couve de Murville and British Foreign Secretary George Brown. I wrote that Israel's intention not to acquiesce in the blockade was "solid and unreserved. It is essential that President Nasser should not have any illusions."

I instructed our ambassador in London, Aharon Remez, to add orally: "Our decision is that unless attacked we shall not move against Egyptian forces unless or until they attempt to close the Straits to Israel-bound shipping. They have not yet done so."

No reply was to come from Paris until after the blockade of the Gulf had begun. The British government, in a letter from Harold Wilson to Eshkol, aligned itself with the American view that any action by Israel should depend on a prior act by the UAR establishing the blockade. Wilson wrote:

> *I am on public record as saying that the Straits of Tiran constitute an international waterway which should remain open to the ships of all nations. If it appeared that any attempt to interfere with the passage of ships through the waterway was likely to be made, we should promote and support international action through the United Nations to secure free passage. We stand by this statement. We think it important however that attention should be concentrated on free passage and not on the shore*

positions. If we are to give you the international support we wish, it must be based on your undoubted rights.

Our intention to regard the closing of the Straits as a *casus belli* was communicated in similar terms to the foreign ministers of those states which had supported international navigation in the Straits in 1957 and thereafter. There can be no doubt that these warnings reached Cairo. One thing was now clear. If Nasser imposed a blockade, the explosion would ensue not from "miscalculation," but from an open-eyed and conscious readiness for war.

Could the peace be saved with Egyptian troops established at the entrance to the Straits of Tiran? It needed a sanguine temperament to believe this possibility. But it had to be explored. Some years before, Dayan had publicly suggested that Israel should actually work for the removal of UNEF in the hope that our maritime rights would be secured by the power of our own deterrence. His argument was that it would be a greater achievement to send our ships through the Gulf with Egyptian troops acquiescing in their passage than to rely on a temporary and symbolic international presence. I had thought that this was too optimistic. I could never conceive of Egyptian officers at Sharm el-Sheikh waving Israeli ships and tankers indulgently on their way if they had the physical power to stop them.

If Nasser had not recoiled before the brink, he was not likely to retreat from the position he had taken some distance beyond it. Any residual prospect of a peaceful issue now depended on a firm and, therefore, improbable show of international resolution. Would the powers which had promised to support Israel in resisting the blockade inform Cairo convincingly that their pledge stood intact? Would the United Nations register the wrath and apprehension of peace-loving mankind?

All these questions were to be answered in complete negation. International retreat comes a close second to Arab hostility among the parent causes of the 1967 war.

Nothing that any of the powers did in the third week of May increased Nasser's anxieties. Fervent Soviet support of Arab hostility was not accompanied by any serious Western gesture on Israel's behalf. There was complete silence in Paris, and cautious generalization in Washington and London. On May 20, Israeli representatives at the United Nations and in Washington were told by U.S. representatives that London and Paris seemed about to evade or repudiate their obligation to act under their 1950 declaration. On May 21 the

Foreign Ministry in Paris and the Foreign Office in London confirmed this prediction; they laid the whole burden on the United Nations which was manifestly incapable of bearing any burden whatsoever. The central point of the 1950 Declaration was the undertaking to act "outside the United Nations" if the international bodies were deadlocked or inoperative. The letters sent by Eshkol and myself to President de Gaulle and Couve de Murville on May 18 and 19 about the Straits of Tiran were to go unanswered until several days after the blockade was imposed. Britain's promise of "action through the United Nations" was in our experience a way of promising no action at all. The United Nations is a forum; it is not an instrument of action. Indeed, it can "act" only in the histrionic sense. It is a theater in which important drama is sometimes enacted; it is not in itself a source of power.

All now hinged on the major powers. If any of them addressed strong admonitions to Cairo between May 14 and May 22, their efforts still remain shrouded in modest reticence. On May 18 President Johnson wrote to Eshkol: "I am sure that you will understand that I cannot accept any responsibilities on behalf of the United States for situations which arise as the result of actions on which we are not consulted." A few days later the United States informed us and the world that "we and our friends have done all that we can to make amply clear both to Cairo and Damascus that there is an urgent need for the cessation of terrorism and the reversal of military movements of the type which we have witnessed during the past week."

I received these ominous signs of caution together with the text of an American statement of May 22. A close study of this document and of accompanying press briefings deepened my concern. The phrase employed was that Washington would *"support* suitable measures in and outside the United Nations." President Kennedy's declaration of May 1963 had stated that if Israel was threatened with aggression, the United States would also *"adopt* other courses of action of our own." The difference between adopting courses oneself and supporting other measures is not trivial. It is the distinction between responsible initiative and mere "joining." It was impossible to believe that the change was inadvertent; the approach of danger always lends precision to the diplomatic art. The conclusion was plain: the powers were giving a most cautious interpretation to their commitments. The United States, traumatically affected by the refusal of its allies to support it in Vietnam, was making its policy dependent on a concerted international enterprise; it was reluctant to act alone.

We left the door open for Nasser's retreat until the very end. On Monday, May 22, Eshkol addressed him from the Knesset rostrum.

The speech was firm but unprovocative. Israel planned no attack on Arab countries and did not seek to undermine their security, attack their territory or challenge their legitimate international rights. There was no shred of truth in talk of Israeli concentrations on the Syrian frontier. Israel was still ready "to participate in an effort to reinforce stability and advance peace in our region." The powers were invited to promote a reciprocal reduction of troops. Israel's army was ready for any trial and the nation's right would be defended.

The moderation of this address was designed to give Nasser a last possibility of face-saving retreat from the temptation of blockade. From Washington, London, Paris and even Moscow, Nasser had heard the most precise, formal and drastic Israeli warnings that the closure of the Straits would be regarded by Israel as an act of war. It was not necessary or prudent for Eshkol to close his retreat by public challenge.

International apathy now created a vacuum in which the hope of peace could no longer breathe. If the flight of the Powers from their commitments was implicit and private, the abdication of the United Nations was explicit and overt. When Eshkol spoke on May 22, the United Nations action was still centered in the Secretary-General. Precious days had gone by since his journey to the Middle East had first been proposed. On May 18 I had invited U Thant to visit Israel as well as Cairo, but he decided not to come to Israel. He would make his effort in Cairo alone. By the time Nasser "allowed" him to set out, the expulsion of UNEF was an accomplished fact, the troop concentrations were vast—and all international presence had been banished from what U Thant himself, in a report on May 19, had described as "the two sensitive points" of Gaza and Sharm el-Sheikh. Above all, Nasser's arrogance was riding high. While his ruthless pressure on Israel was arousing indignation in international public opinion, it was met by an obsequious deference among governments. When U Thant flew from New York on May 22, his journey had become too little and too late. By the time he reached Paris he heard of Nasser's speech at Bir Gafgafa, imposing a blockade in the Straits of Tiran.

I myself heard the news at dawn. Shafts of light were streaming through the curtained windows when, a little after five o'clock on May 23, the telephone rang. A minute later I knew that nothing in our life or history would ever be the same. There was no audible emotion in the voice from Army Headquarters in Tel Aviv. It told me dryly that President Nasser had announced the closure of the Gulf of Aqaba to Israeli shipping and to all other vessels bound for Israel with "strategic materials" aboard.

An hour later my senior advisers were assembled in the downstairs living room. They found me listening to Nasser's recorded words.

He was utterly resolved to have his war—and to be satisfied with nothing less. He had written years before of "a hero's role searching for an actor to play it." Now the dream would unfold, with himself in the central part and with the whole world as stage. He presented the blockade not as a single stroke of malice, but as a challenge to total combat. The choice for Israel was drastic—slow strangulation or rapid, solitary death:

> We are in confrontation with Israel. In contrast to what happened in 1956 when France and Britain were at her side, Israel is not supported today by any European power. It is possible, however, that America may come to her aid.
>
> The United States supports Israel politically and provides her with arms and military matérial. But the world will not accept a repetition of 1956. We are face to face with Israel. Henceforward the situation is in your hands. Our armed forces have occupied Sharm el-Sheikh. . . . We shall on no account allow the Israeli flag to pass through the Gulf of Aqaba. The Jews threaten to make war. I reply: 'Ahlan wa sahlan'—'Welcome!' We are ready for war. . . . This water is ours.

The speech had been made to officers of the Egyptian air base at Bir Gafgafa in Sinai, a hundred miles from Israel's southwestern border. A few days later the commanders of this airfield, and of others, received operation orders listing the targets in Israel which they were to bomb. To their valor and efficiency, yet unproved, Nasser had committed the outcome of his most daring enterprise. He owed them whatever a leader's authority could do to enlarge and galvanize their powers. But far beyond his fervent audience in the baking desert heat, he was appealing to the whole domain of Arabism, calling its sons to such display of union, sacrifice, hate, resilience and selfless passion as they had not shown since the ferocious days of their early history. His declaration of war was unique in one respect: it contained no specific charge or grievance against his adversary. After all, there had been no collision of forces, no spark of active violence between Egypt and Israel for ten full years. This was beside the point. In Nasser's view, Israel's mere "existence" was an offense which could only be expiated by destruction. The macabre vision of Israel's demise had been nourished in speech and sentiment during all the years of suspense. Now, suddenly, the dream seemed ripe for fulfillment, and what had brought it within reach was Israel's apparent solitude. Nasser had always considered Israel incapable of independent resolve. All her successes were ascribed by him to the intervention or sustaining influence of external powers. It followed that if Israel were now left alone, she would be inhibited not only from action, but even from decision. Nasser had never sought to probe the sources of Israel's autonomous vitality. This had always been, and was again to be, his central error. Once he had scanned the international prospect and found no ally at Israel's side, his course was plain. An opportunity little imagined a few weeks before had somehow taken form and substance. If lost, it might never be reborn. Turning his back on a whole decade of prudence, he now uttered a courtly and exultant welcome to the approaching war: *"Ahlan wa sahlan."* It was as if he were greeting the unexpected appearance of a beloved and long-absent guest.

By eight o'clock I was on the road to Tel Aviv. Prime Minister Eshkol had called his colleagues and military leaders into urgent consultation. Those who greeted me from vehicles and roadsides along the way managed to give their gestures an implication of anxiety. Only a month before, the national mood had been as close to normalcy as could be expected by a people born in war and nurtured in siege. Now the crisis was upon us. As countryside and townships sped past the window, I was gripped by a sharp awareness of the fragility of all cherished things. For the whole of that day in Tel Aviv, and far into the night in Jerusalem, our minds revolved around the question of survival; so it must have been in ancient days, with Babylon or Assyria at the gates.

There were no cheerful faces around the table in the Ministry of Defense in Tel Aviv at nine o'clock in the morning of May 23. With General Rabin came the Chief of Operations, General Ezer Weizman, and the chief of military intelligence, General Aharon Yariv. The Prime Minister had asked leaders of all major parties to join our counsels soon after they began. Helicopters swarmed toward us, bringing them in ones and twos. We passed in stages from official deliberations in the Cabinet Defense Committee to intimate talks in less formal groups.* Eshkol solved the emotional problem by a deliberate tone of understatement: "We have news on the political front. I don't know if you have all heard it. It requires consultation and, probably, action as well." The peril was taken for granted; it stood in no need of rhetorical adornment. The accent was placed on clarity of decision. A great doom was in the making and it seemed to be coming on relentlessly.

And yet, our military reports were still restrained. The Egyptian

---

* In addition to ministers, those who participated in our talks on May 23 were the following Members of Parliament: Golda Meir, David Hacohen, Moshe Dayan, Shimon Peres, Menahem Begin, Aryeh Ben Eliezer, Chaim Landau, Elimelech Rimalt, Yosef Serlin, Yosef Almogi and a Mapai leader, Shaul Avigur.

battle order was not yet in full offensive array. Airfields in Sinai were being made ready, but their technical preparedness was still deficient. Nothing yet moved on the Jordan front. (Indeed, the next day Jordan broke her diplomatic relations with Syria in reaction to a terrorist raid which had cost fourteen Jordanian lives). In the north the Syrians, who had lit the flames of impending war, now seemed to be recoiling from the heat. The most ominous reports, apart from Nasser's blockade, were those which described the ecstatic mood sweeping over the Arab world. Masses of people, long elated by dreams of vengeance, were now screaming for Israel's blood.

There was no doubt that the howling mobs in Cairo, Damascus and Baghdad were seeing savage visions of murder and booty. Israel, for its part, had learned from Jewish history that no outrage against its men, women and children, was inconceivable. Many things in Jewish history are too terrible to be believed, but nothing in that history is too terrible to have happened. Memories of the European slaughter were taking form and substance in countless Israeli hearts. They flowed into our room like turgid air and sat heavy on all our minds.

Before my turn came to speak, I noticed that our military colleagues had made no proposals for immediate action. General Rabin, accompanied by Colonel Efrat, had visited me in my Jerusalem home on May 21 to discuss the likelihood of an Egyptian takeover at Sharm el-Sheikh. Moshe Raviv was with me. Rabin was very tense, chain-smoking all the time. He pointed out that Israel's military preparedness for ten years had always been related to the northern and eastern fronts, with little attention to the south. When I asked what the diplomatic establishment could do to help, he had said, "Time. We need time to reinforce the south." On May 23 Rabin was confident of ultimate victory, but he warned that there would be "no walkover."

The difference between 1956 and 1967 was sharply sketched in his words to the assembled ministers. Eleven years before, Israel had been flanked by two major powers, and Egypt was its only adversary. This time Israel would be alone while Egypt might have Syria, Jordan and contingents from other Arab countries at her side, and the Soviet Union in full political support and geographical proximity. Our military advisers could make no comforting predictions about the scale of Israeli losses. The candor of their words left a chilly aftermath.

The ministerial meeting was brief and to the point; in the formal conversations our discourse was fuller. My own expressions of opinion all through that day began with what I called an unquestioned premise: if Israel did not break the ring of blockade and encirclement, her deterrent power would be destroyed and her international position brought to ruin. There was thus no possibility for us to adopt a doctrine of peace at any price. I went on to say that the blockade in the Gulf sundering Israel's connections with the Eastern world was legally and politically equivalent to a truncation of our territory. We must henceforth behave and think like a nation whose soil had already been invaded. The only possible sequel must be Nasser's retreat by whatever means it could be achieved. If the threats uttered at Bir Gafgafa could be brought to nothing, it was doubtful that Nasser could survive. The issue was sharply drawn—either he or we would be broken. The question was not whether we must resist, but whether we must resist alone or with the support and understanding of others.

I was, of course, particularly concerned with the international context. We could not forget the Soviet role in creating the threat to our existence. Whether or not the USSR had approved every phase of Nasser's audacity, it now stood firm in his support. If the Soviet Union had in fact provoked a war, would it agree to lose it? We had no more right to evade this question than to take a complacent view of the Egyptian military preparations. Our predicament was now international, not regional. We must look across the Atlantic toward the only power that could neutralize a Russian menace. The Soviet boasts that "Israel would pay a heavy price for resisting Arab assaults" might be no more than conventional rhetoric, but who could be sure?

Here I turned to an analysis of Western and especially American reaction. I pointed out that although France had taken the most vigorous stand of all in 1957, our messages to Paris had now gone unanswered.

Washington, on the other hand, was in ferment. At midnight of May 22–23, Ephraim Evron, the minister in our embassy, had been summoned to the State Department to discuss Nasser's speech at Bir Gafgafa. We were told that President Johnson was sending urgent messages to Cairo, Damascus and Moscow, urging de-escalation of troop movements and respect for free navigation in the Gulf of Aqaba. In the meanwhile, Israel was urged to abstain from unilateral action for a few days. I read out a cable from Evron conveying a formal request to this effect from the United States government. Israel was asked to make no decisions for forty-eight hours, and during that respite to take counsel with the United States. We were told that the President would take no responsibility for actions on which he was not consulted. Here were disquieting echoes of 1956. I thought that a determined effort must be made to secure a warmer American understanding. Otherwise, I said to some of my colleagues, we could well win a war and lose the victory.

None of our advisers thought that any military prospect would be lost at that stage by acceding to the American request for a few days' respite. I considered that if time was available, it should be used for two purposes: we should explore Soviet intentions in close communion with the United States, and we should remind the Western powers that not only Israel's destiny but the credibility of their own commitments was at stake. If we didn't do it, I said, they would say afterward that we missed an opportunity to solve our problem in cooperation with them. For generations we would not be able to explain to ourselves and others why we did not put these promises to the test.

It was clear to all of us that the humble port from which Israel looked out onto the Red Sea had become the focal point of international tension, and our options were few. It was impossible to violate Israel's interests at Eilat without touching her sovereignty at its most sensitive point. It was here that we must do or die.

I noted that I had heard no proposal for immediate military action which would open the Straits; there might be other proposals of shorter range. My view was that any operation, however successful, which left Nasser in command of Tiran would be a strategic failure even if it was a tactical success. For example, some of our advisers proposed an attack at Gaza or in northern Sinai; I thought that this would be absorbed and shrugged off. If Nasser remained in possession of the southern key to Israel, his political triumph would not be canceled by any physical blow elsewhere.

The debate went on in deep gravity. Most were agreed that the moment for military reaction was not yet ripe, and that a political phase must first ensue. The story of a conflict on May 23 between counsels of immediate reprisal and of prior political action has become something of a legend, diffused in many books. It is without any substance. No proposal of immediate riposte was made that day.

I saw no need to point out that during the forty-eight hours requested by the United States, there would almost certainly come a request for additional respite. The Minister of Finance, Pinhas Sapir, thought realistically that "forty-eight hours would become seventy-two hours or more." We were agreed that our efforts should be focused on Washington. The Minister of the Interior, Moshe Shapiro, considered that I should make contact with leaders of the Western powers in their capitals. Such a journey could be important, in Israel Galili's words, if it was designed to explore the whole prospect, and not merely the next step. Dr. Zerach Warhaftig, the Minister of Religious Affairs, took a long political view. Our aim should be to introduce another anti-Nasser factor into the struggle. If this took two or three weeks, it was worth doing. Egyptian preparedness would decline. There would be a weakening in their tension and a growth in ours. Events were to confirm this insight.

In my own ministry the consensus was in favor of my going to Washington only. In the informal May 23 discussions, there were some party leaders who even questioned this course. Might it not invite American pressure on Israel to weaken or abandon our mood of imminent resistance? I disagreed, pointing out that even in advance of any high-level encounter, the United States was already pressing us to show "restraint" without any outspoken defense of our position on the blockade. My arrival in Washington to invoke the 1957 commitment would make it more difficult for the United States to urge the renunciation of our rights. Golda Meir emphasized the need to solve the mystery of France's attitude. After all, it was French equipment that stood between us and disaster; we would need French understanding if the battle became prolonged. Later in the day there was an idea of sending an unofficial emissary to the United States, such as Mrs. Meir herself, who could make demands while evading any requests for official commitment. Nobody supported this course. Mrs. Meir rejected it most strongly of all, and it never came to a point where there was a necessity for my reaction. Eshkol felt that we had to face our friends and foes alike as government to government, in the most formal and solemn confrontation.

Dayan's view was that we should accept the U.S. request for a respite since it did not prejudice our security, but we should reject any general principle of prior consultation. It might be necessary to take lonely decisions for which it would not be realistic to expect American approval in advance. Dayan added that only the United States was physically able to force the Straits of Tiran. If it did so, he would be gratified and surprised, but he would be prepared to forgo national pride and give the honor to others.

Before we dispersed, I circulated the first formal proposal made by a minister since the imposition of the blockade:

> The Government of Israel decides to give effect to the policy which it announced on 1 March 1957, namely, to regard any interference with shipping as an aggressive act against which Israel is entitled to exercise self-defense.

The majority view was that we should take a few days to explore the political ground, but without giving any impression of indefinite resignation to the blockade.

Our ministerial meetings ended with a formal decision on Eshkol's proposal, which was made without dissent. It was based on my own draft, with Eshkol's addition on the need to consult Washington:

1. *The blockade is an act of aggression against Israel.*
2. *Any decision on action is postponed for 48 hours, during which time the Foreign Minister will explore the position of the United States.*
3. *The Prime Minister and Foreign Ministers are empowered to decide, should they see fit, on a journey by the Foreign Minister to Washington to meet President Johnson.*

In the late afternoon our movement flowed back toward Jerusalem. I found cables from Walter Eytan, our ambassador in Paris, telling us of an important meeting of the French Council of Ministers to be held the following day. Eytan thought that he might be received by De Gaulle. Eshkol felt that the General should, if possible, also receive a direct impression of the agony and suspense in Israel. Eytan's only hesitation concerned the possibility that the request to receive me would raise greater problems on the protocolar side than the confirmation of a routinely arranged ambassadorial audience. In Jerusalem we thought it unlikely that De Gaulle would want to miss an opportunity to hear Israel's aims and calculations at first hand. I arranged with the Prime Minister that I would set out for Paris in the early hours of the morning, and after conferring with President de Gaulle, go on to Washington. I would not take part in the United Nations Security Council meeting which had been called by Canada and Denmark. We had nothing to expect from that body despite the good intentions of the two governments which had convened it. I further agreed with the Prime Minister that I would speak frankly of Israel's resolve not to yield to Nasser's aggression.

This policy came to expression in Eshkol's speech to a tense and crowded Parliament that evening. When he and I came into the Chamber, its temper was already at a high pitch. The air of emergency was unconcealed. We had advised President Zalman Shazar to return from his state visit to Canada, which he had begun on May 20, and Eshkol had reluctantly cut short the visit of Finnish Prime Minister Rafael Passio, who had arrived on May 21.

Members of all parties had spoken that afternoon of impending ordeals which would demand national unity. Spokesmen of the religious parties had movingly prayed at the rostrum "for the survival of Israel's remnant." But the nobility of the hour was being reduced by those who thought it more urgent to change the government at home than the situation abroad.

The Prime Minister's words were few but heavy: an international commitment was now in the balance at an hour fateful for Israel and the world. Egyptian forces in Sinai had grown from 35,000 to 80,000. Israel was mobilized against all eventualities. The Israeli government would carry out the policy which it had announced to the United Nations General Assembly on March 1, 1957. This was a clear allusion to our decision to fight against a blockade.

At three-thirty in the morning on May 24 I set out from Lod Airport to Paris with my political secretary, Moshe Raviv, in an otherwise empty Boeing 707 chartered from El Al. At seven in the cool morning we touched down at Orly and checked in at the Airport Hotel. There had been no sleep for me since the telephone call from Tel Aviv at five o'clock the previous morning.

13

Negotiations in Three Cities 1967

I HAD SPENT THE JOURNEY TO PARIS READING SOME OF DE GAULLE'S LOFTY prose. ("All my life I have given myself a certain idea of France. Sentiment inspires me no less than reason. France is only herself when at the highest rank.") The encounter which lay before me stirred my imagination. From early youth I had held a romantic notion of France. The cadence of the language had taken me in thrall. I had spent many years and journeys to perfect some mastery in its use.

The fearful laceration of France in war and under Nazi occupation had evoked my deepest anguish. Charles de Gaulle, as a slim, tall general, had once passed across my line of vision when I was an officer on leave in Cairo in the summer of 1943. His solitary demeanor bore witness to the tragedy into which France had fallen and from which he was seeking her recuperation. When he returned to office in 1958 and began to revive his nation's purpose, he seemed to prove that no cause is lost—as long as perseverance endures.

The adherence of this strong figure to Israel's cause had given us great pride during the nine years of his regime. The question now was how our new predicament would affect him. I had recently become uneasy about some gaps in the structure of French-Israeli relations. Early in 1966, on taking office in the Foreign Ministry, I had written a memorandum drawing the attention of our embassy and of senior officials to signs of exaggerated French discretion and reserve. I pointed out that none of our ministers had ever been formally invited to Paris. No French minister in office had visited Israel. On the other hand, an increasingly ceremonial atmosphere now surrounded French-Arab relations. And at the United Nations, French delegates gave little expression to the special solidarities which inspired the direct relations between Paris and Jerusalem. Moreover, since the departure of the eloquent and learned Ambassador Jean Bourdeillette, no resounding public expression of French-Israeli amity had come even from the French embassy in Israel.

These twinges of disquiet were not widely shared. Our embassy had advised me not to worry. When I reached Paris in February 1966, our military and supply missions had shown me impressive lists of helpful French actions in fields vital to our security. Economic, technological and cultural cooperation were also in full spate. What did protocol matter in comparison with such things? Eminent Frenchmen concerned with our relationship, such as the Gaullist parliamentarians Pierre Schmittlein and Diomède Catroux, were even more emphatic to me in their reassurance. They thought that any expressions of nervousness from us would create the very situation that we wanted to avoid. To put De Gaulle's assurances in doubt would invite resentment—and not from him alone. Verbal gestures were admittedly scarce, but aircraft and other equipment were flowing copiously. A new agreement for fifty Mirage V aircraft had been signed in the summer of 1966. This seemed to show that France valued the substance of things above their form. True, De Gaulle had reacted with irritation in May 1963 to Ben Gurion's plea for an official alliance, but a year later he had reiterated to Eshkol that France was still Israel's "ally and friend." If the French relationship was rich in content but sparse in outward expression, was this not better than if the opposite were true?

I had scarcely had time to pursue my doubts or to put the reassuring counterarguments to test by the time the 1967 crisis came. Since early May, my disquiet had grown. The Secretary-General of the French Foreign Ministry, Hervé Alphand, visited Arab capitals in mid-May. He announced in Beirut that there was no contradiction between French recognition of Israel's existence and France's friendship with Arab states. This was impeccable as far as it went, although most states expect more from their friends than mere recognition of their "existence."

On May 23 French official spokesmen had reacted with lack of excitement to the withdrawal of UNEF and the imposition of the blockade. We knew that American and British leaders were preparing statements criticizing the blockade and recalling their own commitment to oppose it, and both governments had replied affirmatively to my notes of May 21. No similar response had come from Paris. Officials there had even hinted that there were juridical obscurities about Israel's navigation rights. They spoke as if Ambassador Georges Picot's March 1, 1957, speech had never been made, and in official talks we had been asked if the economic value of our Red Sea outlet was really enough to justify war.

Moreover, a few hours before Nasser had made his menacing speech at Bir Gafgafa, French and British Foreign Ministry spokesmen had announced that the 1950 Tripartite Declaration opposing force in the Middle East was no longer valid. There was room for different views about the strength or weakness of the 1950 declaration; Israel had never regarded it as an effective guarantee. But to choose May 22, 1967, as the occasion for declaring it invalid could only have one meaning; two of the signatories were abandoning a commitment at the very moment when it might have to be invoked.

In Paris the current of French opinion seemed to run strongly against the tide of official reserve. As I read the Paris newspapers in the Orly Airport Hotel I could feel the strength of the public mood in our behalf. I resolved to present Israel to General de Gaulle in the terms and language of his own struggle. He had always held that dignity and greatness are more worthy than base and convenient courses, that independence of decision is the hallmark of sovereignty, and that in moments of solitude a nation can redeem its past and save its future by refusing to come to terms with the violation of its rights.

I reached the Elysée Palace with Ambassador Eytan a few minutes before noon. As we entered the courtyard I saw some twenty identical Citroëns drawn up in precise formation. The Council of Ministers was evidently still in session, as always on Wednesdays. I wondered if I would not find myself already confronted by decisions which no argument of mine would be able to bend this way or that. On entering the presidential quarters, I was told that the Cabinet meeting would be brought to an end in time for General de Gaulle to confer with me.

When I was ushered in, accompanied by Eytan and Couve de Murville, General de Gaulle received me with grave courtesy. Authority flowed from him like a steady tide. Even before I was seated near his desk—uncluttered by papers or telephones—he said loudly, "Ne faites pas la guerre." At that moment we had not even been introduced. We then exchanged greetings and the General went on as if completing his previous sentence, "At any rate, don't shoot first. It would be catastrophic if Israel were to attack. The Four Powers must be left to resolve the dispute. France will influence the Soviet Union toward an attitude favorable to peace."

After these brief sentences, quietly spoken, the General awaited my exposition. I summarized our views in a few minutes. I said that Israel had reached a turning point in her history; we therefore wished to consult our country's great friend. The tension was composed of three factors: Syrian-based terrorism; Egyptian troop concentrations in Sinai after the departure of the United Nations forces; and the blockade of the Straits of Tiran. The third of these measures was not merely a "threat" of aggression; it was an aggressive act which must be rescinded. We would like to hear an expression of France's attitude. In 1957 France had given the most energetic definition of Israeli rights in the Gulf of Aqaba. The French declaration had even included recognition of Israel's title to defend herself physically against blockade. In 1957 our rights in the Gulf had been only a title and a prospect. It had since become a geopolitical reality expressed in hundreds of sailings under dozens of flags and in a new commercial and communications complex. Across this new artery Israel had developed her relations with the Eastern world and would thus not have to limit her relations to the West alone. This was an innocent and creative enterprise. Israel without Eilat would be stunted and humiliated. "Israel without honor is not Israel. Our nation faces a stern choice."

The last two words seemed to shake the President. He interrupted me with an anxious question: "What are you going to do?" "If the choice lies between surrender and resistance," I replied, "Israel will resist. Our decision has been made. We shall not act today or tomorrow, because we are still exploring the attitude of those who have assumed commitments. We want to know whether we are to be alone or whether we shall act within an international framework. If Israel fights alone (and she does not recoil from this), she will be victorious, although the price in blood may be heavy. If the powers act in accordance with their engagements, Israel will harmonize her resistance with theirs. It is only in order to explore this prospect that we have not yet put our rights to the test."

General de Gaulle listened to me attentively. His own sentences were equally brief and definite: Israel should not make war. At any rate, she should not be the first to do so. I replied that we could not be the first to "open hostilities," since these had already been opened: Nasser's blockade and declaration were acts of war. Whatever Israel did would be a reaction, not an initiative. A state could be attacked by many methods apart from gunfire. Civil law recognized no distinction between assault through strangulation and assault through shooting. Nor did international law.

De Gaulle evidently did not accept this definition. "Opening hostilities," in his view, meant firing the first shot. He admitted that France's declaration of 1957 on freedom of navigation was correct juridically, but 1967 was not 1957. Picot's statement had reflected the "particular heat" of 1957. Today it must be understood that "there are no Western solutions." The Soviet Union must be associated in a concerted effort by the Four (*"Il faut que les quatre se concertent"*). "The more Israel looks to the West, the less will be the readiness of the Soviet Union to cooperate." When I pointed out that the Soviet Union had condoned and, indeed, fomented all the Arab pressures against Israel, De Gaulle replied that Moscow's attitude had been negative in principle, but the USSR had, in fact, reconciled itself to Israeli passage in the Gulf of Aqaba. He thought that U Thant had acted correctly in removing UNEF at Egypt's request, although it might have been wiser to wait for consultations with the Four Powers.

At this point his tone softened. The General admitted that the blockade and troop concentrations "could not last" and that Israel "must reserve its position." But for the present, at any rate, Israel should not act. Time must be given for France to concert the action of the Four Powers in order to enable ships to pass through the Straits.

I said that the voice of France had not even been raised against Nasser's action of May 22. It was important that this be done. The President reaffirmed that he upheld the freedom of the seas and that an international agreement on the Straits should be sought "as in the Dardanelles." He added that since 1957 there had been "incidents," of which the blockade was the latest. Israel had not always "pampered" (*ménagé*) the Arabs, and tension had grown. I said that I was not sanguine about a positive Soviet role. After ten years of Egyptian quiescence on the frontiers, the Soviet Union had incited Egypt to put pressure on Israel. The General expressed skepticism about Western naval demonstrations. He said that Israel's adversaries were hoping that Israel would open hostilities. Israel should not satisfy these expectations.

After repeating that we would not accept the new situation created by Nasser, I said that French help and friendship had meant much for the reinforcement of Israel's strength and spirit. General de Gaulle replied that it was this very friendship which now moved him to give the advice which he had formulated. Israel was not "sufficiently established to solve all her problems herself." She should not undertake never to act, but in the meantime she should give a respite for international consultation. France would still work for a strong Israel. I pointed out that sometimes inaction is more dangerous than action. The reply was solemn. "De Gaulle understands the dangers which arise from inaction, but I advise you now not to be precipitate. Do not make war." As I rose to take my leave I found myself for a moment alone with General de Gaulle, out of earshot of Couve de Murville and Eytan. I conveyed Eshkol's personal respects to the General. "I remember what I said to him when he sat in this chair," he mused. "I said that the essential thing is that Israel should exist and develop."

As I went down the Elysée staircase with Ambassador Eytan I tried to digest what I had heard. The three salient points were: the emphatic advice to abstain from active resistance; the diminution, almost to vanishing point, of the 1957 maritime commitment; and the constant accent on the "Four Power" solution. France had once recognized Israel's right to fight if Egypt imposed the blockade or renewed terrorist raids. All this had now vanished. De Gaulle had said blandly that 1967 was not 1957.

To representatives of the French and international press gathered on the steps of the Elysée, I said, "I have told President de Gaulle that the blockade of the Gulf of Aqaba is an act of aggression. Israel is in a posture of preparedness but not of alarm. Her forces are capable of defending the vital interests and the territory of the State. The blockade is a piratical act. A world which resigned itself to such acts would be a jungle."

The Israeli ambassador in London, Aharon Remez, had heard that morning that the British government would like to exchange views with me if I could pass through London on my way to Washington. When I left the Elysée, I was told that the Prime Minister would see me without fixed appointment as soon as I arrived in London. I instructed Moshe Raviv to cable a few main headings to Jerusalem of my talk with General de Gaulle, including his ominous advice that it would be "catastrophic" if Israel acted without giving the Four Powers time to consult. I thought it urgent that this grave development in our position be known in Jerusalem at once. I asked Eytan to prepare a more detailed cable from his notes. President de Gaulle spoke in a measured and stately fashion, and Eytan had been able to write a very precise account. The next morning the Israeli government had before it a record of seven hundred Hebrew words in terms hardly less precise than if a tape recording had been made. There was not the slightest room for any conclusion except that France was disengaging herself from any responsibility for helping us if we chose early resistance. The expressions of friendship were general; the advice to us not to act was specific and almost brutally direct.

My intuition that the issue had all been decided before our conversation was now to be confirmed. While I was at the Elysée, the

French Minister of Information, Georges Gorse, was already telling correspondents of the conclusions reached in the morning Cabinet session. The communiqué said that France was "deeply preoccupied by recent developments, especially those concerning free passage in the Gulf of Aqaba." It went on to say that the Four Powers should take all measures to influence *both parties* to avoid taking any action which might prejudice peace. In reply to questions, Gorse said that responsibility would rest on whichever party was "first to shoot." When asked what France's attitude would be if Egypt were to open fire on an Israeli vessel in the Straits, he replied that in the present tension the appearance of an Israeli vessel in the Straits of Tiran would be a provocative act.

My visit to London, although casually conceived and improvised, now took on more significance. The rhapsodic quality which had marked Israel's relations with France had never touched our dialogue with London—not even at the height of the Suez crisis, when we had a common foe. But British opinion was now in ferment. A weekly paper not usually friendly to our cause had even written of "Israel's agony." When UNEF had suddenly been removed, the most pungent, emotional and forthright comment against Nasser had unexpectedly come from Foreign Secretary George Brown. He had said that a force which could be withdrawn in the hour of tension was a "mockery." I could not forget that there had always been a considerable British component in our defense equipment, especially in armor. This might be an important element in a prolonged war. On the other hand, Britain was in full momentum of disengagement from military commitments east of Suez, although her naval presence was still strong. In 1957 British support of Israel's right of navigation in the Straits of Tiran had been firm, although less vehement than that of France. My best hope in London seemed to lie in the heavy influence of public opinion on official policy, and on Harold Wilson's personal understanding of Israel's predicament.

From the airport in London, I drove with Ambassador Remez to Downing Street. The London air was charged with familiar symptoms of crisis. The British public has a strange ritual at such times: it assembles in Downing Street and stares with silent gravity at those coming in and out of No. 10. As a rule the crowds merely gaze contemplatively at the simple black door and at the policeman on guard, who returns the stare with defiant solemnity. As our car drew up, the Conservative leaders Edward Heath and Sir Alec Douglas-Home were walking away. After much photography on the celebrated doorstep, I entered the residence for the first time in my life, and registered the usual surprise at its spacious dimensions of which no hint is given by the external façade.

Everything in style and atmosphere was different from the Elysée Palace. I sat alongside Mr. Wilson in the middle of the Cabinet table, drinking strong tea and receiving pungent assaults of smoke from his pipe. His demeanor was solid and assured. Our dialogue was on a low, pragmatic key with no attempt at rhetoric or stylized discourse; I seemed to have crossed the Channel into the twentieth century. There was also a current of unembarrassed sympathy, which had been absent in my morning talks. Traditional roles were reversed. I had gone starry-eyed to Paris and more skeptical to London, but it was in London, not in Paris, that Israelis could feel a decent respect for their predicament.

The Prime Minister asked me about my talk with President de Gaulle, whose proposal for a Four Power consultation had come to him over the wires. Wilson seemed doubtful about the feasibility of the idea, but he had preferred to react affirmatively, if only to put it to the test. He feared that George Brown's talks in Moscow and the proceedings in the Security Council would show that the Soviet Union was in no mood to concert action with the West on behalf of an Israeli interest or of regional peace. (Only a few hours were to pass before the Soviet Union rejected De Gaulle's plan, refusing even to conduct Four Power talks at United Nations headquarters. Moscow's view was that there was no crisis to discuss. With Israel encircled, humiliated, blockaded and embattled, the situation in Soviet eyes was as "normal" as could be.)

To Wilson I expounded my belief that Israel's three choices were: to surrender, to fight alone, or to join with others in an international effort to force Nasser's withdrawal from his present course. Israel would not live without access to Eilat or under the threat of Egyptian encirclement. Therefore the only choice was resistance, whether Israeli or international. My purpose was to examine, within a brief time, whether there was any serious intention of the maritime powers to act in accordance with their engagement.

Wilson's reply was forthright. The Cabinet had met that morning and had reached a consensus that the policy of blockade must not be allowed to triumph; Britain would join with others in an effort to open the Straits. Wilson said that I would be surprised if I knew who had supported firm British action in the Cabinet and who had opposed it. The implication was that the pro-Israelis such as Crossman had advocated a passive British stance. (This has since been confirmed in Richard Crossman's diaries.)

The Prime Minister handed me the copy of a speech that he had made at Margate that morning. He had also sent the Minister of State, George Thompson, to Washington to see if a detailed plan could be worked out for common action; the talk in Washington would be of "nuts and bolts." Wilson asked if I believed that Western action on the Straits should be limited to the United Nations. I said that the United Nations, with the Soviet veto, was a blind alley.

The Prime Minister showed a close interest in the mood prevailing in Israel. I said that the atmosphere was grave but that "we will win if we have to fight." I exchanged views with him on our appraisal of Israel's strength and morale. Summing up, he said that Britain would work with others to open the Straits and was seeking an agreement with the United States on how to proceed. The emphasis was on collective international responsibility. I told him of our undertaking to Washington to refrain from action for forty-eight hours. Wilson suggested that I see George Thompson if he was still in Washington when I arrived; he would cable him accordingly. He saw me to the door of No. 10. There was more picture-taking—presumably designed to see if I had changed physically within the past fifty minutes. I went back to the hotel.

I noticed that Harold Wilson had confined himself to an analysis of Britain's position and had not given me any counsel one way or the other whether Israel should resist by armed force. I found this lack of exhortation realistic and mature; it was also prudent, since those who advised us not to act would obviously be assuming a heavy responsibility which they might not be able to discharge. I thought that Wilson was showing a distinguished statesmanship. He was prepared for the maximum degree of commitment compatible with his country's real strength and responsibility. These were not as broad as they once had been, and Wilson moved with assurance and precision within their limits.

A detailed telegram of my talk in Downing Street was sent to Jerusalem by Raviv. I warned my colleagues that although Wilson's views strengthened the chance of international support, their effectiveness would obviously depend on what was concerted in Washington.

It was now late for air passage to America; nor could I hope to have talks there before the following afternoon (Thursday May 25). I had no course but to stay the night. As I dined with some members of my family that evening I was overcome by a sudden exhaustion, which sent me back to the hotel for my first sleep in forty hours. The war atmosphere in the Middle East was evident from the heavy security guard outside my door at the Savoy Hotel. The British radio and television, which I turned on briefly before retiring, were full of sympathy for Israel, but they had a distinctly funereal air. I spent a totally sleepless night in a mood of deep national and personal solitude.

After seven hours' flight I reached Kennedy Airport in New York where I was met by UN Ambassador Rafael and Minister Evron. To the assembled newspapermen I repeated what I had said in Paris: Israel would resist the aggressive design now being woven around her; within a day or two we would know if we were supported by those who had committed their honor to our cause ten years before. When asked about the possibility of an Egyptian armed attack, in addition to the blockade, I said that "Israel would not expect American soldiers to lose their lives on Israel's behalf." This was a sensitive point for Americans, already convulsed by the agonies of Vietnam. I added that I had come to seek understanding and common counsel —and to ask how the United States now regarded its 1957 commitment on the Straits of Tiran. An hour later I was in Washington; the decisive stage of my mission had been reached.

Ambassador Avraham Harman began to brief me orally and through documents as we drove from the National Airport to the Mayflower Hotel. President Johnson had made an emphatic speech that morning, condemning Egypt's blockade as "illegal and fraught with danger." The President was now on an official visit to Canada and would return later that day. It was already plain to the embassy that my talk with him would only be feasible on Friday noon at the earliest. All indications from the White House were that Johnson was disturbed by Nasser's moves, especially by the blockade. He was also keeping a close eye on Soviet policies and measures. The United States was supporting the Canadian-Danish attempt to convene the United Nations Security Council: the Congress and the American people would insist on exhausting this procedure before considering any action outside the United Nations. A *New York Times* correspondent had been told in the White House that Israel could only be held back "for a matter of days" and that therefore the United Nations procedure should be followed rapidly to its inevitable deadlock. Our embassy had been informed by officials that a plan for breaking the blockade was being devised together with Britain, but that it was essential first to exhaust UN remedy.

At this stage the direction and thrust of my mission were changed by a cabled message that reached me from Jerusalem. It had followed me from London and New York, and I studied it with Ambassadors Harman and Rafael in my hotel suite in deep anxiety. The cable, signed by Eshkol, described our military posture in terms more alarming than those which I had heard in Tel Aviv two days before. Egyptian armor had crossed the Suez Canal eastward. Enemy troop concentrations in Sinai were dense. Airfields were on the alert and there was every reason to expect a surprise attack, even before we decided to challenge or resist the blockade. I was asked to convey this appraisal to Washington in the most urgent terms, and to ask if the United States would regard an attack on Israel as an attack on itself.

I considered briefly whether I should seek clarification of this directive. According to its wording, I would be asking the United States if it would do what I knew that its President had no constitutional power to promise. I feared that I might be exchanging an attitude of military self-confidence for one of apparent weakness. Instead of asking for specific political support and deterrence in the matter of the blockade, I would, in effect, be saying that Israel felt her life to be at Egypt's mercy unless there was an American intervention beyond the limits of the Gulf of Aqaba problem. I found it hard to understand how such an extreme change could have come over our military positions since I heard our generals report in Tel Aviv on May 23. I debated with myself whether I should find out more about the sudden nervousness behind the cable. At this point another cable reached me from Jerusalem reinforcing the first in even more emphatic terms.* The issue was so grave that I felt no capacity to argue. What would my responsibility be if, while I delayed my action, a "surprise attack" did take place during the delay? I asked for my talk with Secretary of State Dean Rusk to be advanced a few hours before the scheduled hour.

Dean Rusk and I had known each other for twenty years in varying circumstances of harmony and divergence. His approach to Israel's problems had sometimes been inhibited. He often seemed perplexed by the motives of Israel's existence and action. But his fidelity to presidential policy was absolute, and an austere intellectual honesty often created common ground with those whose views differed from his own. International statecraft is a less impersonal business than many people believe: a background of understanding and trust helps quick communication—especially when danger looms.

I conveyed what I had received from Jerusalem about an imminent possibility of surprise attack and our request that the United States deter it. The tone of the message came as a surprise to Rusk, as

* Eshkol's clarification of this development was published by him in an interview in *Ma'ariv* (New Year, September 1967).

well as to Eugene Rostow and Lucius Battle, who accompanied him. The Secretary immediately broke off our conversation, presumably in order to communicate my words to the President with all urgency. He asked whether we had made similar representations in London and Paris. I had no answer to this. Rusk said that I had raised questions which involved the American constitutional position. He could tell me that the trend of discussion in the Senate Foreign Relations Committee that morning had been in favor of supporting Israel's cause, but only on condition that the United States would not be alone. Rusk then arranged for us to meet again at greater length that evening.

An hour later, accompanied by Harman, Rafael and Evron, I was back in the State Department for a "working dinner" with leading American officials. On the American side there were Eugene Rostow, who was Undersecretary of State for Political Affairs; Fay Kohler, an expert of Soviet affairs; Lucius Battle, who was in charge of Middle Eastern and South Asian problems; Joseph Sisco, director of the United Nations department; George Meeker, the legal adviser; and Townsend Hoopes, who represented the Pentagon. I began by explaining the acuteness of Israel's peril; her total resolve to emerge from it; and her conviction that freedom of passage in the Straits of Tiran was "a paramount and unconditional national interest."

From the dinner table I returned to Secretary Rusk's office. He had evidently conferred at length with President Johnson and was able to give me a detailed summary of the President's views. At one-thirty on Friday morning I sent my impressions to the Prime Minister. I told him that in my view, the President was likely to discuss a program for opening the Straits by the maritime powers led by the United States, Britain and perhaps others. The plan in its present form was based on the idea of a joint declaration by maritime states, including Israel, concerning their resolve to exercise freedom of passage. The second stage, according to what had been said to us, would be the dispatch of a naval task force which would appear in the Straits. Some officials had predicted that the President would make a pledge that the Straits would be opened, even if there was resistance. Some press reports were appearing in the same sense. I had told them that after my talk with the President, I would fly home at once and bring the thoughts of the United States government to the knowledge of my colleagues; in the meantime, I had no authority to define any attitude during the present short visit. My efforts were limited to inducing them to make their proposals in the fullest detail, including a time-table and a method of carrying out any plan, so that our government should be able to determine its attitude one way or the other. I had emphasized that in the absence of an immediate plan for opening the Straits, there would, in my opinion, be no escape from an explosion. Since their plan included a certain reliance on the United Nations, I expressed a deeply skeptical appraisal of its effectiveness. They would continue to work on the details of the project.

Friday, May 26, was a crowded day for me. It began at nine-thirty when Secretary Rusk telephoned. He asked whether I would still be in Washington on Saturday morning, when the results of U Thant's report would be known. The leisurely implication of this question gave me great alarm. At nine forty-five I called Rusk and told him that I intended to leave Washington that night. There was a Cabinet meeting on Sunday which I had to attend, and ahead of which I would have to consult. This could be one of the most crucial Cabinet meetings in our history. Our decision would largely be based on what President Johnson conveyed to me today; U Thant's report was not the decisive factor in our eyes. I told him frankly that I thought we were in for hostilities next week. "There is an act of blockade which will be resisted." I doubted whether anything at this stage could change this outlook. What had depressed me most was all the talk about the United Nations. This conjured up nothing but a vista of delay and procrastination. The Secretary replied "I get you" and hung up.

After this tense episode I went to the Pentagon, where Secretary of Defense Robert McNamara was attended by the nation's senior military advisers, including General Earl Wheeler, the Chairman of the Joint Chiefs of Staff. I was accompanied by Harman and our military attaché, Aluf Mishne Yosef Geva. Evron stayed in the embassy to await communication from Jerusalem. Conversation had scarcely begun when a cable was handed to me from Jerusalem reiterating the military appraisal that had reached me the night before.

There was a frank exchange of evaluations with the American defense chiefs about Israel's security problem. Our political attitudes seemed to be harmonious; but now our military appreciations diverged widely. The professional American view was that Egyptian forces were still not arrayed in a posture indicating an early assault. Nasser, having imposed the blockade and carried out the troop concentrations, would lay upon Israel the onus of an armed response which he felt able to repel. He had already taken the strategic initiative and would now wait. This seemed to be the logic of his military dispositions. My interlocutors did not think that Nasser would take the next step, unless he saw what Israel intended to do. Despite American skepticism about an early Egyptian move, the Egyptian ambassador had been called in the previous evening and warned against any reckless act. The United States had done this because of the urgent tone of my message from Jerusalem, not because it really believed that Nasser would push his tactical success further at this stage.

I feared that the Jerusalem cable had caused me to lose the first round. We had elicited from the United States a purely diplomatic gesture, probably superfluous, and had created a position which would be ambiguous if we ourselves felt obliged to engage Egyptian troops pre-emptively.

The American defense establishment obviously had a different picture of the immediate military prospects than that which I had conveyed from Jerusalem that morning. They pointed out that any question of American action would, of course, require a presidential decision on which they were not competent to pronounce judgment. (President Johnson later published the fact which he told me about that day—that he had asked three teams to examine the results of a possible war.) All the American defense chiefs could do was to give a professional view on what the results would be if a conflict broke out between Israeli and Egyptian forces. Their studies all pointed toward Israeli success if there was a war. They thought that this would be the case no matter who took the initiative in the air. That question would affect the time and the size of our casualty list, but not the result itself. The days and hours that were passing did not, in their view, increase the inability of Israel to defend herself successfully. On the contrary, it was the Egyptian forces who were increasing their vulnerability by extending their lines of communication. All reports from the area indicated a logistic confusion in the Egyptian camp. The American military view was that Israel's immediate security was in good shape, and that time, in the short terms at least, was not working against her. Israeli mobilization was becoming effective, while Egyptian difficulties would grow every hour. Israel's lines of supply and communication were short and efficient; Egyptian communications were a nightmare of distance and complexity. The Pentagon leaders made it plain that they were speaking purely as specialists; they were not recommending that we acquiesce in the present situation. But the idea that Israel was being outmaneuvered in the military domain, and would have to act in a mood of "now or never," seemed to them so remote that they would be interested to know on what such appraisals were based.

When I went back to the embassy, news reached us from the

State Department that a detailed study was being made of the Eisen-
hower-Dulles commitment to Israel on freedom of passage in the Gulf
of Aqaba. I had brought the relevant documents with me from
Jerusalem. The most impressive were the minutes of a conversation
which I had conducted in Secretary Dulles' home on February 24,
1957, after arriving in Washington from consultations in Jerusalem.
These minutes had been checked by me in the United Nations Division
of the State Department before they were sent to Jerusalem on or about
February 26, 1957. Harman now had this document photographed
and sent to the State Department for study; it proved how firm and
detailed our understanding had been in 1957.

By midafternoon there was still no confirmation from the official
spokesman that my talk with the President would take place that day.
At the same time I was receiving a shower of telegrams from Jerusalem, telling me that it was essential for domestic as well as for
international reasons that I be back home by Saturday night. Conversations were afoot about the enlargement of the government coalition.
And our military circles evidently did not share the optimistic appraisal that time was working in favor of Israel's security. I had the
impression that if further hours were to pass, vital decisions would be
reached in Jerusalem without my presence. Accordingly, I asked Evron
to make urgent inquiry. On reaching the White House, Evron
received a frank explanation of what the difficulties were. Canadian
Prime Minister Lester Pearson had published in his Parliament certain things that he had heard in a conversation with President Johnson. The President was put out; matters could be grave unless publicity was concerted ahead of my talk. There would have to be a clear
understanding that we agreed beforehand on anything that would
be said to the press about American intentions. Evron gave immediate assurance that I had no interest in publicity and would be prepared to say nothing except that I had had serious discussions with
the President and the Secretaries of State and Defense.

On hearing these reassuring words from Evron, the White House
official telephoned President Johnson, who asked Evron to be brought
in to see him. Evron received a frank and full preview of what I
would be told officially later on. He had spent more than half an
hour alone with the President by the time I arrived with Ambassador
Harman. Out of respect for the President's inhibitions concerning
publicity, we made our way to the Executive Mansion by a circuitous
route and ended up at the White House at an unexpected point of
entry, to be suspiciously received by a disturbingly well armed White
House guard. At seven o'clock I began a conversation with President
Johnson which lasted for an hour and forty minutes. Of the nine par-

ticipants, six were American: President Johnson, Secretary McNamara, Walt Rostow, Eugene Rostow, Joseph Sisco and George Christian. I was accompanied by Ambassador Harman and Minister Evron.

It is hard to convey the tension which gripped my heart. It was clear that Israel faced a hard choice. But it was no less clear that her success would depend not only on her own valor, but also on the understanding that we could now achieve with our strongest friend. I remembered what I had said to my colleagues on Wednesday morning, "It is quite possible that we may win the war and lose the peace." My mind went back to the parallel occasion ten years before.

Indeed, two days before, a link had been forged between 1956 and 1967; Ambassador Harman had gone to Gettysburg, Pennsylvania, on May 24, for a meeting with former President Dwight D. Eisenhower. Our ambassador's purpose was to ensure that the former President would support his successor in honoring the American commitments that had been concluded a decade before. Eisenhower told Harman that he was not accustomed to making statements, but if asked by newspapermen, he would say that the Straits of Tiran was an international waterway. This had been determined in 1957. He would repeat the attitude which he and Secretary Dulles had then taken. He would add that a violation of the rights of free passage would be illegal. His friends in the Republican Party had already been in touch with him and he was going to tell them exactly what he thought. Eisenhower strongly critized the United Nations role in recent weeks. Referring to U Thant's present conversations in Cairo, he said that Nasser had created an illegal position and there should be no compromise with illegality. He asked Harman about the positions of France and Britain. Eisenhower, ruminating on the past, said that he still regretted that they had not taken steps of a concrete nature in the Suez Canal similar to those which had been adopted with regard to the Straits of Tiran. General Eisenhower, on hearing Ambassador Harman's report of President Johnson's speech of May 23, said that he hoped the President's position would be strongly maintained. He said that when he was President, the Russians tended to believe his strong statements because he had been a military man. General Eisenhower concluded by saying, "I do not believe that Israel will be left alone."

Two days had passed and now the President of the United States was seated opposite me with his eyes very close to mine, staring gravely into my face. Johnson's manner was courteous, but his demeanor was graver than I had ever known it before. My mind went back to our first meetings in the mid-fifties when Lyndon Johnson was the Majority Leader in the Senate. In those early days I had felt that he came hesitantly to our concerns. His mind and heart were then turned inward toward the forces which shaped American society. Yet, in the early fifties, a sharp concern for Israel's future already gripped large sections of the American people and forced its way into the Senate's halls. Accompanied by a friend from Houston, Jim Novy, who had first introduced us, Lyndon B. Johnson had come to my Washington residence in 1952 in an effort to find out everything essential about Israel in the briefest possible time. His interrogation had been avid, detailed, implacable and seemingly free of sentiment. He had the air of a man parsimonious of time and jealous of every minute not devoted to a functional end.

He thus had some interest in Israel's destiny by the time he entered the White House on the dark evening of President Kennedy's assassination in November 1963. Within a few months he had established with Prime Minister Eshkol the kind of intimate confidence that had never before existed between heads of American and Israeli governments. We no longer had to use the back door for access to the center of American policy. In February 1966, when I became Foreign Minister, I had taken up the thread of my previous acquaintanceship with Lyndon Johnson by completing the negotiation of an agreement on the Skyhawk aircraft. I found that his intuitions about Israel had filled out and deepened since our tentative conversation in 1952—and even since the troubled days of 1956.

All this came to memory on May 26 as we began to talk. I opened by saying that there had never been a moment for my country such as this. Israel was on a footing of grave and anxious expectancy. I had come to discuss the question of the Gulf of Aqaba. But, meanwhile, an even graver issue had arisen. Here I gave the President the essence of what had reached me from Jerusalem late the previous day. I pointed out that we faced a total assault on Israel's existence. The maritime blockade was not in itself the whole of our crisis; it had, however, been a turning point in the growing chain of violence.

Discussing the Straits of Tiran, I said that what Nasser had done would change the entire character of our country. I reminded the President that ten years before there had been a solemn pact between the United States and Israel: we had agreed that the Straits of Tiran would be open to all shipping, including that of Israel. What had then been a mere prospect had now become a legal situation and an economic fact, enshrined in the 1958 Law of the Seas, and in hundreds of sailings under dozens of flags, in trade with Asia and Africa and in vital economic and political interests. Did Nasser really think that he could cancel all this out in five minutes? Our case was that the act of aggression had already been committed.

Some people had asked why we had not yet reacted to this. I could say in all frankness that when we met on May 23 to discuss the matter, we realized that we were faced with a clear-cut choice between surrender and resistance. We were unanimous in the decision that we could not and would not surrender. If we had to fight, this was an issue on which we could make a legitimate stand. "It might be a bloody business but we would win." However, in the light of cables from Washington, we thought it worthwhile to have a look at the possibility that Israel's resistance might take place within the framework of an international effort.

We now looked to the United States to see if it would take a special initiative, I went on. If the President would tell me that the Straits were going to be opened again, and if he would make common cause with Israel on this matter, then there was still a possibility that Nasser would retreat, and a victory would be won for legality without war. I told him that I had spoken to President de Gaulle, who had raised the question of a Four Power agreement; I hoped that by now this expectation was out of his mind. The Soviets were clearly not in a mood for harmonious action with the Western powers. Despite disturbing aspects of my conversation in Paris, the armories of France were open to us, and we were still being given every help. In London I had been pleasantly surprised by a readiness to act; but obviously, this would only have serious effect if it were concerted with the United States. I emphasized repeatedly that there was an explicit American commitment. Indeed, there had been a joint American-Israeli effort in 1957 to open up a new avenue of the sea for international communication. All our links with Africa and Asia depended on this.

I added that there was no doubt on the part of my government about what American policy was. The President had given it forceful expression within the past few days. The policy was there; the question to which I had to bring the answer was: Does the United States have the will and determination to carry out that policy, to open the Straits?

I now went back to the problem of Egyptian troop concentrations. On my arrival in Washington I had been apprized by the Prime Minister of a change for the worse in the situation since I left Israel. I had received a series of most urgent messages, advising me that Nasser was ready for an imminent attack together with Syria. I had never received documents from my Prime Minister as urgent as those.

The President had listened to me with total concentration. There was a pause before he spoke. He said that he had found it necessary to say publicly that an illegal arbitrary action had occurred, and to make quite clear that the Gulf of Aqaba was an international waterway. That statement had perhaps not yet had the effect that he thought it would have. He felt very strongly on this issue and had stated what he felt to the American people and to the world. The question was: What to do and when to do it? He could only help us if his Cabinet, Congress and people felt that Israel had been wronged and that neither the United States nor Israel had precipitated the situation. Here the President involved me in the complex problems of time and patience. "I can only tell you that the best influence of the United States will be used to get that waterway open."

He expressed some robust views about U Thant's withdrawal of UNEF. Nevertheless, he clearly believed that the United Nations channel must first be exhausted. "If it becomes apparent without filibuster that the United Nations cannot do the job of opening that waterway, then it is going to be up to Israel and all of its friends, and all those who feel that an injustice has been done, and all those who give some indication of what they are prepared to do, and the United States would do likewise. The United States has had some experience in seeking support of friendly states, but Israel should put its embassies to work to get support from all those concerned with keeping the waterway open. The British are willing and the United States is trying to formulate a plan with them. It is unwise to jump the gun." Here the President mentioned his efforts with other countries, including Canada and various European states. Prime Minister Pearson had received and published the impression that the President was in favor of "a Four Power arrangement." This was not so; but more substantive was a Canadian indication that "they may give a ship or two." What is needed in a very short time is Israel's initiative and British help to evolve an international effort with some effectiveness. How soon and how effective depends on events. Everything that the United States has ever said in relation to Israel, from Truman through Eisenhower and Kennedy has been reviewed. "All effort is important, but is not worth five cents unless I have the American people with me. Therefore we must see what comes out of the statement of the Secretary-General and the Security Council meeting. We should get busy to talk to those nations who had come out in support of freedom of navigation. If your Cabinet decides to do anything immediately and to do it on their own, that is for them. The United States is not going to do any retreating. I am not forgetting anything I have ever said."

The President was frank about his constitutional position. For example, to say that an attack on Israel was an attack on the United

States was beyond his prerogative. But he wanted to be in a position to help. "I know that Israel's blood and life are at stake. My own blood and life are at stake in many places and may be in others. I do not believe that the procedure outlined for building up an international task force is going to take too long. The purpose is to see to it that the Israeli ships go through. I have been into all the aspects of Israel's security situation. I am aware of what it is costing us today; but it is less costly than to precipitate the matter while the jury is still out and to have the world against you. All I can tell you is what you have heard—friendship. I have spent hours of work on this and I have the determination; but it is essential before anything else to thrash this out in the United Nations and to try to work out some kind of a multilateral group. Other nations can and should help. There should be no doubt about my objective. It is to get Israeli shipping through the Gulf. I have said in my statement that the Gulf was an international waterway. [Here the President referred to his statement of May 23.] What you can tell your Cabinet is that the President, the Congress and the country will vigorously support a plan to use any or all measures to open the Straits. But we have to go through with the Secretary-General and the Security Council and build up support among the nations." Here the President said with great emphasis: "Israel will not be alone unless it decides to go alone." He repeated this three times. It was to become his public watchword for the next week.

His discourse then took on a personal emphasis. He recalled that he had had a great deal of association with me personally, and knew our Prime Minister and President and many others. He could not imagine that we would make a precipitate decision. He was going to do what was right if he was permitted to. "I am not a feeble mouse or a coward and I am going to try. What is needed by the United States is a group, five, or four or less, or if we could not do that, then on our own." He had publicly said that the blockade by Egypt was illegal; no one in America had come out against that position.

I then discussed Nasser's hostile references to Israel's oil supplies through Eilat. I pointed out that most of our tankers were not under Israeli flag. President Johnson insisted on the need to establish Israeli shipping. "I am not going to say that it is all right if the rest go through, but Israel cannot."

I said to the President, "Can I tell my Cabinet that you are going to use all efforts in your power to get the Gulf of Aqaba open to all shipping, including that of Israel?" The President said "Yes."

I returned again to the more urgent problem created for us by Egyptian troop concentrations and the possibility of an attack. From the President's reaction, it appeared to me that his experts believed that there was no imminent attack to be expected, and if there was, Israel would succeed. There was a general conviction that Israel had a right to be worried and could not be expected to live indefinitely under an illegal siege. But the official American belief was that Israel could afford to wait and was not pressed for time in terms of hours or days.

Dusk was falling when I rose to take my leave. Ambassador Harman had made a very detailed record of the conversation; and the President had constantly referred to a paper which he gave me as an *aide-mémoire:*

> *Regarding the Straits we plan to pursue vigorously the measures which can be taken by maritime nations to assure that the Straits and the Gulf remain open to free and innocent passage of all nations. I must emphasize the necessity for Israel not to make itself responsible for the initiation of hostilities. Israel will not be alone unless it decides to do it alone. We cannot imagine that Israel will make this decision.*

The President and I walked alone toward the White House elevator. On the way he said to me, "What do you reckon will be the result in Israel of what I have said?" I replied that things were moving so quickly at home that my intuitions of yesterday had no real relevance. The real question was what I told my colleagues about the President's attitude and resolution. "Again, Mr. President, can I tell my Cabinet that you will use every measure in your power to ensure that the Gulf and Straits are open for Israeli shipping?" The President said "Yes." He shook my hand with such a paralyzing grip that I doubted that I would ever regain the use of it—and after seeing me into the elevator, he turned back into his room.

My impression was that a new potentiality was only now beginning to grow in American-Israeli relations, and that it would be worthwhile to give it time to reveal itself. Whether an international effort to run the blockade would be mounted was in my mind a matter of doubt. In any case, a week or so would make this plain one way or the other. Of more importance was the clear American recognition that Israel had been wronged, that the situation created by Nasser should be reversed and not allowed to congeal. At its highest level of responsibility, the United States saw itself as charged with a commitment which could not merely be allowed to languish and die. None of these elements had existed in American policy in 1956.

I went with Ambassador Harman straight to National Airport, where we emplaned for New York. There we took rooms in the Kennedy airport hotel, and Ambassador Harman immediately began to dictate to a secretary the full minutes that he had written. We felt it essential that our Cabinet, when it met, should have the whole wording and flavor of the President's words. It was not every day that a President of the United States spoke to us in such lucidity and depth about a grave international situation in which our country was involved. Later Harman sent a short account of our conversation to Jerusalem, together with a résumé of Evron's preliminary talk with the President and the assurances that Rusk had given us about a prospect of support by Britain, Holland, Australia, Canada and other states for a proposed multilateral action to assert freedom of navigation. Leaving Harman and Raviv at the airport hotel, I drove into New York for a conversation with Ambassador Arthur Goldberg at his suite in the Waldorf Towers; he has a calm rationality always which shines forth in moments of crisis.

He said that the proceedings of the Security Council were already petering out. The Secretary-General had virtually brought nothing back with him from Cairo, apart from Nasser's assurance that he did not plan an armed attack. I said that I found this assurance convincing. Nasser did not want war; he wanted victory without war. Goldberg listened attentively to what I told him of our Washington conversations. It was clear that he had already been briefed personally from Washington. He urged me to draw a very sharp distinction between what the President had said personally and what I had heard from other sources. The American choices were now so grave that only presidential commitments mattered. I found Goldberg skeptical about the logistic aspects of the naval task force; he feared that it would be an "amateur show" unless a stringent presidential directive got the plan off the ground. Goldberg tended to attach subsidiary importance to the problem of "multilateralism." Of far greater consequence, in his view, was the President's absolute need to rely on congressional backing. The Vietnam war had generated an atmosphere of caution, even about the most limited commitments. Many in the Congress would wonder whether a small and innocuous-looking effort in the Red Sea might not escalate into a major American engagement in the Middle East. Goldberg emphasized that nobody knew whether anything would come of an international attempt to secure freedom of navigation and de-escalation of troop concentrations. The essence of the matter, in his view, was whether I had helped to convince President Johnson of Egypt's culpability and of Israel's innocence. This was of crucial importance; if it was established in the American mind that Egypt's action was illicit, then Israel could hardly lose. Either she would gain international support against the blockade or if she acted alone, she would have the United States committed to the doctrine of Israel's rectitude and Cairo's guilt.

From the Waldorf Towers I returned to Kennedy Airport, where my plane was due to leave at midnight. Harman had meanwhile edited his notes on the talk with the President. Confiding a copy to me and one to Raviv, he took leave of us. On boarding the El Al plane, I found that the emotion of the past fifteen hours had taken a full toll of my energies. I fell fast asleep and woke up seven and a half hours later at Orly Airport in Paris. In the official lounge I gave a short and cautious interview, stating that the object of my visit to three capitals had been to inquire whether the powers which had accepted solemn commitments in Israel's support ten years before were still mindful of what they had then undertaken. In Washington I had found support for my contention that Israel was the victim of an illegal and irresponsible act, but I could not say what practical conclusions would ensue. I would be bringing my impressions back to my government. I was enigmatic about how I envisaged the future course of events. The room contained many Israeli newspapermen who were certain that "there would be a war in a few days," and that they would follow it from Paris.

At first sight, nothing in my talks in Washington had made Israel's tasks lighter or her dilemma less sharp. Historians and biographers think of President de Gaulle as a stronger personality than President Johnson. Like many conventional images, this one may be false. President Johnson, like De Gaulle, sometimes allowed emotion to invade policy. To say this is merely to confess that he was human, and yet his response to Nasser's action had its realistic aspect. It was inspired by a coherent philosophy about America's place in the world. Like all his predecessors from Franklin Roosevelt onward, he believed that predominant strength created particular responsibility. He had a strong contempt for the illusion that American peace and prosperity could flourish for long without simultaneous peace and prosperity across the world. He rejected isolationism not merely because it was ignoble, but also because, in the final resort, it was ineffective. He was not widely traveled and did not have a very detailed knowledge of foreign countries, but he had a spacious vision of the world, and in that vision America had a large role. There may have been something romantic in the notion that the United States, like the knights in the period of chivalry, was compelled by honor and duty to save whatever weak nation was threatened by the dragons of aggression. Like many men who put on a hard-headed front and who speak in masculine expletives, Johnson had a soft core.

Nasser's actions and the role of the Soviet Union in inspiring them were a clear threat to the aims of international stability and order which are the better side of America's foreign policy. For this reason, he was not going to dishonor the pledge which he had inherited from Eisenhower ten years before. Here the President came face to face with the inhibiting factors at work in American policy. A President who went out to incur risks could no longer count on the loyalty of allies or on a national consensus at home. In Southeast Asia, an American commitment had been defended in a most uncongenial arena—and thereby the principle itself, and all that hung upon it, had been brought into jeopardy. But for that very reason, the Egyptian-Israeli crisis seemed to offer the United States an opportunity of rehabilitation. To act firmly in defense of principle and commitment in the Middle East would be more effective than the Vietnam intervention in restoring respect for engagements. Here the American risk was minimal. Israel was strong, resolute and united; she therefore represented an asset which had no counterpart in the Far East. The likelihood of Soviet or Chinese intervention was infinitely less than in Vietnam. The tactical objective—the cancellation of the Eilat blockade—was limited in scope and entirely feasible. To honor American promises in the Straits of Tiran was perhaps the easiest possibility that an American President would ever have for resisting aggression and demonstrating fidelity to commitments.

Lyndon Johnson's perceptions were sharp enough to grasp all these implications; what he lacked was the authority to put them to work. Less than three years after the greatest electoral triumph in American presidential history he was like Samson, shorn of the symbols and reality of his previous strength. In his own country and especially in his own party, the Vietnam trauma had set up a reaction not only against the Vietnam war, but against the notion of commitment itself.

Johnson may have been misguided in his confidence that with time he could overcome the obstacles. But we had an interest in granting him the time. It turned out that with every passing day the obstacles became greater and the will for action diminished.

Yet by May 24, 1967, it was already evident that the Middle East was going to be one of the better chapters in Lyndon Johnson's presidency. He was clear about his aim, honest in the recognition of principles and inventive in the search for means to vindicate them. In short, he was ready for leadership. But in his blunt, unadorned way, he had put his finger on the crux of his difficulty: "What a President says and thinks is not worth five cents unless he has the people and Congress behind him. Without the Congress I'm just a six-feet-four Texan. With the Congress I'm President of the United States in the fullest sense."

Ambassadors Eytan and Remez, who had met me in Paris, equipped me with documents which had come to hand while I was in the air across the Atlantic. First, there was the full text of Nasser's speech on May 26. This vividly revealed the strategy with which we were confronted. Everything seemed to be flowing in Nasser's direction. A neatly calculated series of steps had opened up prospects which, until recently, had appeared to be unreal. He had said:

> We were waiting for the day when we would be fully prepared. I say nothing aimlessly. One day two years ago I stood up to say that we had no plan to liberate Palestine. This was at the Summit Meeting. Recently we felt strong enough, that if we were to enter a battle, with God's help, we could triumph. Taking over Sharm el-Sheikh meant confrontation with Israel. Taking such action also meant that we were ready to enter a general war with Israel. It was not a separate question. Actually, I was authorized by the Arab Socialist Union's higher executive to implement this plan at the right time. We have sent reconnaissance planes over Israel. Not a single brigade was stationed opposite us on the Israeli side of the border. All Israeli brigades were confronting Syria [sic]. . . . The battle will be a general one and our basic objective will be to destroy Israel [emphasis added]. I probably could not have said such things five or even three years ago. Today I say such things because I am confident.

NASSER THREATENS TO DESTROY ISRAEL was now the headline in thousands of newspapers throughout the world. The concentrations in Sinai gave it a deadly resonance; nobody could now torment himself with questions about what was at issue. Whatever was left obscure in Nasser's speech had been illuminated in an article published by Mohammed Hassanein Heykal in *Al-Ahram* on the same day. He had written: "An armed clash between the UAR and Israel is inevitable. This armed clash could occur at any moment, at any place along the line of confrontation between the Egyptian forces and the enemy Israeli forces on land, air or sea, along the area extending from Gaza in the north, to the Gulf of Aqaba and Sharm el-Sheikh in the south."

After analyzing Israel's economic interests in the Gulf of Aqaba, Heykal went on:

In my personal opinion, all these important economic matters and questions are not the decisive factor which will influence or dictate the Israeli reaction to the closure of the Gulf of Aqaba. The decisive factor in my opinion is the psychological factor. From this aspect there is one answer. Yes; it is in the light of the compelling psychological factor that the needs of security, of survival itself, make Israel's acceptance of the challenge of war inevitable. One thing is clear: the closure of the Gulf of Aqaba to Israeli navigation, and the ban on the import of strategic goods, even when carried by non-Israeli ships, means first and last that the Arab nation, represented by the UAR, has succeeded for the first time vis-à-vis Israel, in changing by force a fait accompli imposed on it by force. This is the essence of the problem regardless of the complications surrounding it and future contingencies. Therefore, it is not a matter of the Gulf of Aqaba, but of something bigger. It is the whole philosophy of Israeli security. It is the philosophy on which Israeli existence has pivoted since its birth and on which it will pivot in the future. Hence I say that Israel must resort to arms. Therefore I say that an armed clash between the UAR and the Israel enemy is inevitable.

Heykal concluded with an almost intoxicated candor:

In short, Egypt has exercised its power and achieved the objectives at this stage without resorting to arms so far. But Israel has no alternative but to use arms if it wants to exercise power. This means that the logic of the fearful confrontation now taking place between Egypt, which is fortified by the might of the masses of the Arab nation, and Israel, which is fortified by the illusion of American might, dictates that Egypt, after all it has now succeeded in achieving, must wait, even though it has to wait for a blow. Let Israel begin; let our second blow then be ready. Let it be a knockout.

He made no provision for the possibility that the "knockout" might come from Israel with the first blow, not from Egypt with the second.

14

Days of Decision June 1967

IT WAS PAST TEN O'CLOCK AT NIGHT ON MAY 27 WHEN I REACHED LOD
Airport. I was met by Prime Minister Eshkol's secretary, Aviad Yafeh,
who told me that a ministerial meeting was then in session. I could
feel that the mood had grown even more dramatic since I left the
country on Wednesday, May 24. On the way to Tel Aviv, Yafeh informed me of the trend that the meeting was taking. Our preparedness had advanced rapidly; nothing was left of the tentative spirit that
had existed on May 23. There was now a feeling close to alarm about
what would happen if Egyptian concentrations in Sinai were allowed to become further consolidated. On the other hand, it would
now be feasible, as it was not on the previous Wednesday, to make
a heavy riposte to the Egyptian forces now arranged against us. Even
if the Straits were not opened at once, the blow to the Egyptian
forces would be so hard that Egypt's capacity to maintain the blockade
would be prejudiced. The issue that the ministers were deliberating
was, in essence, one of political timing. Had we created political
conditions in which a victory, if achieved, would be ratified by political success? Or, conversely, would the political advantages of some
further diplomatic action outweigh the physical dangers inherent in
delay?

Nor were these the only points at issue. Internal political complications had now invaded the arena in full force. There were many
who would support military resistance only if the Cabinet's composi-

tion was changed. The National Religious Party, although moderate in its security policies, was in a mood of estrangement from the Prime Minister. It was putting forward two ultimatums: first, that the coalition be widened to bring in both the main opposition groups (Gahal and Rafi), and second, that the Prime Minister divest himself of the Defense Ministry and make it available to General Moshe Dayan, who enjoyed a broader public confidence than did the Rafi Party, of which he was a member. At the same time, Gahal and Rafi leaders were striving to depose Eshkol, at least from the Defense Ministry.

The public temper was deeply affected by the prolonged mobilization. Israel had been used to short and sharp campaigns; the agony of waiting had never been part of our military experience. The pressure of this impatience was being brought to bear by reservists at the front on their families at home. There was no clear political and military horizon, and the national spirit might well sink down in contention and bitterness unless it would be rallied by decisive leadership.

When I reached Tel Aviv, Yaacov Herzog told me how General Rabin had expressed a sense of despondency and self-accusation about the national danger, and how General Weizman had held the fort for some days until the Chief of Staff recovered from what was called nicotine poisoning, but which seemed to have been a severe bout of tension. Rabin was now back in command.

I learned that while I was journeying to three capitals, the Soviet Union had been busy in Middle Eastern cities. During the night of May 26–27 Ambassador Dmitri Chuvakhin had aroused Eshkol from his bed in the early hours of the morning to deliver a communication from Prime Minister Kosygin. There was less invective here than was usual in Soviet communications to Israel and a perceptible note of anxiety could be read in Mr. Kosygin's words:

> Guided by the interests of peace and the aspiration to avoid bloodshed, the Soviet Government has decided to send you this appeal. We wish to call upon you to take all measures in order that a military conflict should not be created—a conflict that would have grave consequences for the interests of peace and international security. We turn to you in order that there should not be created in the world a new center of war which would bring unlimited suffering to the nations. We think that whatever the position may be in the border areas of Israel, Syria and the UAR, and however intricate that problem may be, it is essential to find means to settle the conflict by non-military means. It is easy to light a conflagration and difficult to put out the flame. Indeed, to put

out the flame would not be as simple as those people may think who are pushing Israel over the precipice of war.

When I reached the Cabinet Room, I reported briefly on the conversations in Paris and London and more comprehensively on those in Washington. Accounts by our ambassadors of the talks with President de Gaulle and Mr. Wilson had been in the hands of my colleagues for nearly three days, while the exact formulation of President Johnson's views would be new and crucial material. Nevertheless, I found it necessary to portray the extreme vigor with which President de Gaulle had opposed any idea of Israeli military resistance.

I read out verbatim substantive parts of Ambassador Harman's detailed report. I also placed the document in its entirety in the government file for immediate perusal by whoever wished to read it that night. I said that I would not commit myself to the view that the international patrol would ever come to anything. But I was strong in emphasizing that the President's assumption of responsibility for the effort must have an inhibiting effect on us for some days, and that if it failed, despite our patience, new political possibilities would open out in the American-Israeli relationship.

Finding the ministers arrayed in two groups—one arguing for immediate action, the other for a further period of waiting—I made a compromise proposal for a forty-eight-hour period of disengagement, after which we should resume our consultations and make our decision. (This suggestion was the only restraining proposal that I submitted at any stage of the 1967 crisis before, during or after the Six-Day War.) Contrary to what had been written in speculative books and articles, no vote was taken that evening; that we might have split 9 to 9 is a conjecture based, presumably, on the general tenor of the speeches.

I left the Cabinet Room at Eshkol's request to brief the Knesset Defense Committee, which was assembled downstairs. In my absence my proposal for the interposition of a forty-eight-hour delay was amended by the Prime Minister. He told me later that a divided and fatigued Cabinet would not be in a position to take responsibility for drastic decisions. He suggested very humanely that we all get a few hours' sleep and assemble the following day. It was clear from the tenor of his discourse that unless new considerations came to light by then, he would argue in favor of immediate resistance.

At the risk of further disruption of a prevalent myth about the May 27 discussions, I must emphasize that its atmosphere was calm at every stage. The conjecture in some books that I pressed my views to the point of threatening resignation is the most far-fetched of many fictions that imagination and intrigue have woven around the May 27 meeting. At no point was I swimming against any tide; there was no violent argument and counterargument between the military leaders and myself. Many supported my view that we had to some extent limited our capacity for immediate military action by asking for a restraining American démarche in Cairo. The unambiguous words which President Johnson had used to sustain the justice of our cause also made a strong impression. Eshkol said that all doubts about the utility of my mission should now be dissolved; whatever the future held we would face it in a stronger political posture than was likely before.

By the time the ministers assembled again in the afternoon of Sunday, May 28, Washington had made intensive efforts to secure a further respite. The first development on May 28 was a visit by Ambassador Walworth Barbour to Assistant Director-General Moshe Bitan, who was in charge of North American affairs, partly for the purpose of ensuring that there was mutual uniformity in reporting. The American ambassador had received an official State Department account of my talks on May 25 and 26, which he was instructed to convey to us in the cause of precision, and also because inaccurate newspaper speculation had been made in both countries.

According to the State Department report to Barbour, I had been warned that the maritime plan would undoubtedly go through many permutations and changes as the experts worked it over. The central ideas were simple. There would be three stages:

(a) *The United Nations proceedings;*
(b) *A current declaration by the maritime powers on freedom of passage in the Gulf;*
(c) *The preparation of a plan for naval presence which hopefully would be enough to deter the UAR from interfering with freedom of passage in the Straits if the United Nations proceedings failed.*

The State Department continued that "Eban's main source of concern was being bogged down in endless UN proceedings. He thought that the point could be established by a relatively short exercise. He felt confident that the United States would never be challenged if it announced that it was going to exercise its undeniable rights to the other side."

The State Department message to Barbour described my meeting with Rusk and McNamara and my "long meeting with the President." It went on to say that the President had told me of his determination to make the international maritime plan work and his "fealty" to this commitment he and his predecessors had made. The Department further informed Barbour that in response to my query if I could tell the Prime Minister that "Johnson had decided to make every possible effort to assure that the Straits and the Gulf would be open to free and innocent passage," the President had replied "Yes."

This unexpected message from Washington was of personal importance for me. The advocates of immediate military action, as well as my political adversaries, were conducting a whispering campaign about the accuracy of my report of the talk with President Johnson. Had Johnson *really* given strong support to Israel's case on the blockade? Had he *really* promised to "use every possible means" to keep the Gulf open? Had he *really* talked with any seriousness about a naval plan to deter the blockade? If so, the political accord that I had secured with the United States was impressive in itself, and the case for giving some time for Johnson's policy to be put to the test was correspondingly strong.

I had good reason to resent the malicious reflections on my reporting—which were later to find a place in some of the more demagogic Israeli books on the Six-Day War. I have always understood the difficulty of simultaneously conducting a conversation and reporting on it. Therefore I have always separated these functions. I have never agreed to go to an important talk alone, unless there was compelling reason. The reports of what De Gaulle and Johnson told me were accurately conveyed to the Cabinet in the words of Ambassadors Eytan and Harman, not of myself. Nevertheless, the whisperers went on whispering.

But here was the American ambassador bringing us a report identical with what I had conveyed to my colleagues about the depth of Johnson's involvement in the Israeli cause. My report about Washington's commitment had erred—if at all—on the side of reserve. We had now been informed of a "determination to make the international maritime plan work." The project was not described any longer as a "British plan" but as an enterprise to which the United States had committed its resolve.

A few hours later a presidential communication came to Eshkol from Washington conveying a message from the Soviet Union which was clearly designed for Israeli ears. Moscow had told Washington that the Soviets had information about Israel's being prepared for military action, which would provoke a conflict fraught with grave consequences. The Soviet Union had asked the United States to take all measures to ensure that there be no military conflict. President Johnson's message went on to refer to his talk with me at the White House on May 26 and to America's interest in the safety and vital concerns of Israel. He now told Eshkol that as Israel's friend, he must repeat more strongly what he had said to Eban: Israel just must not take preemptive military action and thereby make itself responsible for the initiation of hostilities. In his reply to the Soviets he would of course take up his and our view about the international character of the Gulf of Aqaba and the Straits of Tiran.

More decisive than this text was something which Secretary Rusk instructed his ambassador to convey. In a written addendum to the President's letter Rusk said that Eshkol and I should be told that the British and the United States were proceeding urgently to prepare the military aspects of the international naval escort plan and that other nations were responding vigorously to the idea. The Dutch and Canadians had already joined even before a text was presented to them. With the assurance of international determination to make every effort to keep the Straits open to the flags of all nations, unilateral action on the part of Israel would be irresponsible and catastrophic.

This prospect was soon to fade. But an Israeli government receiving such a message had very few options. On the negative side, to ignore it would open Israel to the charge of having refused a chance for international action which, through the sheer weight of deterrent power, might have brought about a peaceful opening of the Straits. On the positive side, the international interest in opening the Straits was so assertively stated as to give Israel's position an impression of unusual support.

Eshkol, as he subsequently revealed, had intended to ask for a drastic decision on May 28, but the representations from Washington put a new aspect on his dilemma. He was particularly impressed by Rusk's statement concerning the progress of the naval escort plan. He was now prepared to advise the Cabinet to give the United States and others a chance over the next two weeks to bring the project to fulfillment. One minister after another followed him in this course. It was not the Soviet warnings, but the American show of resolution which won the delay. My colleagues were clearly impressed by the reinforced confirmation of what I had transmitted the previous night. Of the eighteen ministers only one—Moshe Carmel, the Minister of Transportation—was now prepared to vote for immediate military action. His argument was that with every passing day the possibility of an Egyptian surprise attack would grow.

However, I had noticed some reports which confirmed a different appraisal. Although our military advisers understandably portrayed every passing hour as an increase of Israel's danger, some of the material now reaching me gave growing representation to an opposite view. Stories of chaotic dislocation among Egyptian forces in Sinai were becoming more frequent and authoritative. At the same time, we were receiving reports from our Ministry of Defense that equipment previously ordered from Europe was reaching us every day. I was unconvinced by the vehemence with which some of our advisers were telling us that time was working against us and was likely to bring about "the destruction of the Third Jewish Commonwealth." Eshkol has revealed that on meeting the senior officers late on May 28, he listened patiently to their sincere and tenacious lecture, and ended by shrugging his shoulders and saying, "You are exaggerating quite a lot."

Few decisions in Israel's history have been the object of such contentious comment as the resolution taken almost unanimously on May 28. Many months later, when Israel had emerged safely from her ordeals, the public mind continually reverted to this theme. Was the decision wise or catastrophic? Had we come out safely through a stroke of fortune or by the inherent wisdom of our timing? What did the May 28 decision have to say about the moral and mental fiber of the seventeen ministers who adopted it?

The first thing to be said is that a governmental decision must be judged by its consequences. These were to vindicate our May 28 decision. It was nearly a unanimous vote, and it was not made in panic. On the contrary, our military advisers were by now fervent in the promise of victory. True, their buoyancy was somewhat deflated by the contrary thesis that a brief delay would convert certain triumph to certain ruin. To me it seemed unlikely that we could be assured of utter victory if we acted on May 28—and of complete rout if we waited a few days. It is a primary ministerial function to be skeptical of expert advice, however sincere, just as it is the duty of military commanders to overestimate and never to underestimate the adversary's potential.

It is true that the expectation of victory was overshadowed by fear of terrible casualties. Zalman Aranne, the Minister of Education, had spoken eloquently of the fearful toll of war and of the moral need to do everything possible to avoid it. He was a man of refined consciousness and strong individualism. He was always more likely than anyone to give utterance to feelings which other ministers held discreetly in their hearts. The Minister of the Interior, Moshe Haim Shapira, was in consultation with Ben Gurion, who also thought that a military challenge by Israel without allies by her side would be exorbitant in blood. Eshkol was to write a few months later: "Had we not received Johnson's letter and Rusk's message, I would have urged the Government to make the decision to fight; but their communications pointed out not only that unilateral Israeli action would be catastrophic but also that the United States was continuing with its preparations for multilateral action to open the Gulf to shipping of all nations. I could not forget that the letter was signed by the President who had once promised me face-to-face: 'We will carry out whatever I ever promise you.' I did not want him to come afterwards and say: 'I warned you in advance and now you cannot make any claims whatever on the United States and its allies.' "

Eshkol was here acting under the influence of the 1957 trauma, which had also haunted me at every stage. We were both using time as currency to secure ultimate political support. Either the multilateral naval action would collapse, in which case the United States would have little right or cause to restrain Israel's independent action, or if it succeeded, Nasser would, for the first time, believe that Israel had political backing as well as military strength. We must remember that our only aims in the Egyptian context were to break the blockade and disperse the troop concentrations. The idea of a new boundary for Israel was not in the air at the end of May; it was only later that the Jordanian and Syrian interventions brought the whole Arab-Israel territorial structure under question. To defeat Nasser's blockade and troop concentrations in May by a combination of military preparedness and political pressures would be no less honorable, and in the long run, no less significant than to bring him low by an actual trial of strength. That the seventeen ministers were dominated not by "confusion" or panic but by a mature political calculation also emerges from the observations made by some of them after the war. Moshe Shapira has been quoted as saying: "I thought strongly that we should keep our promise [on May 23] and wait 48 hours, even though it was obvious that they would turn out to be longer. When President Johnson spoke to Eban about a further delay I thought we should continue to wait. If the war came it was essential that Lyndon Johnson should not be against us. If we had not waited we would still have conquered in the field of battle; but we would have lost in the political arena. The United States would not have stood by our side in the way that she did. We must remember that the general mood of those days was that we could not reasonably expect the emphatic victory which ensued. I said then and it is clear to me today that if we had begun war too early, we would have shown a lack of responsibility for our future. This has now been proved. The United States is giving us support such as we have never known before. I believe that a Superior Force directs our history. There is a destiny that shapes our ends."

With President Johnson, May 1967.

Leading the Israeli delegation to the UN after Six-Day War in 1967, with Gideon Rafael and Golda Meir, member of the Knesset.

Israel and the Arabs look at Resolution 242 from "different angles." Cartoon by Zeev, Ha'aretz, November 24, 1967.

"Jews everywhere saw something historic in this handshake." Rome 1969.

First visit to Germany, with Chancellor Willy Brandt, 1970.

My biggest audience: 20,000 New Yorkers, October 1973.

The Great Synagogue in Bucharest, November 1973.

Golda Meir's last Cabinet, January 1974. Sitting: *Golda Meir, President Ephraim Katzir, Deputy Prime Minister Yigal Allon.* Standing: *Pinhas Sapir, Shlomo Hillel, Shimon Peres, Yehoshua Rabinowitch, Gideon Hansaez, Abba Eban, Yosef Burg,*

With Senator Edward Kennedy.

Moshe Kol, Yitzhak Rafael, Chaim Zadok, Shlomo Rozen, Haim Guati, Israel Galili,
Yitzhak Rabin, Aharon Uzzan, Aharon Yariv, Moshe Dayan, Haim Barlev,
Michael Arnon (Cabinet Secretary).

With Henry Kissinger, May 1974.

At home 1977

In later months the decision to postpone our military resistance in order to reinforce our political bulwarks exposed me to virulent attacks. The paradox is that seventeen ministers, not one, voted for that decision, and the campaign against the decision came after the war, when it had proved to be utterly triumphant. It was as though something in the national character made Israel intolerant of her own success. We refused to take yes for an answer. Yet I felt that public opinion, unlike the press, was strongly in support of careful diplomatic preparation. By the end of 1968 every reference by me in public meetings to the "Hamtana" (waiting) was ardently cheered. In March 1969, General Rabin said publicly that but for the "Hamtana" decision and the diplomatic activity between May 23 and June 1, "it is doubtful if Israel would have been able to hold firm at the cease-fire lines and in the political arena two years after the war." In August 1969 a reputable poll showed that 63 percent of Israelis considered that the "waiting period" was an act of wise statesmanship, while only 24 percent ascribed it to hesitancy and indecision. My own judgment has never wavered; the May 28 decision was an expression of political intelligence and moral strength. I am proud of having defended it through stormy days. Of the many international verdicts in favor of the "Hamtana" decisions, I select one by an extremely nonpacifist friendly commentator on the Six-Day War: "The efforts of Israeli Foreign Minister Abba Eban, although the subject of derision and deprecation by many of his countrymen and even some of his colleagues in the Cabinet, had managed to secure for Israel in his two weeks of peregrinations backwards and forwards to Washington, London and Paris, a climate of opinion in which it was possible for Israel to take *decisive* action." *

Before evening fell on May 28, the Cabinet had communicated its nearly unanimous decision to the heads of all parties in the Knesset and to members of its Security and Political committees. In transmitting the decision to the Knesset Foreign Affairs Committee, I listened carefully for any hint of opposition. None was expressed. On behalf of Gahal, a formal reservation was entered, asserting that responsibility for the decision to wait lay with the Cabinet alone. Not a word, however, was said substantively against the decision itself.

Eshkol immediately convened senior military officers and informed them of the Cabinet's policy. He had gone through a busy and exhausting day; he was now called upon to defend a decision whose justification lay substantially outside the military sphere. Prime Minister Eshkol, together with Yigal Allon, the Minister of Labor, put up a

* *The Six-Day War,* Randolph and Winston Churchill, 1968.

373

strong defense of the Cabinet's decision. Most of the officers accepted it with disciplined serenity, but some showed a lack of confidence in the possibility of success unless resistance was made immediately. Their fear was that a further lapse of time, however short, would have a catastrophic effect on the military balance.

It is certain that the tiring ordeal to which Eshkol had been submitting himself had its effect on him when he went on the air that evening. Modern history tells us much about the importance of rhetoric in national crises, and this power is now enlarged by the range of mass communications. That day in May, the whole Israeli adult population had its ear fixed on the radio sets, which were its main link with what the government was going to decide. The Prime Minister's statement was brief, unsensational, and in its content, somewhat defiant. He said that it had been decided to maintain full military preparedness. The government had noted with satisfaction the valiant spirit of the people and of the Israeli Defense Forces. It had also expressed the opinion that the closing of the Tiran Straits to Israeli shipping was tantamount to an act of aggression toward Israel. Eshkol went on: "We shall defend ourselves against this in the hour of need in virtue of the right of self-defense to which the State is entitled." Eshkol then said that the Cabinet had listened carefully to my report. He went on: "The government laid down principles for the continuation of political activities. These are designed to induce the international factors to adopt effective measures to safeguard the freedom of international shipping in the Tiran Straits. Lines of action have also been adopted for the removal of military concentrations from Israel's southern border and for action to safeguard our sovereign rights and security on the frontiers and the prevention of aggression. The government declares that the Israeli Defense Forces are strong enough to defeat any aggressor and to ensure Israel's sovereign rights. Tomorrow I shall have an opportunity to explain the government's position in a speech before the plenary session of the Knesset."

The rational interpretation of this speech was that the hour of trial was near and that the government was not surrendering any of its rights, but that it was postponing resistance in order to win more international support. It was here, however, that a technical fault destroyed the effect of the government's action. An adviser—to this day prudently anonymous—had for some reason counseled Eshkol to go on the air and deliver the government communiqué as though it were a speech. The dry, legalistic formulation was bound to disappoint expectations. Moreover, Eshkol, like many other eminent prime ministers, had never cultivated the rhetorical arts. Elementary foresight would have demanded a recording in which any errors of diction or failures of tone could have been eliminated. Heavily burdened by fatigue and responsibility, and deeply stirred by his tempestuous meeting with the generals, Eshkol read the speech in a painful and stumbling manner. Whereas the nation had expected a call to action, or at least a stoic promise of blood, sweat and tears, it was now tormented by an impression of hesitancy and exhaustion. Eshkol's opponents exploited the consequent despondency to the full. A morning newspaper, which went to press a few hours after the broadcast, published the letter of an anonymous reader calling for Eshkol's resignation on the grounds of the unhappy broadcast. Many wondered how such a communication could have reached a newspaper office between the hour of the broadcast and the closing of the printing press; those who believed this were forced to ascribe to Israel's postal services a miraculous rapidity for which they had never been distinguished.

The weekend of May 26–28 was the only spasm of time during which international action against Nasser's excesses seemed even contingently possible. In the next seven days, international agencies and foreign governments were all to retreat from danger and duty. Israel's solitude would emerge for all to see. Yet from the tension of a week's delay, Israel would reap a good harvest. Her resistance would be borne along on the wave of a universal public opinion mounting day by day toward a climax of support. Her military position would become predictably better, and that of Egypt unexpectedly worse, than on May 28. The Arab states would vastly enlarge their own vulnerability. Most important—the offer to the United States and Britain of an opportunity which they were not to seize, would give Israel a strong claim to their political support on the morrow of victory.

But all these benefits lay in the future; they would emerge slowly and painfully from the clouds. Meanwhile, in a single week, Israel was to endure a stress of agonies and disappointments which would put her nerve and judgment to a fearsome test. One setback succeeded another. Eventually the choice would lie between docile resignation and a stern eruption of resistance.

It was in the United Nations Security Council that the air of demoralization was heaviest. In the years after World War II, this body had seemed for a short hour to be the incarnation of a new international order. Its charge was to exercise "primary responsibility for international peace and security." No international institution had ever held a more concentrated—or a more illusory—aggregate of power.

The impression of omnipotence soon passed. By 1967 the Security Council had become deprived not only of a capacity for action but even of the ability to define an issue with justice and reason. With the Arab states permanently represented by one of their own members or by their closest kin, and with the Soviet Union standing ready to ensure that no proposal uncongenial to Arab policy could ever be accepted, the Security Council had become a one-way street. During the fifties the Security Council had refused to criticize Egypt's blockade, Syria's attempt to strangle our water development, Syrian efforts to make the killing of Israelis a legitimate pursuit, constant threats by all Arab states to bring about Israel's liquidation, and even the direct invasion of Israeli lives and homes by the shells and bullets of armies across the frontier.

After the event, it is difficult to read the proceedings of the Security Council in the final week of May 1967 without a gasp of disbelief. We must remember that the meeting took place two days after the imposition of the blockade in the Gulf of Aqaba. Powerful Egyptian concentrations, including armored columns, were pouring into Sinai. Military airports were being made ready for the assault. Two speeches had been delivered by President Nasser, which, by any classical definition, would have been regarded as declarations of war. The aim of bringing about Israel's annihilation had been frankly stated. Israeli mobilization in reaction to the Egyptian movement of troops had taken momentum. After ten years of sentinel duty, the United Nations forces had been humiliatingly banished. Secretary-General U Thant had gone on a desperate journey to Cairo in an effort to salvage the declining peace. Arab masses in the streets were hanging Israel in effigy. The entire Israeli nation was laying down the tools of peace to take up weapons of defense. Vast demonstrations of public ardor in Israel's cause surged through streets and cities on every continent. At no time since World War II, except during the Cuban crisis of 1962, had the headlines of newspapers everywhere expressed a sharper accent of tension.

In these conditions of emergency, the Security Council convened on the initiative of Canada and Denmark at ten-thirty on the morning of May 24. The first words spoken by the representative of the Soviet Union were almost beyond belief:

> The Soviet delegation deems it necessary to stress that it does not see sufficient grounds for such a hasty convening of the Security Council and for the artificially dramatic climate fostered by the representatives of some Western Powers which are probably counting on an exaggerated effort in the staging of this meeting.

As soon as the Canadian representative, Ambassador George Ignatieff, recovered from his stunned surprise, he calmly set out the reasons why the Security Council should meet. He seemed incredulous that the question could even be asked:

> We are suggesting that this Council should exercise its responsibilities under the Charter to deal with the threatening situation which the Secretary-General has reported to the Security Council . . . That situation as the Secretary-General rightly reported has shown signs of increasingly dangerous deterioration. In the face of this rising and dangerous state of tension the means for bringing influence of moderation to bear in the area through the United Nations, far from being increased, have actually been decreased at the very moment of crisis by the withdrawal of the United Nations Emergency Force.

To this, Ambassador Nikolai Fedorenko, for the Soviet Union, replied with quiet cynicism. He saw nothing in the international situation which required the highest body of international security to show any active concern. To the Canadian representative he quoted an obscure Oriental proverb: "You show him the moon but all he looks at is your finger." Obsequious laughter came from the Bulgarian table.

Once the Soviet utterance had been duly translated into French, the representative of Mali said:

> In the opinion of my government it is doubtful that this abrupt convening of the Security Council can in any way lessen tension in the region in question if that is really our concern. My delegation feels that meeting at this time can only be most inopportune.

He was followed by a remarkable character, Milko Tarabanov of Bulgaria, who, without movement of his impassive features, declared:

> The delegation of the People's Republic of Bulgaria believes that at the present moment there is really no need for an urgent meeting of the Security Council. Such a meeting is designed only to dramatize artificially a situation to whose creation the western countries and some of their representatives contributed by their previous activities. My delegation believes that the holding of a Security Council meeting at this time will only serve the interests of the forces of intervention and aggression in the Middle East. There is no reason to avoid holding a useless and perhaps even dangerous meeting at this time.

The Indian representative then stated with bland solemnity:

The situation on the ground while potentially dangerous is still not clear, therefore an urgent and immediate discussion is unwarranted.

And so the debate droned on. One representative after another asserted that the mere imminence of war was no reason for convening the tribunal charged with the preservation of peace. Ambassador Roger Seydoux of France was extraordinarily patient. "My delegation," he said, "has expressed doubts on the usefulness of an urgent meeting of this Council." The eloquent British representative, Lord Caradon, maintained an unusual silence. For the United States, Ambassador Arthur Goldberg put a reasonable view:

This Council meeting cannot "dramatize" the situation which at this moment is at the center of the stage of world concern.

There is nothing more bizarre in the history of international institutions than the fact that the Security Council on May 24, 1967, showed reluctance in holding a discussion on an issue of which the urgency did not seem compelling in its eyes! Eventually, after further talking to and fro, the chairman, representing Nationalist China, caused the agenda to be adopted. Ambassador Hans R. Tabor of Denmark took the floor to ask:

What should be our attitude in the face of this grave danger? Should the Council just stand by, see what happens and hope for the best? That is hardly, I believe, what world public opinion would expect of us.

The harsh fact is that by this time, world public opinion expected the Security Council to perform any folly of which human beings are inherently capable. At one-fifteen the Council rose—having done nothing except adopt its agenda.

The Security Council was to hold meetings intermittently until June 3. Not for one hour did its proceedings rise above the ineptitude and cynicism established in its first session. Even a mild Canadian-Danish draft resolution expressing "full support for the efforts of the Secretary-General" and requesting "all member-States to refrain from steps which might worsen the situation" could not be put to the vote. It was simply not polite to the Arabs to ask for the situation not to be "worsened." Mohammed Awad El-Kony of the United Arab Republic insisted with vehemence that there was nothing in the

Middle Eastern situation which justified international intervention. This plea for detachment reflected the high level of military confidence that must then have dominated Nasser's mind. On May 22 he had said: "We are ready for war, our armed forces and all our people are ready for war, we have built a strong national army and achieved our objectives."

After doing nothing on May 24, the Security Council adjourned until the afternoon of May 29. For almost a week, the crisis mounted from stage to stage without United Nations action or even comment. In Greek tragedy the chorus would at least express consternation about events which it was powerless to affect. Here we could not even hope for a mild expression of concern. Israel was being told in the plainest possible terms not to expect any assistance or even moral support from the United Nations. The fragility of the United Nations as a source of security was one of the traumatic lessons which Israel would carry into her memory and policy—long after the summer of 1967 had passed away.

The burden of action now lay on the maritime powers which had committed their honor to us so deeply over ten years before. Few assurances could have been as promising or vigorous as that conveyed to the Israeli government from Washington on the morning of May 28. But the prospect of international action against Nasser's piracy was to glow with a brief flame, and then flicker out.

In Israel and throughout the world, it was believed that our decision of May 28 gave two weeks during which the confrontation would either subside or come to a new point of explosion. But this assumption implied more restraint in Cairo than Nasser was prepared to show. He seemed bent on stretching the elastic of his good fortune as though it had no possible breaking point. The abstinence expressed in Israel's decision of May 28 evoked nothing but a brutal scream of triumph and menace in Cairo. Addressing members of the National Assembly on May 29, Nasser took the conflict far back beyond the maritime context to place the question mark squarely on Israel's survival:

> *Now eleven years after 1956 we are restoring things to what they were in 1956. This is from the material aspect. In my opinion this material aspect is but a small part, whereas the spiritual aspect is the great side of the issue. The spiritual aspect involves the renaissance of the Arab nation, the revival of the Palestine question and the restoration of confidence to every Arab and to every Palestinian. This is on the basis that if we were able to restore conditions to what they were in 1956, God will surely help and urge us to restore the situation to what it was in 1948. Preparations have*

*already been made, we are now ready to confront Israel. The issue
now at hand is not the Gulf of Aqaba, the Straits of Tiran or the
withdrawal of U.N.E.F., but the rights of the Palestinian people.
It is the aggression which took place in Palestine in 1948 with the
collaboration of Britain and the United States. . . . They want to
confine the issue to the Straits of Tiran, U.N.E.F. and the right of
passage. We are not afraid of the United States and its threats, of
Britain and its threats or of the entire Western world and its par-
tiality to Israel.*

Scarcely had Nasser's tirade been digested in Jerusalem than we
suffered another and more decisive blow to peace. On May 30 King
Hussein flew to Cairo, where he signed a mutual defense pact between
Jordan and Egypt. Israel was now not only blockaded but also encircled. All the conditions which had induced her to erupt against
the siege of 1956 were now reconstructed in a more alarming context
and without the alleviating effect of alliance with other powers. By
his journey to Cairo on May 30, Hussein had made it certain that war
would break out and that it would not necessarily be limited to the
Egyptian-Israeli front. Israel's plans for resistance, which had been discussed in detail since May 22, had all made provision for leaving
Jordan scrupulously alone. Hussein had now thoughtlessly renounced
this immunity.

King Hussein's own account leaves many of his motives and calculations obscure. My impression is that he was swept into disaster
by the blast of emotion and euphoria raging across the Arab world.
In his book *My War with Israel*, he has recorded that he made his
decision on May 29 on hearing Nasser's speech before the National
Assembly. He immediately summoned the Egyptian ambassador in
Amman, Osman Nurie, and asked for a prompt meeting to be arranged
with Nasser to "coordinate means of defense against the Israeli
threat." King Hussein writes: "The desire to meet Nasser may seem
strange when one remembers the insulting, defamatory words which
for a whole year the Cairo radio had launched against the Hashemite
monarchy; but from every point of view we had no right nor could
we decently justify a decision to stand aside in a cause in which the
entire Arab world was determined unanimously to engage itself."

On reaching Cairo, the King had gone to Koubbeh Palace, with
Nasser escorting him from the airfield. Here is King Hussein's account:

*We went straight to the point. Our mutual relations, the situ-
ation which we were going to confront, the necessity for a serious and effective coordination, the measures to be taken. Then
Marshal Abdel Hakim Amer, Vice-President of the UAR and*

Commander-in-Chief of the Egyptian armed forces, joined us, followed by my Prime Minister, Saad Jouma, and other Egyptian and Jordanian officials. I proposed that we utilize the framework of the United Arab Command. "No objection," replied Nasser. "But it is difficult to make the Command function in the light of my agreement with Syria. I suggest another solution: we could immediately make a pact between our two countries."

At my demand, he sent for a file containing the bilateral Egyptian-Syrian defense pact by which those two nations had been linked since April 1967. I was so anxious to reach an agreement that I contented myself with a rapid perusal of the text and said to Nasser: "Give me another copy; let us replace the word Syria by the word Jordan and the matter will be arranged."

Having thus sealed his people's future with a disastrously casual stroke of the pen, King Hussein flew back to Jordan, burdened with the embarrassing company of Ahmed Shukeiry, the PLO commander whose departure from Cairo to Amman had Nasser's whole endorsement. Shukeiry had a unique capacity for causing relief in any place by the mere act of leaving it.

The Egyptian-Jordanian agreement made it plain that we would probably have to fight on three fronts, with a special vulnerability in the coastal strip, where a successful advance by an armored column could cut the nation's vital artery in two. Arab unity, which had seemed an unsubstantial mirage a few days before, was now becoming impressive. At a meeting of heads of departments in the Foreign Ministry on May 31, I said that the assumption of two weeks' respite must now be revised, and that our dialogue with the United States must be modified accordingly. On May 31 Kuwaiti and Iraqi forces arrived in Egypt. The next day Jordan celebrated her reconciliation with Syria by the resumption of diplomatic relations. On the Baghdad radio we now heard the strident voice of President Abdel Rahman Aref addressing air-force officers: "Sons and brethren, this is the day of the battle to avenge our martyred brethren who fell in 1948. It is the day to wash away the stain. We shall, God willing, meet in Tel Aviv and Haifa."

We could feel Ahmed Shukeiry breathing down our neck from the Old City of Jerusalem; in the new circumstances he seemed much less ludicrous than before. International television and radio stations now took him seriously enough to accord him interviews; in one of these he was asked what would happen to the Israeli population after the Arab victory. His prescription was plain: Israelis who had been born elsewhere would be "repatriated." When it was pointed out to him that nearly half of the Israeli population had been born in Palestine, he replied with nonchalance, "Those who survive will remain in Palestine, but I estimate that none of them will survive."

To much of the outside world, accustomed to the flights of Arab rhetoric and touchingly respectful of Israel's military powers, this may have sounded like mere verbiage. But as Israelis looked at the changing strategic map, the threat of massacre now had a more deadly resonance. Tens of thousands of Israelis still live closely with the memories of the European holocaust. Others recall how in 1948 the gates were left open, amid international indulgence and impotence, to an attempt by Arab armies to carry out what the Secretary-General of the Arab League, Azzam Pasha, had predicted would be a "Mongol massacre." Israel bears both the nobility and the servitude of Jewish history. Experience had taught her people that the sheer business of staying alive had been the major Jewish preoccupation for centuries past. Whether they understood it or not, the Arab leaders were here playing on Israel's most sensitive nerve. Even the consoling solidarity of world opinion did not dispel the dark visions which now crowded in upon us. Indeed, much of this world sympathy had an ominously valedictory note. Thousands of letters came in offering us blood donations, imploring us to send our children for shelter abroad, and requesting our attention to verses and prayers by poets and priests in which a note of last unction could be clearly detected. I remember feeling, with typical Israeli perversity, that if our friends were so concerned about us, we must indeed be in a sorry situation.

At the same time, Arab embassies in all countries in diplomatic relations with the UAR were distributing a memorandum which denied Israel the right not only to free passage in the Gulf of Aqaba but even to possession of the town of Eilat, where Israel had exercised unchallenged jurisdiction for the whole nineteen years of her existence. This memorandum was the highest peak of effrontery to which Nasser rose. It referred openly to a "state of war between the so-called Israel" and the Arab League countries, but emphasized that Israel had no right to fight! It went on to say that the blockade of the Gulf of Aqaba by the UAR, together with the Arab countries, is legitimate and justified. It stated that "Israel during the first week in May has moved thirteen complete brigades towards the border of Syria and its troops will march on Damascus." It "revealed" that this plot had been exposed (presumably by the Soviet Union) on May 14, when the U.S. Sixth Fleet was on maneuvers in the Mediterranean. "The Israeli aggression against Syria was planned for May 17 and Nasser . . . took the well-known appropriate measures." As a crowning sentence, the memorandum said: "The occupation of the Israelis of the harbor of Eilat was illegal." The hint was that Egypt's blockade would be followed by a seizure of Eilat, and her military dispositions made this a credible threat.

Thus, within three days, Arab belligerency had leaped far ahead of any attempts to contain it. In Washington an interdepartmental team was laboriously wrestling with the intricacies of the maritime task force. At noon on May 30 a cable reached me on a conversation between the State Department and the Israeli embassy the previous night. Our representative had been given to understand that a declaration by the maritime powers would be drafted and opened for adherence by other nations. It would contain no threats of force, but it would be a basis for action by any signatories who wanted to act. The United States had sent yet another letter to Moscow affirming the American and universal interest in the international character of the Straits of Tiran. On Wednesday, June 1, consultations would begin with congressional leaders with the aim of securing a joint resolution of both houses. In the meantime Israel would be offered economic aid to compensate her for the strain imposed by the period of mobilization and waiting.

The United States and Britain were contacting eighty capitals in an attempt to obtain signatures within the next few days on a declaration of intent to enforce free passage in the Straits. A resolution for adoption by both houses of Congress was in preparation; Vice-President Hubert H. Humphrey would be assigned the task of securing its adoption. London and Washington recognized that Israel's adherence to the declaration, including the determination to "assert its rights" on behalf of ships under Israeli flag, would give the declaration a special dramatic force.

This was, on the face of it, a busy program of action, but within twenty-four hours the picture had become transformed. With the exception of Israel, the idea of resisting Nasser became steadily less appealing to all governments. Ambassador Harman had cabled me on May 28 about a talk with a White House official who had told him that the President's mood was somber and that he could see no way out of the crisis. Our direct news from Ottawa made it clear that the hopes expressed to us in Washington about Canadian participation in the task force were not going to be realized.

Wherever we looked, we now found growing signs of hesitation. We were told that Robert B. Anderson, who had been Secretary of the Treasury in the Eisenhower Administration, was meeting with Nasser in Cairo. It was not certain that the mission had official status, but it was probable that this initiative would aim at a face-saving compromise—and that the face to be saved would be Nasser's, not

Israel's. For us the importance of denying Nasser political and psychological victory had become no less important than the concrete interest involved in the issue of navigation.

On May 30 Prime Minister Eshkol had consulted with me about a new attempt to gauge the American posture in the light of what had occurred since my talks on May 26. Many believed that the United States was less disposed than a few days before to assume responsibility itself, or to take responsibility for restraining Israel from action. We had jointly decided on sending a high official to take counsel in Washington. His cabled reports showed that an attempt was still being made to concert the naval plan, but that the barriers were growing hourly more difficult to surmount. On the other hand, a strong tide of public feeling was now running in Israel's favor. Many Americans were becoming resigned to the feeling that if the United States was unable to act quickly, it would not be able to demur strongly should Israel take independent initiative. The official whom we had dispatched to Washington reported to Jerusalem on June 1 that at the end of his first round of talks in Washington, his conclusions were that we should still wait for a few days in order to give a chance for the operation of forcing the Straits. Public opinion was on our side, he went on, and so were many people high up in government. The time left to us should be used to prepare public opinion and to plow a deeper furrow. From hints and scattered facts that he had heard, he got the impression that the maritime-force project was running into heavier water every hour.

On the morning of Thursday, June 1, I decided to make a new appraisal in the Foreign Ministry on the basis of recent reports. I was then in Tel Aviv in order to remain close to the Prime Minister and the Defense Ministry. In a telephone conversation, the Deputy Director-General of the Foreign Ministry, Arthur Lourie, told me that senior officials would respond willingly to a suggestion that we reopen our minds and hearts. I asked them to come from Jerusalem as soon as possible. While awaiting their arrival, I received a document in the late afternoon which had a decisive effect on my attitude. An American, known for his close contact with government thinking, had described the situation to one of our friends in Washington as follows: "If Israel had acted alone without exhausting political efforts it would have made a catastrophic error. It would then have been almost impossible for the United States to help Israel and the ensuing relationship would have been tense. The war might be long and costly for Israel if it broke out. If Israel had fired the first shot before the United Nations discussion she would have negated any possibility of the United States helping her. Israelis should not criticize

Eshkol and Eban; they should realize that their restraint and well-considered procedures would have a decisive influence when the United States came to consider the measure of its involvement." The American friend whose thinking seemed typical of the current Washington view understood that "time was running out and that it was a matter of days or even hours." But he believed that "if the measures being taken by the United States prove ineffective, the United States would now back Israel."

What I found new in this information was the absence of any exhortation to us to stay our hand much longer. Our restraint in the past was strongly praised; its continuation in the future was not suggested. At the same time, there came over the wires a report of one of Secretary Rusk's press comments. He had been asked whether, in addition to American plans for action in the United Nations, any efforts would be made to restrain Israel from precipitate action. The Secretary brusquely replied, "I don't think it is our business to restrain anyone."

When my senior officials had assembled, I requested a meticulous scrutiny of all the cables and conversations that had taken place with the United States in the past forty-eight hours. It emerged that since the communication which had reached us on the morning of May 28, no responsible American leader had assumed the authority to urge Israel to wait for any length of time or to place excessive reliance on international action. There were some in our military establishment who went further; they believed that it might be American policy to "unleash Israel," since our independent action would cause less complication than an international armada which would be resisted by Egypt and the Soviet Union.

I now came to the conclusion that I must take a decisive step that very day. It seemed that the diplomatic and political exercise on which we had been engaged since May 23 had reached its maximal result. The United States was less confident about its own action and less inclined to take responsibility for restraining Israel than a few days ago. The draft declaration by the maritime powers languished unhonored and unsigned. The naval task force was becoming a figment. The encircling net was being drawn tighter around us. The opinion of the humane world was enlisted in our cause. I felt that in friendly capitals throughout the world, a solitary eruption by Israel from the agony of siege would be greeted with satisfaction on two counts: our success would be applauded for its own sake, and the fact that we had not involved others in the risk of life or blood would evoke a universal relief.

I went to the Dan Hotel for a conversation with the most intimate of my advisers, Arthur Lourie, who urged me strongly along the course which I was contemplating. Both of us thought that the hour was now ripe to pick up the fruits of our patient efforts of the past ten days. I returned to our Tel Aviv office and asked the Director-General, Aryeh Levavi, to accompany me across the lawn to a meeting with the Chief of Staff, General Rabin, and the chief of military intelligence, General Yariv. I told them that I no longer had any political inhibitions to such military resistance as was deemed feasible, necessary and effective, and that if we were successful, I believed that our political prospects were good. We would not be set upon by a united and angry world as in 1956.

To explain the decisive nature of this step, I must refer to the special position of a Foreign Minister within the Cabinet system at a time when peace and war are in the balance. In constitutional theory the Foreign Minister is one of many whose votes have equal weight; in practice, however, his vote, if given for military action, has the strength of many. It is, after all, his business to exhaust peaceful remedy. If he believes that this is no longer feasible, and that diplomacy can only express itself after an assertion of physical strength, it is unlikely that any other minister will be more concerned than he with international reactions. I had lived with the knowledge that if I withdrew my inhibiting hand, military resistance with its incalculable visions and prospects would become certain.

There comes an hour when everything must be weighed and determined. It took but a few sentences for me to say to the two generals what was on my mind. I told them, without specific details, that I believed the waiting period had achieved its political purpose; that its advantage would unfold in the coming days and weeks; that there was nothing now for which to wait; that the need to withstand the throttling grip of Arab aggression was paramount; and that any decision on methods and timing should now be reached on military grounds alone. There was talk of possible times and occasions, all close at hand, at which Egyptian pressure would invite total response.

When I left their room, my step was lighter than when I had entered.

As I crossed over toward my own office I found Prime Minister Eshkol waiting silently on the lawn. He told me of tense debates that he was having with senior officers concerning the grave implications of any further waiting. I told him of the step that I had just taken with the General Staff; his relief was unconcealed.

For the first time since the crisis had erupted, I was now free to give thought to our internal convulsions. Until Thursday, June 1,

I had not understood how violent the crisis had become. On my return from Washington I had reported extensively to the Foreign
Affairs Committee of the Knesset; this had been during the memorable
night May 27–28. My account, with its implicit counsel of a further
short period of waiting, had been sympathetically received and scarcely
challenged at all. One member, Yaakov Hazan of Mapam, had said
that whether or not the maritime project took shape and substance,
to have elicited such undertakings from President Johnson was in
itself something of a political victory.

A less harmonious meeting had taken place with members of the
Labor Alignment in the Knesset on the evening of May 29. I told them
of the mission which I had carried out by express and formal Cabinet
decision. I said that the price paid for this political effort was by no
means exorbitant. I pointed out that a military action which left
Nasser in possession of his blockade would be a political and psychological failure, no matter what other loss was inflicted on the Egyptian
forces. There was military as well as political logic in choosing our
time. No contentious debate followed this report, but on my way out
of the committee room two members, Undersecretary of Education
Aharon Yadlin and Undersecretary for Trade and Commerce Liova
Eliav, met me with gloomy words. Their information was that we had
no time to lose and nothing to gain by letting time pass. They painted
the catastrophic picture of an Israeli military defeat that might arise
out of any further delay. They thought that if we waited another week
or two we would be finished. I replied that if we fought in another
week or two, our military prospects would be just as good as now, while
our political prospect would be better.

On May 23, after the announcement of Nasser's blockade of the
Straits of Tiran, the idea of enlarging the national coalition had
gained a new momentum. Eshkol's agreement to have opposition leaders join the meeting of the Cabinet Defense Committee showed that
he, too, was moved by a natural instinct to share responsibility. A
further development came on May 22 when Shimon Peres and Men-
achin Begin conversed before boarding the helicopter which was to
take them to our deliberations in Tel Aviv. Begin asked Peres whether
he thought that Ben Gurion, who had now passed his eightieth year,
would be willing and able to take the leadership of a broadly based
national government. When Peres gave an affirmative answer, Begin,
with candid courage, decided to make a direct approach to Eshkol.
On the afternoon of May 24, while I was in Paris, Begin had called
on Eshkol to ask whether he would step down and serve as Deputy
Prime Minister in a government headed by Ben Gurion, who would
also be Minister of Defense. In a tactful reference, Begin said that he

knew what bitter words and events had passed between Ben Gurion and Eshkol, but over the years he himself had been involved in a much sharper personal tension with Israel's first Prime Minister, who had even developed the habit of walking out of the Chamber when Begin rose to speak. Begin urged that this was the time for putting all such memories aside in the national interest and emergency.

Eshkol's reply, as could be anticipated, was sternly negative. He had no reason, in the light of his achievements, to doubt his ability to carry the nation through its trials. Moreover, he knew much more than Begin about recent developments in Ben Gurion's mood and capacity. While Ben Gurion's physical energies were enviable for a man in his eighty-first year, no one who had spoken with him or had watched his public appearances could believe that he had the power of objective analysis which had distinguished him in the past. His main weakness was in the realm where he used to be the strongest; he did not always put large and small things in their due balance, and his mind was now obsessed with personal rancors on which he tended to build political judgments. Eshkol spoke with justification of the intimacy and trust which prevailed between him and the Army High Command. Moreover, much would depend in the next few weeks on the relations between the United States and Israel. Never had Ben Gurion been able to establish with an American President the kind of confidence which had grown up between President Johnson and Eshkol.

It says much for Eshkol and Begin that their unusual conversation left no personal bitterness behind. Thereafter, as the days grew darker, the opinion in favor of a broad coalition went forward in greater strength.

It is not surprising that amid his international concerns Eshkol should have lost touch with developments in his own party. Much of what was being organized against him had begun to flow from those whom he had regarded as his steadfast supporters. A sharp change in the mood and policy of the Labor Alignment had developed after Eshkol's unsuccessful radio broadcast on May 28. Before that time, Mrs. Meir had given a strong lead in favor of maintaining the authority of the existing Cabinet, which she thought would be strengthened in two ways: by asking Minister of Labor Yigal Allon to assist Eshkol in preparing the national defense, and by developing informal consultation with the opposition without exposing the country to the turmoil of Cabinet changes.

If the national morale had not been deeply affected by the May 28 broadcast, these measures would have carried the day, but by the morning of May 29, any possibility of holding the line without Cabinet changes had been dispelled. The morning paper *Ha'aretz* wrote: "If we had confidence that Mr. Eshkol was capable of guiding the ship of our State in these days, we would willingly follow him; but this confidence does not exist. It seems to be disappearing amongst more and more of our citizens. . . . He is not built to be Prime Minister and Minister of Defence in the present situation." (The events of June were to disprove this dark prediction.) In a similar spirit, though less emphatically, other newspapers, especially *Ma'ariv* and *Yediot Aharonot,* called for governmental changes. Articles in the Labor Party organ *Davar* suggested the retention of Prime Minister Eshkol at the head of a War Cabinet which would include Generals Dayan, Allon and Yadin. At a meeting of the Labor Party members of the Knesset on the evening of May 29, two members, Professor Sadan and Mordechai Zar, called for the co-option of Dayan to the Cabinet. Further discussion of this idea had been postponed to the next day.

For Eshkol, the adherence of Speaker Kaddish Luz to the demand for his relinquishing the Defense Ministry caused the sharpest pang. The Prime Minister had no closer friend than his neighbor from Degania. He left the meeting in anguish. Pinhas Sapir and Golda Meir, Yigal Allon and Israel Galili, who might have rallied the dissidents, were absent—Sapir in the United States, Golda Meir in Tel Aviv, Allon and Galili outside Jerusalem. My own position was at least as much in contention as Eshkol's; someone other than he or I should have spoken candid words on his behalf and mine. In a scribbled chit to me, the Prime Minister had written: "I don't intend to answer all the personal references. I ask you not to. Let us both hear and see where and who our comrades are."

The hard fact is that they were nowhere to be heard or seen. A strong doubt about Eshkol's ability to combine the heavy burdens of the premiership with the simultaneous leadership of the Defense Ministry in an imminent war had seized much of the nation. All his colleagues were being inundated with expressions of opinion about this. On May 30 two senior scientists at the Weizmann Institute, Professors Amos de Shalit and Schneour Lifson, came to me to urge that Dayan or Allon be given the Defense responsibility, since Eshkol's broadcast had given them an impression of fatigue. They expressed the view that Israel's existence was in danger. I told them that peace, not Israel, was in danger and that "Nasser would have the beating of his life," but with this reservation I accepted the sincerity of their concern. (De Shalit said publicly in 1969 that this was the first optimistic appraisal of our military prospects that he heard that week.)

The sentiment for a change might have been satisfied a few days before if Eshkol had agreed to the suggestion of seconding Allon to assist him as Defense Minister; now it was too late for such simple remedies. The call was for a total extraction of the Defense Ministry from his hands. Eshkol's own grievance was deep. Of his two offices he held the Defense Ministry in greater affection than the premiership. His nature expanded more in action than in direction. He had once called me in, a few weeks after assuming his two offices, when I was his Deputy Prime Minister, to ask me in a querulous voice "what being a Prime Minister means." He had been used to the executive role of a Finance Minister whose hands were full of detailed work. He preferred this world of specific, tangible, defined tasks to one in which he could only give general leadership while others had the concrete satisfactions of fulfillment.

On Wednesday, May 31, it was plain that the government in its previous composition could not endure. The National Religious Party, the Independent Liberals and Gahal insisted on Dayan's appointment to the Defense Ministry. Their motives were varied and complex; the most creditable among them had to do with morale. If war was near, we would have to fight it with the equipment, the operational plans and the manpower which Eshkol and his associates in the Defense Ministry had carefully put together in the previous four years. More would depend on the commanders, officers, pilots and soldiers in the field than on a new civilian direction of the ministry. But in the Middle East and across the world, the appointment as Defense Minister of a soldier whose armies had once swept across Sinai and opened the Straits of Tiran would sound a note of defiance, memory and warning. Dayan had, in the past decade, been more of a politician than a soldier, and in the political arena he had never been, or claimed to be, a unifying force or an enthusiast for "party work as a member of a team." But the salient memories were now of his military leadership and his influence on the nation's youth.

These thoughts were to clash and interact with one another during the incessant meetings on May 31. At eleven o'clock in the morning we assembled in the Political Committee of the Labor Party at Tel Aviv. To most of us it was plain that a new Minister of Defense must be appointed. Many thought that Allon would bring to that office all the specialized qualities which it demanded, together with a chance of working harmoniously with Eshkol and his senior colleagues.

At this stage one of my colleagues, Minister of Justice Yaacov Shimshon Shapira, suggested in open session, and with no prior consultation, that Allon's appointment as Defense Minister be accompanied by Dayan's appointment as Foreign Minister and my own "elevation" to the post of Deputy Prime Minister. He prefaced this proposal with sincere eulogy of my work, and especially of my efforts in Washington which had got the United States more involved in support of our cause than had previously seemed conceivable. He doubted "if anyone else could have secured this result." He said that he proposed the change not because he thought that Dayan would be a good candidate for the job of Foreign Minister, but because he wanted to prevent the Defense Ministry being removed from Eshkol's control. There was a brief but embarrassed silence. In a note to Eshkol I said that I had no ambition to stay in the Cabinet if my presence obstructed "arrangements" necessary to him, but that I would not accept a titular office or stay in a government with an inexperienced Foreign Minister whose talents were remote from the international sphere and whose heart and mind lay elsewhere. Allon, Golda Meir and Eshkol severely rejected any proposal for a change in my ministry. Many in the country seemed to have received word of this idea before I had, for while we were in session, word reached Eshkol from the National Religious Party, the Independent Liberals and Mapam that they would strenuously object to this proposal. Their six ministers had supported all my moves, as indeed had eleven of my twelve Labor colleagues during the crucial vote on May 28. That nearly unanimous decision had not been proved wrong in any way. Thus, the proposal for any change involving the Foreign Ministry died a swift death an hour after it was submitted.

Our meeting ended with a decision to offer the deputy premiership to Dayan and the Defense Ministry to Allon. That afternoon Eshkol formally made the proposal to Dayan; he rejected it firmly. If he was not to be Defense Minister, he would prefer to go back to military service and take the Southern Command. The war, after all, would be won or lost on the Sinai front, which he knew more intimately than anyone else. He added that even if he was appointed Defense Minister, he would spend most of his time at the Negev front and very little of it in the ministry.

This unconventional proposal was adopted by Eshkol. But its lease was short. Gahal, the National Religious Party and the Independent Liberals were not interested in merely separating the premiership from the Defense Ministry. Their objective was to secure a broader coalition, not just a new division of functions among the existing Labor ministers. Allon's appointment would not broaden the Cabinet's base. This aim could be served only by the adherence of Rafi and Gahal—and that adherence would only be achieved by Dayan's appointment to the Defense Ministry.

At a meeting of the National Religious Party that evening, impatient voices were heard. There were threats to leave the Cabinet unless Gahal and Rafi could be co-opted and the Defense Ministry given to Dayan.

On Thursday, June 1, I stayed away from the early part of the Secretariat meeting in order to consult with Foreign Ministry officials on my future course. It was during that morning that the news from Washington and other capitals convinced me that the time was ripe for early resistance, and that we had lost nothing by the delay. In the meantime, Eshkol was making a dignified address to the Party Secretariat. When I joined the meeting toward noon, he was in full spate; I felt that his colleagues were in his confidence for the first time that week. When he came to discuss recent events he spoke sadly about comrades whose support he had expected in vain. "If our own party had a little more iron," he said, "we would have maintained our responsibility intact and avoided the complexities and antagonisms of recent days." He went on to describe how Allon had patriotically asked to be excluded from consideration as Minister of Defense when he had heard how this would increase internal difficulties. Eshkol then went on to say that he had reached a firm decision to bring the whole discussion to an early end. He now proposed to offer the Defense Ministry to Moshe Dayan as representative of Rafi, and to suggest the inclusion of Gahal representatives in the government. He was calling a meeting of the Cabinet later that evening, and the coalition government in its enlarged framework would set to work at once.

Eshkol's statement was well received. The way was now open for the nation to face its ordeals in unity. By midnight on Thursday, June 1, the Cabinet was in session with Begin and Dayan in attendance, although they had not yet been sworn in at the Knesset. By that time, as we have seen, I had already told our military advisers that I would support whatever response they thought necessary to break the ring. On the morning of Friday, June 2, we were all given a briefing by the General Staff. One officer after another took the rostrum to urge the necessity for immediate resistance; whether they knew it or not, at this point they were preaching to the converted.

As we looked around us we saw the world divided between those who were seeking our destruction and those who would do nothing to prevent it. Nasser had by now crossed the boundary of arrogance into a realm where all proportion or restraint was lost from view. Even the maritime declaration being worked out by Washington and London was too much for him to endure. On June 2 he stated: "If any power dares to make declarations on freedom of navigation in the Straits of Tiran, we shall deny that power oil and free navigation in the Suez Canal." As if to force Israel's hand and to make certain that she would not act differently from his own prediction, the irrepressible Hassanein Heykal stridently repeated in *Al-Ahram* that "the Jews of Israel have no escape except war." He went on to point out that even this was not an escape, but one of the available routes for Israel's annihilation.

Our government was facing an acute dilemma about what it should do to boost public morale. We had every reason for inculcating a sense of alertness and common sacrifice; on the other hand, there was a real danger that the sheer exuberance of the Arab voices would bring about a paralyzing depression. On June 1 General Chaim Herzog, the chief military spokesman, discussed the extent of our air-raid precautions. Not only were shelters being dug, but women and children were being instructed in defense against gas warfare. Herzog, having made a detailed estimate of the Arab forces in the region, discounted the possibilities of a successful blitz and strongly doubted that the Egyptians could penetrate Israel's air defenses at all. "Knowing the facts, I can say that if I had a choice between sitting in an Egyptian aircraft set to bomb Tel Aviv, and sitting in a house in Tel Aviv, then I would prefer, for the good of my health, to sit in Tel Aviv." The subsequent failure of the Egyptian air force was to bear out this prediction. At the time, it sounded too good to be true. By sheer numbers and proximity of aircraft, the Arab states seemed to have an alarming capacity for causing bloodshed and havoc. The nation gritted its teeth and prepared to fight for its life.

In our review of the situation on Friday, June 2, my advisers and I paid special attention to the attitude of the Soviet Union. As the West became increasingly timid, Soviet militancy grew more intense. I had told my colleagues and advisers the day before that in my view the Soviet Union would not intervene militarily in the impending conflict, and that "the shorter the clash the less likely Soviet intervention would be." On the other hand, Moscow was playing a skillful game of intimidation. I could observe with some irony that while many in Israel regarded me as the main factor in the decision for a short period of restraint, I was being portrayed in Moscow as the leading hawk! The Soviet Union had clearly caught the import of my press conference on May 31, and on the morning of June 2 the Kremlin delivered a note to us through our ambassador attacking my statement that Israel could only wait a short time for her demands to be met; that this waiting period would be a question of days or weeks, since inaction was a form of action; and that Israel herself would open the Straits of Tiran if the Great Powers did not eliminate the blockade. It was a fact, the note said, that my declaration could serve as official confirmation of information testifying to the reckless activity initiated by warmongering circles in Israel who aspired to dictate a line of action to the government and people of Israel; a line of action that would apparently end in a position which would be irreparable from Israel's point of view . . .

At our June 2 meeting I told my senior Foreign Ministry associates how I had informed the military leaders the previous day that I saw no political reason for inhibiting our resistance; in consequence, we could probably expect a unanimous government decision for resistance within a few days. My own reading of the Washington position told me that if we were successful, the United States would feel relieved at being liberated from its dilemma, and would not support international pressures against us.

While I was in consultation with ministry officials, a telephone call came from Washington; Ambassador Harman was about to leave for Jerusalem to report, and he asked that any "decisions" be held up until he arrived. From the cautious hints exchanged during our conversation, I understood that he had no good news to bring of his talk with Secretary Rusk that afternoon.

There was a strange ambivalence in Israeli life during the Sabbath of June 3. Everyone in responsible positions knew that the die had been cast. Ample chance had been given to international organizations and the maritime powers to check Nasser in his headlong course; the chance had been explored, sniffed at tentatively—and emphatically renounced. Nobody of fair mind would now be able to say that there was a serious alternative to Israeli resistance. Yet, since May 28, there still lingered a general impression that a week or two were still in hand. The beaches and picnic grounds in Israel were crowded with officers back on short leave from the front. In a cautious press interview General Dayan had stated that June 2 was either too early or too late for action; it was too late for an instant reaction to the Aqaba blockade—and too early to regard diplomatic measures as exhausted. It was evident that much would depend on the atmosphere in the Cabinet meeting and ministerial consultations scheduled for the following day.

Before the Sabbath was out, Ambassador Harman came from the airport at Lod to consult with me at my home. His conversation with Secretary Rusk had done nothing to change our impression that there was even less international disposition to act against Nasser than a few days before. Vice-presidential visits would probably be exchanged between Cairo and Washington. Secretary Rusk had told Harman that measures to be taken by the maritime powers were still under consideration, but that "nothing had been firmly decided." This was a far cry from Rusk's positive statement delivered through Ambassador Barbour only five days previously, on May 28, speaking of military preparations "having reached an advanced stage."

In the evening I went over to the Prime Minister's residence, taking Ambassador Harman with me. We were joined by Dayan, the army chiefs, Minister of Labor Yigal Allon, General Yigael Yadin and the official of the Prime Minister's office who had been dispatched to the United States. We were unanimous in our interpretation of the position in Washington. It was now clear that the United States was not going to be able to involve itself unilaterally or multilaterally in any enforcement action within a period relevant to our plight. But we all felt that if Israel found means of breaking out of the siege and blockade, the United States would not now take a hostile position.

Before we separated, it was clear that Eshkol, Allon, Dayan and I would take similar attitudes in the Cabinet and the ministerial meetings planned for the next day. Ambassador Harman's realistic report strengthened our certainty that there was nothing for us to expect from outside. Our military plan was concerned with Egypt alone; we would not fight against Jordan unless Jordan attacked us. As I walked the short distance to my own residence in the still night, I came across groups of workers building shelters near the schools. In conformity with the general mood, my wife, son and daughter had put sticking tape inside the windows of our home, as protection against explosions. Everyone in Jerusalem was doing this, but I had to ask my long-suffering family to spend some hours peeling the tape away, since television teams were going to arrive to record interviews with me: I thought that visible evidence of defense preparations in the Foreign Minister's own house would give too sharp a hint of impending war.

On Sunday, June 4, ministers were in session for over seven hours. There was a regular Cabinet meeting, a preparatory committee review, and many consultations of ministers in smaller groups. The atmosphere was now strangely tranquil. All the alternatives had been weighed and tested in recent days; there was little remaining to do except plunge into the responsibility and hazard of choice.

It seemed as if our adversaries, by their hatred—and our friends by their impatience—had narrowed our options down to a single compulsion. Everything in Arab utterance and posture confirmed our impression that our physical survival was at stake, and the attitude of the powers clearly proclaimed our solitude.

The brunt of Egyptian preparation lay in Sinai. There were now some 100,000 troops strung out across the wilderness, organized in seven divisions. The Second and Seventh divisions had dug themselves in deeply in the northeast corner of the peninsula. It was here that our chief danger lay: the forward armored units of the Egyptian army were but a few minutes from populated centers in the northern Negev. And if the Israeli forces opposite them, commanded by Brigadiers Israel Tal, Avraham Yoffe and Ariel ("Arik") Sharon, were to take the offensive, they would find the enemy deeply entrenched in bunkers and foxholes. It was this process of fortification which had caused some of our military leaders such anxiety that they had openly chafed at having to wait for the past ten days. The Egyptian battle order was at its strongest and most self-confident along the few roads which an Israeli thrust would have to follow.

Behind the 100,000 Egyptians mobilized in Sinai, there was a small reserve not exceeding 60,000 men. Some 80,000 Egyptians were still held down in Yemen. The Egyptian army in Sinai had 1,000 tanks, most of them, including the Soviet T-54s and T-55s, in forward positions. But it was in the air that our enemy's superiority seemed most marked. He had the advantage of overwhelming numbers and of alarming proximity to our most sensitive nerve centers. The air base at Bir Gafgafa was within a few minutes of Tel Aviv, while there was no vital Egyptian target in similar range of an Israeli airfield. The Egyptian air force had some 400 interceptors and fighter-bombers, and 75 to 80 medium and light bombers which seemed capable of creating enormous havoc in Israeli cities.

Those foreign military experts who took a dark view of Israel's prospects were mainly impressed by our deficiency in attacking aircraft. Except for a few Vautour light bombers, we were entirely dependent on French-manufactured fighters and fighter-bombers, some of them obsolete. We knew that on this slender thread hung the full weight of our history and the sole chance of our survival. With the best will in the world, it was difficult to avoid quoting the celebrated rhetoric about the many who owed much to the few.

And the peril from Egypt was compounded by the adherence to the Egyptian design of the manpower, armor and air force of other Arab countries. None of these amounted to a decisive danger in itself, but the combined strength of all, as well as their strategic disposition along Israel's frontiers to the north and east, would inevitably prevent us from putting all our strength to work against the main adversary.

That Syria would participate in the war against us was taken for granted. This meant that we had to reckon with a Syrian army of 50,000 men, with at least 200 tanks of operational capacity, and 100 Soviet aircraft, including 32 modern MIG-21s. Political estimates were not unanimous about whether Jordan would actively enter the fighting, but our military plans had to take this prospect into some account. There was a Jordan army of some 50,000 to 60,000 men, whose main strength lay in 250 Patton and Centurion tanks. It was only in the air that Jordan was relatively negligible. She could count on some two dozen British Hunter fighter-bombers; American Starfighters had begun to arrive but had not yet been put under Jordanian control— indeed, we heard that they had been quietly removed on orders from Washington. An Iraqi division was taking up its positions on Jordanian territory in accordance with the UAR–Jordanian Defense Agreement, to which Iraq had officially adhered.

These were the stark facts of our enemy's numerical superiority, which was enlarged by his geographical advantage and sharpened by a higher morale than the Arab world had known in all our modern experience. The frenzy in Arab streets belonged to the tradition of hot fanaticism which, in earlier periods of history, had sent the Moslem armies flowing murderously across three continents. Reports were reaching us of Egyptian generals and other leaders straining hard against the tactical leash which Nasser had imposed upon them. His idea of absorbing the first blow and inflicting a "knockout" in the second round was receding before a simpler impulse which told Egyptian troops that a first-blow victory was possible and that there was no need to "absorb" anything. The correspondent of the London *Observer* told how tens of thousands of young men across Egypt were forming societies with the aim of forcing Nasser's hand so that even if he wanted to control them, it could be only for a short time. After the war this version was to be supported by an account from Eric Rouleau, a French writer known for his zealous support of Arab causes. In his words, the Cairo atmosphere could be summed up in simple terms: "We have waited long enough. It serves no useful purpose to wait any longer. Let's finish with Israel and be done with it. No more words; prompt action is needed. Forward to Tel Aviv!"

After the military appraisal, it became my duty to sketch the political environment in which we now moved. I told my colleagues of the letter which Eshkol had received from President Johnson the morning before. Johnson had explained that he was pursuing efforts through the United Nations and was simultaneously making concerted diplomatic efforts with Britain to secure a declaration by the principal maritime powers asserting the right of passage through the Straits. As he told me, there was doubt that other powers would be willing to take steps unless and until UN processes were exhausted. American leadership was unanimous that the United States should not move in isolation.

These were cautious words. In spirit and atmosphere they marked a retreat from Johnson's message and Rusk's addendum of May 28. But I could now report that a tide of solidarity with Israel was sweeping across every free community in the world. In my opinion, important circles in the United States and other free countries would not be surprised if Israel felt obliged to act. There were different appraisals of Soviet intentions, I added. Most of them indicated that the Soviet Union would not intervene militarily, especially if the campaign was brief. My conclusion was that if we acted and triumphed, many would not regret it. If there were prolonged hostilities, there would be much pressure to bring about a cease-fire as early as possible. I observed that for several days the British government had not spoken to us about restraint. My impression of the American position was that they had a certain dialectic which compelled them not to spur us on or encourage us, but what happened after we took action would depend largely on the degree of our success and our ability to keep public opinion in a state of intense emotional support. My interpretation of the Soviet attitude was that we could expect hostility in the political arena, but that there was nothing to indicate the eventuality of armed intervention.

I then spoke of France. President de Gaulle was still firmly wedded to the formula of Four Power consultations, even though this had been contemptuously rejected by the Soviet Union. Foreign Minister Couve de Murville had told our ambassador that, in his view, the most dangerous course for Israel would be to go to war. He said that we had the choice between war and the path indicated by France. The choice was in our hands and he agreed that it was a difficult one.

I reported how Ambassador Eytan, having heard that normal military supplies to Israel had been held up at the ports, had gone to see a high official in the Elysée Palace who habitually dealt with these matters. To Eytan's surprise the President himself, who was in an adjoining room, had invited him for a talk. It soon became clear that General de Gaulle's attitude had hardened further within the mold fixed by his talk with me on May 24. He believed that a war would be disastrous for Israel even if she won. There would be enormous losses; the Arabs would bomb Israeli cities; and in the end, no problem would be solved—indeed, hate would be increased. If the present crisis could be surmounted without war, he thought that it would be possible to solve some of the basic questions, beginning with navigation in the Gulf. The General advised Israel not to rely too much on the United States; he thought that America might support us at the beginning, but would soon come up against problems of oil and the Suez Canal and would cool off, notwithstanding the sympathy felt for Israel, "especially in New York." When

Eytan spoke of the harsh impression made in Israel by the French statement of June 2, President de Gaulle replied that the essential point in that statement was that France wished Israel "to exist as a state and not to disappear."

De Gaulle went on to say that while France wished Israel to survive, the position was no longer as it was in 1957. At that time he had not been in power and things had changed. France had renewed her relations with Arab countries and was interested in their development. He thought that this could be of use to Israel as well; there would be at least one power to whom both sides would be willing to listen. Eventually Eytan reached the crucial point of the embargo. He was told quite plainly that the ban would remain in force "as long as it is not clear if you will go to war." Afterward it would be resumed as before. Eytan said that France was denying Israel arms in order to exercise pressure not to go to war, but such methods sometimes engender situations of despair and thus make war more probable. To this cogent point, there was no reply. President de Gaulle ended by saying that the Eastern question always arises in history and always finds its solutions by the powers. The same powers have always been involved—Russia, France and Britain, and now the United States had been added. I linked his reference to the "Eastern question" with what he had said to me about the Dardanelles. He seemed to be living in a previous world—the world of his youth.

I could see that this report from Paris had a strong effect on all my colleagues. The appraisal of our military authorities must now be considered in a new dimension. Not only had we reached the peak of our danger, we had also marked the zenith of our military capacity; and if more weeks went by, the arms balance would deteriorate. Supplies were pouring into the Arab states from the Soviet Union, while Israel's main supply artery had been cut.

When the reports were finished, the silence was deep and long. Eshkol's glance went around the table as if to ask each minister to declare his view. My own advice was that our decision should be that the government authorize our defense authorities, together with the responsible ministers, to decide on any action necessary to break the enemy's stranglehold, and that the timing should be determined in accordance with military necessities alone. I went on to express the conviction that the Egyptians would continue to move against us and encroach by land and sea. I agreed with my colleagues that we should make a total response to the next encroachment, and we should tell the world frankly that what we were answering was not Egypt's immediate movement alone, but the outrage inherent in her aggressive design of encirclement and blockade. I added that if our military resistance was successful, I thought that after the first strike, our political position would grow stronger. On the American attitude, I said I thought that we had involved them very deeply. That week their political and moral responsibility was much greater in the eyes of the people and the President than it was before I was sent there. I did not believe that we would repeat the situation of 1956, when the United States refused to speak to us.

In the dense pressure of business, I had not had time to consult with other ministers who, like myself, had been in favor of restraint a week before. I could see that some of them were surprised that I had now left them behind. The two Mapam ministers, Barzilai and Bentov, seemed to be taken aback by my attitude in favor of resistance. On the other hand, they did not dissociate themselves from it; they said that they would consult their senior colleagues in the party concerning their vote, which would have to be registered at a later time. It came through a few hours later—in favor of resistance.

The afternoon was wearing on, and nothing new remained to be uttered. There is often something casual about the way in which great decisions fall. Eshkol asked in a sober voice for a show of hands on the proposal that the Defense Minister, in consultation with the Prime Minister and others concerned, should be empowered to decide when and how to resist the Egyptian aggression. Of the eighteen hands entitled to vote, sixteen went up at once. The other two, belonging to the Mapam ministers, were added before the day was out. We decided to remain in daily session and to meet the next morning in Tel Aviv, where we would be nearer our operational headquarters.

Of those who sat together in Jerusalem on June 4, four have passed on: Eshkol, Moshe Hayim Shapira, Israel Barzilai and Zalman Aranne. The rest of us are joined together with them in the covenant of memory; we have known the sharing of great things by men set apart from ordinary concerns. Once we voted, we knew that we had expressed our people's will, for amid the alarms and fears of mid-May, our nation gave birth to new impulses within itself. All the conditions which divide us from each other and give our society a deceptive air of fragmentation, all the deeply rooted Jewish recalcitrance toward authority now seemed to have been transmuted into a new metal which few of us had felt before. There had, of course, been some fear, as was natural for a people which had endured unendurable things. Many in the world were afraid that a great massacre was sweeping down upon us. And in many places in Israel there was talk of Auschwitz and Maidenek. The anxiety expressed by friends outside told us that our apprehension was not vain. Yet, as the last days of May were passing into the haze of memory, the people were gripped by a spirit of union and resolve. Men of military age silently laid down their work in factory, office and farm, took up their files of reservist papers and disappeared toward the south.

Hospital beds by the hundreds were made ready with a quiet and almost macabre efficiency. Trenches and shelters had been dug all over the land. Industrialists, noted in better days for their hard-headed thrift, donated legendary sums for the national defense. As the days of suspense rolled on, the radio brought touching messages exchanged between soldiers at the front and their young wives at home. There were homely references to children about to be born, or anxious allusions to the oven having been left burning in the haste of departure. The simplicity of these exchanges held a pathos hard to bear. There had been a sudden rearrangement of values with human affections rising to the top.

The Jewish dispersion, too, was in ferment of a more dramatic kind. There were, of course, ardent rhetorical demonstrations. But there also came more tangible evidence of solidarity. Thousands of young men were crowding the offices of Israeli consulates and Jewish Agency institutions throughout the world, asking to be sent to Israel for immediate service. Nor was excitement limited to Jews alone. In Stockholm some members of Parliament discussed resignation so as to make themselves available to fight in Israel. A blind man in Brooklyn tried to send me the money that he had accumulated over twenty years to buy a house, stating that if Israel went under there would be no point in living anyway, and that if we succeeded, he would certainly get his money back. An elderly Christian spinster in northern Scotland announced that she could do very little by way of fighting, but that few people could drive an army truck as well as she.

Had the ensuing battle not been so short, the voluntary convergence of men and women to help Israel's defense would have been without parallel in the history of modern war. Amateur technologists sent their obsessive plans for secret weapons which would cause the Egyptian hosts to crumble into dust. Even sophisticated newspapers like the *Times* of London, the *Guardian,* the *Economist,* the *Observer,* the *New York Times* and *Le Monde,* which for long had been preaching nothing but Israeli restraint and concession, were suddenly admitting that one of the possible ways of dealing with aggression might be to resist it. There was something in our predicament which touched sensitive human chords. In the moment of danger, Israel stood high in the trust and anxiety of peace-loving mankind.

From some newly liberated African states came scores of messages from young men who had spent some weeks or months in Israel's training courses, and for whom we had become an alma mater—the nurse and architect of their skills. In the churches of Holland, prayers were being uttered for Israel's survival. In Israel, the normal asperities were now softened by individual acts of tolerance and sympathy which, in normal days, most of our citizens would have been too shame-faced to offer or to accept. In the Druze villages of Galilee, a traditional militancy found expression in heavy volunteering. Synagogues all over the land seemed fuller than usual. The air was quiet with courage and simple rectitude. The nation, which was supposed to have lost its youthful idealism and pioneering virtues, now looked back to the old unifying visions. Israelis and Diaspora Jews found one another anew—and rejoiced in the mutual discovery.

At our meetings on June 4, we saw no reason to galvanize Cairo into a premature alert. We decided that in order to defuse the atmosphere, we should transact some ordinary business for public notice. Out of this discussion came the following communiqué:

> The Cabinet heard reports on the security situation from the Prime Minister and Minister of Defence-designate; and a report on the political situation from the Foreign Minister. The co-option to the Cabinet of Ministers Menahem Begin, Moshe Dayan and Yosef Saphir was approved. It was agreed that the new Ministers would be sworn in before the Knesset on Monday afternoon.
> Legislation was approved: (a) Issue of new debentures of the State of Israel (Second Development Loan 1967); (b) Security Tax (1967); (c) Floating of Security Loan (1967). . . .
> Agreements were ratified: (a) Technical Co-operation between the Israel Atomic Energy Commission and the Atomic Energy Commission of Peru; (b) Cultural Agreement between Israel and Belgium; (c) Agreement with Great Britain on Legal Procedures in Civil and Commercial Matters.

The Cabinet Secretary was to add that Ambassador Harman would return to Washington "to continue diplomatic efforts." The communiqué, which was literally true, though not comprehensively accurate, sent many unperceptive foreign correspondents back to their countries in despair of ever seeing a war. A technical agreement with Peru did not sound like a trumpet call. If in confusing the enemy we also confused a few friends, the price was not high.

On Monday, June 5, I awakened early in the Dan Hotel in Tel Aviv, of which I was almost the only occupant that night. The morning heat lay heavy on the streets. At seven-fifty, while I was driving the short distance to the Ministry of Defense, the air-raid sirens set up an unfamiliar howl. Men and women going to work and children hurrying to their schools gave no immediate attention to the sound. Only when policemen began to move tensely among them did they sense that something more was afoot than the familiar testing of the warning system. The roads began to clear as the crowds moved awkwardly and dubiously toward the few shelters which existed.

When I reached the Prime Minister's room, I learned that Egyptian planes advancing toward us had been sighted on the radar screens. In accordance with our decision of the previous day, our own aircraft had gone out to meet the advancing force. But this time our airmen's mission was not tactical or limited as before; they had embarked on a total counterattack against the Egyptian air force wherever it could be found. Shortly afterward the Egyptian ground forces in the Gaza Strip had bombarded Israeli settlements. Our armored forces were instructed to make a total response.

The action to which Nasser had been goading us for three intolerable weeks had now erupted. Israel was hitting back in the air, and from the beginning there was a glow of victory on her wings. Even before the first results of our air action were known, I was overcome by a vast relief. Everything that could be done to defend honor and interest without war had been exhausted.

In legal terms, Israel was exercising the inherent right of self-defense recognized for all states in Article 51 of the United Nations Charter, and this involved certain prescribed procedures. It was now two o'clock in the morning in New York; I asked Yosef Tekoah, the deputy director-general in charge of international affairs, to make a telephone call to our permanent representative at the United Nations, Ambassador Gideon Rafael. His orders were to ask for an urgent meeting of the Security Council, before which he was to unfold the design of Egyptian aggression and report on Israel's resistance. By ten o'clock in the morning on June 5 we were receiving reports of excited headlines, radio bulletins and television stories all over the world reporting Egyptian aggression and Israeli defense. Most of them spoke of Israel's peril in the face of overwhelming odds; the Arab radio stations told of sensational Egyptian victories which augured Israel's early liquidation.

By eleven o'clock Israel's destiny had been turned upside down. Reports came in of unbelievable successes in the air. All the Egyptian airfields had been attacked and most of their planes destroyed on the ground. These included the TU-16 jet bombers which, alone among the Egyptian aircraft, would have been able to wreak havoc on our densely populated cities. Although Nasser and his generals had been talking openly of "inevitable war" and had even suggested June 5 as its probable beginning, their vigilance had fallen below the level of their foresight. By flying low out to sea to evade detection by Egyptian radar and then turning around to come in from the west, our squadrons had scored a complete tactical surprise. By noon the number of Egyptian aircraft destroyed ran into hundreds.

All our aircraft had been committed to action. Planes would set out for their targets in Egypt, return to their bases and be prepared for a new sortie within minutes. The ardor and efficiency of the ground crews were hardly less impressive than the more spectacular valor of pilots in the air.

But the elation of military success did not absolve us from urgent political duty. There were heavy tasks before us. The first was to ensure that Soviet intervention would be deterred. This meant that we could not long afford to be out of communication with the United States. Our second aim was to ensure that even when Egypt was totally engaged, and Syria, as expected, had joined the combat, Jordan would still be given a chance to avoid involvement. A three-front war had always been Israel's darkest nightmare.

In the early morning I helped Prime Minister Eshkol draft letters to the heads of friendly states. I myself asked the American, British, French and Soviet ambassadors to come, one after the other, to my temporary office in Tel Aviv. Ambassador Walworth Barbour said that he would be accompanied by one of President Johnson's associates in the White House, Harry McPherson, who had arrived from India that morning for a visit of which we had been given notice a week before. McPherson was an improbable name for an American Jew—but there it was. President Johnson had commended McPherson to Eshkol in a letter written a few days before in a mood of deep emotion about Israel's ordeal. He had written: "May God give us strength to protect the right."

When the ambassador and his guest had departed, Eshkol heard my report and even went over my draft of his message to President Johnson. This began with a description of the dangers facing Israel since mid-May right up to the Egyptian bombardment of Kisufim and Nahal Oz that morning. "All of this," it went on, "amounts to an extraordinary catalogue of aggression abhorred and condemned by world opinion, in your great country, and amongst all peace-loving nations." It then expressed the hope that everything would be done by the United States to prevent the Soviet Union from exploiting and enlarging the conflict. "The hour of danger can also be an hour of opportunity. It is possible to create conditions favourable to the promotion of peace and the strengthening of freedom in the area."

In transmitting this document, we had indicated to the United States through diplomatic channels that the sentence about the Soviet

Union was the most crucial point. The hint to our greatest friend was courteous but frank. The United States had not been able, despite sincere efforts, to help us in our previous ordeal and anguish. We had taken a solitary responsibility. But its leader now had the opportunity, which belongs to Presidents of the United States alone, to ensure that a regional conflict was not enlarged by the intervention of a Great Power. This, after all, had been one of the main themes of my talks in Washington on May 25 and 26, and most of President Johnson's communications to us since then had concentrated on the Soviet prospect. The question whether Moscow, having done so much to initiate the war, would allow its clients to lose it, now lay as a heavy cloud between us and our brighter hopes.

Similar communications went out to Prime Minister Wilson, President de Gaulle and the heads of most friendly states. As the morning wore on, the prospect of Jordanian intervention took on a more grave and urgent aspect. Eshkol's letter to Harold Wilson, after reiterating the points made to President Johnson, contained this paragraph: "Our Foreign Minister has told your Ambassador of our attempt to avoid any engagement with Jordan, unless Jordan makes conflict irresistible. I hope that this can still be avoided."

The hope was rational enough, but the Middle East is so constructed that the least likely things to happen are those which reason dictates. Our efforts to prevent a Jordanian military assault were not confined to the writing of letters to friendly states. We used all our channels to give explicit assurance to Jordan that we would abstain from any attack if King Hussein and his government stayed out of the war. Our military authorities fully supported this course. Faced by eleven Jordanian brigades on the West Bank of the Jordan and in the area south and east of the Dead Sea, they had made the most modest provision for a holding action. The experience of 1956, the constant hostility between Nasser and Hussein ever since, and the fragility of Jordan's army had all led to the conclusion that King Hussein would not enter the fray; and that an unexpected decision to enter it would involve him in long deliberations, giving us time to make effective provision.

All these calculations were shattered when at ten o'clock Jordanian forces opened a heavy bombardment all along the front. Even then, there was a theoretical possibility that King Hussein was making a formal gesture of solidarity with Egypt. We decided to give King Hussein an ultimate chance to turn back. Arthur Lourie was asked to make immediate contact with General Odd Bull, chief of the General Staff of the United Nations Truce Supervision Organization, requesting him to convey a message from Eshkol to King Hussein.

The message reached its destination but was contemptuously rejected. King Hussein himself has written the story:

> It was then that I received, while at the operational head-quarters of our Air Force, a telephone call coming from Jerusalem. It was General Odd Bull of the United Nations who communicated a message. It was shortly after 11 o'clock [10 A.M. Israel time]. In this message the Norwegian General representing the United Nations observers in the Middle East informed me of an appeal from the Prime Minister of Israel addressed to Jordan. Mr. Eshkol told us that Israeli operations had begun that Monday morning against the United Arab Republic but "if you do not intervene, you will not suffer any harm."
>
> However, we were already fighting in Jerusalem, and our planes had already taken off to go and bombard the Israeli air bases. I therefore replied to Odd Bull: The Israelis unleashed hostilities. They are therefore now receiving the reply of our Air Force. In three waves our Hawker Hunters attacked the base at Natania in Israel without loss. In addition, our pilots reported having destroyed more enemy aircraft on the ground—the only ones which they found not in the air. For their part, the Iraqis bombarded the aerodrome of Lydda. The Syrians addressed themselves to the air base of Ramat David and the refineries of Haifa.

The message that Israel "will not attack any country which does not first launch an attack against us" had been approved for broadcast on our Arabic radio as soon as the first air strike against Egypt began. The Jordanian reply had been a formidable bombardment of western Jerusalem. Eshkol's communication to King Hussein through General Bull was:

> We shall not initiate any action whatsoever against Jordan. However, should Jordan open hostilities, we shall react with all our might, and the King will have to bear the full responsibility for all the consequences.

The response to this statement was not only an intensification of shelling in Jerusalem, but also bombardment of the outskirts of Tel Aviv. Even so, we decided to make no move until one o'clock. It was at that hour that the die was cast. Jordanian forces captured Government House in southeast Jerusalem, where the United Nations Truce Supervision Organization had its headquarters. Early in the afternoon the Jordanian army began moving its tanks opposite northwestern Jerusalem. Thus, within a few hours, a danger to our security had arisen from the most unexpected quarter and at the most vulnerable place. In a swift redisposition of forces, the central sector was reinforced. Amman radio was now making bloodthirsty statements in the name of King Hussein, announcing that all Israelis should be "torn to bits." The fact is that on that day, Monday, June 5, more casualties were being inflicted on us by Jordan than we were sustaining on the Egyptian front. Our forces were now ordered to resist without inhibition, and shortly after two o'clock our air force attacked the airfields at Amman and Mafrak, where nearly all Jordan's air fleet of twenty Hunter aircraft was destroyed. In a swift counterattack, Government House was recaptured and Jordanian forces expelled.

Israel has no cause to regret that even under Jordanian fire she gave King Hussein the opportunity of prudence. It was to become evident after the war that the King was not really free to apply his own discretion or to consult his own interest. Egypt's most formidable soldier, General Mahoud Riad, had been appointed to command the Jordan sector, and on the evening of June 4 he had installed himself with an Egyptian staff at operational headquarters in Amman. King Hussein has described how the Egyptian General Staff calmly took Jordan into its military possession, without taking her into any truthful confidence. He writes:

> *We were the recipients of false information about what had happened in Egypt since the attacks by Israeli air forces on the air bases in the U.A.R. A new message from Marshal Amer informed us that the Israeli air offensive was continuing. However, it went on to affirm that the Egyptians had destroyed 75% of the Israeli Air Force! The same communication told us that the Egyptian bombers had counter-attacked with a crushing assault on Israeli bases. Amer continued with the information that Egyptian ground forces had penetrated Israel through the Negev. These reports (which were fantastic to say the least) contributed largely in sowing confusion and distorting our appreciation of the situation. At that point when our radar signalled to us that machines coming from Egypt were flying towards Israel, no doubt crossed our mind. We were instantly persuaded that it was true. They were Israeli bombers returning after carrying out their mission against Egypt.*

So by noon we had a war with three Arab armies, which would soon be reinforced by contingents from more distant Arab lands. But by the time the grave news of Jordan's initiative came to us in

Tel Aviv, we had the compensating knowledge that we had won a decisive battle against Egypt's main striking force. Cairo's failure was one not only of technique and valor, but also of arrogance.

The result of the Israeli-Jordan war makes it almost impossible to believe that Jordan had entered the battle with bold determination —and Israel with strong reluctance. But this was the truth. The Jordanian Prime Minister, Sa'ad Jum'a, had said in his morning broadcast: "For many years we have been waiting for this battle which will wipe out the shame of the past." In a contrary spirit, it could be said that Israel, for many years, had nourished the hope that Arab-Jewish coexistence would find its first expression in a settlement with Jordan. The meeting of Faisal with Chaim Weizmann in 1918, the direct negotiations with King Abdullah at Shuneh in 1949, and occasional symptoms of realistic moderation in King Hussein's policy had all contributed to the positive image which Israel carried of the Hashemite dynasty. There was nothing here of the inhuman virulence which marked the attitude of other Arab nationalists toward Israel's existence. Even in wars, an unspoken assumption of ultimate accord hovered over the relations between Israel and Jordan. General Uzi Narkiss, commander of our central front, described the first artillery bombardment of Monday morning in his diary as a "salvo to uphold Jordanian honor." But the Jordanian capture of Government House, together with the encirclement of Israeli positions on Mount Scopus, had a far more serious effect. Unlike the dispatch of shells, these measures changed the strategic position to Israel's peril. By early afternoon an Israeli armored brigade, held back in reserve, was moving from the Tel Aviv area up the hills to Jerusalem.

Having explained our case and position to the world press, to the ambassadors of major powers, and through our embassies, to all friendly governments, I felt that my own work in Tel Aviv was done. At about three o'clock, I set out for Jerusalem. As we drove up from the coast we found the road thick with ministerial cars. War has its own idiom and postures to which peaceful men adapt themselves only with reluctant difficulty. Thus, many incongruous things happened on the afternoon of June 5. The news that a special Knesset session would convene in Jerusalem at four o'clock had obligingly been broadcast by our national radio station to the Israeli public— and to the Jordanian artillery. We had thus made our seat of government a precise and inviting target.

As our car reached the Bab-el-Wad Valley, which marks the confluence of the coastal plain with the Judean Hills, we found ourselves in an absurd encounter between civilian parliamentarians on their way to the Knesset, and Israeli tanks and infantry engaging the enemy across the hills north of Jerusalem. The situation became even more picturesque when we were joined by David Ben Gurion in a traffic jam of impossible intricacy at the very heart of the battle area. Somehow, the military and civilian police sorted us all out, sending the parliamentarians on their way and leaving the soldiers to get on with their task. Entering the city, we could see the advance columns of Colonel Mordechai ("Motta") Gur's Paratroop Brigade moving towards Jerusalem from the south in a convoy of buses such as those which usually carried schoolchildren on excursions across the countryside.

Eshkol's speech that night to a tense and crowded Chamber, like his radio broadcast to the nation, was to be enigmatic about our military progress. He concluded with a restrained and implicit reference to Jordan:

> *Again we announce we shall not attack any state as long as it does not wage war against us. But anyone attacking us will meet with our full power of self-defense and our capacity to defeat his forces.*

Our assumption on June 4 had been that Tel Aviv and the coastal area would be front-line positions with civilians sustaining heavy casualties from Egyptian air attacks, while Jerusalem would be a tranquil oasis far behind the lines. King Hussein's decision had changed those perspectives. The Knesset itself had now become a target for Jordanian artillery, which was also raining shells on other buildings in northwestern Jerusalem, including the Hebrew University and the National Museum. When darkness fell, the Cabinet convened in one of the Knesset's air-raid shelters. While waiting for the Prime Minister to arrive, we heard a report from a briefing officer, Brigadier General Ze'evi of the General Staff. His main theme was our phenomenal triumph in Egypt and the destruction of the main body of the Jordanian and Syrian air forces. He ended his otherwise factual account with the sensational words: "Israel is now the only air power in the Middle East."

We began our official session with as much formality as our cramped physical conditions would allow. It was clear that our main concern was with Jerusalem. The crash of falling shells was ominously near. When one minister asked to draw the attention to the Jordanian bombardment of Jerusalem, there was a moment of humorous relief. We should all have had to be deaf to have our "attention" focused on anything else. It was now well understood that the defense of western Jerusalem would involve the need to capture the eastern part; that once an Israeli army entered the Old City it would be historically and emotionally impossible to relinquish it to Jordanian hands again; and that unlike any other sector of the front, this one involved international repercussions which would carry the war far beyond its regional context. Some ministers began to speculate on what our attitude should be to the political future of Old Jerusalem if its capture became inevitable. My own proposal was that we should now act in response to the needs of security, and leave the political consequences for later discussion. The problems of the city's juridical status and of the Holy Places of Christianity and Islam were far too intricate to be made the subject of decisions before the Old City was in our hands. This approach commended itself to most of our colleagues, and the Prime Minister summed up, with Menachem Begin's endorsement: "We are going to take the Old City of Jerusalem in order to remove the danger of the bombardment and the shelling incessantly being carried out by Jordan."

Cables now began to reach me from United Nations headquarters in New York. The Security Council had come into session to hear Ambassador Rafael's account of Israel's resistance to Egyptian aggression. The Egyptian representative, Ambassador Mohamed El-Kony, had stated that "for several hours now the Israeli armed forces and the Israeli air force have again committed a cowardly and treacherous aggression against my country." This was rather hard even for Security Council members to take; after all, scarcely four days had passed since Mr. El-Kony had announced that Egypt regarded itself as "in a state of active war" with Israel and asked nothing of the United Nations except that it keep its nose out of the whole affair. El-Kony now went on: "My country has no other choice than to defend itself by all means at its disposal, in accordance with Article 51 of the Charter of the United Nations." Ambassador Rafael had made eloquent response. But his cables informed me that some delegations, including those of France and India, were beginning to formulate resolutions which would call both for a cease-fire and for withdrawal of forces to the positions held the previous day.

Israel was living the military hour and there was little thought for political complexities. Nobody in our country was paying much heed to the Security Council, which had done everything during the previous two weeks to forfeit any title to international deference or Israeli respect. Yet I could not expel from my mind a sense of fatal, historic repetition. Here again we were breaking out of the closing circle of Arab aggression, and here again plans were being laid to see that our neck was restored as soon as possible into the encircling noose. It was all very well for some Israelis, in the hour of victory, to believe that nothing could now happen abroad that would affect our purpose and destiny. The stark fact remained that on the only occasion—in 1956—on which we had been pressed by a unanimous world to give up the fruits of victory without obtaining peace, our response had been to yield, and not to resist. The prospect that we might lose at the conference table what was being gained on the battlefield would, within a few days, become an obsessive Israeli anxiety. By virtue of my special responsibility and particular memories, I was already in the grip of that possibility. That there would be a call for cease-fire was inevitable, and if things went on as they were going, the time was near when Israel could reconcile herself to it. But a unanimous international policy for restoring the previous lines was a far graver matter. If such a resolution was adopted, Israel would either be pried loose of her gains without peace or, at best, be left to possess them in a situation of international isolation, boycott and political blockade.

It was a normal United Nations practice to accompany a cease-fire resolution with a call for restoration of previous lines. A special effort of imagination and intellectual resourcefulness would be needed if these two concepts were to be separated. My own task was to ensure that a cease-fire resolution was not accompanied by any automatic restoration of the territorial status quo. Eshkol thought that I should go to New York to appeal to world opinion on the righteousness of our resistance, and above everything else, to ensure that the military victory now taking shape would not be frittered away by a call for withdrawal without a negotiated peace.

I made my short way home, amid the noise of shells and mortar bombs. Suzy and the children had been taking up their position in the air-raid shelters which, to my unexpected benefit, my predecessors had integrated into the Foreign Minister's residence. My eleven-year-old daughter thought that the air-raid shelter was much more fun than her regular bedroom on the second floor. Here was a wonderful new world of candles and paraffin lamps, of emergency food supplies and telephone cables and switchboards, designed to keep the minister in touch with the world from his subterranean confines. The shells and bombs were now getting louder. In the midst of the collective triumph, there was much individual tragedy. Many of our young men were falling in the sands of northern Sinai, and the hospitals in

Jerusalem were filling up. Much death, damage and loss had been inflicted on Musrara, the poorest of Jerusalem's Jewish quarters, and if the Old City had to be stormed within the next day, many young lives would be snuffed out. The knowledge that calm diplomats in New York were arranging for all our sacrifices to become worthless and our gains to be annulled without the compensation of peace filled me with a sharp rage and a corresponding determination.

It was past midnight on June 7 when I said farewell to my children in the shelter. Suzy came out of the front door to say goodbye on the doorstep. As we drew apart from our embrace, we both felt a rush of wind passing between us at face level. Neither of us could give it any explanation. I was on my way to the coast when the experienced policeman gave my wife the engaging information that a sniper's bullet, or, alternatively, a piece of shrapnel, had neatly bisected the few feet of space between our heads.

My journey from Jerusalem to Lod Airport took the best part of three hours. I embarked with Moshe Raviv on a twin-engine aircraft of the Arkia Company. It had an unconvincing look about it. Our problem was that a small part of the Syrian air force still existed, with radar facilities intact, and none of the international companies was flying in or out of Israel. Our pilot proposed to go to Athens at the lowest possible altitude compatible with flight, until we were outside any reasonable range. Once in Athens, we would explore the feasibility of getting to New York. As dawn broke in poignant flash of scarlet beauty, the Acropolis came into my view. The Distinguished Visitors' Lounge at the Athens airport had an air of normality in comparison with the flames and din which I had left behind. After complex discussions around the desks of major airline companies we discovered that our best chance of getting to New York in time for me to have an effect on the Security Council discussions lay in a KLM airliner which would stop over in Amsterdam and then continue across the Atlantic.

We had given our ambassadors in major European capitals some notice of my itinerary. When I reached Amsterdam I was greeted by Ambassador Daniel Levin, our representative in The Hague; Ambassador Remez from London; and Ambassador Eytan from Paris. There was also a forest of television cameras trying to probe my knowledge and my mood. I referred them to a broadcast by Generals Rabin and Hod (which they had made a short time before my departure from Israel) outlining the full extent of Arab air losses. Three hundred enemy aircraft had been destroyed between dawn and dusk. Nothing of the kind had ever happened in the history of air warfare. I said less about the battle on land. Weeks later the Netherlands Foreign

Minister, Dr. Josef Luns, told me that he had scanned my features on the television screen and had adduced from them, for the first time, that the talk of Arab victories in press communiqués were either fictitious or beyond my knowledge. European and American newspapers were still publishing victory statements from both sides, and world opinion was plunged in doubt and confusion.

15

A Political Success 1967

WE FLEW IN DAYLIGHT WESTWARD FROM AMSTERDAM TO NEW YORK. IT WAS the evening of June 6 and I received hourly reports from the pilot's radio of continuing Israeli advances. When I left Jerusalem, we had already passed from anxious defense of the western City to an assault on its eastern part, from which so much death and ruin had afflicted us. Jordanian forces were retreating in the West Bank, and Israeli armor was advancing in Sinai with its main thrust toward the west, and a vital push southward toward Sharm el-Sheikh. It came to my mind that if the Arab governments had any rationality, they would now try to secure international pressure for a cease-fire, together with withdrawal to the previous armistice lines. This seemed to be so logical that I thought that on reaching New York I would find a cease-fire–plus-withdrawal resolution already drafted. I could hardly assume that our adversaries would match their military failure by political improvidence. I knew that Ambassadors Rafael and Harman were working busily to avoid a premature withdrawal resolution in the Security Council, but I did not know what progress they were making in Washington or at the United States mission in New York.

We were three hours from New York when a telegram from Ambassador Rafael reached me through the pilot's cabin. It told me that the Security Council debate was taking place under the massive scrutiny of the world mass media, that no resolution had yet been adopted and that I would be expected to make an address as soon as I landed. The hospitable Dutch steward and air hostess made me comfortable in a separate cabin with a wooden table on which I began to scribble notes for the address that I would make to the Security Council.

At Kennedy Airport, Ambassador Rafael and members of the Israeli mission conferred with me rapidly. There had been much discussion in Washington and New York about whether to accompany the cease-fire resolution with a clause about withdrawal. The decision now lay in President Johnson's hands.

I made immediate contact by telephone with Ambassador Arthur Goldberg to reinforce Rafael's insistence on an unconditional cease-fire which would leave other matters open for later and more deliberate discussion. I then made my way to the United Nations, where I conferred with the chairman of the Security Council, Ambassador Hans Tabor of Denmark, who promised to give me the floor immediately.

Throughout June 5, consultations among members of the Security Council had failed to develop a consensus. France and India had suggested formulations which would have linked the cessation of hostilities with a withdrawal of forces to the June 4 positions. This would mean that 80,000 heavily armed Egyptian forces would have to be re-established on Israel's southern border, and that the Egyptians would return to control Sharm el-Sheikh and blockade the Straits of Tiran! This was very strong meat, probably too strong in its anti-Israel bias even for the tolerant digestion of the Security Council. I learned from my colleagues that the Soviet Union, throughout the whole of Monday, June 5, had shown no urgency about any Security Council action on a cease-fire. Ambassador Fedorenko had been unavailable for many hours, and when he was found, he insisted on a draft which would include a violent condemnation of Israel's aggression. Since no majority at the Security Council could be mobilized for such a text, the effect and, probably, the intention of the Soviet move was to delay the call for a cease-fire, presumably because Moscow believed that Nasser was winning.

The deadlock seemed complete. The Soviet Union refused to accept a cease-fire without a condemnation of Israel, while the United States would accept a cease-fire only if it contained no condemnation and no paragraph on withdrawal. So Ambassador Tabor produced a consensus calling "upon the governments concerned as a first step to take forthwith all measures for an immediate cease-fire and for a cessation of all military activities in the area."

I felt that Israel had gained an important first round, but no more. The danger of international pressure for restoring the Egyptian troop concentrations and blockade had been averted for the moment. But it was clear that once the cease-fire was in effect, the Arabs and Soviets would return to the matter of withdrawal. The Arab delegations were torn in conflict between dream and reality. According to the official version in Cairo, Amman and Damascus, Arab armies were sweeping forward deep into Israeli territory. If Arab delegations now acquiesced in a resolution for cease-fire and withdrawal, they would be telling their people a new and unpalatable truth. Victorious armies seldom plead for their own withdrawal and they are in no hurry about cease-fires. As so often in the policy of our neighbors, rhetoric and pretense overcame concrete interests. The Egyptian delegation, in particular, refused to accept the cease-fire unless it was accompanied by a condemnation and a call for Israeli withdrawal. During every minute of this obstinacy, Sinai sands were being swallowed up by Israel's advance.

In these conditions I addressed the Security Council and millions of listeners in the early-morning hours of June 7. My first sentence was greeted with audible surprise: "I have just come from Jerusalem to tell the Security Council that Israel, by its independent effort and sacrifice, has passed from serious danger to successful and glorious resistance." For multitudes of people, puzzled by contradictory communiqués, this was the first outright assertion that Israel was winning the war.

I went on to describe how a few days ago "Israel was being strangled in its maritime approaches to the whole eastern half of the world." I portrayed the Jordanian assault, the shells falling on institutions of health and culture in the city of Jerusalem, the arrival of Iraqi troops to reinforce the Jordanian front, and the convergence of Algerian and Kuwaiti troops toward Egypt. Syrian units, including artillery, were bombarding Israeli villages in the Jordan Valley. "In short, there was peril for Israel wherever it looked. Its manpower had been hastily mobilized, its economy and commerce were beating with feeble pulse, its streets were dark and empty. There was an apocalyptic air of approaching peril, and Israel faced its dangers alone."

I groped for some way of identifying these countries with Israel's predicament on the blockade. I glanced around the table at which the countenances of diplomats emerged behind flags bearing their countries' names—the United States of America, Canada, United Kingdom, France, Denmark, Brazil, Japan, India. I decided to give a concrete representation of Israel's dilemma: "To understand how Israel felt, one has merely to look round this table and imagine a foreign power forcibly closing New York or Montreal, London or Marseilles, Toulon or Copenhagen, Rio or Tokyo or Bombay harbor. How would your governments react? What would you do? How long would you wait?"

I briefly refuted the Soviet accusation of Israeli "aggression" and turned my eyes in conclusion directly to Nasser:

> *As he looks around him at the arena of battle, at the wreckage of planes and tanks, at the collapse of intoxicated hopes, might not the Egyptian ruler ponder whether anything was achieved by that disruption? What had it brought him but strife, conflict and the stern criticism of progressive men throughout the world? Israel in recent days had proved its steadfastness and vigour. It is now willing to demonstrate its instinct for peace. Let us build a new system of relationships from the wreckage of the old. Let us discern across the darkness the vision of a better and a brighter dawn.*

It was long past midnight when I regained my hotel room. All the messages reaching me told me that Israeli forces were rushing from one victory to another. Our political fortunes were also high. Telephone calls and cables were reaching my hotel and our UN mission through the night, indicating that my speech had reached a massive audience and had apparently evoked strong reactions.

President Johnson had let us know bluntly that the American attitude on withdrawal would be strongly influenced by the reaction of public opinion to Israel's case. If he were to hold firm against pressures for our withdrawal, he could only do so on the foundation of strong public support for Israel. His advisers had told us that it "was up to Israel to win support." I therefore studied the American press on June 7 and 8 with anxiety. It soon became clear that in this respect my mission had not failed. The *New York Times* reported the unprecedentedly large audience which had been glued to television and radio sets all over the world. It wrote generously of my exposition: "Abba Eban took honors for mastery of phrase-making and drew applause from the gallery. A primary feature was Mr. Eban's composure compared with the indignation of Arab representatives over a cease-fire that would cost them the territory already won by the Israelis. Last night was one of television's finest moments." A chain of thirty major newspapers in the Midwest wrote that "Americans who listened to Israel's Foreign Minister Abba Eban's address at the historic session of the Security Council on Tuesday night heard one of the great diplomatic speeches of all time. Eloquent in its phrasing, brilliantly devastating in its array of facts against the Arab enemy, Eban's speech at the same time avoided any semblance of boasting over Israel's sensational military triumphs." The Chicago *Tribune* went so far as to call my address enthusiastically "one of the great speeches of modern times." Ralph McGill wrote in a widely syndicated column that I "had cut up the Egyptian delegates with the sword of truth." A Washington paper remarked that "Eban flew out of the bleeding, war-tortured Jerusalem to make a remarkably eloquent defense of the nation's response to Arab provocation. He spoke from a position of strength, but with the magnanimity and wisdom that gives hope for the future." Columbia made a record of my speech which quickly sold tens of thousands of copies and I donated the royalties through B'nai B'rith to the Emergency Fund of the United Jewish Appeal.

When I turned to consider how all this was being received in Jerusalem, I saw the fantastic contrast between the atmosphere surrounding me in the political arena abroad and the climate of politics in Israel itself. When I spoke to Suzy and some of my Foreign Ministry associates by telephone on Wednesday morning, they reported that a determined attempt was being made to use my absorption in the political struggle to bring about my removal! Newspapers were being persuaded to underestimate or ignore the international support generated by my speech on June 7. Few of them confessed that there was any significance in the fact that withdrawal resolutions had been presented and defeated. I had to face the fact that a speech which hundreds of the world's newspapers had hailed as the vindication of Israel's struggle was reported scantily and without comment in my own country. Before I left Israel, two major newspapers had written that I ought not to have gone abroad to worry about what the powers and the Security Council might do, since this no longer had any importance. As a result of the "Hamtana" period before the war, our military triumph was now being crowned by political success. Yet partisan journalists were demoralizing our public by assertions that the political action taken by the Eshkol government before and after the fighting had been superfluous, and even harmful.

Many Israelis were still under the traumatic sensations to which they had been subjected. Amid the triumph, the memories of the preceding agony lingered on. Logic told Israelis that unless we showed political vigilance, our military gains could be blown away like cobwebs. But emotion had put logic to flight and set up waves of intolerant rancor. Israel's "finest hour" had lasted in its full radiance for no more than two days. There was still a joyous air surrounding Israel abroad, but at home the knives were out. I wished to curtail my stay in New York. On the other hand, I reflected that Israel would look remarkably foolish if, the day after my departure, a resolution on withdrawal to the previous lines was adopted.

When the Security Council assembled at one o'clock on June 7, Soviet Ambassador Fedorenko asked for the "condemnation of Israel." This was eccentric, since Israel was now basking in the sun of admiring world opinion. He went on to propose a new cease-fire resolution with the additional demand that a time limit be fixed for compliance. The deadline was to be at 2000 hours (8 P.M.) on June 7, 1967, which would be midnight in the Middle East.

I thought it wise to be in close touch with Ambassador Goldberg to find out how American policy was evolving. He proposed to present an American draft to the Security Council, looking beyond the cease-fire toward the horizons of political stability:

> *The Security Council calls for discussions promptly thereafter amongst the parties concerned, using such third-party or United Nations assistance they may wish, looking towards the establishment of final arrangements and comprising the withdrawal and disengagement of armed personnel, the renunciation of force regardless of its nature, the maintenance of vital international rights and the establishment of a stable and durable peace in the Middle East.*

The text had gone through an interesting evolution before it reached this point. In one of its versions it called not for the establishment of a stable and durable peace, but for "a revitalized armistice." I have rarely argued with more passion against any proposal than I now used in the attempt to eradicate the "armistice" concepts from the American draft. I pointed out that we were at a turning point in Middle Eastern history. We should banish all concepts of armistice from our minds, our hearts and our vocabulary. Cease-fires, truces and armistices had been tried for two decades. They had all burst into flames. The only thing that had never been tried was peace. I urged Goldberg to seek approval for a resolution in which the cease-fire be succeeded not by an armistice, but by the higher vision of a permanent peace.

These views were duly communicated to Washington. By the morning of June 8 I heard to my relief that the United States had approved the idea of calling for a negotiated peace. Armistices, "revitalized" or otherwise, were no longer in vogue.

Meanwhile the Soviet and Arab representatives were arguing against the American proposal at long-winded leisure, as though it mattered nothing to them that Israeli armies were still on the advance. At this point the Soviet Union suffered an unexpected setback. It could hardly be a convincing champion of the Arabs if it turned out to be more Arab than the Arabs themselves. Yet this is what now happened. The scope of their military disaster had become fully understood by the Arab governments. The Egyptian delegate, who, a few hours before, had been resisting any cease-fire resolution unless it was accompanied by Israeli withdrawal, was now told by Cairo to get a cease-fire as soon as possible. An air of humiliation was written deep on the face of Ambassador El-Kony as he announced to the Security Council that Egypt accepted a cease-fire without conditions. He then went to the small lounge behind the Council Chamber, where he was seen unashamedly dissolved in tears.

It was clear to me that my immediate mission in New York had been accomplished. The cease-fire had been separated from any call for withdrawal so that our military victory would now be the starting-point for the next stage in the question for a solution. I had also been able to help secure an American position, based on a forward-looking approach. The idea of leaving the armistice behind and moving forward to peace had taken root.

And yet, hostilities on the Syrian front had still not been suspended. The cease-fire had not been accepted by the Syrian armed forces, and it was probable that only a few days would pass before the Arab states and their Soviet allies would regroup for a political counteroffensive to bring about Israeli withdrawal. In the meantime, my friends and family in Jerusalem were urgently pressing me to return home. Our military and political fortunes were at a high pitch, but the domestic scene was complex. Many had forgotten that we had often won military victories in the past, but had never been able to conserve them long enough to translate them into a new reality of peace and security. A leading Israeli scientist had written an article suggesting that Israel's posture should be one of contempt for international opinion: "We should just bang on the table and say that we had won the war, and that was that."

I could not deny that it would be satisfying to adopt this somewhat unscientific counsel, but how could I forget that on the previous occasion ten years before, when a unanimous world had called for our retreat, a government headed by an admittedly militant Prime Minister had folded its tents and agreed to withdraw within forty-eight hours? If there was now a possibility to have much of the world on our side in our refusal to withdraw without peace, it seemed reckless to neglect the prospect.

Our dialogue with the United States had not been unclouded.

During the fighting an American signal ship, the *Liberty*, had been inadvertently attacked and damaged by Israeli aircraft. Thirty-seven of those on board had been killed, and heavy damage sustained. It was plain that the vessel had entered the fighting area to keep Washington in touch with the course of the war. In view of the global responsibilities of the United States, this was fair enough, but it seemed inevitable that those who took risks might sometimes incur tragic sacrifice.

I had intended to spend a day in Washington to learn the direction of American policy at first hand. I now abandoned this decision and contented myself with long telephone conversations in which I exchanged views with leading officials in Washington. One White House adviser informed me that Mr. Johnson had watched and heard my speech in the Security Council with appreciation. He thought it "worth several divisions" to Israel. Clearly, the President still deemed it important for Israel to have a positive impact on American opinion. The official went on to reflect that it seemed strange that Syria, the originator of the war, might be the only one which seemed to be getting off without injury. Might it not turn out paradoxically that less guilty Arab states such as Jordan would have suffered heavy loss while Syria would be free to start the whole deadly sequence again?

I deduced from these remarks that official Washington would not be too grieved if Syria suffered some penalties from the war which it had started, so that Jordan's moderate posture up to June 1967 should not seem to be penalized.

On the evening of June 8, I set out for home. With me, in addition to Moshe Raviv, were two friends from the newspaper world, Theodore White, the celebrated chronicler of American presidential elections, and Dick Clurman of *Time-Life*. Apart from us, the plane was mostly occupied by young men and women who had registered their names for voluntary service in Israel.

It was midafternoon by the time that we reached Lod Airport. As we flew over the runway I could see long convoys comprising every kind of vehicle, military and civilian, winding their way up towards the north. The accent of crisis had clearly shifted to the Syrian front.

When I reached the Prime Minister's office in Tel Aviv shortly thereafter, discussions about the Golan Heights were in full spate. After abortive attempts on the second day of the war to invade Dan, Dafna and Sha'ar Yishuv with infantry and tanks, the Syrians had returned to their forts on the Golan Heights from which they were bombarding our settlements in the plain. The question was whether we should storm the heights or not. Eshkol explained to me that the strongest hesitation had come from Dayan, who feared that our forces would become overextended and that the Soviet Union would be more likely to intervene on Syrian's behalf than in any other sector. Unexpectedly the Mapam ministers, with their intimate concern for the kibbutzim in Upper Galilee, were urging a reluctant Dayan to force the heights. It was my duty to report that some people in Washington would not be put out if Syria were denied a posture of immunity and success. It was plain to me that an Israeli military success on the Syrian front would not incur displeasure in Washington.

All this time General David Elazar, commanding the northern sector, had been in suspense while he, his fellow officers and the farmers' representatives pleaded their case at army headquarters and in interviews with ministers. Eventually Dayan acceded to the proposal for forcing the heights and went over to a characteristically vigorous prosecution of the plan.

The fighting was savage and our losses of valiant young men tore at the nation's heart. The battle followed the classic pattern of infantry engagements, including hand-to-hand combat in which all the advantage belonged to the Syrians embattled on the heights. Yet by nightfall on June 9 General Elazar had penetrated the heights at many points, and the road to Kuneitra lay open to the extreme north of the front.

June 10 was full of suspense as our forces pressed onward across the heights. In Tel Aviv I was bombarded by anguished cables from United Nations headquarters, where the Security Council was in permanent session. The Soviet Union was attempting to defend its Arab protégés by heavy political pressure. Resolutions calling for the immediate observance of the cease-fire were put before the Council one after the other; a stage was reached at which Soviet threats became so concrete that the United States was thrown into a global alarm. Goldberg, through Rafael, was conveying to us President Johnson's urgent request that we cease fire immediately. American representatives were openly hinting to us that Soviet intervention no longer seemed inconceivable. The hot lines were at work.

By the time Kuneitra was in our hands and the road to Damascus open, we all felt that the political reasons for calling a halt were compelling. The cease-fire became effective at 1800 hours (6 P.M.) on June 10, and with it, the Six-Day War had come to an end. In less than two days of intense fighting on the Syrian front, we had lost 115 killed and 322 wounded. Syrian casualties were estimated at 1,000 killed, 600 captured and many thousands more wounded.

Clearly, the Soviet Union had not given very effective protection to the Syrian regime. There was rage in Moscow. In the Security

Council debates on June 9 and 10, Fedorenko had warned that our diplomatic relations with the Soviet Union would be broken if we did not halt in our tracks. By the time Kuneitra had fallen, the Soviet commitment to break diplomatic relations had become too explicit for dignified retreat.

On the afternoon of June 10 Ambassador Chuvakhin, accompanied by his counselor, stormed into my temporary office in Tel Aviv. In a trembling voice the ambassador read out a note in a sonorous Russian, which his associate translated into excellent Hebrew with an even more indignant intonation:

> *News has just been received that Israeli armed forces, in disregard of the cease-fire resolution of the Security Council, are continuing warlike actions carrying out the conquest of Syrian territory and moving towards Damascus.*
>
> *If Israel will not immediately cease warlike acts, the Soviet Union, together with other peace-loving states, will adopt sanctions with all the consequences arising therefrom.*
>
> *The Government of the USSR announces that in the light of the continued aggression by Israel against the Arab States and the flagrant breach of the Security Council's resolutions, the USSR Government has adopted a decision to break diplomatic relations with Israel.*

My short service as Foreign Minister had not included any experience of breaking relations with Great Powers. I replied to the excited ambassador that Israel had no intention of "moving towards Damascus." I added that Syria, with Soviet instigation, had been the originator of the war. I expressed regret that the Soviet Union during the ambassador's mission had shown such little understanding of realities in Israel. I added that the fact that a sharp conflict existed between us should encourage us to intensify our diplomatic dialogue, not to break it off: "Surely diplomacy is needed when there is conflict, not when there is harmony." Chuvakhin replied that this sounded logical; however, he had not come to argue about logic, but to announce his government's intention of breaking off relations. To my surprise and embarrassment, I noticed that his eyes were filled with tears. I could not deduce whether this was due to nostalgic regret at leaving Israel or some apprehension about the nature of his welcome in Moscow. It was well known that the Soviet embassy in Israel had been reporting that Israel was unlikely to fight, and that if she did, would not show much unity or prowess.

Other Communist states in Eastern Europe swiftly followed the Soviet Union in breaking diplomatic relations with us. Only Rumania held out. The rupture with Moscow was received in Israel with remarkable placidity. There was and is no need to regret the serious efforts I had made in the past few years to improve relations with Communist Eastern Europe. Not to have made them would have been sheer neglect.

In any case, Israeli life was being lived at a pitch of emotion above the reach of diplomatic events. The public joy was clouded by hundreds of private tragedies, and our relations with the Middle East were now being enacted on a new level of experience. The departure of Ambassador Chuvakhin had a curiously trivial dimension amid so many large events. The barbed wire which had stretched as an ugly scar across Jerusalem had been removed, and thousands of Arabs and Jews were now coming together in a strange mixture of political interest and intellectual fascination. The Defense Minister, Moshe Dayan, and the Mayor of Jerusalem, Teddy Kollek, had opened the city to free movement. They had given the unity of Jerusalem an imaginative expression. Great convoys of buses and taxis were bringing thousands of Israelis up to Jerusalem every day to look with exaltation at the Wailing Wall. We had come back to the cradle of our nationhood to stay there forever, and the reunion was watched across the world with awed respect. Beyond Jerusalem, too, Israelis were feeling their way toward a human contact with the cities and villages of the West Bank. Those of middle age and beyond who had known the undivided Palestine of the Mandatory regime recovered their links with Hebron, Ramallah and Nablus, Jericho, Jenin and Bethlehem. Some of the names were saturated with Jewish memories. The generation born and bred since 1948 saw a chance to break out of the claustrophobic isolation which had separated them from the Arab world. The strange thing was the deference of the conquerors to the vanquished. A world hitherto closed in mystery was now open before us, and the old rhetoric about Arab-Israeli coexistence became more concrete. And so, Israelis took in the unique sounds and smells of Arab cities and villages, with their braying donkeys and bustling markets and the ever-present smell of strong coffee, spices and home-baked bread. They bargained cheerfully in Arab markets, contemplated landscapes familiar from Biblical and pre-Israeli history, and marveled at the new variety and spaciousness of our environment. Having satisfied themselves with these sights and being assured that they were theoretically available, most Israelis were to show a diminishing interest in the West Bank as the months went by.

The Arab population received our scrutiny with phlegmatic calm.

Those Arabs who were politically conscious thought of themselves as passing through a bad dream, which would soon end in the usual way, with the United Nations sending Israel back to previous positions, putting the barbed-wire fences neatly into place and avoiding any nonsense about Jews and Arabs living together. For the Arab masses with their simpler shape of minds, the change had been too quick to be absorbed. Villages and small townships lived on in their typically self-contained structure, calmly, independent of central institutions. But there was a psychological change. Neither Jews nor Arabs saw in each other the monstrous characteristics with which propaganda had made them familiar. There was as yet no terrorist movement to shake the Arabs in the administered areas out of their docility. Palestine Arab leaders, mayors and heads of religious communities spoke to us frankly about the iniquities of Arab governments which had persistently led them into war and then left them to their fate. In many places Arab populations had believed that Israelis would do to them what Arab armies would certainly have done to Israelis had the fortune of battle gone the other way. They now knew that they were safe. But many who had feared the worst had concluded that prudence and safety lay across the Jordan. There was also a fear that the river would come down as a barrier, separating the Palestine Arabs on its West Bank from access to relatives, bank accounts and centers of Arab sovereignty.

It was the general belief of Israelis as well as of Arabs that great events would soon unfold in the international arena and that the situation created by the war would not endure for more than a few weeks. For Israelis, the military hour had ended and the political hour had begun. In objective truth the political struggle had begun at the Security Council meetings, but in the heat of battle, Israel had been almost the only country in the world not to have been gripped and stirred by the Security Council debates of early June.

I was naturally the focus of this tension. In the Security Council debates I had tentatively sketched out a policy which saw the existing cease-fire lines as our starting point and a contractual peace settlement as our objective. I had been acting more on intuition than on specific Cabinet decisions. I felt that if we returned to the strait jacket of the demarcation lines and failed to win a permanent peace, the sacrifice of the past week would have been recklessly squandered. At the same time, I thought that it would be wrong for us to be swept away in such a wave of emotion as to regard the new cease-fire lines as the permanent boundaries of Israel. My conclusion was that we should stand firm while keeping options open for a negotiated peace. In press conferences in the second week of June, I said, "What Israel wants is very simple, security and peace. But," I added, "security and peace do have some territorial implications."

Although the Arabs and Soviets had been unable to get the cease-fire resolution accompanied by a withdrawal order, their failure was not necessarily final. Sure enough, on June 13 the Soviet Union asked the Security Council to adopt a resolution vigorously condemning Israel's aggressive activities against Arab states and demanding that "Israel should immediately and unconditionally remove all its troops from the territory of those states and withdraw behind the armistice lines."

The adoption of these paragraphs would mean that our military victory had been followed by swift political defeat. In contacts with Washington I urged a strong and negative response to the Soviet assault. It was quickly forthcoming. Ambassador Goldberg said on June 13, "If ever there was a prescription for renewed hostilities, the Soviet draft resolution is that prescription." Goldberg then went on to advocate a movement away from the tense past toward a better future. The object must be "the conversion of the armistice agreements of 1949 into a permanent peace."

The Security Council's meeting on June 14 was a significant political victory for Israel. When the Soviet resolution came to the vote, only four states—Bulgaria, India, Mali and the Soviet Union—supported the operative paragraph "condemning" Israel's "aggressive activities." The second paragraph, calling for "the withdrawal behind the armistice lines," obtained only 6 votes instead of the necessary 9.

Many Israelis could hardly believe their eyes or ears. In contrast to 1956, our victory in 1967 was not condemned by an international body. Nor was there any pressure to have its results rescinded by a withdrawal to the previous lines. I felt justified in believing that this result was at least partly due to our "Hamtana" preparations and to the spectacular meeting of the Security Council on June 7. It was clear that both the Arabs and the Soviets had underestimated the depth of support which Israel had won in world opinion.

Moscow now reached the conclusion that it would stand a better chance of success in the broader arena of the General Assembly. Accordingly, the Soviet Union initiated steps for bringing the General Assembly into special session.

We were obviously in for a hard time in a parliamentary forum hopelessly weighted against our cause. To prevent hostile resolutions for condemnation and withdrawal from being adopted, we would have to mobilize between forty and fifty countries. Any realistic possibility of achieving this would require close cooperation with the United

States. In the General Assembly, however, the United States does not have the same power to frustrate undesirable resolutions as it does in the Security Council.

The difficulties which I confronted abroad were now compounded by domestic complications. If I believed that my adversaries were limited to the Soviet and Arab worlds, I would have been guilty of innocence, which is a politician's gravest sin. As I sought to rally our slender forces for the international struggle, I found myself beset by a virulent campaign at home. On June 13 in Jerusalem I had worked round the clock in a successful attempt to defeat the withdrawal resolution in the Security Council, telephoning, cabling and writing to our United Nations mission and capitals. That morning the newspaper *Ha'aretz* helpfully rewarded my efforts by calling for the appointment of a new Foreign Minister! This was a strange interpretation of patriotic duty.

The argumentation of the editorial writer was complex. He began by confessing that Israel had in fact gained great advantage by waiting a week or two before embarking on military resistance, and added that the reward for this prudence was now being reaped in the form of international opposition to our withdrawal. So far, so good. Things had worked out well. But, he went on, darkly, things might well have turned out otherwise if Israel had waited longer! The Foreign Minister was, in theory, one of twenty-one ministers and in reality would have to bear a special burden of responsibility in leading the nation's international defense. Now came the punch line: "Since *Ha'aretz* does not have faith in Mr. Eban's ability to carry out this task, a new Foreign Minister should be appointed." The implication was that to enjoy the faith of *Ha'aretz* was a constitutional necessity, rather like a parliamentary vote of confidence, without which an Israeli government had no right to function. The editorial went on to say generously that if we had a strong Prime Minister like Mr. Ben Gurion (who had "strongly" opposed our resistance on June 5), I could have served my ministry with efficiency. Since, however, we had "only" Mr. Eshkol (who had led the nation in the most victorious war of its history), a change in the Foreign Ministry was essential!

This article was so clearly partisan that it could not do its intended victim very much harm. The Labor Party *Davar* seized an unusual opportunity to rally sane opinion in an article that summarized the 1967 war with great lucidity. It went on to say:

Every intelligent and unprejudiced man knows very well that the Government's line of action has, so far, justified itself to a total degree. There was a war in which we won a glorious victory and which evokes enthusiasm across the entire world. The period of waiting has justified itself from the military viewpoint as well. We now enjoy a favourable public opinion such as we have never had before. To this day, the United States has not uttered a single word against our military actions. And its representative in the United Nations has struggled with intensity and success against Soviet attempts to get a resolution condemning Israel and calling for the withdrawal of her forces. This magnificent achievement is the fruit of the "hesitation" of the Government. Let us hope that this achievement will be prolonged.

Nevertheless, domestic politics continued to intrude on our international struggle. The press and the public, which had been apathetic about United Nations' actions in early June, were suddenly seized with panic in face of the forthcoming General Assembly session. This reflected a traumatic memory of the 1956 Sinai Campaign, when the General Assembly had been the arena of Israel's enforced retreat from its conquered territories. A debate now broke out in the press about the composition of the Israeli delegation to the Emergency Assembly. It was suggested that I should be "accompanied" to the United Nations by other ministers, including Dayan and Begin.

In a frank private conversation with the Prime Minister on June 15, I pointed out that the political struggle in the next few weeks would be as fateful as anything that had happened in our recent history. If the Prime Minister wanted me to carry the burden and to proclaim Israel's message to the world, he must liberate me from domestic intrigues. It would be as grotesque for two or three ministers to lead a delegation to the General Assembly as it would be for two or three generals to be in simultaneous command of an armored division. I told Eshkol that I had no intention of going to the United Nations if other ministers were sent, either as watchdogs or as publicity gimmicks.

Eshkol always responded well to candor. He promised to oppose any proposals which would divide my authority. His promise was kept. All the Israeli newspapers on June 16 carried the decision to put our delegation to the emergency session of the General Assembly unreservedly under my command.

The atmosphere surrounding the special session was becoming more dramatic by the hour. An announcement in Moscow said that Prime Minister Kosygin himself would head the Soviet delegation; that the heads of states and governments in socialist countries would represent their nations at the General Assembly; and that the Soviet Union hoped that President Johnson, President de Gaulle, Prime Minister Harold Wilson and other Presidents and Prime Ministers would come to New York, thus converting the Special Assembly into a universal summit meeting for the purpose of forcing Israel back to the armistice lines. Most Western governments declined to give Kosygin the satisfaction of sending their heads of government obediently in response to his summons.

On June 17 I set out for New York with my head of bureau, Emanuel Shimoni. At Kennedy Airport I learned that President Lyndon Johnson was to make a public speech on Monday morning ahead of the General Assembly session. He would not come to the United Nations meeting, for he did not wish to give recognition or deference to Kosygin's hostile initiative. From the White House came a message that a better symbolic impression would be made if the Monday-morning discussion, on which hundreds of millions of eyes would be turned, were to be held between the Soviet Union and Israel alone. The "David and Goliath" image would have a strong appeal to the chivalry of the American people.

Goldberg told us that the General Assembly was meeting under unprecedented publicity. The impact that the Israeli cause would make on public opinion would largely determine the course of American policy. Goldberg thought that the Soviets would try for a quick withdrawal within a week to ten days, and that our voting position was not good.

Goldberg's appraisal, as usual, was realistic. On the battlefield the confrontation had been between Israel and the Arabs, with the Soviet Union hovering in contingent menace over the scene. In the political arena, the roles were reversed. The struggle would be waged under Soviet leadership, with the Arabs in a secondary role. By coming himself with his own Foreign Minister and all the Communist Prime Ministers, Kosygin had ensured that whatever happened, the results would be crucial for the Soviet Union. In a week or two, Soviet prestige in the world would either have risen high or sunk low, according to the success or failure of its efforts to obtain the condemnation of Israel and an unconditional withdrawal of forces.

I sat up for most of the night of June 18 preparing my speech for the next morning. The question whether the United Nations is or is not an important forum cannot be answered simply. Everything depends on the context in which it works and on the power balance which it reflects. The United Nations is like a stage on which anything can be enacted—from high drama to sordid farce. Many of its activities in recent years had been marginal and trivial. But there have been moments in its career during which it has been the decisive arena in which nations contend for high stakes under the gaze of world opinion.

These thoughts came to me as I worked away into the night, writing and dictating, correcting, redrafting, destroying, mutilating and expanding, to the despair of patient secretaries who kept moving in an unceasing procession of coffee and sandwiches. At two o'clock I broke off to read cables from Jerusalem containing the usual roundup of press comment. The personal campaign against me seemed to have died down. But there were also one or two attacks of hysteria. In *Ma'ariv* on June 18, an Israeli scientist had published a venomous article affirming that if we had lost the war, those like myself who had voted "shamefully" for some delay on May 28 would have been responsible. The impact of this malice in the middle of the night, a few hours away from my duel with Kosygin, was so maddening that I had the absurd idea of deciding not to appear in the General Assembly at all. With some effort I put exaggerated sensitivity behind me, and at five o'clock, when the dawn was coming up over Central Park in the summer haze, I committed my final manuscript to the typists and snatched a few hours of sleep.

Although the General Assembly was to convene at eleven, the first round in the struggle would take place a little earlier. On my arrival on Saturday night I had been told something of the way in which President Johnson's mind was moving. I had even been able to have contact through Ambassador Harman with some of those who were advising the President on the formulation of his address. I was anxious to ensure that the thrust of his policy would remain riveted on the future, and that he would make clear that Israel's withdrawal from the cease-fire lines could not take place without a peace negotiation in which boundaries would be fixed by agreement.

The President came on the television screen at ten. After a brief allusion to the Vietnam conflict, he plunged into a definition of principles for peace in the Middle East.

This document has had a remarkable effect on the Middle Eastern crisis ever since. In the conditions of that morning, his speech stood out as an exercise in lucidity and international courage. He committed the United States to five principles: "First, the recognized right of national life. Second, justice for the refugees. Third, innocent maritime passage. Fourth, limits on the wasteful and destructive arms race. Fifth, political independence and territorial integrity for all."

The principles seemed general and innocent. Of more decisive interest was the specific interpretation that Johnson gave to them. He described the dispute in terms of a contrast between the past and the future. Peace would not be obtained by going back to the "fragile and often violated armistice." The principle of a "recognized right of national life" as well as "political independence and territorial integrity for all" brought the United States in headlong collision with the central theme of Arab nationalist ideology. After all, the nonrecognition of a separate, independent Israeli nationhood had been the foundation on which Arab belligerency had been nourished for twenty years. The principle of "justice for the refugees" was stated without any prejudicial material. The accent was not laid either on repatriation or on resettlement. "Innocent maritime passage" was enunciated on the basis of a specific assertion that violation of this principle had played a major part in more than one war.

It would be wrong to say that President Johnson's statement brought the United States into full identification with the Israeli position. But since Israel was attempting a negative result—to prevent a resolution for unconditional withdrawal—the Five Principles of June 19, 1967, gave us an important international opportunity.

With this encouragement I made my way to the United Nations building and forced my way through a forest of television cameras to the Israeli desk in the General Assembly Hall. At my side were Gideon Rafael and other veterans of our UN struggle. Around me were members of our special parliamentary delegation, including Golda Meir, at that time a member of the Knesset and Secretary-General of the Labor Party. The hall was crowded, with ten prime ministers in attendance, and almost every other delegation headed by its foreign minister. But beyond the visible audience I was aware of millions of listeners throughout the United States and across the world whose attention was focused on the podium toward which masses of television cameras glared hungrily down.

Kosygin, on ascending the tribune, must have been aware of the enormous public interest in him at that moment. If so, he seemed to be deliberately attempting to make the least of his opportunities. He was, of course, handicapped by his need to speak a tongue incomprehensible to most of the millions watching him throughout the world. Listeners on the television and radio heard a halting translation, appended without intonation to his moving lips. Although his voice was calm, the contents of his remarks were harsh. He asked the General Assembly to condemn Israel; to order the unconditional withdrawal of its forces back to the armistice lines; and even to demand the payment of compensation by Israel for the damage inflicted by the war. To all of this, he added a threat: "No country can be indifferent when a local war is likely to cause a great world war, whose consequences would be disastrous." He went on to criticize the United States, Britain and, with superb irrelevance, the Federal Republic of Germany, for "encouraging Israeli aggression." Kosygin's only meaningful concession to objective opinion in the Assembly was the acknowledgment that the Soviet Union did not support the Arab doctrine of Israel's illegitimacy. He said:

> *Every people enjoys the right to establish an independent national state of its own. It is on this basis that we formulated our attitude towards Israel as a State when we voted in 1947 for the United Nations decision to create two independent states, a Jewish one and an Arab one, in the territory of the former British colony of Palestine. Guided by this fundamental policy, the Soviet Union was later to establish diplomatic relations with Israel.*

At the end of his speech Kosygin recited the terms of the draft resolution. This would have the General Assembly "condemn" Israel, determine that we had acted "aggressively," demand that we immediately and unconditionally withdraw all forces to the armistice demarcation lines and make good, and in the shortest possible period of time, all the damage inflicted by our "aggression" on the United Arab Republics, Syria and Jordan. I would not have been surprised if he had gone on to suggest that Israel should disband all its arms and equipment and distribute them on Christmas Day, together with all her territories and currency reserves, to each of the neighboring Arab states in proportion to the violence of their hostility.

It was exactly noon when I went to the tribune. I began with a few sentences designed to give the debate its context:

> *The subject of our discussion is the Middle East; its past agony and its future hope. We speak of a region whose destiny has profoundly affected the entire human experience. In the heart of that region, at the very center of its geography and history, lives a very small nation called Israel. In recent weeks, the Middle East has passed through a crisis whose shadows darkened the world. This crisis has many consequences, but only one cause. Israel's right to peace, security, sovereignty, economic development and maritime freedom, indeed its very right to exist, has been forcibly denied and aggressively attacked. This is the true origin of the tension which troubles the Middle East. The threat of Israel's existence, its peace, security, sovereignty and development has been directed against her in the first instance by the neighboring Arab states. But all the conditions of tension, all the impulses of aggression in the Middle East have been aggravated by the policy of one of the Great Powers which, under our Charter, bear primary responsibility for the maintenance of international peace and security. I shall show how the Soviet Union has been unfaithful to that trust. The burden of responsibility lies heavy upon her.*

At the end of these two minutes, I looked up and was encouraged by a feeling that I had the audience with me, and beyond this audience, the vaster one to which my words were going out. I spoke in narrative form of Israel's embattled history, of the background of the Holocaust, of the implacable nature of Arab hostility, of the way in which the arrangements made in 1957 had been violated through continued blockade and the action of terrorist groups. I spoke of the period between May 14 and June 5, during which the clouds had gathered fast around us:

> On the morning of June 5, our country's choice was plain. The choice was to live or perish; to defend the national existence or to forfeit it for all time. From those dire moments, Israel emerged in five heroic days from mortal peril to glorious resistance. What should be condemned is not Israel's action, but the attempt to condemn it. Never have freedom, honor, justice, national interest and international morality been so righteously protected.

I now came down from these emotional flights to discuss the Soviet Union's role. I reacted with special violence to Kosygin's charge that Israel had acted in a "Hitlerist" manner:

> The USSR has formulated an obscene comparison between the Israel Defense Forces and the Hitlerite hordes which overran Europe in the Second World War. There is a flagrant breach of human decency in this comparison. Our nation never compromised with Hitler Germany. Our nation never signed a pact with it as did the USSR in 1939.

As I felt television cameras zooming in upon me, I thought that this was the time to illustrate the confrontation between an indignant Israel and a Soviet Union which, having provoked the war, was now taking an attitude of superior virtue. I paused until I could find the desk at which Prime Minister Kosygin and Foreign Minister Gromyko were sitting. Pointing a finger straight at them, I said:

> Your Government's role in the stimulation of the arms race, in the paralysis of the Security Council, in the encouragement of an unfounded suspicion in the Arab world of Israel's intentions, your constant refusal to say a single word of criticism of Arab statements threatening the violent overthrow of Israel's sovereignty and existence—all this undermines your claim to objectivity. You come here in our eyes not as a judge or as a prosecutor, but as a legitimate object of international criticism for the part that you have

played in the events which have brought our region to a point of explosive tension.

The spectacle of a very small country pointing its accusing finger at its gigantic adversary sent a wave of surprise and emotion through the Assembly Hall, and among millions outside. It was a few seconds before I could collect my voice for the final part of my speech:

> *The Arab states can no longer be permitted to recognize Israel's existence only for the purpose of plotting its elimination. They have come face-to-face with us in conflict. Let them now come face-to-face with us in peace.*

When I came down from the rostrum, the approval from the public galleries and the delegates' tables reminded me of a similar occasion, in 1956. Back in my hotel I was awakened by a telephone call from Jerusalem by Eshkol, who had listened to the speech on the shortwave radio and wished to convey his emotion. Late that night I anxiously bought the following morning's *New York Times*. It had an article by James Reston:

> *Mr. Kosygin's request that the United Nations should pretend that two and a half million Israelis were a menace to eighty million Arabs and should be punished like a race of moral monsters, set the stage for the Israeli Foreign Minister, Abba Eban, who talked like a Cambridge Don and who came through like a tank commander. It is easy to understand after listening to this debate between Kosygin and Eban why the Russians are suspicious of free speech. Eban worked through Kosygin's arguments with all the gentility of General Dayan's tanks in the desert.*

Later the New York *Post* came on the stands with a comment by James Wechsler:

> *Kosygin inadvertently set the stage for one of the most impressive rhetorical performances in the annals of the United Nations or any other major parliament, the speech of Israeli Foreign Minister, Abba Eban. All of Israel's heritage seemed blended yesterday in the lyrical, Churchillian cadences that Eban brought to the finest hour of his life. The cause of a lonely, encircled nation, born of centuries of travail, achieved new dignity and drama in the UN Hall and on millions of TV screens. Listening to him, one had the sense that almost every day of his life had been prepared for*

this interlude when he would summon all his resources to articu-
late the anguish and glory of a people so long under siege.

Wechsler went on to draw attention to a paradox:

> *Perhaps the largest footnote of irony in yesterday's events is*
> *that Eban, a prophet less than fully honored in his own country,*
> *could not even have the satisfaction of knowing that his historic*
> *address was being televised to Israeli homes. Only a limited edu-*
> *cational TV network exists in his country at this juncture, but the*
> *word, one hopes, will get around in many places that few men in*
> *our time have spoken with such distinction under such momentous*
> *circumstances, even commanding Mr. Kosygin's recurrent atten-*
> *tion, for sixty-four minutes.*

I could hardly be unmoved by such a response. Yet I knew that
no nation can live by speech alone. I still faced two questions. First,
we had evidently overwhelmed Kosygin in debate, but could we defeat him in the vote? Second, would the surge of favorable opinion
outside the United Nations break into its walls, so as to thwart an
international policy calling for our retreat?

I began a series of talks with prime ministers and foreign ministers,
beginning with Prime Minister Aldo Moro of Italy and Prime Minister Jens Otto Krag of Denmark. At a party at the Waldorf-Astoria
I met the normally imperturbable Dean Rusk who told me that in
watching the television together with the President and some of his
advisers, he had been brought to deep emotion. I heard that Radio
Moscow, having fully televised President Kosygin's speech, had turned
the broadcast off just before I reached the rostrum. On the other
hand, West European, Latin and African newspapers reaching us
within the next few days uniformly approved Israel's cause. I got
about twenty lines in *Pravda*. Most of the Israeli press threw off all
partisan inhibitions and associated itself proudly with what I had
declared in Israel's name on June 19.

The problem now was to work in concert with the United States
to ensure parliamentary success. It was hard to imagine that harmony
could be secured unless we had a close understanding of each other's
policies. At this stage I received cables from Jerusalem informing me
of the decisions adopted in our Cabinet after its discussions on
peace terms. These were very close to the views that I had expressed
in the earlier sessions in which I had participated before leaving
for New York. I was surprised by the spacious approach which Esh-

kol now authorized me to communicate to the United States for transmission to Arab governments.

Meeting with Secretary Rusk, Ambassador Goldberg, Undersecretary Eugene Rostow, Assistant Secretary Joseph Sisco and others in the Waldorf Towers, I outlined Israel's proposals for a final peace. I told Rusk and his colleagues that Israel would be prepared to sign peace treaties with Egypt and Syria "based on the former international boundaries with changes for Israel's security," subject to the demilitarization of the evacuated areas and a special agreement for Sharm el-Sheikh. I pointed out that there was no similar consensus concerning the future peace terms between Israel and Jordan. This question raised problems that transcended strategic interest. Our government would continue to give attention to that problem as well.

I could see that Rusk, Goldberg and their colleagues could hardly believe what I was saying. Here was Israel, on the very morrow of her victory, offering to renounce most of her gains in return for the simple condition of a permanent peace. This was the most dramatic initiative ever taken by an Israeli government before or since 1967, and it had a visibly strong impact on the United States.

A few days later replies came back through Washington stating that Egypt and Syria completely rejected the Israeli proposal. Their case was that Israel's withdrawal must be unconditional. It must not bring about any reward for Israel or any change in the previous system or the previous juridical relationships. In Goldberg's sarcastic words, the Arabs wanted the film to be played backward in the projector.

Some of the burden of our defense was now taken off my shoulders by the addresses of Ambassador Goldberg, acting with President Johnson's authority. The United States insisted that the objective of the General Assembly "must be a stable and durable peace in the Middle East to be achieved through negotiated arrangements with appropriate third-party assistance." The American draft followed the trend of the five points mentioned in President Johnson's address on June 19. It added that the "just and lasting peace" referred to in the resolution would have to be based on "mutual recognition of the political independence and territorial integrity of all countries in the area, encompassing recognized boundaries and other arrangements including disengagement and withdrawal of forces that will give them security against terror, destruction and war."

The United States did not have an easy time in getting the support of its allies. The diversity of views in the Western world came to expression on June 21 when the British Foreign Secretary, George Brown, made his address. Brown had an original and lucid mind, as well as an unpredictable range of emotional reaction. His logic and humanity were sometimes obscured by a stormy temperament of which he, himself, was engagingly conscious. He had no excess of false modesty. He sincerely believed that there was no middle course between George Brown's views and plain stupidity. He also had a somewhat embarrassing tendency to abuse his subordinates in my presence. But he was an exciting personality who gave zest to the diplomatic adventure. His speech gave general support to the American view that withdrawal could not be requested unless it was accompanied by a total renunciation of warlike policies. On the other hand, he emphatically stated that no nation should secure "territorial aggrandizement" by war. I recalled that Britain had not objected to the "aggrandizement" of the Kingdom of Jordan as a result of its annexation of the West Bank and eastern Jerusalem during the fighting of 1948. What Israel was asking for was not "aggrandizement," but a rational territorial and security system that would make us less vulnerable than in the dark days of May and June 1967.

George Brown went on to make an emotional comment on the position in Jerusalem. He separated this from the general context and called for the withholding of international recognition from Israel's unification of the city.

This part of the British speech had one inadvertent effect. We had achieved the union of Jerusalem during the fighting on June 7. Our ministers were still divided about whether we should immediately give this any formal juridical expression. There was some sentiment in favor of postponing such action for a week or two in order to make things easier for us in the United Nations debate. George Brown's speech, however, sounded a premature alarm. It strengthened the feeling of Israeli ministers that it was urgent to affirm our position on Jerusalem's unity before it became too late.

We drew little comfort from France. General de Gaulle had issued a statement roundly accusing Israel of aggressive initiative. His Foreign Minister, Couve de Murville, adopted cooler formulations. He even stated that "only a freely negotiated settlement accepted by all the parties concerned and recognized by the international community would, one day, solve these problems as a whole." In the meantime, Couve de Murville suggested that the four major powers should exercise their special responsibility for the maintenance of peace and security.

General de Gaulle's belief that there were four powers of roughly equal weight and status, responsible for the future of mankind, did not seem to be shared in other quarters. When I had gone to see President Johnson on May 26, I told him that General de Gaulle had said that "the Four Great Powers ought to get together." The President had given me one of his belligerent looks. "The Four Great Powers? Who the hell are the other two?"

Haggling about the texts of resolutions went on for some days. After a week in which our delegation seemed to be holding its own, the prospects darkened. A tidal wave of anti-Israeli resolutions suddenly loomed before us. The change did not arise through anything that had happened in the General Assembly; it sprang from events in the Middle East. On June 27 the Israeli Parliament voted in favor of adding Jerusalem to the area of Israeli sovereignty. Before this happened, an unusual development had taken place. All the members of our parliamentary delegation, including Aryeh Ben Eliezer of the Herut Party, had joined in a cable to Jerusalem drawing attention to the adverse effect which an initiative in Jerusalem would have at a time when the General Assembly was debating the general problem of withdrawal. They urged that we should be allowed to do our work in the General Assembly without any external impediment and that the measures proposed for Jerusalem should be taken as soon as the Assembly adjourned. In a telephone conversation with me from the Cabinet meeting on June 27, Eshkol explained that there would have been no difficulty in holding the matter up for a week or two, but that George Brown's speech had raised the specter of preventive international action. In other words, the longer we waited, the stronger would become the international pressure against giving full effect to Jerusalem's union. I did not contest this view. After all, the union of Jerusalem was ultimately more important than whether or not our parliamentary struggle would be more difficult. George Brown has had more to do with the Israeli unification of Jerusalem than he might have wished.

This development naturally evoked some international concern. On top of it came news of an exodus of Arabs from the West Bank. The television screen was full of pathetic pictures of refugees, including women and children, trekking across the River Jordan in great numbers with their meager possessions on their backs. The combined effects of our Jerusalem legislation with the exodus from the West Bank created a public climate uncongenial to our cause. I suddenly felt our front crumbling on all sides. I instantly asked Eshkol to make some decisions that would have a reassuring effect. He responded with understanding to this urgent appeal. The Cabinet empowered me to promise the restoration of Government House in Jerusalem to the UN cease-fire supervisors and to announce that any pressure for eastward migration of Arabs would be stopped. He even added a provision for allowing the new Arab refugees to return.

As a result of these alleviations, I was able to rally our delegation for a renewed assault on hostile resolutions. The most dangerous text was presented by Yugoslavia. This draft skillfully omitted condemnatory references, but called for Israel's total withdrawal without any reciprocal action by the Arab states.

Another anxiety lay in the prospect that American defense of Israel's position would be weakened as a result of talks scheduled in Glassboro, New Jersey, between President Johnson and Mr. Kosygin. It turned out that these fears were exaggerated. Kosygin's statements to President Johnson were apparently no less harsh than his public addresses. But President Johnson had countered the Soviet request for Israel's unconditional withdrawal by expounding his own doctrine, according to which there should arise in the Middle East "a mosaic of peace" composed of the elements which he had mentioned in his speech, including the determination of permanent boundaries, freedom of navigation, and a solution of the refugee problem. I was told that the American participants in the Glassboro talks had got the impression that the Soviet Union would not intervene militarily in the Middle East unless it had a strong international basis for such intervention. It was absolutely vital to deny the Soviet Union a parliamentary success.

And yet, it was not easy for us to emerge from the prospect of imminent defeat. There was confusion in the friendly Western camp. Our European and Latin friends were laying greater emphasis on withdrawal and less emphasis on the need for establishing peace. It was not even certain that Britain would vote against the Yugoslav resolution. The French-speaking African group had begun to weaken and I arranged to meet them collectively the next day in order to win back their support. King Hussein's appearance on the rostrum had strengthened the Arab position.

Never since our historic lobbying effort in November 1947 had Israel made such a far-ranging attempt to secure a parliamentary result as that which we now invested in our effort to prevent adoption of the withdrawal-without-peace resolution. The French-speaking delegations of West Africa told us sardonically that Mr. Gromyko had ignored them year after year, regarding them as mere "tools of French imperialism." Suddenly the foreign ministers found themselves invited to tea at the Soviet delegation with unusual frequency. And in addition to blandishments, there were threats. Members of the Soviet delegation were putting it around freely in many capitals, as well as in the General Assembly, that if the Yugoslav resolution was adopted, the Soviet Union would "help to implement it." A possible implication was that the USSR would regard the Yugoslav text as a political basis for direct military intervention. The effect of these menaces was electric. If we had any reason before to wonder if the United States was putting its full weight behind the defeat of the Yugoslav resolution, these doubts were set at rest. The United States now reinforced its action in the General Assembly by purposeful diplomatic efforts in many of the world's capitals.

In the meantime, it was essential to hold the French-African front. The most influential figure among the French-speaking African states was President Felix Houphouet-Boigny of the Ivory Coast. In an effort to enlist his energetic support I asked Golda Meir, who was then at a socialist congress in Paris, to seek him out. It emerged that the President was resting somewhere on German territory. It was not easy for Mrs. Meir to overcome profound inhibitions of principle and emotion which had so far prevented her from setting foot on German soil. Nevertheless, she agreed that the success of our struggle in the General Assembly demanded a special effort. The meeting with the African statesman took place and contributed perceptibly to the strengthening of our position in what had then become the crucial sector of our parliamentary front.

When we assembled in the afternoon of July 4, our estimates of the parliamentary situation were not firm. In an atmosphere of deep tension, the Yugoslav text was put to the vote. It received 53 in its favor by the Arab states, the Communist states, the Moslem countries and, incongruously, France. The 46 votes against the proposal comprised the entire Latin American bloc, the United States, Great Britain, most of Western Europe, Israel, the senior Commonwealth countries Australia, Canada and New Zealand, and African delegations including Botswana, Gambia, Ghana, Togo, Liberia, Lesotho, Madagascar and Malawi. The resolution had fallen massively short of the required two-thirds majority. There was no doubt that Israel had gained one of the greatest political victories of her international career.

As if to make this even more emphatic, the Soviet Union called for a vote on its own resolution, which was an even more extreme form of the anti-Israeli policy than Yugoslavia had proposed. One by one the familiar paragraphs on "condemnation," "withdrawal" and "compensation" by Israel were voted emphatically down. By the time all the roll calls were completed, the condemnation of Israel had been rejected six times, and the concept of withdrawal to the June 4 lines had been specifically turned down four times. The stunned expressions on the faces of Mr. Gromyko and the Arab foreign ministers gave us an almost sensual satisfaction.

For me, it was a moment to be cherished for many years to come.

Against the combined weight of the Soviet and Arab world, despite our relative weakness in territory, population and resources, we had obtained a certificate of legitimacy from the General Assembly for our continued presence along the cease-fire lines until such time as the Arab governments were ready for peace.

By nine o'clock that evening we were assembled in my suite at the Plaza, drinking enthusiastic toasts to ourselves and to each other. I got through on the telephone to Jerusalem, where, at three in the morning, I aroused my Director-General, Aryeh Levavi, from his bed. He received the news with incredulity. The general feeling in Israel was that the Yugoslav resolution would be adopted, either as it stood or with some trivial amendments. That every call for condemnation and withdrawal should have been rejected was a political triumph which the skeptical Israeli public had not expected to hear.

I arrived back in Israel on July 7 to find the country in a mood of political celebration. I found a large and enthusiastic welcoming party at Lod Airport, headed by Mrs. Meir, whose presence was a special gesture, since she had been in poor health. Minister without Portfolio Israel Galili was also present. The atmosphere surrounding me domestically had now been transformed. A public opinion poll published in *Ha'aretz* revealed that 89 percent of those canvassed wanted me to be their Foreign Minister, while the next candidate was supported by 3 percent. Newspapers which only two weeks before had suggested that I be accompanied to the United Nations by two or three ministerial supervisors now began to eat their words in varying degrees of pain or relish. *Ha'aretz* published an editorial expressing surprise at the enthusiastic fidelity of the Israeli public to its leaders, but accepting the verdict with excellent grace.

My report to the Cabinet on July 9 was preceded by congratulatory words from the Prime Minister, and at a meeting of the Secretariat of the Labor Party, my entry was greeted by a burst of nonproletarian applause which violated our party's traditions of reticence. Apart from the human satisfactions, I found that the new possibility to devote all my emotion to our international struggle made the ministry's work more effective than during the period when so much energy had to be given to sheer political survival.

Meanwhile our government took a step designed to create a better feeling in the Christian world and in the international community concerning our attitude on the problem of Jerusalem. It was beyond my understanding why anybody in the world should wish to restore East Jerusalem to a regime which had fallen so far short of its minimal trust toward religious freedom and sanctity. In a letter to the Secretary-General I defended the changes which had come about in the city. "Where there had been an explosive military frontier, there is now unity. Where there had previously been strife, there is now peace. Where there had been sacrilege and vandalism, there is now a decent respect for the rights of all pilgrims to have access and free worship at the shrine which they revered." At the same time my letter of July 10, drafted together with two ministerial colleagues, Menachem Begin and Zerach Warhaftig, opened the way to a compromise between Israel's national rights in Jerusalem and the interests of the world community. We stated that Israel "does not claim unilateral control or exclusive jurisdiction in the Holy Places of Christianity and Islam, and that in the peace settlement we would be ready to give appropriate expression to this principle." This was the first time in the history of Jerusalem that a government in control of the city had offered the custodianship of Holy Places to anyone outside its total jurisdiction. We hoped that by offering to remove the mosques of Omar and El Aqsa from our exclusive jurisdiction, we might be creating an "enclave" possibility which would help a political settlement with Jordan at a later stage.

A few days later I was back on my flight to the General Assembly. Finding themselves unable to secure a general withdrawal resolution, the Arab and Soviet delegations, under Pakistani sponsorship, managed to get a reiteration of the General Assembly's position against Israeli annexation of East Jerusalem. At the same time they made a new exploration of the possibility to produce General Assembly pressure for Israeli withdrawal to the pre-war lines. Their efforts came to nothing. The Arabs and Soviets would not pay any price at all for the "total withdrawal" on which they had set their minds. On the other hand, the United States together with the forty-five nations who had rallied to us a week before, declined to call for any withdrawal without a certainty that the conflict would come to a final end. The emergency Assembly, which had seemingly perished on July 4, was now being kept alive by artificial diplomatic respiration. When July 17 came, President Abdul Pashwak gave the dying Assembly three further days of grace. Unless agreement was reached by July 20, Kosygin's unprecedented diplomatic initiative would expire in deadlock.

On the morning of July 20, when members of our delegation were assembled in my hotel suite about to leave for what we thought would be the final session of the emergency General Assembly, a call came from Joseph Sisco, who was Ambassador Goldberg's chief assistant in the American delegation. What we heard from him was disconcerting. Meetings had taken place on July 18 between Goldberg and Soviet Ambassador Anatoly F. Dobrynin, and on July 19, between

Goldberg and Gromyko. We had not been taken fully into the confidence of the United States about the content of these exchanges. Sisco now informed us that various tentative drafts had been discussed, and that the United States would agree to a twenty-four-hour postponement of the final session. I was invited to come over to the United States mission, together with Rafael, to hear what all this was about.

There now took place one of the most embarrassing discussions which the United States and Israel had ever held. The confrontation was all the more painful in view of the close political and conceptual harmony which had prevailed in our relations since June 5. It appeared that Gromyko and Goldberg had been able to reach agreement on the wording of a proposal which they might both support in the General Assembly. When I saw the text, I knew that we were in serious trouble. The operative paragraphs read as follows:

Affirms the principle that conquest of territory by war is inadmissible under the United Nations Charter and calls on all parties to the conflict to withdraw without delay their forces from the territories occupied by them after June 4, 1967.
Affirms likewise the principle of acknowledgment without delay by all member states in the area that each of them enjoys the right to maintain an independent national state of its own and live in peace and security, as well as the renunciation of all claims and acts inconsistent therewith are expected.*

I pointed out with indignation that our American friends seemed to be giving up all the results achieved in the past six weeks of common struggle. The withdrawal of forces was no longer to be conditional on peace with secure boundaries. It was stated explicitly that the June 4 lines should be restored. We considered this remarkable in view of the eloquent speeches by President Johnson and Ambassador Goldberg describing a return to the previous position as "a prescription for the renewal of hostilities." Furthermore, instead of Israel withdrawing to agreed boundaries in return for peace, we would be withdrawing to the old boundaries without anything like peace. The only recompense would be "acknowledgment" of the general rights of states. Even the fatal word "Israel" did not appear, so that the Arab states would have no difficulty in making a general statement and then claiming its nonapplicability to Israel. I said that I could see no difference between this formulation and Kosygin's

* This text was publicly outlined by Ambassador Goldberg in a speech on July 27, 1967, published in the *State Department Bulletin*. See *The UN and the Middle East Crisis, 1967*, by Arthur Lall (New York: Columbia U. Press, 1968, page 312).

call for unconditional withdrawal against which the United States and Israel had battled so hard. I pointed out that if this text was presented and voted on, Israel would find herself in the tragic position of having to flout a joint American-Soviet proposal endorsed by the General Assembly. The United States, according to this text, would have detached itself from Israel and allied itself to the Soviet Union without prior consultation on our most vital interests.

Our American friends were acutely uncomfortable. Rafael and I left them in no error about our belief that the allurement of an accord with the Soviet Union had uprooted them from their own principles and set them on a course incompatible with Israel's security and with the interest and dignity of the free world.

We were obviously approaching a crisis. A Soviet-Arab-American alignment against us had been prevented during six weeks of suspense. It now threatened to come about almost casually in a hurried attempt to grasp the fiction of a Great Power agreement which was, in essence, an agreement to surrender to Soviet and Arab demands. I said that Gromyko must at this moment be the happiest man on earth.

Just then a telephone call came to the United States delegation. One of the American officials left the room and returned with a message, which he passed to Ambassador Goldberg's hands. It appeared that the Arab states had rejected Gromyko's advice to accept the proposed tentative formula! Under the influence of Algeria and Syria, Egypt had given a negative reply. The Arab states wanted the full withdrawal of Israel's forces, without even giving a meaningless rhetorical gesture acknowledging "the rights of all states in the area." Goldberg said that the vehemence of our criticism would, in any case, have required him to seek presidential reconsideration of the initiative, but the Soviet-Arab rejection of the proposed formula had virtually put it out of court.

Now that the Arab states had rejected the Goldberg-Gromyko formula, Moscow insisted that the draft be regarded as a tentative working paper, which, having failed to produce agreement, should be regarded as null and void. On hearing this news from Goldberg and Sisco, we could not conceal our relief.

But the international debate had been suspended, not concluded. The next stage would be the General Assembly meetings scheduled for September 1967. On the other hand, there was a growing willingness to restore the discussion to the Security Council. Nothing had been gained by interrupting the Council's work during the second week in June in favor of the spectacular international conference which had left everything unresolved.

Meanwhile the heads of Arab states came together at Khartoum at the end of August. In strong defiance they tied their governments' hands by a series of negative resolutions adopted with great rhetorical flourish. The Khartoum decisions were: no negotiations with Israel; no peace with Israel; no recognition of Israel; no bargaining concerning any Palestinian territory. Some newspapers and governments in the world made light of this development, ascribing it indulgently to the Arab love of slogans. In my own report to the Cabinet, I expressed the view that the Khartoum conference was an important event. Not only had the Arab governments refrained from exploring a peace settlement, they had closed every door and window that might lead to one in the foreseeable future. Even if the Khartoum proposals had been accepted in a spirit of rhetorical intoxication, the Arab governments which had voted for them would find it very difficult to revoke them.

Nasser's defeat had created some convulsive effects in Egypt. At the height of the fighting, Nasser had staged his own resignation, together with a "spontaneous" pressure by cheering masses calling on him to stay at his post. Thus consolidated, he had accepted the resignation of the defense leaders, Field Marshal Abdul Hakim Amer and Defense Minister Shams ed-din Badran. He now went on to dismiss other heads of the armed forces. In effect Nasser was, therefore, turning the popular indignation against the military leaders, whom he replaced with new and loyal staff members.

In Israel during the summer I could feel a sense of relief at having emerged unexpectedly from the most dangerous stage of our political struggle. This feeling found expression in a discussion which I opened in the Knesset on July 31 and which was concluded on the following day. The Knesset even went so far as to praise me personally in a formal resolution on August 1, in which it called for the establishment of peace treaties by direct negotiations. Until such peace was established, we would hold the present lines.

The Knesset's resolution implied territorial concessions in return for peace. It gave no real support to the slogans of the extremist groups. But those groups enjoyed support in the national press. Since it is easier to attack persons than ideologies, the extreme territorialists conveniently presented me as their target.

As the soldiers returned to their civilian occupations, the country was gripped by a moving dialogue on the implications of the war. It was claimed that the rank and file of the army had kept its purpose steady and its spirit compassionate. There was very little boasting about military conquest, and a great deal of moral anguish about the implications of killing the enemy. A book called *The Warriors*

Speak contained moving expressions of moral torment and human tenderness from the lips of young men, mostly in the kibbutz movement, who had returned from their encounter with death and bloodshed.

In our own government and public opinion, views were divided between those who thought that we could afford to let the Arabs take the initiative for opening a peace dialogue and those who believed that the responsibility lay with ourselves. Defense Minister Moshe Dayan had said that Israel needed simply to wait for "Hussein to call up on the telephone." This was vivid language, but many of us thought that the imagery simplified the problem. It might have been valid if Israel had to live with the Arab world alone. The truth was, however, that Israel was much more dependent on the opinion of states beyond the region than on the policies and emotions of her immediate neighbors. Among friendly governments there was an expectation that the victors should actively pursue a peace settlement and join in the exploration of its terms. Following the audacious initiative we had taken in June toward Egypt and Syria, I was empowered by the Cabinet to explore what Jordan's reaction would be to a peace treaty in which the indivisibility of Jerusalem as Israel's capital would be preserved and some territorial changes in our favor would be made along the Jordan, but in such manner as to restore to the Hashemite kingdom the great bulk of the populated areas of the West Bank. The first reaction of Jordan was one of interest. But when the conception behind our policy found expression in a map attributed to Minister of Labor Yigal Allon, the Jordanian attitude became adamant. It was clear that King Hussein would rather leave Israel under international criticism in possession of all the West Bank then take on himself the responsibility of ceding 33 percent of it to us.

Nevertheless, the fact remains that by the spring of 1968, Israel had offered the restoration of the great bulk of the conquered territories. The Arabs had rejected this opportunity. I said on a television program: "This is the first war in history which has ended with the victors suing for peace and the vanquished calling for unconditional surrender."

Although there were some who felt that Israel had nothing to do but sit back virtuously and taste her victory, my own feeling was there would be no long respite. The Khartoum conference had been grave enough. Another blow to the prospects of peace was now delivered by the Soviet Union through its armament program. When the cease-fire had come into effect in mid-June 1967, the Egyptian, Jordanian and Syrian armies had been either destroyed or shattered to the point of demoralization. Israel was the major military power in the Middle East. Her surviving strength in mid-June outweighed that of the Arab states. It was the first time that this had been true. The air fleets and tank forces at our disposal were more numerous than the forces which some of the greater powers maintain in our part of eastern Mediterranean. Europe was suffering economically· from the closure of the Suez Canal, but in the political and strategic balance, it benefited from the reduction of Soviet prestige in the Mediterranean. The United States had emerged with greater credit than the Soviet Union. It had, for a change, been on the winning side, both of the military campaign and of the political struggle.

The frustration engendered in Moscow by this situation explains its decision to rearm Egypt on a massive scale during the summer months. Moscow understood that without military power it would be difficult for Egypt to win a parliamentary victory at the United Nations and that such a victory, if won, would have no more than a symbolic and propagandist value. The only hope for the Soviet Union to re-establish its position was by ensuring that its Arab protégés recovered their military strength.

16

Jarring, Lyndon Johnson, Richard Nixon and "242" 1967-1970

OUR POLITICAL STRUGGLE IN 1967 FLARED UP ANEW IN NEW YORK ON September 17 with the termination of the emergency session of the General Assembly and the transfer of the Arab-Israel conflict to the Security Council.

The United Nations was now in an acute dilemma. It was unable to solve the problem and unwilling to disengage from it. Lord Caradon, the British representative, suggested ways of keeping the UN in contact with the Middle Eastern question while removing it from sterile public debate. The central idea was for the Security Council to appoint a representative to help the governments of the area toward a peace agreement.

The idea that the United Nations should aspire to a new era of stability gained ground in the discussions that I now held at the Security Council. In September and October, Canada and Denmark, as well as the United States, showed understanding of the Israeli position. They proposed that withdrawal should take place not to "armistice demarcation lines" but to "boundaries worked out in negotiation." In the meantime King Hussein had again visited London and Washington after consulting with Nasser in Cairo. He gave the impression that he would be willing to negotiate on the basis of a Security Council resolution acceptable to Israel and most Arab states. Hussein believed that he had Cairo's support for this course. Accord-

448

ingly, the United States began to draft a proposal to which Israeli-Jordan acquiescence would be sought in advance.

I went to Washington to meet President Johnson again on October 24. He reviewed the events which had unfolded since our meeting on May 26. He insisted that if we had given him "a little more time," he would have taken measures that would have made our armed resistance unnecessary. I did not feel that there was much conviction in his voice. He did admit that once Israel had made her decision, we had acted with drive and resolution. He was now firmly resolved not to weaken the position which he had outlined on June 19. An "edifice of peace" would have to be built. He was alert to Soviet intentions, and as we parted he told Harman and me that my speeches in June 1967, which he had watched on television, had moved him more deeply than anything since Churchill's 1940 orations.

We clearly had a firm basis of support in American policy, but Ambassador Goldberg warned me that British support was still not assured.

I had accepted an invitation to fly from New York to London to address a meeting in the Royal Opera House marking the fiftieth anniversary of the Balfour Declaration. I thought that this would be a useful occasion for probing the British attitude and paving the way for a Western policy which would satisfy our major interests. On November 6 I had talks with Foreign Secretary George Brown and Prime Minister Harold Wilson. They were in general agreement with an American proposal that had been discussed in New York, but they were not yet instructing Lord Caradon to support it. I found this disquieting. The implication was that Britain would hold back so that, should the occasion arise, she could propose a policy closer to the Arab view than that which the United States was willing to initiate. The essence of the American draft was that the establishment of peace should be accompanied by withdrawal to secure and recognized boundaries without making any quantitative judgment on the scope of the withdrawal or of the territorial change. My talk with an ebullient George Brown at his country residence at Dorneywood yielded one important result. He told me with clarity that Britain would only advocate Israeli withdrawal in a context of permanent peace, to secure and agreed boundaries which Israel would find satisfactory for its security. Officials in attendance took this all down with precision, while I withstood George Brown's resolute attempts to induce me to drink more Scotch than I needed. I felt that it was no small thing to have an American and British commitment to the principle of agreed territorial change in the transition to peace.

After another transatlantic journey, I was met in New York by Ambassador Rafael. He told me that the Egyptian representatives, headed by their Foreign Minister, had been suspiciously watching King Hussein's move for a resolution based on Israeli-Jordanian acquiescence. Before an American text embodying this aim could be brought to formulation, the Egyptians had called for an urgent meeting of the Security Council. India, Mali and Nigeria had submitted a resolution calling for a complete withdrawal, together with a complete absence of peace. Cairo was undermining any chance of an Israeli-Jordanian compromise.

When the Security Council debate opened in November, the alignment of forces was clear. All of us were prepared to accept the appointment of a United Nations representative who would have the parties explore the possibilities of peace. It was clear that there was no escape from some mention of the principle of withdrawal. Here the demarcation was between the United States, Israel, Canada and Denmark, which insisted that withdrawal should be accompanied by peace and secure boundaries—and the Soviet Union, together with the Arab and Third World states, which wanted the Arabs to get withdrawal without paying the price of recognizing Israel's legitimacy and right to security.

When Ambassador Goldberg took the floor on November 15, it was plain that we had made a major breakthrough. For the first time a major power was advocating not only a change in the political relations between Israel and the Arab states but also a doctrine of territorial revision. Ambassador Goldberg pointed out that there had never been agreement on any lines as the permanent territorial boundaries between states, and that the armistice demarcation lines of 1949 had been specifically defined by the signatories as provisional lines based on purely military considerations. These lines, he said, stood to be revised as a part of the transition to peace. He pointed out that neither the armistice demarcation lines in force on June 4, 1967, nor the cease-fire lines that had emerged from Israel's victory could be regarded as territorial boundaries: "Since such boundaries do not exist, they have to be established by the parties themselves as part of the peace-making process."

During my visit to London, Harold Wilson and George Brown had indicated that they were in general agreement with the American approach, but since Britain now had tolerable relations with Egypt, Brown felt able to conduct a relatively autonomous policy. Thus, just when it seemed depressingly probable that a Latin American text would be adopted fixing the June 4, 1967, frontier as the point of withdrawal, British intervention created a new and more flexible situation.

Lord Caradon came to my hotel suite on November 18. The British government felt that the American draft had no chance of success. To get a majority, it would be essential to state the principle of the "nonadmissibility of the acquisition of territory by force." This, however, would be a preambular reference. The operative element in the proposed resolution would be that in return for Israeli withdrawal, the Arab states would have to make a "just and lasting peace" and agree on "secure and recognized boundaries." Israel, in order to get peace, would have to withdraw from the cease-fire lines to a territorial boundary to be established in a peace negotiation. Thus, there would be a balance of incentives. Neither party could get what it wanted without moving toward the other.

The first draft presented by Lord Caradon did not meet our minimal claims. It virtually gave the United Nations' representative the power to dictate a settlement. I urged that his role be limited to an attempt to "promote agreement" between the parties. Moreover, in the first British draft there was no adequate provision for leaving the secure boundaries open to negotiation. I told Lord Caradon that we could not accept this draft.

The United States had informed the British delegation that it would not support a resolution which did not have Israeli as well as Arab acquiescence. Under these pressures and in a strong personal and national desire to achieve an agreed solution, Caradon worked away assiduously for several days. When his text came to the Council table, it contained some alterations designed to meet our apprehensions. First, it was stipulated that any UN representative would have to "promote agreement between the states of the region." This would safeguard us against attempts to dictate solutions from outside. Second, the objective of the resolution was now stated to be the establishment of a just and lasting peace to which all other provisions, including the withdrawal of forces, would be subordinate. On the boundary question, there was a perceptible loophole for our cause. The "armistice lines" or the "lines of June 4, 1967" were not mentioned in the text. The withdrawal would not be from "all the occupied territories" or even from "the occupied territories," but from "occupied territories" whose scope and dimension were left vague.

The question whether the Security Council's resolution as presented by Britain in November 1967 authorized territorial revision was to be the subject of unceasing international discussion in the months

451

and years ahead. Israel's case was to be reinforced by the interpretations of those who had drafted the original and responsible resolution. Goldberg's distinction between the old "armistice lines" and the future "peace boundaries" was endorsed by the United States in a series of statements culminating in a speech by Secretary of State William P. Rogers on December 9, 1969:

> *The boundaries from which the 1967 war began were established by the 1949 armistice agreements, and have defined the areas of national jurisdiction in the Middle East for twenty years. Those boundaries were armistice lines, not final political borders. The Security Council resolution neither endorses nor precludes the armistice lines as the definitive political boundaries.*

Since the British government sponsored the resolution, its interpretation of the territorial provisions has special weight. In the House of Commons on October 29, 1969, the Foreign Secretary, Michael Stewart, made it clear that the withdrawal envisaged by the resolution would not be from "all the territories." He stated that the omission of the word "all" was deliberate. Some years later, in his book *Out of My Way*, George Brown made the same point with full personal authority. Before the adoption of the final text, there was much interchange between Washington and Moscow about whether the resolution should leave the door open for any territorial change. The Arab states and the Soviet Union tried to close it tight. They first insisted on a formulation which would speak of withdrawal from *"all* the territories occupied during the hostilities of June 1967." As a last resort, they were prepared to settle for a text calling for withdrawal of Israeli forces from *"the* territories occupied in the hostilities."

The little definite article became a source of international contention during the 1969 debates at the summit. The argument came to a head on November 21 when, in response to an urgent plea from Kosygin for the United States to "interpret" the resolution as referring to "all the territories" occupied in 1967, President Johnson made a typically firm reply, insisting that the noncommittal text be left as it was.

When we assembled in the Security Council on November 22, there was tense speculation about the Soviet attitude. Moscow was in a dilemma; if it vetoed the British resolution, the Security Council, like the General Assembly, would disperse, with Israel in possession of the field and with no resolution endorsing the principle of withdrawal. The Soviet Union accordingly announced its support of the resolution on its own "understanding" that withdrawal from territories meant withdrawal from "all the territories." The Indian delegation made the same "assumption." Lord Caradon stated emphatically that any such interpretations did not bind the Council as such, and that the resolution meant what it said and not a word more.

While Resolution 242 could not be described as an Israeli victory, it certainly corresponded more closely to our basic interests than we could have dared to expect from the United Nations a short time before. At best, the resolution could become the basis for a peace negotiation. At worst, if the Arab governments persisted in their refusal to make peace, there would be international justification for maintaining our position on the cease-fire lines.

Security Council Resolution 242 was based on the assumption that world opinion urgently required peace in the Middle East. But Arab nationalism drew no such lesson from its failure in war. The Arab reaction to defeat was not to assume that the anti-Israeli policy had failed, but rather that it had not been sufficiently applied. The hope of early revenge was nourished with virulence by the Palestinian organizations, especially El Fatah. After some eruptions of military action in 1968 and occasional acts of spectacular piracy against airlines, these movements shifted their emphasis to the political domain. Their device was to elevate the concept of "Palestine" to the point at which "Israel" would disappear. As long as the struggle seemed to lie between Israel and the Arab world, sympathy went to Israel. It was enough to compare our sparse territory with the huge Arab expanse in order to conclude that Arab nationalism did not have much to complain about. But when the contest was presented as being not between Israel and the Arabs, but between Israel and the Palestinians, the perspective changed. All the gains of Arab nationalism in nearly two dozen states outside Palestine were taken for granted as though they had no effect whatever on the balance of equity between Arab and Jewish rights to independence. Israel was now portrayed as powerful, sated, established and recognized, while the Palestinians were, by contrast, dispossessed, bitter, dissatisfied and implacable. The current of world opinion flowed away from the embattled victor toward the defeated aggressor. We found ourselves transformed from David to Goliath overnight. Israel had committed the dark sin of survival.

At the Foreign Ministry in Jerusalem, my main business was to ensure some diplomatic mobility. The period between 1967 and 1973 is often portrayed as years of deadlock in Israeli policy. Nothing could be further from the truth. There was a more intensive Israeli quest for peace after 1967 than in any other period of our history.

Yet those of us who wished to explore a compromise did not have an easy task. We were hemmed in on one side by our own political right-wing, and on the other side by an Arab nationalism that did everything possible to frustrate the hopes of Israeli moderates. For the first two years of this period I was intensely occupied with the mission of Gunnar Jarring, whom Secretary-General U Thant had appointed as UN Representative for the Middle East under the terms of Resolution 242.

There was an unusually thick fall of snow in Jerusalem on the day of Jarring's first visit to my home. Snow fell again ten days later. Jarring must have thought that Israel and Sweden had unexpected climatic affinities. During the first part of his mission he developed the shuttle technique that Henry Kissinger was later to make more famous. Jarring managed to convey an air of tranquil deliberation even in a frenzied schedule of flights between Jerusalem, Amman, Cairo and Beirut.

Since the Syrians refused to accept Resolution 242, they took the logical course of boycotting the Jarring Mission. There was nothing inconvenient for Israel in this attitude, since it exempted the delicate question of the Golan Heights from our complex and crowded agenda.

Jarring, who was the Swedish ambassador in Moscow, was a man of scholarly attainments and high integrity whose greatest virtue may have been his major defect. His mind moved strictly within the rational limits of European humanism. He assumed that nations, like individuals, guided their actions by reason. He later came to learn that logic played a very small part in the history of the Middle East. The passions and sensitivities, the instincts of wounded pride and frustrated hope, together with deeply traumatic memories of persecution, domination or oppression, had sharpened the intensity of our region's emotional life. Israelis, more than Arabs, could manage to temper emotion with logic. All that Jarring could do was to ask Israel to be less rational and the Arabs less emotional.

It was not easy for me to draft moderate proposals in a Cabinet composed of all parties, including Gahal, whose representatives professed to believe that peace treaties could be obtained without any territorial sacrifice at all. Eshkol discreetly and quietly gave me his backing for formulations that were not always pleasing to Begin and his colleagues.

On December 27 I communicated to Jarring a proposal that Israel and the UAR should, as a first step, discuss an agenda for peace. I then made a similar proposal for an agenda for peace with Jordan.

In his report on the first phase of the Jarring Mission, presented on January 4, 1971, Secretary-General U Thant said:

The United Arab Republic and Jordan for their part insisted that there could be no question of discussions between the parties until the Israeli forces had been withdrawn to the positions occupied by them prior to June 5, 1967.

This is an accurate summary. The slogan "withdrawal now, peace perhaps later" was not likely to win much support in Israel, especially after we had secured its defeat in the United Nations.

Yet for a brief period during February and March 1968, we seemed to be on the verge of a negotiation. I had suggested to Jarring that instead of trying to get agreement on semantics, he should convene a conference between the parties under his chairmanship similar to that which had taken place under Bunche's auspices at Rhodes. Despite a vehement assault on me in the extremist sections of the Israeli press, I told Jarring that Israel would not "object to this indirect approach to negotiations, provided that it was designed to lead to a later stage of direct negotiation and agreement." Eventually Ambassador Jarring drew up a document for which he sought the agreement of Egypt, Israel and Jordan. It called for agreement on a letter of invitation under which Israel would attend a conference with Egypt and Jordan under Jarring's auspices in Cyprus to discuss the implementation of Resolution 242.

To Jarring's disappointment, this text was rejected by the Egyptian Foreign Minister on March 7. On March 10 Jarring showed me the document informally. He would not present it to me formally, since, according to his concept, the agreement of all parties was necessary before it would have any official status. I told him that in my view it would be fully acceptable to my government if it was also accepted by the other side. Subsequently Jarring was informed of Israel's official acceptance of the text without conditions. Later he amended his proposal to one for meetings between him and the parties at New York. This made the proposals less attractive to us, since it meant that he would merely hold separate meetings with permanent representatives at the UN, thus avoiding any impression of a specific Arab-Israeli "encounter." Nevertheless, the change of venue was not objectionable to us in principle. The most that Jarring could elicit from Egypt was an expression of readiness "of our Permanent Representative to the UN in New York to meet with you to continue the contacts which you have been conducting with the parties concerned in accordance with Security Council Resolution 242." The idea of a "conference with Israel" had disappeared.

At one stage Jarring had thought of going to New York and sending an invitation to the parties to meet him in accordance with an agreed-upon text, without seeking their agreement in advance. I fully supported this idea. After all, Bunche had not asked the parties to the Armistice Conference in 1949 to agree in advance to the terms of his own invitation. I wondered whether Egypt would really refuse a United Nations invitation to come to New York for discussions with the UN Special Representative and thus incur international opprobrium for obstructing a peace settlement. U Thant reported: "In consultations with me, he [Jarring] considered issuing a formal invitation along the lines of his proposal, but with the venue at New York. But, it was felt that a forced acceptance obtained by such an invitation would not be helpful."

I believe that this was another of the missed opportunities of progress toward peace after the 1967 war.

Later I instructed our Permanent Representative, Yosef Tekoah, to state in the Security Council on May 1, 1968:

> *In declarations and statements made publicly and to Mr. Jarring, my Government has indicated its acceptance of the Security Council resolution for the promotion of agreement of the establishment of a just and lasting peace. I am also authorized to reaffirm that we are willing to seek agreements with each Arab state in all matters included in that resolution.*

U Thant's report laconically says that "this statement was not regarded as acceptable by the Arab representatives."

Thus Jarring came and went, to and fro, between Nicosia, in Cyprus, and the Middle Eastern capitals. On one occasion I went to meet him at Nicosia myself in the hope that I might coincide with the Egyptian Foreign Minister so that Jarring's "conferences" might be simultaneous and less laborious than the shuttle procedures which were beginning to wear him down. The Egyptians had got wind of my plans and deliberately arranged their own absence. My compensation lay in an interesting talk with President Makarios, who discoursed sadly on the difficulty of maintaining a binational state.

The truth was that the Arab states wanted full withdrawal without any peace. They were not prepared to pay the smallest price for the restoration of their territory. On the other hand, no Israeli government could be persuaded that Israel should give up security assets without the compensation of a peaceful relationship, which was, after all, not our privilege but our right. In an effort to win a better world opinion, I made a detailed statement to the UN General Assembly on October 8, 1968, containing a nine-point peace plan. In this statement I gave the most moderate possible formulation to Israel's position on 1) the establishment of peace; 2) secure and recognized boundaries; 3) security agreements; 4) the open frontier; 5) navigation; 6) refugees; 7) Jerusalem; 8) acknowledgment and recognition of sovereignty, integrity and right to national life; and 9) regional cooperation. One of my proposals was that a conference of Middle Eastern states should be convened, together with governments contributing to refugee relief, and the Specialized Agencies of the United Nations, to work out a five-year plan for the solution of the refugee problem in the framework of a lasting peace, and the integration of refugees into productive life. I suggested that this conference be called in advance of peace negotiations. I reiterated that "Israel does not seek to exercise unilateral jurisdiction in the Holy Places of Christianity and Islam." I said that we should work out a "boundary settlement" compatible with the security of Israel and with the honor of Arab states.

For at least a year after the nine-point peace proposal, Israel was immune from charges in the international press about her obduracy and intransigence. Hundreds of newspapers across the world told the Arab states that the ball was in their court. But it is characteristic of the pull between international interests and domestic pressures that my speech on October 8 was challenged in our own Cabinet by Gahal members, who had to be defeated in a vote called for by Eshkol. Moreover, the day after my address to the General Assembly a prominent opposition leader, Shmuel Tamir, arrived in New York and held a press conference in which he poured public scorn on our government's peace proposal. I had ended my peace plan with the words:

It may seem ambitious to talk of a peaceful Middle Eastern design at this moment of tension and rancor, but there is such a thing in physics as fusion at high temperatures. In political experience, too, a consciousness of peril often brings a thaw in frozen situations. In the long run, nations can prosper only by recognizing what their common interests demand. The hour is ripe for the creative adventure of peace.

As far as the Arabs were concerned, it was clear that the hour was not "ripe" at all. But my address had another purpose, which was amply fulfilled. President Johnson had given tentative assurances to Prime Minister Eshkol in January 1968 concerning the supply of

Phantom jet fighters to Israel. This was a crucial matter for our security, since the categories of arms available to our neighbors were escalating under Soviet supply and stimulation. On the day after my peace plan was announced in the General Assembly, Johnson published his decision to make the Phantoms available.

Johnson was now nearing the end of his term in office. It was known, however, that a presidential commitment would certainly be honored by his successor. Richard M. Nixon and Vice-President Hubert H. Humphrey, who were the two major candidates, had given assurances to that effect. But President Johnson had told me that in order for his announcement to be made, it was essential that Israel have a peaceful posture in American opinion. A few days after my General Assembly speech with its nine-point peace program, Johnson announced his intention to supply the Phantom aircraft. A little later in the month I had my last meeting with him in his capacity as President of the United States.

It was an impressive experience. The presidential power was beginning to ooze out of Johnson's massive frame, but his habit of dominating still filled the room. There was now a note of sadness in his demeanor and discourse. He had begun his presidency after the assassination of Kennedy in a mood of national shock. He had immediately administered a therapeutic dose of harmony. He had then put his vast energy to work to get the Congress to adopt legislation which took America into the age of the welfare state. At the center of his laws and programs was the underprivileged American: youngsters growing up illiterate on Southern farms; old people wasting away without dignity through lack of social concern; families of the sick whose resources were being cruelly bled by medical expenses for which no public insurance was available; populations living in areas in which racial discrimination was unrestrained by law. If he had been able to concentrate on these measures, Lyndon Johnson would have ended his presidency, or even prolonged it, in an atmosphere of domestic and international respect. But across his horizons had come the Vietnam war. The few military "advisers" sent to Saigon by Eisenhower had been vastly expanded by Kennedy in the flush of his "imperial" presidency. Johnson had not had the courage to break away from the momentum which his martyred predecessor had initiated. By 1968, American involvement had become bulky and untenable, and yet there was no easy extrication. With American loss of life growing more alarming, and the American reputation assailed throughout the world, the President had reached the conclusion that he could no longer express or elicit a national consensus. Moreover, most Americans doubted the morality as well as the utility of the war.

In the early part of 1968, he had announced his intention not to submit himself for re-election.

As we sank into leather armchairs in his office on that October morning, I noticed how his love of gimmickry had affected the interior decoration. There were three television sets, which he could work separately or simultaneously without moving from his seat. As he opened a flap on the arm of the chair I noticed a whole system of buttons and gadgets. One of the buttons seemed to be a direct line to some far destination, perhaps Moscow. Another said "Coffee" and a third "Fresca." I devoutly hoped that his aim and eyesight were accurate.

The President began by reaffirming his intention to sign the agreement for the supply of Phantoms. He then told me that both candidates for the Presidency had' agreed to honor this commitment. He wanted me to tell Eshkol that Lyndon B. Johnson had kept his word.

After hearing my account of our peace explorations with Jordan, the President went on to speak frankly about his own sentiment on leaving the White House. He had come there with a social purpose vital to his country's future. The affairs of the world had diverted him into problems of international conflict. What disturbed him now was not so much that the United States would fail, for the first time in its history, to win a military objective. More serious was the new American attitude to the world. Like Roosevelt, Truman, Eisenhower and Kennedy, he had represented the idea of "American responsibility." But now there was an effort to turn America's back on the world and to retreat into an illusory isolation. The President seemed to feel that his own party was the focus of the new isolation.

He then gave me remarkably frank and somewhat picturesque character sketches of his adversaries: Senator J. William Fulbright, Senator Wayne Morse, Walter Lippmann and—in a sad and resigned tone—Frank Church of Idaho. All these had been leading advocates of restricted American commitments. Walter Lippmann wanted the United States to limit American defense commitments in the Pacific to Australia and New Zealand while maintaining alliances with Western Europe. President Johnson wondered whether it was an "accident" that all the beneficiaries of this protection "happened to be white."

He told me that he had spoken to Nixon and Humphrey not only about Phantoms but about the American concern for Israel. He thought that we could be reassured about the future. Either of his possible successors, for different motives, would keep faith with the commitment to Israel's security and independence. On the other hand, if the Congress and public opinion continued to develop an isolationist trend of thought in other contexts, a situation would be created in the United States in which "Israel will go down the drain." He thought, therefore, that Israel and her friends had an interest in supporting an American policy of commitment. He added wryly, "A bunch of rabbis came here one day in 1967 to tell me that I ought not to send a single screwdriver to Vietnam, but on the other hand, should push all our aircraft carriers through the Straits of Tiran to help Israel."

I did not feel that this parallel was valid. But his concern for Israel was so deep that I did not feel that I had a special duty to defend American liberals against his charge of neoisolationism. I was watching the political collapse of a man born with all the attributes of command who had lost control of his own vision. I admired his conclusion that it was useless for him to pursue his presidency beyond the point of its relevance.

On returning to Jerusalem in November, I put the Foreign Ministry to work preparing papers and policies for our future contact with the Nixon Administration. As I speculated about the new President's attitude to Israel, I became aware of apprehension in Israel and among American Jews. Israel's best experiences in American-Israeli relations had been linked with the names of Democratic Presidents. The Eisenhower Administration had given us five years of anxiety and only two or three years of friendship. And many Israelis and American Jews were influenced in their attitude to Nixon by their own tendency to be on the liberal side. The Secretary-General of our party, Golda Meir, had legitimately expressed her hope that Hubert Humphrey would be elected. The Israeli Labor Party has traditionally adopted ideological positions that the Israeli government itself cannot articulate.

But in February 1969 a sudden change came over our domestic scene. Levi Eshkol's health had been declining rapidly in recent weeks. He seemed exhausted by the weight of his ordeals. One heart attack had succeeded another. Early in the year Eshkol had published a courageous interview in *Newsweek* indicating a willingness to give up territory west of the Jordan in return for final peace. This had brought upon his head a violent assault from opposition parties. He felt that some of his own colleagues in the Labor movement had not given him full support. A vote of no confidence in his Administration had been defeated during his absence on a sick-bed, but he told me that he could have wished the support of his position in the Knesset by Deputy Prime Minister Allon and Labor Party Secretary-General Golda Meir to have been somewhat more fervent.

On February 26 I was having breakfast at home with the Minister of Tourism, Moshe Kol, when a telephone call came from Yaacov Herzog. He told me in a shaky voice that the Prime Minister had passed away a few minutes before.

I had seen Levi Eshkol the previous day during one of our periodic consultations, and was quite unprepared for this news. I went at once to his house in Rambam Street, reflecting that, against every expectation, this unassuming, humane, easygoing man had built the most successful record of all Israeli leaders. He had victoriously come through the ordeals of war. It had been his careful accumulation of weapons and resources that had made Israel's victory possible. He left behind a secure nation, a strong army, a solid majority in Parliament and a united Labor movement—though none of these achievements was destined to survive his death for more than a few years. Israelis who had been skeptical about Eshkol as Prime Minister had grown to respect his firmness as well as his capacity to transcend the disruptive elements in our national character by his own harmonizing force. The national grief was profound and sincere. For me personally, it was the loss of a friend under whose tolerant leadership my own work had been able to develop to its fullest potential.

For some years it had been assumed that the competition for succession to Eshkol would lie between Dayan and Allon but I had never fully accepted this logic. At a dinner in London when Harold Wilson asked me which of the two would be likely to succeed, I had told him that in my opinion this was a race between two "nonstarters." The relations between these men and their supporters were so acute that the victory of either might have portended a loss of party unity. A few months before Eshkol's death, Finance Minister Pinhas Sapir had asked to have an intimate talk with me. He told me that Eshkol's physicians were pessimistic about his ability to survive another attack such as that which he had weathered after the election in 1965. Sapir had said that since there would have to be an election anyhow in 1969, we should have a plan for maintaining continuity of leadership in the event of the Prime Minister's incapacity. He thought that Golda Meir might accept the task, but that such willingness would depend on the agreement of all members of the Cabinet to retain their present functions. In the contingency that we were discussing, the Cabinet would remain intact, with a change only at the top. I was being asked to express approval.

I did this without hesitation. Besides Golda Meir's experience and strong roots in the public confidence, there was also the circumstance that she represented the central element in our party's structure, whereas Allon and Dayan still represented the two minority factions. Thus, the prospect of keeping our party united coincided with other considerations in favor of Mrs. Meir's candidacy, failing which I would then have supported Allon. I was not surprised when, within a few weeks after Eshkol's death, Sapir was able to secure the vote of our party's Central Committee for Mrs. Meir's election.

The last matters that I discussed with Eshkol before his death had concerned my forthcoming visit to Washington, where I would meet the new President and his Secretary of State, William P. Rogers. I set out on my journey before Mrs. Meir was sworn in.

My talks with President Nixon and Secretary Rogers were harmonious. The obligation to keep Israel strong was reiterated with great sincerity. So also was the American attitude in favor of maintaining the cease-fire lines until they could be replaced by a permanent peace. I spent many hours with the new American leaders and I felt that I had helped lay the foundation for good relationships in the coming four years. Ambassador Rabin, who accompanied me on these conversations, enthusiastically cabled back to Israel that "the talks of Foreign Minister Eban with the President and Secretary of State have created a firm basis for positive relations with the Nixon Administration."

On the other hand, I could see a few clouds on the horizon. The first visit of President Nixon abroad had been to Paris, where he came under the spell of General de Gaulle's commanding personality. (The new chairman of the National Security Council, Dr. Henry A. Kissinger, had initiated the President's regime by according priority to Paris in the hope that the United States could overcome the French inhibition which had weakened the Atlantic Alliance.) President de Gaulle talked much of the Middle East. He had never recovered from the Soviet rebuff to his proposal for a Four Power consultation and he still believed that a new concert of Europe, based on the "Big Four," was a better formula for international stability than the despised United Nations, or the "hegemonistic" idea of an American-Soviet dialogue that would leave the rest of the world as a mere spectator of the Great Power discourse. President Nixon had accepted the idea of Four Power talks on the Middle East. He assured me, however, that I need not take this as a serious threat to our interests. The United States would keep close control and would veto any proposal that it thought inimical to Israel's security. Moreover, the talks would be held by United Nations ambassadors in New York. This was a notoriously weak level of authority in the minds of the Nixon Administration, which took a hard-nosed, skeptical view about the role of an international organization in a world dominated by nuclear powers.

Nixon had been cordial, but still seemed insecure in his new eminence. He greeted me with the words "We've both gone up in the world since we last met." Our last meeting had been in 1965 on a Constellation shuttle from Washington to New York. He had lost his campaign for the governorship of California three years before and was practicing law in some obscurity in New York. The stewardess approached us and asked for my autograph—not his. He seemed to be a rejected politician with no horizon ahead, but within three years he had clambered back to the summit. In March 1969 I found him lucid, competent and authoritative. He took me into the Rose Garden for a few moments, despite the cold March winds, to ask me earnestly why "Israel's friends" in America did not have more faith in his concern for Israel's interests. He assured me that he would never let Israel down. I did not understand, until some years later, why the Rose Garden was regarded as a more intimate arena than the Oval Office.

My sense of reassurance was only partly secure. In one of the working papers that Secretary Rogers gave me there were some adverse innovations in comparison with previous formulations by the Johnson Administration. The most that Johnson had ever said about withdrawal was that it should be to "secure and recognized boundaries" which should not "reflect the weight of conquest." Rogers now added the stipulation that any changes agreed upon in the 1967 boundaries should be "minor." He also proposed that while Jerusalem should remain united, provision should be made for a "civil and religious role" for Jordan. Johnson had spoken only of the "Holy Places in Jerusalem," not of the city as a whole. Even those of us who were not ambitious about territorial revision could not help feeling that our bargaining position was weakened when our greatest friends made restrictive references to Israel's territorial hopes and, simultaneously, entered a dialogue with Three Powers, none of which fully shared the American concern for Israel's security.

The first year of a new U.S. Administration has always been a delicate period for us. This is the hour of the perfectionists—the interval during which an incoming government believes that all things can be quickly changed. Yet, I did not have any apocalpytic fear about what the Four Power talks were likely to produce. My feeling was that the gap between the American and Soviet positions was too great to allow agreement. Back in Jerusalem, however, I found Mrs. Meir intensely worried by the Four Power exercise. At a meeting with her and some senior colleagues I felt that they regarded me as insufficiently pessimistic about the Nixon Administration. My prediction that the Four Power talks would peter out harmlessly was not very well received by the press. Most Israelis prefer their clouds without silver linings.

Despite the ambassador's optimistic appraisal, which I shared in its general outline, 1969 was to be a stormy year in Israeli-American relations. The Four Power talks between representatives at United Nations headquarters petered out, as I had anticipated, into inconclusive tea parties. The Jarring Mission was now confined to polemical exchanges. Israel and Egypt made statements with an eye to their propaganda effects. Not a single reticent diplomatic exchange took place at any stage. In Washington it was feared that a conference of Arab leaders at Rabat in December would adopt proposals hostile to Western interests. To prevent damage to American interests, the State Department, under Secretary Rogers, decided to make a placatory gesture to the Arab world. Rogers published a statement of policy on December 9 in which he advocated an Israeli withdrawal to the pre-1967 lines in favor of Egypt and Jordan within the framework of a peace settlement. At the most, his plan made provision for minor adjustments. He thus weakened Israel's bargaining power in an eventual negotiation on boundaries. Even those of us who were far from being territorial extremists resented this pressure. The diplomatic balance, always weighted against us, was now hopelessly unstable. The Johnson Administration had never made a formal commitment on the dimensions of the projected Israeli withdrawal, and had thus kept alive an Arab incentive for negotiation. The Rogers plan was undoubtedly one of the major errors of international diplomacy in the postwar era. It had arisen out of another attempt to secure American-Soviet agreement.

Our government and Parliament were almost united in rejecting the proposal. Our protests did not bring about the withdrawal of the Rogers proposals, but they did induce some restraint. The United States made no attempt to give operative effect to the Rogers proposals, and the bilateral relations between us were not affected.

In any case, the military situation on the Suez Canal soon superseded the preoccupation of the United States with diplomatic gestures. The fact that Israel had rejected the Rogers plans did not mean that the Arabs accepted them. The central reality was that Nasser hoped for military vengeance which would expunge the memories of the Six-Day War. Artillery bombardments with air action across the Suez Canal were causing us severe losses of life as well as a constant wastage in our strength. Yet, Nasser was suffering losses far greater than he was inflicting. Our policy was one of controlled response. We would hit the Egyptian forces sufficiently hard to make their assault unrewarding. At the same time we would avoid globalizing the conflict by provoking Soviet intervention in defense of Egypt.

This view, however, was not uncritically accepted, and one of the most decisive debates in Israel since 1967 took place in the late weeks of 1969 and the early days of 1970. At the outset, ministers were divided between those willing to take the risks of a deep penetration of Egypt's air space for massive attacks on Cairo, and those who feared that this would bring the Soviet Union to Egypt's defense with a consequent disturbance of the strategic balance.

A decisive element in this discussion was the advocacy of a militant approach by our ambassador in Washington. Rabin bombarded us with cables urging escalation against Egypt and other Arab states. He clearly believed that there were some people in Washington who might react sympathetically to such a course. I did not believe that this analysis, however tempting, corresponded to international realities. My resistance to his appraisal engendered a tension which was to cloud Israeli domestic politics for some time to come. Yet Rabin's strong advocacy certainly helped to bring about a majority in favor of more intensive Israeli air action across the Canal. The Washington embassy was unexpectedly strengthening the hawks at home.

On January 7, 1970, Israeli bombers crossed the cease-fire line, which we had been able to penetrate easily since the capture of Soviet radar by Israeli commandos ten days before. Our Phantoms now carried the war into the deepest parts of Egyptian territory. Bombs fell in areas less than twelve miles from Cairo. The rest of the story has been described by Heykal. Faced by the humiliation of an undefended capital, Nasser made a secret trip to Moscow. The Soviets, initially reluctant, agreed not only to supply more sophisticated air-defense equipment but, more significantly, to send Soviet advisers and military personnel to man the equipment and to instruct Egyptians in their use. Although the Soviet forces were to be expelled by Sadat in 1972, their work until then gave the Egyptian forces a technical competence that was to make Sadat's Yom Kippur decision more feasible.

There is no evidence, in my view, that the United States ever wanted us to escalate the war. At any rate, in March 1970 its attitude was cool: Secretary Rogers gave a delaying answer to Israel's request for additional aircraft. This caused disquiet in Israel, since our losses were beginning to mount. I shall never forget a meeting late at night at Golda Meir's house in which Dayan made apocalyptic predictions of what would happen if American arms supplies were not forthcoming. My own belief was that we would get the arms—but a little later than we had hoped.

Although the war was having a more devastating effect on Egypt than on us, it was still a fact that we were losing lives and planes. Without the assurance of ongoing supplies of Phantoms and other equipment, our military command would not have the confidence with which to take essential tactical risks. This was my main concern when, in May 1970, I had a discussion with President Nixon in the White House. He was accompanied by Kissinger and Sisco. The main question was whether we could expect a favorable response to our arms request in the near future. The President began with a significant question. Was it still Israel's policy that American troops would not be involved in any foreseeable development of the war in the Middle East? When I gave a positive answer, Nixon immediately replied, "Well, in that case, you will get the stuff, so long as you don't insist on too much publicity." He then instructed Kissinger and Sisco to discuss delivery schedules with us.

When the minister at the embassy, Shlomo Argov, drafted his cable to Jerusalem, I felt that I could expect an expression of relief. But skepticism was so deeply embedded in Israeli minds that even the President's formal announcement to me was not regarded as final. The public mood about the Phantoms was becoming obsessive. Israelis would not believe that they would get the planes until they actually landed on an Israeli airstrip. My own feeling was that a presidential commitment such as Nixon had given was, in fact, irrevocable. When I reached home, I could feel blasts of skepticism flowing toward me across the Cabinet table. I had the foresight to send a note to my friend and neighbor, Pinhas Sapir, saying: "I predict that the Phantoms will be delivered in September. Please keep this chit and open it at the end of September." Sapir played this game with a perfectly straight face. He informed me on October 1, after the Phantoms had arrived, that "to the surprise of some of our colleagues," I had not been optimistic in vain.

American policy, however, was now on a double course. It sought to strengthen Israel, but also to bring the fighting to an end. The United States began to work actively for a cease-fire. President Nixon had told me this in our conversation in May. He had added, in quiet parenthesis, that "we might do something on the political side, but you won't have to worry. We shall consult you before we take any steps." In the ensuing weeks the Foreign Ministry constantly asked our embassy to find out what was being planned on the political level. The response was that since Nixon had promised to consult us ahead of time, we had no need to push. On June 24, however, on my return from West European capitals, I was met by Director-General Gideon Rafael, who said that Ambassador Barbour was seeing the

Prime Minister at her house with a message. I drove straight to the meeting.

On Rogers' behalf, Barbour presented us with a proposal consisting of three parts: first, the acceptance of a cease-fire on the Egyptian front for a period of three months; second, a statement by Israel, Egypt and Jordan that they accepted the Security Council's Resolution 242 and, specifically, the call for "withdrawal from occupied territories"; third, an undertaking to negotiate with Egypt and Jordan under Dr. Jarring's auspices when the cease-fire came into force. One of the important provisions of the cease-fire was to be a "standstill." Neither Egypt nor Israel would be able to bring missiles or artillery closer to the front than before. It was obvious that if Israel accepted a cease-fire and Egypt brought its anti-aircraft missiles forward, we would simply be offering Egypt a shelter from which to pursue the war of attrition with greater effectiveness when the cease-fire expired after three months.

The time had now come for another major decision. It was obviously going to have domestic effects. Although we had previously accepted Resolution 242 in general terms, a specific commitment to withdraw in the context of a Jordanian negotiation would create a dilemma for the Gahal Party, which had been our coalition partner since the eve of the Six-Day War. To disrupt our national coalition was a heavy sacrifice to ask of our party, and especially of Prime Minister Meir. Her first response to Barbour had been negative. But in the ensuing weeks President Nixon deepened his commitment to Israel's security in several ways. He let us understand that his undertaking to me about the Phantoms should be taken seriously, and he gave assurance that Israel would not be expected to withdraw a single soldier from any of the cease-fire lines except in the context of a contractual peace agreement which Israel would regard as satisfactory for its security. There was also an undertaking to use the American veto power in the Security Council to resist resolutions calling for a complete withdrawal to the pre-1967 lines. Thus, in late July, when we surveyed our situation in all its aspects, we felt that the risks of accepting the American cease-fire proposal were less than the dangers of rejecting it. The rejection of the cease-fire would mean the continuation of savage war with Egypt, the prospect of involvement with the Soviet Union, and diminishing American fidelity to Israel. Begin and his supporters argued that the United States would be willing to accept the part of the proposal that was congenial to us, namely the cease-fire, without giving the Arabs a prospect of political negotiation in return. The rest of us found this hard to believe. We believed that anybody who wanted a cease-fire would have to accept its conditions: Resolution 242 and the resumption of the Jarring Mission.

After tense discussion, Begin led his party out of our coalition, despite the wish of nearly half of his supporters to remain. A memorable period in Israel's national history came to an end.

We were now free to explore peace settlements without the constant threat of a veto by the Herut Party. And the Labor Party had maintained its unity. The formula announcing our readiness to withdraw to secure and recognized boundaries in the context of peace with Jordan or Egypt was actually drafted by Moshe Dayan, on whom Herut had probably relied for support. The National Religious Party also accepted our August 1970 decision in the knowledge that we were talking of withdrawal on the Jordanian as well as on the Egyptian front.

The departure of Begin and his able colleagues, Ezer Weizman, Rimalt and Landau, left the Cabinet table more compact and tranquil. But the spice and zest of intellectual combat were reduced. Begin's talent flourished more on large parliamentary occasions than in more intimate Cabinet encounters. I had the feeling that he exchanged the Cabinet table for the Knesset rostrum with a measure of relief.

Begin and his colleagues had acted with logical rectitude in resigning their posts. They assumed correctly that the government would be willing to renounce large areas of the West Bank in the context of a peace settlement with Jordan. In later years some members of our party were to pretend that this had never happened at all. The fact is, however, that August 1970 was an important date in the evolution of Labor Party policy. One of its consequences was to illustrate the issue that separated us from our rivals in Gahal (and later Likud). We were back to the partition logic. We did not believe that a unitary structure west of the Jordan could be permanently reconciled with our international interests, with our democratic nature or with the basic Zionist concept of a Jewish state saturated with Jewish identity and associations.

The cease-fire was received in Israel with satisfaction. When Mrs. Meir announced it on television, the public reaction was almost as if a peace settlement had been secured. No longer would the hourly news bulletins begin with the sad voice of the radio announcer telling us the names of young Israelis fallen in battle. The toll of life and of precious equipment had made the war of attrition costly for us.

It had been even more disastrous for Egypt. Many Israelis believed that if this was the best that Nasser could achieve by military methods, his empirical temperament might bring him around to the idea of restoring Sinai territory by negotiation and peace. This, however, was by no means his immediate reaction. But soon after the cease-fire agreement, we were involved in a disappointment that gave ammunition to the opposition and anxiety to those of us who had advocated the cease-fire in good faith.

The "standstill" was for us a crucial part of the cease-fire agreement. Neither party was entitled to reap military advantage by bringing missiles forward. While the exchange of fire had gone on across the Suez Canal, the Egyptians had not been able to build any new missile sites close to the cease-fire line. If they were now to do this under the cover of a cease-fire, they would be in a better position to resume the war successfully after the lapse of the three-month period. Within a few days of the conclusion of the cease-fire agreement, our head of military intelligence, General Aharon Yariv, was reporting to Chief of Staff Chaim Bar-Lev and to responsible ministers that the Egyptians had begun to move their missiles forward as soon as the ink was dry on the cease-fire agreement. This was obviously being done with Soviet encouragement.

The first American reaction was evasive. The United States had taken a grave responsibility in causing us to adopt a decision that had disrupted our parliamentary cohesion. Washington at first professed not to know that the violations were taking place. Since we depended on the United States for the surveillance of the agreement, our frustration was deep. But ten days after the violations had been attested by Israeli minds, Ambassador Barbour came to see me in the Dan Hotel. He told me with characteristic sincerity and bluntness that Israel was right. Aerial reconnaissance had revealed that the Egyptians had committed a violation. The United States would consult with us on how to meet the new situation. We decided to delay our resumption of talks with Jarring until Egypt moved its missiles back.

Insofar as we could find any compensation for the Soviet-Egyptian action, it lay in the improvement of our relations with the United States. We had learned from President Kennedy's reaction to Gromyko in the Cuban crisis that the last thing that any American President likes is to be made to look foolish by Soviet promises. The Nixon Administration, too, reacted sharply to this deceit. The credibility of Soviet assurances to the United States is a vital element in the world security system. Although Israel was the immediate victim of the Soviet-Egyptian violation, American interests were also at stake. We were thus able to get American understanding for our refusal to resume discussions with Egypt under the Jarring Mission unless Egypt withdrew the missiles that had been moved up contrary to the cease-fire agreement.

In the United Nations debate that opened in September, the United States alone justified Israel's refusal to resume the Jarring Mission until the Egyptian violation was corrected. But the General Assembly voted for the unconditional resumption of the Jarring Mission, thus condoning the Egyptian violation. It also stressed the need for early withdrawals from occupied territories without an equal stress on the need for a peace treaty. In 1968 and 1969 I had managed to avoid debates in the General Assembly by ensuring that an operative diplomatic process should be on foot, either through the Jarring Mission or in the Four Power talks. Once a vacuum was created, the General Assembly moved into it with a massive pro-Arab majority working against us. It was not until 1973 that I was able to avoid the annual autumn debate by insisting that the Geneva Conference be planned for the end of the year. We thus successfully argued that an Assembly debate would sabotage a more constructive diplomatic effort.

No sooner had the General Assembly debate, with its adverse conclusion, come to an end in December 1970 than I was disconcerted in New York to read reports that Dayan was advocating that we should "jump into the icy waters" of the Jarring Mission. This report was published on the very day that I was telling Rogers and Kissinger at Mrs. Meir's request that Israel would not agree to resume the Jarring Mission without the Egyptian violation being corrected. If we were going to jump into the icy waters, I thought that we might just as well have done so before the General Assembly debate, which had created an adverse international jurisprudence for us. Rogers and Kissinger seemed to be just as surprised by Dayan's initiative as was Golda Meir. But it was no part of their business to be more Catholic than the Israeli Popes. Although Dayan's press briefings and speech at Haifa could be formally presented as an individual expression of a view not endorsed by the Cabinet, American representatives assumed that if Dayan had predicted our unconditional return to the Jarring talks, this would become the official Israeli policy in the near future. As usual, they were right. I saw no harm at all in Dayan's idea of giving the Jarring Mission another chance, but I was worried by the fact that what we had been saying in Washington and the United Nations for several weeks had lost credibility.

17

The Twilight Years
1971-1972

THE YEAR 1971 WAS A PARTICULARLY BUSY TIME FOR ISRAELI DIPLOMACY.
In its early days the Jarring Mission was resumed. As a result of our
Cabinet's decision of August 1970, I was able to transmit to Egypt and
Jordan separate proposals for the conclusion of peace treaties based
on the termination of all acts of hostility and "withdrawal of Israeli
forces to secure and recognized boundaries to be determined in the
peace negotiations." I could not have used this language before August 1970. Moshe Dayan had helped to draft this formula, and the Religious Party acquiesced. Since August 1970 the Israeli position has
been firmly rooted in the principle of territorial compromise in the
West Bank as well as in other sectors.

Unfortunately, the Arab governments were no more willing to take
advantage of this development than of our far-reaching peace proposals in June 1967. Their response was that there was no territorial
issue to be discussed. Israel had to return to the June 4, 1967, lines
with all their inherent vulnerabilities intact. While they were clear
about what Israel should do about withdrawal, the Arab governments
were not specific about what they would do in the direction of peace.
There had been no effective change in their positions since the Khartoum Conference in 1967.

The Jarring Mission thus came to a permanent end. It had become
evident that any attempt to pass from total hostility to total peace
involved too drastic a transition for Arab states to undertake. There

would obviously have to be movement in stages. In early February, Israel took an unexpected initiative which arose out of long meditation by Defense Minister Moshe Dayan. He had been reluctant for Israeli forces to reach the Suez Canal in the first place and had been deeply apprehensive thereafter about the consequences of staying there. This position differentiated him sharply from Ministers in the Likud Party, and even some of my own colleagues, who believed that our command of the Suez Canal waters gave Israel a particular weight in international strategy. Dayan felt that we would be better off at a cease-fire line established somewhere near the Gidi and Mitla passes, which we had reached in the 1956 campaign. The conflict would then be drawn between Israel and Egypt alone. If we stayed at the Suez Canal, we would always be in sharp tension not only with an Arab state but with all countries that depended for their commerce on an open Canal, and especially with the Soviet Union, which had no other way of trading with East Africa or Asia, except from Vladivostok. But the fact that Soviet warships had no access to interoceanic traffic gave quiet satisfaction in the United States. It was assumed by some Israelis that the Americans would prefer a closed Canal. My own feelings was that the Soviet Union and Israel had come so close to direct clash in the later stages of the war of attrition in 1970 that the United States must surely have had a serious scare. I shall not soon forget the day when it became known to us from radio intercepts that Soviet pilots were engaged in air combat with Israeli aircraft over the Canal fighting zone. I felt that even if the United States secretly wanted a closed Canal for reasons of long-term strategy, its short-term interest would dictate a preference for an open Canal as a guarantee against renewed military confrontation.

In the early weeks of 1971 Dayan continued to develop the idea that Israeli forces should withdraw from the Canal to enable it to be opened for international traffic. We would naturally require assurances about the security of our forces at a new line east of the Suez Canal.

This idea was discussed with the United States in January. President Sadat's first response on February 4 seemed to be promising, but before we could put the idea to an operative test it was frustrated by the independent initiative of Jarring, who, on February 8, 1971, publicly addressed Israel and Egypt with his own proposal. He suggested that Egypt should give a list of assurances on peace, recognition and the end of the state of war, while Israel should make an undertaking on the withdrawal of her troops to the previous international boundary. In order to correct any impression that the future of Gaza was still open, Jarring added that Gaza should be restored to Arab rule and not left in Israeli hands. He was thus giving full endorsement to the Arab territorial claims, leaving Israel no opportunity to negotiate even the smallest territorial adjustment. There was not even an opening for the maintenance of an Israeli military position under "lease" at Sharm el-Sheikh, as Secretary Rogers had once proposed.

The United States now exercised strong pressure on Israel to accept this proposal as it stood. In our discussions we decided to applaud Sadat's readiness to talk for the first time about a "peace agreement" with Israel, but we added that the terms of the peace agreement, including its territorial terms, must be negotiated between both parties and not dictated by one of them. We expressed willingness to withdraw to secure and recognized boundaries, the location of which would not correspond to those of June 4, 1967, but would be agreed in the negotiating process. Some of us, including Allon and myself, wished to formulate our rejection of the June 4 boundaries in measured terms by explaining that they were not secure or defensible. The Cabinet, however, opted for a categorical refusal to restore the previous line, thus giving our reply a more peremptory tone.

The Jarring proposal was a windfall for Egyptian diplomacy. It naturally reduced Egypt's incentive to accept a more practical and limited withdrawal at the Suez Canal. A few weeks later, however, it became apparent that the proposal had misfired. Israel had no intention of signing away her right to negotiate on boundary and security arrangements, and her adversary was not prepared to be satisfied with a peace engagement concerning Sinai alone. Egypt insisted on an Israeli undertaking to withdraw from the Gaza Strip and from all other "Arab territories" to the boundaries that existed on June 4, 1967. It also entered a reservation in favor of Palestinian rights.

Nevertheless, the decision of Jarring and of the United States to regard the Israeli reply to the February 8 memorandum as negative has always seemed to me to have been mistaken. The fact is that in their replies, the Egyptians made more progress toward the idea of a peace agreement, and the Israelis made more progress toward the concept of withdrawal, than at any other previous stage. The wise reaction would have been for Jarring to stress not the gap that still remained, but the distance that had already been bridged. He should have tried to elicit the range and motive of Israel's reservation on full withdrawal. He should also have explored the prospect of bringing Egypt's declaration on peace closer to what Israel would accept. He chose to regard the first replies of each party as final answers and failed to notice our offer to negotiate. The United States was fully behind this erroneous reaction and must share responsibility for it.

To the extent that the idea of an overall settlement receded, the possibility of an interim agreement on the Suez Canal came more vigorously to life. Some ministers had thought that Dayan's readiness to "jump into the icy water" of the Jarring Mission had been premature while we were still attempting to secure the withdrawal of Egyptian missiles as a condition for resuming the Jarring talks. By mid-March, however, this was obviously academic. It was clear by then that the Egyptian missiles would not be withdrawn. We would have to seek compensation through an American agreement to strengthen our defenses so as to meet our new vulnerabilities. We succeeded in this plan and the way was now open for an intensive exploration of a Suez Canal interim agreement.

On March 22 the Israeli government, at the initiative of Moshe Dayan, took another of its important decisions. It virtually renounced the principle (to which American adherence had been obtained) that not a single Israeli soldier would be withdrawn from cease-fire lines except in the context of a contractual peace settlement. Dayan suggested that this far-reaching American assurance be abandoned in favor of a limited withdrawal from the Canal in return for something far less than peace. He proposed that in return for a limited pullback, enabling Egypt to open the Canal, Israel should ask for undertakings that the state of war be ended, that future withdrawals would be subject to negotiation, and that a normal civilian situation would be created in the Canal area. Once the waterway was opened, the cities and villages near the Canal—Suez, El Qantara, Ismailia and Port Said —should be restored to normality. Another condition was that the United States should make binding engagements on long-term military support of Israel, and should supervise the demilitarized character of the territory that we evacuated. Dayan's idea was that Israeli forces be withdrawn some thirty kilometers from the Canal up to the western edge of the Gidi and Mitla passes.

At its March 22 meeting, the Israeli Cabinet accepted the principle of a partial Israeli withdrawal in return for something less than full peace. I was engaged at that time in talks with Secretary Rogers and Dr. Kissinger in Washington. They showed great interest in the Israel Cabinet's initiative. I suggested to them that the United States take active steps to explore the Egyptian reaction and that we should avoid placing this matter in the hands of Jarring or any other United Nations agency. It would thus be accurate to say that in March 1971 a new era in Middle Eastern diplomacy began. The concept of a partial interim settlement replaced the previous "all or nothing" approach to peace. And the idea of American "good offices" super-seded the previous concept of UN mediation.

Unfortunately, our government, although united on the principle of a Canal withdrawal, was in some discord concerning its application. The fact that Dayan had originated the idea may have played some part in creating resistance to it on the part of his political adver-saries. There was a cautious approach to the Canal withdrawal, not only on the part of Galili and Allon, but more surprisingly from the moderate Sapir, who now supported the view of General Bar-Lev that the Israeli withdrawal should not be for more than ten kilo-meters from the Canal. This limited withdrawal would enable us to ensure that Egypt would not be able to cross the Canal in military strength and create a jumping-off ground for assault. It would also enable Israel "to shoot its way back" to the Canal area if Egypt vio-lated the agreement.

These views were reflected in a memorandum that we submitted on April 15. It was not communicated to Cairo. Our objective was merely to ensure that the United States, in its mediatory capacity, did not go beyond what Israel could accept. On this basis Secretary Rogers and Joseph Sisco set out for an exploration of the interim agreement idea in May 1971.

Our discussions with the United States in Jerusalem opened un-promisingly with a sharp exchange between our Prime Minister and the American Secretary of State. Rogers seemed to have been con-vinced in Cairo that Sadat was genuinely in search of peace, while Golda felt that the Secretary had been unduly credulous. In this some-what sterile discussion, the practical issue of the interim Canal agree-ment was lost from sight. Dayan, who was still the main advocate of the agreement, suggested a private clarification between himself and Sisco the next day.

In Dayan's talk with Sisco, he explained that there were two possible approaches to the settlement. One was the cautious approach based on a ten-kilometer withdrawal with the option of "shooting our way back to the Canal." This was the logic of the April 15 agreement. Dayan, however, did not disguise that there was another approach which he himself preferred, namely a permanent renunciation of Israeli access to the Canal and a willingness to go back as far as thirty kilometers. Dayan believed that no Egyptian government would open the Canal under the very eyes of an Israeli army and within range of Israeli tactical artillery some ten kilometers away. I had no doubt that he was correct.

When the results of this conversation returned to the broader ministerial group, Dayan came under criticism for what some of his colleagues regarded as excessive flexibility. I sent him a note asking whether he would put this idea to a vote in the Cabinet, in which case not only would I support him but, in my view, other ministers too, especially from the Mapam and Independent Liberal Groups. Dayan replied that unless the Prime Minister accepted his proposal, he would not even put it up for discussion and would, in fact, deny that the proposal had any official status at all. Since there was no consensus for a thirty-kilometer withdrawal, Dayan reluctantly let the matter drop. I have always regretted that he did not show his usual tenacity in support of this imaginative proposal, which could have averted the Yom Kippur War.

There was now a dangerous atmosphere of deadlock. The Jarring Mission was in abeyance, and Israeli initiative for an interim Suez settlement had reached a dead end. Sadat had promised the Egyptian people that 1971 would be "the year of decision." While it was not necessary to take this threat with complete seriousness, it was obvious that total diplomatic immobility would make the cease-fire precarious. There was also the chance that if Sadat had nothing to show in the political sphere, it might be succeeded by a more militant Egyptian leadership. Immobility also had grave disadvantages for our international position. While world opinion respected our aspirations for peace, it was not reconciled to our inflated map. European liberals found it hard to reconcile themselves to a prolonged Israeli control of a million Arab noncitizens of undefined civil status. In Africa our territorial conflict with Egypt, a founding member of the Organization of African Unity (OAU), threatened to create grave tensions. Both in Africa and in Europe, there was a general support of Israel's sovereign rights, but there were sharp reservations about our territorial condition. The absence of any progress toward a settlement worked more against us than against the Arabs, since the disputed territories were in our hands, not theirs.

I therefore recommended that we take the risk of reacting positively to an African move in the early autumn of 1971. The main author of this initiative was one of the most interesting of African statesmen, Léopold Sédar Senghor, President of Senegal. He had brooded long and seriously on the parallel mysteries of Moslem and Jewish history. Just as "negritude" had been an inherent condition of suffering, so also was Jewishness. This gave him an initial sympathy for Israel's aspirations. On the other hand, Islam, unlike Judaism, was a solid and integral part of African history. Senghor embodied the paradox of a Moslem state with a Christian leader. His African nation was headed by a man whose cultural roots and style were embedded in the French idiom. It was reasonable for him to think that the special contour of his personality gave him a conciliatory role. He developed the idea of a mission to Israel by four heads of African states with whom we had close relations. They would wear the mantle which Jarring had discarded and which the United States had not yet fully assumed. They would try to see whether a basis could be created on which the Jarring Mission could be resumed.

The four Presidents designated by the OAU for this mission were Senghor of Senegal, Josef Mobutu of Zaïre, Ahmadou Ahidjo of Cameroon and Major General Yakubu Gowon of Nigeria. The first three were known to me from my visits to their countries. Each of them was a strong idiosyncratic personality. It would be hard to think of four leaders more sharply divided in temperament and personality. In this they conveyed the richness and variety of African leadership. I had met Mobutu on each of my visits to Kinshasa and had been impressed by his sense of authority in a country whose area and structure seemed recalcitrant to any form of central control. The major link between Israel and Zaïre was the training of a mobile Zaïre parachute force by Israeli officers. This enabled Mobutu to transfer a unifying power quickly from one part of his huge country to another without maintaining a burdensome standing army. He had a great admiration for Israel's military record and for our robust resistance to Soviet intimidation. One of his prophetic apprehensions was that the weakness of the West, and especially American indifference, might open the way to a Communist hegemony in Africa. Léopold Senghor had a deeply analytical mind. His cultural experience was so sharply defined that he found it difficult to react to anything that was not said or written in French. This gave me some advantage over my principal colleagues when it came to the need to explain complex ideas to him.

With Ahmadou Ahidjo I had an even more intimate personal link. I had first met him in the United Nations in 1959 toward the end of my mission in Washington and at UN headquarters. One of our able diplomats, Aryeh Ilan, later to be ambassador in Burma, had suggested that I take an active role in a discussion on the future independence of Cameroon. The leader of the Cameroon National Movement, Ahidjo was disconsolately pacing the UN corridors in an effort to break through procedural difficulties that impeded his success. He was a small, sad-faced man in a foreign environment giving little sign of the authority that I saw in his demeanor in later years.

Nearly every other African state had achieved independence without any difficulty at the UN. In Cameroon, however, there were disputes about where the legitimate authority of the national movement lay. In particular, there was a claim by a group supported from Cairo which denied Ahidjo's legitimacy. The bilingual character of Cameroon, her complex history of domination first by Germany and then by France, created unusual intricacies. I took an interest in the problem and was able, with the use of our long and turbulent UN experience, to offer some advice on how the Cameroon case might be successfully presented. After all, Israel was one of the few states that had ever needed to fight its way from anonymity to UN membership. Ahidjo remained personally grateful to me for many years and received me warmly when, as Minister of Education and Culture, I made an official visit to his country in 1962. To this day his huge elephant tusk presented to me in Yaounde graces the entry to my home.

We had, naturally, been apprehensive about the visit of the African Presidents. But during several days of intensive talk we seemed to have made a strong impression on them. In a report to the General Assembly they stated that the Israeli and Egyptian positions, although still separated, were not so incompatible as to make the resumption of Jarring's mission impossible. In this courageous judgment they were virtually criticizing Jarring himself, as well as the United States, which had drawn excessively drastic conclusions from our reply to Jarring's February 8 memorandum. The reports from the African Presidents elicited a statement of our views supporting the principle of withdrawal from occupied territories and making clear that in determining our border with Egypt we would be guided not by any expansionist aims, but by considerations of free navigation and security alone.

This favorable report by four African Presidents came as a bombshell to the Arab states, and especially to Egypt. Instead of condemning Israel for unilateral intransigence, the African Presidents were putting Egypt and Israel on the same footing as having made legitimate reservations to the Jarring memorandum. Mahmoud Riad, the Secretary-General of the Arab League, rushed to UN headquarters in December 1971, where he found himself engaged in an extraordinary fight against the acceptance by the General Assembly of an African report favorable to Israel. The Arab steam roller was successful. The General Assembly voted—ridiculously—against Senghor's proposals. Another peacemaking prospect had been frustrated by international irresponsibility.

And yet it had seemed rational enough at the beginning of 1972 to believe that war was not probable. Egypt seemed too weak to undertake either a general or a limited offensive, and her relations with the Soviet Union were becoming tense. Egypt could still count on total diplomatic support from Moscow, but arms deliveries, although still large in quantity, seemed to lack the particular items which would have given her a sense of offensive power. The Soviet military mission, now fifteen thousand strong, was becoming more of a burden than a grace. It gave Sadat's government a dubious image in the eyes of the non-Communist nations in the West. It prejudiced Egypt's status in Africa, where a non-African military presence on African soil seemed to violate the entire spirit of the African liberation movement. The spectacle of Russian officers in the streets and clubs of Egyptian cities evoked memories of the British occupation, against which Egypt's national movement had fought so long. Egyptian pride was injured and there was no adequate compensation in other fields.

All these tensions exploded in the jubilation which seized Egypt in July 1972 when Sadat ordered the withdrawal of all the Soviet military personnel stationed on Egyptian soil. Paradoxically, many Is-elis shared the Egyptian relief. The general belief was that Sadat had obtained an emotional satisfaction at the expense of his strategic and political power. The disruption of the military organization in which the Soviet officers had played such an important role would surely weaken the Egyptian order of battle along the Suez Canal. Egypt, deprived of the Soviet presence, also appeared less formidable as a political adversary. Moscow felt humiliated by Sadat's sudden initiative. It even began to show a certain parsimony in the dispatch of spare parts and new equipment. Sadat had made American-Israeli relations more comfortable than before. As long as Soviet personnel was present in the Canal zone, the Egyptian-Israeli conflict was always in danger of becoming a Soviet-Israeli confrontation. In that contingency, the United States would have to face grave problems about its commitment to Israel's security and to international equilib-rium in the Middle East. Along with that, there had been an obsessive fear in Israel that Washington would exercise pressure for a settlement which would relieve it of the menace of global war. From now on, this nightmare seemed to have faded. With the departure of Soviet troops, the powder keg was defused. The United States exercised no pressure on Israel. Administration spokesmen in Washington spoke of an accord between the Arabs and Israel as a long-term aim, demand-ing slow and prudent progress.

This comfortable view was not universally shared. In interdepart-mental meetings, the Director-General of the Foreign Ministry, Gid-eon Rafael, raised the possibility that Sadat's expulsion of Soviet forces might herald his desire to make the war option more concrete. The Soviet Union might have been regarded by Sadat as an inhibiting factor rather than as a potential supporter of military action.

This was the minority view. The general feeling was that a new respite had been won. The Arab states could still win victories in international organizations. By threatening a restriction on the flow of oil, Arab countries could also count on compliance whenever they pressed European or African governments to support the withdrawal of Israeli troops from positions occupied since the 1967 cease-fire. This, however, was small consolation for the Arabs compared with the fact that there was no concrete action likely to lead to early Israeli withdrawal. Thus, the Arabs won their triumphs in the field of rhetoric, while Israeli forces entrenched themselves more firmly in their positions. The Israeli government developed the exploitation of the oil resources in the western Sinai and built apparently impregnable fortifications called the Bar-Lev Line east of the Canal.

All political activity concerning the Middle Eastern conflict was now suspended. The Jarring Mission had ceased to function. The Four Powers had dispersed. Worse still, from the Arab point of view, the summit meeting in 1972 between President Nixon and Brezhnev ended with a vague reaffirmation of Resolution 242. The Arab leaders had reason to fear that their case was not so much rejected as forgotten.

The accent in Israel's national concern shifted from military preparation to antiterrorist activity. There had been violent explosions of terrorism at the airports of Athens and Rome, and hijackings and murders in Washington and Cyprus. But the climax of terrorist action came in September 1972 when the civilized world heard with horror about the massacre in cold blood of eleven Israeli athletes under the shelter of the Olympic flag in Munich. The United States and the UN Secretary-General made an intensive but brief effort to secure action by the UN General Assembly against terrorism, but the Arabs and Soviets were able to mobilize enough votes to frustrate any international action against brutality and piracy.

There were times when antiterrorist measures seemed to preoccupy us far more than the more basic questions of the military balance. Some Israelis might have come to think that the grenades and mortars of the terrorists represented a greater threat to the national existence than the concentration of armies and air forces which were taking place in Egypt and Syria. In this sense the intensity of antiterrorist preoccupation in Israel may have weakened our security by giving the nation a false idea of its priorities.

At the General Assembly in 1972 I gave full support to Secretary Rogers and Secretary-General Waldheim in their efforts to secure a United Nations convention against terrorism. Another of my preoccupations was with our relations with Europe.

As early as September 1967 I had addressed the Council of Europe in Strasbourg about the relevance of Europe's example to the Middle East predicament. I outlined the prospect of a peace settlement which would give the Middle East a "community" structure. I suggested that Israel and her neighbors to the east and north might develop a relationship similar to the Benelux Agreement, which had been the forerunner of the European community. Could not Israel, Lebanon and Jordan establish a relationship like Belgium, Holland and Luxembourg? Europe had discovered a formula for reconciling the separate sovereignty of states with a large measure of integration and of mutual accessibility across open boundaries. At the same time I struggled hard to develop our initial relationship with the European Economic Community into a preferential agreement similar to association.

The chief obstacle to our developing relations with the EEC had been created by France. Paris understood that signature of a preferential agreement between Israel and the EEC would reinforce our international position and thus run counter to France's Arab policy. Surprisingly, the break in the deadlock came from the French Foreign Minister, Maurice Schumann, whom nobody in Israel had ever regarded as a friend of our cause. I had many conversations with him, and reached the impression that his reputation for hostility to Israel might have been exaggerated. In 1971 Schumann had suddenly announced that France would support a global Mediterranean approach by the EEC under which preferential agreements would be simultaneously available to Israel and any Arab state that wished to take advantage of the opportunity. Many people in Israel thought that this was an elegant way of closing the door to us. Would not the Arabs withhold their own adherence in order to prevent Israel from strengthening her relations with the EEC? Once again I was in the embarrassing position of suggesting a more optimistic diagnosis than that which was prevalent in the Israeli government. I believed that some Arab countries, especially in North Africa and on the eastern littoral of the Mediterranean, would be anxious to take advantage of this opportunity so that Schumann's "parallelism" could solve our own deadlock. Sure enough, as the months went by, it became apparent that Schumann's formula enabled us to enter negotiation for a meaningful agreement which would make us something close to a partner of the EEC, both in trade relations and in technological and financial development.

In June 1970 I had signed our first substantial agreement with the EEC in Luxembourg. The president of the EEC under its system of rotation was Pierre Harmel, the Foreign Minister of Belgium. It was an impressive experience to sit behind the Israeli sign with all the six representatives of the EEC represented at high levels. The agreement that I signed with Harmel provided for an even more significant stage of negotiation that was to take effect within three years. We were on our way into Europe.

In Luxembourg I was invited to meet the Foreign Minister of Spain, López Bravo. My tactical plan in the EEC had been to ensure that an agreement between the Community and Spain would be resisted by countries friendly to Israel unless there was a parallel agreement with Israel. This policy exercised pressure on France, which greatly desired the Spanish agreement. It was probably this, more than anything else, that led Maurice Schumann to seek a constructive solution of the deadlock. Foreign Minister López Bravo seemed interested in our meeting becoming known to the press. The encounter may have improved Spain's image in the progressive and socialist movements in Europe.

I confess to a weakness for small countries. I had been charmed by the special atmosphere of Iceland during my official visit in 1968, and I now succumbed to the appeal of Luxembourg. Here were tiny communities which resolutely maintained their national identity and also expressed a deep solidarity with Israel. Luxembourg, like Iceland, had supported all the international decisions which had helped Israel's integration into the international community. Luxembourg had a Ruritanian quality about it. Verdant scenery, mountains and ancient buildings give an air of peaceful contentment. My partner in the Israeli-Luxembourg dialogue was Gaston Thorn, a young statesman (now Prime Minister and Foreign Minister) whose capacities went beyond those ordinarily required for so small a country. The European Community and later the United Nations General Assembly, of which he became president, were to be a larger arena of his talents.

The Community's negotiations with Arab countries were slowed down by such complexities as the sale of Moroccan and Algerian wine in France. Accordingly, our own agreement was delayed. I therefore signed an agreement in January 1973 with the new Belgian Foreign Minister, Van Elslande, containing a firm promise to safeguard our commercial interests during 1973, and thereafter to give the EEC Commission a mandate to negotiate a preferential agreement with us.

Our own Foreign Ministry was at its specialized best in the European question. We had to bring six—and later nine—governments with disparate interests into line on a series of detailed conditions relating to our trade. Some of the difficulties were not political but material. For example, the orange growers of South Italy had reservations about an agreement that would open the European market to Israeli citrus. I established a special European Community Department in the Foreign Ministry under the able direction of Isaac Minervi. I also strengthened our staff in Brussels, where the energetic ambassador, Moshe Allon, was accredited both to the Belgian government and to the European communities. By the beginning of 1973 all the members of the Community, as well as the three new candidates for admission—Britain, Denmark and Ireland—agreed that Israel would be a constructive partner in the European adventure. In my official visit to Scandinavian countries in the summer of 1972, a further strengthening of our European links took place.

A significant experience for me was the first visit of an Israeli Foreign Minister to the Federal Republic of Germany. Both Chancellor Willy Brandt and Foreign Minister Walter Schell greeted me cordially. I had previously been to Bonn only for a ceremonial occasion—the funeral of Konrad Adenauer, which I attended in April 1966 together with David Ben Gurion. I now trod on soil full of tragic memories for my people. I had obtained the permission of my hosts to begin my visit with a tour of the concentration camp in Dachau. Some of the sharp pangs of emotion that I had undergone at Auschwitz in 1966 came back to me here. Again I found myself reciting an emotional *Kaddish* for multitudes of Jews who had been the victims of the Holocaust. My visit took place in 1970 despite reservations of ministers of the Gahal party in Israel. It was significant, however, that Gahal was divided on this issue. General Ezer Weizman and Dr. Elimelech Rimalt supported my decision to undertake the voyage. Brandt, Schell and other German statesmen did not pretend that the future of German-Israeli relations was already detached from the heritage of the past, but by the exercise of tact and historic imagination they enabled my visit to take place in an atmosphere of truth and candor. Thus, the groundwork was laid for a return visit by the Chancellor himself in 1972. The fact that Willy Brandt had been a determined resistance fighter softened the Israeli reaction to his presence. No other German Chancellor could have made an official visit with so little abrasive effect on the wounded memory of countless Israeli citizens.

By the end of 1972, there was hardly a country in Europe with which we had not exchanged official visits at prime-minister or foreign-minister level. They included Britain, Germany, Italy, Austria, Switzerland, Belgium, Holland, Luxembourg, and all the Scandinavian countries. And yet it was in Europe that the Palestinian terrorists made their strongest impression. I shall never forget the terrible night of suspense when the members of our Olympic team of athletes were captured in Munich. The German government decided not to yield to terrorist extortion. When the terrorists escorted the Israeli athletes to the Munich airport, ostensibly as part of a deal for the release of Palestinian Arab saboteurs in Israel, the German forces opened fire on them. The operation, although conceived in a brave and friendly spirit, misfired tragically. Although the German commandos were able to kill most of the terrorists and capture the others, there was a moment of suspense and hesitation in which one of the terrorists brutally killed all eleven Israeli athletes, who were bound and gagged in the helicopter.

The most macabre element for Mrs. Meir, myself and our other colleagues was a false radio report announcing that all the Israeli athletes were safe. Our ambassador in Bonn, Eliashiv Ben Horin, earnestly exhorted us not to believe the good news unless or until visible evidence was obtained. Ben Horin turned out to be right. When the news came that all eleven had in fact been killed, one by one with shots in the head, a fearful cold silence descended upon us in Golda's office.

The terrible symbolism of this murder of Israelis in the city associated with the Hitler curse cast a pall of indignant fury over Israel and the Jewish world. There ensued a period of coolness in German-Israeli relations. We had been fully in accord with the basic decision of the Brandt government to deal firmly with the terrorists, but we could not fail to be enraged by the clumsy failure in the execution of the plan.

The Israeli emphasis on antiterrorism as the central theme of our security now became stronger than ever. Despite these setbacks, 1972 ended with Israel's international position ostensibly strong. Our flag flew in nearly ninety embassies across the entire world. Although our relations with East European states had not been repaired, the whole of non-Moslem Africa and all of Europe and Latin America were linked to us by strong diplomatic, economic, cultural and human ties. The Munich massacre, the indecent support given to the assassins by Arab leaders, including President Sadat, the gloating that ran riot across the Arab world with the honorable exception of King Hussein, all fortified Israelis in the feeling that peace with the Arab world was an Israeli dream that evoked no echo in the Arab heart. At the same time, the Munich attack had reduced the international pressures upon us to make concessions to an adversary who seemed impervious to any human impulse and unreconciled to Israel's identity as a legitimate and sovereign state. Yet while it was evident that terrorism would increase, the general feeling in Israel was that the favorable military balance, the strong support of Israel by the United States, and the weakening of Egyptian-Soviet relations, all made the outbreak of war with our neighbors a remote contingency.

18

Year of Wrath
1973

ALL ISRAELIS NOW DIVIDE THEIR EXPERIENCE BETWEEN WHAT HAPPENED before October 1973 and what befell them thereafter. Yet there was no air of drama in the year's beginning. It opened for me, as usual, with a conference of the foreign press in Jerusalem. My theme was that a long political deadlock would drive the Arabs to war and that we should strive "urgently" to make 1973 "a year of negotiation."

"Urgency" was just about the last quality that anybody could then discern in the public mood. Israeli forces were established on the cease-fire lines from the Suez Canal to the River Jordan and the Golan Heights. After five and a half years, these positions seemed to be gaining a measure of legitimacy. President Nixon had declared that no Israeli soldiers should be withdrawn from the occupied territories until a binding contractual peace agreement satisfactory to Israel had been achieved. Even the Soviet Union, while urging Israel's return to the previous borders, conceded that the withdrawal could only take effect on the conclusion of a peace accord.

Meanwhile, the million Arabs in the West Bank and Gaza seemed reconciled to a prolonged Israeli control. They lived with us, sullen but tranquil, in a strange ambivalence of harmony and discord. But while the harmony was one of the immediate concerns of daily life, the conflict was about remote political goals. It was therefore possible for many Israelis to indulge an illusion of stability. Seventy thousand Arab workers from the administered territories came daily into our towns and farms, taking back earnings which enlarged the prosperity of their villages. Hundreds of thousands crossed the Jordan for family visits each summer. Now and again, Israelis were alarmed by diplomatic initiatives which threatened to remove them from the administered territories without a peace settlement, but these all came to nothing.

In 1969–1970, the representatives of the Four Powers had met periodically at United Nations headquarters. But the intervals between their conversations became longer, and by 1971 the exercise had quietly perished. Dr. Jarring's mission had been paralyzed since his February 1971 memorandum, in which he had endorsed Egypt's territorial claims—and thereby lost Israel's confidence. American and Soviet leaders still came together at summit meetings. Israelis, who remember the American-Soviet "steam roller" of 1956, always reacted nervously to these encounters, but the Nixon-Brezhnev meeting in June 1973 ended with no more than a ceremonial reference to Resolution 242, after which the ripples subsided and the diplomatic waters became still once more. The Arabs could generally win victories in United Nations votes and international conferences, but this consolation was wearing thin. The votes and speeches made loud headlines, but they moved no Israeli troops from their positions. So Arabs and Israelis settled down into a curious distribution of satisfactions; the Arabs got the resolutions, while Israel remained in the territories.

The impression of stability became even stronger when Moscow and Washington agreed to define their relationship in terms of "détente." Even if the reality fell short of the dream, it was unlikely that the Soviet Union would provoke American resentment by actively inciting the Arabs to war. The Soviets were no great admirers of Arab military prowess and they had no desire to see Russian weapons discredited again by inefficient use. There were even rumors of parsimony in the rate and scope of Soviet arms supplies to Egypt and Syria. In Israel, Soviet policy excited resentment without alarm, while in Arab countries it provoked approval without enthusiasm.

But while the Arab armies were passive, the Palestinian terrorists exploded again and again into murder and violent blackmail. For a time they seemed able to disrupt public order in Europe, to make international aviation precarious everywhere, and to extort vast sums of money in exchange for hostages. However, they had little impact in the Middle East itself. In all the territories west of the Jordan, Israeli security measures were generally effective, and the Palestine Arab population, immensely weary of wars, rarely gave the terrorists any shelter or welcome.

Israeli "hard-liners" seemed to have good evidence that their policies were well founded. Moshe Dayan no longer talked, as he sometimes had in the past, of a need "to give up a lot of territory" for a final settlement with Egypt and Jordan. He now believed that there was an inherent stability in the situation that had developed since 1967. There would be neither imminent war nor early peace. His doctrine came to frequent expression during the summer of 1973. He believed that the relations between the United States and the Soviet Union were in a sort of balance that favored a mutual "hold-off" in the Middle East. The Arab armies would be too impressed by Israel's military strength to risk an offensive. The terrorists could kill and maim some Israelis, but their assaults would not eliminate the Israeli state or even change its boundaries. They were, therefore, politically marginal. Accordingly, Dayan thought that Israel's task was not to explore the "remote prospects" of peace but rather "to draw the new map of Israel" by "creating facts" of resettlement in Judea and Samaria. He saw no point in leaving options open for peace negotiation. On May 14, 1973, he said in a television interview on the BBC that "Israel should remain for eternity and until the end of time in the West Bank." If the Palestine Arabs did not like this idea, they could "go and establish themselves in an Arab country—Jordan, Syria or Iraq." On July 30 he said to *Time* magazine, "There is no more Palestine. Finished." In April 1973 in a ceremony on the peak of Massada he had proclaimed the vision of "a new State of Israel with broad frontiers, strong and solid, with the authority of the Israel Government extending from the Jordan to the Suez Canal."

In all these statements, Israel's armed strength and expanded boundaries figured as the only components of national security. There was silence about the idea of peace, and nothing was said about any of the nonmilitary ideals or values that Israel was born to serve.

The unusual aspect of these declarations was that they had little to do with the government's official policies. We had officially accepted the Security Council Resolution 242, which involved withdrawal to secure and recognized boundaries. Indeed, in August 1970 Dayan himself had drafted the Cabinet's decision for negotiating with Jordan and Egypt on the basis of such withdrawal. The result had been that Menachem Begin and his party had withdrawn from the government coalition in the correct belief that the government was committed to surrender the West Bank territories to Jordan in a peace settlement. Yet by 1973 the idea of territorial compromise in the West Bank had disappeared from Dayan's view. In an interview with the *Times* of London in March 1971, Prime Minister Golda Meir had expressed her opposition to the annexation of the West Bank and Gaza as demanded by Gahal and the National Religious Party. But it was Dayan with his insistent concern for the "new map" who created the image of our policy in Israel, the Middle East and the world. There was a gap between the official formula and the public consensus.

All this time, the Israeli defense strategy was frankly attritional. The logic was that if the Arabs were unable to get their territories back by war or by Great Power pressure, they would have to seek negotiation and to satisfy some of Israel's security interests. This view made no provision for a third Arab option—neither docility nor negotiation, but a desperate recourse to war in the hope that even an unsuccessful attack would be more rewarding than passive acceptance of the cease-fire lines.

The 25th Anniversary parade in Jerusalem in April 1973 was conducted in an atmosphere of exuberant national pride. If anything, the self-confidence was too extreme to be attractive. At a meeting of Israeli ambassadors in Europe which I convened in Jerusalem a few months later, some of the envoys asked our military leaders to comment on the possibility of an Arab attack designed not to win military victory, but to break the political deadlock. The response of our intelligence chiefs was adamant: the Arabs would not risk an attack which they knew would be suicidal; and even if they did, they would be flung back so quickly and with such violence that Israel's deterrent power would, if anything, become even stronger than before.

By the summer of 1973 it was expected that two of our former military commanders, Generals "Arik" Sharon and Yitzhak Rabin, would soon enter our political struggles. Whatever personal innovation they would bring to our politics, it was clear that they strongly supported the prevailing mood of military self-confidence. Sharon urged Israelis to remember that "there is no target between Baghdad and Khartoum, including Libya, that our army is unable to capture" and that "with our present boundaries we have no security problem" (*Ha'aretz*, September 20, 1973). And on July 13 Rabin had published an article in *Ma'ariv* which seemed designed to give Israelis a strong sense of reassurance. This was a lucid defense of the prevailing concept of Israel's security up to the Yom Kippur War:

> *Our present defense lines give us a decisive advantage in the Arab-Israel balance of strength.*
> *There is no need to mobilize our forces whenever we hear Arab threats, or when the enemy concentrates his forces along the cease-fire lines. Before the Six-Day War, any movement of Egyptian*

forces into Sinai would compel Israel to mobilize reserves on a large scale. Today, there is no need for such mobilization so long as Israel's defense line extends along the Suez Canal.

We are still living within a widening gap of military power in Israel's favor.

The Arabs have little capacity for coordinating their military and political action. To this day they have not been able to make oil an effective political factor in their struggle against Israel.

Renewal of hostilities is always a possibility, but Israel's military strength is sufficient to prevent the other side from gaining any military objective.

In an address on the "Strategy of Peace," Deputy Prime Minister Allon stated that there was no need for Sadat to fear that an interim Suez agreement would reduce his military option, since "Egypt has no military option at all" (*Yediot Aharonot,* June 4, 1973).

Some Israelis were troubled by this military euphoria. And yet, all the evidence seemed to support the optimistic mood. For several years whenever Israel's power had been put to the test, it had come out triumphant. Israeli forces could wrest a Sabena airliner from armed hijackers, cross into Egypt to bring back a new Soviet tank or radar installation, enter Beirut in April 1973 to make a street-by-street search for terrorist leaders, and inflict heavy casualties on Arab aircraft which they met on patrol. Whenever the Israeli army or air force moved, there was always a sense of mastery and command. All was quiet west of the Suez Canal, where Sadat had not revived Nasser's futile "war of attrition." King Hussein, acting in his own interest but to Israel's consequent advantage, was blocking any westward movement of Palestinian terrorists across the Jordan. All in all, Israel was in possession of the field, and the barometer pointed to stability rather than change.

It seemed perverse to disturb this serenity, but from 1972 onward, I found myself expressing a minority view. In many speeches and articles I emphasized that a security doctrine based on unlimited confidence would degrade the tone and quality of our life, and that the impression of durability might be illusory. Why should we expect the Arab governments to abstain from military action if they had no hope of gaining something in the diplomatic field?

I brought these anxieties to expression many times, and especially in an address at Haifa University on February 26, 1973. I pointed out that there was "much talk of Israel's physical map, but little attention to the problem of her moral frontiers." A note of arrogance in the press and in the public rhetoric had made the Israeli voice discordant. "A strong nation does not have to beat the drums every morning in order to illustrate its power. It does not have to be constantly proving its virility. The unsolved question about Israel does not concern its courage or resourcefulness. These are generally taken for granted. The question relates to Israel's human quality. The problem is to emphasize freedom, tolerance, equality, social justice and humane values as the salient features of a strong and serene society."

I recalled how some Israeli newspapers and broadcasts had been callous in discussing the dead passengers on a Libyan airliner mistakenly shot down by the Israeli air force on the unlikely assumption that the plane was on its way to attack the Dimona research reactor. There had also been many signs of public intolerance toward legitimate dissent. I asked, "Is it just a coincidence that the national style has become strident just when annexationist pronouncements proliferate?" I recalled Ben Gurion's statement that to wish to dominate the Palestine Arabs betrayed a "Hottentot mentality." "The problem is not merely to proclaim our own valid historic rights to this land," I added, "but to bring those rights into balance with the rights of others—and with our own duty of peace. Since our national experience has sharpened the emotional, passionate, mystical and metaphysical elements in the Israeli character, the task of the intellectual community is to contribute the balancing dimension of rationality." I concluded, "Reason without passion is sterile, but passion without reason is hysteria."

This speech, and others in similar vein, had a strong resonance, and I received many expressions of support, mainly from the kibbutzim and the universities, and also from officials in many ministries. But it was a disquieting indication of the Israeli political climate that not one of the professors who exhorted me to go on speaking out like this ever said a word of encouragement in public when I came under attack from the embattled "hawks." The Haifa speech and other addresses and interviews of similar tone were a personal attempt to break out of a dilemma. As Foreign Minister, I had to articulate the collective policies of the Cabinet more precisely than anyone else. Nor was there anything immoderate in the official formulations. The trouble was that influential ministers spoke more abrasively than our official platform entitled them to, so that the more conciliatory formulations of our policy lost credibility. To restore the balance of the domestic dialogue, I tried to register my individual philosophy. I was in favor of such frontier changes as were essential to ensure our defense and deter a new war. But I emphasized that these should be confined to the minimum required for security. To our party's "Young Leadership" I said in August 1973, "The fact that we cannot give a hundred percent of self-determination to the Palestinian Arabs is no excuse for offering them zero percent." I urged that our security should be "based on a peace settlement, buttressed by a balance of power, shielded by demilitarization, reinforced by limited territorial change and supported by a broad international consensus."

My anxiety about the public mood was drowned in the dominating atmosphere of contentment, and it was in an uneasy frame of mind that I set out early in August on a series of official visits to South America. There had been signs of hostility to Israel among African states, including some that Israel had helped on the road to development. Latin America, on the other hand, was not vulnerable to Moslem solidarity and was much less exposed than Europe to Arab oil pressures. My visits to Brazil and Bolivia ended with strong reaffirmations of support. The Bolivian capital is 14,000 feet above sea level, but I managed to live without much oxygen for three days despite the exertions involved in Spanish oratory. I was also encouraged by the support of my Brazilian hosts, President Emilio Medici and Foreign Minister Barbosa, but could not forget that they would be succeeded by a new Administration within a few months. In Lima the Foreign Minister of Peru, Señor de la Flor, who was both a general and a socialist, gave me a moving account of his government's attempt to draw closer to the Third World without weakening the traditional friendship with Israel.

My Latin American journey had been planned some months ahead and could not have been postponed without giving offense, but as I got farther from home my enjoyment of new landscapes and friendly people was marred by the feeling that the distance between my colleagues at home and myself was growing wider. I was in a hotel in Rio de Janeiro when I got two reports which made me wonder if our government was still in full contact with international reality.

On August 10 a Lebanese airliner had taken off from Beirut on a scheduled flight to Teheran. On reaching cruising altitude, it was intercepted by Israeli jet fighters and ordered to land at a military airport. The pilot complied. For some hours Israeli security officers interrogated the puzzled passengers. Finally the airliner was allowed to go on its way. Our intelligence services had believed that the most savage of the Palestine terrorist leaders, George Habash, was aboard the plane. The intention had been to arrest him and, presumably, to bring him to trial before an Israeli court.

Apart from the fright and risk of interception, the passengers and crew of the airliner had suffered no injury. And yet, a shock went through Israel and the world. Here was a civil aircraft subjected to an act of force, not by terrorist "revolutionaries," but by a sovereign government. Until then we had always been passionate crusaders for aerial freedom. In condemning Arab hijacking, we had sought to place civil aviation on a special peak of immunity, removed from all vicissitudes of political conflict. And now a planeload of travelers, representing a cross section of innocent and vulnerable humanity, had been placed in risk. There was a feeling across the world that but for the pilot's compliance, there might have been a tragedy similar to the Libyan aircraft incident in 1972.

It turned out that the interception had been approved in a rapid consultation between three ministers. It had opened Israel to a hostile reaction in world opinion, especially in the United States. I felt that our decision makers might have made a wrong calculation about the techniques of antiterrorist combat. What could we have done with our "success" even if Habash had been aboard? He would surely have used an Israeli court as a forum for expounding the "Palestine revolution" in a mood of martyrdom to a world audience. His very presence year after year in an Israeli jail would have provoked a new series of kidnappings with the aim of getting him released.

I sent a telegram to the Prime Minister from Brazil strongly criticizing the interception. I expressed the fear that the principles defended by Israel in her struggle against hijacking would now be undermined and that even our closest friends would condemn our action.

All these forebodings turned out to be well founded. In discussions of the Security Council and the International Civil Aviation Organization, Israel reached the nadir of her isolation, while Arab governments exulted. In Israel, there was more press criticism of the interception than of most other security decisions since 1967. One of the nation's most fervent "hawks," the novelist Moshe Shamir, wrote trenchantly against the operation.

On the home front, too, there was disarray. The Labor Party was formulating its plans for development in the West Bank and Sinai for the next four years. Most Labor ministers were reluctant to go beyond the selective and cautious policies that we had followed since 1967. Only a few thousand Israelis had established themselves beyond the old armistice lines, most of them in Jerusalem or close to the previous borders where we seemed to have a prospect of limited territorial change under a peace agreement. There was no objective need to make noisy formulations of long-term settlement goals. The Israeli government had full control and could always move empirically as conditions dictated. But as De Tocqueville once wrote: "Democracies only do external things for internal reasons"; in this case, the judgment was well founded. Dayan was hinting that he might not be a Labor Party candidate in the election unless commitments were made for an accelerated "creation of facts" in the territories. Galili was accordingly asked to draft a document which would bridge the gap between the views of Moshe Dayan, who favored increased settlement in the West Bank and Sinai, and those of Pinhas Sapir and others among us who did not.

The Galili document was published on August 23, and the next day I anxiously telephoned Sapir in Kfar Sava from Rio de Janeiro. He gave me the impression that he had emerged victorious from the engagement. He told me that very few binding commitments were contained in the Galili text and that everything was hedged in with political and financial reservations. He thought that the document by itself would not generate any additional settlements and that everything still depended on individual Cabinet decisions. This was literally and formally true, but while the document said very little in substance, its psychological effects were far-reaching. Sapir may have triumphed on the strict language of the document, but Dayan had won in its spirit and impression. Internal politics, not for the first time, had laid a heavy burden on our diplomacy.

The Dayan-Sapir compromise as drafted by Galili was interpreted across the world as a reinforcement of annexationist tendencies. In my conversation with him from Rio de Janeiro, Sapir told me that he was afraid that if Dayan left the Labor Party and fought on a separate ticket, he might pick up twelve to fifteen seats at the expense of the Labor Alignment. He said that I ought to bear this in mind and judge the document as a domestic necessity even if there was some international inconvenience.

It is impossible to understand Moshe Dayan's strong hold on our policy without reference to his unique position in the national leadership between 1967 and 1973. Although he was not the head of the government, he was certainly its most powerful member. The general admiration of the armed forces after 1967 naturally "rubbed off" on the Minister of Defense, whose departmental budget was as great as that of all the other ministries combined. Between 1967 and 1969, Dayan's administration of the newly conquered areas had been supervised by a ministerial committee under the chairmanship of the Prime Minister. But with Eshkol's death, this committee was disbanded, and Dayan, in effect, held solitary control over the million Arabs under military rule. It was, of course, possible to defeat some of his proposals by a Cabinet majority, but there was always an apprehension that if this was done too often, he might resign with the support of enough Knesset members to destroy the government's majority. One influential minister, in private conversation with me, used to say that "a large Cabinet majority without Dayan is not really a majority."

This abnormal position was sustained by a warm favoritism toward Dayan in other sectors of public life. Newspaper correspondents and commentators showed him a deference that the rest of us had good reason to envy. Between 1967 and 1973 most papers reverently published full texts of Dayan's addresses even when they reiterated his established views and formulations time and again. If Dayan changed his views, he was praised for intellectual resilience. If he was obdurate, he was praised for stability. He thus got the benefit of every doubt. This is not to say that dissent from Dayan was suppressed; it was simply treated as a harmless eccentricity. When Dayan said publicly in April 1973 that "those who believe that Israel's control of Judea and Samaria is temporary should stop teaching the Bible," I chose the annual Bible Conference in Jerusalem to retort that we should stop brandishing the Bible in our political discussions. I added that "the Bible deals not only with geography and place-names but also with ideals of peace, social justice and humility." Dayan, who sat in the front row, received these observations with smiling good humor. My remarks were featured in the press—and that was that. The habit of invoking Holy Writ on behalf of territorial claims continued unabated.

How did a single minister wield such vast influence? There are three explanations. First, there was the fact that Dayan and his supporters had the arithmetical power to overturn the coalition majority. Then there was the undeniable appeal of a dominant and original personality. Finally, and above all, there was a popular sentiment that whatever they thought of Dayan in other respects, Israeli citizens could sleep soundly at night, knowing that the defense system under his responsibility was at a high pitch of vigilance and efficiency. It was only when this last assumption collapsed in October 1973 that Dayan was assailed by a resentment almost as intense as the adulation that preceded it.

By the summer of 1973, the charge of Israeli "expansionism" was giving us particular trouble in Africa. At the conference of the Organization of African Unity at Algiers in early September, President Sadat made a strong impression. We expected that Moslem African nations would act in solidarity with Egypt; and we knew that some poor countries in West Africa were being simultaneously threatened and tempted by the opulent governments of Libya and Saudi Arabia. But even our loyal friend President Mobutu of Zaïre was now reported to be contemplating a rupture of relations. This was not because of any failure in our diplomacy, but because, unlike Egypt, we were not members of the African "club" and had no claim on continental solidarity.

West European states still set a high value on their relations and affinities with Israel, but they, too, had a growing need of Arab oil and an aversion to "occupation," however liberal. Their compromise was to support Israel's independence and to intensify our direct contacts, but at the same time to oppose Israel's minimal claims on the matter of secure boundaries.

I felt that time was now working against us. Accordingly, in an interview with the newspaper *Davar* on September 29, I revived my assault on the solidity of the status quo. I said that "deadlock is not an American ideology and should not be an Israeli objective . . . We should be concerned to unfreeze the situation, not to perpetuate it." But there was nothing to indicate that most of our political and military leaders saw anything wrong in the idea of deadlock. The New Year editions of our newspapers were saturated with cheerful statements about our impregnable security. On September 26 the *Jerusalem Post* editorial had stated: "There was never a period in which our security situation seemed as good as now." The same mood had been reflected in an interview with General Rabin in *Yediot Aharonot* on September 18. The headline was: "Golda has better boundaries than King David or King Solomon." The text was a warm celebration of the cease-fire lines, of the existing stability and of the Nixon Administration. The lesson seemed to be that patience and strength together would bring their due reward.

All this time, the rhetoric of confidence continued to be backed by military superiority. On September 13, Israeli and Syrian aircraft clashed just off the Syrian coast. Thirteen Syrian aircraft were brought down with the loss of one Israeli plane. Amid all the jubilation, I recalled our air victory against Syrian MIGs in April 1967 and the growing Soviet hostility up to the eruption of the Six-Day War. With this memory it was hard for me to celebrate this latest triumph with a full heart.

Throughout August and early September I made many speeches for our party ticket in the Histadrut and Knesset elections, as well as in support of Yehoshua Rabinovitch's unsuccessful candidacy for the mayoralty of Tel Aviv. One of my constant themes was a criticism of what was called the Yamit project. Moshe Dayan had advocated that we should not be satisfied with a military or paramilitary position at Rafah—the crossroads of the classic invasion route from Egypt into Israel. He advocated the construction of a seaport at Yamit, and a densely populated urban center deep within Sinai. My view was that this would be tantamount to closing our options of territorial concession in a large part of Sinai. I advocated "more pioneering in Galilee and the Negev, and a lesser obsession with settlement in areas of doubtful political future." I believed that we should be satisfied with a mobile and limited presence at the Rafah salient and not plan a massive urban development at Yamit.

Despite the new vogue of toughness at home, I hoped to repair some of our political bridges when I set out for the United Nations General Assembly at the end of September. The annual reunion of foreign ministers in New York is a useful international ritual which has very little to do with the United Nations meetings themselves. Most foreign ministers make policy statements from the rostrum. These usually pass directly from ministerial lips into complete oblivion, unless they come from a Great Power or from a country like Israel, whose dramatic history invites permanent attention from the media. Beyond the "general debate" there is the opportunity to settle business at foreign-minister level without the toil of constant travel. My own schedule included meetings with Latin American and European ministers, talks with the African states, with most of which we still had widely ramified relations, and discussions with the foreign ministers of France and Rumania, who had told us of their decision to invite me for official visits in their capitals in the next few months. But the focal point of my activity would, as always, be a comprehensive review with the American Secretary of State. Henry Kissinger had just been appointed to that office.

Some people have suggested that foreign ministers could very well meet every year in New York without going through the tedium of United Nations debates. The answer is that if important things have to be done "behind the scenes"—you have got to have "scenes." The main price has to be paid in social agony. The first few weeks of the General Assembly are crowded with luncheons and cocktail receptions at which the same people say the same things to one another around the same tables under rotating auspices of hospitality. The United Nations building becomes something like a cruise ship, self-contained and self-propelling, with hardly any link to the world outside. There is no more disadvantageous arena for Israel than a General Assembly of which twenty member states are Arab, another dozen are Communist and a further twenty are committed by Moslem solidarity to the Arab cause. But I had no reason to renounce whatever opportunity existed for expounding our policies and interests to friendly ears.

Historians who read the Israeli newspapers published in the first days of October will be startled to find that there was no hint of any crisis, let alone of imminent war. The headlines were seized by a few Arab terrorists who had assaulted a train carrying Soviet Jews to

Vienna in transit for Israel. Two of the immigrants were kidnapped and threatened with death. Austrian Chancellor Bruno Kreisky insisted that the terrorists give up their hostages, but he also yielded to their main demand by promising the early closure of the transit camp at Schönhau, where Soviet Jewish immigrants assembled for their onward journey to Israel. He offered compensating transit facilities elsewhere.

In May 1973 I had paid the first official visit of an Israeli Foreign Minister to Austria as the guest of Foreign Minister Kirschläger. One afternoon my wife and I had gone out to Schönhau to meet a hundred Soviet Jews who had left Russia a few days before. Their voices and faces told a dual story of suffering and hope. I was moved to find that many of them had heard me speaking for Israel in UN debates to which they used to listen in clandestine groups; and they spoke to me now with deep intensity. The Schönhau camp gave most Austrians a sense of humane pride which they valued with special force against the melancholy background of the Nazi years. Kreisky's apparent acceptance of the terrorists' demands hit Israel with violent impact. It seemed that whenever Arafat's murderers chose to strike, they could produce an instant erosion of Israel's rights.

Prime Minister Golda Meir was then on a visit to Strasbourg to address the Council of Europe. This was a relatively modest chore for a Prime Minister and it illustrated how far the Israeli government was from any premonition of crisis. She decided to go personally to Vienna to urge Kreisky to rescind his decision. The world's newspapers, including those of Israel, were giving their central attention to this drama—none at all to the troop concentrations on the Egyptian and Syrian cease-fire lines.

On October 4, I talked in New York with Secretary Kissinger, who was making the rounds in the United Nations to meet his colleagues for the first time. He had met Arab foreign ministers at a dinner party a few days before. In the American ambassador's suite at the Waldorf Towers, Henry Kissinger was jocular and relaxed. He recalled our conversation in the Israeli embassy residence in Washington the previous August when we had spoken of the need to replace the diplomatic vacuum by "some form of negotiation." He now came back to this theme, but there was no panic or urgency in his mood. He was aware that Israel was to have an election at the end of October. He told me that he knew of Egyptian and Syrian troop concentrations. He asked me what our intelligence services had to say. I replied by reciting the military intelligence appraisal which I had sought from Jerusalem that morning. Our experts confirmed that the concentrations in the north and south were very heavy, but they gave no drastic interpretation of their purpose. They spoke of "annual maneuvers" on the Egyptian front, and of a hypochondriac Syrian mood which might have made Damascus apprehensive of a punitive Israeli raid. Syria was the base of the terrorist movement, and her government might well expect Israel to punish the Vienna outrage by striking in that direction. It would thus be normal for Syrian troops to be in heavy defensive posture. Our military advisers believed that without a prospect of aerial advantage, Egypt would not risk storming the Suez Canal and the Bar-Lev fortifications. The Israeli military report referred in learned vocabulary to "inter-arm maneuvers, which are due to end on 7 October."

It seemed that American intelligence experts confirmed the Israeli view, and Kissinger was tranquil. Nevertheless, he doubted that Israel could indefinitely enjoy a stable cease-fire, occupation of all the administered territories, and freedom from any international pressures. This seemed too unrealistic for comfort. "Well, you have your election soon," he concluded. *"In any case, nothing dramatic is going to happen in October.* Can you be back here sometime in November? I have reason to believe that the Egyptian Foreign Minister will be here. I would then like you both to come to Washington so that we may discuss how a negotiation may be set afoot."

The Secretary's idea that Egypt be the first candidate for negotiation was also congenial to us. An Egyptian-Israeli negotiation would, of course, require concessions in Sinai, but these would not evoke the passionate reaction involved in territorial concessions in Judea and Samaria. I told Kissinger that if our party was returned to power, I expected to come back to the United States in early November and would welcome the opening of "a negotiating process."

I remember leaving Kissinger's apartment in the Waldorf Towers in a mood of relief. At last there was some promise of movement. Israel's international position could only be improved by a process of negotiation. The contagion of hostility in Africa might be checked. Our credit in Europe would be restored. And the atmosphere of our own national life would be transformed if our essential military power was supplemented by an active diplomacy in which we and the Arabs would be talking about mutual compromise.

From Kissinger's suite I went to that of President Felix Houphouet-Boigny of the Ivory Coast, one of Israel's most faithful friends. He was worried about the effects of Moslem pressure on Israel's position in Africa. But his own attachment to us seemed unimpaired. He was also worried that Washington was leaving Africa to Moslem and Communist influence without any balancing assertion of American interest. He even asked me to do what I could to make American leaders more conscious of Africa's needs.

It had been a strenuous day, and I hardly found time to change into formal clothes for my own reception for delegates and the dinner party marking Kissinger's assumption of office as Secretary of State. It was held, unexpectedly, in the Metropolitan Museum of Art. It was hard to imagine any of the Secretary's predecessors choosing such an environment. But Kissinger was not a conventional politician, and he was celebrating his new eminence with candid relish. His mind had been shaped in Europe, but it was only in the atmosphere of American pluralism that a Jewish immigrant could rise to such sudden prestige. He was now the leading statesman in the world community, and the foreign ministers and ambassadors passing along the receiving line seemed to be united, whether reluctantly or willingly, in a tribute to American predominance. I sat in a corner at the museum hall between Kissinger's parents, embarrassingly close to the sculptured posterior rotundities of a Greek goddess, who seemed more at home in the museum than the elegantly accoutered diplomats. The elder Kissingers exuded a silent impression of Jewish and personal pride.

All I remember of the after-dinner speeches is that none was very brief and few contained any particular radiance of thought or expression. Kissinger himself spoke dutifully about the importance of the United Nations. I felt that he was allowing courtesy to triumph over candor, since I knew him to be as skeptical as any man could be about the pomposities of conference diplomacy. All in all, there was little tension in the air that evening, and certainly no warning of possible shock. The Soviet representatives, led by Gromyko, were stretching their faces sideways very hard to convey a determined amiability. China was not yet a United Nations member, but we knew that it was on the threshold. The traditional Cold War was giving way to new attitudes and vocabularies. Such talk as there was of the Middle East that night was mainly about the outrage at Schönhau and the prospect of checking the terrorist movement. Not a single minister or diplomat spoke to me of the Egyptian and Syrian troop concentrations.

Nor did my agenda the next day give any indication of an approaching storm. I had scheduled meetings with foreign ministers of African states, of which the most important for us was Nigeria. President Mobutu of Zaïre had gone directly from the liner at New York harbor to address the United Nations in a fervent speech, at the end of which he announced that Israel had been a loyal friend of his country—and that he was now breaking relations with it. His explanation: a man can choose his friends but he cannot choose his brothers. It was the same with nations—the Arabs had been unfriendly to Zaïre in its ordeals but they were African kinsmen, whereas Israel had been a staunch friend but was not one "of the family." He must therefore put kinship above friendship and do what the Arabs wanted.

The next day, October 5, while we were with Foreign Minister Orikpu of Nigeria at his mission, my political secretary, Eytan Bentzur, was called to the telephone. A message had come to me from Jerusalem saying that I might have to request another talk with Secretary Kissinger in New York that day. Nothing was said about the issue to be discussed, but I assumed that it had something to do with the troop concentrations in the north and south. I was asked not to fix the interview until material on the subject of our talk reached me through our embassy in Washington. If Kissinger was in Washington, the material should be conveyed to our *chargé d'affaires*, Mordechai Shalev.

Hours went by and no reports arrived. Finally a telegram came from Mordechai Gazit, the director-general of the Prime Minister's office, saying that it would not be necessary, after all, to trouble Kissinger for another meeting; it would be enough if our appraisals were brought to his knowledge in writing.

It was nearly six o'clock when Shalev called me to say that the "new material" had come in. It turned out to be a more detailed version of the intelligence appraisal that I had received the day before, ascribing the Egyptian troop concentrations to "maneuvers," and those in Syria to a fear of Israeli action. This document was accompanied by a personal message from the Prime Minister to Kissinger, asking the United States to assure Cairo and Damascus that Israel had no intention of attacking. If the Arab troop concentrations were based on anxieties about an Israeli attack, said Mrs. Meir, the United States could set them at rest, but she added that if Egypt and Syria or both intended to attack, Israel was vigilantly posed for a response. Shalev did not recite or send the whole text of the cable to me in New York before Yom Kippur. In any case, the decisive weight of Mrs. Meir's communication seemed to be in the enclosed intelligence document. This gave an accurate description of how Egyptian and Syrian troops were aligned, but it concluded with the official intelligence judgment that "the probability of war is low."

I understood in strict logic why it had been decided by Jerusalem to cancel my proposed talk with Kissinger, a busy man whose closest friends have never praised him for monumental patience. He would not like to be asked for an emergency meeting simply to be told that our government in Jerusalem did not see very much to worry about. Like all foreign ministers at the United Nations, Kissinger was in almost constant movement from one meeting to another. Shalev told me that he had passed the Jerusalem reports to Kissinger's deputy at the National Security Council, General Brent Scowcroft, who was in permanent communication with the Secretary from the White House. We could assume that Kissinger would get our documents before nightfall. (I later learned that he had received them very soon after six o'clock.) Looking back with hindsight, I believe that it may have been a mistake for Jerusalem to have canceled my proposed meeting with Kissinger. The confident tone of our documents may have reassured him, but a personal probing by both of us together might have provoked some twinge of concern and led to an earlier American decision to find out what was going on.

Several months after the Yom Kippur War, I asked Kissinger how he had reacted to the documents that were submitted to him on the eve of the outbreak. He replied that he had gone to sleep peacefully. He had naturally asked American intelligence agencies to give their own appraisal, but they tended to concur with Israel's judgment. Mrs. Meir's cabled suggestion that the United States make soundings in Damascus and Cairo seemed reasonable, and Kissinger intended to act on it the next day. In the meantime, the evening closed in on Israel—and on Israelis in New York—in the somber tranquillity of the Day of Atonement.

Yom Kippur is a unique day in the calendar of the Jewish people. In Israel all secular activity is suspended while the nation turns inward for prayer and reflection. Television and radio stations are closed, and no vehicles are heard or seen on the streets. Most Israeli soldiers can count on a day's leave except in the most crucial positions at the front, and even there the lines are usually lightly manned.

Something of this repose affects the lives of Israel's representatives abroad. I remember saying to Suzy late on October 5 that we could count on not being disturbed for twenty-four hours—a rare prospect for us. This optimism was mocked when I heard a firm knock on my door at the Plaza Hotel very early in the morning. I opened the door to find Eytan Bentzur holding a telegram just received from Jerusalem. It was signed by Israel Galili, on the Prime Minister's behalf. It stated bluntly that *"to our certain knowledge"* the Egyptians and Syrians would launch a combined and coordinated attack later that day with the aim of seizing positions at the Suez Canal and on the Golan Heights.

It was clear that what we faced was not a "contingency plan" but an act of war timed precisely for October 6. A violent armored and air assault would be made simultaneously from the north and south. The time of the assault was not specified, but there was an implication of early evening. For reasons that have never become clear, several hours seem to have passed between the receipt of this hard intelligence in Tel Aviv and the official communication of it to the United States through Ambassador Kenneth B. Keating and myself.

There was some additional information in Galili's message to me. The Prime Minister was in conversation with the American ambassador at the moment that the telegram was sent. He had been told that Israel had decided not to take any pre-emptive action. Our forces would absorb the first blow and hit back.

I quickly phoned Secretary Kissinger at the Waldorf Towers only a few blocks away. When he came on the line, he said gravely that he was just about to call me. He had been studying a report of our Prime Minister's talk with Ambassador Keating. He noted the Israeli decision to abstain from pre-emptive action. He wanted to put on record with me that this was an Israeli decision conveyed to the United States after it had been taken. He personally believed it to be the right decision, but the United States had no need to give advice on an issue which Israel had already determined for herself.

I pointed out to Kissinger that our knowledge of the Arab war plan might still be used to prevent it from taking effect. Clearly, the Egyptians and Syrians were counting on the advantage of surprise. If they could be convinced that surprise was no longer available, might they not recoil from their intention? It was a very slender chance, but worth trying. The Secretary said that he was going to contact Cairo, Damascus and Moscow, to see if the threatened war could be prevented.

When Kissinger called back a few minutes later, he was in an even more agitated mood. He had not learned about Soviet intentions, but the Egyptian Foreign Minister had told him that Israel had started a naval battle at Za'afaran near the Gulf of Suez. "It makes no sense," Kissinger said. "I frankly don't believe the story. But all governments, even yours, sometimes do strange things! I ought to get your specific denial."

Ten minutes later I was on the phone to the Prime Minister, reporting the Egyptian accusation. Golda assured me that the Egyptian version was a complete fabrication. I called Secretary Kissinger again. His reaction was mixed. On the one hand, he expressed relief at the Prime Minister's reply, to which he gave full credence. On the other hand, it was obvious to both of us that unless Egypt had war in mind, she would not speak of Israel having struck the first blow. And he added, "I am deeply disturbed. Can you find out where the places are at which the naval battle is alleged to be taking place and, especially, if there are any UN observers?" He suggested that we both consult with Secretary-General Kurt Waldheim at United Nations headquarters. I told him that I would speak to the president of the Security Council as well as to the Secretary-General. They both informed me that the Arab delegates to the UN seemed to have disappeared and that it was impossible to contact them. I asked Ambassador Yosef Tekoah to come to my hotel, but first to find out exactly where the UN observers were stationed. On arrival, he was able to tell me that there were no UN observers anywhere near the area of the alleged "naval battle." The Egyptian motive was plain: Cairo was gaining time for the assault by alleging a pretext which could not even be checked, let alone formally refuted.

I called Secretary Kissinger to discuss what I called "the invisible naval battle." In the meantime the second telephone rang on my desk. Avraham Kidron, the Director-General of the Foreign Ministry, was now speaking in an excited voice: "The war is on. The attack was launched ten minutes ago. It comes simultaneously from Egypt and Syria. We are fighting hard. I cannot say anything yet about operations. We shall establish a special direct line of communication with you during the day." I glanced away from the telephone toward the television screen, on which telex cables were being relayed. There was an announcement of an Egyptian and Syrian assault which the news agencies were describing as "the greatest military operation in the Middle East since the 1967 war."

Duties now pressed upon me so heavily that I had little time to reflect on the collapse of all the appraisals that had dominated the Israeli security doctrine for over six years. The war which our intelligence experts had defined as of "low probability" had erupted in sensational violence. The perfection of surprise, the seizure of initiative, and the early success of a complex amphibious operation all proved—as we later discovered—that there had been effective preparation by Egypt for many weeks before. The Israeli deterrent had simply not deterred, and the Israeli intelligence had not detected. The idea of driving Egypt to a polarized option between accepting the status quo or changing it by negotiation had proved baseless. There had been a third option—that of military assault—and it had been seized by Sadat in an operation full of guile and conspiracy just when the negotiating option had become real.

And yet, in the first few hours these hard thoughts were balanced by more sanguine hopes. After all, the Israeli security doctrine had been based on two assumptions: that our adversaries would hesitate to make war unless they had a prospect of victory, and that even if the Arabs took military action, the Israeli response would be so crushing that they would be suing for a cease-fire within a few hours. The latter was the more important of the two elements in the Israeli security doctrine, since it was the one over which Israel had direct control. We could not ensure that the Arabs would not make war, but we could ensure that they would lose it heavily. The memories of 1967 were still vivid in our minds. Everything that had occurred since then had confirmed the impression of Israeli superiority—thus, our first impulse on receiving news of the war was to console ourselves for the shock of its eruption by the expectation that it would be short and triumphant.

Not many hours passed before this hope, too, fell to the ground. The tickertape on my television set spoke of conflicting claims—by Egypt of having crossed the Canal in force, by Israel of having "resisted" the first wave of Egyptian attack. In the north, it was confirmed, the Syrians had made a slight encroachment on our position, but there was no impression yet of deep penetration. I drove down to the Israeli delegation at the UN to meet press representatives and give television interviews. As the day went by without convincing news of Israeli success, my apprehensions mounted high.

In Orthodox and Conservative synagogues in America, news of the war was by now passing from mouth to ear, while less observant Jews across the country were drinking in every word and picture from the television screen. The choice of Yom Kippur for the Arab attack seemed at first to be diabolic; it added the crime of sacrilege to the sin of aggression. Yet in the secular atmosphere of modern international life, it carried very little odium for the Arab governments. Nor did that particular choice of date give them any military advantage. In fact, it later emerged that the Arab leaders who planned the war had not been aware of Yom Kippur at all. They had thought of such things as the full moon, the rate of flow in the Canal, and Israeli preoccupation with the election. While our Day of Atonement was not in their consciousness, it was in fact imprudent for them to choose the day in which Israeli mobilization would be quicker than at any other time. The call-up of Israeli reserves faces two logistic difficulties: delay in locating reservists, and congestion of communications. On Yom Kippur, an Israeli reservist can be found either in his home or in a synagogue; and the roads are open and free.

By midmorning many delegations at the United Nations were anxiously asking me for news. To Sir Donald McIntyre of Australia, the president of the Security Council, I gave all our information, which he acknowledged in laconic tones through which I caught a hint of anxious sympathy. The Arab delegates, mindful of 1967, were reticent and confused. They had learned from experience that it was unwise to be exuberant too soon about prospects in the battlefield.

For a few hours after the first assault, the spirit that I felt from Jerusalem was of traditional buoyancy. I received a message from Golda Meir stating that we would not agree to a cease-fire until the status quo was restored—on both fronts, our intention was to strike until we had driven the last Egyptian and Syrian soldier back across the cease-fire line. We would try to inflict heavy blows on both armies. We would direct our blows to military targets alone and would take care not to injure civilian concentration. The army's spirit was high. The Cabinet was now assembling to hear reports. The cable also told me that the Egyptians had used a FROG and an ICELET missile. It seemed that our civilian population might not be spared the sufferings of war this time.

Mrs. Meir's words in this message were characteristically brave, but many hours went by without our troops being able to give them effect. The evening telegrams told me of military briefings by the Israeli command to the American military attaché. Behind the optimistic phrases there was some obscurity about concrete results. The bulletins were silent about our own losses while giving full play to those of our adversaries. This was unprecedented. In the 1967 campaign and thereafter, the Israeli army had always chosen a policy of candor. Bad news had been conveyed austerely, without euphemism or obscurity. It had seemed more important to maintain credibility at home and abroad than to elevate morale by artificial displays of complacency.

We later learned how in the first few hours of the war the Bar-Lev Line, too lightly manned, began to crumble; how the Israeli tank force in Sinai was diminished beyond the point of national safety; and how scores of Israeli aircraft, attacking in mass formation, were brought down by new missiles of unexpected accuracy. By nightfall Egyptian helicopters carrying commando troops had seized strategic points east of the Canal. Boats and bridges had begun to carry 70,000 troops and 1,000 tanks across the water. In the north, 40,000 Syrians with 800 tanks had driven deep into the Golan Heights. Soon they would be able to cross the river and fork out toward Safed and the lower Jordan. Yet very little of these dangers came across in the first official broadcasts to a stunned and confused nation. In a television address Mrs. Meir announced: "The army is fighting back and repelling the attack. The enemy has suffered serious losses. Our forces were deployed as necessary to meet the danger." Dayan was much more sanguine: "In the Golan Heights perhaps a number of Syrian tanks penetrated our line, but the situation in the Golan Heights is relatively satisfactory. In Sinai, on the Canal, there were many more Egyptian forces. The Egyptian action across the Canal will end as a very dangerous adventure for them."

The question in my own mind was not how it might end, but how it had begun. Israeli military specialists had clearly overrated the difficulty that the Egyptians would encounter in crossing a water obstacle with heavy equipment. Months of Egyptian preparation had obviously gone into amphibious training. The so-called maneuvers were being expanded into a total assault. By the end of the first day, everything in the field had gone against us, and the shadows were growing long.

On Sunday, October 7, Secretary Kissinger and I spoke many times on the telephone comparing notes on the military situation and discussing how America and Israel could deal with a possible Security Council appeal for a cease-fire. We agreed that the time was not ripe for any such move. United Nations resolutions only bring hostilities to an end if there is a mutual interest in a cease-fire. Nothing at that time seemed more disastrous for Israel, or corrosive of its deterrent power, than to cease fire with the Egyptians and Syrians well beyond their previous lines. On their part, the Arabs would wish to pursue their advantage. Thus neither party had an interest in a cease-fire on October 7. In my talks with Kissinger, we developed a joint policy of making our agreement to a cease-fire dependent on withdrawal to Friday's positions. There was, of course, no chance that this would be accepted unless we had some military success. The Arabs and the Soviets were still in a buoyant mood. Their official policy was to refuse a cease-fire unless Israel evacuated the whole of Sinai, Golan, the West Bank, Gaza and East Jerusalem. I told Kissinger that this attitude, ridiculous as it sounded, had a good chance of being adopted by a majority of the Security Council. Kissinger's reply was: "Such a resolution is impossible; we are against it."

Early on Sunday evening it was plain that we were in military disarray. There was no longer an Israeli denial of Egyptian claims to have moved massively across the Canal with tanks, guns and missiles. News reports of heavy Israeli losses in aircraft and tanks were coming on the air without any denial. American Jews were catching these indications with sharp sensitivity. The previous evening Jewish leaders, led by Sam Rothberg, had come to my office at the Israeli delegation. I recorded a broadcast to Jewish communities, calling for solidarity in a difficult hour. My listeners must have noticed that I did not claim any victory in the early fighting. On Sunday hundreds of Jewish leaders assembled in the Plaza Hotel to hear my account of the Israeli struggle. A mass demonstration of New York Jews and sympathizers had been called for the next day.

By evening Israeli military spokesmen could be seen on TV screens explaining that an "initial" breakthrough of Arab forces had been "inevitable." Such vast forces could hardly be deployed in an armored thrust without establishing a base east of the Canal and somewhere within the Golan area. The Israeli tactics were now being explained in the following terms: Israel's army was based on reserve strength. A relatively thin line of manpower had been ordered to blunt the first assault and to yield as little ground as possible; the Israeli "fist" would then come into action. The plan seemed logical, but this time the Arabs were not acting in conformity with our logic. The "blunting" operation had simply failed to blunt. There had been a deeper Egyptian and Syrian penetration than anyone in Israel had predicted. But by Monday or Tuesday, Israel would be at peak strength, with all armies deployed. At that stage we could expect a turn of the tide, and Egyptian forces east of the Canal would either be thrown back or destroyed. General Chaim Herzog, our most trusted military spokesman, was reporting Israeli success in destroying the pontoon bridges across which the Egyptians had come. It followed that they had no line of retreat. Since they were bottled up in a narrow corridor, they would not be able to deploy for serious operations. This description was accurate in itself, but it made no provision for the extraordinary speed with which Egyptian engineers could now repair or replace damaged bridges.

A message from Mrs. Meir on Sunday asked me to remain in the United States for possible action by the Security Council and in other political arenas. Late that day we felt the harshest psychological blow that Israelis had endured in recent years when we saw films from Damascus on television showing dozens of young Israeli soldiers sitting dejectedly on the ground, blindfolded, with their hands on their heads in the demeanor of surrender. Many of them were in slovenly dress as though they had been taken unawares. Some were wounded, with bandages covering their heads, faces and arms. How different this was from the image of Israeli soldiers who had been so victorious in 1967 and had established a reputation of invincibility ever since!

In the next forty-eight hours the cables from Jerusalem came to me thick and fast. Dayan had flown to the front in a helicopter and had returned to Tel Aviv to meet the Cabinet and to brief the Committee of Newspaper Editors. It was only a few days later that I learned that he had unfolded a somber vision of Israel's danger and had recommended a withdrawal to the Milta Pass in the south and to a position several miles within the Golan Heights. The majority of the Cabinet, led by Mrs. Meir, overruled these harsh proposals. The decision was to contain the Egyptian bridgehead until it could be attacked, and in the meantime to transfer the main Israeli counteroffensive to the Golan Heights. The battle front at the Suez Canal was remote from Israeli centers of population. Sinai offered room for a war of movement, and an Egyptian advance of a few kilometers here or there would not threaten vital Israeli targets. On the other hand, a further Syrian thrust of more than five kilometers would put the most savage of our enemies in control of roads leading to Safed and Haifa. They would also be able to bring the settlements in Upper Galilee and the Jordan Valley under fire. So it was the Syrians, not the Egyptians, who now threatened the security of our state. The battle of the Golan Heights had first urgency, and as long as it was being waged, there would be no surplus of strength to uproot the Egyptian bridgehead.

At a tense meeting of the United Nations General Assembly on Monday I said that it was our intention "to throw the attacking forces back to the cease-fire line whence they had come." Twenty-four hours later this appeared to be a remote ambition. When the Israeli Cabinet and defense chiefs surveyed the scene after three days of war, they found a position that would have seemed fantastic to any Israeli a week before.

The Arab success could not be denied. Our military command had, incredibly, left no more than about 400 troops and 30 tanks at the front line to face hundreds of thousands of Egyptians in full array a few hundred meters across the water. From Jerusalem I now learned that on Wednesday, October 3, four ministers—Golda Meir, Yigal Allon, Moshe Dayan and Israel Galili—meeting with senior military officers, had discussed the Egyptian and Syrian troop concentrations for over two hours. They recalled how in May similar Egyptian concentrations had dispersed without firing a shot, so that millions of pounds had been wasted on Israel's massive mobilization. This episode had bequeathed a feeling of superiority to those intelligence officers who had argued against the mobilization; to them, General Elazar, who had insisted on mobilization in May, had obviously been excessively pessimistic. This precedent may have been alive in their minds on October 3, when, under the emphatic persuasion of our military leaders, the four ministers accepted the appraisal that on this occasion the probability of war was minimal. They concluded their meeting by accepting Allon's proposal to discuss the security situation at the regular Cabinet—on Sunday, October 7.

The October 3 meeting will haunt Israeli history for many years to come. It was certainly the central episode in what came to be known as "the failure." But General Elazar had not been fully reassured. He had ordered a fairly high state of alert throughout the armed forces.

The next evening, October 4, General Eli Zeira, the chief of military intelligence, had reported to the Chief of Staff that Soviet families were being evacuated from Egypt and Syria. Even this news led to no operative conclusions. Early on Friday morning the military correspondents of Israeli newspapers were briefed "not to exaggerate" the significance of reports about large Arab concentrations along the borders and to stress that the Israeli Defense Forces were taking the necessary precautions. Later on October 5 the intelligence chiefs were still telling the Prime Minister and the General Staff that the probability of war breaking out was "the lowest of the low."

Mrs. Meir had briefed those ministers who happened to be in Tel Aviv; she did not wish to disturb those who lived in Jerusalem, Haifa or kibbutzim. But at four o'clock in the morning on October 6 General Zeira was startled to receive a message which moved him to call Defense Minister Moshe Dayan, Chief of Staff General Elazar and Deputy Chief of Staff General Israel Tal with the information that war would certainly break out on both fronts, probably toward sundown. Two hours later General Elazar asked the Minister of Defense to authorize general mobilization and a pre-emptive strike against Syria. Dayan rejected the proposal for a pre-emptive strike and authorized a more limited mobilization than Elazar demanded—one division for each of the north and south commands. Since Elazar was tenaciously advocating more stringent measures than Dayan was willing to approve, the matter was referred to the Prime Minister. Dayan still opposed the general mobilization which General Elazar emphatically requested. Dayan said that the United States or world opinion would regard this as provocative. This argument is described in the Agranat Report as "cogent" (see next chapter). I do not recall any cases in which a precautionary mobilization of our forces has ever had any adverse international effects or has ever been opposed by a Foreign Minister on those grounds.

Prime Minister Meir was now closer to the Chief of Staff's urgent view than to that of Dayan. She had authorized the mobilization of about 100,000 reserves; in point of fact, General Elazar ordered an even larger call-up.

Dayan had yielded reluctantly to the Prime Minister's ruling. He was clearly convinced, as were most Israeli leaders, that the Israeli forces already on the ground would be adequate to stem the first assault, so that massive mobilization could safely be postponed until after an attack took place. Elazar made a proposal for a pre-emptive air strike against Syria. The Prime Minister and later the Cabinet supported Dayan's opposition to a pre-emptive air strike against Syria on the grounds that nobody would believe its "pre-emptiveness." After all, only a few hours had passed since Israel had been telling the United States that the Syrian concentrations did not portend war at all. Moreover, our security doctrine since 1967 had been based on the belief that the new cease-fire boundaries, unlike the old armistice lines, enabled us to absorb a first blow and thus to avoid a pre-emptive strategy. To pre-empt from those lines would disprove our military doctrine.

And so it came about that the Israeli Cabinet had been in constant session between midday and two o'clock on Yom Kippur when General Israel Leor, the Prime Minister's military aide, pushed the door open to announce that the war had begun—four hours earlier than the intelligence chiefs had emphatically predicted. When I received the startling cablegram on October 6 in New York, I had no knowledge of the preceding days of confusion and unpreparedness. Nor did the Israeli people then know that a junior intelligence officer, Lieutenant Benjamin Siman Tov, had been submitting documents on October 1–3 in which he despairingly demonstrated that the "maneuvers" in Sinai were, in fact, a camouflage for an impending attack. This theory was so heretical in the eyes of his seniors that it was never passed upward to the General Staff or even included in the Southern Command Intelligence report.

The news about the procedure of consultation in the first week of October came to my knowledge in New York a few days after the outbreak of the war. Those of us who were carrying on the diplomatic struggle had little time to ask ourselves how the national peril had been allowed to develop. All that we could see was the jubilation of Arab delegates parading their success in United Nations corridors—and puzzled faces of American officials wondering what had happened to the legend of Israel's invincibility.

Nevertheless, the early setbacks were still regarded in Israel as a tragic accident from which our forces would recover within a few days. The hopeful rhetoric of our spokesmen was not a mere tactic designed to reinforce morale. It really represented the official mood. The Prime Minister was indomitable in her confidence. On Monday evening, October 8, she sent me a reassuring message saying that she wanted to strengthen my hands for the forthcoming political struggle. It was vital, she said, that I should know the precise position. The Cabinet meeting had just ended. The Chief of Staff had surveyed the situation on all fronts. The general trend of the discussion following his report was that we were now about to pass from a holding action to a counteroffensive both in Sinai and the Golan Heights.

The cable went on to tell me of our General Staff's belief that there was a strong prospect that our forces would be able to make good progress in throwing the enemy back beyond the cease-fire line in the Golan Heights and also to make perceptible progress in uprooting the enemy forces which had crossed into Sinai. Our offensive in Sinai was now at its height. Mrs. Meir referred to the danger that once our position improved, pressures would be exerted upon us to expedite a cease-fire while the enemy was still on our side of the cease-fire lines, especially Sinai. We could not possibly conceive carrying out a cease-fire resolution so long as the enemy forces had not been repelled. Mrs. Meir hoped that in the course of our counteroffensives, we should be able to seize military positions across the Canal and beyond the previous line in the Golan Heights, with the aim of ensuring ourselves against new assaults of the enemy and of strengthening our position in the political negotiation. There was no controversy among ministers about the desirability of these two aims. In the present conditions, therefore, we had no interest in risking any confrontation with the Security Council or with our friends. The Prime Minister thought that "the United States will understand the risk that we have taken on ourselves by our decision not to make a pre-emptive strike."

It turned out that any fear of premature Security Council action was unfounded. The Egyptians and Syrians had their tails up and were in no mood to call a halt. The optimism which our commanders had expressed to the Prime Minister was not yet confirmed by military results. The operations of our forces on Monday were immensely heroic, but when night fell, little impression had been made on the Egyptian bridgehead, which was becoming further consolidated every hour. In the north the Syrians had been checked, but not thrown back, and Israeli losses were high.

Tuesday, October 9, was the black day, made darker for us in New York by a sense of impotence. We could not ask for a cease-fire with Arab forces deep into our lines, and we had no clear political aims as long as our military fortunes were low. So, for many hours, I alternated with Ambassador Tekoah at fruitless meetings of the Security Council in which we discussed Arab complaints about Israel bombing raids near Damascus, Ismailia and Port Said. This reached a high peak of paradox even in the quaint jurisprudence of the United Nations: the Arabs were waging war, refusing a cease-fire— and loudly complaining that Israel was hitting back!

We were in close communication with the United States government, but in the first seventy-two hours of the war, we had no ambitious requests to make. But since we were telling Washington that the Egyptian and Syrian advances were going to be crushed in a few days, there was not yet any solid reason for Washington to prepare an emergency supply operation. This condition only changed when the disappointing results of Monday's engagements became known. Once our reserves had been mobilized and moved into position, the Israeli commanders on both fronts had ordered massive attacks with huge waste of planes and tanks; they were clearly concerned to make up for the days of unpreparedness. The initial Israeli tactic was to fling the Egyptian and Syrian forces back by the sheer intensity of armored and air counterattacks.

But they were now confronted with a surprise. The Soviet Union had supplied Egyptian and Syrian forces with anti-tank and anti-aircraft missiles of such mobility and simple deployment that they could be effectively used even by troops not specially qualified in advanced weapon techniques. There was now a lethal anti-tank missile which could be operated from the shoulder, like a somewhat bulky rifle or machine gun. These new devices, and men trained to use them, were deployed in such mass that the Israeli air and tank forces wilted under the intensity of the Arab assault.

By the fourth day of the war, Israel's losses both in first-line planes and in tanks were so heavy that our commanders were inhibited from throwing further forces into new attacks. The slender shield of steel that stood between the nation and its direst peril had quite simply grown too thin. It was now essential to ask the United States for immediate reinforcement of lost material.

No preparations had been made for such a contingency. For several years the expectation had been that if war broke out at all, it would be swiftly ended by the superiority of Israeli arms. The idea that Israel would not be able to deal the Arabs a fatal blow with its existing weaponry had not entered anybody's head. On the second and third day of the war Israel had asked the United States somewhat tentatively for the replacement of ammunition and even of blankets and drugs. The nature of these requests hinted that our military logistics had not been very effective. Buoyed up by memories of swift victory in 1967, Israeli commanders had not absorbed the idea that our country would be threatened so drastically as to need an emergency infusion of air and armored strength.

It therefore took some time before the notion of an American airlift struck root. On Monday, October 8, the prevailing Israeli view still was that the total expulsion of Egyptian and Syrian forces was only a few days away and that when this occurred, a cease-fire would be established. A message from Mrs. Meir to Secretary Kissinger that evening stated that our military people, on whose appraisal and judgment the Prime Minister relied completely, had told her that we were involved in very difficult battles, but that when our reserves in manpower and, especially, in equipment came into play, there would be a change in our favor. She added that our military leaders had never misled either themselves or the national leadership. Mrs. Meir agreed with Kissinger's view concerning the uselessness of an early Security Council meeting. On the other hand, if the Security Council convened on Wednesday or Thursday, there was good cause to assume that we would then be in a posture of attack instead of defense, so that there was more chance of our opponents' agreeing to an acceptable cease-fire.

Thus, all that the Israeli government was asking of the United States in the first days of the war was to have confidence in our early triumph and to avoid complications in the Security Council for a few days. Within forty-eight hours it was plain that the expulsion of the attackers was not in sight, least of all from their bridgehead east of the Suez Canal. By Tuesday evening the Prime Minister had asked General Aharon Yariv to appear on television to give a less complacent picture of our military condition than had been prevalent a few hours before, when General Elazar had bravely promised "to break the enemy's bones." The harsh truth was that it was Israel's bones which were not fully intact. The fractures were serious, though not beyond remedy. An urgent supply problem was now high on the Cabinet's agenda.

Even then the need of massive reinforcement from the United States grew slowly in our official consciousness. It was first suggested from Jerusalem that Boeing civilian planes of the El Al Airlines be allowed to land in the United States to carry off such equipment as could be brought together at American airports. But when the full extent of our needs became known, it was realized that Israel would need reinforcement not only in ammunition and small arms but also in the most vital armored and aerial weapons. This was revealed to President Nixon on Tuesday, and by evening, to our enormous relief, his affirmative decision had been given.

The relief of the Cabinet and the General Staff was deepened by our parallel knowledge that European countries, including Great Britain, were falling back in panic before the Arab threat to withhold oil supplies. European governments were not only denying Israel new armament; they were even forbidding the export of ammunition and spare parts necessary to put existing equipment to work. The decision of Edward Heath and his government in London came as a specially harsh blow to Israel at the lowest point in her ordeal. The quantities at stake were not vast, and the material effect was perhaps not decisive, but the British example affected other European countries. Moreover, British leaders should have been the first to recall the crucial influence of morale and solidarity in lonely hours. Some months later when a British minister, Sir Keith Joseph, came officially to Israel for Ben Gurion's funeral, he admitted to me that the Conservative Cabinet never understood how deep a wound its embargo would leave in Israeli opinion. It was only when Harold Wilson's Labour government came to power that the scar in our relations began to heal.

There was a much better response to Israel's supply needs in Germany, until publicity about the arrival of an Israeli ship in Bremen caused hesitation and temporary stoppage. It became more and more evident that the crucial verdict for the supply of Israeli armies in the field would have to come from Washington. But it also became increasingly clear that the presidential directive was not enough to set the arms flowing. Our representatives in Washington found themselves wandering in a bureaucratic maze. There were no precedents to guide their action, nor were even the friendliest American agencies able to refer to any preconceived contingency plan. There was a traditional American inhibition against sending weapons under U.S. flag into areas of conflict. Since the El Al solution was inadequate, Secretary Kissinger's mind turned to the idea of encouraging American charter companies to make their aircraft available to carry arms to Israel. On Wednesday and Thursday these and other devices were explored, but nothing moved. All the charter companies were "otherwise engaged."

It is not surprising that by Friday, October 12, there was a note of alarm in the cables from Israel. Ambassador Simcha Dinitz, too, was no longer certain that all was going well. He was finding it necessary to employ a more urgent tone in his contacts with officials in Washington. The presidential directive was still barren of results. The battered Syrian armies were being reinforced by Iraqi and Jordanian contingents. Israel was approaching a scarcity in vital arms without any imminent certainty of replenishment.

When I arrived in Washington on Friday evening I had two grave themes for discussion with Secretary Kissinger. I had been urgently asked from Jerusalem to express our concern at the absence of arms shipments even after President Nixon's favorable directive—this was to be the primary purpose of my intervention in Washington. What I had not anticipated was a message I had received a few hours before leaving New York. It spoke of Israeli consent to a possible cease-fire "in place."

The United States and Israel had hitherto refused to have anything to do with the idea of a cease-fire "in place." This would have legitimized Egyptian and Syrian positions seized since Yom Kippur. It was precisely because we rejected a cease-fire "in place" that we had not wished the Security Council to adopt a resolution. I was therefore surprised when I received a cable from Mordechai Gazit, the director-general of the Prime Minister's office, saying that the Cabinet had decided to acquiesce in a cease-fire "in place" if it could be achieved. The reasons were starkly realistic. There was no early prospect of expelling Egyptian forces in the south, while in the north we had reached the peak of our success and might not be able to push the Syrians farther, now that fresh Iraqi and Jordanian contingents were coming into the line.

Early on Saturday morning, I went with Dinitz to see Secretary Kissinger, convinced that we had reached the turning point in the war. I began by pointing out that during that Friday night we had made gains in the north, but an effective push in the southern front was not feasible. We had been unable to advance on both fronts because of the slowness and paucity of American supplies. When we received news of the President's decision on Tuesday night, there had been immense joy in our Cabinet. The expectation then was that the supplies would reach Israel without delay. None of us conceived that the actual results would be so meager. I gave details of the numerous Soviet transports that had reached the Arab side. Kissinger lifted his telephone and spoke to officials in the White House, the Pentagon and other departments, calling for rapid action and suggesting ways of overcoming obstacles.

When Ambassador Dinitz and I reiterated that our military difficulties arose from the absence of anticipated American supplies, Kissinger made no attempt to demur. It was obvious from his exposition that he found the existing military position adverse to basic American interests. It gave the Soviet Union excessive prestige, and it contained no incentive for a cease-fire, still less for negotiations. Unless Israel improved its military position, American diplomacy had no basis on which anything could be built. He summed up by saying that before the day was out, three methods of supply would be at work. There would be direct flights to Israel by C-3 supply aircraft and C-130s; there would be flights by chartered planes; and there would be a first supply of replacement military aircraft to Israel via the Azores. He showed annoyance at having been unable to get things moving earlier. He went on to say that American foreign policy depended on creating a military position which would constitute "an incentive for a cease-fire." I pointed out that the delay in the promised supplies had prevented us from creating that incentive, and had thus frustrated both American and Israeli policy. The Secretary made further telephone calls in my presence, from which I learned that he was working hard to overcome whatever obstacles had prevented arms supplies from moving to Israel. He said that "before the night is out, I shall know if we have broken through." We later learned that President Nixon had ordered the great airlift at this meeting.

We went on to discuss the diplomatic situation. In accordance with my instructions just received, I told Kissinger that we saw no reason to delay the procedures leading to an early cease-fire. He had had some talks with the British government on this the previous night. I told him of my cable from Jerusalem. He looked surprised and somewhat concerned and left the room, saying that he was going to telephone the British Foreign Secretary, since the United States, in view of its previous positions, would not wish to sponsor a cease-fire resolution "in place." When he came back, Kissinger told me that the British government was not prepared to take the initiative, since it had learned that Egypt did not want a cease-fire at this stage. It seemed to me that this reply from London angered him. The idea apparently had been to secure acquiescence in a cease-fire proposal after it was submitted, not to receive endorsement of it in advance. He had, however, arranged for another talk with Sir Alec Douglas-Home, and if the British government still refused to sponsor a resolution, he would consider probing the Australian delegation if it was all right with me. I gave my consent to this, and embarked on some discussion of possible parliamentary tactics in a cease-fire debate. Kissinger asked what the Israeli reaction would be if the Security Council called for a cease-fire and a standstill in present positions. I said that my instructions from Jerusalem would compel me to say that we still stood for the restoration of the October 5 lines, but that if there were a new proposal, I would consult my colleagues.

I asked Kissinger what the U.S. reaction would be. He replied that the United States would still express a preference for the restoration of the previous positions but would not veto a cease-fire "in place" on both fronts. He had said this to Douglas-Home, who had raised the possibility of a broader resolution calling for UN troops and a peace conference. Kissinger thought that this was too complex at this stage, and that we should first concentrate on an acceptable cease-fire formula. I pointed out that even if one could be agreed upon, we could not implement it unless there were absolute assurances of a prisoner-of-war exchange. Kissinger agreed that the slowness in conveying supplies to Israel was disturbing and he would now go to the White House, where there would be a decisive meeting. (It later emerged that the "breakthrough" conference at the White House took place late on Saturday morning, October 13.)

From the Secretary's office I went back to our embassy, where I spoke to Prime Minister Golda Meir in Tel Aviv on a direct line. I said that Secretary Kissinger seemed to be putting his full weight behind the airlift, but that in any case we should know by the evening to what extent his intervention had been effective. Mrs. Meir expressed relief and asked Dinitz and me to lay special emphasis on the urgent need for certain specific weapons required to stem Arab tank assaults on both fronts. I gathered that there were signs of greater stability in our military position, but that it would take a day or two before we could honestly say if the tide had turned.

Ambassador Dinitz and Shalev spent the next few hours at the departments and agencies to which Kissinger had spoken in our presence. They found strong and direct echoes of his intervention. The administrative machine was conscious, at all levels, of Kissinger's emphatic insistence on immediate action.

Toward evening I took a shuttle to New York to be prepared for a possible cease-fire "scenario" in the Security Council. A few hours later a call came through to me from Secretary Kissinger in New York. He said that he had given Ambassador Dinitz the information that he was now communicating to me, but in view of our conversation in the morning, he wanted me to hear directly that some sixty huge transport aircraft were now in the air and would be landing within the next twenty-four hours at Israeli airports. The Secretary hoped that the arrival of this great transfusion of strength would reinforce Israel's spirit as well as her physical strength.

Before I had time to thank him for these tidings, the Secretary went on to tell me about the fate of the "cease-fire scenario." The British reply had been negative, and the Soviet Union would not cooperate if the sponsorship of the cease-fire was Australian rather than British. Therefore, unless Israel wanted a cease-fire so badly as to desire American sponsorship, the whole prospect was now in abeyance. I told the Secretary on my own responsibility that I was certain that the Israeli government would not wish the United States to go back on its declared position in favor of restoring the October 5 cease-fire position. I would, however, let him know.

An extensive literature has grown up on the responsibility for "delaying" the American airlift, and there has been much tendentious analysis of motivation. In this case, the facts are simpler than the legends. In my judgment and knowledge, there was no prolonged "delay" in the airlift at all. As late as Monday night, Israel was telling the United States that we were on the verge of a victory and a cease-fire. The need for massive reinforcement only became evident on Tuesday. The President ruled favorably that same night. There was no contingency or logistic plan, since nobody had imagined since 1967 that an Arab attack would be unrepelled for several days. If everything had gone smoothly, supplies should have begun to flow on Thursday or Friday. By Saturday, the operation was in full swing. I had the impression that the driving force in surmounting the obstacles was Kissinger, who knew that there could not be a cease-fire, let alone a negotiation, unless the military situation gave an incentive to stop the fighting. For those who know bureaucratic ways in Washington, the astonishing fact is that the airlift was in massive motion about three days after the idea of it was first conceived.

On returning to New York from Washington, I had found a message on my desk from our consul-general in New York, David Rivlin. The Jewish leaders were worried and confused. They, too, had been told by the Administration that President Nixon and Secretary Kissinger had decided to give Israel massive reinforcement. On the other hand, friends of Israel in the Congress were telling them that the presidential promises were not sincere and that no arms were moving toward Israel at all. Many heads of Jewish organizations wanted to break their restraint and to launch a pressure campaign against the Administration. A few of the leaders of major Jewish organizations were assembled at their headquarters at 515 Park Avenue under the chairmanship of Jacob Stein. In the consul-general's view, it would be crucial for me to come and clarify the situation. Jewish leaders were entitled to know what the position was and exactly what the Israeli government wanted from the United States.

When I met the small group of Jewish leaders that evening, I was in a dilemma. On the one hand, several of them were convinced that the arms supply, although authorized, had in fact been deliberately frustrated. I myself knew that this was no longer the case. On the other hand, with transport aircraft on the way to Israel at that very hour, I did not wish to give the meeting a precise account of my recent talks with the Secretary. It was even possible that premature publicity about massive arms supplies would restrict our chances of receiving them. I therefore said that whatever the situation had been in early morning, it had now been repaired, and that processes were afoot which would make hostile demonstrations against the Administration on Israel's behalf not only futile, but unjust. "I might not have been able to say that twenty-four hours ago," I added.

The next morning, Sunday, October 14, all mystery was dissipated.

Washington had apparently decided that having given Israel vast shipments of arms, it might just as well reap the deterrent value of its action by elevating its "low profile." All the Sunday newspapers were carrying stories about Secretary Kissinger's disappointment at the lack of Soviet restraint in arms supply to the Arabs. He had hoped that Soviet arms shipments would remain "moderate." Indeed, he had raised the art of understatement to new levels on Friday, October 12. Discussing Soviet incitement of other Arab states to join Egypt and Syria in fighting against Israel, Kissinger had said that this was "not exactly helpful." Events during the weekend showed that the Soviet Union, pleasantly surprised by the initial success of Arab arms, was moving to increase its advantage by massive arms supplies. The United States would now have to choose: it must either vindicate or dishonor its policy of preserving the balance of power. Accordingly, the American people was now being told frankly that American arms were flowing copiously to Israel.

It was still my duty to find out what the Israeli government wanted me to do about the idea of a cease-fire. I had been surprised by the readiness for it on October 12–13. I did not know if it reflected a fleeting moment of despondency or a deliberate design to cut losses and bring the war to an early end. The answer was not slow in coming. The messages reaching me on Sunday morning from Jerusalem were suddenly buoyant and hopeful. We had, at last, scored some authentic military successes and looked forward to more. A massive Egyptian assault designed to widen the bridgehead east of the Canal had been thrown back with heavy casualties to the attacking force. The Egyptians had lost more than 200 tanks, against only 16 Israeli losses. In the north our troops continued to advance. A telegram to me from Jerusalem referred to the immense encouragement that the American airlift had given to the morale of the Cabinet and the General Staff. In these conditions, I decided to leave the cease-fire problem alone. It was evident that if our military situation continued to improve, an Arab interest in a cease-fire would soon emerge.

The literature on the Yom Kippur War has already been prolific, but it is relatively silent on the October 13 cease-fire proposal. President Sadat had shown great astuteness before the war and in its early stages. But to our relief he made an immense blunder in declining the cease-fire available to him on October 13. The hostilities would then have ended before any Israeli crossing west of the Canal, and at a time when the Syrians still held a few positions in the Golan Heights. The legend of Arab "success" in the Yom Kippur War would have been more convincing if the war had ended when Egypt was in an optimal military position. Like gamblers at a roulette table, the Arabs preferred not to put their gains in their pocket, but to bank everything on another turn of the wheel. Sure enough, their gains now began to dwindle. After October 14, all their counterattacks were to fail and all Israeli operations would succeed.

Israelis who now speak regretfully of the cease-fire on October 22, with Israeli troops close to Suez and Ismailia and pressing on the suburbs of Damascus, are inclined to forget how close they were to accepting a cease-fire in much less advantageous conditions only ten days before. October 13 was an authentic turning point in both the military and the political sense. When the day dawned, Israel had no assurance of sufficient arms and was ready for a chastening cease-fire. By midnight the arms were flowing and our forces were moving from one triumph to another.

The sense of having reached a new landmark came clearly through the report that I received from Jerusalem after the Cabinet meeting on Sunday morning. I was told that on the southern front we were at the height of a general offensive by the enemy. Egypt had thrown three divisions into a battle which was expected to be of decisive significance. The Cabinet had been praying that the enemy would make an all-out attempt to erupt eastward, and this, the report went on, is what he was doing. It seemed that we were in a position for a well-contrived and daring operation. Morale was very high, and a heavy armored force had been assembled. Air support would be used. In the north, the position was good. The Chief of Staff looked and sounded optimistic, and hoped for a good result. The discussion on political steps would take place later.

All talk of a cease-fire had now become obsolete; it would not be revived until Egypt's consciousness caught up with its military reality. As I had expected, Jerusalem confirmed what I had told Kissinger: we would not welcome an American initiative for a cease-fire resolution "in place." We could now wait for the military situation to create a mutual incentive for a cease-fire. Sadat had missed his best chance. Under intense air cover, Israeli columns had cut in behind the central Egyptian force on the way to the Gidi Pass; we had struck the mass and scattered the remnant. About half of the armor committed by the Egyptians that day had been destroyed or put out of action.

In a cable to Jerusalem on October 13 I had said that our political position would be improved if there were some places at which Israeli forces pushed beyond the October 5 cease-fire lines. This would give us something to give back in cease-fire negotiations. I had no way of knowing in New York whether this was anything but fantasy. But reports coming in on Sunday indicated that the defeat of the Egyptian attack that day made it possible for the Cabinet to consider a plan submitted by General Arik Sharon for seizing a bridgehead across the Canal. Sharon's plan was to attack the Egyptians westward from Tassa toward Ismailia with one brigade, to loop anticlockwise with another, which would then attack from the south ostensibly in an attempt to break into the Egyptian bridgehead. Simultaneously, Major General Avraham Adan ("Bren") would take an armored force to the west bank of the Canal.

Sadat's political mistake in refusing the cease-fire on October 13 was now compounded by the military miscalculation of his High Command. There was a total failure for nearly thirty-six hours to comprehend the scope or purport of the Israeli crossing. When Egyptian communiqués spoke contemptuously of "a few Israeli commando units" that had crossed west of the Canal, they were not merely uttering propaganda; they were giving a sincere appreciation of the position as they saw it. Obscurity in the Egyptian mind about the dimensions of the Israeli crossing persisted for most of October 15 and 16. The main preoccupation of the Egyptian General Staff still lay east of the Canal, where their tank forces were reeling after their unsuccessful Sunday assault, while in the south, Egyptian brigades were threatened with encirclement by advancing Israeli forces. It has been suggested that if the Israeli generals had made a tactical retreat to lure Egypt farther eastward, the Egyptian defeat would have been even more conclusive. But the disasters of the first three days had understandably created a cautious mentality in our General Staff, and there was no disposition to give any ground for tactical purposes. Even so, the Egyptians, while still in control of the east bank of the Canal, had passed the peak of their success. General Bar-Lev had pulled together a formidable Israeli force with four fully mobilized divisions. In the north, the Syrian attempt to recapture the Golan Heights had failed and everything was ready for a decisive Israeli success in the south.

But our commanders were now at odds about the precise timing of the major push westward to reinforce Sharon's bridgehead. General Sharon, justifiably anxious lest a Security Council or Great Power cease-fire might come too soon, had wanted to go forward quickly, irrespective of his supply lines. His commanding officer, General Gonen, who advocated caution, was much junior to him in service and experience, and Sharon showed little deference to his formal rank. In the end, Sharon had been overruled by Bar-Lev and Elazar, who thought it advisable to let Egypt push more of her armor eastward across the Canal, leaving the west bank thinly defended. They also insisted on a firm supply line for the westward crossing. Without this they feared that there would be the danger of a romantic but costly fiasco.

The Israeli thrust had begun in the late afternoon on Monday, October 15. Throughout Tuesday the Egyptian response had been defused. The Egyptian planning had been rigorously precise up till then, but it had taken no account of the contingency that Israeli troops would cross the Canal in strength. It was only on Wednesday afternoon, when General Adan's division went across the Canal with heavy pontoon bridges to reinforce Sharon's bridgehead, that the Egyptians began to react with alarm. They could no longer pretend that Sharon's forces were across the Canal for a mere "commando raid". It was obviously a major offensive which, if it was allowed to develop, would bring the road to Cairo under peril.

As the news of these battles reached us in New York on October 17, it became obvious that a new political phase was drawing near. The Arab governments would now have to abandon the lofty condescension with which they had been refusing cease-fire proposals a few days before. Our task was to be on guard against adverse political conditions that might be attached to what now seemed the inevitable approach of a cease-fire. Late in the day Ambassador Dinitz sent me a message in New York from Washington. Kissinger's deputy, General Brent Scowcroft, had called him to a meeting to discuss the contingency of an early cease-fire resolution at the United Nations. Late on October 16, the day before, the Soviet Union had asked the United States what the American attitude would be to a cease-fire linked to Security Council Resolution 242. It was possible that the Soviets might in the end agree to a cease-fire "in place" even if their rhetorical position still spoke of a return to the June 4, 1967, lines. The United States had told the Soviet Union that it was not opposed to a cease-fire in principle, but would have to see a specific proposal before making any comments. It was already known that Prime Minister Kosygin was about to visit Cairo, and his inquiries from Washington were presumably related to that trip.

Later that Wednesday evening I had a telephone call from Kissinger, who told me that the Soviets had not yet presented any cease-fire draft and would probably not do so until the end of Kosygin's visit to Cairo. Kissinger reiterated that the United States would have nothing to do with any Soviet proposal that linked the cease-fire with a return to the pre-1967 boundaries.

While our armies were now advancing on all fronts, I thought it wise for the Israeli government to make some tentative planning for a cease-fire discussion. In a cabled memorandum on October 17, I raised many contingencies. First, would we be willing to have a cease-fire "in place"? I presumed that in principle we would soon be in a position to answer this affirmatively. Nevertheless, I assumed that we would now be interested in gaining time, since the military prospects were constantly improving. Second, would we be willing to mention Resolution 242? I thought that it would not be realistic to avoid such a reference in view of our acceptance of this resolution in the past; I also had the impression that the Americans had conceded this point to the Soviets already. Third, should we wait for the Soviets to present a proposal to which the United States would react? I thought that it would be dangerous for us to accept this procedure. I still had a traumatic recollection of the Goldberg-Gromyko draft of July 1967. I thought that it would be better for the United States and Israel to agree on a contingent text in advance. Fourth, what should the sponsorship of such a resolution be? Here I gave detailed reasons for opposing a British or European initiative. In the light of the European embargo and many signs of obsequious attitudes toward Arab oil producers in London and elsewhere, I felt that we could not rely on a European initiative. To the surprise of my colleagues, I suggested that we propose an American-Soviet sponsorship of a resolution that would be agreed upon by us, since this would be the only way to tie the Soviet Union to the United States and to immunize ourselves against undesirable Soviet amendments. At the same time I urged that we remain firm in making a prisoner exchange one of the conditions of implementing a cease-fire.

Late in the evening of October 17, Ambassador Dinitz reported to me cheerfully by wire on his telephone conversation with Jerusalem about the situation on the southern front. We were now fighting on both banks of the Canal; October 17 had been a successful day in every respect. If this trend continued, the political prospect would change. One of our important assets was that even now the Egyptians did not seem to grasp the full implications of our presence west of the Canal, and for this reason, we were keeping a "low profile" in our military bulletins. In this situation we had no reason to accelerate international discussions. The military momentum would make a cease-fire proposal realistic in due course.

I could see that the Israeli government would soon be in a position to review its political options in a more positive atmosphere than could have been imagined a few days before. Late on October 18 the Prime Minister told me by cable that the Cabinet must soon hold a crucial discussion. She thought it essential that I take part in the Cabinet meetings that would discuss the cease-fire prospects. She therefore asked me to inform Kissinger that I had been called home for

Cabinet consultations, and that until these consultations were held, we would not be in a position to reply to the queries that General Scowcroft had raised.

I made arrangements immediately for returning home by the overnight El Al plane. At four o'clock that Thursday, Kissinger called me from Washington. He said that despite its soundings on October 16, the Soviet Union had still made no serious cease-fire proposals. The position at this moment, therefore, was that the cease-fire issue was still not operative. The Secretary had heard that I had been asked to go home for a Cabinet meeting. He would appreciate it if I could bring back a full picture of the trends of thought and conclusions in Israel. In the meantime there was the problem of how to deal with Resolution 242 in a cease-fire resolution, and he hoped he would hear all our proposals and considerations on this point. He asked me how I saw the question of timing.

I replied that the time factor was certainly no longer working against us, and I hope that this consideration would be in the mind of the United States. He replied, "Certainly. I don't believe that anything will move unless all parties have some incentive for a balanced cease-fire." I replied that we were creating incentives for them every hour. I thanked him for the support that the United States had given us in the past week. "Be assured yourself and tell your Prime Minister and colleagues," Kissinger replied, "that the principles which guided United States policy in the last two weeks of the war will continue to guide it." He added that he had enjoyed the experience of working with me in these critical days and hoped that we would be able to cooperate in easier times.

Kissinger then said, "I don't know anything that is not known to you, and it is in that spirit of candor that I will remain in touch with the ambassador." He said that it might well be that the Soviet Union would soon present concrete proposals. I repeated that there need be no hurry in responding. "If time is not pressing on you, there are more options than otherwise," Kissinger replied. He then added, "There is more happening on the Soviet side than I can talk about. My inhibition in talking to you more about this is the fact that we are now on the open telephone." I said that if he would keep in touch with the ambassador at every point, it would be greatly appreciated.

As soon as I had finished this conversation, I prepared to make a dash for the airport to catch the late flight. As I was leaving my hotel room a call came from Ambassador Dinitz saying that he was sending important information to me to New York which could not be relayed on the open line. He hoped that this would get through before my plane left. I waited another half-hour, but it was now apparent that my choice was whether to miss the plane or to await the message. I decided to begin my trip to Paris and asked the ambassador to transmit to me there whatever news there was to tell me.

At Kennedy Airport a tragic aspect of the war burst upon me in an intimate personal context. I was told that our Ambassador in Paris, Arthur Ben Nathan, did not yet know that his son had fallen in action. By the time I arrived, this news might be in his possession. The last few days had been clouded for all of us by the alarming lists of casualties. It was already clear that the final toll would go well over the two-thousand mark, while the number of heavily wounded also grew steadily day by day.

On reaching Paris six and a half hours later, I was told that Ambassador Ben Nathan had been given the grievous news and had left the airport for his residence. I sent him a message of consolation, knowing how futile it was to hope to be useful in such a terrible hour.

I then telephoned Ambassador Dinitz. He told me that Secretary Kissinger, when he had spoken to me before I left New York, had already known that the Soviet leaders had asked him to come to Moscow right away, presumably to discuss the conditions for a cease-fire. Since the American response had not yet been decided, he had been unwilling to commit this information to the open telephone line, except in the most cryptic way. In the hours that had elapsed since I had taken off from Kennedy Airport, the Secretary had decided to respond to the urgent invitation from Moscow. He was, in fact, already on his way.

I could not understand the American haste in responding to the Soviet request. I asked Ambassador Dinitz in perplexity, "What was his hurry?" It later emerged that Prime Minister Kosygin, on reaching Cairo, had found a military situation that surpassed his worst expectations. With Israeli forces closing in on Ismailia and Suez, and the Egyptian Third Army virtually encircled, Moscow faced stark options: either to wait passively for a crushing Egyptian defeat or to threaten its own intervention in the hope of scaring the United States. There was no doubt in the Soviet mind that Egypt was facing a military disaster, the full scope of which Cairo had not yet been willing to confront. President Sadat's mind was still obsessed by the memory of October 6. The ecstasy of that military success blinded him to the new perils arising from Israel's westward thrust. The Soviet Union was under no such illusion. It knew that a cease-fire was urgent. It was not realistic to imagine that the United States would refuse to discuss a cease-fire with Moscow, but I was unable to grasp why Secretary Kissinger could not have agreed to go to Moscow on the morrow rather than on the same day. It seemed to me that the twenty-four hours thus gained would not have entailed any risk of Soviet reaction, while they might have helped to improve Israel's negotiating position in a cease-fire discussion.

Dinitz said that in his last talks with Kissinger before the Secretary's departure, he had been told that the Soviet Union was still clinging to its formula for a cease-fire to be conditioned by an Israeli declaration of intent to return to the pre-1967 lines. The American response to this was still negative. It was therefore accurate to state that at the moment of the Secretary's departure for Moscow, no cease-fire proposal was before us. On reaching Lod Airport, I told correspondents that the American-Israeli cooperation in the past twelve days had been intimate and constructive. I added that while we should be alert for the results of talks in Moscow, the fact was that at *that particular moment* what we faced was not a cease-fire but a continuation by Egypt and Syria of savage battles in which we should push our success to the maximal limit. "Our job *at this moment*," I said, "is not to speculate about a cease-fire which has not yet been offered, but rather to put to good use the massive reinforcement which the United States has given us."

It was late on Friday when I reached home. Less than four weeks had elapsed since I had set out, in mid-September, for what had then promised to be a routine meeting of the United Nations General Assembly. Yet the Israel to which I was returning was living in a new epoch. The streets were blacked out, able-bodied men of military age were nowhere to be seen, cafés and movies were empty, and the lists of casualties reaching us at our ministries threw up one name after another with poignant closeness and familiarity. But the national mood was surprisingly calm. The shock of the October war had not yet been fully absorbed. Only when the fighting had ended would the volcanic elements in the public emotion come to the fore. The Prime Minister and her senior colleagues were in continuous session. I was astonished by her tranquillity and resilience. On the other hand, it was probably easier for me than for others who had been in contact with them day by day to observe the sharp difference in the demeanor of our defense leaders, including Dayan and the generals. They were now recuperating from early disasters, but the shock of the first few days was clearly marked in their muted expression.

In the small villa of the Prime Minister's office at Hakirya in Tel Aviv I now joined my colleagues in two converging dramas. One was on the banks of the Suez Canal, where Sharon's and Adan's forces were moving westward. The other was in Moscow, where through most of the Sabbath and the early part of Sunday a strange silence had descended. The line of communication from Secretary Kissinger to the Israeli government went from Moscow to Washington and, via our ambassador, back to us in Tel Aviv. Dinitz was being constantly called to the White House, but for many hours was receiving little but procedural information. It was clear that hard bargaining was going on. After all, the two major powers took their starting points from sharply polarized positions. The Soviet Union, despite the collapse of Egyptian positions, was clinging to its demand for an Israeli declaration of intent to return to the June 4, 1967, lines. The United States had rejected this idea even when Israel's military fortunes were low; it was certainly not going to yield to it when our armies were pushing forward on all fronts. It seemed obvious that a compromise position would be sought in terms of a "cease-fire and standstill."

But the problem was not only how the cease-fire would be described in terms of geography. The question was how its political conditions would be identified. I recalled how in June 1967 I had been able to persuade the U.S. government to call for a cease-fire without any accompanying political conditions such as withdrawal to previous lines. As a result we had then obtained a cease-fire without conditions, and the political discussions in November 1967 took place with Israel established in favorable positions. This time it was inconceivable that a cease-fire would be proclaimed without any political conditions at all. It would, at the very least, have to be described as a first stage toward a permanent peace in accordance with Resolution 242. The question was whether the pressure of their military plight would force the Arabs to make some concessions by also accepting the principle of negotiation. Our expectation was that Kissinger would consult us on all these matters before concluding an American agreement with the Soviet leaders.

On Sunday, October 21, in Tel Aviv, I reported to the Knesset Committee on Foreign Affairs and Defense. I described the American reaction to the war, the events leading to the airlift, the turning of the tide after October 14, and the background for Kissinger's visit to Moscow. I repeated that while it was very likely that the two powers would seek some formula at Moscow, the position as I had left it in Washington and New York could be simply described: "While the conditions for a cease-fire now exist in the field, the conditions attached by Moscow and Washington to a cease-fire resolution are so widely separated that we should be thinking at this moment of how to use every hour to improve our position."

At the moment that I was giving this information, which was entirely accurate at the time, a message came to me from the Prime Minister's office. After long hours of telex silence, the machines were clicking briskly. Lengthy documents from Moscow via Washington were coming over the wire. I curtailed my report to the committee and joined the vigil in the Prime Minister's office. A full Cabinet had been called for two hours later.

The messages that we now received told a vivid story of the Moscow negotiations. Kissinger had arrived in Moscow late on Friday and had wanted to rest in order to pursue the negotiations intensively the next morning. His Soviet hosts, however, did not relent their sense of urgency. Kosygin had been alarmed by the swift turn in the military balance since the Israeli bridgehead became consolidated on October 17. A realistic understanding of Arab dangers set the Soviet leadership to political motion on October 18. Moscow may well have been surprised by the rapidity with which Kissinger had responded to its invitation, but having got him into their ambit, they were not going to let another twelve hours be frittered away. Nevertheless, they felt compelled to defend the Egyptian and Syrian positions during useless negotiations throughout Saturday, when they went on asking for an Israeli return to the June 4, 1967, lines.

Kissinger countered with a proposal for a cease-fire "in place" to be followed by negotiations between Israel and the Arab states for a peace settlement on the basis of Resolution 242. With the Arab position deteriorating on both fronts hour by hour, the Soviets finally yielded. At nine-thirty in the evening of Sunday, October 21, Brezhnev instructed his ambassador, Vladimir Vinogradov, to see President Sadat in Cairo, requesting him to agree to an immediate cease-fire and attaching the draft of the resolution which America and Russia intended to sponsor at the Security Council. There is no doubt that Egyptian agreement had already been obtained by the time Nixon and Kissinger made an identical communication to us in Israel. The American message even stated that the Security Council would be asked to convene at ten o'clock that evening (New York time) and would adopt the resolution around midnight.

When we assembled at ten o'clock for a Cabinet session that was to last through most of the night, our sentiments were mixed. On the one hand, there was real indignation about the procedure that had been followed. Instead of coordinating its political moves with us, the United States had presented us with a draft on a "take it or leave it" basis. Once the Soviet Union and Egypt had given their consent, it was not likely that they would improve the text to meet Israeli apprehensions. The precedent seemed ominous. It seemed to herald future occasions on which the two powers would formulate proposals on matters no less vital to us than the precise time for cessation of hostilities.

On the other hand, when we turned from procedure to substance, we realized that we had a chance of emerging successfully from what had seemed only a few days before to be a grave peril to our security. In military terms, the Yom Kippur War was an Israeli triumph, despite an Israeli refusal to admit this fact. The cessation of hostilities was to take place with Israel far beyond any positions she had ever held before. We had also achieved what we had been seeking for many years —Arab acceptance of the principle of negotiation. Even the Security Council Resolution 242, which called for the establishment of a just and lasting peace, had not explicitly committed the Arab governments to a "negotiating" process. It had instead appointed a mediator whom the Arabs regarded as responsible for ensuring that the resolution was "implemented." Thus the proposal now being made to us kept our military victories intact and added an important political gain.

The main consideration on the other side was the prospect that with a few more days of advance, we could bring about a decisive humiliation of the Egyptian army. Even this chance was questionable. Any fighting that went on far beyond the appointed hour of the cease-fire would incur the opposition and, perhaps, the resistance of the Soviet Union without the compensating support of the United States. Thus Israel would be risking an isolation more drastic than any that she had known before. We could not realistically exclude a prospect of Soviet military intervention. There might at least be a threat credible enough to bring about an alarmed Israeli cease-fire decision as in 1956.

Finally, and above all, there was the price to be paid in Israeli lives. The news of casualties already suffered was streaming into our ears day by day and hour by hour. All that we could elicit from our military advisers was that if they could pursue their westward push, they could achieve the encirclement and starvation of the Third Army. But they could not deny that some hundreds—perhaps a thousand— Israeli dead might be the price of a new advance.

The more our Cabinet looked at these options, the heavier it leaned toward accepting the American-Soviet proposal. The balance of risk was too heavy to be ignored. Some of us even felt that the only solid gain from pursuing the conflict—a decisive humiliation for Egypt —might not necessarily work in our favor. Nothing, after all, could have been more humiliating than the Egyptian defeat in 1967. The result had been not to bring Cairo to the peace table, but to create an emotional inhibition against any encounter or compromise with us. Might the infliction of a further humiliation not give us another decade of Arab obduracy and refusal? If the war ended now, the cease-fire map would still reflect an Israeli military victory. On the other hand, the Arabs would retain some memories of a fleeting success in the first three days. Perhaps the ambivalence of the military result would be more conducive to a negotiated peace than if we were to trample the Egyptians into the dust.

Many arguments flowed into our decision, but the most decisive was probably the prospect of losing a thousand dead who would never return, in order to capture a mass of Egyptian prisoners whom we would have to restore to their homes in short time. It is Israel's strength and weakness that we are always impelled by our history and conscience to give priority to the humane consideration. After all, the Jewish people does not have much blood left to lose.

Within a few days we were to hear this unanimous Cabinet determination described by the opposition in Parliament and the press as "surrender to a diktat." The truth is that the Israeli Cabinet itself saw a balance of advantage in bringing the fighting to a halt where it stood. As I look back over all Israel's wars, I recall that there was never a cease-fire about which it could not be said that "with a few more days" we might have improved our situation. There comes a time, however, when it is wiser to put gains into one's pocket than to gamble on another speculative chance. At stake here was not a gamble, but the lives of our sons and daughters, the relations of our country with its friends in the world, and somewhere in the distance, the remote but glowing prospect of a negotiated peace.

At any rate, no proposal for rejecting the cease-fire came from any minister. Nevertheless, we knew from experience that cease-fires on the ground seldom took effect at the appointed time; I also noticed that contrary to most United Nations cease-fire resolutions, the text presented that night made no provision for any machinery or supervision. This omission itself would probably engender some delay.

The Security Council was merely the theater in which the cease-fire scenario would be enacted. In point of fact, the United Nations had no effective role in the negotiation of the cease-fire, which, like all important security developments, had to be conducted outside its walls. Since it was vital for our action to be coordinated with our agreements with the United States, I took the unusual step of dictating to Ambassador Tekoah the full text of the speech that he was to make. I included the provision that a cease-fire would not be valid for Israel unless it contained an agreement for the release of prisoners and the ending of blockade practices at Bab el Mandeb, the straits where Israeli shipping trying to enter the Red Sea from the Gulf of Aden had been stopped for many days. This news, however, had been kept under censorship, so that most Israelis learned of the existence of the blockade for the first time through the formulation in Tekoah's speech.

The text of the American-Soviet resolution was:

The Security Council

(1) Calls upon the parties to the present fighting to cease all firing and terminate all military activity immediately, no later than twelve hours after the moment of the adoption of this decision in the positions they now occupy.

(2) Calls upon the parties concerned to start immediately after the cease-fire the implementation of Security Council Resolution 242 in all its parts.

(3) Decides that immediately and concurrently with the cease-fire, negotiations will start between the parties concerned under appropriate auspices aimed at establishing a just and durable peace in the Middle East.

(Resolution 338)

The Security Council debate was completed within the deadline fixed by the Americans and Russians in Moscow so that the duration and content of the speeches there had no effect at all.

Resolution 338 was accepted by the Israeli government not only because of pressure by the powers, but on its own sovereign judgment and without much reserve. But the fact that the text and the "scenario" had all been set up without any prior coordination continued to rankle in our hearts. It was important to deter such procedures in the future. Accordingly, Prime Minister Golda Meir was strongly urging Secretary Kissinger to come to Israel before returning to Washington. This was accepted by President Nixon, and Kissinger arrived at Ben Gurion (formerly Lod) Airport in the morning of October 22. Extending his hand to Ambassador Keating and myself, he said apprehensively, "I expect that Golda is mad at me. I'll explain to her exactly why I had to act as I did."

We entered the ambassador's car and drove the half-hour to the Prime Minister's vacation office near Tel Aviv. On the way, the car bearing the American flag was greeted with respect and sympathy from passers-by. Kissinger was being received by the Israeli people as a friend in need. This was his first visit to us since the American airlift had begun to reach Israel, less than ten days before. The supply aircraft were still coming in. Whatever differences might later emerge, this was a moment of special harmony between Israel and the United States. Kissinger interrupted the narration of his Moscow experiences by saying to me with a mischievous smile, "Judging by the crowd, Israelis are not mad with me, after all."

In a more serious vein he explained his predicament. Throughout Saturday the Soviets had insisted on making the cease-fire conditional on an Israeli withdrawal to the pre-1967 lines. Kissinger had resisted this firmly. Then, without warning, the Soviet Union had withdrawn its extremist proposals and announced its acceptance of the American position on a cease-fire "in place." These sudden transitions are characteristic of totalitarian diplomacy.

Kissinger had gone on to the offensive, stating that it would not be enough merely to mention Resolution 242. It was vital to commit the Arab states and Israel to negotiate a settlement on the basis of the Resolution. The Secretary had won this point. Knowing what the Israel position had always been, he hoped the Israelis would regard the result of his talks as a substantial gain. The road would now be open for negotiations in conditions far better than any foreseen a few days before. What, after all, was the alternative? Nothing but the maintenance of the conflict with losses day by day, across Egyptian territory which, in any case, would one day be returned. Kissinger hoped that Israel would regard the substantive result as more important than any resentment about procedure. He said that there had been difficulty in communicating to Israel from Moscow, where he had been at the mercy of Soviet electronics. For some crucial hours, the American telex system had been inoperative.

Kissinger spent a long hour—which I did not envy him—explaining all this to the Prime Minister. After two hours he and Mrs. Meir emerged for a working lunch attended by Dayan, Allon, myself and our military commanders. After the meal, which was not a notable gastronomic success, we went downstairs for a prolonged military briefing. There was a moving moment when the Chief of Staff, "Dado" Elazar, and the Air Force commander, General Bennie Peled, expressed laconic but sincere gratitude to the United States for the supply of weapons at difficult hours. As I accompanied Kissinger back to the airport he spoke frankly of his impressions and hopes. His impression was that the Israeli commanders were in good spirit, but were very strained by the intensity of their ordeals. His hope was that the cease-fire, agreed upon in principle the night before, could come into effect within a day or two.

He then spoke of the prospect beyond the cease-fire. He hoped that I would come to Washington sometime in November so that a negotiating process could be discussed. He then told me for the first time of plans for a Geneva Conference, of which he had apprized Mrs. Meir in their conversation earlier that day. The idea was that Israel and the Arab states would confer under the chairmanship of the United States and the Soviet Union. It was vital for the Middle Eastern problem to be discussed in a framework more compact than the General Assembly and the Security Council. Kissinger felt that the United States would have a determining role at a conference of this kind. He knew that Israel was preparing for an early election. But he felt it vital that the Geneva Conference should convene before the end of the year. Otherwise, he feared that Egypt, under pressure from more radical Arab governments, would withdraw its consent. The opportunity of committing the Arabs to the negotiating principle might then be wasted. He thought it best for the conference to have an opening session and to adjourn without going into substantive bargaining before the Israeli elections.

When I got back from the airport to Tel Aviv, the messages reaching me from the fronts indicated that hostilities, far from ceasing, were in fact growing more intense. I knew from experience since 1948 that this was the usual result of a cease-fire injunction. Each of the parties would hastily try to improve its positions on the ground before the cease-fire took effect. This tradition was now working in Israel's favor. Our forces were completing the encirclement of the Egyptian Third Army. We were also pushing farther eastward in Syria. The Israeli armies were now completely liberated from the confusion and bewilderment of Yom Kippur; they were acting everywhere with their old mastery and resilience. Some days before, General Bar-Lev, whose steady hand had helped to turn the tide, had sent a message to Jerusalem reporting that both the Israeli and Egyptian armies were at last behaving "in accordance with their 1967 reputations."

Ministers were closeted with the Prime Minister for most of October 23 and 24. The messages reaching us were ambivalent. Dayan, Bar-Lev and Elazar were now reporting encouraging developments from the southern front almost every hour. On the other hand, our very success was precipitating a delicate international situation. The Soviet leaders were exercising strong pressure on the United States. The Americans, after all, had jointly sponsored the cease-fire resolution. The Soviet Union was hinting that Washington, "in collusion" with Israel, was delaying the implementation of the Moscow agreement so that Israel could win a decisive victory after the cease-fire. The Soviet Union would do everything within its power to prevent such an outcome. It was now receiving desperate pleas from Egypt. Sadat and his generals were fully aware of their plight. Indeed, we later learned that one of them had died of a heart attack at his headquarters on hearing the full story of the Egyptian rout. Frenzied messages were going from Cairo to Damascus, explaining why a cease-fire was urgent and why there might even have to be a political price for its attainment. How things looked on the Egyptian side toward the end of the war has since been vividly described in Mohammed Hassanein Heykal's book *The Road to Ramadan:*

> *By the evening of October 19, Israel had established a formidable bridge-head on the west side of the Canal, which included four tank brigades, one mechanised brigade and a parachute brigade. It was probably the day before this on Thursday, October 18, that President Sadat saw the extent of Israel's thrusts across the Canal, because that day Kosygin was able to produce aerial photographs of the battle area which had been flown to him. Kosygin left next day convinced that Egypt was ready for a peace conference.*

Heykal goes on to describe a meeting between President Sadat and his leading generals late on October 19:

> *At this vital meeting, a difference of opinion showed itself. [Chief of Staff] General Shazli, who had seen the situation on the spot, realised its extreme gravity. He felt that some of the reinforcements that had been sent to the east bank should be withdrawn. He also advocated withdrawing some tanks and anti-tank missiles from the east. Unless these measures were taken, he feared that the Third Army might be encircled and the Second Army threatened.*

After the war a report was published indicating that Egypt's deteriorating military situation had demoralized General Saadeddin Shazli to the point of a nervous collapse. It is clear that within the week of October 13–20, Egypt had passed from a contemptuous rejection of a cease-fire to a desperate need for an end to hostilities. But the war now had its own momentum. It continued to rage on all fronts with armies interlocked with each other and no concrete arrangements for a cease-fire. And with every passing hour, the plight of the Third Army became graver.

As the Israeli thrust developed, the United States became increasingly alert to the possible Soviet reaction. I do not believe that Nixon and Kissinger ever regretted Israel's military recovery. They must have known that the more the Arab states got tired of the war, the greater was the chance of winning a cease-fire and an eventual negotiation. On the other hand, the American relationship with the Soviet Union was now at issue. It was not only the question of saving the détente; there was always the haunting fear that the Soviet Union might not sit back passively while Egypt suffered further defeats. So the messages to us from Washington now became more irascible and insistent. It was known that President Nixon had given President Sadat an assurance that the Third Army would not be reduced or starved out after the cease-fire; it was unlikely that Washington would allow Israel to frustrate this pledge. We also learned that the United States attached real credibility to rumors that the Soviet Union was preparing aircraft and helicopters to bring supplies to the Egyptian Third Army.

Thus, by the evening of October 24, the Middle East came to the brink of its most acute crisis. Moscow decided to embark on global intimidation. Brezhnev sent a message to the United States suggesting that the two major powers use their forces in the Middle East to "keep Israel in order." But the Soviet letter went on to say that if for any reason the United States was unwilling to play this role, Russia would have to consider doing it herself.

The letter passed through the White House and the State Department like an electric shock. It was believed that the Soviet Union would not hesitate to land supplies by helicopter to relieve the Third Army. The Soviet Union would then be physically involved in the war against Israel, and it would become necessary for the United States to think long and hard about its own commitment to regional stability and to Israel's security. In a word, a local conflict would be globalized. This was the American nightmare. Nevertheless, after many hours of tormented consultation in the White House, it was decided to stand up to Soviet threats.

No Israeli minister who took part in the all-night meeting on October 25 will ever forget the tension that gripped us. Would the United States defy Soviet threats at dire risk or would it prefer to join the Soviet Union in direct pressure on Israel? When we knew that the United States had decided on a deterrent alert, we were profoundly heartened and impressed. On the other hand, our need to take American wishes into account was now more acute. American-Israeli relations were clearly in the balance. Kissinger had given us plainly to understand that while the United States had shown readiness to go to the brink, "it was not prepared to go over it."

The Israeli government now had to choose. Should we attempt the strangulation of the Third Army at the risk of Soviet intervention or should we ensure American support and the saving of Israeli lives by putting the cease-fire into effect? If our major national goal was the subjugation of the Third Army, we would have to risk conflict with the Soviet Union without compensative American support. Once the issue was clearly seen in this light, our options were greatly narrowed. It was hard to believe that to capture 20,000 Egyptian soldiers (whom we would have to return soon after in a prisoner-exchange agreement) was an aim of such importance as to justify military confrontation with the Soviet Union with no parallel protection from the United States.

The key was in the American hands. Before the October 22 cease-fire, Kissinger had acted swiftly to ensure Israeli military recuperation. It is just as certain that by October 25 he did not desire a complete rout of the Egyptian armies. American policy was that Israel should be successful without being overwhelmingly predominant. Washington may have had two ideas in mind. On the one hand, it was convinced that if the Egyptian defeat was total, there would be no psychological context favorable to negotiation. But I felt that Kissinger's more decisive calculation concerned the Soviet Union. By initiating the cease-fire jointly with the USSR, Washington had virtually made a kind of pact with Moscow. If the cease-fire collapsed as a result of American consent to further Israeli advances, there would be a danger of Soviet military action and a destruction of whatever remained of the détente. The sources available to us confirmed the American belief that Soviet units had been put on the alert at various points in Eastern Europe. The prospect of Soviet intervention was not a mere figment.

On hearing that our forces were approaching the suburbs of Suez, Kissinger began to send us insistent messages. He was frank enough to state clearly that the United States could not allow the Third Army to be starved out by military action taken several days after the cease-fire. If this was Israel's policy, the United States would have to "dissociate itself" from it.

By Wednesday morning, October 24, the United States seemed to estimate that four divisions of Soviet airborne troops were on the alert. This meant that 50,000 soldiers were ready to move, and Soviet naval concentrations in the Mediterranean were increasing as well. By early afternoon Egypt was openly calling for a joint Soviet-American peacekeeping force in the Middle East. Soviet representatives at the United Nations were supporting the idea of intervention "by both Powers, and if this were not possible, by the Soviet Union alone."

Brezhnev's warning of unilateral action had impelled the United States to move on two fronts. Every pressure would be put on Israel to stabilize the cease-fire and to open a supply line to the Third Army; at the same time the threat of Soviet intervention would be met by a tough American posture. This was the logic behind the instructions on October 24 alerting American forces, ground, sea and air, including units with nuclear weapons. This decision was not published, but it was clearly intended that the troop movements should become known in Moscow. In view of previous complaints by NATO allies of American failure to consult them, Kissinger now informed the British government separately, and the other NATO countries collectively, of what was afoot. Thus, by the morning of October 25, knowledge of the American alert had spread throughout most of the world.

Whatever the effects were on the Soviet Union, it is certain that the Americans had frightened themselves. Drastic fluctuations took place in the stock market. There were also uneasy stirrings on the domestic political scene. Many American newspapermen and politicans suspected that the alert was not a sincere response to an international challenge, but an effort to divert attention from the Watergate scandals and to create an impression of presidential indispensability. Kissinger replied indignantly to this charge.

In Israel we had no doubt about the reality of the Soviet danger. There was no reason to question the American warning that if the Soviet Union dropped supplies to the Egyptian Third Army, the United States could not oppose its action. We unanimously decided to open a controlled supply line through United Nations checkpoints, enabling the Third Army to receive humanitarian aid while ensuring that no weapons would pass through.

As a result of this decision the Yom Kippur War virtually came to an end on October 25. It had lasted for eighteen days, and our victorious military posture at the end could not have been predicted in its terrible first hours. But we were still worried about the future development of relations with the United States. It was therefore decided to respond to the suggestion that Mrs. Meir visit Washington on October 31. At the same time, the Egyptian Foreign Minister had invited himself to the United States.

Our Prime Minister's contacts with President Nixon were reassuring. A deep personal harmony had grown up between them. But some of the difficulties that had arisen in the American-Israeli dialogue were too grave to be solved by semantic formulas. Egypt was demanding an Israeli return to what it called the "October 22 lines." For Israel, it was hard enough to order the end of fighting on October 24. To bring about a unilateral withdrawal without any mutual concession was beyond our domestic possibility or our international duty.

In fact, the positions of the armies in the field were so acrobatically intertwined that nothing but direct contact between commanders could stabilize the front. A further point at issue was the prisoners of war. The record of Arab governments, and especially of Syria, in the treatment of prisoners had caused horrified reactions in Israel at many stages of the conflict. There was no chance that an Israeli government would sign an agreement beyond the cease-fire unless it received assurances on this point.

While Mrs. Meir was in Washington in November, the Egyptian Foreign Minister, Dr. Ismail Fahmy, arrived there, apparently by coincidence. The Deputy Foreign Minister of Syria, Mohammed Ismail, also reached the United States. He was ostensibly bound for United Nations headquarters; his real intention was to open communications with the United States which had been cut off since 1967. Thus, during three tense days in Washington, the United States was in the center of a diplomatic circle with lines radiating out to Israel, Egypt and Syria at high levels of responsibility. There could be no better illustration of the predominance which the United States had inherited as a result of the war.

Mrs. Meir's task was difficult. She had to resist the possibility that the United States would support Egyptian proposals involving unilateral withdrawal of Israeli troops under the pretext of "returning" to the October 22 lines. Instead of such a unilateral Israeli withdrawal, Mrs. Meir proposed a six-point program which would satisfy Israeli requests for an Egyptian-Israeli meeting and for an immediate implementation of the prisoner exchange. Kissinger and Mrs. Meir parted in an atmosphere of some coolness, with the American Secretary of State skeptical about the prospect of these points ever being accepted in Cairo.

The lines of diplomatic movement were now becoming more complex. While Mrs. Meir was in Washington I received an urgent request from the talented Rumanian ambassador in Israel, Kovaci, to call on me at my home in Herzliya. He carried a message from President Nicolae Ceaucescu urgently requesting me to make an official visit to Bucharest. The ambassador pointed out that what was at stake was not only the development of Rumanian-Israeli bilateral relations but also the need for Israel to hear the Rumanian President's account of dangers looming on the Middle Eastern horizon. Israel had learned to set a high value on the fidelity of Rumania to the maintenance of her ties with Israel. Despite the awkwardness of leaving the Cabinet table in Israel, at which emergencies were arising every half-hour, I decided, with Mrs. Meir's cabled approval from Washington, to go to Bucharest.

It turned out to be a moving encounter. Courtesies were exchanged at lavish banquets given first by my opposite number, Macovescu, and then by myself. My wife and I were also the objects of warm Rumanian hospitality at industrial enterprises. We spent what should have been a tranquil thirty-six hours in the neighboring mountain area. But my own peace of mind was disturbed by the consciousness that events of much greater centrality would soon unfold between Jerusalem, Cairo, and Washington. Yet in a conversation of four hours with President Ceaucescu, I was able to gain many new insights. He was aware that the proximity of the Egyptian and Israeli armies on the ground made a stable cease-fire very improbable. He supported the Egyptian proposal for an Israeli withdrawal from the area west of the Canal. On Israel's behalf, I was able to accept the principle of disengagement— but only if it were carried out with some reciprocity.

It was clear to me that President Ceaucescu's anxieties extended beyond the Middle East. He may have felt that if fighting broke out again, American and Soviet involvement might escalate the conflict. He also saw a prospect that the forthcoming Arab-Israeli negotiation would not be a sovereign encounter between independent Middle Eastern states, but a "diktat" arising out of the hegemony of Great Powers.

Before leaving Bucharest, I had an experience that I shall never lose from memory. I went to the Great Synagogue, where the redoubtable Chief Rabbi Dr. Rosen presided over the remnant of Rumanian Jewry. Although no official notice had been given of my arrival, the streets to the synagogue were lined with enthusiastic Rumanian Jews, cheering in passionate solidarity with Israel. The synagogue itself was almost choked by an agonizing Jewish nostalgia. Opening the Ark with great ceremonial dignity, Rabbi Rosen courageously called for prayer in memory of Israelis who had fallen in the battle for the nation's survival. I then addressed the throng in Hebrew while Rabbi Rosen translated each group of sentences into Rumanian with great oratorical flourish.

We left Bucharest toward evening and landed in Israel early one November morning. On reaching the airport, we were told that Secretary Kissinger, during his visists to Saudi Arabia, Egypt and other Arab countries, had asked his deputy, Joseph Sisco, to detach himself from the party in order to bring a message to the government of Israel. Hastening from Ben Gurion Airport to Mrs. Meir's offices in Tel Aviv, I found the Prime Minister with other colleagues and the Chief of Staff in a mood of unexpected relief. Mrs. Meir's proposal for the first stage of disengagement, about which Secretary Kissinger had been so skeptical, had in fact been accepted by the Egyptian government. As Kissinger magnanimously admitted, Israel had shown a clearer perception of Egyptian attitudes than the United States. The way was now open for meetings to take place at high military level in a tent at Kilometer 101 on the Suez–Cairo road in Sinai, sixty-three miles from Cairo, for stabilizing the cease-fire and discussing the next stage of disengagement.

The text of the six-point agreement for disengagement appears in retrospect to be technical and even subsidiary, but it had great importance at the time. It reversed the cycle of conflict and set up a process of negotiation. The very spectacle of Major General Aharon Yariv for Israel and Lieutenant General Mohamed Abdel Ghany el-Gamasy for Egypt, in hard but courteous bargaining, seemed to augur a more rational order of relations in the Middle East.

Once the Kilometer 101 talks had been initiated, I set out for the United States, where I had been asked to help mobilize the support and solidarity of American Jews. I was accompanied this time by Meir Ronen, a young member of my bureau. It had been stipulated that during this visit I would resume discussions with Secretary Kissinger.

In November 1973 I found the American Jewish community in ferment. Its emotions had been torn to shreds by the fluctuations of the previous three weeks. It had followed the struggle of the Israeli army through danger into security. It now saw the toll that the war had taken, primarily of young lives, but also of our morale and of our economic resources. Years of patient construction had been swept away by the crushing costs of the war. The Israeli people would also have to face a new period in its history, scarred and tormented by a great volume of bereavement. It was confused by the expected collapse of the military euphoria that had lasted since 1967.

I had never faced a more electrically charged Jewish assembly than that which I found assembled in New Orleans under the auspices of the Council of Jewish Welfare Funds. Having flown in from Jerusalem straight to the meeting, I was more weary than I could ever remember. I began by pointing out that whatever it said on the clock in the United States, for me it was 5 A.M. and "none of the great orations in history have ever been delivered at five o'clock in the morning." But as I proceeded, I could feel a great swell of Jewish anxiety. At the end of my address I asked:

> *I have come here to tell you that our burdens are heavy. . . .*
> *We cannot bear them alone.* Why should we bear them alone?
> *After all, whatever we have created and built and defended in*
> *Israel these twenty-six years we have defended, created and built,*
> you and we together, *in the service of a common responsibility*
> *and a common pride. So, the people of Israel looks out across the*
> *debris of the war, across the graves of its sons, and asks itself*
> *whether American Jewry will stand with us in helping us bear*
> *these burdens. That is the question that Israel asks of you. The*
> *answer is in your hands.*

At that point the assembly of over three thousand rose in solidarity and emotion, with a tearful applause beyond which I had neither the ability nor need for further speech.

After a few more addresses in the southern and central parts of the United States, I reached Washington on November 14. I learned from Ambassador Dinitz that things were not going well. Talks at Kilometer 101 had gone on daily but without result. There was the danger that they might break down and that this would mean a renewal of war. Kissinger, whom I met the next morning, told me that in his view the decisions to be made at Kilometer 101 required political authority, not merely military understanding. This applied specially to the Israeli proposal under which we would withdraw from positions west of Suez in return for a liquidation of the Egyptian bridgehead east of the Canal. The United States did not believe that Sadat would ever agree to remove Egyptian troops from their cherished gains in western Sinai, but some compromise by way of reduction of forces on both sides might be feasible, and a prisoner exchange could be envisaged. Beyond this, however, it was useless for General Yariv to ask General Gamasi to give answers. Things were not run in Egypt at that level. Kissinger therefore advocated that the issues not resolved at Kilometer 101 be transferred to the opening session of the Geneva Conference.

He urged me to influence our Cabinet in two directions. First, he wanted us to agree that a session of the Geneva Conference be held in advance of the Israeli elections. If this was not done, there would be a diplomatic vacuum in which the cease-fire would collapse. The second suggestion was to allow the Geneva Conference to take up the proposals that were being exchanged at military levels at Kilometer 101.

Flying straight from Washington to Jerusalem on November 23, I made for the Prime Minister's Jerusalem residence, which I reached in the late evening. Mrs. Meir was remarkably calm as she went about the business of making coffee for the two of us. She decided that we should cooperate with the United States in both the directions that Kissinger had suggested to me. Looking back over the turbulent events since October 6, the Prime Minister had at that stage grown to trust Secretary Kissinger's good will. He had brought the airlift into being, had led American resistance to Soviet intimidation, and had enabled us to obtain a prisoner exchange at an expectedly early stage in the postwar negotiations.

The Israeli Cabinet accepted my proposal for Israeli participation in the Geneva Conference. Kissinger had asked that this representation be at foreign-minister level, and that the Secretary-General of the United Nations be enabled to take part. I had seen Secretary-General Kurt Waldheim before leaving America. While there were fears in Israel that the United Nations, with its Arab majority, might "take over" the conference, Waldheim was prepared realistically to confine himself to an unobtrusive role at the convening stage. I felt that his presence might even be helpful. It would enable us to resist the inundation of the conference by states from the Third World and Europe.

The Cabinet accepted the draft letter of invitation which would go from Secretary-General Waldheim to Israel and the Arab states, inviting them to attend a peace conference to be convened by the UN Secretary-General on the basis of the Security Council's Resolution 338. Membership in the conference would be confined to the belligerent states. The participation of any other state or group, such as a Palestinian organization, would have to be agreed upon between the United States and Israel. The conference would be held on December 18.

After our affirmative response, followed by corresponding replies from Cairo and Amman, Secretary Kissinger set out for the Middle East on December 13. One of his tasks was to ensure that Syria accept a prisoner exchange as a condition of its participation in the Geneva Conference. We were in deep agony at the news reaching us about the ill-treatment of Israeli prisoners in Damascus. Moreover, the Syrian regime had violated the Geneva Convention by not even giving us a list of the prisoners in its hands. We felt it urgent that Secretary Kissinger should come back into the area a few days before the conference was convened. I met him at Lod Airport on December 16, and he briskly told me of his experience in Riyadh, Cairo and Amman, which he had visited in the previous three days. We were now—at last—in a negotiating rhythm.

The Geneva Conference
Disengagement and
Cabinet Changes
1974

"IF WE ACCEPT THE CEASE-FIRE, IT IS BECAUSE OUR ULTIMATE TARGET IS peace, not the destruction of Egypt. The cease-fire will be worthwhile if there is a proper move towards negotiations." These words in the *Jerusalem Post* of October 23 summarized the view of Israelis who supported our cease-fire decision. There was a contrary opinion, more vehemently formulated. "The Moscow agreements were made behind our backs and the haste with which they were put together was dictated by a desire to save the Arabs from defeat. It would be advisable that both the Government and the Israeli Defense Forces should not use a stop-watch in observing the cease-fire but rather redouble their efforts on the field of battle." Here the evening newspaper, *Yediot Aharonot,* was reflecting the militant view.

On the whole, the idea of a peace conference between Israel and the Arab states had a strong grip on the national imagination. No such encounter at a high political level had even taken place. We could reflect that the sacrifices of the Yom Kippur War might not be as politically sterile as many Israelis believed. After all, never before October 1973 had Arab governments agreed to negotiate with Israel for the establishment of a "permanent peace."

Yet during five days in the Middle East, in mid-December 1973, Kissinger had many obstacles to overcome. The Arab states wished the conference to be held under the aegis of the United Nations, in which they held a permanent majority. They also wanted an invitation to be extended to the Palestine Liberation Organization. And Syria showed no intention of carrying out the Geneva Convention on the treatment of Israeli prisoners of war. On our side, we could not have an Israeli Foreign Minister sitting with a Syrian colleague while our prisoners were outside the protection of the Red Cross and undergoing indescribable torture.

It was in order to explore the Syrian position on prisoner exchange and disengagement that Secretary Kissinger made his first contact with President Hafez al-Assad. The significance of the encounter lay in the fact that it could take place at all. No Arab country had been more intense in its struggle against Israel, or in its vendetta against the United States, than Syria under the Baathist regime. The conflict between the Arab states and Israel was evidently giving American diplomacy a new field of strength. By the time he left the area, Kissinger had maintained his record of success. He had persuaded the Arab states to renounce the appearance of a Palestinian delegation at the opening session at Geneva. He had secured their agreement to a text which made the participation of additional representatives at the conference dependent on the consent of all the "founder members." And he had established the principle of American-Soviet chairmanship, with the Secretary-General of the United Nations participating at the convening stage to represent the interests of other member states. On our part, we had won American understanding of our refusal to confer with Syria until it began to carry out the Geneva Prisoner-of-War Convention.

In later months, the Geneva idea was to fall into eclipse. It is therefore important to recall the seriousness with which it was taken at the time. The Israeli Labor Party, in the throes of a national election, had made Geneva the primary plank in its platform. We told the electorate at the end of 1973 that a Likud majority, dedicated to rejection of any territorial compromise, would make Israel's role in the peace conference virtually impossible. It was primarily on this basis that we sought a mandate from the voters.

We agreed with Kissinger that the first session of the conference would deal with a general exposition of policies, and with the establishment of machinery for disengagement negotiations. But my belief was that after our elections, the conference would really get down to substantive work on a peace settlement. Accordingly, in the weeks between November 21, when I first heard Kissinger explain the conference idea, and December 21, when I set out for Geneva, I had worked to establish files and briefings for a full peace conference. Interdepartmental committees had been established to study the problems of a peace treaty—its juridical provisions, its political and economic implications, and some of its territorial aspects. I took to Geneva the draft of a peace treaty that we would be prepared to sign with Egypt, Jordan and Syria. The salient point was that peace consisted of more than the absence of war. It was not merely a list of abstentions from firing, terrorism, hostile propaganda, boycott and blockade. It also entailed affirmative acts of cooperation. Every peace agreement signed in our generation has something to say about diplomatic, economic, commercial, cultural and human relations. Our aim was not merely to add a new document to the archives but to establish a new order of regional relations, with free movement across open frontiers.

It was evident that for the Arabs to pass from decades of hatred to the kind of peace that I had spelled out in my draft treaty would involve them in a radical transformation of their attitudes and policies. I thought that we should be responsive if they replied that it was beyond their emotional capacity to make the journey in a single leap. We should then be prepared to work out stages of progress toward the goal.

In preparing our papers for the peace conference, I sought the cooperation of Israeli experts in Oriental, political and juridical studies from our institutes of research and higher learning. Since the idea of an Arab-Israeli peace conference had captured the interest of the world's information media, we knew that some seven hundred representatives of newspapers, agencies and television and radio stations would be assembled in Geneva. It would be beyond the capacity of our small delegation to make contact with all of them. Accordingly, I asked a group of Israeli professors to be available in Geneva.

In view of our internal domestic situation, I decided to submit the main points of my speech for the scrutiny of my colleagues. I thought it vital that whatever public reaction ensued from my Geneva address should engage the responsibility of all our coalition partners, including the National Religious Party.

As I prepared my text on the night before my departure, I knew that it was unlikely that any of the foreign ministers of the Soviet Union, the United States, Israel, Jordan and Egypt would change their policies because of the others' speeches. But I also felt that beyond the Palais des Nations, there was a great world of opinion imbued with a basic friendship for Israel and yet anxious to see the quest for peace pursued with greater vigor. I also knew that this was going to be an important personal test for me. It was an intellectual challenge no less sharp than the one that had faced me on June 19, 1967, when Kosygin had opened the dramatic session of the General Assembly after the Six-Day War. Lest I should be tempted to think about myself with excessive solemnity, destiny struck me with a fierce tooth infection.

A Jerusalem dentist was so overpowered by the thought that the first Israeli address to a peace conference "for two thousand years" lay in his power that his hands shook on the drill, with no increase of relief for me.

Geneva was full of its old pomp and importance when I landed there toward noon on December 20. Anyone prone to nostalgia would have thought that Eden, Briand, Litvinov, Beneš and Stresemann were about to arrive. My delegation included Ephraim Evron, one of the most astute and experienced diplomats in Israel's service; Dr. Meir Rosen, a Sorbonne graduate whom I had appointed as legal adviser a few months before; Zalman Divon, who presided over our Middle Eastern Department and also spoke fluent Russian; Mordecai Kidron, a skilled veteran of our UN struggles; Ze'ev Shek, head of my bureau, whose easy Viennese charm was clouded by sharp recollection of his experiences as an inmate of Teresienstadt concentration camp; and my political secretary, Eytan Bentzur, my loyal and capable companion throughout all my service in the Foreign Ministry. Ahead of me I had sent the head of our Information Department, Aluf Hareven, a man of original mind, under whose guidance Israel's information services had greatly expanded in budget, staff and variety of techniques. I found him at work amid a throng of newspaper correspondents and television crews converging on our headquarters at a Geneva hotel. There was a sense of occasion in the air. Nobody believed that a conference could by itself overcome the deep rancors that had scarred Arab-Israel relations for so long. But the innovation was unmistakable.

After a tooth extraction by a calm Swiss dentist the previous night, I began the morning of December 21 with breakfast with Secretary Kissinger and his familiar retinue. I told him what our objectives at Geneva were. I wanted to make a frank statement of our international policies in a mood and style likely to conciliate world opinion. Beyond this, I would record Israel's conviction that the essence of the conflict now lay in the question of peace, not of territories. There was an official and overt Israeli consensus for territorial concession. But was there a corresponding Arab consensus for establishing peace with Israel? There was yet no evidence of this. A third Israeli aim at the conference was to develop possibilities of encounter, if possible with Arab delegates but certainly with the Soviet Union, from which we had been cut off since 1967. Fourthly, in order to ensure the continuity of the conference, after the opening session, we wanted to establish a link to the future by setting up committees for disengagement negotiations, first with Egypt and then with Syria. Kissinger told me that none of these aims was at variance with American policies. His chief aim was to get the rhetorical stage over as soon as possible and bring about a concrete discussion on disengagement.

Making my way to the Palais des Nations, I called on Secretary-General Waldheim to check that all was in order for the conference procedure. Here a snag developed. The Egyptian Foreign Minister, Dr. Ismail Fahmy, was bristling with sensitivity. There was discomfort in militant circles in Cairo about the fact that President Sadat had agreed to take part in what was specifically called a "peace conference." Syria had decided to be absent from the conference. This left Egypt alone with Jordan, whose company did nothing to elevate Egypt's position in the "progressive" world. Furthermore, a picture taken recently of General Gamasi and General Yariv shaking hands at Kilometer 101 had caused discomfort to the Egyptian general and to his superiors. Fahmy was petrified by the thought that he himself might be caught in such a compromising posture with me. He insisted on having an empty table demonstratively placed between those of the Egyptian and Israeli delegates!

I told Waldheim that although I was not very interested in wrangles about prestige, I felt that a political principle was here at stake. Could anything be more ridiculous than to open a "peace conference" with a visual message that the two countries which were supposed to make peace with each other could not even sit normally around a table? I told Waldheim that I would refuse to accept a seating arrangement with a hint of Israeli ostracism, as if we were afflicted with leprosy. For one thing, the quarantine table would get all the media coverage and the conference would be a public failure before it began.

There were agitated consultations to and fro while we waited in the ornate anteroom. Kissinger then entered with a compromise. Secretary-General Waldheim would sit in the middle with myself on his left and Egypt on his right. My left-hand neighbor would be Gromyko, while Kissinger would be on the right of Fahmy. Beyond the Soviet delegation would come the empty Syrian chair and finally the Jordanian delegation, headed by Prime Minister Zaid al-Rifai. There would thus be no atmosphere of ostracism.

The half-hour of seeming triviality had, in my opinion, not been wasted. We had established that no decisions, whether procedural or substantive, could be taken at the Geneva Conference without the unanimous consent of the participants.

The speeches of Waldheim, Kissinger and Gromyko were all predictable, but they had some interesting undertones. I have always felt that negotiations do not merely photograph existing positions; they often lead to their modification. And indeed, at the opening of the

Geneva Conference all the participants tried to present themselves in the most moderate light. Kissinger expressed a strong preference for moving quickly into a practical stage of negotiation. He urged the parties to forget their past rancors. "As the Arab proverb says: *'llli fat mat'*—'That which is past is dead.' The United States calls the people of the Middle East to think of future cooperation rather than of past conflict."

It was astonishing for me to hear an eminent historian describe the past as dead. In the Middle East, alas, it is often more passionately alive than the present or the future. But this was a minor discomfort, soon to be forgotten when Gromyko took the floor. From him we heard familiar accusations, charging Israel with an endemic love of territories for their own sake. On the other hand, I detected a new tone. The Soviet Union was criticizing Israel's policy—not its existence. Gromyko came out strongly for a restoration of the pre-1967 lines, which he described as Israel's "legitimate boundaries." While this made no provision for any territorial adjustment, it at least marked an advance on previous Soviet positions. It refuted maps published in Soviet reference works showing Israel within the narrower boundaries of the abortive 1947 partition scheme. The Soviet Union was catching up with reality, even if it was still one step behind. I also noticed that Gromyko made a sharp reference to the need for respecting the independence and integrity of all states in the region, including Israel. He was thus putting some distance between the Soviet doctrine and that espoused by the Palestine Liberation Organization and similar movements whose programs were based on the idea that Israel's very statehood was at issue.

I had intended to postpone my speech until the next day. I thought that it might thus get more cover in the press. But when I heard the speeches of Egypt and Jordan, I changed my mind. Both Fahmy and Rifai had spoken as though they had come not to a peace conference, but to an all-out wrestling match. They had given the world a bitter catalogue of Arab grievances. I could not allow the media the next day to be taken up exclusively with vehement attacks on Israel by Jordan, Egypt and the Soviet Union, mitigated only to some extent by a balanced address from Kissinger. I asked Waldheim for an opportunity to address the conference in the afternoon.

I later learned that this decision had deep effects at home. A quaint electoral regulation in Israel decrees that once the lists of Knesset candidates are published, none of them shall ever appear on the television screen until after election day. The effect of this bizarre enactment is that even when the Prime Minister is received by foreign statesmen abroad, or the Foreign Minister addresses an international forum, he may not be shown on our national television, although he can be heard on radio. The implication that the physical graces of senior ministers have a more seductive effect on the voters than their words or voices seemed to me unduly flattering. If the rules had been strictly observed on this occasion, the Israeli public would have been able to learn what the Egyptian, Soviet and Jordanian foreign ministers thought about them, but would have no chance of seeing their own representative presenting their cause. At it was, a gleam of rationality suddenly lit up our domestic political scene, and all Israeli television sets were tuned in to hear my speech.

When I entered into the hall shortly before three in the afternoon, I found Gromyko sitting at his desk. I decided to greet him. After all, I was a member of a conference of which he was one of the chairmen. Scores of cameras were focused upon us. I knew that I ran the risk of a spectacular rebuff that would resound in the world, and especially in Israel. Gromyko rose, shook my hand long and cordially and said that he would be glad to see me for a discussion in the evening at the Soviet delegation headquarters. This was not a complete surprise. On my arrival in Geneva I had asked Secretary Kissinger to find out whether Gromyko would respond to an approach from me. When the response was favorable, I had asked Ze'ev Shek to suggest to the Soviet delegation that a meeting take place. I was now receiving the answer.

I began my address by stating that "millions of people across the world are hoping that we shall somehow succeed to break the cycle of violence, to give a new purpose and direction to Middle Eastern history and to bring a halt to the spreading contagion of force." I pledged that Israel for her part was resolved to seize the chance. "We cannot ignore experience, but nor are we committed to its endless reiteration. Israel comes to Geneva in the conviction that there is room for innovation, initiative and choice."

Before stating our political objectives, I replied to what Arab delegates had said about Israel's basic "illegitimacy":

> It will be necessary for political and intellectual leaders in the Arab world to reject the fallacy that Israel is alien to the Middle East. . . . Israel is no more nor less than the Jewish people's resolve to be itself, to live, renewed, within its own frame of values, and to contribute its particular shape of mind to the universal human legacy. That is what Israel is all about, and all this is much too deep and old and strong to be swept away.

I pledged Israel's support of the Security Council Resolution 338 and to continued observance of the cease-fire on the basis of reciprocity. I then went on to propose a peace treaty defining the terms of coexistence between Middle Eastern states:

> Peace is not a mere cease-fire or armistice. Its meaning is not exhausted by the absence of war. It commits us to positive obligations which neighboring states owe to each other. The ultimate guarantee of a peace agreement lies in the creation of common regional interests in such degree of intensity, in such multiplicity of interaction, in such entanglement of reciprocal advantage, in such mutual human accessibility as to put the possibility of future wars beyond any rational contingency.

I spoke of the specific provisions that the peace treaty should contain, including the permanent elimination of all forms of hostility, boycott and blockade. On the crucial matter of boundaries, I said:

> We are ready for a territorial compromise which would serve the legitimate interests of all signatory states. In this matter, as in others, there must be a basic readiness on all sides to make such concessions as do not threaten vital security interests. Security arrangements and demilitarized areas can supplement the negotiated boundary agreement without, of course, replacing it.

I went on to state that "the specific identity of the Palestinian and Jordanian Arabs should find expression in the neighboring state in peaceful cooperation with Israel. Separate political sovereignties need not rule out a large measure of economic and social cooperation. We aspire to a community of sovereign states in the Middle East, with open frontiers and regional institutions for cooperation." On Jerusalem, I said that "Israel does not wish to exercise exclusive jurisdiction or unilateral responsibility in the Holy Places of Christendom and Islam, which should be under the administration of those who hold them sacred. We would be willing to discuss ways of giving expression to this principle, as well as working out agreements on free access and pilgrimage."

Nevertheless, I was aware that these visions could not be realized in a short time. They were also mocked by the current reality in which hundreds of thousands of Egyptians and Israeli troops in the south, and similar numbers of Syrian and Israeli forces in the north, were tied up with each other in such tangled proximity as to make the cease-fire untenable. Accordingly, I said: "Israel would support a proposal to discuss a disengagement agreement with Egypt as first priority when the conference meets after this inaugural phase." And I concluded:

> Our common ancestor, Abraham, shocked all his contemporaries by breaking the idols and suggesting something new. That is what we now have to do—to smash the idolatries of war and hate and suspicion, to break the adoration that men give to their traditional attitudes and, above all, to their traditional slogans, to strike out towards a horizon uncertain—but better than the terrible certainties that face us if we stay behind. Our Holy Book puts it simply: "Nation shall not lift up sword against nation, neither shall they learn war any more." It is put with equal simplicity in your Holy Book: "If they incline to peace, then turn towards it and put your trust in God."

I quoted the last sentence from the Koran in Arabic.

I had barely finished before I received a warm congratulatory note from Secretary Kissinger, but the Egyptian Foreign Minister had been fidgeting irritably in his chair. Fahmy now took the floor for a virulent assault on Israel. It was later explained that Egypt's very presence at a "peace conference" was so offensive to Arab radicals that Fahmy had to atone by a show of militance. Since he was not making a very favorable impression with his virulence, I decided to leave him with the last word.

While the opening statements of the parties had not concealed the gap between them, they had all been formulated in some flexibility. The Arabs had not closed the door on peace. Israel had spoken of maximal territorial concessions compatible with vital security interests. The Soviet Union had given its expected support to Arab territorial demands, but it had stated more openly than ever before the need for respecting Israel's independence, integrity and security. Apart from Fahmy's outburst, I thought that this was a promising beginning.

But there was still much work to do. The situation in Sinai and Golan was so volcanic that no diplomatic discussions were feasible unless short-term relief was found. Disengagement was the urgent theme. We decided that the five foreign ministers would go into a working session the following morning, without the press, in order to establish the machinery for such a discussion.

I went back to our delegation headquarters to brief the Israeli and international press. I told them to their astonishment that I would be meeting Gromyko at eight o'clock. The result was that the television bulletins in Israel that evening opened with the news that the

Moscow-Jerusalem dialogue, broken off seven years before, would now be resumed.

Accompanied by Evron, Shek and Bentzur, I came to the spacious grounds of the Soviet embassy at the United Nations headquarters near Geneva. I again had occasion to observe the taste of Soviet leaders for opulence in their official environment. On entering the Foreign Minister's room with my associates, I found Gromyko surrounded by Vladimir Vinogradov, his ambassador to Egypt, and by three other officials.

Nobody who watched the expression on their faces would ever have assumed that the Soviet Union had angrily broken off relations with Israel seven years before, and had maintained hostility toward us ever since. I had always wondered whether Soviet policy, with its special rigidities, ever allows its spokesmen to develop any personal sentiments. I had seen Soviet diplomats make the transition from the cordiality of 1948–1950 to subsequent hostility without showing much emotion at either stage. But Andrei Gromyko was a special case. It was he who, in 1947 and 1948, had electrified our people by a sudden abandonment of Soviet anti-Zionism in favor of unswerving support of Israel's struggle for admission to the international family. It seemed impossible that he could be unaware of this lineage, or that he could have forgotten the hours of common counsel that he and I had spent together in the decisive stages of Israel's national struggle.

He began in a facetious mood. He said that very often while sitting at international gatherings, he had said to himself, "What does Israel think and especially what does Minister Eban think?" This time he reached the conclusion that instead of asking himself, he would ask me. He had intended to suggest that we meet, and he was very glad that it turned out to be possible.

I told him that we appreciated the initiative of the Soviet Union in joining with the United States to convene the peace conference as co-chairmen. Israel attached hopes to the conference as a framework which might enable us to emerge out of deadlock. "Israel wins its wars, but would much prefer to prevent them." Gromyko said that he was glad to hear what I had said. "It is always easier to take a negative position than to reach agreement. The Geneva Conference is an important step in the right direction if the parties will show readiness to make progress towards a measure of understanding, even if not to complete agreement." The conference had already made it possible for him to meet me. This indicated that it had value in the promotion of encounter.

I told him that we ought not to underestimate the differences between Israel and the Soviet Union, but neither should we exaggerate them. I wanted to know if it would be right to say that there was no change in the Soviet position of 1947–1948 about the principle of Israel's legitimacy as a Jewish state, and that the Soviet Union did not intend to go back on that position. On the boundary question, I said, "We do not want to swallow territory simply out of appetite for a big map; but security requires selective adjustment of boundary lines. Even if the Soviet Union thinks otherwise, there are many countries who differ in their conceptions. This does not require rupture or confrontation."

Gromyko replied that since Israel's establishment in 1948, the Soviet Union had adopted a constant attitude and I would not be able to quote a single sentence which would indicate its retreat from the support of an independent State of Israel. The Soviet Union was still in favor of a sovereign and independent Israel living in peace and security. The USSR was ready to put all its weight on the balance in order to settle the conflict and to promote a solution which would guarantee the boundaries of states and their integrity in the area. This included Israel. That was and had always been the Soviet attitude. He added that it would be wrong to say that the Soviet policy consisted of blind adherence to the Arab cause. "We take an independent and logical line of which the main principles are: First, the Soviet Union recognizes that Israel has an undoubted right to exist like any other independent state in the world. If anybody violates this principle, we will oppose that with great force, since that would be against our basic policy. Second, the Soviet Union believes that security ought to be sought not by the acquisition of the territories of other states." He then sat back and asked me to comment on these principles.

We went on for some time discussing the admissibility of agreed-upon territorial changes. I asked how war could be avoided by reconstructing the very situation out of which it had so often erupted. I adduced the parallels of the European settlement in which the Soviet Union had insisted on territorial revisions far larger than any that Israel would demand. Gromyko was adamant. What happened in Europe and what should happen in the Middle East were "different."

I felt that we were endlessly defining our positions on boundaries without bringing them closer together. I therefore came back to the problems at our doorstep. I told him that we had given our consent to the United States and to Egypt to negotiate a disengagement agreement as the first step toward peace. But the Israeli delegation would not be in a position to conclude any agreements before the election at home. Kissinger had asked us to bring military officers to Geneva to commence the discussions and give the impression of continuity. I had consulted my Prime Minister on this. Gromyko drew me back to the central issue. He wanted to tell me in all frankness that the Soviet Union regarded the June 4, 1967, lines as secure and recognized boundaries of Israel. If we agreed to withdraw to them, we could expect important progress.

In good humor, he looked at Vinogradov and his other associates and said, "I have a feeling, Mr. Eban, that your friends and mine have a desire to go for a talk in the next room." Our respective "friends" took the hint and left us alone for twenty minutes.

The conversation turned, on Gromyko's initiative, to the question of Soviet-Israeli relations. He explained that "in principle" there was no bar to diplomatic relations. In 1948 the USSR had been the first country to establish them fully with Israel, but to renew them now would only become possible if there was "important progress in the work of the Geneva Conference." My efforts to clarify the term "important progress" met with no response.

It was obvious that the Soviet Union was vitally interested to secure our agreement to a disengagement accord with Egypt and thereafter with Syria. It was therefore showing as amiable a countenance to Israel as its basic policy allowed. I also noted that Gromyko did not make the renewal of relations with Israel dependent on a full peace settlement in the Middle East. Moscow evidently wished to keep several options open and to indicate to Israel that an improvement of its relations with the Soviet Union was a realistic objective. Gromyko went further and said that not only were diplomatic relations possible, "Everything that normally takes place between two countries in relations with each other can in principle be envisaged. For example, an exchange of visits between Chairman Brezhnev and Mrs. Golda Meir." All this, however, could be "envisaged only if important progress were made in carrying out the tasks of the Geneva Conference."

We parted courteously. The resumption of the dialogue between the Soviet Union and Israel at a high level raised strong echoes in world opinion and in Israel itself. Before I left, Gromyko said that we should continue to meet whenever international conferences or gatherings brought us together. At that time the expectation was that the Geneva Conference would be active during many months of the year. Moreover, the General Assembly of the United Nations would meet as usual in September. The Soviet Union seemed prepared not just for a one-time conversation but for a continuous dialogue, despite the evident differences in our policies.

The next morning I received a warm message from Golda Meir, praising my speech at the opening session, which had been well received in spite of the suspicious election climate. When we assembled in working session at the Palais des Nations, the atmosphere was more relaxed than on the previous day. The television cameras and the army of press correspondents had vanished. The five foreign ministers and their assistants were meeting alone around the table, with Waldheim presiding. The absence of the news media induced a visible relaxation. This confirmed my impression that much of the virulence of Israeli-Arab exchanges at international meetings results from publicity. Faced by the bright lights and the hovering pencils, statesmen are more likely to strike poses of heroic virility than to be revealed in flagrant compromise and reconciliation.

Thus the compactness and intimacy of the Geneva meeting enabled our working session to take some steps away from war in a short time and without much rhetoric. The United States proposed that the conference approve the establishment of joint committees to work out disengagement agreements. The intention was to begin with the Egyptian-Israeli front and then to seek disengagement in the Syrian-Israeli sector. Gromyko supported this proposal. So did Fahmy for Egypt.

By the evening the conference was able to announce the establishment of a "military committee." I cabled Mrs. Meir, recommending that Israeli officers come to Geneva at once, in spite of the inhibitions imposed by our elections. It was clear that these officers would not be able to do much during the remaining days of December. But their arrival would symbolize our serious approach to the conference's work. It would apparently be of great assistance to Sadat if he was able to say that concrete procedures had been worked out. The Soviet Union, in its turn, had made it clear to me through Gromyko that it would appreciate the gesture of beginning the work of the Geneva Conference before the Israeli elections. I had a telephone call from Kissinger, urging this in the strongest possible way. Before the evening was out, Mrs. Meir had given the Cabinet's assent, and General Gur and Colonel Tsiyon arrived the next day.

I flew back to Israel to take up my share in the election campaign. The fact that I came fresh from the Geneva Conference, which had been televised and broadcast throughout the country, resulted in a huge flood of requests for me to address meetings all over the country. The Labor Party's Information Department, for reasons that were then obscure, seemed unwilling to take full advantage of this opportunity by scheduling meetings in the main urban areas. Nevertheless, the Geneva Conference was now the primary theme of the campaign. Sapir was later to express the opinion that the Geneva Conference, and the echoes raised by my televised speech, brought our party the extra four or five seats which prevented it from losing control of the Knesset and the Coalition. It was the only element in our appeal which had a "forward look" and gave some premonition of change.

Before leaving for Geneva, I had taken an active part in formulating the Labor Alignment platform on peace and security. I had told Sapir that I would only join the platform committee if I could initiate the first draft that would form the basis for the platform. Time and again during my years as Foreign Minister, the entire foreign service had been called upon to rescue our political position from "hard-line" statements conceived for the sole purpose of ensuring party unity. The Galili document had produced harmful effects, not so much by its content as by its tone. The reason for formulating any long-term proposals on settlement in the West Bank and Gaza was that without such a formulation, Moshe Dayan hinted that he might not appear on the party list. The Galili document was thus designed for domestic, not for international purposes. But all this had been before the Yom Kippur War. Now there was a chance to formulate principles without having the "Oral Law" and the Galili document tied like millstones around Israel's neck.

The platform adopted by the Labor Alignment, known as the 14 Points, deviated very little from my first draft. We stated the principle of territorial compromise in all sectors. We spoke specifically of the Geneva Conference as the main arena in which Israeli diplomacy would be deployed. And, for the first time, we gave recognition in our party platform to the right of the Palestinian Arabs, not merely to economic benefits and autonomy but to the "expression of their national identity" in the state which would arise on Israel's eastern border in an Israeli-Jordanian peace settlement.

Taken as a whole, this platform had a more flexible tone. It contained no specific geographical reference. Thus, our negotiators would have their hands freer than before.

The election campaign of 1973 was now going forward on a somber note. For the first time, more importance was given to television than to public meetings, most of which were sparsely attended. However, I was still one of the few who seemed able to draw large crowds, and the reputable public opinion polls, which showed a decline in the ratings of some of my colleagues, revealed no such tendency at work in my case.

I spent the night of the election returns as usual in our party headquarters in Yarkon Street, together with Mrs. Meir, the party's secretary-general, Aharon Yadlin, and others. It soon became certain that our strength would be reduced. Quite apart from the circumstances of the war, we had suffered depletion through the influence of a new party founded by Shulamit Aloni, a vigorous Labor member who had been excluded from our list of candidates by Sapir's committee on the grounds that her appearance on the list might irritate the Prime Minister. We paid a heavy price for her exclusion. Mrs. Aloni received over 30,000 votes, most of which would have accrued to our party if she had not established her separate list.

Under these conditions it was not unimpressive for Mrs. Meir and her colleagues to secure fifty-one seats for the Alignment, together with three seats for Arab voters affiliated to us. The protest movements that had been so voluble in the streets obviously commanded less support in the nation's homes. While the voters had narrowed the gap between the Labor Alignment and the opposition Likud, our party still held the field. No other group could build a majority. In an "inquest" on the election results in the party's leadership bureau, I said that the results had been "worse than we had hoped, but better than we had feared." There had certainly been no landslide or collapse. The voters had refuted the drastic idea that we were a "government of failure."

Before the Cabinet could even be constituted, it had to negotiate a disengagement agreement with Egypt. We therefore had the paradox of an outgoing caretaker government negotiating an agreement of vital importance for the country's future. Our constitutional tradition imposes no limitations on the executive power of a Cabinet, even after its formal resignation. In any case, it seemed evident that the main functions in the Meir Administration would not change hands. A day after the election, Dayan as Defense Minister was in Washington exploring the possibility of a more stable cease-fire line between Egyptian and Israeli forces, while I embarked on new enterprises in our foreign relations in the conviction that a new period of my tenure lay ahead.

But however promising these prospects were, it was evident that progress in disengagement was the condition for any repair of Israel's international situation. It was this that would occupy me throughout the first months of 1974.

Although disengagement had been decided in principle by the Geneva Conference, the main brunt of negotiating it was to fall on Kissinger. There now began a remarkable period of achievement in American and Israeli diplomacy. The "shuttle" era had begun.

It may seem at first sight that the excitement was exaggerated. The Egyptian-Israeli disengagement agreement was of limited scope in relation to the Middle Eastern problem as a whole. Yet the negotiation was attended by great suspense. We knew that even if success would not bring peace, it was certain that failure would mean war. On each side of the Suez Canal, masses of troops, tanks, missiles and artillery were locked together in tangled positions. Even if there had been good will between the two governments, it would hardly have been possible to prevent a dangerous eruption. In the prevailing bitterness, there was no hope at all for the cease-fire to remain intact. Sadat would not for long be able to conceal the proximity of Israeli forces to his major cities, or the beleaguered condition of the Third Army. Israel was condemned to an almost total mobilization of her manpower, with a consequent paralysis of her economy so long as her forces were strung out across long lines of communication, reaching into the heartland of Egypt. The presence of Israeli troops on the soil of Africa raised hostile reactions through that continent. Nearly all African governments had broken relations with us, most of them from the date of our crossing the Canal into African territory.

During five weeks of disengagement talks, the pendulum swung wildly to and fro. Israel was prepared, if necessary, to give up her newly won positions west of the Canal, but she could not forget that many lives had been lost in capturing them. Many Israeli soldiers were still missing, and an Israeli government would have to give a dire account to its people if it accepted the kind of withdrawal that would make war probable again. If we were to move from west of the Canal, while allowing the Egyptians to remain east of it, we would have to seek a drastic reduction of Egyptian forces and weaponry east of the Suez waterway. On the other hand, it would be difficult for Sadat to persuade his exuberant army to move so many units backward.

During January, Kissinger developed his technique of "shuttle diplomacy" for which the diplomatic textbooks showed no precedent. The procedure was dictated very largely by his taste for centralized responsibility. He showed a candid lack of reverence for the professional skills at the disposal of the State Department. Although the disengagement issue looked small on the map, it would have large international consequences, so that the Secretary's personal involvement was fully justified. Moreover, the structure of Arab governments, with all decisions taken by one man at the top, required the United States to operate at a similar level of hierarchy.

The shuttle had exhausting effects on my own physical and political strength. Kissinger would arrive at Ben Gurion Airport early in the morning from Alexandria. On the road to Jerusalem I would hear the main issues that he had solved—or left unsolved. He would pay almost no attention to the surrounding landscape or to its Biblical or historical associations. Arriving in Jerusalem, he would be received with applause by a group of hotel guests, composed largely of

Jewish tourists from the United States. Our conversation would continue in the crowded elevator, spill out into the corridor and culminate in his suite on the sixth floor, where we would be revived by the pale stimulus of diet soft drinks. In the meantime, his large body of officials, headed by Undersecretary Joseph Sisco and the uncannily reticent Ambassador Ellsworth Bunker, would be wearily disposing themselves along the rest of the sixth floor. On leaving Kissinger's apartment with Ambassador Dinitz, I would arrange for Mrs. Meir to be informed on how the negotiations stood after the last Alexandria visit. There would be a brief period for refreshments, after which the Secretary would arrive—usually late—for a summary of the negotiations. There would then be the plenary sessions attended on our side by Mrs. Meir, Allon, Dayan and myself, together with the Chief of Staff, military officers and officials from our ministries. There would be at least eight or nine on the American side. These sessions would take place around the dinner table at my official residence, or at the Prime Minister's office, about ten minutes' drive away.

At these sessions Kissinger's narration would be lively and expansive. It would include character sketches of the statesmen he had met across the border. His technique was to avoid making "American proposals." He would ask us to put ourselves into the skins of our adversaries. He would give a picture of how their minds worked, what their complexes were and how far they could operate within the terms of their domestic authority.

I am certain, that he gave a similar picture of Israeli predicaments when he reached the other side. He would try to ensure that there were always Egyptian and Israeli suggestions on the table. He would "merely" seek to close the distance between them. After the plenary sessions he would make his way back to Ben Gurion Airport for another visit to Alexandria. Sometimes the itinerary would be Egypt–Israel–Egypt–Israel within a single day. And since there were many cross-currents of policy within the Arab world, he would often make tangential jumps to Riyadh, Damascus or Amman. The atmosphere was permanently dramatic. There were always cameras, tape recorders and microphones massed outside the building in which the disengagement negotiations took place. Sometimes the tumult would be swollen by demonstrators from the Likud and Religious parties, warning the government against the evil intentions of the outside world in general, and of the American Secretary of State in particular.

As the weeks went by, the street demonstrations became uglier. Virulent slogans on placards and violent phrases shouted through microphones would portray Kissinger as an emissary of evil, hypnotizing Israel into a betrayal of its central interests. The climax came when anti-Semitic slogans such as "Jew Boy" were introduced—by Jews in Israel!—into the arsenal of invective. This was an allusion to some of the unsavory expressions used in the Nixon Watergate tapes. Israel, paradoxically, became the first foreign country in which Kissinger would be invidiously reminded of his Jewishness. Now and again, some of us tried to reason with the demonstrators. It usually turned out that they were people of mild nature, whose actual demeanor bore no resemblance to the ugliness of their slogans. Others were tied down by a religious fundamentalism so dogmatic as to be beyond rational discussion. There is no evidence that the demonstrators expressed the basic national temper, but they had their effect on the news media and, perhaps, subconsciously on some of the Israeli negotiators themselves. However strongly we rejected what they were saying, their presence reminded us that we would have to fight hard for a domestic consensus in favor of compromise.

The negotiations neared their climax in mid-January. The opposition demonstrators now took to the major streets and squares of large cities, where they denounced the disengagement agreements as an apocalyptic disaster for the Israeli people. General Arik Sharon was particularly emphatic on this matter. The public recalled his intimate knowledge of the Sinai terrain, as well as the audacity and sweep of his recent operations across the Canal. His case was that positions captured by Israel at poignant expense of life were being bartered away for little benefit. It was not difficult to make this case, since the negotiation was never symmetrical. All the territorial gain was being made by Egypt. What Israel sought in return was more intangible: a movement away from war; the ability to release our productive manpower from military tasks far from home; the possibility of exploring new horizons of coexistence. It was one thing for the opposition to state that they thought the disengagement unwise; it was quite another to pretend that if Israel were to be twenty instead of six kilometers from the Suez Canal, our national security was doomed. Nor did the opposition take any serious account of the fact that we were negotiating not only with Egypt, but with America. It seemed to make no difference to them whether we ended up with no arms or economic assistance from the United States—or whether we faced our new dangers with a powerful ally in our support.

By the third week in January, the issues had been narrowed down. We had reached accord on the depth of the Israeli withdrawal west of the Canal, and from certain positions east of it. It was accepted that the buffer zone between the two armies would be manned by

United Nations troops. It was mutually understood that weapons would be so placed that no fire from the guns, tanks or missiles of one party would be physically able to reach the cease-fire lines or the air space of the other.

The unsolved issue was now the reduction of forces. The hope of agreement would stand or fall on this. Israel, after all, was giving up hundreds of square miles of territory that it had occupied on both sides of the Canal. The waterway would be opened with Egyptian sovereignty and control on both banks. These concessions would be intolerable unless we could be assured that the evacuated areas would not become jumping-off grounds for a new assault upon us. The question was how far Sadat would be prepared to go in reducing his forces in Sinai.

We lived many gloomy days in which Kissinger predicted that he would never get Egypt to go below a level of 250 tanks. We knew that the presence of Egyptian forces in such strength east of the Canal would make "disengagement" farcical. So Kissinger set out for Alexandria for what I feared would be the last stage in an abortive mission. When he returned that evening, he told me at the airport that Egypt would have no more than 32 tanks in Sinai. I could hardly believe my ears. He had induced Egypt to reduce her tank force in Sinai from 700 to a few dozen, her manpower from 70,000 to 7,500, with corresponding reduction of artillery missiles and other arms. This meant that he had virtually secured a substantive demilitarization of areas captured by Egypt in the Yom Kippur War.

Sadat had undertaken, reportedly against the advice of some military commanders, to withdraw masses of troops, tanks and missiles which had triumphantly crossed the Suez Canal in the first days of October. It was this decision by Sadat that led me, for the first time, to reflect that a substantive change of direction might have taken place in Egyptian policy.

The end of the negotiations came amid blinding snowstorms that swept through Jerusalem streets and made it impossible for us to hold meetings with Kissinger except through the use of jeeps and snowplows. Riding with Dayan and General Elazar on a snowplow to the King David Hotel made me feel as if I was somehow involved in the last stages of the Russo-Finnish war.

On January 18 the snow had melted, and so had our remaining crisis points. I announced Israel's agreement in a television and radio press conference at the King David Hotel at 9 P.M. This was synchronized with announcements from Alexandria by President Sadat and from Washington by President Nixon, who sorely needed something favorable to announce. His Watergate troubles, as we now know, were beyond remedy, but he still hoped against hope that they could be transcended by international successes.

The next day, since the road from Jerusalem to Lod was still blocked by ice and snowdrifts, I traveled with Kissinger on a train which, with all respect to Israel Railways, lacked some of the lavish amenities attributed by Agatha Christie to the Orient Express. Nevertheless, it was possible for us to talk at length. Kissinger clearly felt that Egypt had embarked on a new course in her international orientation. Sadat was determined to move away from dependence on the Soviet Union into a closer relationship with the United States. This would have a moderating effect on Egypt's attitude toward Israel. It also meant that Sadat was ready to alienate the Arab extremists all the way from Baghdad to Tripoli. The problem now was how to maintain "momentum" in the negotiation. Although an agreement with Syria was not stipulated in the text of our disengagement agreement with Egypt, it was understood by Sadat that he could not long remain isolated as the only Arab leader to have entered a new contractual relationship with Israel.

Kissinger hoped to negotiate a disengagement agreement between Israel and Syria early in 1974, and then to turn to the problem of the Jordanian-Israeli sector. Since there had been no war on the Jordanian-Israeli front, there was no real military motive for disengagement. On the other hand, I recalled Zaid Rifai's speech at the Geneva Conference. He seemed to be saying that if King Hussein was left out of the disengagement process, he would be discredited and lose his position as a negotiator on the future of the West Bank. The result would be an increase of prestige and status for Arafat and the PLO. Kissinger had shown a remarkable persuasive power. I felt that if he wanted to sell us a car with a wheel missing, he would achieve his purpose by an eloquent and cogent eulogy of the three wheels that remained. But the first priority was still disengagement with Syria.

"And now we can all relax," Kissinger said as we left the train and walked to his plane, but for me the next few months were to hold everything except relaxation. The three major themes were the rise and fall of Golda Meir's last government; the election of a new Israeli leadership; and the negotiation of the Israeli-Syrian disengagement agreement. All these were overshadowed for me by my mother's last illness and death.

On June 4, 1974, I was destined to sign documents annexed to the Syrian Disengagement Agreement in the morning, to leave the outgoing Cabinet in the evening, and to march toward an uncharted political and personal future.

None of these events could have been foreseen in January. After his journey with me by train to Lod, Kissinger had flown to Damascus. In accordance with our prior arrangement he stopped at Ben Gurion Airport on his way back to America. Dayan and I waited for him there, but on the arrival of Yigal Allon, Dayan recalled a previous speaking engagement and left the airport before the Secretary's arrival. Kissinger showed Yigal Allon and me a map explaining Syria's ideas of a disengagement. They were so exorbitant that in any area but the Middle East they would have been regarded as the collapse of negotiations before they had begun. Assad had not only demanded the abandonment by Israel of the salient captured in the October 1973 fighting, he also wanted us to remove ourselves completely from the Golan Heights without any semblance of peace. He seemed to be talking like a victor laying down a dictated peace rather than as the head of a state which had suffered a military defeat. Kissinger had refused to be intimidated by this "opening gambit." For him, the important thing was Assad's agreement to the principle of disengagement rather than the unrealistic nature of his first proposal. At any rate, there was something to talk about, and Kissinger looked forward to discussing the prospect first with myself and then with Dayan when he visited Washington in March.

But before any new diplomatic move could begin, we had to set our political house in order. Mrs. Meir had won a mandate in the December 1973 election empowering her to form a new Administration. The process this time was inordinately slow. The reduced strength of the Labor Alignment made it more dependent than before on the support of other groups. There was also an explosive turbulence within the Israeli society itself. The shock of the Yom Kippur War was being absorbed in spurts and spasms. There was a constant likelihood that war would erupt again. Disengagement with Egypt had, paradoxically, produced greater tension on our domestic scene. Thousands of troops came home from the Nile Delta and Sinai, bringing stories of the neglect and disorder that had led to vast casualties in the early days of the war. The full lists of killed and wounded had been published. The country was aflame with urgent questions. Why had our intelligence services been taken by surprise? How was it that the Israeli deterrent had not deterred? Once the Egyptian attack had erupted, why had it not been flung back across the Canal in a day or two, as all experts had predicted? How did the General Staff and Defense Ministry explain the inefficiency of communication, the staggeringly light manning of the Bar-Lev Line, the emptiness of our forward positions, the absence of tanks where they should have been, and their presence where they had no business to be? Why had generals indulged their savage rivalries at the very height of the war? How about the predictions that the Arab armies would not be able to dent the cease-fire lines, to coordinate their operations or to bring the oil weapon to effective use? Was no minister specifically responsible for the military unpreparedness which had had such agonizing political and psychological effects? Why had there not been a single dismissal or resignation?

These perplexities flowed through Israeli society like hot lava. All the sources of national confidence seemed to shrivel up. The whole government and establishment came under the assault, but it focused with particular sharpness on Moshe Dayan and to a lesser extent on Golda Meir, who had overriding responsibility for the national security.

Protests, demonstrations and calls for ministerial blood gave Israeli politics a more venomous aspect than ever before. Many forgot that an electoral verdict had been given at the end of December 1973, when the course of the war had been fully known. While the voters had penalized the Alignment for the misadventures of the first week of the war, they had certainly not shown any enthusiasm for the other parties, or any decline in the belief that Mrs. Meir and her chief colleagues should retain their responsibilities.

The successful negotiations with Egypt had done something to alleviate domestic tensions; and by early March Mrs. Meir had been able to turn to the intricacies of coalition-making. They seemed insuperable. Dayan, enraged by the virulent assault on him, mostly from within his own party, had announced that he would not serve in the new Cabinet. Shimon Peres had stood loyally by his side. The Minister of Justice, Yaacov Shimshon Shapira, had earlier voiced a demand for Dayan's resignation. When Mrs. Meir denied this appeal and reiterated her confidence in Dayan, Shapira had himself left office. The National Religious Party was refusing to join the coalition unless there was an "Emergency Government," including the Likud opposition. The Labor Party recognized that this would paralyze our diplomacy. We would have to seek obscure formulas to cement our unity instead of making the painful territorial compromises called for in the Alignment platform.

The result of all these crosscurrents was that early in March, Mrs. Meir was able to constitute an Administration with a slender statistical basis. It would have only fifty-eight supporters in the Knesset; it could survive only if its opponents failed to combine on any single issue. The Prime Minister's antipathy toward Shulamit Aloni was so strong as to exclude the three members of the Civil Rights Party from her Cabinet. The Alignment's only partners would thus be the

Independent Liberal Party. Since Dayan and Peres had refused participation, Yitzhak Rabin would be Minister of Defense, and Aharon Yariv Minister of Transportation.

When she presented her list to the Labor Party Knesset members on March 3, Mrs. Meir spoke severely about the rumblings of nonconfidence that had reached her from several Labor Party leaders, including Cabinet members. She did not feel that there was sufficient unanimity for maintaining a minority Administration in power. She had particularly noted the tendency of some members of the Knesset, such as Liova Eliav and Yitzhak Ben Aharon, to deny us their votes on crucial occasions. Therefore she proposed her list of ministers with one change. She suggested that a new Prime Minister be found!

The consternation was immense. A stream of persuasive delegations began to flow toward Mrs. Meir's house in Rehavia. Most Labor Party leaders went in to urge her to stay in office and emerged to tell the television cameras and microphones about their persuasive efforts. After much thought, I decided not to join the procession. It seemed to me that when a political leader proclaimed weariness at the age of seventy-seven, it was time for her party to respect her statement and to have a new look at itself. It was true that Mrs. Meir's authority and firmness would be missed, but it was also true that we would one day have to seek leadership from somebody at least a decade younger. On the other hand, we were then in the midst of crucial negotiations with Syria. I thought that we should ensure a continuity of responsibility at least until the Syrian agreement was concluded. Until this happened, we could not accurately say that the Yom Kippur War had ended, or that the simmering volcano would not again erupt. I expressed these views frankly in a handwritten letter that I sent over to Mrs. Meir, who responded with a cordial telephone call to my home.

Mrs. Meir yielded to public pressure and the national need. She reluctantly agreed to present her new Cabinet without Dayan and Peres for the President's ratification and the approval of the Knesset. Here came a dramatic turning point. At a meeting of the Labor Party Central Committee, Dayan sat waiting for expressions of support. Very few of these came, except from the Prime Minister herself. Rabin's address evoked a favorable response; the party seemed quite willing to have the Defense Ministry under his control. Nevertheless, the Party Central Committee voted a strong appeal to Dayan and Peres to revoke their refusals to take office. At this point Dayan was told of new troop concentrations on the Golan front. These were not any more intimidatory than usual, but this time Dayan and Peres went to Jerusalem to tell Mrs. Meir that in view of what they described as a "national emergency" created by the tension on the Syrian front, they had changed their minds. They would be willing to join Mrs. Meir's Cabinet. The Prime Minister received this news ecstatically. She appointed Dayan Defense Minister, Peres Minister of Information, and restored Rabin to the role of Minister of Labor.

While welcoming the consolidation of our ranks, many of us thought that the process of achieving it was dubious. There were not a dozen Israelis who seriously believed that any "emergency" had occurred sufficient to explain the decision of ministers to join a government which they had rejected so strongly a short time before. The National Religious Party, now awakening to the same "emergency," ended weeks of suspense. It favored joining Mrs. Meir's Cabinet so as to assure it a solid majority.

Much newspaper gossip in Israel and abroad had spoken of the likelihood that I would not be included in the new Cabinet owing to my frank dissent from some of the Cabinet's decisions, especially in the matter of the Lebanese aircraft and Yamit. I had decided not even to discuss my own position with Mrs. Meir, still less to lobby for any post. When she announced her list of Cabinet officers at a public session of our party, I learned for the first time that my own position was intact.

I frankly wanted to continue my task for the next two or three years. For the first time since 1948, the Arab states had accepted the principle of a negotiated peace settlement. In the Geneva Conference I had helped to create a normal framework for peace discussions. Unlike the Six-Day War with its total Israeli victory and utter Arab defeat, the Yom Kippur conflict had ended with a chastened mood on both sides. We had made an astonishing recovery, but it could no longer be said that the Arabs were too humiliated to come to the table or that the Israelis were too confident to accept compromises. There was now enough buoyancy in the Arab world and enough realism in Israel to create a negotiating atmosphere. The vision of an Arab-Israeli peace had filled my heart and mind for many years. Moreover, the negotiating effort would be directed by the United States, where I was widely known.

I also wished to follow up some symptoms of diplomatic recovery in Europe. In January 1973 I had taken our negotiations with the European Economic Community to an advanced stage by signing a protocol committing the EEC to work out an agreement for a Free Trade Area with Israel by the end of the year. After a long period of estrangement I had negotiated an agreement with Foreign Minister Michel Jobert of France elevating our dialogue to foreign-minister level. It was now agreed that I would go on an official visit to

Paris on May 15. This would be close to the seventh anniversary of my talk with De Gaulle on the eve of the Six-Day War. It was clear to me from the attitude of the electorate during the campaign and after the Geneva meeting that the Israeli public still wanted to see me at my post. Accordingly, once the Cabinet had been presented to the Knesset, I felt able to turn to the urgent business of the Syrian agreement, without any sense of personal vulnerability.

When I saw Kissinger in Washington in early March he again urged us not to take the initial Syrian proposal as anything but a bargaining maneuver. Yet he was convinced that unless Syria obtained the salient that we had taken in 1973 as well as a symbolic foothold beyond the old cease-fire line at Kuneitra, she would not be able to sign an accord. Militant Syria could not appear more flexible than Egypt, which had gained from the disengagement agreement more than her armies had won in the field. The Egyptian agreement set the parameters for what Syria could or could not accept. This logic seemed realistic to me. I concluded that we should strive to achieve with Syria a fairly exact replica of the Egyptian agreement.

Much of Israeli opinion was not prepared for such a course. The idea that Syria should obtain any foothold in the Golan area aroused resentment. I knew that Dayan was more lucid on this point than most of our colleagues. His view was that if we were unwilling to concede Kuneitra to Syria, we might as well give up the idea of a disengagement agreement and save ourselves and the United States the acrimony of a sterile debate.

While I was discussing these matters with Kissinger in Washington on March 20, a note was passed to me telling me that a telegram awaited me at the embassy. From this and a subsequent telephone call I learned that my mother's condition had become desperate. I had seen her twice during her terminal illness. The first time was on a special trip from Israel to London the day after the new Cabinet was confirmed by the Knesset. She had responded so cheerfully to my visit that the doctors believed some miraculous prolongation might be possible. She said with deep pathos how relieved she was to know that my position was "assured for the next four years." On my way to Washington I had seen her again, this time in weaker condition. With a realism that I found intolerably poignant, she had discussed the eighty-two years of her life with quiet satisfaction and pride. There had been many moments of travail in the early years. But there had been so much fulfillment since then! Her valediction was as serene as if she were discussing the end of a successful vacation that had turned out better than anticipated.

This had been two weeks before. Now as I flew back to London from Washington on March 21, I knew that the end was near. It came twenty-six hours later in the Westminster Hospital. The gentle memory lingers. I think of many things in terms of how she would react to them.

I remained in London for the week of special mourning, spending much time revisiting boyhood haunts with which my mother's memory was associated. The first message of concern that reached me just before my mother's death came from Harold Wilson, a humane gesture that I especially appreciated, since he was then in the midst of a governmental reconstitution after his recent victory at the polls.

In my private grief, during the sad details of internment and memorial, I was naturally cut off from rumors in Israel about attempts to get me out of the Cabinet. In his book *Road to Jerusalem,* Walter Laqueur speaks of "the special virulence of Israeli political life." It is hard to contest this verdict. Some members of the Labor Party had been disappointed by the composition of Mrs. Meir's Cabinet. Three of them in particular, Aharon Yadlin, Moshe Baram and Avraham Ofer, were waiting eagerly for what might be a last chance to take their place at the Cabinet table. It was clear that this chance would increase if established ministers such as Sapir and I could be eliminated. On the left of the party, Liova Eliav was brooding over his exclusion from the national leadership. The continued dominance of Dayan as Minister of Defense after the Yom Kippur War irritated many party leaders who felt that he was the Prophet Jonah—inviting our electoral shipwreck by his very presence aboard. Others believed that he was still a formidable asset to our campaign. Thus a precarious atmosphere surrounded Mrs. Meir's government from its earliest days. Throughout all these weeks, a Commission of Inquiry slowly pursued its probing into the conduct of the war. It was headed by the Chief Justice, Dr. Simon Agranat, and included two former Chiefs of Staff—Yigael Yadin and Chaim Laskov, as well as Justice Landau and the state comptroller, Dr. Nebenzahl.

The publication of the Agranat Commission's Report in April was like a cloudburst, bringing the heavy, hot tension to the breaking point. It told a tragic story of deficiencies, neglect, false appraisals and inadequate reactions in the terrible days that followed the Egyptian and Syrian attacks. The conclusions, however, did not seem to accord with the narrative. The commission recommended the dismissal of the Chief of Staff, General "Dado" Elazar; the chief of military intelligence, General Eli Zeira; and other high officers, including General Gonen, who had commanded the Sinai front. But it found mitigating explanations for the conduct of their minister, Moshe Dayan. And while the commission obviously thought that it had been unwise to avoid mobilization in the first days of October, it paid generous tribute to Mrs. Meir's strong nerve and sense of direction during the actual conduct of military operations.

The public was deeply shocked by the dissonance between the dismissal of leading officers and the effort of the Agranat Commission to avoid charging the Defense Minister with responsibility for what his subordinates had done or omitted. At a stormy Cabinet meeting, some ministers were even inclined to reject the report. The Minister of Labor, Yitzhak Rabin, proposed that it be sent back to its authors for further consideration. The general public could not understand how a Defense Minister could continue on his course while his leading associates were penalized for actions taken with his full knowledge and approval. To make the situation even more bizarre, it emerged that in the crucial days before the outbreak of fighting, General Elazar had vainly tried to persuade Dayan to take precautionary measures of full mobilization. Although Dayan had formally satisfied the Agranat Commission, he had not satisfied the deeper national intuitions. His formal exoneration only intensified the public clamor for his removal from the Defense Ministry.

The Agranat Commission's Report is still a controversial document in Israel despite the respected status of its authors. It dealt with the first half of the war—not with the entire drama of peril and recuperation. Its assessment that it was legitimate for a Defense Minister to adopt attitudes which were culpable if adopted by the Chief of Staff seemed to violate the principle of a ministerial responsibility. I had a strong liking for Dado, whom I often met after his resignation, and I was shocked by his sudden death a year and a half later. If I had remained in the Foreign Ministry, I would have offered him a senior diplomatic appointment.

On April 15 there was a tense meeting of the Labor Party, which had met to consider how to respond to an opposition motion of no-confidence in the Cabinet in the light of the Agranat Report. Mrs. Meir, after a moving speech, now announced her decision to resign. Although this had happened before, there was now an air of authentic finality. It was clear that her five-year reign was ending. It had begun in very high promise. Israel's position in the world community had been proud and confident. The cease-fire lines had been effectively held and the unity of the Labor movement had been solidly entrenched. Five years later, the cease-fire lines were breached, Israel's repute for invincibility had been shattered, with a consequent collapse of its international position and the beginning of a virulent internal dissension. It would take much time and energy to achieve recovery. The cease-fire and the Disengagement Agreement lay to the credit of Mrs. Meir's Cabinet as the possible beginning of a new era of regional stability. But she was not prepared to wait for the return of public confidence. Her most distinguished talent was her capacity to impose a moral and emotional domination over any scene in which she moved. There was also the individual tenacity of her devotion to the causes that she served and led. She took a nation's respect into her retirement.

The Labor Party was now compelled, with brutal suddenness, to face the problem of succession. Golda Meir's last team (Allon, Eban, Dayan, Sapir, Zadok, Rabin, Yariv, Peres) was perhaps the strongest our party had ever had. Mrs. Meir's action disbanded the group and opened the way for unrestrained rivalries. It was a turning point in our party's history. The central figure was now Pinhas Sapir. Despite some reservations about his capacities in the international field, there was no doubt that he could have had the prime-ministership for the asking. He rejected this opportunity. In Israeli political folklore, political leaders have to portray high office as an intolerable burden, only to be undertaken at personal sacrifice and under strong pressure. But the more vehemently an Israeli politician disclaimed an ambition for the premiership, the more he was regarded as aspiring to it. Sapir's many talents did not include clarity of expression, and many ambiguities still surrounded his attitude. Some of us believed wrongly that if he was sufficiently pressed, he would take up the challenge. We failed, however, to take one thing into account. The only persuasive voice that would have impelled him to accept the leadership was that of Golda Meir. In many conversations that I had with Sapir, the absence of endorsement from the Prime Minister, whom he had projected into the leadership five years before, came up with obsessive emphasis. I was one of a delegation of a dozen Labor leaders who made a final attempt to prevail on Sapir to rescue the party and the nation in its predicament. At a meeting in his office in the Finance Ministry, he gave us a reply of such emphatic negation that we knew we had lost hope of changing his mind. The vacuum of leadership yawned before us like a chasm.

The day after Sapir's refusal, I received telephone calls from Aharon Yadlin, the secretary-general of the Labor Party, and later from Moshe Baram, the leader of our party in the Knesset. They each suggested that I submit my candidacy as the party's nominee for the premiership. The only candidate whose hat was already in the ring at that time was Shimon Peres. He was gathering much support through his dynamism and capacity for organization. Yet it seemed unlikely that he could lead a united party. As the central figure in the Rafi secession, he had aroused intense hostility among leaders of the Mapai and Achdut Ha'avodah factions. Sapir was fiercely antagonistic to him. Peres had held Cabinet offices less weighty and responsible than those that I had occupied. Moreover, he had given such absolute fidelity to Dayan that his own political identity was not yet fully established in the public mind. It was generally assumed that if Sapir remained firm in refusing the leadership himself, he would support a candidate from the Mapai group in our party such as Chaim Zadok or myself.

While Peres steadily wooed the support of members of the Central Committee, Sapir pursued an eccentric course. First he used heavy persuasion to discourage Zadok's candidacy. He then explained to me that it would be unwise for me to let my name go forward at this stage. There was no chance of forming a new coalition in the present Knesset, since the National Religious Party would insist on a broad composition including Likud, which our party would not accept. The natural course would be for Golda Meir's Cabinet to continue in office until October. The leadership problem should therefore wait until the late summer. Moreover, if I ran for the premiership after Peres and Rabin had secured so many commitments, I would at most get about 100 of the 600 votes, and it would not befit my "dignity" to come in third in such a contest. At this stage Sapir did not admit that he was committed to Rabin's candidacy.

The Central Committee with its six hundred members convened on April 21. At a Cabinet meeting that morning Allon passed me a note seeking my support for his proposal to allow the Meir government to continue in a caretaker status while new elections were prepared for October. Allon argued that it would not be democratic for a new leader to inherit Mrs. Meir's mandate for nearly four years without seeking a popular mandate. When I told Allon that I would vote for his motion, he indicated that this was not enough: it was important that I should make a strong speech which might sway votes, since the issue was open and narrowly poised.

When I reached the Central Committee meeting on the afternoon of April 21, the names of Peres and Rabin were firmly in the ring. My own name had not been withdrawn, although I was not actively canvassing. Some members were asking me if I intended to be a candidate or to withdraw. In the latter case they would be influenced by my preferences between the two remaining candidates. I told the Secretary of our Tel Aviv branch and members of the Labor Youth Movement that I would prefer Peres' candidacy to that of Rabin, and that if they wished to be guided by me, they should act in that direction.

When I took the floor to support Allon's proposal for new elections, I seemed to kindle a sudden fire. I spoke with vehemence against the procedure whereby a few people under Sapir's authority virtually arranged the voting results by pressure on the voters. The party should rid itself of its oligarchical habits and present itself to the voters. The Central Committee ought to get itself renovated before it sought to "renovate" the government. The electorate had voted for Meir-Allon-Eban-Dayan-Sapir. If the party intended to change that decision, it should go back to the people.

There was very intensive applause for this address—more than I had ever earned at a party meeting. The *Jerusalem Post* of April 22 spoke of the audience as "spell-bound." The evening paper *Yediot Aharonot* commented that if I had spoken as vigorously as this before in party meetings, the leadership issue would have been decided in my favor. At midnight the television was still including me among the candidates, but a few minutes later I formally announced that I was not running. I let the press know that I would support Peres.

At seven-thirty the next morning Peres came to breakfast with me at the Dan Hotel. He was optimistic about his chances. I was less sanguine. I knew that Sapir had been working all night to rally votes for Rabin. He had enrolled others to help him in the task, many of whom told me later that they did not know Rabin at all, but were acting on the assumption that "Sapir knows best." Peres spoke to me soberly and imaginatively of the innovations of policy and style that he would try to introduce if he was elected. He would regard me as his senior partner.

My inability to support Rabin against Peres was not a matter of personal prejudice. It arose from my close knowledge of each candidate. Hardly anybody else among our leaders had such an intimate experience of working with them. I believed that even if a candidate could not possess all the attributes ideally required of an Israeli Labor Prime Minister, he should approach a fair number of them. He should have experience in parliamentary work and a respectful attitude to parliamentary authority. He should be capable of creating an atmosphere of confidence between himself and members of a diverse team. He should have a unifying, not a divisive personality. He should be firmly rooted in Jewish humanism, and capable of bringing Jewish communities to enthusiastic response and warm reaction. He should have respect for intellectual values.

I thought that these qualities were not so prominent in Rabin's record as to justify his elevation to the central place without the party and the public first having a chance of observing him in a less decisive role. General Ezer Weizman had caused a sensation by circulating his memories of Rabin's somewhat depressed reaction to the sudden crisis of May 1967. I believed it tasteless for this to have been done in the context of an electoral campaign, but even those who criticized Weizman's initiative did not assert that it was factually inaccurate.

The Central Committee had voted by secret ballot on April 24. The vote surprised the country: Rabin 289; Peres 245. For the first time the "machine" candidate had nearly been overthrown. The procedural precedent was far-reaching. It was unlikely that we would ever return to the tradition of unopposed election of leaders after consecration by party chieftains in a smoke-filled room. Henceforward, the race would belong to the swift.

My first inclination was to announce that in view of my strong preferential stand in the leadership discussion, I would not take office in the Cabinet that Rabin would compose. I believed that by its choice of leader the party had made an error and that there would be no stability ahead. It would be best for me to disengage. But there was strong dissuasion from Peres. He called me from Tel Aviv at my Jerusalem residence to thank me for my part in bringing many votes to his column. It was the unexpected strength of his showing that ensured him the second place in the hierarchy. The next morning he visited me in Jerusalem. He urged that I accept the continuation of my service under Rabin. I said that this was unlikely to be offered. Peres disagreed. He believed that Rabin would find it necessary to offer me membership in the Cabinet in order to heal wounds and ensure a balance. A Rabin-Peres-Eban team in the political arena would have a special equilibrium and a broad resonance. I could not deny that it was the practice in parliamentary countries for Cabinets to be formed among those who had taken contrary attitudes in the leadership ballot. I decided to let matters take their course. My resolve was to apply all my thought and care to my part in the Syrian-Israeli disengagement negotiations. Kissinger was about to resume his journeys in the Middle East. If this effort failed, the precise composition of our new Cabinet would become a marginal issue amid the ruin and grief of renewed war.

The Syrian demands for disengagement were an ultimatum calling for an Israeli withdrawal so deep as to put the northern part of our country at Syria's mercy. But Kissinger was right in his assumption that an attritional diplomacy would deflate Assad's claims. At an early stage Dayan and I were united in our willingness to regard disengagement as a national objective of sufficient value to justify the sacrifice of Kuneitra. The list of Israeli gains was long: the saving of lives on the Golan Heights; the return of prisoners; the prospect that our economy could swing into full momentum; a chance for the Israeli Defense Forces to recuperate in equipment and strategic planning; the advantage of closer relations with the United States; the strengthening of American influence in Damascus; the corresponding weakening of Soviet prestige; and, perhaps, the first glimmer of some new horizon in Syrian-Israeli relations. There was also the calculation that our agreement with Egypt could become stable only if Sadat was taken out of the solitude which he had incurred in the Arab world by his agreement with Israel.

These were solid advantages, but they looked less solid on the map than the visible, concrete territory gained by Syria. The fact that we were exchanging territory for nonterritorial advantages should have been self-evident to Israeli opinion. Was this not the rationality under which we were holding territories beyond our previous lines? Yet the lack of symmetry between our concessions and our advantages made it easy for our opponents at home to ridicule the transaction on which we were embarked. The fact that Dayan and General Mordechai Gur, who led the defense establishment, adopted a flexible approach to the Syrian negotiations was of decisive weight. It refuted the opposition theory that the proposed withdrawal was a sacrifice of permanent security needs to temporary diplomatic convenience. The unity of our diplomatic and military arms also made it easier for us to overcome the dark predictions of General Arik Sharon and his Likud colleagues that there would be catastrophic results for our security if we gave up Kuneitra. The same applied to the nonsensical theory, of which we heard much in some religious quarters, that giving up Kuneitra would lead us down a slope, at the bottom of which we would be abandoning the Western Wall. "If I forget thee, O Kuneitra, may my right hand forget its cunning" was my ironic response to the zealots who argued in this way.

But the withdrawal of our forces from the new salient and from Kuneitra made it necessary for our generals to bargain hard for the surrounding hills. Kissinger even became exasperated by what he called our "Himalaya complex," as well as by the fact that he had to commute between Jerusalem and Damascus "like a carpet-seller peddling a hundred meters at a time." On one of our innumerable journeys to the airport, I explained that what Americans might regard as minute topographical detail could mean life or death for many Israelis in the north of our country. Despite occasional outbursts of impatience, the Secretary soon returned to his familiar tenacity. It was an arduous ordeal for him. He went to Cairo to enlist Sadat's support, and to Cyprus for a meeting with Gromyko. The Soviet Union was resentful of the spectacle of the "revolutionary" Syrian regime drawing closer to the United States as a result of

Kissinger's mediation. When Gromyko asked Kissinger to press Israel to be more "flexible," Kissinger neatly responded with a suggestion that Gromyko fly to Jerusalem to try his luck. The truth is that the Soviet Union was reaping the disadvantages which I had predicted to Ambassador Chuvakhin when he came to announce the rupture of relations in my office in Tel Aviv in June 1967. Kissinger believed that he had softened Soviet opposition to a disengagement agreement. He had also been led by Gromyko to believe that in the interest of détente, the Soviet Union would liberalize the exiting of Jews from the USSR to the extent of 60,000 a year. This proved to be an illusion.

When the negotiations about the disengagement line came to an end, we were still not in sight of a haven. Assad was reluctant to establish a real buffer zone with hundreds of UN troops; reluctant to have Mount Hermon demilitarized after Israel's withdrawal; reluctant to have Israeli troops on the hills even after we conceded Kuneitra. Meanwhile, the Palestinian terrorists struck such an evil blow that all else was put aside. On May 15 they crossed the northern frontier and seized the schoolhouse at Ma'alot, where they held dozens of children and teachers, mostly from Safed, who were on an excursion during the summer vacation. We were in Cabinet session all day while the terrorists sought to bargain through the French and Rumanian ambassadors for the release of some of their saboteur colleagues held in Israeli prisons. In the end, on Dayan's initiative, the Israeli forces stormed the building and killed all the terrorists, but not before one of them had turned his machine gun for a split second on the children, killing twenty-four of them as well as one soldier. Despite this tragedy, most Israelis agreed that the decision to attempt a forcible release was correct. It embodied an important antiterrorist principle which had succeeded with the Sabena aircraft hijacked in 1972, and was to have triumphant results at Entebbe in July 1976.

While the suspense and agony of the Ma'alot attack were enacted, Kissinger awaited events in his Jerusalem hotel. He had now been joined by Nancy Kissinger, who added her personal grace and intelligence to the informal contacts of Americans and Israelis between our official sessions. The shuttle operation became more and more like a "cliff hanger." Time and again it appeared as if the effort was doomed to failure. On one occasion I had actually made arrangements for a hall to be hired at Lod Airport in which Kissinger would announce the "suspension" of the negotiations. We had even worked out a communiqué to this effect. He would not admit defeat. He would say that the gap between the parties had been narrowed, but that events in Washington, where the Vietnam crisis was reaching its culmination, demanded his presence. He would rely on the parties to think over their positions and to try to overcome remaining differences within a few weeks.

Yet we all knew in our hearts that if the talks were broken off, they were unlikely to be renewed. Apart from the rumblings in Southeast Asia, the final stages in the Watergate crisis were holding the American people in a grip of suspense. This made President Nixon almost fanatically avid for success in the Middle East. Time and again when Kissinger believed that his own dignity, as well as the prestige of his country, obliged him to abandon his efforts, a message from the White House would exhort him to go on trying beyond any rational point of hope.

Once the disengagement line and the UN buffer zone were agreed upon, we came to the question of thinning out troops and weapons on either side of the line. This did not have as much significance as with the Egyptian agreement; the distances were so small that even if the parties respected their signatures, it would be a matter of a few hours before large troop concentrations could be brought into close proximity again. We spent two or three days attempting to overcome Syria's refusal to make a commitment, analogous to that of Sadat, for preventing terrorist activity across the disengagement and cease-fire lines. Assad, who was then the main protector of the Palestinian terrorists, refused to include any such provision. Kissinger's solution was to give us an American-backed promise that if terrorists attacked us from Syria, Israel's forceful reaction would be regarded as justified; the United States would veto any proposal in the UN Security Council directed against Israel for exercising its right of self-defense.

On May 29, 1974, we were able to sink back with a sense of relief. With my colleagues in the Foreign Ministry, I was up all night helping to draft the agreement, the accompanying protocols and various U.S.-Israeli exchanges designed to compensate us with American political support and arms supplies for what we had not been able to get from the Syrians. At a reception to mark the end of the negotiations, Golda said, "Today all our efforts that seemed impossible are crowned with success. From today on, I hope that quiet will prevail on the northern borders, a day when mothers and children both in Syria and Israel will be able to go to sleep quietly."

It now remained for us to arrange for the return of our prisoners. Before the discussion entered its first operative stage, Kissinger had brought us a list of over sixty prisoners who were being held in a Damascus jail. Grim rumors had been circulating to the effect that not more than twenty of them were still alive. The relief of families and of the whole country was immense.

As I worked away at the final drafting of the agreement, I had the sensation that an important gain for sanity and proportion had been won. When I reflected on the temper of the Syrian regime, on the harshness of Syria's first proposals, and on the daily toll of young Israeli lives on the Golan Heights, I could not fail to respect the U.S. role in this development. American-Israeli relations reached their peak that day. We had not secured peace, but we had moved away from the volcanic imminence of war. The controversies between Washington and Jerusalem had often been acute, but their general effect was to bring us closer together in mutual confidence.

Kissinger's success was enthusiastically celebrated in America and across the world. The improbable achievement of bringing Israel and Syria to agreement gave him a "superman" image in world opinion to which he probably now looks back with nostalgia. In Israel the tumult of opposition died down once the Israeli government made its decision with the full concurrence of our military leaders. There was a sense of drama when on Friday, May 31, 1974, Israeli and Syrian military delegations sat around a table in Geneva under the chairmanship of Major General Ensio Siilasvuo, the head of the UN Observer team, in order to sign the agreement. The Syrians refused any photography and were, of course, adamant against any exchanges of courtesy between the signatory delegates. Nevertheless, the contractual atmosphere that had grown up in our agreement with Egypt had now been consolidated. The way seemed open to an agreement with Jordan or a new stage at the Geneva Conference.

There had been a strange convergence between our international negotiations and our domestic power struggle. The Israeli negotiating team, composed of Golda Meir, Dayan, Allon and myself, had been reinforced since April by Rabin and Peres, who were destined for the highest offices in the next Cabinet. It was thought wise to ensure continuity of both knowledge and responsibility. Rabin was reticent during the negotiations. Peres participated more actively, especially in explaining the complexities of the discussions to the public in his capacity as Minister of Information. But they each gave their assent to the final compromise. Thus the competence of the outgoing Administration could not be challenged by referring to its brief lease on life.

The negotiations were so voracious of my time and energy that I could spare little thought for what was happening on the internal front. As a result of our Central Committee's decision in April,

Rabin had been charged with assembling a new coalition. The contacts between party leaders were so protracted that they brought us very near the date after which Rabin would have to report to President Katzir on his inability within the prescribed time limit to present an Administration that could win the confidence of the Knesset. The main difficulty was the refusal of the National Religious Party to join a coalition without the accompanying presence of the militant Likud under Menachem Begin. But there were also maneuvers, posturings and even intrigues about the posts to be held by Labor ministers.

After Peres' talk with me late in April, I had decided not to close the door on my possible participation in a new Cabinet, but I would respond concretely only if concrete proposals were made. During all those weeks, emissaries claiming to speak for Rabin kept giving assurances that I would be asked to remain in the new Cabinet. Other party leaders hoped that I would respond. On one occasion there were rumors that Allon was being suggested for my post; but without prompting from me, he had sent me a note at the Knesset table asserting that this was not true, and that he would refuse to supersede me. He then went to London in May for what was supposed to be a protracted absence. He had been recalled because of the Ma'alot raid; as Minister of Education he had been responsible for the safety of the children who became victims of the PLO. On June 1 Rabin asked if he could come and see me the following day to discuss the new Cabinet and my own place within it. I agreed, and a meeting was fixed. But on the morning on which it was due to take place, I turned on the radio at seven o'clock to hear an announcement of the new line-up; Allon was to be both Deputy Prime Minister and Foreign Minister, with Peres as Minister of Defense and myself as "Minister of Information"!

It was clear that without my knowledge Rabin not only had offered Allon the portfolio which I was holding but had also closed other doors by awarding Allon the deputy premiership as well. Moreover, I had heard all this for the first time on the radio. I had always maintained, as was later to become evident to Shimon Peres and Aharon Yariv, that a separate Ministry of Information was not viable within a Cabinet system under which all department heads were responsible for informing the public about their own responsibilities and problems. A separate Information Ministry was bound to fail, as it subsequently did after Yariv's brief tenure.

An hour or so after the radio announcement, as we sat around the table at the Cabinet session, I passed a note to my neighbor, Allon, asking him if the radio report was true. With some embarrassment he replied in writing: "Yes." I immediately drafted a statement for the radio and the press stating that I had not been approached nor had I agreed to accept the position allotted to me in Rabin's Cabinet, and that in view of what had transpired, I would not now wish to take office under Rabin at all.

The repercussions within our party became more serious. Sapir, on hearing the results of Rabin's hesitations about my place in the Cabinet, publicly announced that he had no intention of joining the new Administration. On the radio he asserted that my exclusion was a primary factor in his decision.

The discomfort created by the radio announcement did not easily abate. Rabin insisted on meeting me in spite of a note that I had sent him stating that this would be unnecessary, since the Cabinet was already announced. When he came to my residence in Balfour Street, only two or three hours remained before our party was due to ratify the list of its own representatives in its Cabinet. Rabin said that he would like me to be in his Cabinet and asked me if I had anything to suggest. I replied that it was surely for the Prime Minister–designate to make specific offers, and not for me to make requests. Rabin agreed that this was correct. He went on to add that he understood my objections to the Information Ministry, and no longer made that proposal; all he had come to say was that he wished me to be in the Cabinet and would like to know what I thought I could do. An hour later, the party convened and voted for Rabin's Cabinet. A few minutes before the vote the party secretary-general, Aharon Yadin, came to ask if I would agree to be a minister and leave the definition of my task till later. I declined.

The events of the last few days, beginning with the radio announcement, had strangely put me at peace with myself. My last action as Cabinet minister was to propose and secure the adoption of a decision for the establishment of a new Research and Planning Department of the Foreign Ministry. This had been recommended by the Agranat Commission as a means of ensuring that an Israeli government would have more than one source of appraisal about Arab intentions and policy trends among the powers. In previous years my predecessors had not been able—and perhaps not particularly keen—to obtain budgetary resources enabling them to "compete" with the powerful Mossad and Military Intelligence, whose large staffs probed the complexities of Middle Eastern politics. The total failure of Military Intelligence to predict or follow Sadat's war plan through the many stages of its evolution had deflated the Israeli "intelligence legend." The small research division in my ministry had given more serious indication of Egypt's bellicose intentions, but its small voice was scarcely heard, and I doubt if the Prime Minister or Defense Minister read its modestly mimeographed reports. Although the American intelligence failure proves that even a multiplicity of sources is no guarantee of successful appreciation, I believe in the avoidance of monopoly and the value or diversity in all intellectual domains, and I was pleased to launch this new enterprise.

The final Cabinet session which I attended was ceremonial and valedictory. Nostalgic speeches attended Mrs. Golda Meir on her departure. There were some references to my own Cabinet career, mostly from ministers who had not always been in accord with my views. Shimon Peres to my surprise said of me briefly, "The Jewish people has had many voices in its history but it has never had a voice that reverberated from one end of the world to another with such resonance as this."

On June 4 I assembled my personnel on the Foreign Ministry lawn. I could see that they were quite emotional. Many of them had long been my disciples in international politics and diplomacy. I told them that Israel's cause could be represented either with moral incisiveness and intellectual elevation, or with routine, prosaic dullness. In the former case, our policies would have a strong resonance among the Jewish people and throughout the world. It mattered very much not only what Israel's policies were, but how they were expressed. I wished the Ministry success in its future responsibilities, then walked away from the Foreign Ministry building, which I have not entered since that day.

I was now in an unfamiliar situation. Since joining the Zionist service in 1946, I had been in continual harness. Of the twenty-six years that had passed since the establishment of Israel, I had spent eleven in senior diplomatic posts and nearly fifteen as a Cabinet minister. Apart from a six-month interval between the end of my embassy mission in 1959 and the formation of the Cabinet at the end of that year, I had borne the challenge and burden of office in the public eye. I had played an intense role in our party's electoral struggle on four separate occasions. From the early fight for independence in 1948 right through to the Geneva Peace Conference in 1974, I had been a leading participant in Israel's international battles. I had traversed the whole world in this cause, from Buenos Aires to Wellington, from Scandinavia to East Africa. The satisfactions had come from the bite and thrust of conflict and from the general upward curve of our national history. The price had been paid in human terms, in long separations from my family, in an implacable series of tensions, in the strangling effects of security precautions and protocolar fuss. The simple pleasures of walking down a city street, of driving into a countryside, of dropping haphazardly into a theater or shop, of visiting friends without the accompanying panoply of office, had all been unknown.

More important, I had lacked the freedom of self-expression. I always had to remember that I was speaking not for myself but for a country, a government or a party which might not want to be committed to everything that I believed or said. Now and again, especially in the two years before the Yom Kippur War, I had broken out of these limitations, to present a clear picture of my personal viewpoints. This, however, was not a luxury that I could often afford. My fellow countrymen and many well-wishers across the world had only been able to see and hear me through the screen of reticences that surrounds a Cabinet minister and, especially, a Minister for Foreign Affairs. In my books *Voice of Israel, My People* and *My Country* I had set out my views as a writer and scholar without any sense of official reservation. But these works dealt with matters in which most Israelis were in harmony. On issues held in controversy, the image of my thought and character had been blurred by the restraint of office and collective responsibility. I could now bring it to light.

On the first Sunday after the formation of the Cabinet without my membership, I awakened with a sense of void. There was almost a spontaneous inclination to rush from a hurried breakfast into my car, up the coastal road from Herzliya to Jerusalem for the Cabinet meeting. Instead, I crossed my back garden into the swimming pool of the Sharon Hotel and began to taste the tranquillities of leisure. A Knesset colleague, sitting at poolside, shouted to me in the water, "Well, isn't it nicer like this?" I frankly agreed with him. The next day in the Knesset I occupied the traditional place, just behind the government benches, reserved for former ministers.

In a sense, I was beginning a parliamentary career for the first time. Although ministers are members of the Knesset, their parliamentary role is necessarily circumscribed. They hardly ever have a chance of following general discussions on matters outside their competence.

Yet my first human feeling on abandoning office was an intense passion for change. I wanted to get out of the environment of intrigue and shock in which I had lived during the past few weeks.

I had some reason to feel resentful at my party; it had laid every possible burden upon me. It had never found me wanting; yet it had now acted toward me with a lack of normal courtesy. Thus, when cables began to come in offering me new opportunities to use my experience, I could not fail to be moved. The University of Haifa asked me to accept a visiting-professorship; at the same time I received a moving communication from American universities, including Columbia. President William McGill invited me to spend a whole year reading, writing and teaching, and giving the university body the benefit of my experience and thought. I was tempted to take this invitation at its full scope and go away for a year. This, however, would have meant resigning my seat in the Knesset and thereby removing myself from parliamentary and party life. I saw no reason to give so much comfort to my rivals and adversaries. Why should I not remain in the field? This would be salutary for them, and in some degree, emotionally rewarding for myself. I therefore agreed to teach at Columbia for one semester, between September and mid-December 1974. More than half of this period would, in any case, fall within the Knesset recess, so that my parliamentary absence would be a matter of a few weeks during which I would decide, if necessary, to fly back for crucial votes.

After correspondence with Harvey Picker, dean of the School of International Relations at Columbia, I decided to teach a postgraduate course on "multilateral diplomacy" and to hold a seminar on "Deterrence and Miscalculation in War as Illustrated by the Middle Eastern Conflict 1948–1973." Suzy and I took a two-week vacation in Europe and returned home to prepare for our new adventure. We arrived in New York on the eve of Labor Day and prepared for my professorial career, taking up residence in Meyer Weisgal's apartment on Central Park South.

Despite my inclination to have a period of silence, I had found it necessary to express some views on public policy after leaving office. The Palestine terrorists organized within the PLO were making headway in gaining international recognition. When President Nixon and Secretary Kissinger visited Israel in June, their dialogue had been held with our new government. I had attended a reception in Nixon's honor in the Chagall Hall of the Knesset. As I passed him in the receiving line he said, "You've been trying for years to get me to come to Israel. I remember your suggesting this at my first dinner in your home in Washington more than fifteen years ago. And now that I come here, I find that you're no longer Foreign Minister."

I had a feeling that his political future would henceforth be shorter than mine. But he had a strange air of confidence for one so close to the brink.

The next day I had a talk with Secretary Kissinger, who expressed concern that the new Israeli government would feel bound to adopt a less mobile diplomacy than its predecessor. The test case was an interim agreement with Jordan. We had to decide whether we wanted King Hussein as our partner in negotiating the future of the West Bank and Gaza territories. If we were not willing or able to make a favorable decision, Kissinger said, "You will have to deal with the PLO and not with Hussein." He indicated a strong American preference for an integral Jordanian-Israeli-Palestinian negotiation, but he exercised no strong pressure. He clearly thought that the Israeli, rather than the American, interest was most intimately involved.

Prime Minister Rabin's first statements had concentrated on the theme that "the heart of the Middle Eastern problem" was the relationship between Israel and Egypt. The problems of Jordan and the Palestinians were, according to this view, subsidiary, and in any case, not urgent.

Writing in *Ma'ariv* and *Ha'aretz*, I took issue with this analysis. It was, of course, true that the decision to make war, to cease fire, to sign armistice and disengagement agreements had all been initiated by Egypt, which is the natural center of Arab culture and politics. On the other hand, the core of the dispute lay in the unresolved conflict between Israel and the Palestinian Arabs. In a sense, we were still fighting what I called the War of the Palestine Succession. The refusal of the Palestine Arabs to share sovereignty and territory with Israel had erupted into violence. Egypt and Syria had entered the arena not through any concern for their particular national interests, but in obedience to Arab solidarity. In a sense, therefore, the participation of the Arab states outside the Palestine area, although spectacular in scope and degree, was secondary in the strict sequence of logic. The first link in the chain of tragedy and discord lay within the area between the river and the sea.

I suggested that we now give priority to a Jordanian-Israeli agreement parallel with those concluded with Egypt and Syria, even if this meant giving Jordan a foothold across the river at Jericho to create an analogy with the Syrian gain of Kuneitra. I added: "If our Government says that it is impossible to make the transition to peace with Egypt and Syria in one leap without going through intermediate stages, why does this logic expire when we come to the problems of Jordan and the West Bank?" I specifically made clear that even if there was no military justification for disengagement, we ought to pursue that aim so as to prevent the PLO from monopolizing responsibility for representing the Palestinian cause.

These suggestions were rejected. I later learned that Yigal Allon had pressed views similar to my own. When he reached Washington and began conversations with American leaders, it was reported that Rabin had instructed him to keep off the subject of Jordan on the grounds that we could not have an election just because of Jericho. This was a subordination of international needs to domestic requirements. There was also a tendency to work for a new period of immobility. My view was that if a withdrawal from any part of the area west of the Jordan required a consultation of the electorate, our party and government should prefer that result to a new period of immobilism which would reinforce the PLO and weaken Israel's international position.

A second theme on which I dissented from the new government's policy concerned the Geneva Conference. In *Ha'aretz,* late in August, I criticized the abrupt discontinuity of the Israeli attitude on this point. What the Labor Alignment had portrayed in 1973 as a hopeful turning point had by the end of 1974 become a sinister peril in the eyes of our new leadership. Rabin took an apprehensive posture about the idea of a peace conference in which the conditions of a general settlement would be explored. It was argued that the Geneva Conference would produce a deadlock with the Arabs, and an inevitable conflict of views with the United States on the boundary question. It was said that an Israeli peace proposal, no matter how moderately conceived, stood no chance of Arab acceptance.

I felt that these objections were not convincing. A transition from an enthusiastic celebration of the Geneva idea to a panic-stricken evasion of its continuance was bound to weaken credibility at home and abroad. An imaginative Israeli plan, balancing a rigorous demand for peace with a readiness for territorial concessions, might well be rejected by the Arabs. But even in that case, we would gain a valuable by-product in terms of a closer understanding by world opinion of Israel's cause.

The Middle Eastern crisis, after all, persists not because of an Israeli refusal to evacuate territories, but because of an Arab refusal to make peace. Yet this truth would only become convincing if it emerged in an operative diplomatic test. If our primary aim was peace with the Arab states, with a "fall back" aim of winning international support, what valid objection could there be to a peace proposal which would hit at least one of those targets? In expounding this policy, I added that since we would inevitably have to seek American support for our minimal boundary modifications, it would be better to make the attempt before 1976, when presidential sensitivity to Israel's interests would be at its height, than to wait until 1977, when American policy makers would attach less weight to Israeli influence. The alternative to an Israeli peace initiative now would be a prolonged deadlock followed by "peace plans" put forward by other parties to which we would have to respond defensively.

The Rabin Government went a different way. The "Egypt First" doctrine was advanced in every speech. The "noncentrality" of the Palestine issue became an article of official faith. Geneva was shunned.

It was clear that the diplomatic momentum generated by the Meir government between the cease-fire in October 1973, through the six-point agreement and the Geneva Conference, up to the Egyptian and Syrian disengagement accords of 1974, would now slow down. Fourteen months were to elapse before a new interim agreement with Egypt was concluded. In the ensuing vacuum, the PLO leaped forward to broad international recognition, Jordan's role was eclipsed, and the United Nations adopted resolutions in favor of the PLO and against "racist Zionism" that would have been inconceivable a year or two before. The entry of the National Religious Party, including its radical wing, into the Cabinet, and the subsequent resignation of two moderate ministers, Shulamit Aloni and Aharon Yariv, and the appointment of General Sharon as the Prime Minister's national security adviser, accentuated the drift toward hawkishness.

I was now a spectator or—at most—a commentator of these events. At Columbia University I was warmed by the courtesy and friendship of the faculty and the student community. My inaugural lecture on "Multilateral Diplomacy" on September 9 was staged like the première of a new film. My three public lectures filled the McMillan Auditorium, and my classes and seminars went forward in a creative intellectual tension. I was strengthened in my belief that the study of international relations at universities is enriched when empirical experience is joined to theoretical investigation. Universities in America are more successful in achieving this balance than anywhere else.

The months I was spending in the United States were a welcome relief from the tensions of the political arena. It was a novel experience to move about in freedom, to develop my reflection and thinking in the shelter of a great university, to meet large audiences all over the United States in lectures and discussions in which I was free to express my personal views without the inhibition or obscurities of diplomacy. I was not by any means anonymous. I could still not walk down a street or enter a cab without Americans engaging me in intense and friendly dialogue about Israel, the Middle East, or more embarrassingly, about myself. The public seemed puzzled about the circumstances that had led to my absence from the international arena. On the day in November when Arafat was obsequiously applauded in the United Nations General Assembly, a strong current of despondency pervaded the minds of Jews and other friends of Israel in New York. The world seemed to belong to our foes.

I received many telephone calls asking if there was no chance of my joining Israel's team in its vigorous struggle in the United Nations and of attempting my own formulation of Israel's vision. Since no call came from the Israeli government, I said nothing and quietly went ahead with my weekly seminar. But when the major Jewish organizations planned a mass demonstration against the United Nations' invitation to Arafat, and requested me to address it, they received "a negative reaction" from the Foreign Ministry in Jerusalem. At this point, the docility of the Presidents' Conference expired. As Rabbi Israel Miller and Yehuda Hellman quietly said to me, "We told the embassy frankly that in this matter we shall not accept the Israeli government's advice. We're not going to have a demonstration of Jewish solidarity downtown and you in New York not taking part." Their view prevailed, and in a very short address to a hundred thousand demonstrators I was heartened by a cordial response.

It was not easy to take leave of Columbia University or to reject a generous offer from Johns Hopkins University to accept a visiting professorship in international organizations at its Institute of Advanced Studies in Washington. But toward the end of the year the emotional and intellectual pull of home and country had begun to work on me too strongly to be denied. There were also parliamentary and political challenges ahead.

Back in Israel at the beginning of 1975, I plunged into activity in the Knesset and the party. I became the chairman of Beit Berl, the Labor Party's education and research bureau, named after Berl Katzenelson. On the Beit Berl grounds there is also a college specializing in the social sciences and attended largely by students who could not possibly afford to study at the Hebrew University or Tel Aviv University. It is the nucleus of a workers' university, the establishment of which owes much to the persevering efforts of its director, Nahum Shamir. But my own decision to accept the chairmanship of the Berl Katzenelson Foundation was motivated less by the desire to intervene in the college—which was developing well—than by an ambition to increase the intellectual energy of the Labor movement.

For the party had virtually ceased to function after the 1974 leadership struggle. The rank and file in local branches was not being consulted on the national issues. I decided to try to add three dimensions to the party's activity: the establishment of a forum in which the major political and social problems were discussed; the publication of a monthly journal; and the constitution of "think teams" which would analyze and renovate the Labor movement's political doctrines. By the end of 1975 all these enterprises were in working order. The Beit Berl discussions on Middle Eastern policy, Israel's economic problems, Zionism and the Israeli Arabs, drew large crowds and did something to rehabilitate our image as a party dedicated to serious thought, not only to the rivalries of power. The monthly journal *Migvan,* edited by Asher Maniv, a leading thinker in the kibbutz movement, set a high standard of comment and public dialogue; and the "think teams" generated some intellectual energy within a movement which had almost ceased to ask itself any questions beyond the major interrogative of maintaining power.

The paradox was that I was now contributing more directly to the party which had, in a sense, "rejected" me from its service than I had been able to do when I held high offices of state. My conviction was that with all its defects, the Labor Party was still the only viable and coherent source of leadership in an otherwise fragmented political arena. While some leaders outside its ranks such as Begin, Sharon and Yigael Yadin commanded varying degrees of support, the Labor Party could still claim the broadest "gallery" of men able to elicit public confidence. The trouble was that since Mrs. Meir's resignation, the leading personalities had split into individual domains of thought and action. There was no authority sufficient to convert them into a team driving the nation toward visible goals.

The result was that less than two years after the election of a new leader, the leadership question was still open. The Prime Minister was unable to secure the implementation of his own decisions, such as the establishment of a Ministry of Social Security; or to ensure the execution of Cabinet decisions, such as the removal of a settlement established provocatively at Kaddum in the populated area of the West Bank by a group of political zealots belonging to an organization called Gush Emunim. He had also committed an error in nominating for Governor of the Bank of Israel an official—Asher Yadlin—who was already under investigation and was later imprisoned for bribery.

The economy was afflicted by unchecked inflation. A measure of salutary tax reform was instituted, but the dynamic task of promoting economic growth was not fulfilled. The old economic leadership of Eshkol and Sapir was not always distinguished by a methodical approach, but it was inspired by an instinct for movement and growth. It was believed that it was better to build many things of which some might fail than to build nothing out of a fear of failure. The new Cabinet team did not manage to reach an intimate partnership with Diaspora Jewry, such as its predecessor had maintained. Rabin became publicly alienated from his own colleagues, including Minister of Defense Shimon Peres. He had launched verbal assaults on the entire teachers' community and had called on the nation to accept in June that which he had strenuously opposed in March, namely, a withdrawal from the Abu Rodeis oil fields in Sinai and the passes of Mitla and Gidi without an Egyptian decision to abandon the claim of a "state of war." The interim agreement negotiated by Kissinger and concluded in September 1975 gave stability and depth to the 1974 disengagement agreement, but even those like myself who strongly supported it were disturbed by the weakening of Israel's credibility through so sudden a change of position from virulent rejection to self-congratulatory acceptance a few months later.

The decline of public morale was arrested by an extraordinary feat of arms by the Israel Defense Forces on July 4, 1976. An Air France plane had been hijacked in Athens by Palestinian terrorists and taken to Entebbe in Uganda. There were over a hundred Israelis among the hostages. The non-Israelis were released, and we were left with the nightmare situation of knowing that our fellow citizens were under the fragile mercy of terrorists who, in their turn, were being granted the protection of our savage foe President Idi Amin. At first the Israeli government agreed to negotiate the exchange of these hostages for the release of PLO terrorists, including Akomoto, the Japanese assassin of passengers at Lod Airport in 1972, and Bishop Capucci, who had exploited his sacred immunities to smuggle weapons for the Fatah terrorists. But when the defense authorities proposed a military solution, this was daringly approved. An armed expedition of airborne troops flew from Israel to Uganda, forcibly rescued the Israeli hostages from their captors and flew homeward to the proud relief of all Israelis and the incredulous admiration of the world. It was hard to recall a military exploit of greater daring, skill and human resourcefulness. Israelis, unduly depressed by the Yom Kippur War, suddenly felt a new surge of self-confidence. The typically Israeli qualities of resilience and verve had, after all, not been eclipsed or lost.

For this very reason the nation longed for a more sustained feeling of self-assurance. In 1976 many party leaders began to canvass the idea of my return to the Cabinet. I declined these overtures out of a feeling that a nondepartmental minister could not do anything effective in the declining months of Rabin's term. My conviction was that we needed not a mere cosmetic correction of the Cabinet's image but a fundamental opening of the whole question of party and national leadership. Most of my friends advised me to consider myself as being in reserve for the highest position rather than as a mere addendum to an uncongenial team. I therefore announced my intention to stay free, to exercise my critical judgment as effectively and usefully as possible, and to be available for a return to the national leadership at a more effective level.

In 1977 I entered the arena of combat again. I was successful on the level of party support, winning third place—after Peres and Allon—on the party list with a personal vote of 80 percent. But the Labor movement's long command of Israeli politics was at an end. Instead of joining my former colleagues at the Cabinet table, I was to join them on the opposition benches as Menachem Begin led his Likud Party to power.

In Retrospect

MY EIGHT YEARS AS FOREIGN MINISTER TOOK ME TO ALL FIVE CONTINENTS and brought a rich harvest in human experience. The center for my work was the Foreign Ministry complex in West Jerusalem, a collection of motel-like huts surrounded by green lawns and slim asphalt roadlets. The flat profile was disrupted only by one building that "towered" for all of two floors, and accommodated the minister, the director-general and a few of the senior ministry officials. Every year an eminent architect would show me the plans for the ultimate and permanent edifice in which the ministry would come into its full splendor. And every year economic difficulties put the plan back into the filing cabinet. So we lingered on in the temporary durability of our little motel. It would be impossible to conceive or contrive an arrangement more hostile to administrative efficiency.

Yet within this unpromising framework there had grown up across the years a family of professional diplomats who could rival the best of their colleagues in other lands. My own directors-general, Gideon Rafael and Mordechai Gazit, were men of sharp analytical mind and with a skeptical view of what Israel could realistically expect of a self-interested world. There was a rich diversity of linguistic talents. The ministry had come into existence with improvised haste in 1948, and Moshe Sharett had inevitably chosen men and women with a knowledge of Western languages, especially English. His successor, Golda Meir, has written about her discomfort at working with so many people from a nontypical and somewhat uniform environment and during my tenure the foreign service was naturally in constant replenishment, with the original "Anglo-Saxons" giving way to a broader variety of Israeli representation drawn from all sectors of our society. This came about partly because of the growing number of new nations. I was not always convinced that we really needed over twenty separate embassies in Africa—more than all but the greatest powers, but one of the advantages was that a young Israeli foreign-service officer could realistically dream of an ambassador's portfolio if he was willing to give a dozen years to a foreign-service career.

Diplomacy has developed across the centuries as a sacred calling requiring early discipleship and constant devotion. Its members live in a kind of subsidized international aristocracy whose lavish style and studied mannerisms have long been irrelevant to twentieth-century life. In our foreign service we attempted some informality of speech and dress, but in the last resort, there is no escape from the need to accept the international norms. The diplomat faces the danger of alienation. Like a scientist, he tends to develop a closer sense of affinity with professional colleagues across the world than with fellow citizens who do not practice his special arts. On the other hand, the Foreign Minister is a vehement champion of his own national interests. Indeed, his basic function is to get as much as possible for his country while giving as little as possible in return. He is more obliged than any of his colleagues to perceive the limitations of national positions and to seek legitimacy for national policies in terms of a broader ideal. Public opinion and his own colleagues are liable to make the Foreign Minister the scapegoat for the nation's inability to get its own way. Thus, diplomacy suffers from an incurable remoteness from popular understanding. I have noticed that when celebrated foreign ministers have moved on to the premiership—Spaak, Lester Pearson, Eden, Couve de Murville, Willy Brandt—they have seldom been able to assume the note of earthy, solid provincialism that makes for full authenticity.

There is also a constant need for self-defense against intrusion. Since war is everybody's tragedy, diplomacy is everybody's business. I often had the sensation of being one of twenty foreign ministers, since nearly all my colleagues gave vent in their oratory to their divergent views on our international relations. Most Israeli ministries are closed systems into which there is no penetration by other ministers. Theoretically, the Prime Minister has a right to overall supervision, but in Israel this is exercised only in the heat of crisis. During my tenure as Minister of Education and Culture, Ben Gurion sent me about six notes or inquiries in three years. This was regarded as an unusual degree of frequency; it meant that Ben Gurion was exceptionally interested in educational problems. It was natural for the Foreign Ministry to be more exposed to the Prime Minister's interest. Both Eshkol and Golda Meir, however, confined themselves to issues on which the fate of their Cabinet might depend, such as the outcome of our relations with American Presidents. Contrary to much legend and gossip, there were no jurisdictional tensions, and no attempt by ambassadors to sidetrack the Foreign Ministry in the communications network.

I would begin my day at seven-thirty with a voracious consumption of daily newspapers in my residence at Balfour Street. (This was a fairly imposing structure built in the 1930s by an Egyptian Jewish magnate with an appetite for spaciousness that must have seemed eccentric in the pioneering days. There was even a swimming pool on the roof which had never known a single gallon of water but which gave a symbolic sense of affluence.) There are too many daily newspapers in Israel by any relevant standard, and international politics is their favorite theme.

At the office I would begin by reading extensive cables from our missions, and consulting with the director-general and department heads. It is normal for government officials to complain about ministers who give them too much to do. The complaint against me was that I gave them too little to do. I suppose that I was the victim of my own professional training. I preferred to draft cables and directives to our leading envoys personally, and I wrote my own speeches in Hebrew, English, French and Spanish, thus reducing some of my associates to large frustration and imposing an unnecessarily heavy load upon myself. I tried to compensate by regular policy discussions with senior members of the ministry staff. Here the intellectual climate was utterly free. Nobody had any compunction about differing from the view of the minister or of the Cabinet as a whole. I was told that in the days of my formidable predecessor, Golda Meir, few dissenters were eager to rush in where angels feared to tread.

I did not succeed in my ambition of forcing ambassadors to curtail their cables. Nor did I ever receive a dispatch from an ambassador about an encounter in which he came off second-best.

The office routine was broken by regular Cabinet meetings and ministerial consultations. After 1967, the accent in Cabinet sessions was firmly placed on political and security matters. The National Unity Coalition had come into existence as a result of the war, and the Gahal members, especially Menachem Begin, had shown no more than a subsidiary interest in matters not directly concerned with our military and political struggle. They also had a chronic suspicion that

the "compromisers" at the head of our foreign relations would commit
the government to territorial concessions. I was therefore called upon
to report on our diplomatic contacts at greater length and detail than
I would have wished. My personal relations with Begin were cordial.
I opposed his views but respected his constancy and sincerity as well
as his record as a daring resistance fighter. When the Gahal ministers
left the Cabinet in 1970, my reports became more concise and sporadic.
Nevertheless, whenever I had visited Washington or another major
capital, the Cabinet wanted to hear a detailed narrative. At one
stage there was a ludicrous practice whereby ministers who had been
abroad on fund-raising missions would give their "impressions" at
length and in a somewhat touristic vein. This practice subsided under
Eshkol's businesslike administration and shriveled up completely
under Golda Meir.

Most Cabinet members had long sat together and had become
familiar with each other's individual quirks. We all knew that at the
end of an intricate debate Israel Galili would get out a piece of paper
and attempt to formulate the results, often with clinical objectivity, as
though the art of formulation was an end in itself, irrespective of his
own views about content. The Independent Liberals were represented
by Moshe Kol, a talkative and effervescent character who, in the
opinion of some colleagues, stressed the obvious too often and gave
rather full play to his range of Biblical quotations, though most of
his positions were balanced and lucid. He always had the courage
of his convictions and was not deterred by prime-ministerial frowns
or by the irritated fidgeting of the hawkish school.

For some years the head of the National Religious Party was Moshe
Haim Shapira, with whom I had a strong friendship. He would often
determine the balance of a vote. I used to visit him at his home at
Ahad Ha'am Street in Jerusalem on Saturday night to rehearse possible
scenarios that might occur in the Cabinet the next morning. He was
a slow, solid, sensible man, the authentic symbol of the best bourgeois
virtues.

I developed similar habits of consultation with the senior Mapam
minister, Israel Barzilai, a kibbutz leader of Polish origin with a
taste and talent for music who seemed to me to represent the Zionist
pioneer tradition in its purest form. When I had something difficult
to propose, I could usually rely on Barzilai, Kol and Shapira to give
me support in favor of political moderation.

The embarrassing fact, however, was they did not belong to my own
party. I could not forget Moshe Sharett's experience in winning
Pyrrhic victories over Ben Gurion by getting votes against him with
the aid of other parties. I therefore attached great value to my relations

with my Labor colleague Pinhas Sapir. His mind ranged simultaneously across dozens of preoccupations. These rarely included our international relations, but he had emphatic views on peace and security, which were closer to mine than to those of the two Prime Ministers, Eshkol and Golda Meir, whom he had done so much to bring to their positions of leadership. He was skeptical of the long-term value of the territories that we had administered since 1967. On the other hand, he set a high value on rigorous and vigilant preparedness in the Israel Defense Forces. He would vote with me against the more extreme proposals for military reprisal, but neither of us could fairly be described as pacifists. We understood that Israel's existence in the eyes of the Arabs was, at best, an enforced reality to which they would not reconcile themselves unless they were so compelled. Sapir was in frequent conflict with Moshe Dayan and later with Shimon Peres. I sometimes felt that his personal antagonisms weakened his objectivity. He would even vote against an underground railway for Tel Aviv if Peres was the Transport Minister who proposed it.

In the edifice of our coalitions, Sapir was the cohesive force. He did not allow dissent from Golda Meir to go to the point of threatening the Cabinet's authority. He was a master in the preservation of harmony with coalition partners. He was bulky, ponderous, chronically overweight, so bald that it was impossible to believe that he had ever had any hair to shed. There was a natural dominance in his posture and attitude. He seemed to hold the entire economy and domestic and political system in the palms of his huge, hairy, gorillalike hands that looked perfectly capable of strangling any unfortunate adversary. His voice was deep, gruff, ironic and indignant. Throughout all the years of my association with him, I could hardly remember him having completed a grammatical sentence. Names, ideas, and, above all, statistics would splutter from him like water from a tap in need of repair. Sometimes nothing would come out, and then a sudden irregular spurt of grunts and vague allusions which only the practiced expert could ever interpret. But he was precise in his intentions even if he was vague in his technique of expressing them.

His willingness to accept responsibility was unlimited. This was his greatest attribute—and perhaps his ultimate defect. There was no trouble in which the nation, the government, the coalition, the party or any individual colleague could find himself in which Sapir would not be willing to involve himself fully. This made it inevitable that multitudes of people in Israel, and later throughout the Jewish world, would lean upon him. In spite of his irascible voice and tongue, he was at heart a sentimental man incapable of prolonged anger. On the negative side, he took so much responsibility for so many things,

great and small, that the pattern of his life became chaotic, and great
areas of ambivalence crept into his management of affairs. As long as
there was integrity and loyalty around him, there was no great harm
in this. But since he had a somewhat childish trustfulness, it was not
difficult for questionable characters to flourish in the administrative
environment that he created and inspired. However, when all is said
and done and written, he remains an essentially creative memory.
Things would grow rapidly around Sapir—cities, suburbs, development
towns, agricultural settlements, schools, hospitals, cultural centers,
village synagogues, clinics, kindergartens, universities would all pass
under his auspices, moving from hopeless vision to concrete fulfillment. He had a special power of persuasion, not so much with large
audiences, who were somewhat perplexed by his incoherence, as with
individuals, especially Jews of newly made wealth with an East
European background behind them. These, whether in Israel or in the
United States or Europe, responded eagerly to his touch.

During moments of crisis for Israel, especially during our wars,
Sapir's invitations to Jewish leaders were regarded almost as commands. His lack of method in organizing himself often took its toll.
He would work through the day from six in the morning to past midnight, dividing his agenda into quarters of an hour. Some of these inevitably spilled over beyond the allotted time. The result was that his
appointment book and, even more, his waiting rooms, would be
crowded with jostling holders of appointments falling over one another in chaos. He trusted few memories other than his own, dealt with
far smaller matters than those that should occupy a senior minister,
had very little idea of delegation, and as a result, lived in a frenzy of
preoccupation. Even on his many missions abroad, once he checked
into a hotel, he would commence to organize his twenty conversations
a day on the same unorganized basis by which he directed his life in
Israel. Any idea of recreation or leisured reflection was foreign to his
impatient mind. Since he never made a systematic division of his
energies, he would often tend to be alert and dormant at the wrong
times; full of life and vigor at three-thirty in the morning when he
would make a telephone call to a disconcerted party branch leader in
Beersheba, but totally exhausted during Cabinet meetings or ministerial committees, during which he would quite simply and unashamedly
fall asleep. He was, in fact, the only man I have ever met who could
sleep not only during speeches made by others, but during speeches
made by himself. As a neighbor around the Cabinet table I used to
leave him undisturbed in slumber but would shake his sleeve on
behalf of governmental decorum when he began to snore. Even when
he was ostensibly in a deep torpor, the quotation of some relevant

financial statistic would bring him to sharp and often indignant reaction. He had a proprietarial and paternalistic approach to the Jewish people, the State of Israel, the government and the party, and his authority was respected even by those who were in sharp dissent with his economic policies. He was a kind of institutional Robin Hood, canalizing Jewish wealth from its centers of excessive accumulation to the broad pyramid of social needs in an immigrant community.

The Israeli Cabinet has never been adequately systematized, and my own upbringing made me somewhat impatient of its untidiness. I may have had a subconscious desire to see it working in accordance with the textbooks of Bagehot, Ivor Jennings and others. For example, it is my conviction that in the Israeli Cabinet there is too little communication by writing and too much by speech. One of the results is a proliferation of ministerial meetings, sometimes on matters which civil servants could well settle or at least prepare for ministerial decisions. Another consequence of this method is a lack of precision. I have always believed that submitting a proposal in writing commits a minister to a more rigorous exercise of self-criticism than remarks around a Cabinet table require. During one period I attempted to circulate documents setting out a policy decision in terms of tabulated pros and cons, with references in support of factual assumptions. When it turned out that these were not being read, I went back to verbal reporting.

On matters involving foreign affairs, my views and proposals often conflicted with those of Moshe Dayan, but despite our differences, the atmosphere of our relations was correct. We had been in the same "league" and age group and both of us could count on a wide range of support and familiarity beyond Israel's shores. Our policy dissensions were sharp but did not prevent a degree of mutual respect.

With Yigal Allon I had a strong harmony of political and tactical perception, so much so that I can hardly recall an instance in which I did not assist him in what he was trying to achieve. He was often under strong assault by numerous adversaries and he needed any support that he could get. My record with him was so consistent that his unwillingness to take any account of my position or to share responsibility with me in June 1974 was hard to explain.

The task of our Ministers of Justice was to ensure some order and decorum in the atmosphere of improvisation in which our Cabinets were conducted. The three men who held this office sequentially, Dov Joseph, Yaacov Shimshon Shapira and, toward the end, Chaim Zadok, played this role in different circumstances of temperament and character. Dov Joseph was slender to the point of emaciation, severe, ascetic, of puritanical disposition and generally unsmiling. Shapira, who succeeded him in 1963, seemed to be making a purposeful effort to be the opposite of his predecessor in every respect. He was large, corpulent, alternately genial and irascible, expansive and frankly at ease with the amenities of existence. He made us feel that it was possible to be legally correct without an exaggerated sense of suffering. In our political debates he would normally adopt a moderate and pragmatic course. So did Zadok, who was always incisive, detailed and specific in argument and invariably calm in disposition.

Over this variety of temperaments, Golda Meir presided with un-challenged authority. She intervened very little in the departmental concerns of ministers, placing the accent of her activity on the two or three points in which her interest was engaged. Her premiership was primarily an exercise in crisis management. There was always some conflagration to be put out, some peril lurking on a close horizon. She disliked long analytical processes and tended to reach conclusions ahead of the arguments in favor of them. She lived and planned for today and the immediate tomorrow, not for a future so remote as to seem abstract and unreal. Ben Gurion and Eshkol had also worked more through intuition than through analysis.

The method of operating in our Cabinet was empirical. There was no cumbersome Secretariat, and all efforts to establish "think tanks" or any other sophisticated process of analysis and decision were swept away by skeptical prime ministers. The result is that our Cabinets have been better at dealing with sudden emergencies than with deeper currents of development. They are more prone to react than to initiate. To secure real attention in an Israeli Cabinet it is not enough for an issue to be important; it also has to be visibly urgent. And after such emergencies or failures, there would be a search for fashionable remedies. Thus the 1973 crisis set off a debate about the merits of a small Cabinet in preference to a bulky table of twenty-one members. The fact is that intimate consultation among a few ministers is essential to the Cabinet system. Critics have talked darkly about a "kitchen," as though five or six ministers meeting on matters within their particular responsibility constituted a form of conspiracy rather than a normal aspect of Cabinet organization. Too much has been made of technicalities in our internal controversies. For example, the Agranat Commission, of which Professor Yigael Yadin was a member, chastised the Golda Meir Cabinet for not meeting in plenary session early in October 1973 to discuss the Arab troop concentrations. Yet when the terrorist action took place at Ma'alot, Yadin, by now a party politician, criticized the Cabinet for holding a bulky plenary session instead of delegating the matter to the few ministers concerned.

It is almost impossible for ministers ever to be right about procedure, and the mechanisms of a Cabinet are probably less important than the degree of confidence among its members.

With all its imperfections, Israeli Cabinet meetings were impressive occasions. They were inspired by a sense of gravity. And they drew us all together in a covenant of great things shared and heavy ordeals jointly surmounted.

It was natural that I should pay more than one visit a year to the United States apart from annual attendance at the United Nations. Israel has a fairly unique tradition in this respect. There has never been an instance in which an Israeli Prime Minister on an official visit to a foreign capital has been accompanied by the Foreign Minister. Similarly, the Foreign Minister has always made his own independent excursions into foreign capitals. Whenever the Prime Minister or Foreign Minister is abroad, the other is at home. I believe that this procedure has its advantages. For one thing, it gives the government a double chance of high-level negotiation abroad. It also enhances the dignity of the Foreign Minister, who appears in foreign capitals in his own right and not as somebody "in attendance." Each Israeli Prime Minister has had a Foreign Minister of independent international status and has probably, for that reason, not wished to confine him to a manifestly subsidiary role.

There is nothing in modern international relations quite like the American-Israeli relationship. What makes it incongruous at first sight is the immense disparity between the size and power of the partners. But this is outweighed by a deep harmony of values, memories, spiritual affinities and democratic loyalties. The two nations share a common belief in the creative power of a free society. And yet a hypochondriac fear of an imminent collapse in American-Israeli relations follows Israelis across all the years. When they see the immensity of Arab resources in territory, population, multiplicity of states, mineral and monetary wealth, Israelis often wonder why the United States should bother about them at all. I have heard my own countrymen say, "In America's position, we would not care if Israel lived or died." The paradox is that Americans rarely say this. In the United States, despite some doubts about Israel's policies and especially her present territorial status, the validity of the commitment to Israel is almost unquestioned. Americans believe that if the United States were to let Israel fall through lack of American support, there would be no confidence in American commitments to other countries. And it is on the credibility of the American deterrent that the security of the United States itself largely depends.

There were ups and downs. I can never forget that immediately after our admission to the UN in May 1949, the State Department, sometimes with presidential support, sent us fierce notes calling for concessions to the Arabs at the expense of our basic security. A few weeks later—all would be calm again. This pendulum swing has often been repeated over the years.

Since the Vietnam crisis, I have felt that Israel's position in the United States has, if anything, become more secure. Vietnam taught American Presidents that any true definition of the national interest must include a capacity for reconciling the domestic consensus with foreign policy. There is no other country in which public opinion catches up with official policy more quickly or sternly. There is also the feeling that a humiliating defeat for Israel in the Middle East would be a Soviet victory of such strength and resonance that it would leave the United States enfeebled. There is thus a basis of concrete interest and not only of sentiment on which our partnership can rely. To honor the commitment to Israel, it is not necessary for Americans to be pro-Israeli. It is enough to be pro-American.

All the Presidents with whom I dealt, from Truman to Nixon, were at ease with the special nature of Israel's hold on American opinion. I was thus less nervous than many of my colleagues when crises developed in American-Israeli relations. Anyone reading the Israeli newspapers since 1948 would get the impression that America and Israel have been in such constant opposition that one would be forced to wonder where all the military, economic and political support came from.

American Secretaries of State and their department, laden with a multiplicity of Arab contacts, bombarded by two dozen U.S. embassies in Arab capitals, have found it more difficult than their Presidents to accommodate themselves to the weight of Israeli reality in American policy. They are, after all, less concerned than Presidents with the domestic consensus. Yet, there is not one among them whom I would ever have called an adversary of Israel's basic interests. Some of them, especially Kissinger, deserved more Israeli appreciation than they received.

During the decades of my experience in the American-Israeli relationship, new generations have taken over in the leadership of the Senate, the Congress and the public life, without any negative effects on the American-Israel partnership. American senators from states in which the Jewish electorate is small have not fallen behind their colleagues from areas with large Jewish populations in support of Israel. If congressional leaders from Idaho, the State of Washington, Oregon, Alabama and the rest of the Deep South join representations on Israel's behalf, it is surely not because their electoral prospects are at issue. I do not find that the new generation of American congressional leaders are any less devoted to Israel's interests than their veteran predecessors. Insofar as an Israeli can ever feel at home outside Israel, it is in America that he feels less alienated from his environment than anywhere else.

While the Dulles and especially the Kissinger secretaryships stand out in my memory for the sharpness of their intellectual challenge, many people at a lower level also have left an imprint on my memory. Some diplomats such as Joseph J. Sisco accumulated an experience of Israel which surpassed that of many Jews. In the American-Jewish community I always found a warm welcome but I often felt that while they listened to me, American Jews had one eye directed to the gentile audience whom I was trying to convince. Their pride was often a function of Israel's capacity to impress non-Jewish Americans. With all the intimacy of American life, the Jews of the United States still feel that they need an external interpreter of their heritage and their particularity. My feeling was that we Israelis owed them an elevation of their confidence. They seemed to have everything else—security, economic opportunity, cultural vitality, the sense of belonging to a powerful, tolerant society. All they lacked until Israel's establishment was a certain dimension of dignity; this is precisely what Israel has been able to contribute. But by giving them this, we have paradoxically made their life in America psychologically more comfortable than before. We may even have removed one of the possible incentives for their emigration to Israel. If they can get their wealth and opportunity from America and their pride from Israel, there is very little that American Jews lack.

Thus the Carter Administration builds its policy toward Israel on a basis firmly laid across three decades. Late in 1966 I discussed the outlook at my home in Herzliya with Zbigniew Brzezinski, who later became the President's National Security Adviser. My feeling was that there would be many tensions between us and Washington, but no drastic break.

Among European statesmen whom I have known, some have stood out in the special preoccupation that Israel evoked in their hearts. Harold Wilson is pre-eminent among these. Whenever I came through London, he not only would want to know about our international fortunes, but would also show a detailed curiosity about our domestic relationships and rivalries. To be frank, he enjoyed Israeli gossip. Yet when I came away from him, I could never recall a malicious word. He was usually regarded as a cerebral rather than an emotional man. However, he was capable of strong fidelities that sometimes got him into trouble but were, in general, an ennobling dimension of his character. He and his colleagues came to terms with Britain's dwindling power in the Middle East and gave short shrift to the "Arabists" who still dreamed of a Pax Britannica sustained by friendly Arab clients.

For other European statesmen, like Joseph Luns of Holland, the Belgian Premier Eyskens and his Foreign Minister Harmel and, above all, Willy Brandt, Israel had an appeal and emotion that were not explicable in terms of our size or our weight. Canadians, Australians and New Zealanders seemed to be endemically pro-Israel, as though an understanding of our enterprise came to them from the very air of their pioneering experience.

In its Middle East policy, Europe since 1967 has been caught up in a constant struggle between its values and its interests. Its values, including the Holocaust memories, drive it toward Israel; its interests, especially those concerning oil and financial reserves, pull toward the Arab side. The balance oscillates and has never come fully to rest. Europe usually solves the issue by strong support of the pre-1967 Israel, her dreams, her enterprise, her social aspirations and Zionist vision, while withholding support of the territorial change that took place in 1967.

By the time I left office in 1974 I felt that I had played a role of some effect in the development of European-Israeli relations. I had initiated an intense rhythm of reciprocal ministerial visits, and I had made a special effort to draw Israel into the European community. In September 1972, addressing the Council of Europe, I had frankly said that the European attempts to harmonize separate sovereignty with economic integration held an important lesson for the Middle East. The Benelux relationship, under which states could be separate in the juridical sense but united in human accessibility and multiplicity of contact, is a good example for a future relationship between Israel, Lebanon and the Jordanian-Palestinian State. The twentieth-century boundary does not have to be a barrier; it can also constitute a bridge. There need be nothing hermetic about it. If this "community" vision sounds Utopian, were not Jean Monnet and the architects of the European Economic Community regarded as hopelessly visionary when they suggested the establishment of the Common Market amid the recent wounds of World War II?

There is such a thing in physics as fusion at high temperatures. The very intensity of a conflict may produce a sudden emergence of new thought and feeling. Whenever I am asked if Israel is European, African or Asian, my answer has always been that Israel is none of these. It is a Mediterranean state. It is across the Mediterranean that

Israel has sent and received her particular message. Mediterranean waters wash the shores of three continents—Europe, Asia and Africa—with each of which Israel has special links. There is thus no need for an exclusive continental definition of Israel's identity.

As I look back on my African experience, since my first initiative at the Rehovot Conference, I recall a capacity for common understanding with leaders who have shared my own humanistic background. In Nairobi, Accra, Abidjan and other capitals, I found that a common basis in Western humanism and in the mystique of national independence gave me a special link with African leaders. The obvious exception was, of course, Idi Amin Dada. He was my host for many hours during my official visit to Uganda when he was Chief of the Army under President Obote, and I came back to my home in Jerusalem bearing mementos of his lavish hospitality, including a large zebra skin to adorn a staircase. I have since removed it, in revulsion against its donor's savagery. When Amin became President, I was often at Lod Airport meeting his bulky figure, resplendently uniformed, as he descended from the Israeli-constructed jet aircraft which took him on his voyages. But the eccentricity of his character became apparent to me even before his alienation from us. Indeed, the trouble probably began because we refused him his "toys." I recall a conversation in 1972 in Moshe Dayan's home when President Amin suddenly told us that he wanted Israel to give him a couple of squadrons of Phantoms. He added as an afterthought that as he had no pilots, we would have to provide these as well. When I asked tentatively what he needed them for, he replied, "To bomb Dar-es-Salaam." He then stated that it was essential for Uganda to have an outlet to the sea. Turning to Dayan, he asked, "How long does it take to force an outlet to the sea? Six days, I understand." Dayan replied to me in surreptitious Hebrew that the man appeared unbalanced and could I get him out of there. I decided on a more diplomatic approach. I reminded the President that Israel was bound by treaty with the United States not to discuss the transference of such equipment without the approval of the original donor. I hoped at least to win time but he seemed to be irritated, and Israel never heard a friendly word from him again.

A short time afterward, when a British minister came on an official visit to Israel, he told me that an extraordinary thing had happened to him in London. Amin had told him that Israel had refused to give him Phantoms and that he must therefore ask for Harrier aircraft. When his British host inquired what the object of this was, he seems to have replied with consistency, "To bombard Tanzania." The classic

British reply is said to have been, "Mr. President, would you like another cup of tea?"

The fact remains that it was thereafter against Israel and Britain, who had refused him his weapons, that Amin was to direct the full blast of his vengeance. I am certain that most enlightened African leaders were not proud of the figure that Amin cut in the world. And yet, his capacity to heap insult and humiliation on Western statesmen may have evoked an underlying sympathy in the hearts of Africans who remembered how the Western colonial powers used to deal with them. One of the major problems of African nationalism is to avoid too sharp a pendulum swing. There is a danger that justified grievance against the humiliations of colonialism may lead to an inverse racialism under which anything white or Western would be regarded as alien and hostile. Statesmen such as Kenyatta, Houphouet-Boigny, Kenneth Kaunda, Hastings Banda and others can be relied upon to uphold a vision of a multinational society and not to allow past persecutions to generate a corresponding revenge. The lesson of Africa is not that decolonization came too early, but that it came too late, and with an inadequate degree of Western support which might have created a new and equal harmony in place of the injuries of the colonial decades.

The life of nations is not governed by their temporal memories alone. I developed a special fascination with the idea of cementing our relations with the Vatican. In this I was strongly supported by my friend and colleague Yaacov Herzog. Toward the end of his tenure, late in 1969, our ambassador in Rome, Emil Najar, proposed that he should seek to obtain an official encounter for me with the Pope. I gave him full encouragement, and Najar pursued his mission with tenacity. On a memorable day in October, my car with its Israeli banner drove through the Vatican gates. I confess that my mind was flooded with historic emotion. It had taken so long for the Church of Rome to accommodate itself to the persistence of Jewish identity, let alone to that of Jewish sovereignty in the Holy Land. Even though full diplomatic relations were not yet envisaged, my meeting seemed to mark a turning point. My talk with Pope Pius gave me a glimpse of the intense spirituality of his mind. His vocation seemed more religious than political. Yet his desire for innovation in the dialogue between the Church and the Jewish people came to expression. "The period of the Crusades is ended," he said to me. "It is now a question of harmony and coexistence." The photograph in which we exchanged our handshakes had symbolic significance for Jews everywhere. For the first time Israel and the Church were meeting in reciprocal understanding of their sovereignty. Three years later, this contact was elevated to prime-ministerial level when Golda Meir had a conversation with the Pontiff. It was a far cry from the Pope's journey to Israel through Megiddo in 1964, when he made such an intense effort to avoid giving his visit any implication of political recognition.

In that encounter the theme was not Israel as a Middle Eastern state, but the Jewish people as a universal nation. This dimension of experience was always central in my consciousness. I believe that it gave me a particular capacity for intimate discourse with Diaspora Jews. I often met difficulties and discords at home in Israel, but my relationship with Jews outside Israel has been constantly "romantic." It may be because I have never been in a competitive relationship with them, whereas the element of competition is never absent in Israeli politics. A deeper reason lies in the earnestness of my effort to interpret Israel to them in a spirit of common responsibility and mutual pride. Israel could make no greater error than to live within the limits of her geography rather than within the enlarging dimensions of her history and culture. Although I was active in the enterprises that brought many hundreds of millions of dollars to Israel, I always regarded my contacts with Jewish audiences primarily as occasions for dialogue about our common Jewish identity.

While the eight years of my stewardship at the Foreign Ministry and the preceding decade at Washington and the UN are, of course, the major landmarks, they do not monopolize the whole of my recollection. There was nothing particularly dignified about the way in which my party dispensed with me in the summer of 1974, but I did gain the opportunity to delve into the prosaic realities of Israeli society, and especially of the Labor movement. The fact that I was now able to speak with frankness and occasional bellicosity seemed to improve my relationship with the Israeli public. I no longer had to declaim careful formulas. Politicians and diplomats sometimes utter sentences as though they are laying eggs; everything comes out in uniform and predictable shape. Now I could say what I thought in the way that I deemed best, and the response was sometimes electric.

When the contest for the party leadership was renewed in the early months of 1977 I gave my full endorsement to Peres, whom I had supported back in 1974. He often acknowledged that by bringing him many supporters of the Mapai wing in our party, and also among those who held moderate political views, I had given his candidacy a weight that it would not otherwise have possessed. I doubt that he would have achieved a vote of 49.7 percent against Rabin in the party conference without my support, and but for this impressive showing, he would not automatically have succeeded to the party leadership when Rabin resigned in 1977. I have never sought to disguise the differences of policy and temperament that divide me from Peres, but Israeli leadership is always an exercise in synthesis. It must always be diverse, never monolithic—it is a question of balance. What is important to me in an Israeli politician is not his formulations about territories, but whether he has a sense of innovation rather than a habit of reaction; whether he believes in some of the intangible elements in Jewish experience such as the power of science, intellectual effort and social originality. I feel more at home with the intellectually adventurous than with the temperamentally cautious, and it is this that gave me common ground with Peres when Rabin's unhappy era of leadership came to an end.

The Labor movement had never become fully at ease with the Rabin team, and the leadership struggle was renewed when the election year 1977 dawned. By that time the United States was moving into its new era under President Jimmy Carter. Free from domestic preoccupation, America could resume its mediatory role in the Middle East. The savage Lebanese war, in which Israel had combined military restraint with humanitarian aid to refugees from South Lebanon, no longer held priority in Arab preoccupation. The Arab leaders were evidently resolved to seek a political showdown by inducing the United States to press Israel for massive withdrawal. In the background they kept their two intimidatory weapons ready: a threat of an oil embargo and a threat of renewed war.

The Labor Party seemed to have ample time to rally its forces for the impending foreign and domestic struggle. The elections were scheduled for October 1977. A new spirit of contest and competition was now at work in our party. Rabin would clearly have to defend his leadership against a renewed challenge from Peres, and I decided to offer a third option by presenting my own candidacy. Many leading members of our party were abandoning it in order to join a new movement established by Professor Yigael Yadin, under the name of "Democratic Movement for Change," but I believed that with a few months of careful planning, in which we could reorganize our party branches and elect new delegates, we would have a good chance of maintaining our strength. Our home in Herzliya became the center of intense party activity. Eli and Gila had finished their army service and were away from home, and I was free to devote myself to political activity. Suzy pursued her functions as president of the Israel Cancer Society in which she had been nothing short of triumphant, expanding the Society's financial resources in vast degree.

The decisive moment came when in January 1977 Rabin suddenly dismissed the ministers of the National Religious Party and offered the resignation of his own government. The legal motive was the failure of the Religious ministers to support a vote of confidence in their own government after a violation of the Sabbath at a ceremony for receiving F-15 aircraft. (Similar deviations had been forgiven by Golda Meir without disrupting governmental stability.) The effect of this move was that of a snowball that becomes an avalanche. The election date was put forward to May 1977. At an impressive party conference in February, Rabin was elected by a tiny majority (50.3 percent against 49.7 percent) in a contest with Peres for the party leadership. Before anything could be done to consolidate this tiny advantage, Rabin visited Washington, where President Carter made ominous remarks about the American hope of a full withdrawal of Israeli forces in a peace settlement.

Rabin, naturally eager for the impression of triumph on the eve of an election, may not have told the Israeli people the whole truth about the new American attitude. But his main trouble arose from a relatively minor incident—the discovery that his wife and he were maintaining bank accounts abroad without the prior declaration and permit prescribed by law. On April 7 Rabin renounced his leadership of the party while continuing to serve as Prime Minister in a caretaker government. In the subsequent meeting of the party's Central Committee, Peres was elected to the leadership. Members who had served in the Knesset for more than two parliamentary sessions were required to secure a vote of at least 60 percent in order to present their candidacy again. I received a vote of 80 percent, which was an impressive demonstration of party confidence.

But for some weeks I was diverted from my tasks by an utterly false charge (propagated by an Israeli émigré in New York who had been dismissed from the Foreign Ministry some years before) that I had maintained my bank accounts abroad without due authorization. This absurdity was totally refuted by an official inquiry that gave me complete vindication, but not before my family and I had endured a preposterous McCarthyist press campaign, from which we emerged intact, but with a sober understanding of the diminished quality of Israeli public life.

Since Allon was promised the Defense Ministry in the event of a Labor victory, it is fairly certain that I would have returned to the Foreign Ministry under a Peres Administration. But the Labor movement, after twenty-nine years in office and a badly organized electoral campaign, lost its majority. The Likud Party under Menachem Begin became the leading party for the first time. There had been a sharp swing toward political militance and social conservatism in Israel. The Left and Left Center were repudiated, and Israel faced the world under Likud leadership with overtones of religious dogmatism and rigidity on territorial issues. A few days later Moshe Dayan, who had sought to be included among the top members of the Labor list, accepted Begin's invitation to become Foreign Minister in the Likud Party, against whose election he had fought! He had no mandate from the public for such a step. Dayan's disregard of all the fidelities linking him to the Labor movement had been carried to its final point of culmination. Yet it must be confessed that the Labor Party had shown no sign of readiness to find an arena for his talents. I had been the Likud's adversary for many years, but in July 1977 Begin and Dayan asked me to undertake a mission to Washington in an effort to strengthen Israel's position in America.

I was warmly and respectfully received by an American public and a Jewish community that had not been accustomed to see me in an "opposition" capacity. I pointed out to my audiences that in a parliamentary system, opposition was an honorable function—even if it was the only honor that politicians did not actively seek. I felt that the reinforcement of Israel's position in world opinion, and especially in America, was a supreme national interest overriding party divisions. Anybody who can make a special contribution to that end has no right to withhold his service.

At the same time I was disturbed by the excessive emphasis that Diaspora Jewry places on the question of "image." This obsessive concern arises out of a special Jewish experience. What other people have thought about Jews has often been an issue of life and death. But in Israel's context there is an inherent conflict between the negotiating interest and the interest of image-making. To succeed at the negotiating table, it is sometimes necessary to be obdurate and tenacious. But this is bad for the image. To succeed in image-making, it is better to be always flexible. But then there is damage to the concrete interests defended at the negotiating table. Other nations consistently subordinate transient popularity to concrete interests; never the other way around. In Israel's case the situation is more complex, since a degree of international support for our image is itself a "concrete" interest. Israel, on the whole, appeals more to the conscience and values of the world community than to its utilitarian interests. Yet I cannot forget that Israel proclaimed her independence on May 14, 1948, in a solitary decision for which support and respect were secured only after the decision was made. Our international posture cannot exclude the capacity to stand alone for certain periods of time when a vital interest is at stake. It is important to be popular—but even more important to be alive. If you are alive, you can work hard to reconstruct your popularity, whereas if you are dead, you will be conspicuously popular during the funeral oration, but the consolation will be transient and brief. The test for Israel's friends in the world lies in the readiness to respect our solitude of responsibility for determining what the minimal conditions for our security are. Despite all our victories, Israel is the only nation that stands or falls in history by the manner in which the Middle Eastern conflict is resolved. No similar mark of interrogation hangs over the head of the Arab nations.

At this stage of my story, Israel is not the same society whose rise from a vulnerable birth I have followed from the earliest days. It has lost its rhapsodic sense. It is an anxious people, consumed by fear of the immense growth in Arab power; fear of erosion in American support; fear of its incapacity to achieve a stable economic order; fear of the long-term effects of a loss in magnetism, reflected in a dwindling immigration and a disquieting flight of manpower from the country. The lucid, visionary but empirical doctrine of the Labor movement is in eclipse. I believe that the popular reaction against a party too long in power is not the final answer, and that Israel will regain the balanced view by which she has surmounted the tempests and push on, forward and upward, to new spurts of creativity. Some writers have defined anxiety as the essence of the Jewish condition. The question is whether we shall make our anxiety fertile or whether we shall squander it in self-pity and despair. In political terms, the issue is whether and for how long we can reconcile the idea of a "Jewish" state with our present demographic and political structure.

The central theme in the doctrine of the Likud is that Israel can indefinitely maintain her rule over the million Arabs, non-citizens of Israel who came under our jurisdiction in June 1967. I cannot sustain this belief. The military victory of 1967 has failed to have any marked effect on the sharp duality of experience between the Jordan River and the Mediterranean. To pass from the area of Israeli law into the realm of military administration is to undertake a voyage of drastic transition. On the one side is a parliamentary society totally saturated with Jewish memories and dreams, with Hebrew speech and social-democratic ideals. On the other side of the line there is no parliament, no government by consent, no Jewish affinities, no Hebrew, no Zionism. Not for one second in the twenty-four hours of each day do the million Arabs in the West Bank and Gaza share a common emotional experience, a common dream or vision with Israelis on our side of the line. The territories are Judea and Samaria—but this does not make the Arab inhabitants Samarians or Judeans. There is no political structure in the modern world marked by such a sharp and total discontinuity as that which describes the relations between the area of Israeli law and the area of military administration. Neither of these two human worlds seeks harmony with the other through any compromise of its separate nature. Our task must be to seek a political separation with the highest possible degree of mutual contact: to be neighbors—neither ruling each other, nor being ruled. The essential territorial changes will have to be selective if this result is to be secured. But in the final account, Israel's security may depend more on her compact but ardent population than on an overextended territorial shape.

I have fought hard for Israel to be physically strong, but it is the intellectual and qualitative element in Israel's life that has the greatest hold on my heart. The only greatness that we can achieve lies in those domains in which matter and quantity can be transcended by mind and quality. Our country has its defects—and we have no lack of friendly counselors to point out exactly what they are. Indeed, the very fulfillment of our aims sometimes creates a sense of vacuum. I remember asking Edmund Hillary, the first man to climb Everest, what exactly he felt when he reached the peak. He replied that the first sentiment was one of ecstatic accomplishment. But then there came a sense of desolation. What was there now left to do? The great ambition had been fulfilled, and with fulfillment, it left a void behind. Were there any Everests left to conquer? The paradox of Israel is that there was more zest in striving for the goal than achieving it. The problem now is to seek new Everests, new points of elevation.

But when all is said and done, it has been an unusual enterprise. I have known both the pains and the contentments, and may well know them both again; however, there is no other journey that I would have wished to make, and the continuation of it is still my strongest hope. Zionism and Israel made great promises to the Jewish people. They may even have promised too much. There has always been a Utopian element in our national movement. The higher the expectation, the greater the possibility of disappointment. Yet, many of the goals have been approached. We have restored our nation's pride. We have given the Jewish people a renewed sense of its collective creativity. We have created a sanctuary in which our special legacy can be preserved and enlarged. We have taken Jewish history out of provincialism and caused it to flow into the mainstream of human culture. We have given mankind a special communication of social originality and intellectual vitality. We have revealed an immense power of Jewish recuperation. Above all, we have fulfilled our human vocation by redeeming hundreds of thousands of our kinsmen from sterility, humiliation and death. So Israel has no cause for comprehensive apology. It is a society inspired by a positive vision, a nation in which tomorrow is more vivid than yesterday, and in which it seems more important to build than to destroy. We have thus been immune to some of the nihilistic currents in contemporary culture. Israel can only be safely led from positions firmly rooted in Jewish humanism, intellectual progress and social idealism.

Our landscape is not sufficiently cherished, our environmental instincts are undeveloped and the texture of Israeli life reveals a weak esthetic sense. In the search for directness and normality there is a tendency to revolt against the lofty and humane elements in the Jewish tradition. In some sections of our society, to be tough is mistakenly regarded as a substitute for being strong. Political competition goes on in an atmosphere more vindictive than in most free countries, and no nation anywhere has the least cause to envy the strident personal tone that gets free rein in some of our journalism. Jewish material, scientific and intellectual power still lies more in the Diaspora than in Israel. And yet, it is in Israel alone that the Jew can face the world in his own authentic image, and not as a footnote in the story of other societies. It is only as a nation in its own soil, its own tongue and its own faith that the Jewish people can hear what it has to hear, say what it has to say—do what it has to do.

My main satisfaction is that many people across the world may have learned from me that the Jewish story, with its culmination in Israel's statehood, is a brave and noble adventure. My road from London through Cairo and Jerusalem to New York and Washington and back to Jerusalem again has been long and eventful. Many lifetimes have been crowded into a few decades. My hope is that the Jewish people will be enabled by its experience of freedom to rise beyond the sufferings of the past and the frustrations of history into the assertion of its unique spirituality.

Index

Young Men's Christian Association
(YMCA), 48, 78
Young Zionist (publication), 12
Youth Aliyah, 280
Yugoslavia, 44, 49, 80, 91, 99, 214, 227,
439-40, 441

Zacharias, Jerrold, 278
Zadok, Chaim, 570, 571, 596
Zaghlul, Saad, 39
Zaire, 477, 494, 499-500
Zar, Mordechai, 389
Ze'evi, Brigadier General ("Gandhi"), 409
Zeira, General Eli, 509, 568
Zionism, 3, 7, 39, 48, 61, 151, 161, 288,
468, 586, 593, 601, 608, 609; Balfour

Declaration and, 8-9; Basel Congress
(1946), 68-69, 92, 103; Eban and, 10-14,
18-20, 22-24, 26-29, 31, 32, 43, 49, 51,
52, 60, 63, 65-66, 68, 73, 74, 78-79, 87,
126, 580; in France, 73-74, 133; Geneva
Congress (1939), 28-29; Hebrew language and, 6; higher-education development (in Israel), 283; Political
Committee, 13; Suez crisis and (in U.S.),
213, 214; United Nations and, 72, 74,
75, 76, 585; Zurich Congress (1937), 27
Zionist Actions Committee, 84
Zionist Executive, 84
Zionist General Council, 84
Zionist Group (Cambridge University), 19
Zionist Office (London), 8, 22-25
Zorea, Brigadier General Meir, 277